Law, Governance and Technology Series

Issues in Privacy and Data Protection

Volume 45

Series Editors

Serge Gutwirth, Brussels, Belgium
Gloria Gonzalez Fuster, Brussels, Belgium

Issues in Privacy and Data Protection aims at publishing peer reviewed scientific manuscripts that focus upon issues that engage into an analysis or reflexion related to the consequences of scientific and technological developments upon the private sphere, the personal autonomy and the self-construction of humans with data protection and privacy as anchor points. The objective is to publish both disciplinary, multidisciplinary and interdisciplinary works on questions that relate to experiences and phenomena that can or could be covered by legal concepts stemming from the law regarding the protection of privacy and/or the processing of personal data. Since both the development of science and technology, and in particular information technology (ambient intelligence, robotics, artificial intelligence, knowledge discovery, data mining, surveillance, etc.), and the law on privacy and data protection are in constant frenetic mood of change (as is clear from the many legal conflicts and reforms at hand), we have the ambition to reassemble a series of highly contemporary and forward-looking books, wherein cutting edge issues are analytically, conceptually and prospectively presented.

More information about this subseries at http://www.springer.com/series/13087

Marek Zubik • Jan Podkowik • Robert Rybski
Editors

European Constitutional Courts towards Data Retention Laws

Springer

Editors
Marek Zubik
Department of Constitutional Law, Faculty of Law and Administration
University of Warsaw
Warsaw, Poland

Jan Podkowik
Department of Constitutional Law, Faculty of Law and Administration
University of Warsaw
Warsaw, Poland

Robert Rybski
Department of Constitutional Law, Faculty of Law and Administration
University of Warsaw
Warsaw, Poland

ISSN 2352-1902 ISSN 2352-1910 (electronic)
Law, Governance and Technology Series
ISSN 2352-1929 ISSN 2352-1937 (electronic)
Issues in Privacy and Data Protection
ISBN 978-3-030-57188-7 ISBN 978-3-030-57189-4 (eBook)
https://doi.org/10.1007/978-3-030-57189-4

This Springer imprint is published by the registered company Springer Nature Switzerland AG.
The registered company address is: Gewerbestrasse 11, 6330 Cham, Switzerland

About This Book

The turn of the century brought a revolution within the scope of information exchange. Since then the space for the possibilities of human functioning and shaping interpersonal relations has expanded visibly. Means of distance communication have become widespread. All these phenomena are undoubtedly connected to the development of civilisation and technology, as well as the reduction of costs of participation in the global flow of information. It is hard to deny that these changes have increased the possibilities of exchanging thoughts, views, and ensuring the transparency of public life and social control of public authorities, the provision of public services, the purchase of goods and services, and the development of scientific research. They have also brought new opportunities to ensure the safety of people and their property, enabling the monitoring of people and places or their electronic supervision, thanks to which—regardless of some random events—even geographical location is possible.

Increasingly sophisticated technologies seem to have diminished citizens' awareness of the effects of their exertion. Our dependence on technical devices, various types of applications and social forums, as well as the specialists who support them have extremely increased. Moreover, technically advanced mechanisms incur the risk of the phenomenon of civilisation exclusion of social groups which are not prepared for the use of new civilisation inventions. It can be also sometimes noticed—not without connection to fears of losing control over one's privacy, the way of living, or more broadly one's freedom—a phenomenon of a conscious abandonment of the pursuit of modernity.

Human privacy has now undoubtedly become a commodity desired by various entities or corporations of a private nature. More or less consciously, citizens have begun to pay for their participation in cyber reality. The protection of privacy and freedom from advertising or profiling has become a luxury, for which one just has to pay money. Cyberspace has also become a place of rivalry between states and international non-state creations, or even a subject of an impact on social life in other countries.

Not only do new technologies give public authorities new forms and ways to perform their functions, but they also create the opportunity to interfere in the privacy of their citizens. They can be used for a very broad acquisition of knowledge about the behaviour of citizens which is beyond an effective social control. This also refers to the content and forms of provided information, as well as the processing of these data and their subsequent use.

However, technological changes have not changed the human nature, which has got its darker sides, too. New technologies make it also easier for people who violate the law to contact each other. The increasing availability of means of communication increases the risk of using them to commit crimes or trespass. On the one hand, technological development has led to the emergence of new forms of committing 'traditional' crimes. The Internet and means of distance communication are to become a new, specialised tool in the hands of criminals, existing somehow parallel to the techniques having been in use so far. On the other hand, some new, previously non-existent types of crimes have emerged which can be committed only by using new technologies (the so-called cybercrime).

The awareness of the expansion of the area of freedom and citizens' activity and the emergence of new threats have forced public authorities to react. The process of incorporating new technologies into public decision-making procedures has begun, giving the citizens new opportunities for social participation. Legal problems related to the spread of new forms of communication go far beyond the issue of processing subscribers' telecommunication data by private operators and then the acquisition of such data by public authorities. It is necessary to consider in which way new forms of communication and the conclusion of various types of contracts may have a reference to the existing legal culture. The key question is whether we are dealing with completely new manifestations of human freedom, including freedom of contract, or whether these are typical activities but carried out in virtual reality. Key problems have arisen, such as the question about the place and time of the conclusion of contract, sufficient consumer knowledge about a product, the risk of using electronic means to conclude a contract, the use of new value media (cyber money), or how to protect effectively sensitive information, especially regarding human health and other forms of privacy, and not to lead to new discrimination phenomena against this background. It is necessary to introduce new legal solutions, civilising legal transactions with the usage of new technologies. After the first period of enthusiasm, when it seemed that the new media would bring only positive effects, also for democratic life of open societies, the original optimism has already worn out. As social media have become more widespread, the realism about the existence of their harmful face has also increased. Political discussions mainly among anonymous strangers have turned out to be often more emotional and less respectful towards people having different views than such discussions carried on in the real world; extreme views can spread more widely and rapidly; disinformation campaigns have appeared, denying more than once scientific evidence, etc.

These general observations already show the scale of problems and challenges democratic legislators have to face. It appears therefore a very significant problem. It has become the key issue to this publication. Namely, the question has to be answered how to set limits for the interference of public authorities in the framework of the use of new technologies by citizens, including in cyberspace. It has been quickly realised that one needs to search for the possibly widest recognised standards. However, cyberspace is poorly prone to modalities set by political boundaries. Freedom of communication exists and is protected by public authorities, and the state interference in this sphere respects the general principles of limiting freedom allowed in a democratic state or the state uses cyberspace for social manipulation. Conversely, maintaining general, democratic standards for the protection of human dignity and human freedoms and rights must be at some point met with the need to maintain public security or to protect the freedoms and rights of others. The use of modern technologies in the course of terrorist attacks has shown how urgent it will be to determine the appropriate limits for the gathering and processing data created while using modern forms of communication by citizens. An open question is also the issue of the need to ensure a proper education so as not only to prevent the already mentioned phenomenon of civilisation exclusion among various social groups, but also to show sufficiently the threats and challenges which users usually face when using new channels of communication.

We have never had any doubts that the issue of legal regulations regarding the consolidation and use of telecommunication data is socially significant. The book is the result of work of a number of lawyers from different countries and at least in two dimensions. The first one—and the most obvious—the studies have been written and developed by lawyers. The second dimension—but not less important—court rulings and their justifications were also made as a part of the judicial service of lawyers. All these elements—legal norms, court rulings, and statements of the law literature—reflect the legal framework of freedom of communication in the digital age.

In the book, we have tried to capture the essence of the development of legal thought on the subject of the legal mechanism adopted in European Union countries, which are also members of the Council of Europe. This mechanism consisted of the legal obligation of private telecommunication network operators to record information about the communication of their customers, excluding the content of messages, and it also sets the legal framework for the acquisition and use of this information by public authorities. Legal solutions adopted at the level of the European Union and in particular member states have quickly begun to be questioned. Matters related to them have ended up on the agenda of the national constitutional courts and the Court of Justice of the European Union itself. The longer they have been in force, the more doubts have been growing about the compliance of these regulations with human rights and the rule of law.

The undoubted turning point for the existence of joint solutions regarding the consolidation and acquisition of telecommunication data by public authorities was the judgement of the CJEU of 8 April 2014 in case of Digital Rights Ireland, which annulled the directive of the European Parliament and of the Council of 15 March 2006 on the retention of data generated or processed in connection with the provision of publicly available electronic communications services or of public communications networks. Nonetheless, we put forward the thesis that the CJEU's approach to such a decision would not be so obvious if it were not preceded by a series of judgements of the ECtHR related to the protection of privacy in the digital age, and in particular the judgements of the national constitutional courts proclaiming the unconstitutionality of provisions implementing this directive. The general social reluctance to the excessive interference of public authorities in the cyberspace has certainly also been not without any significance for these decisions.

The book we give to the reader consists of two parts: One of them is an attempt to capture the basic way of seeing standards for the protection of individual freedoms and rights and balancing it with ensuring public safety by the national supreme judicial authorities of the EU countries in which constitutional courts or supreme courts ruled on the provisions regulating the mechanism of telecommunication data consolidation. This is presented in studies written by lawyers from particular countries. The second part constitutes an attempt to reconstruct the common European standard for the protection of freedom of communication in the digital era, as well as to show how the exchange of thoughts and views between national courts, the ECtHR, and the CJEU has taken place. One could say, it is a practical exemplification of the phenomenon that is referred to as 'judicial dialogue'.

The publication can undoubtedly serve as a source of information for those who want to acquire knowledge about legal solutions in force in several countries and about particular court decisions made towards them. The reader can learn the history regarding the assessment of national provisions on the collection of telecommunication data and their use by public authorities. At the end of the book, there are extensive fragments of judgements, which should enable the reader to refer to the source of the case-law (not only for the analytical study itself). Particular studies, however, are not focused on the mere analysis and assessment of judgements, but rather on the search for a common standard for the protection of freedom of communication within a common area of the European legal culture while preserving the constitutional achievements of particular member states.

We have tried to find the actual shape of emerging constitutional and international standards for the protection of freedom of communication in the aspect of telecommunication data retention and processing. Largely devoted to the latter issue is the last study, which is our summary of analyses focused on particular countries and the jurisprudence of the ECtHR and the CJEU. Professor dr. habil. Marek Zubik (retired judge of Poland's Constitutional Tribunal), dr. habil. Jan Podkowik and dr. Robert Rybski.

We are aware that the publication shows the state of development of legal thought at some historical point. Whether the outlined development will persist or collapse over some time, it depends on many factors, not only legal ones. This thesis can be only verified in the future. We hope, however, that the book could serve as a valuable help in further scientific research conducted on both standards for the protection of freedom of communication, as well as cooperation and judicial dialogue in the best way.

The book has been composed as a part of the project "Impact of jurisprudence of European constitutional courts and of the Court of Justice of European Union on forming universal content of freedom of communications in Europe in the era of technological development" conducted at the Faculty of Law and Administration of the University of Warsaw, financed by the National Science Centre in Poland (project No. 2015/17/B/HS5/01408).

Contents

Part I
Data Retention in Europe

Data Retention in the European Union

Barbara Grabowska-Moroz

Abstract Global security challenges after the 9/11 terrorist attacks have revolutionised national approaches on the fight against public security threats. The broad and open-ended concept of terrorism has allowed national legislatures to adopt extraordinary measures to face these undefined threats. Their impact on human rights (personal freedom, freedom of movement, right of privacy, freedom of information) has led to the development of case law, which is aimed at balancing safeguards against unknown threats and the belief that human rights remain binding. One of such security measures—the retention of telecommunication data—was harmonised by the European Union in 2006. Since then it has been one of the most vividly discussed topics in European law involving both political and business issues. This paper aims at analysing the judicial debate held by the Court of Justice of the European Union on the constitutional and international limits of the Data Retention Directive (Directive 2006/24/EC of the European Parliament and of the Council of 15 March 2006 on the retention of data generated or processed in connection with the provision of publicly available electronic communications services or of public communications networks and amending Directive 2002/58/EC.).

1 Data Retention Directive: Scope, Aim, Consequences

The European Commission proposed a Directive on data retention[1] in September 2005, two months after the London bombings. Despite the lack of unequivocal competence in the field of national security, the European Union decided to regulate this issue as an internal market matter. The proposal noted that different retention

[1]Proposal for a Directive of the European Parliament and of the Council on the retention of data processed in connection with the provision of public electronic communication services and amending Directive 2002/58/EC {SEC(2005) 1131}.

B. Grabowska-Moroz (✉)
University of Groningen, Groningen, The Netherlands

M. Zubik et al. (eds.), *European Constitutional Courts towards Data Retention Laws*, Law, Governance and Technology Series 45,
https://doi.org/10.1007/978-3-030-57189-4_1

requirements binding in Member States could constitute obstacles to the internal market for electronic communication and therefore needed to be harmonised. However, the European Commission argued that such differences also limited law enforcement's access to data thus impeding the fulfilment of their duties including "preventing and combating organised crime and terrorism."

The Directive was adopted in 2006 and imposed a duty of retaining telecommunication data by service providers and obliged Member States to ensure access to data by "competent national authorities."[2] The scope of the data covered by the Directive was broad and included information regarding the sources of communication; the date, time and duration of a communication; type of communication; and the location of mobile communication equipment. Specific elements of access to the retained data (e.g. procedure) were to be regulated by Member States "in accordance with necessity and proportionality requirements." It constituted a clear exemption from the general rules of data protection established in Directive 2002/58 regarding privacy and electronic communications,[3] which imposed significantly stricter limits on data protection.[4] The Data Retention Directive also constituted a challenge in light of the European Court of Human Rights (ECtHR) case law, since ECtHR required proportionate and strictly tailored measures that would protect not only public security but also respect the essence of right to confidential communication, private life and freedom of speech.[5]

The Irish government initiated the first judicial challenge of the Directive before the EU court based on the assumption that Directive 2006/24 was not appropriately and legally adopted, and that it was an internal market Directive based on Article 95 EC instead of the precedent decision adopted on Title VI of Treaty of European Union (TEU) regulating judicial cooperation and fighting crimes. Determining competence demarcation between the first and the third pillar and clarifying the appropriate body entitled to act—the Union or the Community[6]—resulted from the pre-Lisbon Treaty legal framework that currently is not as relevant as it previously was. However, focusing attention on the issues of procedure and competence instead of the merits detracted from the main arguments analysed in Advocate General Bot's opinion and the Court's ruling. Consequently, the Court found that "Directive 2006/24 covers the activities of service providers in the internal market and does not contain any rules governing the activities of public authorities for law-enforcement

[2] Directive 2006/24/EC, Article 4.

[3] Directive 2002/58/EC of the European Parliament and of the Council of 12 July 2002 concerning the processing of personal data and the protection of privacy in the electronic communications sector.

[4] CJEU in *Tele 2/Watson* stated that "retention of traffic and location data is the rule, whereas the system put in place by Directive 2002/58 requires the retention of data to be the exception" (para. 104).

[5] Breyer (2005).

[6] Poli (2010), p. 138.

purposes."[7] Although the Court referenced the 9/11 terrorist attacks, which motivated national legislators to impose obligations on service providers regarding data retention, it analysed the EU's data retention obligations through the "internal market lens". The Court found that the Data Retention Directive regulated the retention of data and not its access or use by law enforcement.[8] For most stakeholders it was obvious that the chief aim of imposing data retention obligations mainly affects security; however, it also undoubtedly and directly affects service providers in the Member States. Nevertheless, applying an internal market approach to regulating this issue might have undermined human rights protections.[9]

In 2011, the European Commission recommended the amendment of the Data Retention Directive and regulation of data retention as a security measure and not merely as a tool harmonising the internal market.[10] The Commission also emphasised the need to strengthen personal data protection within the scheme of telecommunication data protection by shortening the periods of mandatory data retention, ensuring independent supervision of requests for data access and retention, thereby reducing the data categories to be retained.[11] The Commission directly referred to the standard established by the ECHR in the *S and Murper v. UK* ruling,[12] which balanced an individual's concerns about data collection against the public safety and security.

2 The Constitutional Road to *Digital Rights Ireland*

Ireland v. European Parliament was a first step in challenging data retention obligations; however, the challenge failed due to the Irish government's and subsequently the Court's formalist approach. Nevertheless, it was indisputable that future judicial challenges of the Directive would inevitably follow. Implementation of the Directive differed between Member States providing various mechanisms of control and different interpretations of the vague proportionality standard established by the Directive. Therefore, the Court's decision in *Ireland v. European Parliament* did not end the discussion about the Data Retention Directive.

---

[7]Judgment of 10 February 2009, *Ireland v. European Parliament and Council of the European Union*, C-301/06.

[8]Judgment of 10 February 2009, *Ireland v. European Parliament and Council of the European Union*, C-301/06, para. 80.

[9]Herlin-Karnell (2009), p. 1667.

[10]Report from the Commission to the Council and the European Parliament – Evaluation report on the Data Retention Directive (Directive 2006/24/EC) Brussels, 18.4.2011 COM(2011) 225 final, p. 31.

[11]Report from the Commission to the Council and the European Parliament – Evaluation report on the Data Retention Directive (Directive 2006/24/EC) Brussels, 18.4.2011 COM(2011) 225 final, p. 32.

[12]Judgment of 4 December 2008, applications No. 30562/04 and 30566/04.

Instead, the discussion shifted to the national level where national constitutional courts analysed the implementation of the Data Retention Directive following their national constitutions. In those cases, the courts attempted to properly balance the concerns of law enforcement against the desires of individuals residing in democratic states for data protection. Such an analysis was a new step because the Court of Justice did not analyse the merits of the directive's provisions. National constitutional reviews of data retention in light of the Directive's obligations triggered judicial dialogue between the courts.[13] It was nearly impossible for the Court of Justice of the European Union (CJEU) to ignore national constitutional reviews while adjudicating the Directive. The main arguments against the Directive's retention scheme dealt with the broad scope of retained data and their effectiveness in fighting against serious crimes (Czech Republic). However, the national constitutional courts had to also consider the relation between national and the EU law (Germany, Cyprus).

In 2014, CJEU eventually discussed the constitutional arguments in the *Digital Rights Ireland* decision.[14] Preliminary references—from both the Austrian and Irish courts—addressed whether the Directive was compatible with the human rights expressed in the EU Charter of Fundamental Rights, including the rights to privacy and protection of personal data. The Court followed the typical ECtHR approach used in cases concerning alleged violation of Article 8 European Convention on Human Rights (ECHR) and applied a three-prong proportionality test.[15] The interference with "privacy rights" (rights to privacy and protection of personal data) resulted from two elements regulated by the Directive—(1) the obligatory retention of "data relating to a person's private life and to his communications" and (2) access to data by national authorities. The Court found the interference to be a "particularly serious" one, especially due to the lack of notice, which could lead to "constant surveillance."

Nevertheless, the Court concluded that a "particularly serious interference"—meaning the fight against serious crime to maintain public security—is legitimate because "data relating to the use of electronic communications are particularly important and therefore a valuable tool in the prevention of offences and the fight against crime."[16] However, the Court did not articulate the effectiveness of the entire legal framework for storing and using telecommunication data. It appears that when applying the balancing test, the Court did not fully consider a data retention system's legitimate purpose and failed to specifically explain it. The Court referred to neither the Commission's evaluation of 2011 nor to other sources reviewing the effectiveness of a data retention system.

[13]Vedaschi and Lubello (2015), p. 23.

[14]Judgment of the Court (Grand Chamber) of 8 April 2014, *Digital Rights Ireland Ltd v. Minister for Communications, Marine and Natural Resources and Others* and *Kärntner Landesregierung and Others*, C-293/12.

[15]Tracol (2014), p. 742.

[16]*Digital Rights Ireland*, para. 43.

Nevertheless, the "particularly serious interference" with an individual's right to privacy led the Court to apply a "strict" standard of review.[17] The Court expressly noted shortcomings with the following: interference to both the retention and access to data; no relation between data retention and serious crimes; overly broad data retention covering the entire European population; lack of procedural safeguards regarding access to retained data; vague and ambiguous definition of "serious crime"; and concerns regarding the safety of retained data.[18] The overall shortcomings of the Directive led to the conclusion that the Directive "has exceeded the limits imposed by compliance with the principle of proportionality in the light of Articles 7, 8 and 52(1) of the Charter." Consequently, the Court found the Data Retention Directive invalid.[19]

The Court's decision in *Ireland v. European Parliament* revealed that the criminal and law enforcement concerns played a secondary role to the internal market concerns, whereas in *Digital Rights Ireland* internal market concerns were not the primary focus.[20] The Advocate General referred to the "dual function" of the Directive and stated that it was "manifestly disproportionate" with respect to the goal of internal market harmonisation.[21] Nevertheless, the *Digital Rights Ireland* decision revealed the growing importance of the EU Charter of Fundamental Rights, despite the Court's lack of a detailed legal analysis of the interference with the right to protection of personal data,[22] instead mostly referring to the right to privacy, whereas AG made clear distinction between those two rights.[23]

The Court's ruling caused to some extent legal uncertainty of national legislation implementing the Data Retention Directive. It remains clear that the EU continues regulating personal data protection via Directive 2002/58, which allows for the limitation of data protection rules.[24] Consequently, the EU Charter would apply to national laws implementing this aspect of the EU law, including national data retention schemes. Despite the set of rulings relating to data retention issued by national constitutional courts, it was the *Digital Rights Ireland* decision that was described as a "game changer" in judicial discussions about the EU data retention scheme.[25] This decision elaborated the main disadvantages of the whole data retention system.[26] For this reason, national courts have implemented this decision

[17] *Digital Rights Ireland*, para. 52.

[18] *Digital Rights Ireland*, para. 68.

[19] Advocate General suggested however to suspend the effect of Directive invalidation (para. 158).

[20] Guild and Carrera (2014), p. 7.

[21] Opinion of AG Cruz Villalon of 12 December 2013, Case C-293/12, para. 100.

[22] Tracol (2014), p. 743.

[23] AG opinion, paras. 64–65. The Court cleared it up in *Tele-2/Watson* ruling by stating that data protection does not have any equivalent in the ECHR.

[24] Rauhofer and Mac Sithigh (2014), p. 126; Boehm and Cole (2014), pp. 92–93.

[25] Rauhofer and Mac Sithigh (2014), p. 127.

[26] Rauhofer and Mac Sithigh (2014), p. 127: "the ECJ has now sharply removed the sticking plaster that up to now has held a creaking system together".

when reviewing national legislation following the Data Retention Directive.[27] Although it remains unsettled whether the European Commission would propose a new directive in this respect, it remains obvious that the new EU legal framework and national laws implementing exemption from Directive 2002/58 must meet the criteria discussed by the CJEU.[28]

3 National Legislation on Data Retention Under Scrutiny: *Tele-2/Watson* Develops the *Digital Rights Ireland* Findings

Between the two possible scenarios at the EU level[29]—legislative intervention and judicial challenge—the latter provided clarity sooner. National legislation in Sweden and in the UK was challenged before national courts, which referred their cases to the CJEU for redress of privacy questions with regard to national law.[30] The common denominator in the questions referred to CJEU in *Tele2/Watson* was whether national legislation providing mandatory telecommunication data retention was compatible with the EU law, particularly with Article 15 of Directive 2002/58 and with the Charter of Fundamental Rights (Articles 7 and 8).

Advocate General (AG) Bot's analysis was closer to the approach used by the Court in the *Digital Rights Ireland* decision.[31] The opinion underlined the need of procedural safeguards established by *Digital Rights Ireland* ruling concerning law enforcement's access to retained data rather than the broad scope of data storage by service providers.[32] The AG's analysis was described as a "pragmatic solution" because it followed an analysis similar to the one adopted in *Digital Rights Ireland.*[33] The AG concluded that the general retention of telecommunication data can be compatible with the EU law if certain criteria are met.

Instead of applying the safeguards on access to telecommunication data established in *Digital Rights Ireland*, the CJEU concentrated solely on data retention systems established by Swedish and British law.[34] The Court found that Directive 2002/58 is applicable to national legislation on mandatory data retention[35] because

---

[27]E.g. Slovakia, Poland, UK in *Davis* ruling of July 2015.

[28]Vedaschi and Lubello (2015), p. 30; Ojanen (2014), p. 540.

[29]Vedaschi and Lubello (2015), p. 3; Guild and Carrera (2014), pp. 13–15.

[30]*Tele2 Sverige AB v. Post- och telestyrelsen* and *Secretary of State for the Home Department v. Tom Watson and Others*, C-203/15.

[31]Opinion of Advocate General Bot of 9 November 2016, case C-536/15.

[32]Opinion of Advocate General Bot of 9 November 2016, case C-536/15. para. 205.

[33]Gryffroy (2016).

[34]Judgment of the Court (Grand Chamber) of 21 December 2016, *Tele2 Sverige AB v. Post- och telestyrelsen and Secretary of State for the Home Department v. Tom Watson and Others*, C-203/15.

[35]*Tele2/Watson*, para. 81.

retention for combating crimes fall within Article 15 (1) of the Directive.[36] The Court found that the retention of the traffic and location data involved processing them,[37] thus Directive 2002/58 also applies to access to those data by public authorities.[38]

The Court confirmed that the "strict necessity" test is applicable to limitations of personal data protection[39] due to the nature of infringement. The Court followed the findings in *Digital Rights Ireland* that data retention obligations facilitate the precise definition of people's profiles of their private lives.[40] "Very far reaching" and "particularly serious" interference also resulted from the lack of obligatory notice, which is likely to cause a person to feel under constant surveillance.[41] The AG confirmed that the retention of a large amount of traffic and location data can be just as sensitive as access to the actual content of communications.[42] By contrast, in the case of *Digital Rights Ireland* the sensitive nature of data retention did not lead the Court to conclude that the Data Retention Directive breached the essence of individual privacy rights.[43]

According to the Court, such serious limitations of the right to privacy can be justified only by the fight against "serious crime".[44] However, this legitimate goal is not "strong" enough to justify "national legislation providing for the general and indiscriminate retention of all traffic and location data."[45] The Court stated that combatting serious crimes cannot justify indiscriminate retention,[46] otherwise it would become a general rule.[47] Another shortcoming of national regulation was the lack of any relationship between data retention and threats to public security.[48] Furthermore, there were no restrictions on time periods, geographical areas, groups of people likely to be involved or persons who could contribute to fighting crime. Consequently, the national legislation under review exceeded the limits of the "strict necessity" test and was not justified within democratic society.[49]

Nevertheless, the Court noted that Directive 2002/58 and the Charter do not prevent "targeted retention" being limited "with respect to the categories of data to

---

[36] *Tele2/Watson*, para 73.

[37] *Tele2/Watson*, para. 75.

[38] *Tele2/Watson*, para. 76.

[39] *Tele2/Watson*, para. 96; *Digital Rights Ireland*, para. 52.

[40] *Digital Rights Ireland*, para. 27. *Tele2/Watson*, para. 99.

[41] Interference was found to be "very far reaching" and "particularly serious" (*Tele2/Watson*, para. 100).

[42] Opinion of Advocate General Bot of 9 November 2016, para. 253.

[43] *Digital Rights Ireland*, para. 39.

[44] *Tele2/Watson*, para. 102.

[45] *Tele2/Watson*, para. 103.

[46] *Tele2/Watson*.

[47] *Tele2/Watson*, para. 104.

[48] *Tele2/Watson*, para. 106; *Digital Rights Ireland*, para. 59.

[49] *Tele2/Watson*, para. 107.

be retained, the means of communication affected, the persons concerned and the retention period adopted."[50] This approach was considered following the decision in *Digital Rights Ireland* and suggested a possible method for limiting data retention. In *Tele2/Watson* the Court specifically mentioned limitations based on geographical criterion.[51] The approaches established in these cases would allow retention of telecommunication data where the level of crime is high and there is objective evidence to confirm the scope of the area.

On the rules on access to telecommunication data, the requirements established in the *Digital Rights Ireland* decision were confirmed by the Court in *Tele2/Watson*. National legislation must establish "the substantive and procedural conditions" governing the access of competent national authorities to retained data.[52] Fulfilling those conditions shall be reviewed by independent authority.[53] Moreover, the Court clearly expressed the notification requirement after authorities receive access to data to ensure an individual's right to a legal remedy. The Court also noted the requirement of ensuring prior independent review of processing personal data based on Article 8(3) of the Charter. A court or an independent administrative body shall conduct a review into each request for data access, and each request must specify the reasons for data access for verification by the court or administrative body. The goal of data retention and access is limited only to fighting serious crimes including organised crime, terror, or those that pose serious public security threats. However, the Member State must decide which crimes are sufficiently serious to justify data retention and access.

The Court's analysis led to a conclusion that the EU law, specifically Directive 2002/58 and the EU Charter, prohibits the "general and indiscriminate retention of all traffic and location data of all subscribers." Moreover, access to such data collected based on "targeted retention" must meet the following set of requirements: the goal of data access is limited to "fighting serious crime"; data access is subject to prior review by a court and/or independent administrative authority; and the data are retained within the EU. AG clearly stated that the above requirements must be met cumulatively, whereas the Court did not directly address this issue.[54]

[50] *Tele2/Watson*, para. 108.

[51] *Tele2/Watson*, para. 111.

[52] *Tele2/Watson*, para. 118.

[53] *Tele2/Watson*, para. 120.

[54] Pederson et al. (2018), p. 10.

4 Data Retention in the European Union: Where Are We Now?

The ruling in *Tele2/Watson* inevitably constituted a new stage in the evolution of the CJEU approach on mandatory data retention. In *Digital Rights Ireland*, the Court reviewed the EU legislation, whereas in *Tele2/Watson*, the Court clearly referred to national legislation of the Member States.[55] The Court not only analysed the national laws in Sweden and the United Kingdom in light of the Charter but also in light of secondary law. Despite the differences between the subjects of review, *Tele2/Watson* constitutes a "follow-up" to *Digital Rights Ireland*, although *Tele2/Watson* concentrates on analysing the exemption from Directive 2002/58.[56] The Court presented a new approach on data retention, whereas with respect to access by law enforcement, the Court followed the arguments presented in *Digital Rights Ireland*. However, *Tele2/Watson* analysed both aspects—data retention and access by law enforcement—which was often missed at the national level[57] due to separate regulation of each issue. In this sense, *Tele2/Watson* is the decision that fully invalidated the Data Retention Directive. The Court ruled that "Member States may not impose a general obligation on providers of electronic communications services to retain data."[58]

Both decisions confirmed that data retention enables the creation of precise individual profiles, which constitutes a severe interference with privacy rights. Those Member States that did not react to *Digital Rights Ireland* by initiating a review of their national legislation are now likely to do so. Unfortunately, most of the Member States' legislation do not meet the standards that the Court noted in *Tele2/Watson*.[59] Applying the CJEU's high standard of data protection may have posed risks to the effectiveness of the EU law. The consequences of the ruling for the UK regulation[60] will be particularly interesting especially considering the additional changes resulting from Brexit. The requirement that data be stored within the EU could significantly limit the consequences of Brexit.[61]

The notion that unlimited data retention is incompatible with human rights protected by the EU has generated both positive and negative comments. Positive comments have resulted from the CJEU's increased level of data protection in comparison to the standard established in the *Digital Rights Ireland* decision. It noted that requirements must be established in national legislation to ensure that data retention will be limited only where strictly necessary. "In Tele-2/Watson the CJEU

---

[55]Tracol (2017), p. 548.

[56]Cameron (2017), p. 1468.

[57]Privacy International, *National Data Retention Laws since the CJEU's Tele-2/Watson judgment. A Concerning State of Play for the Right to Privacy in Europe*, September 2017, p. 6.

[58]Cameron (2017), p. 1468.

[59]Privacy International, *National Data Retention Laws since the CJEU's Tele-2/Watson judgment. A Concerning State of Play for the Right to Privacy in Europe*, September 2017.

[60]Takatsuki (2017).

[61]Patrick (2016).

not only confirmed the importance of its ruling in *Digital Rights Ireland* but also expanded on that ruling affirming positive requirements that national data retention legislation must comply with both European and international human rights law".[62]

Criticism of the judgment is much more differential. First, it has been suggested that such a high level of data protection in relation to public security has nothing to do with the "classic" vision of the EU focused on internal market collaboration.[63] Second, it has been suggested that "removing a general duty of retention severely undermines the investigative ability of police and intelligence services"[64] due to lack of access to historical data.[65] The *Tele2/Watson* decision was even described as a "radical" one due to the concern it caused among law enforcement in Member States.[66] The opponents of the ruling even stated that it may cause "actual or potential catastrophe."[67] As a result of the decision in this case, data retention systems in Sweden and the UK should be significantly amended. Therefore, this decision is revolutionary.

It has been argued that this decision leads to the elimination of a useful tool in daily law enforcement. The problem of potentially undermining the effectiveness of law enforcement investigations was noted by Europol after the decision in *Digital Rights Ireland*.[68] However, the main problem now concerns the reshaping of the model for data retention and not the conditions that must be met to access data.

The Court found that the untargeted and indiscriminate retention of data of all persons using mobile phones is unlawful. The Court eliminated the Directive's main justification for data retention. The Court found that such a broad collection of data is not "strictly necessary" and is not proportionate. Nevertheless, the Court proceeded to reflect upon the additional standards and restrictions for targeted data retention and access to data in particular.[69] Looking for situations wherein data retention is untargeted is probably the main challenge after *Tele2/Watson* decision.

Some solutions were already proposed, such as removing one category out of traffic data that will not be retained,[70] as well as different time periods and locations for the data traffic. The Court's analysis of national legislation in *Tele2/Watson*

---

[62]Privacy International, *National Data Retention Laws since the CJEU's Tele-2/Watson judgment. A Concerning State of Play for the Right to Privacy in Europe*, September 2017, p. 14.

[63]The EU courts all too often hold the Member States to a higher standard of compliance than the EU institutions extending the EU's ever expanding human rights regime into areas of law that have nothing to do with the EU's classical internal market economic governance competences: Beck (2017).

[64]Cameron (2017), p. 1483.

[65]Cameron (2017), p. 1482.

[66]Anderson (2017).

[67]Hil (2017).

[68]Europol, *An Update on Cyber Legislation*. www.europol.europa.eu/iocta/2015/app-2.html. Accessed 16 August 2018.

[69]Väljataga (2017).

[70]Cameron (2017), p. 1486. The author gives an example of unsuccessful connections as those that could be excluded from the scope of retained data.

allows one to state more easily which elements of a data retention system are not permissible, rather than establish regulations that would satisfy EU Charter requirements.[71] This approach was also presented by the Council Legal Service in February 2017.[72] I. Cameron wondered whether better protection of people with duties of confidentiality would "cure" a general duty of retention.[73]

The Court's suggestion in this respect referred to geographic criteria as a measure to limit and target the scope of retained data. Those geographical criteria would also need to be proved by objective evidence for high crime risk.[74] This idea triggered a set of critical comments afterwards. The main criticism suggests that systems based on territorial delineation may lead to discriminatory profiling of certain areas (e.g. suburbs where low-income migrants live).[75] The second point of criticism suggested that the same goal of targeted retention can be achieved through more simple technical means.[76]

The retention of telecommunication data and their usage for law enforcement investigations or intelligence operations require that one consider the many issues that are at stake, including not only the legal aspects of privacy protection but also a detailed technological knowledge and practice of law enforcement work. *Digital Rights Ireland* and *Tele2/Watson* did not specifically analyse these issues.

I. Cameron argued that the "potential chilling effect" caused by untargeted telecommunication data retention is an "empirical question, only answerable in each Member State."[77] D. Anderson, former UK Independent Reviewer of Terrorism Legislation, suggested that the EU Member States might have different past experience with law enforcement competence on surveillance, which might cause difficulty in establishing one standard common for the whole EU.[78] This would suggest that different historical experiences of the Member States could allow the creation of different legal arrangements of data protection and oversight of law enforcement. It is noted that some EU Member States have already imposed notice requirements, thus providing a guarantee of appropriate control over retained data, whereas the

---

[71]Woods (2016).

[72]Information note of the Council Legal Service to Permanent Representatives Committee (Part 2). https://cdn.netzpolitik.org/wp-upload/2017/05/rat_eu_legal_service_vds_20170201.pdf. 1 February 2017, COREPER (doc. 5884/17) "It is however clear from the operative part of the Tele2 judgment that a general and indiscriminate retention obligation for crime prevention and other security reasons would no more be possible at national level than it is at EU level, since it would violate just as much the fundamental requirements as demonstrated by the Court's insistence in two judgments delivered in Grand Chamber" (p. 6).

[73]Cameron (2017), p. 1488.

[74]Pederson et al. (2018), pp. 10–11.

[75]Väljataga (2017), Woods (2016) and Lynskey (2017).

[76]I. Cameron underlined lack of justification for such an exception; he argued that there are "simpler and more secret ways to get it, most obviously through the use of IMSI catchers.": Cameron (2017), p. 1491.

[77]Cameron (2017), p. 1484.

[78]Anderson (2017).

Court applied an "EU-wide level of (mis)trust in the police and intelligence agencies."[79]

Tele2/Watson also has important implications for the ongoing development of the EU legislation in the field of privacy protection. Particularly interesting are two instruments: the so-called Police Directive[80] and the draft of ePrivacy Regulation that will annul Directive 2002/58. Drafted Article 11 of the ePrivacy Regulation does not specifically mention data retention; however, the EC proposal clearly confirmed that "Member States are free to keep or create national data retention frameworks that provide, inter alia, for targeted retention measures, in so far as such frameworks comply with Union law, taking into account the case-law of the Court of Justice on the interpretation of the ePrivacy Directive and the Charter of Fundamental Rights."[81]

When it comes to Directive 2016/680, it was still negotiated when CJEU ruled *Tele2/Watson*. The Police Directive does not state either a clear notice requirement or a criterion on data access by law enforcement. It also limits its scope of application to the goal of "fighting crime" without clearly defining "serious crimes" established in *Tele2/Watson*.

However, the Police Directive could settle some of the concerns relating to geographic criteria as a basis for "territorial data retention," since the Directive clearly prohibits discriminatory profiling.[82] However, it seems that the requirement of data storage within the EU will be confirmed in an effective law.[83] Nevertheless, the requirement constitutes a challenge for any future international transfer of personal data to third countries.[84]

5 Conclusions

The judicial life of data retention in the European Union can be analysed from different perspectives—the relation between market freedoms and individuals' rights, procedural safeguards against abuse of power by law enforcement, and

[79]Cameron (2017), p. 1481.

[80]Directive (EU) 2016/680 of the European Parliament and of the Council of 27 April 2016 on the protection of natural persons with regard to the processing of personal data by competent authorities for the purposes of the prevention, investigation, detection or prosecution of criminal offences or the execution of criminal penalties, and on the free movement of such data, and repealing Council Framework Decision 2008/977/JHA.

[81]Proposal for a Regulation of the European Parliament and of the Council concerning the respect for private life and the protection of personal data in electronic communications and repealing Directive 2002/58/EC (Regulation on Privacy and Electronic Communications), COM/2017/010 final – 2017/03 (COD), p. 3.

[82]Article 11 of Directive 2016/680.

[83]Article 32 GDPR.

[84]Lynskey (2017).

effectiveness of investigations conducted by law enforcement. The CJEU case law has evolved and emphasised different aspects of the mass collection of telecommunication data. In *Ireland v. Parliament*, the Court concentrated on data retention and noted the connection between the obligation to retain data and the EU's internal market. In *Digital Rights Ireland*, the Court mainly analysed the shortcomings of regulation on access to data retention by law enforcement, whereas in *Tele2/Watson* the Court focused more on the limits of data retention schemes. Ten years after the Data Retention Directive was adopted, the Court concluded that the main idea of the Directive, the indiscriminate and untargeted collection of data traffic, is unacceptable under the EU law. The decision in *Digital Rights Ireland* opened a real judicial discussion about data retention at the EU level, and *Tele2/Watson* certainly did not close it.[85] The discussion may even intensify due to the requirement established in *Tele2/Watson* which provides that there must be "objective evidence" proving that a given data retention system is "strictly necessary."

The EU approach on protecting human rights was mostly perceived as a reflection of ECtHR case law due to limitations established in Article 51 of the EU Charter of Fundamental Rights. The Data Retention Directive saga shows how CJEU evolved and proposed an innovative approach in balancing data protection and national security. However, the main concern is the implementation of *Tele2/Watson* by Member States facing their own shortcomings. The Court certainly did not answer all the questions concerning data retention. Therefore, there are new reasons to discuss it in Member States with respect to other databases, including private ones gathering data on a voluntary basis.[86] The decision in *Tele-2/Watson* expanded the findings in *Digital Rights Ireland* and proposed a new solution—"targeted retention" as a tool able to effectively support the fight against serious crimes.

Member States are in a difficult position—they must defend both in national and the EU courts something that they were obliged to introduce 10 years ago according to the EU law. Because *Tele2/Watson* requires the introduction of limitations to untargeted data retention based on objective evidence independently verified by courts or independent administrative bodies, it is likely that the real discussion about the effectiveness of data retention has just begun.

References

Anderson D (2017) CJEU Judgment in Watson/Tele2. https://www.daqc.co.uk/2017/04/11/cjeu-judgment-in-watson/

Beck G (2017) Case Comment: C-203/15 Tele2 Sverige AB v Post-och telestyrelsen and C-698/15 SSHD v Tom Watson & Others. https://eutopialaw.com/2017/01/13/case-comment-cases-c-

[85] Beck (2017): "the Court implicitly opened the door to further legal uncertainties and future litigation."

[86] Pederson et al. (2018), p. 13.

20315-tele2-sverige-ab-v-post-och-telestyrelsen-and-c-69815-secretary-of-state-for-the-home-department-v-tom-watson-and-others/

Boehm F, Cole F (2014) Data Retention after the Judgment of the Court of Justice of the European Union, Münster/Luxembourg (Study provided by the Greens/EFA Group in the European Parliament), 30 June 2014

Breyer P (2005) Telecommunications data retention and human rights: the compatibility of blanket traffic data retention with the ECHR. Eur Law J 11(3):365–375

Cameron I (2017) Balancing data protection and law enforcement needs: Tele2 Sverige and Watson. Common Mark Law Rev 54:1467–1496

Europol, An Update on Cyber Legislation. www.europol.europa.eu/iocta/2015/app-2.html. Accessed 16 Aug 2018

Gryffroy P (2016) Two years after Digital Rights Ireland: general data retention obligations might still be compatible with EU law. A review of the Advocate General's opinion in Joined Cases C-203/15 and C-698/15. http://jean-monnet-saar.eu/?p=1511

Guild E, Carrera S (2014) The political and Judicial Life of Metadata: Digital Rights Ireland and the Trail of the Data Retention Directive, CEPS Papers May 2014, 65

Herlin-Karnell H (2009) Case Comment Case C-301/06, Ireland v. Parliament and Council. Common Mark Law Rev 46:1667

Hil M (2017) Where to after Watson? The challenges and future of mass data retention in the UK. https://infolawcentre.blogs.sas.ac.uk/2017/05/17/where-to-after-watson-the-challenges-and-future-of-mass-data-retention-in-the-uk/

Lynskey O (2017) Tele2 Sverige AB and Watson et al: continuity and radical change. European Law Blog. https://europeanlawblog.eu/2017/01/12/tele2-sverige-ab-and-watson-et-al-continuity-and-radical-change/

Ojanen T (2014) Privacy is more than just a seven-letter word: The Court of Justice of the European Union Sets Constitutional Limits on Mass Surveillance Court of Justice of the European Union, Decision of 8 April 2014 in Joined Cases C-293/12 and C-594/12, Digital Rights Ireland and Seitlinger and Others. Eur Constit Law Rev 10(3):540

Patrick A (2016) Case Law, CJEU, Tele Sverige/Watson: Who Sees You When You're Sleeping? Who Knows When You're Awake? https://inforrm.org/2016/12/21/case-law-cjeu-tele-sverigewatson-who-sees-you-when-youre-sleeping-who-knows-when-youre-awake-angela-patrick/

Pederson A, Udsen H, Jakobsen SS (2018) Data retention in Europe – the Tele 2 case and beyond. Int Data Priv Law 8(2):160–174

Poli S (2010) The legal basis of internal market measures with a security dimension. Comment on Case C-301/06 of 10/02/2009, Ireland v. Parliament/Council. Eur Constit Law Rev 6 (1):137–157

Privacy International, National Data Retention Laws Since the CJEU's Tele-2/Watson judgment. A Concerning State of Play for the Right to Privacy in Europe, September 2017

Rauhofer J, Mac Sithigh D (2014) The data retention directive never existed. SCRIPTed 11(1):126

Report from the Commission to the Council and the European Parliament – Evaluation Report on the Data Retention Directive (Directive 2006/24/EC) Brussels, 18.4.2011 COM(2011) 225 final

Takatsuki Y (2017) The Tele2/Watson Case: what are the key takeaways?... and what is to become of the New Investigatory Powers Act? http://privacylawblog.fieldfisher.com/2017/the-tele2watson-case-what-are-the-key-takeaways-and-what-is-to-become-of-the-new-investigatory-powers-act/

Tracol X (2014) Legislative genesis and judicial death of a directive: the European Court of Justice invalidated the data retention directive (2006/24/EC) thereby creating a sustained period of legal uncertainty about the validity of national laws which enacted it. Comput Law Secur Rev 30 (6):736–746

Tracol X (2017) The judgment of the Grand Chamber dated 21 December 2016 in the two joint Tele2 Sverige and Watson cases: the need for a harmonised legal framework on the retention of data at EU level. Comput Law Secur Rev 33(4):541–552

Väljataga A (2017) CJEU Declares General Data Retention Unlawful in Tele2 Sverige. NATO Cooperative Cyber Defence Centre of Excellence. https://ccdcoe.org/cjeu-declares-general-data-retention-unlawful-tele2-sverige.html
Vedaschi A, Lubello V (2015) Data retention and its implications for the fundamental right to privacy. Tilburg Law Rev 20:14–34
Woods AK (2016) Implications of the EU's Data Retention Ruling. Lawfareblog. https://www.lawfareblog.com/implications-eus-data-retention-ruling

Freedom of Communication and Data Retention in Judgments of the European Court of Human Rights

Maciej Górski

Abstract This article attempts to analyse how the understanding of the universal freedom of communication expressed in the European Convention on Human Rights (ECHR) has been changing in the context of continuous technological progress. Development of both communication tools and communication itself was a serious challenge for the European Court of Human Rights (ECtHR). Its task was to interpret the provisions of the ECHR in a way that, on one hand, would consider new technological circumstances, and on the other, would guarantee full exercise of freedoms provided for by the ECHR. For this purpose, the article contains an overview of the most important judgments of the ECtHR, in which judges pertained not only to new ways and tools of communication, but also to other functions it fulfils. The text also addresses the problem of potential misuse of technology development in the surveillance by state authorities. Attention was also paid to legal guarantees of freedom of communication, which should assist similar development of surveillance tools. Finally, an attempt was made to forecast in which direction the case law of the Court will follow in the coming years and how the technology development will affect it.

1 Freedom of Communication According to the ECtHR

One of key tasks of the European Court of Human Rights (ECtHR) as an international judicial body—added to its basic adjudication activity involving examination of application lodges—is the interpretation of notions that are of material importance from the point of view of the ECtHR's material competence. Due to the structure and the manner of formulating the Convention for the Protection of Human Rights and Fundamental Freedoms (ECHR), some of freedoms and rights included therein require special judicial activity from the ECtHR.

M. Górski (✉)
Lech Kaczynski National School of Public Administration, Warsaw, Poland

M. Zubik et al. (eds.), *European Constitutional Courts towards Data Retention Laws*, Law, Governance and Technology Series 45,
https://doi.org/10.1007/978-3-030-57189-4_2

The role of the ECtHR with respect to interpretation seems especially important in case of defining the scope of freedoms and rights, the way of exercising which might change significantly together with the technology development. The ECHR had been opened for signature on 10 November 1950, and after obtaining ten ratifications, it came into force on 3 September 1953. Since then, its key parts have remained unchanged, while ECtHR judges were responsible for adjusting their application to changing circumstances. One of the examples of their interpretational endeavours is the evolution of the meaning of freedom of communication.

Freedom of communication is expressed in Article 8 of the ECHR, according to which "Everyone has the right to respect for his private and family life, his home and his correspondence. There shall be no interference by a public authority with the exercise of this right except such as is in accordance with the law and is necessary in a democratic society in the interests of national security, public safety or the economic well-being of the country, for the prevention of disorder or crime, for the protection of health or morals, or for the protection of the rights and freedoms of others."[1]

In the ECHR, the correspondence is broadly understood as communication in various forms to establish contacts with other specifically identified persons, using writing or technical means.[2] In the development of the case law of the ECtHR in this respect, the aforementioned essence of understanding of communication remained, and as a rule, unchanged. However, considering the technology development resulting in a growth in the number and popularisation of tools used in communication, the judges in each case deliberated whether the right to freedom of communication, guaranteed in the ECHR, applies in the particular case.

2 *Klass and Others v. Germany*: Landmark ECtHR Judgment for the Analogue Era

The first judgment of the ECtHR of the crucial importance for the then and the present understanding of freedom of communication was the judgment in the case of *Klass and others v. Germany*.[3] Although it was issued more than 40 years ago, it still retains its precedential character. In this judgment, the ECtHR presented various hypotheses that constituted the base for formulation of the scope of protection of freedom and secret of communication within the meaning of the ECHR. It should be emphasised that the value of the judgment is universal, because based thereon, the ECtHR referred to various issues being basic subjects of its analysis, such as: the

[1]Convention for the Protection of Human Rights and Fundamental Freedoms of 4 November 1950.

[2]Decision of the European Commission of Human Rights of 13 May 1982, *X and Y v. Belgium*, Application No. 8962/80.

[3]Judgment of the European Court of Human Rights of 6 September 1978, *Klass and others v. Germany*, Application No. 5029/71.

definition of a victim of a violation of the ECHR entitled to bring an application, permitted scope of an interference with the right to privacy or the right to effective remedies to protect rights provided for in the ECHR.[4]

The judgment referred to German legislation authorising intelligence service to apply secret measures to obtain information. This is because the special legal situation of Germany after the Second World War was also reflected in the legislation on the surveillance of mail, post and telecommunications. Occupying powers were responsible for this surveillance. As regards the Federal Republic of Germany, neither the entry into force on 24 May 1949 of the Basic Law nor the termination of the occupation regime in 1955 altered this situation.[5] Legal situation in this respect was adjusted not before 24 June 1968, when the Parliament of the Federal Republic of Germany passed new regulations governing the scope of permitted interference by the state with the right to secrecy of the mail.

The law passed assumed that the person, against whom the measures to control mail were ordered, shall not be notified thereof. The mechanism for the verification of the measures taken under the law involved imposing on the competent minister the duty to submit, at least once every six months, a report on the application of the law to the commission appointed by Bundestag.[6]

In the opinion of the applicants, solutions provided by the law were insufficient, and they based their application to the European Commission of Human Rights on the charge that the law allowed applying secret measures without simultaneous obligation of state authorities to subsequently notify persons concerned thereof.

The key issue that must be resolved in the case in question by the ECtHR was whether the individual might effectively claim judicial protection without proving being a victim of secret surveillance. On one hand, the ECtHR emphasised that provisions of the ECHR do not institute for applicants a kind of *actio popularis* and do not allow for *in abstracto* interpretation thereof. However, on the other hand, it must consider the risk of an individual being deprived of the opportunity of lodging such an application because, owing to the specifics of the secret measures, the victim cannot prove that they were actually applied against him.

In the deliberations, the ECtHR concluded that ensuring some possibility of having access to the Commission and submitting application by the individual is of crucial importance. If this were not so, the efficiency of the ECHR's enforcement machinery would be materially weakened. To ensure effective functioning of the protection of the rights granted therein, the ECtHR concluded that an individual may, under certain conditions, claim to be the victim of a violation occasioned by the

---

[4]Shelton and Carozza (2008), p. 292; Brouwer (2008), p. 166.

[5]Judgment of the European Court of Human Rights of 6 September 1978, *Klass and others v. Germany*, Application No. 5029/71, para. 14.

[6]In addition, the law assumed a more immediate control measure involving providing the commission with an account of the operational measures ordered. The commission decided *ex officio* or on application by an interested person, on both the legality and the necessity of the measures in question. If it declared any measures to be illegal or unnecessary, the minister was obliged to terminate them immediately.

mere existence of secret measures or of legislation permitting secret measures, without having to allege that such measures were in fact applied to him. The relevant conditions specified by the ECtHR included: indicating a violation of rights protected by the ECHR, the secret character of the measures taken, and the connection between the applicant and the measure taken.[7]

In the case in question, authorities of the Federal Republic of Germany did not question the conclusion that the application of regulations allowing taking secret surveillance measures constitutes interference with the right to privacy guaranteed by Article 8 of the ECHR. In its considerations, the ECtHR significantly extended the aforementioned supposition, by indicating that: "(. . .) in the mere existence of the legislation itself there is involved, for all those to whom the legislation could be applied, a menace of surveillance; this menace necessarily strikes at freedom of communication between users of the postal and telecommunication services and thereby constitutes an 'interference by a public authority' with the exercise of the applicants' right to respect for private and family life and for correspondence."[8]

In the *Klass* case, the influence of the technology development on the understanding of freedom of communication and mail was also noticed—by concluding that although telephone conversations are not expressly mentioned in paragraph 1 of Article 8, it should be considered that such conversations are covered by the notions of "private life" and "correspondence" referred to by this provision.[9] More importantly, this catalogue will systematically grow together with the development of the ECtHR case law pertaining to freedom of communication.

Although ultimately the judges did not share the position of applicants and unanimously found no breach of Article 8 of the ECHR, just due to recognising the application as admissible, started the evolution of the notion of "freedom of communication" and "correspondence", emphasising the importance of judicial control of the use of secret measures and recognising that their application is sometimes necessary in a democratic societies, the judgment in the case of *Klass and others v. Germany* is considered one of the most significant and meaningful issued judgments in this matter by the ECtHR.[10]

---

[7]Judgment of the European Court of Human Rights of 6 September 1978, *Klass and others v. Germany*, Application No. 5029/71, para. 34.

[8]Judgment of the European Court of Human Rights of 6 Sept 1978, *Klass and others v. Germany*, Application No. 5029/71, para. 41.

[9]Judgment of the European Court of Human Rights of 6 Sept 1978, *Klass and others v. Germany*, Application No. 5029/71. para. 41.

[10]Petaux (2009), p. 164; Lambert Abdelgawad and Weber (2008), p. 123; Christakis (2016), p. 153.

3 Technology Perspective Pertaining to the Prison System

When presenting the evolution of the notion of the freedom of communication in its technological aspect, one should also refer to several ECtHR judgments on prisoners' mail that significantly affected the notion in question. The judgment of 25 March 1983 in the case of *Silver and others v. the United Kingdom*[11] is one of judgments widely commented in the doctrine and important in the context of further line of judgments of the ECtHR. The case originated in a few applications lodged by persons detained in prison (one of these persons was at liberty) complaining about prison authorities controlling their mail. Applicants claimed that an unjustified interference with the right to respect for their correspondence took place. In this case, the ECtHR concluded that "some measure of control over prisoners' correspondence is called for and is not of itself incompatible with the ECHR, having regard to the ordinary and reasonable requirements of imprisonment."[12]

It should be emphasised that in subsequent judgments, in line with the aforementioned approach, the ECtHR admitted that: "(...) it may be necessary to monitor detainees' contacts with the outside world, including contacts by telephone, but the rules applied should afford appropriate protection against arbitrary interference by national authorities with the detainee's rights".[13] In another judgment, the judges presented the following justification for the detailed and prudent assessment of control applied: "In assessing the permissible extent of such control in general, the fact that the opportunity to write and to receive letters is sometimes the prisoner's only link with the outside world should, however, not be overlooked."[14] Additionally, they noted that prisoners should be provided with certain guarantees related to prison authorities monitoring their correspondence: "Where domestic law allows interference, it has to offer certain protection preventing power abuse (...)."[15]

In its extensive case law pertaining to this issue, the ECtHR also criticised preventing correspondence by refusal to supply the prisoner with writing materials,[16] hindering contacts between prisoners and lawyers[17] and the court within the

[11]Judgment of the European Court of Human Rights of 25 March 1983, *Silver and others v. the United Kingdom*, Application Nos. 5947/72, 6205/73, 7052/75, 7061/75, 7107/75, 7113/75, 7136/75.

[12]Judgment of the European Court of Human Rights of 25 March 1983, para. 98.

[13]Judgment of the European Court of Human Rights of 27 April 2004, *Doerga v. The Netherlands*, Application No. 50210/99, para. 53.

[14]Judgment of the European Court of Human Rights of 25 March 1992, *Campbell v. the United Kingdom*, Application No. 13590/88, para. 45.

[15]Judgment of the European Court of Human Rights of 21 October 1996, *Calogero Diana v. the United Kingdom*, Application No. 15211/89, paras. 32–33.

[16]Judgment of the European Court of Human Rights of 3 June 2003, *Cotleţ v. Romania*, Application No. 38565/97, para. 59 and para. 65.

[17]Judgment of the European Court of Human Rights of 20 June 1988, *Schöneberger and Durmaz v. Switzerland*, Application No. 11368/85, paras. 28–29.

meaning of the ECtHR,[18] with journalists,[19] with a doctor[20] or with other entities, such as an ombudsman[21] and NGOs.[22]

In one of the aforementioned judgments, the ECtHR concluded that to effectively exercise rights guaranteed in Article 8 of the ECHR, prison authorities are not only expected to refrain from certain behaviour, but are also expected to implement certain steps to enable the prisoners to effectively exercise their right to communicate. The position of the ECtHR was also repeated in other situations, not related to the prison system.[23]

4 Telephone Tapping

Although in accordance with the traditional understanding of Article 8, letters (written documents) were considered the ordinary form of correspondence, the ECtHR case law that developed over decades has considered the technology progress in this area. In various judgments issued in this respect, the judges not only noticed that communication based on traditional letters is more and more frequently replaced by telephones, but also observed more sophisticated and advanced methods of interference with private life of individuals. For that reason, the development of the case law line has two directions. On one hand, it was examined whether new technical forms of communication are subject to protection under Article 8, and on another hand, attempts were made to reconcile justified needs of authorities to take secret surveillance measures with the right to freedom of communication, to which individuals are entitled.

The main group of judgments of the ECtHR issued before the digital revolution focused on telephone communication and they provided the basis for the standards of freedom of communication formulated at that time. In addition to the judgment in the case of *Klass and others v. Germany*, the judgment in the case of *Malone v. the*

---

[18]Judgment of the European Court of Human Rights of 23 September 1998, *Petra v. Romania*, Application No. 27273/95, para. 37.

[19]Judgment of the European Court of Human Rights of 5 December 2006, *Fazil Ahmet Tamer v. Turkey*, Application No. 6289/02, para. 53.

[20]Judgment of the European Court of Human Rights of 2 June 2009, *Szuluk v. the United Kingdom*, Application No. 36936/05, paras. 49–53.

[21]Judgment of the European Court of Human Rights of 4 July 2000, *Niedbała v. Poland*, Application No. 27915/95, para. 81.

[22]Judgment of the European Court of Human Rights of 24 February 2005, *Jankauskas v. Lithuania*, Application No. 59304/00.

[23]Judgment of the European Court of Human Rights of 18 April 2006, *Chadimová v. the Czech Republic*, Application No. 50073/99, para. 146; Decision of the European Court of Human Rights on admissibility of the application of 16 June 2009, *Benediktsdóttir v. Iceland*, Application No. 38079/06.

United Kingdom of 2 August 1984[24] was one of judgments that significantly affected the case law line.

The applicant was an antique dealer in the United Kingdom, and in March 1977, he was charged with offences relating to dishonest handling of stolen goods. During the trial, it emerged that one of his telephone conversations was intercepted. After being acquitted, Malone, in civil proceedings ineffectively soughed from the police the declaration to the effect that tapping of conversations on his telephone lines was unlawful. When the case was submitted to the ECtHR, the judges had to answer the question whether there was an unauthorized interference by public authorities with the right protected by Article 8, and they also had to assess how "metering" of telephone calls affects freedom of communication. The process known as "metering" involves the use of a mechanism that registers the numbers dialled on a particular telephone and the time and duration of each call.[25]

The ECtHR confirmed its previous position, in accordance to which telephone conversations are covered by the notions of "private life" and "correspondence" within the meaning of Article 8. Additionally, it concluded that "the existence (...) of laws and practices which permit and establish a system for effecting secret surveillance of communications amounted in itself to an interference."[26] British legislation was considered too general and imprecise to consider it as providing sufficient basis for tapping of telephone conversations.

The judges also concluded that: "The records of metering contain information, in particular the numbers dialled, which is an integral element in the communications made by telephone. Consequently, release of that information without the consent of the subscriber amounts to an interference with a right guaranteed by Article 8".[27] Consequently, the ECtHR has noticed new methods of interference, which the authorities began to use, and responded thereto, by extending legal protection available to individuals based on Article 8.

In 1990, the ECtHR issued judgments in two similar cases against France, pertaining to telephone tapping ordered by a court, a tool used in relation to pending proceedings.[28] Based on both these cases, the judges summarised judgments issued until that time and prepared a catalogue of minimum guarantees that must be included in the law providing a legal basis for the use of telephone tapping in order not to consider it contrary to the ECHR. The following was, *inter alia*, indicated: categories of people liable to have their telephones tapped by judicial

---

[24]Judgment of the European Court of Human Rights of 2 August 1984, *Malone v. the United Kingdom*, Application No. 8691/79.

[25]Rainey et al. (2017), p. 413.

[26]Judgment of the European Court of Human Rights of 2 August 1984, *Malone v. the United Kingdom*, Application No. 8691/79, para. 64.

[27]Judgment of the European Court of Human Rights of 2 Aug 1984, *Malone v. the United Kingdom*, Application No. 8691/79, para. 84.

[28]Judgment of the European Court of Human Rights of 24 April 1990, *Kruslin v. France*, Application No. 11801/85; Judgment of the European Court of Human Rights of 24 April 1990, *Huvig v. France*, Application No. 11105/84.

order; the nature of the offences which may give rise to such an order; maximum duration of the application of this control measure; procedure for drawing up the summary reports containing intercepted conversations; the precautions to be taken to communicate the recordings intact and in their entirety for possible inspection by the judge and by the defence; and the circumstances in which recordings may or must be erased or the tapes be destroyed, particularly where an accused has been discharged by an investigating judge or acquitted by a court.[29]

Another interesting issue was resolved by the ECtHR on 25 March 1998, in the judgment in the case of *Kopp v. Switzerland.* The applicant was a lawyer practicing in Zurich, and his wife was a member of the Swiss government fulfilling the function of the head of the department of justice and police. She was under suspicion of disclosing to her husband confidential information that was subsequently used by one of his clients. As a result of these suspicions, she was obliged to resign. Due to the aforementioned suspicion, the President of the Indictment Division of the Federal Court allowed an application by the Federal Public Prosecutor for monitoring of telephone lines allocated to the office of Mr Kopp, except for telephone conversation with the participation of Kopp as a lawyer. After having concluded that the suspicions against the applicant's wife were unfounded, monitoring of telephone conversation was discontinued, recordings were destroyed, and Mr Kopp was notified that his telephone lines were tapped.

In the application to the European Commission of Human Rights, Mr Kopp submitted that the interception of his telephone communications had breached his right to respect for his private life and correspondence. The most interesting element of this case was the issue of effectiveness of protection of legal professional privilege when a lawyer is being monitored as a third party, and the conversation content is not directly covered by the scope of professional privilege. Judges of the ECtHR also had reservations about the fact that the duty to separate materials specifically connected with a lawyer's work, i.e. the ones that could not have been recorded, was assigned to an official of the Post Office's legal department, without supervision by an independent judge. It was concluded that Swiss law did not indicate with sufficient clarity the scope and manner of exercise of the authorities' discretion in the matter, and that there had therefore been a breach of Article 8 of the ECHR.

In this case, the ECtHR also referred to challenges to the freedom of communication resulting from the technology development. The recommendation formulated in judgments in the case of *Kruslin v. France* and *Hudvig v. France* was repeated, in accordance to which: "It is essential to have clear, detailed rules on the subject, especially as the technology available for use is continually becoming more sophisticated."[30] In this context, reflections presented by the judge Louis-Edmund Pettit in

[29]Judgment of the European Court of Human Rights of 24 April 1990, *Kruslin v. France*, Application No. 11801/85, paras. 26–27; Judgment of the European Court of Human Rights of 24 April 1990, *Huvig v. France*, Application No. 11105/84, paras. 54–55.

[30]Judgment of the European Court of Human Rights of 25 March 1998, *Kopp v. Switzerland*, Application No. 23224/94, para. 72.

his concurring opinion, in which he agreed with the verdict, but proposed different arguments, seem interesting. Judge Pettiti admitted that "It is a regrettable fact that State, para-State and private bodies are making increasing use of the interception of telephone and other communications for various purposes."[31] He also stated that "States (...) abuse the concepts of official secrets and secrecy in the interests of national security. Where necessary, they distort the meaning and nature of that term," and described the irresponsible practices of the people running the relevant state services responsible for the communication monitoring as "a sign of the decadence of the democracies and erosion of the meaning of human dignity."[32]

The ECtHR case law line presented in the aforementioned judgments was maintained by judges in judgments issued in last years, among which the following judgments should be, *inter alia*, referred to: *Dragojević v. Croatia*,[33] *R.E. v. the United Kingdom*[34] or *Mustafa Sezrin Tanrikulu v. Turkey*.[35]

5 Other Communication Means

In the development of its case law, the ECtHR often had to answer the question whether new communication tools and platforms are covered by the protection granted by Article 8 of the ECHR. In addition to telephone conversations, other less popular communication methods were also examined, such as, *inter alia*, in the case of *Taylor-Sabori v. the United Kingdom*, where the judges examined the issue of communication with a pager. The issue pertained to the police intercepting messages sent to the pager of the applicant, who was suspected, arrested and ultimately convicted and sentenced for importation and sale of drugs on the territory of the United Kingdom.

The applicant complained that the interception by the police of messages on his pager constituted the interference with the right to privacy and a violation of Article 8 of the ECHR. The ECtHR noted that at that time, in the United Kingdom, there existed no statutory system to regulate the interception of pager messages. It

---

[31]Concurring opinion to the Judgment of the European Court of Human Rights of 25 March 1998, *Kopp v. Switzerland*, Application No. 23224/94.

[32]Concurring opinion to the Judgment of the European Court of Human Rights of 25 March 1998, *Kopp v. Switzerland*, Application No. 23224/94.

[33]Judgment of the European Court of Human Rights of 15 January 2015, *Dragojević v. Croatia*, Application No. 68955/11.

[34]Judgment of the European Court of Human Rights of 27 October 2015, *R.E. v. the United Kingdom*, Application No. 62498/11.

[35]Judgment of the European Court of Human Rights of 18 July 2017, *Mustafa Sezgin Tanrikulu v. Turkey*, Application No. 27473/06.

concluded that there had been a violation of Article 8 of the ECHR, thus admitting that freedom of communication also applies to communication with a pager.[36]

Based on the decision of 27 June 1994 of the European Commission of Human Rights in the case of *Christie v. the United Kingdom*, communication via telex[37] was also classified as covered by the production under Article 8.

The judges were of a similar opinion about the issue of sending letters by telefax, which was assessed by the ECtHR in the judgment of 16 December 1992 in the case of *Niemietz v. Germany*.[38]

The issue of radio communications, examined by the Commission and the ECtHR in the decision of 13 May 1982 in the case of *X and Y v. Belgium* and in the judgment of 16 December 1997 in the case of *Camenzind v. Switzerland*, respectively, was also resolved in the same way. However, it should be added that communication on frequencies available to third parties was treated in a different way.[39]

6 Technology Development as a Challenge to the ECtHR

The technology development is used not only by citizens, but also by entities authorised by public authorities, responsible for communication monitoring and recording, that systematically develop and improve the methods used.

The ECtHR referred to one of the examples of this phenomena in the decision of 29 June 2006 in the case of *Weber and Saravia v. Germany*. The first applicant was a German journalist investigating drug and arms trafficking and money laundering. To carry out her investigations, she regularly travelled to South America. The second applicant was an employee of Montevideo City Council. They both communicated using a satellite phone.

The issue examined pertained to so-called strategic monitoring of telecommunications. In this application, the applicants noted that "(. . .) technological progress had made it possible to intercept telecommunications everywhere in the world and to collect personal data. Numerous telecommunications could be monitored, in the absence of any concrete suspicions, with the aid of catchwords which remained secret".[40] They drew attention to the practice of services involving monitoring of a

[36]Judgment of the European Court of Human Rights of 22 October 2002, *Taylor-Sabori v. the United Kingdom*, Application No. 47114/99.

[37]Decision of the European Commission of Human Rights on admissibility of the application of 27 June 1994, *Christie v. the United Kingdom*, Application No. 21482/93.

[38]Judgment of the European Court of Human Rights of 16 December 1992, *Niemietz v. Germany*, Application No. 13710/88.

[39]Decision of the European Commission of Human Rights on admissibility of the application of 27 February 1994, *B.C. v. Switzerland*, Application No. 21353/93.

[40]Decision of the European Court of Human Rights on admissibility of the application of 29 June 2006, *Weber and Saravia v. Germany*, Application No. 54934/00.

large number of messages sent via various messengers, by using word filters selecting catchwords that might be alarming from the point of view of that services.[41]

When issuing the decision in this case, the ECtHR focused on the issue of the law's foreseeability. It concluded that "(...) foreseeability in the special context of secret measures of surveillance, such as the interception of communications, cannot mean that an individual should be able to foresee when the authorities are likely to intercept his communications so that he can adapt his conduct accordingly. However, especially where a power vested in the executive is exercised in secret, the risks of arbitrariness are evident."[42] The judges emphasised the importance of sufficient clarity of the domestic law in such a situation that "(...) must be sufficiently clear in its terms to give citizens an adequate indication as to the circumstances in which and the conditions on which public authorities are empowered to resort to any such measures."[43] In the case in question, they concluded that adequate and effective guarantees against abuses of the state's monitoring powers existed, and the application was considered ill-founded.

Increasing state capabilities with respect to communication monitoring are without doubt related to greater ability to collect data obtained in this way. The ECtHR emphasised the importance of legislation ensuring proper standards in this respect in the judgment in the case of *Liberty and others v. the United Kingdom* of 1 July 2008. The case pertained to a special unit of the British Ministry of Defence intercepting communications of civil liberties' organisations. The judges confirmed that requirements pertaining to surveillance measures against individual presented in the judgment in the case of *Kruslin v. France* and subsequently often repeated should also be respected within the framework of the generalised strategic monitoring, and the procedure for testing, disclosure, storing and destroying the collected material should be presented in a form accessible to the general public.[44]

A different approach was presented in the case of the Centr*um för rättvisa v. Sweden*. The complaint, lodged by a law firm acting in the public interest, concerned provisions allowing the services to collect data on users of mobile phones and Internet without prior notification on massive scale. The complained provisions did not provide for the possibility of appeal of a person who suspected that he was subject of surveillance. The judges found that the questioned act fulfilled the condition of proportionality, providing sufficient guarantees to prevent the risk of arbitrariness. Moreover, the ECtHR considered that to counteract terrorism, the state must have some discretion in shaping regulations concerning operational control.

---

[41]St Vincent (2017), p. 372.

[42]Decision of the European Court of Human Rights on admissibility of the application of 29 June 2006, *Weber and Saravia v. Germany*, Application No. 54934/00, para. 93.

[43]Decision of the European Court of Human Rights on admissibility of the application of 29 June 2006, *Weber and Saravia v. Germany*, Application No. 54934/00, para. 93.

[44]Judgment of the European Court of Human Rights of 1 July 2008, *Liberty and others v. the United Kingdom*, Application No. 58243/00.

The ECtHR pointed out that the provisions included several guarantees restricting the freedom of services in the application of control. For the application of control measures consent must have been expressed by a court composed of members elected for four-year terms. It could only be applied to data crossing national borders and thus it could not apply to communications carried out only in Sweden. In addition, it could last six months maximally and its extension required a re-examination of the legitimacy of its conduct. Moreover, potential victim was entitled to a wide range of possible complaints, among others to the Minister of Justice, the parliamentary human rights Ombudsman and to the personal data inspector. The ECtHR stressed that the law regulating the surveillance system was sufficiently precise and its interference with the right to privacy was justified in a democratic society, especially considering the state's responsibilities in the area of national security in the context of the current terrorist threat and cross-border organised crime.[45]

7 Freedom of Communication in the Digital Era

The transfer of a significant part of communication to the Internet is one of the consequences of the technology development. Although the technological progress in the context of the understanding of freedom of communication always posed a serious interpretational challenge to the ECtHR, in the digital era it is becoming even more demanding. This is because it requires the judges to analyse the essence of freedom in conditions completely different from those in which the ECHR guaranteeing this freedom was developed. The need to ensure the effective use of rights in digital reality requires the judges to apply a completely different perspective when looking at the communication problem. This interpretation effort is reflected in judgments issued by the ECtHR concerning communication via digital tools.

The judgment of the ECtHR in the case of *Copland v. the United Kingdom* was an interesting judgment from the point of view of the relationship between the technology development and freedom of communication, since it pertained to a few modern forms of communications at the same time. Lynette Copland was employed by a British college, and she complained of the alleged monitoring of her activities on the Internet (dates and times of the visits to the websites), electronic correspondence and usage of the telephone, involving gathering information on the dates and times of the calls, and their length and cost.

The ECtHR confirmed that e-mails sent from work should be protected under Article 8, as should information derived from the monitoring of the employee's personal Internet usage. Additionally, the judges pointed out that the applicant had been given no warning that her calls would be liable to monitoring, therefore she had a reasonable expectation as to the privacy of calls made from her work telephone.

[45] Judgement of the European Court of Human Rights of 19 June 2018, Application No. 35252/08.

The same expectation should apply in relation to the applicant's e-mail and Internet usage.[46]

Similar facts were assessed by the ECtHR in the case of *Bărbulescu v. Romania*. In this case, the judges assessed the issue of the employee's use of the Internet at the workplace. The applicant was dismissed by his employer because of using, for his private purposes, during working hours and in the workplace, the Internet provided by the employer, which was an infringement of the company's internal regulations. The employer monitored, for some time, the applicant's communications via the instant messaging account that was created by the applicant at the request of his superiors, and was to be used to respond to clients' requests and inquiries. The instant messaging account monitoring showed that the applicant used it to exchange messages with third parties, related to personal matters.

On 12 January 2016, the ECtHR issued the judgment stating that there had been no violation of Article 8. In the judgment, it was observed that there were no grounds to conclude that national authorities failed to strike a fair balance between the interests of the individual guaranteed by Article 8 of the ECHR and interests of the employer.[47] The applicant, who was unsatisfied with this judgment, requested the referral of the case to the Grand Chamber, which took place on 6 June 2016.

The Grand Chamber of the ECtHR took a different position. In the judgment of 5 September 2017, the judges observe that the usage of the Internet instant messaging service is just one of the forms of communication subject to protection under Article 8, even if it takes place using an employer's computer.[48] They also noted that the domestic proceedings failed to determine whether the applicant had been notified by the employer in advance of the possibility to monitor his communications via the instant messaging service. National authorities also disregarded the fact that the applicant had not been notified of the scope and nature of monitoring measures applied. In addition, it was not explained whether the employer had legitimate reasons to implement monitoring procedures and whether the aim pursued by the employer could have been achieved by less intrusive methods.

Considering the omissions found in the domestic proceedings, the judges concluded that the domestic authorities had failed to ensure sufficient protection of the applicant's right to respect for his private life and correspondence, and consequently, they failed to strike a fair balance between the applicant's rights and the interests of his employer, which resulted in a violation of Article 8 of the ECHR.

The ECtHR also examines the cases in which the beneficiaries of changes resulting from the digital revolution are the states that use the technology progress to improve their surveillance structures.

---

[46]Judgment of the European Court of Human Rights of 3 April 2007, *Copland v. the United Kingdom*, Application No. 62617/00, paras. 41–42.

[47]Judgment of the European Court of Human Rights of 12 January 2016, *Bărbulescu v. Romania*, Application No. 61496/08, paras. 62–63.

[48]Judgment of the European Court of Human Rights of 5 September 2017, *Bărbulescu v. Romania*, Application No. 61496/08, paras. 74–75.

In one of these cases, the applicant, who was the editor-in-chief of a publishing company and the chairperson of a non-governmental organisation promoting the independence of the media and respect for journalists' rights, claimed that the Russian law requires the mobile network operators to install equipment that permitted the responsible services to intercept telephone communications without prior judicial authorisation.[49,50] Roman Zakharov complained, *inter alia*, of violation of the right to respect for private life and lack of proper guarantees in the Russian law that would ensure protection against unauthorised recording of telephone calls by services. This case was exceptional, *inter alia*, due to the applicant's suggestion that the interference with his rights was not because of the application of any special measures against him, but because of the mere existence of the legislation that allowed a system of secret interception of communications and the risk of interception of his communications.

In its deliberations, the ECtHR emphasised the importance of subsequent notification once surveillance had been ceased, while admitting that such notification cannot be always provided. The ECtHR observed that such notification would be undesirable where it might well jeopardise the purpose of the surveillance and reveal the working methods of the intelligence services or allow identification of their agents. However, where the grounds do not exist, the person considered should be directly provided with the information once surveillance has ceased.[51]

The judges also concluded that the applicant is entitled to claim to be the victim of a violation of the ECHR, although he is not able to prove that he had been subject to a concrete measure of surveillance. They pointed out that it is justified in the situation where the contested legislation institutes a system of surveillance allowing monitoring of telephone calls of any user of domestic mobile telephone network without a need to notify this user thereof, and where the national legislation does not provide for effective measures of appeal for persons who suspect that they were subjected to secret surveillance.

Consequently, the ECtHR admitted that in certain circumstances the applicant would be released from the duty to prove that his or her special situation made it more likely that secret surveillance measures had been applied to him or her. Additionally, it noted that considering the legal regulations binding in Russia, "The effectiveness of the remedies is undermined by the absence of notification at any point of interceptions, or adequate access to documents relating to interceptions."[52]

---

[49]To supplement the aforementioned deliberations, it is worthwhile to note that this refers to the SORM IT system used by the Federal Security Service of the Russian Federation to monitor telephone and Internet activity. Experts in the area compare it to the global electronic surveillance network, Echelon.

[50]Beknazar (2004), p. 485.

[51]Judgment of the European Court of Human Rights of 4 December 2015, *Zakharov v. Russia*, Application No. 47143/06, para. 287.

[52]Judgment of the European Court of Human Rights of 4 December 2015, *Zakharov v. Russia*, Application No. 47143/06, para. 302.

Some representatives of the doctrine considered the judgment in the case of *Zakharov v. Russia* a continuation of the jurisprudential approach proposed in the judgment of 6 October 2015 issued by the Court of Justice of the European Union in the case of *Maximillian Schrems v. Data Protection Commissioner*.[53] It had been issued less than two months earlier and the CJEU judges had concluded therein that the data of European Internet users are not sufficiently protected in the United States from access by United States authorities, and therefore it is necessary to declare the Safe Harbor Agreement between the USA and the EU invalid.[54]

The crucial importance of the judgment in the case of *Zakharov v. Russia* was also recognised by editors of Oxford University Press, who considered it one of top ten developments in international law in 2015.[55]

Less than one month after issuing this judgment, judges of the ECtHR were again resolving a dispute related to surveillance and protection against abuse required by the law.

The application pertained to the legislation based on which an anti-terrorism task force was established within the structures of the police. This task force was given wide prerogatives including, *inter alia*, secret house search and surveillance with recording, opening of letters and parcels, as well as checking and recording the contents of electronic or computerised communications, all this without the consent of the persons concerned.

Máté Szabó and Beatrix Vissy, employees of the Hungarian non-governmental organisation, founded their application to the ECtHR on the alleged violation of Article 8 involving potential application against them of unjustified and disproportionate measures interfering with the rights to freedom of communication and privacy of correspondence. Additionally, they noted that the Hungarian law does not include proper guarantees protecting individual against abuse of power in this respect. They also pointed out that employment with a watchdog organisation, voicing criticism of the government, exposes them to special risk of being subjected to surveillance.

The ECtHR observed that affiliation with a watchdog organisation does not fall within the grounds listed in the law, justifying subjecting a member of such an organisation to surveillance. However, it concluded that under these provisions such measures can be applied against any person within Hungary if their application is deemed useful in preventing threats foreseen by the law. It also emphasised that in the Court's judgments, work for a watchdog organisation has been found similar, in some ways, to those of journalists, as a result of which any fear of being subjected to secret surveillance might have an impact on such activities.[56]

---

[53]Pollicino and Bassini (2016), p. 260.

[54]Judgment of the Court of Justice of the European Union of 6 October 2015, *Maximillian Schrems v. Data Protection Commissioner*, Case No. C-362/14.

[55]Alstein (2016).

[56]Judgment of the European Court of Human Rights of 12 January 2016, *Szabó and Vissy v. Hungary*, Application No. 37138/14, para. 38.

Judges again noted the importance of the technology development in the context of the manner and scope of interference by the services. They also pointed out that the similar development of guarantees provided for by the law should be a proper response to this process: "Given the technological advances since the *Klass and others* case, the potential interferences with email, mobile phone and Internet services as well as those of mass surveillance attract the ECHR protection of private life even more acutely."[57]

The aforementioned thought was developed in further deliberations, in which the position of the ECtHR on this issue was explained as follows: "(...) it is a natural consequence of the forms taken by present-day terrorism that governments resort to cutting-edge technologies in pre-empting such attacks, including the massive monitoring of communications susceptible to containing indications of impending incidents. The techniques applied in such monitoring operations have demonstrated a remarkable progress in recent years and reached a level of sophistication which is hardly conceivable for the average citizen (...)."[58] Consequently, the judges concluded that "(...) the Court must scrutinise the question as to whether the development of surveillance methods resulting in masses of data collected has been accompanied by a simultaneous development of legal safeguards securing respect for citizens' ECHR rights."[59] Additionally, they noted that requirements pertaining to communications interception included in the existing legislation should be enhanced, but not based on this case, since the Hungarian system of safeguards appears to fall short even of the previously existing principles.[60] They also emphasised the particular character of the interference based on the application of state-of-the-art technology, due to which "(...) a measure of secret surveillance can be found as being in compliance with the Convention only if it is strictly necessary, as a general consideration, for the safeguarding the democratic institutions and, moreover, if it is strictly necessary, as a particular consideration, for the obtaining of vital intelligence in an individual operation."[61]

[57]Judgment of the European Court of Human Rights of 12 January 2016, *Szabó and Vissy v. Hungary*, Application No. 37138/14, para. 53.

[58]Judgment of the European Court of Human Rights of 12 January 2016, *Szabó and Vissy v. Hungary*, Application No. 37138/14, para. 68.

[59]Judgment of the European Court of Human Rights of 12 January 2016, *Szabó and Vissy v. Hungary*, Application No. 37138/14, para. 68.

[60]Judgment of the European Court of Human Rights of 12 January 2016, *Szabó and Vissy v. Hungary*, Application No. 37138/14, para. 70.

[61]Judgment of the European Court of Human Rights of 12 January 2016, *Szabó and Vissy v. Hungary*, Application No. 37138/14, para. 73.

8 Conclusion

The impact of the technology progress on the understanding of freedom of communication will be one of the most important interpretational challenges to the ECtHR in the future. Development of new communication tools will require the judges to assess, in each case, whether communication via these tools deserves protection under Article 8. However, keeping in mind that digital progress also supports criminals, the main task will be to strike a fair balance between the individual's freedom of communication and the duty of the states to ensure the security of their citizens, while considering that state services also benefit from the digital revolution by using more and more advanced surveillance methods.

The direction of the case law of the ECtHR in this respect cannot be precisely determined, especially because it depends to a large extent on the unpredictable outcomes of the technology development. However, it is very likely that an increasing number of judgments will refer to modern forms of communication, in particular via the Internet, and judicial activity of judges of the ECtHR in this respect will be interesting not only for legal circles, but also for many users of modern technologies. Consequently, it can be expected that this part of the ECtHR case law will be one of the most closely monitored and widely commented, whereas the issue of freedom of communication will be one of the most important jurisprudence issues in the years to come.

References

Alstein M (2016) Top ten developments in international law in 2015. https://blog.oup.com/2016/01/top-ten-developments-international-law-2015/

Beknazar TB (2004) Country report on Russia. In: Walter C, Vöneky S, Röben V, Schorkopf F (eds) Terrorism as challenge for national and international law: security versus liberty? Springer, Berlin, p 485

Brouwer E (2008) Digital borders and real rights. Effective remedies for third-country nationals in the Schengen Information System. Martinus Nijhoff Publishers, Leiden, p 166

Christakis T (2016) The 'margin of appreciation' in the use of exemptions in international law: comparing the ICJ Whaling Judgment and the case law of the ECtHR. In: Fitzmaurice M, Tamada D (eds) Whaling in the Antarctic: significance and implications of the ICJ Judgment, Queen Mary Studies in International Law, p 153

Lambert Abdelgawad E, Weber A (2008) The reception process in Ireland and the United Kingdom. In: Keller H, Stone Sweet A (eds) A Europe of rights: the impact of the ECHR on national legal systems. Oxford University Press, Oxford, p 123

Petaux J (2009) Democracy and human rights for Europe: the Council of Europe's contribution. Council of Europe Publishing, p 164

Pollicino O, Bassini M (2016) Bridge is down, data truck can't get through... a critical view of the Schrems Judgment in the context of European constitutionalism. In: Capaldo GZ (ed) The Global Community. Yearbook of international law and jurisprudence. Oxford University Press, Oxford, p 260

Rainey B, Wicks E, Ovey C (2017) The European Convention on Human Rights. Oxford University Press, Oxford, p 413

Shelton D, Carozza PG (2008) Regional protection of human rights. Oxford University Press, Oxford, p 292

St Vincent S (2017) Preventing the police state: international human rights laws concerning systematic government access to communications held or transmitted by the private sector. In: Cate FH, Dempsey JX (eds) Bulk collection: systematic government access to private-sector data. Oxford University Press, Oxford, p 372

Part II
Data Retention in Judgments of National Constitutional Courts

Data Retention in Austria

Axel Anderl and Alona Klammer

Abstract The chapter deals with the rise and fall of the Data Retention Directive in Austria. Due to the paradigm shift in the principles of data retention, the Directive received a great media attention in Austria even before its adoption at the European level. In the public discussion, the negative opinions and concerns remarkably outweighed the potential possible benefits of implementation of the Directive into Austrian law. Despite the willful postponement of the implementation, the Directive was finally implemented into Austrian law four years and six months after the respective deadline expired. As long as the preparation and actual implementation took, as short was the lifespan of the regulations: Only few months after the new provisions had been issued, they were legally challenged. A preliminary ruling procedure initiated by the Austrian Constitutional Court among others ultimately led to the repeal of the Directive at the Union level. Finally, the 13 Austrian provisions implementing the Directive were also repealed only two years after their entry into force.

1 Implementation of Directive 2006/24/EC in Austria

In Austria, the discussions on the Data Retention Directive (hereafter: the Directive) started even before the Directive was adopted at the European level. Then, they were intensified in preparation of the required implementation into the Austrian domestic law system.[1] The discussion primarily focused on tensions between the Directive and fundamental rights but also the sudden paradigm shift to the previous Telecoms Data Protection Directive 2002/58/EC,[2] which specifically banned the storage of

[1]Feiel (2008), p. 97.

[2]Recital 22 of the Telecoms Data Protection Directive 2002/58/EC.

A. Anderl (✉) · A. Klammer
DORDA Rechtsanwälte GmbH, Vienna, Austria
e-mail: axel.anderl@dorda.at; alona.klammer@dorda.at

M. Zubik et al. (eds.), *European Constitutional Courts towards Data Retention Laws*, Law, Governance and Technology Series 45,
https://doi.org/10.1007/978-3-030-57189-4_3

data. Under the new regime, Member States had to ensure that operators of public communications networks or providers of public communications services, without cause but also without any right of objection for the parties concerned, retained content and traffic data. Since significant and fundamentally questionable interference with privacy was assumed, in the literature even such term as "spy directive" appeared.[3]

The great importance of telecommunications and communication secrecy has historically led to this area being not only comprehensively protected under constitutional and administrative law, but also under criminal law. Particularly worth mentioning are Article 10 of the Austrian Basic State Law (StGG—*Staatsgrundgesetz*) protecting the secrecy of telecommunication, Article 8 § 1 of the European Convention on Human Rights (ECHR), which according to case law also covers the same area by protecting the right to respect of family and private life[4] and Sec. 1 of the Data Protection Act 2000 (DSG 2000—*Datenschutzgesetz*), as well as several sections of the Telecommunications Act (TKG 2003—*Telekommunikationsgesetz*). They all suggested that the storage of traffic and content data is not permitted without specific cause and in stock without the consent of the parties concerned. Considering the numerous provisions in various laws safeguarding secrecy, experts raised the question as to why such a serious encroachment on this previously highly protected area had to suddenly be tolerated.

There have been many critical comments on the Directive and its specific implementation in Austria. For example, the problem of double storage for both the source provider and the target provider, and the question as to who should ultimately bear the costs for the storage efforts have been challenged in the literature. Further, the vague wording of the directive and legislation as well as the "*rather more than less*" principle in determining the data intended for retention stimulated controversial discussion. For this reason, it has been suggested in statements on the implementation[5] and literature that implementation should be carried out as gently but also as late as possible. In this regard, Austria has actually taken the opportunity provided by the Directive in Article 15 § 3 to postpone its application to the retention of communications data relating to Internet access, Internet telephony and Internet e-mail until 15 March 2009.

But, of course, the greatest doubts were expressed in connection with the fundamental legal problems outlined above, particularly the interference with telecommunications secrecy under Article 8 ECHR. It was put forward that the general and groundless obligation to store data would generate an extremely meaningful data collection. For example, the location data alone might be used to create a very

[3]Otto and Seitlinger (2006), p. 227.

[4]ECHR, 6 September 1978, 5029/71, *Klass v. Germany*, NJW 1979, 1755 highlighted for the first time that telecommunication falls under both private life and protection of correspondence.

[5]See, e.g. the statement on the Ministry's draft by the Austrian Chamber of Labour, pp. 6–7. https://www.parlament.gv.at/PAKT/VHG/XXIII/SNME/SNME_01051/imfname_083527.pdf. Accessed 15 April 2019.

precise movement profile of a person for a very long time.[6] In addition, it would also be possible to draw conclusions about the status of affected persons, such as their state of health because of regular communication to a specific telephone number, e.g. a specific medical centre or a doctor.[7] This would thus also create and affect sensitive data under the applicable data protection regulations. The literature held the opinion that this was an excessive invasion of privacy and therefore could not reasonably comply with Article 8 ECHR.[8] Under this provision, interference with telecommunications secrecy must have a legitimate objective, be necessary in democratic society and finally appropriate and proportionate to the pursuit of the objective. The condition of a legitimate goal caused less of a problem. The prevention and investigation of terrorist attacks and organised crime may certainly be regarded as a legitimate objective and has not been questioned by experts. However, the objective alone is not enough, and the need for suitability and proportionality continued to raise doubts.

The argument in recital 9 of the Directive that data retention in several Member States has proved to be a necessary and effective investigative tool for law enforcement, particularly in serious cases such as organised crime and terrorism, was not convincing in its superficiality for Austrian experts. It was criticised that such a statement needed to be proved by well-founded facts on the success of such data retention. For example, serious studies conducted before the implementation of the Directive could have underpinned that necessity.[9] The mere fact that the availability of traffic and location data in some cases may have contributed to the clarification of criminal offences but may not generally justify the necessity of data retention without any exception.

On the suitability of the directive to pursue the legitimate objective, it was pointed out that data of citizens with no criminal record would be the primary target and would as a matter of fact not contribute to the investigation and prosecution of serious offences. This would be due to the fact that it was precisely the communication services which provided the "desired" anonymity to organised crime and terrorist activities—such as prepaid mobile phones or telephone booths and anonymous user accounts—that were not subject to the retention obligation or could not deliver usable results for prosecution.[10] In addition, it was not clear whether such a large amount of data could be searched effectively to filter the relevant elements for target tracking. Calculations would have proved that using conventional technology,

[6]Statement on the Ministry's draft Austrian Bar Association, p. 1. https://www.parlament.gv.at/PAKT/VHG/XXIII/SNME/SNME_01049/imfname_079592.pdf. Accessed 15 April 2019.

[7]See also the Statement on the Ministry's draft of Telekom Austria AG, p. 1. https://www.parlament.gv.at/PAKT/VHG/XXIII/SNME/SNME_01050/imfname_079854.pdf. Accessed 15 April 2019.

[8]Otto and Seitlinger (2006), p. 227.

[9]Feiel (2008), p. 100.

[10]See the statement on the Ministry's draft of the Austrian Bar Association, p. 2. https://www.parlament.gv.at/PAKT/VHG/XXIII/SNME/SNME_01049/imfname_079592.pdf. Accessed 15 April 2019.

it took about 100 years to search the accumulated data volume of approximately 20,000 to 40,000 terabytes.[11] The ISPA (Internet and Service Providers Austria) concluded that increasing the size of the haystack would not make it easier to find the needle.[12]

Even the opinions that assumed the Directive's general suitability for combating crime criticised the excessively short retention period, as they put it. It was brought forward that a retention period of less than one year, especially with foreign reference, could not lead to the desired search result.[13] However, if the storage time had been extended, the problem of even larger data volumes would have been encountered.

Regarding proportionality, it was noted that the main problem was that there was no differentiation between those affected. The monitoring of individuals was previously permitted only in exceptional cases which would have been quite proportionate, as there was a balance between the interest in efficient prosecution, truth-finding and the interest in protecting privacy. In contrast, the sole possibility of preventing and investigating potential crimes was in no way in proportion to a comprehensive and systematic violation of the rights of all persons who are—by matter of statistics—mainly without any criminal record.

Further, there were not only doubts about the possible violation of Article 8 ECHR, but also about the requirements of the ECHR for adequate and effective protection against misuse.[14] The Directive was said to run the risk of undermining or even destroying democracy on the grounds of its defence. The existing and inherent possibility of abuse was even compared with a system of secret surveillance.[15]

Doubts were also raised as to the compatibility of the Directive with Sec. 1 DSG 2000, which, even in the event of legally permitted restrictions on the right to secrecy, requires the most lenient way to reach the purpose.[16] For the reasons already mentioned, it was also believed that the comprehensive data retention obligation was not the least severe possibility for ascertaining the truth. As a result, the problem was not only that the implementation of the Directive would possibly violate national law, but also that for this very reason it was not possible to implement it at the level of the simple law. Due to the contradiction with Sec. 1 DSG 2000 which protects

[11]Feiel (2008), p. 100.

[12]Der Standard, Ispa: "Größerer Heuhaufen macht Nadelsuche nicht einfacher", 18 October 2005. https://derstandard.at/2212295/Ispa-Groesserer-Heuhaufen-macht-Nadelsuche-nicht-einfacher. Accessed 15 April 2019.

[13]Statement on the Ministry's draft of the Federal Ministry of the Interior, 3 and VAP (Association for anti-piracy of the film and video industry), pp. 3–4. https://www.parlament.gv.at/PAKT/VHG/XXIII/SNME/SNME_01048/imfname_079599.pdf and https://www.parlament.gv.at/PAKT/VHG/XXIII/SNME/SNME_01039/fname_078966.pdf. Accessed 15 April 2019.

[14]Otto and Seitlinger (2006), p. 227.

[15]In comparison to ECHR, 4 May 2000, *Rotaru v. Romania*, ÖJZ 2001/74.

[16]Feiel (2002), p. 343.

data secrecy on constitutional level, the essential provisions of the Directive were also required to be made a constitutional provision.[17]

It was not only the legal literature that highlighted the problems involved in the national implementation of the Directive. Particularly the Telecom provider, directly concerned with carrying out the new tasks, raised the worried voices: Their particular concern was both the vague wording and thus uncertainty as to the extent of the obligations and the question of who would bear the envisaged enormous costs of the data retention obligation. This issue had not been regulated in the Directive but was delegated to the Member States' discretion. Depending on the storage duration and data type, the cost estimates for the implementation of the operators amounted to multi-digit million Euro sums. For instance, the expected additional costs of Telekom Austria amounted to at least 4.5 million euro.[18] Particularly, the adaptation to the new requirements and the establishment of secure operational processes for data retention were considered cost-intensive. But the Ministry's draft did not contain any explicit regulation on who should finally bear those additional costs either. In the event of refusal of cost reimbursement by the state, this might have an enormous impact on Austria as a business location and might led to outsourcing services to non-EU countries[19] or even reallocating operator costs to customers.[20] In this context, particularly the Chamber of Labour feared that the new costs incurred could be passed on to consumers as a consequence.[21] The Chamber concluded that it would not have been reasonable to bear the costs of the surveillance detrimental to their fundamental rights.[22] The Austrian Bar Association drew attention to the fact that this transfer of costs to the operators and ultimately to the consumers interferes with their right to protection of property under Article 1 First Additional Protocol to the ECHR.[23]

Another problem that arose due to the inadequate wording of the Directive was the question as to which crimes should be considered "*serious criminal offences*"

[17]Statement on the Ministry's draft of Telekom Austria, pp. 1–2. https://www.parlament.gv.at/PAKT/VHG/XXIII/SNME/SNME_01050/imfname_079854.pdf. Accessed 15 April 2019.

[18]Statement on the Ministry's draft of Telekom Austria, p. 2. https://www.parlament.gv.at/PAKT/VHG/XXIII/SNME/SNME_01050/imfname_079854.pdf. Accessed 15 April 2019.

[19]Statement on the Ministry's draft of the Austrian Chamber of Commerce, p. 2. https://www.parlament.gv.at/PAKT/VHG/XXIII/SNME/SNME_01044/imfname_079506.pdf. Accessed 15 April 2019.

[20]Statement on the Ministry's draft of Telekom Austria, p. 3. https://www.parlament.gv.at/PAKT/VHG/XXIII/SNME/SNME_01050/imfname_079854.pdf. Accessed 15 April 2019.

[21]Statement on the Ministry's draft of the Chamber of Labour, p. 6. https://www.parlament.gv.at/PAKT/VHG/XXIII/SNME/SNME_01051/imfname_083527.pdf. Accessed 15 April 2019.

[22]Statement on the Ministry's draft of Telekom Austria, p. 3. https://www.parlament.gv.at/PAKT/VHG/XXIII/SNME/SNME_01050/imfname_079854.pdf. Accessed 15 Apr 2019.

[23]Statement on the Ministry's draft of the Austrian Bar Association, p. 3. https://www.parlament.gv.at/PAKT/VHG/XXIII/SNME/SNME_01049/imfname_079592.pdf. Accessed 15 April 2019.

under national law.[24] A reference to Sec. 17 Federal Security Police Act (SPG—*Sicherheitspolizeigesetz*) which covers criminal acts punishable by more than one-year imprisonment was considered both insufficient and excessive.[25] Almost two-thirds of the criminal offences under the Austrian Criminal Code (StGB—*Strafgesetzbuch*) are covered by the definition of Sec. 17 SPG. The use of the stored data for criminal prosecution would therefore no longer be the exception, but the rule. Based on this, the telecommunications secrecy would have factually been abolished. In this context, the legislature was expected to restrict the scope of the Directive either to criminal offences with a considerably higher punishment like, e.g. to Sec. 17 § 1 of the StGB—intentional acts punishable by life-long sentences or sentences of more than three years of imprisonment or to an exhaustive list of the crimes concerned.[26]

Another point was addressed predominantly from a political point of view: The question arose as to how the comprehensive monitoring of the communication of all citizens would affect the development of the society. It was assumed people might behave differently because their data is retained. The common argument that righteous citizens have nothing to hide was rejected, as on many occasions people take actions that are legally permissible, but not intended to be known publicly, e.g. calling a self-help hotline.[27]

Due to wide criticism, especially in many opinions on the Ministry's draft, and the media resistance Austria was not able to timely implement the Directive into national law. The fact that the implementation of the Directive was subject of constitutional review in other Member States triggered hope and a discussion about the possibility of the Directive becoming obsolete and no implementation required. Consideration was also given to the possibility of having the Directive examined for its compliance with fundamental rights in case of infringement proceedings due to non-implementation.[28]

As the transposition deadline had already passed, the Commission actually initiated infringement proceedings under Article 226 of the ECT (now Article

[24]For example, Statement on the Ministry's draft Austrian Chamber of Labour, p. 4. https://www.parlament.gv.at/PAKT/VHG/XXIII/SNME/SNME_01051/imfname_083527.pdf. Accessed 15 April 2019.

[25]Statement on the Ministry's draft of Telecom Austria, p. 2. https://www.parlament.gv.at/PAKT/VHG/XXIII/SNME/SNME_01050/imfname_079854.pdf. Accessed 15 April 2019.

[26]WP 119 (654/06) of 25 March 2006 of Article 29 Group, p. 3. http://www.statewatch.org/news/2006/apr/wp119.pdf. Accessed 15 April 2019.

[27]Statement on the Ministry's draft of the europäisches zentrum für e-commerce und Internetrecht, p. 5. https://www.parlament.gv.at/PAKT/VHG/XXIII/SNME/SNME_01046/imfname_079594.pdf. Accessed 15 April 2019.

[28]Gerhartinger (2010), p. 172.

258 TFEU) against Austria,[29] Sweden,[30] Ireland,[31] and the Hellenic Republic.[32] The Commission considered Austria's position—implementation would only be possible if a political consensus had been reached—insufficient and brought an action against the non-implementation. Austria's appeal to the unlawfulness of the action was unsuccessful since the Court of Justice of the European Union (CJEU) confirmed its previous decisions and denied the basis for examining the legality of the Directive to be transposed in infringement proceedings. Considering some of the substantive proposals from the statements, the Directive was finally implemented by amendments to the Telecommunications Act 2003, the Criminal Code and Federal Security Police Act. It finally came into force on 1 April 2012—four years and six months after the implementation deadline.

2 Proceedings Before the Constitutional Court

After implementation of the Directive, three applications challenging the national implementation were filed with the Austrian Constitutional Court: A claim for examination of lawfulness by the Carinthian state government,[33] an individual petition from a private person and a "collective individual application" involving 11,129 persons.[34]

The Carinthian regional government requested the repeal of the national provisions implementing the Directive for two main reasons: It was brought forward that the Directive would violate the Austrian Constitution's building principles. This would be due to the fact that the provisions of the law in its entirety would "be contrary to the architectural style of a modern state." Furthermore, the government blamed the massive encroachment of fundamental rights as brought forward in the public opinions rendered before to implementation. In particular, it was stated that the protection of privacy under Article 8 ECHR, the fundamental right to data protection in Sec. 1 DSG 2000, the secrecy of telecommunication in Article 10a StGG, the communication secrecy in Sec. 93 TKG 2003, the right to freedom of expression in Article 10 ECHR and Article 13 StGG as well as the presumption of innocence based on Article 6 ECHR were infringed. It was highlighted that the violation of fundamental rights results not only from the use of the stored data, but already from the continuous and groundless retention of communication data of all persons. On several occasions, it has also been argued that the terms of the challenged provisions would be ambiguous and imprecise.

[29] CJEU, 29 July 2010, C-189/09, jusIT 2010/80.

[30] CJEU, 4 February 2010, C-185/09, CELEX 62009CJ0185.

[31] CJEU, 26 November 2009, C-202/09, CELEX 62009CJ0202.

[32] CJEU, 26 November 2009, C-211/09, CELEX 62009CJ0211.

[33] *Antrag* based on Article 140 § 1 No. 2 B-VG (Federal Constitutional Law).

[34] Both *Individualantrag* based on Article 140 § 1 No. 1 lit. c B-VG (Federal Constitutional Law).

The provision on the storage of data was implemented in Sec. 102a TKG 2003. In this context it was essentially argued that the data which shall be retained based on the provision would be in any case personal data within the meaning of Sec. 1 DSG 2000. Such data may not be kept without any justified reasons, otherwise the requirement for confidentiality would be breached. The Carinthian state government conducted in its filing a proportionality test and concluded that the mass retention of data is not the least severe means available for the intended purpose in the sense of Sec. 1 § 2 DSG 2000. Thus, Sec. 102a TKG 2003 would be in contradiction to the constitutional provision of Sec. 1 DSG 2000.

Furthermore, the fundamental right to privacy in Article 8 ECHR would also be infringed as the identity of the conversation partners, the duration of the conversations, the time and suchlike were to be recorded and stored. This intervention would also be unsuitable, unnecessary and disproportionate. The threatened retention of communication data would further be likely to put pressure on the participants and possibly force them to change their communication behaviour without objective reasons or necessities.

In summary, it was also argued that data retention could be easily circumvented by other technical means which is why the actual target group would not be concerned. Further, the data retention would lead to an increase in the risk of misuse of data. Data retention would therefore be unsuitable for preventing or combating serious crime and be overall disproportionately. In total, the arguments of the Carinthian state government predominately reflected and repeated the most frequently voiced criticism of the discussion in the legislation process.

The second claimant against the implementation of the Directive was a private individual. He also asserted the violation of constitutional rights to respect private and family life, the protection of personal data, freedom of communication and equality of all citizens before the law. He thus applied for the repeal of several provisions of the TKG 2003 implementing the Directive, including Sec. 102a and related provision.

On violation of Article 8 ECHR and Article 7 of the Union's Charter of Fundamental Rights (UCFR), he argued that because of the implementation of the Directive he would have to live with constant discomfort as his way of life and his communication would be monitored. Furthermore, he was also concerned that the stored data could be misused, e.g. due to unauthorised access by third parties. This would greatly restrict his legal use of communication services.

In addition, he questioned the pursuit of a legitimate objective by implementation of the storage obligation in Sec. 102a TKG 2003. The declared objective of the Directive, the fight against terrorism, could not be achieved with the national implementation. Instead, the obligation to store data entails a restriction of the freedoms of society that have been fought for over the last centuries. He concluded that the legislation would be an act of submitting to terrorism, rather than the one fighting it. This, together with the lack of necessity and suitability, would lead to the provision not standing up to the proportionality test.

The lack of necessity and suitability again was supported by the already known argument that a user of communication services could prevent the retention of his data within the framework of the Directive and Sec. 102a TKG 2003 by using communication services not covered by data retention. There would be many ways to avoid being subject to the retention either due to usage of communication services offered by providers excluded by Sec. 102a § 6 TKG 2003,[35] simple Internet telephone services or by employing Internet cafes, call shops or prepaid cards. The applicant also argued that the criminals would prefer to use means of communication which are either excluded from data retention or whose evaluation would not allow to derive any usable conclusions. Thus, he also concluded that the data retention would only target data of innocent citizens—like the applicant himself. The stored data would thus not be helpful to solve serious crimes. However, the data retention would increase the risk of any innocent user being exposed to investigation without providing a real reason—for example, if accidentally contacted by a particular number, which is a subject to an investigation.

In addition, claimant argued that in those Member States where the Directive had already been implemented for some time, no significant change in the detection rate was experienced.

Further, the arguments of availability of less severe means, the excessively wide range of criminal offences and the violation of Sec. 1 DSG 2000 were brought forward. Again, the most prominent and most frequently discussed points discussed in the legislation process were stressed.

The third application was referred to as the "*collective individual application*" and was signed by further 11,129 persons in addition to the third applicant. The group consisted of lawyers and IT specialists led by a communications specialist from Ludwig Boltzmann Institute for Human Rights who was also involved in the legal implementation process of the Directive. The group argued more fundamentally and assumed a paradigm shift that could not be justified from a fundamental rights perspective. Due to the retention of data, virtually every citizen was taken under general suspicion.

The arguments of this group of claimants also coincided with those of the filings outlined above. Again, the lack of suitability was underpinned by the fact that the provisions could be easily circumvented by real criminals. Furthermore, it was stated that the pursuit of the objectives by the data retention would be disproportionate to the threatening disadvantages to individuals and society resulting from the regulations. The applicants argued that it would be doubtful that the measures were the least severe and challenged the suitability and necessity of the measures. Thus, they concluded that in this case particularly strict proportionality test had to be carried out. They argued that data retention would have had a positive effect in a few individual cases, only. On the other hand, however, the measures would cause a serious invasion of privacy for the entire population. This would cause a severe disproportionality. This would even be worsened by the broad purposes for which

[35]Small providers not subject to the funding obligations under the TKG 2003 which do not reach a certain turnover volume were excluded from the retention obligation under Sec. 102a § 6 TKG 2003.

the stored data might have been used and the lack of sufficient legal remedies. To support this argument, the claimants referred to a ruling of the German Federal Constitutional Court[36] and a finding of the Austrian Constitutional Court,[37] both stating that actions allowing the usage of the retained data must be predictable and controllable. This requirement would not be met in the specific case since the provisions on the use of data were too ambiguous and too broad.

Claimants also pointed out that data retention led to the violation of Sec. 1 DSG 2000 and Article 8 ECHR: By combining the retained data with other data collected, new information could be generated which allows to draw new conclusions. This would impair the confidentiality interests of the persons concerned and would subsequently lead to intrusion into the private sphere neglecting the constitutional protection. This would also endanger the impartiality of the behaviour. Finally, the storage without a cause would result in intimidating effects.

The claimants suggested that the Constitutional Court should seek a preliminary ruling from the Court of Justice of the European Union on the compatibility of the Directive with the rights under the Union's Charter of Fundamental Rights.

In summary, all three applications were following same argumentation lines as already known from the discussions during the implementation process of the Directive. The main criticism was the possibility of creating personal profiles or inferences on personal data, the possibility of circumventing data retention and the resulting inappropriateness of the provisions to achieve the objective and a violation of Article 8 ECHR by disproportionality.

3 Decision of the Constitutional Court

In its decision, the Constitutional Court dismissed the national provisions implementing the Directive as unconstitutional. In its reasoning, the court asserted an infringement of the constitutional rights of data secrecy in Sec. 1 DSG 2000, Article 8 ECHR and Article 7 and 8 of Union's Charter of Fundamental Rights.

Under Sec. 1 § 1 DSG 2000, everyone has the right to confidentiality of his personal data, insofar as he has a legitimate interest in secrecy especially with regard to protection of his private and family life. Section 1 DSG 2000 contains a substantive reservation which tightens the limits for encroachment on fundamental rights more than Article 8 ECHR or Article 7 and 8 of Union's Charter do: Restrictions on the right to confidentiality may only be imposed to protect overriding legitimate interests of another party. In the case of intervention by a governmental authority any limitation must be based on laws. For the legal basis, Sec. 1 § 2 DSG 2000 requires in addition to Article 8 § 2 ECHR that any data which by its nature is particularly worth of protection may only be used to safeguard important public interests.

[36] BVerfGE, 3.3.2004, 1 BvF 3792, NJW 2004, 2213.

[37] VfGH 28.11.2001, B 2271/00, wbl 2002, 343 (*Feiel*).

Further, any usage is also subject to appropriate guarantees for the protection of confidentiality interests being governed by law. Even if the preconditions are met, any interference with the fundamental right of data protection must only be conducted in the least severe manner leading to the justified objective. Thus, the proportionality of the encroachment on the fundamental right to data protection under Sec. 1 DSG 2000 sets an even stricter standard than that already established by Article 8 ECHR.

The data subject to the Directive are personal data as defined in Sec. 1 DSG 2000. The Constitutional Court emphasised that there is a legitimate interest in confidentiality of those data under Sec. 1 DSG 2000 and that the storage obligation arising from the implementation of the Directive in any case interferes with this interest and thus also with Article 8 ECHR.

The decision pointed out that an intervention in the right of data protection for the fight against crime and terror may be well admissible, but it must comply with the strict requirements of Sec. 1 DSG 2000 and Article 8 ECHR. This also applies to the structure and content of the conditions for data retention and the requirements for data deletion, as well as to the legal measures outlining the possibilities for public and private access to these data. Finally, the Constitutional Court assessed that the contested provisions do not meet these strict requirements mainly for the following reasons:

Considering the rapid spread of "new" means of communication and the expansion of technical possibilities, the fight against crime was ought to face new challenges. This also entails the potential for misuse of recorded data. This would even more be true and severe as the new provisions, although certain precautions have been taken, had not made improper use a punishable offence. Furthermore, the scope of offences allowing data access was considered too broad. The Constitutional Court concluded that the access to retained data was not only possible in cases where ultimately required for the clarification of a criminal offence. The deletion of the data was also held as unclearly formulated due to lack of provisions making a clear statement whether the data will be irrevocably deleted after a certain period.

The Constitutional Court assumed that freedom as an individual's right and the state of a society is determined by the quality of the information network. Although the provisions on data retention are capable of achieving the objective of maintaining law and order and protecting the rights and freedoms of others in an abstract manner, the seriousness of the concrete intervention due to the breadth and nature of the data concerned exceeded the weight and significance of these objectives. In this point, the Constitutional Court explicitly confirmed the above elaborated criticism in the legal process and the arguments brought forward by the applicants. The court did particularly emphasise that the data retention would almost exclusively cover persons who have not given any reason for data retention. The communication services are also mainly used by the population to exercise their fundamental rights such as freedom of expression, information and communication. Therefore, any restriction of the right of confidentiality would in this case be particularly difficult.

As a result, the claimants were to be proved right of the asserted disproportionality. Restrictions on the fundamental right to data protection would only be permissible based on laws that are necessary for the reasons referred to in Article 8 § 2 ECHR and that are sufficiently precise, i.e. predictable for everyone in regulating the conditions under which the identification or use of personal data for the performance of specific administrative tasks is permitted. The provision should also have been applied as the least severe means of achieving the objectives and should have been proportionate in weighing the severity of the intervention against the objectives pursued. These requirements were held not being met by the implemented regulations.

In its decision-making process, the Austrian Constitutional Court followed the request of the third applicant and appealed to the CJEU for a preliminary ruling. In summary, the court asked two questions dealing with the compatibility of Articles 3 to 9 of the Directive with Articles 7, 8 and 11 UCFR and the interpretation of the Treaties. However, since the CJEU already denied compatibility of the Directive with the mentioned provisions, the second question remained unanswered. Since the outcome of the preliminary ruling procedure of the CJEU was essential for the decision of Austrian Constitutional Court, the CJEU's argumentation was also used for the explanatory statement on the incompatibility and the encroachment on fundamental rights.

The case law of the European Court of Human Rights (ECtHR) also played a major role in the decision of the court. Since the contested provisions were examined not only based on the Austrian Data Protection Act, but also on Article 8 ECHR, cases related to surveillance, such as *Leander*,[38] *Amann*,[39] *Rotaru*,[40] *Copland*,[41] *and S. and Marper*[42] had been considered when assessing to what extent the storage and use of data is admissible or interfering with the right to respect for privacy and family life.

The only decision of another national constitutional court of another Member State employed by the Austrian Constitutional Court was the decision 1 BvR 256/08 of the German Federal Constitutional Court.[43] The decision dealt with a constitutional complaint concerning provisions that were introduced or amended because of the implementation of the Directive. In this regard, Austrian Constitutional Court relied on the arguments of the German Court in connection with the gravity of the infringement of the protected legal sphere resulting from data retention. In addition, it agreed with the argument of the German Court that the fact that "only" the name and address of a user who owns an IP address is stored does not change the outcome.

[38]ECtHR, 26 March 1987, 9248/81, *Leander*, § 48.

[39]ECtHR, 16 February 2000, 27.798/95, *Amann*, ÖJZ 2001, 71, § 65 f.

[40]ECtHR, 4 May 2000, 28.341/95, *Rotaru*, ÖJZ 2001, 74, § 43.

[41]ECtHR, 3 April 2007, 62.617/00, *Copland*, EuGRZ 2007, 415, § 43f.

[42]ECtHR, 4 December 2008, 30562/04 and 30566/04—*S. und Marper*, EuGRZ 2009, 299, § 67.

[43]BVerfG 2.3.2010, 1 BvR 256/08, NJW 2010, 833.

4 Consequences and Execution of Judicial Decision

The consequence of the Constitutional Court's decision from 27 June 2014 was the immediate repeal of 13 provisions of the Telecommunications Act and two provisions of the Criminal Procedure Code and two provisions of the Security Police Act (or parts thereof), implementing the Directive. The announcement in BGBl I 44/2014[44] was made three days later, on 30 June 2014.

There were some opinions that the decisions of the Constitutional Court and the CJEU could be interpreted in such a way that it was possible to implement the Directive in accordance with fundamental rights.[45] Although the Directive has been repealed at the European level, there were some discussions in Austria about the reintroduction of a new data retention regime.[46] In principle, the Constitutional Court has in itself qualified data retention as a suitable means to fight and prevent crime, but under the premise that possible new regulations would be subject to clear limitations.[47] Nevertheless, data retention 2.0 has not yet been initiated; and although there have been some amendments to the Telecommunications Act since the Constitutional Court's decision, the repealed provisions have never been replaced.

Considering the recent entry into force of the General Data Protection Regulation (GDPR), however, it is worth mentioning that the new monitoring regulations in the Austrian Data Protection Adaptation Act[48] are subject to strict proportionality testing, which in other words corresponds to what the Constitutional Court pointed out.

References

Feiel W (2002) Wirtschaftsaufsichtsrecht: Zu den Auskunftspflichten nach § 83 TKG, wbl 2002, 343

Feiel W (2008) Datenspeicherung auf Vorrat und Grundrechtskonformität, jusIT 2008, 97

Gerhartinger H (2010) Vertragsverletzung Österreichs wegen Nichtumsetzung der Richtlinie 2006/24/EG über die Vorratsspeicherung der Daten, jusIT 2010, 172

Hattenberger D, Klingbacher K (2015) Bemerkenswertes zur Entscheidung des VfGH zur Vorratsdatenspeicherung, Jahrbuch Öffentliches Recht 2015, 179

Klaushofer R (2014) Normenkontrolle des VfGH und das Grundrecht auf Datenschutz unter dem Eindruck der Vorratsdatenspeicherung, jusIT 2014, 223

[44]Bundesgesetzblatt—Austrian Official Journal.

[45]Hattenberger and Klingbacher (2015), p. 202.

[46]Sulzbacher (2015).

[47]Klaushofer (2014), p. 226.

[48]Datenschutz-Anpassungsgesetz.

Otto G, Seitlinger M (2006) Die “Spitzelrichtlinie” – Zur (Umsetzungs) Problematik der Data Retention Richtlinie 2006/24 EG, MR 2006, 227
Sulzbacher M (2015) Mikl-Leitner will “offene Diskussion” über neue Vorratsdatenspeicherung, der Standard, 25 May 2015. https://derstandard.at/2000016259906/Mikl-Leitnerwill-offene-Diskussion-ueber-neue-Vorratsdatenspeicherung

Data Retention in Belgium

Catherine Van de Heyning

Abstract The implementation of the Data Retention Directive in the Act of 30 July 2013 was applauded by law enforcement as a significant step forward. The Act introduced the retention of subscriber, traffic and localisation data of electronic communication in Belgium. However, in 2015 the Constitutional Court struck down the act following the European Court of Justice's annulment of the Data Retention Directive in the case of Digital Rights Ireland. The Belgian legislator decided not to await a new European initiative and responded with a new legal framework maintaining the bulk retention of communication data but restricting access to these data. In 2018, the Constitutional Court was asked if this new approach did not as well violate the protection of personal data and privacy. Instead of deciding the issue, the court send new preliminary questions to the CJEU on the compatibility of the Belgian approach and the European case law. This contribution analyses the Belgian search for a balanced approach between retention on the one hand and the protection of fundamental rights on the other.

1 Introduction

The retention of communication data was first entrenched in the Belgian Act on Electronic Communication of 13 June 2005 (hereafter: ECA).[1] This Act implemented several EU directives concerning electronic communication and the protection of personal data generated through electronic communication.[2] The ECA

[1]Act of 13 June 2005 concerning electronic communication, Belgian Official Journal, 20 June 2005. For an overview of data retention see Kosta and Valcke (2006), part 6.2 and De Hert and Boulet (2016), p. 131.

[2]Directive 2002/21/EC of the European Parliament and of the Council of 7 March 2002 on a common regulatory framework for electronic communications networks and services, OJ L

C. Van de Heyning (✉)
The University of Antwerp, Antwerp, Belgium
e-mail: catherine.vandeheyning@uantwerpen.be

M. Zubik et al. (eds.), *European Constitutional Courts towards Data Retention Laws*, Law, Governance and Technology Series 45,
https://doi.org/10.1007/978-3-030-57189-4_4

only provided for the retention of telephony data for a period of 12 to 36 months. Given the undefined retention provision, the lack of subsequent execution in Royal Decree, and the limited scope excluding Internet created data, it was clear that the ECA did not meet the requirements of the Directive 2006/24/EC on data retention (hereafter: Data Retention Directive).[3] Only in 2013 and after having received a formal notice of default by the European Commission did Belgium finally implement the Data Retention Directive.[4]

The implementation resulted in an amendment of the ECA providing for bulk retention of identification, traffic and location data of all telecommunication, including electronic communication, for a period of 12 months and up to 24 months for specific categories of data.[5] Belgian law enforcement and intelligence agencies increasingly used and relied on these communication data in investigations and were therefore dismayed when only two years after implementation the provision was annulled by the Belgian Constitutional Court. In its judgement of 11 June 2015,[6] the Constitutional Court relied on the Court of Justice of the European Union's (CJEU) *Digital Rights Ireland* judgment[7] to find that the provision provided for a disproportionate infringement of the protection of personal data and privacy. The current president of investigating judges labelled the Court's judgement "*a black day for justice.*"[8]

Encouraged by law enforcement, the Belgian legislator did not await a new initiative of the European Union. The Act of 29 May 2016[9] amending the ECA

108, 24.04.2002, 0033–0050, Directive 2002/20/EC of the European Parliament and of the Council of 7 March 2002 on the authorisation of electronic communications networks and services, OJ L 108, 24.04.2002, 21–32, Directive 2002/22/EC of the European Parliament and of the Council of 7 March 2002 on universal service and users' rights relating to electronic communications networks and services, OJ L 108, 24.04.2002, 51–77, Directive 2002/58/EC of the European Parliament and of the Council of 12 July 2002 concerning the processing of personal data and the protection of privacy in the electronic communications sector, OJ L 201, 31.7.2002, 37–47 and Directive 2002/77/EC of 16 September 2002 on competition in the markets for electronic communications networks and services, OJ L 249, 17.9.2002, 21–26.

[3]Directive 2006/24/EC of the European Parliament and of the Council of 15 March 2006 on the retention of data generated or processed in connection with the provision of publicly available electronic communications services or of public communications networks and amending Directive 2002/58/EC OJ L 105, 13.4.2006, 54.

[4]Formal notice of 16 September 2012, infringement No. 20122152.

[5]Act of 30 July 2013 concerning amending Articles 2, 126 and 145 of the Act of 13 June 2005 concerning electronic communication and Article 90decies Criminal Code, Belgian Official Journal, 23 August 2013, 56109.

[6]Constitutional Court, 11 June 2015, No. 84/15, available at www.const-court.be.

[7]ECJ, 8 April 2014, *Digital Rights Ireland Ltd v. Minister for Communications, Marine and Natural Resources and Others and Kärntner Landesregierung and Others*, Joined Cases C-293/12 and C-594/12, ECLI:EU:C:2014:238 (hereafter: Digital Rights Ireland case).

[8]NWS, Vernietiging dataretentiewet een zwarte dag voor justitie, available at https://www.vrt.be.

[9]Act of 29 May 2016 concerning the processing and retaining of data in the sector of electronic communication, Belgian Official Journal, 18 July 2016, 44717. Extensively on the new act: De Hert and Boulet (2016), p. 204.

maintained the provision enforcing bulk retention of electronic communication data. However, it provided for additional safeguards as to the period of retention, the period and circumstances in which these data could be requested and relied upon by law enforcement and the safeguards as to processing and storage. With the CJEU's *Tele2/Watson*[10] judgment, the compatibility of these new provisions with the EU law was put into question and new preliminary questions were sent to the Constitutional Court. It was argued by some that the Belgian legislation did not breach Articles 7–8 of the Charter of Fundamental Rights of the European Union (hereafter: the Charter) as the new framework provided of a balanced and proportionate equilibrium between retention, protection and security of personal data through limiting the scope and period of access to and reliance upon these data. Others, however, argued that these safeguards would not suffice to uphold the legislation in the light of the CJEU's case law as bulk retention was ruled out by Luxembourg. As such, the Belgian Constitutional Court's decision on the viability of the Belgian data retention provision in the light of *Tele2/Watson* was eagerly awaited. Much to the surprise of many, the court did not decide the issue, but instead opted to send new preliminary questions to the CJEU. Therefore, the status of bulk retention in Belgium remains *in dubio*.

The following contribution discusses this evolution and particularly the reasoning of the Constitutional Court in both cases. The first part introduces the data retention legislation following the implementation of the Data Retention Directive. The second part goes into the argumentation of the Constitutional Court in its 2015 judgment. The third part outlines the consequences of this judgment for data retention in Belgium, including the new data retention framework as introduced by the Act of 29 May 2016. The fourth and final part considers the Constitutional Court's judgment of 2018[11] and an outlook on the preliminary questions as referred to the European Court of Justice.

2 Implementation of Directive 2006/24/EC in Belgium

Directive 2006/24/EC was to be transposed by 15 September 2007. Belgium relied on provision in the Directive allowing to delay the transposition of the norms on the retention of data created by Internet access (Internet telephony or email) until 15 March 2009. The first attempt by the Belgian legislator to implement the directive had been abandoned after a negative advice from the Belgian Privacy Commission.[12] In 2012, the European Commission send a formal notice to conform Article

[10]ECJ, 21 December 2016, *Tele2 Sverige and Watson*, Joined Cases C-203-15 and C-698/15, ECLI: EU:C:2016:970. See Buono and Taylor (2017), pp. 250–253.

[11]Constitutional Court, 19 July 2018, No. 96/18, available at: www.const-court.be. Accessed 20 July 2018.

[12]Privacy Commission, Advice No. 24/2008 of 2 July 2008.

258 TFEU to Belgium informing the Member State to be in default in transposing the directive and requesting action.[13] At that moment, the validity of the Data Retention Directive in the light of the protection of personal data and the right to privacy had already been called into question. In particular, the preliminary question by the Irish High Court on the validity of the Data Retention Directive pending before the European Court of Justice casted serious doubt as to the viability of the directive, particularly the provisions regarding bulk retention of communication data.[14]

Instead of aligning itself with these critical voices and delaying the implementation of the Data Retention Directive, Belgium decided to put itself in line.[15] The Belgian legislator finally implemented the directive by the Act of 30 July 2013.[16] It introduced a generalised and standardised bulk retention of communication data in Belgium. The parliamentary proceedings refer to the formal notice as justification for the accelerated procedure in parliament implementing the directive.[17] This Act was further executed by the Royal Decree of 19 September 2013.[18] This Decree details what data must be retained and adapts the requirements of storage of the ECA to these specific data categories.

The implementation had a serious impact on the retention of telecommunication data in Belgium. In 2005, the legislator had already introduced a retention provision in Article 126 ECA. It provided for a general retention of subscriber (identification), traffic and localisation data for public operators of telephony services.[19] As such, all communication not wired by telephonic services were excluded from the application. Further, the control, processing and storage of these data was still largely governed by the general privacy legislation.[20] It would go beyond the intent of this contribution to discuss in detail all changes, but the following paragraph will set out the most important, particularly these provisions that were at the core of the legal

[13]Formal notice of 16 September 2012, infringement No. 2012/2152.

[14]Reference for a preliminary ruling from High Court of Ireland made on 11 June 2012—Digital Rights Ireland Ltd v. Minister for Communications, Marine and Natural Resources, Minister for Justice, Equality and Law Reform, The Commissioner of the Garda Síochána, Ireland and the Attorney General, OJ L 258, 25.08.2012, 11.

[15]See the reasoned opinion of Belgium in reply to the formal notice of 30 May 2013.

[16]Act of 30 July 2013 concerning amending Articles 2, 126 and 145 of the Act of 13 June 2005 concerning electronic communication and the Article 90decies Criminal Code, Belgian Official Journal, 23 August 2013, 56109.

[17]Parliamentary proceedings, Parl.St. 53 – 2921/001, 3.

[18]Royal Decree of 19 September 2013 executing Article 126 of the Act of 13 June 2005 concerning electronic communication, Belgian Official Journal, 19 September 2013, 70828.

[19]Provision 126 ECA required the registration and retention of all identification and traffic data of all end users for the investigation and prosecution of criminal facts and the sanctioning of malicious calls to emergency services or the investigation thereof by the Ombudsman. This only applied to operators and providers of active or passive transmission systems and routing devices or other means to transmit signals by wire, radio waves, optical or other magnetic means. Radio and television signals were exempted.

[20]Act of 8 December 1992 as to the protection of privacy on the processing of personal data, Belgian Official Journal, 18 March 1993, 5801.

battle that followed the implementation and the CJEU's judgment on the validity of the Data Retention Directive.

The most crucial feature of the implementation of the Data Retention Directive in Belgian law was by no doubt the extension of the scope from telephony services to all telecommunication, including electronic communication. The data retention obligation as provided in Article 126 ECA applies to providers of publicly available telephony services, of Internet services, access to Internet, and e-mail via Internet, operators of public electronic communication networks and operators providing of one of these services. They are required to retain identification data (i.e. data to identify the user, the subscriber and/or the used device), location (i.e. data concerning the access to the network and the location of the devices) and traffic data (i.e. all data concerning the point of entry to the communication network and duration) for a period of 12 months.[21]

The third paragraph of Article 126 ECA stipulates that the government must further specify the data to be retained specific to each electronic communication service. This paragraph was executed by the Royal Decree of 19 September 2013.[22] The Royal Decree provides in detailed manner all data to be retained specific to the service operated. For instance Article 3 §1 of the Royal Decree of 19 September 2013 provides that landline telephony services must retain the number allocated to the subscriber, the subscriber's personal data, the subscription's starting date or the registration data, the type of landline telephony service used and the types of other services with which the subscriber is registered, in case of number transfer, the identity of the transferring provider and of the receiving provider and the data relating to the payment method, the identification of the payment instrument, and the time of payment for the subscription or for the use of the service.

In so far telecommunication data are not included in the Royal Decree, there is no obligation for providers and operator to retain these data. E.g. there is no data retention obligation for service providers that act as a mere conduit or provide caching and hosting activities. Most significant, there is no obligation to retain content of telecommunication.

Article 126 ECA obliged operators and providers of public telephony services to retain identification, traffic and localisation data for 12 to 36 months.[23] The provision stipulated that the exact period would be determined by Royal Decree after an advice by the Privacy Commission. The underlying idea at the time was that a differential approach on the retention period would be provided in the Royal Decree depending of the nature and use of the data. However, as no such Royal Decree followed, the

[21] A first draft of the act provided that a Royal Decree would settle the period of retention, as was the case in the first version of the ECA. However, the Privacy Commission provided for a negative advice holding that the act itself should settle the duration. Privacy Commission, Advice No. 20/2009 of 1 July 2009, Parliamentary proceedings, Parl.St. 53 – 2921/001, 106.

[22] Royal Decree of 19 September 2013 on the execution of Article 126 of the Act of 13 June 2005 on electronic communications, Belgian Official Journal, 8 October 2013.

[23] This is the same timeframe as mentioned in the 2005 version of Article 126 ECA.

operators and providers were up to the implementation of the Data Retention Directive obliged to retain the data for only 12 months.

At first, the government proposed a retention period of 24 months for the implementation of the directive, being the maximum as provided by the Data Retention Directive. However, in its advice the Belgian Privacy Commission argued that such extended retention period was not substantiated by any underlying rationale or necessity.[24] The commission referred to the neighbouring countries (the Netherlands and France) that equally proposed a retention period of 12 months. The Belgian Institute for Postal and Telecommunication informed that most stakeholders argued for a period of six months. This was rejected by the government as not meeting the needs in the field.[25]

The Belgian legislator therefore followed the advice of the Belgian Privacy Commission and opted to maintain the already applied limitation of 12 months of retention. The ECA provided that in case the evaluation report of the Act determined that the retention period of 12 months is too short for effective investigations, the period could be extended for certain categories of data to a maximum of 18 months. Moreover, the provision even allowed for an extension over 24 months (the Directive's maximum) if required by the outcome of the mentioned report. In such case, the government would have to inform the European Commission.

Article 126 ECA implemented the requirements in the Data Retention Directive on data security, storage and protection requirements, adding certain levels of protection by detailing the specifics of the requirement. The underlying rationale is that the restriction on the protection of personal data by enforcing a data retention obligation should be compensated with an enforced protection of these data as they are vulnerable to illegitimate and unauthorised access and use. First, the provision states that the service providers and operators must ensure that the retained data are of the same quality and guarded with the same protection and security measures as other data in their network.

Second, the providers and operators should take all technical and organisational measures to protect the data against destruction, either illicit, or by loss or accident, any unauthorised or illegitimate access or storage, publication or processing. The providers and operators should, moreover, ensure that the use of the data can be traced to those data requested by the competent authorities. Third, the ECA requires the service providers and operators to render the data illegible and useless to non-authorised persons. (e.g. by means of encryption). Finally, the provision explicitly provides that the data must be retained within the European Union. As such, the ECA ensures that the EU data protection norms fully apply.

Article 126 § 2 ECA lists in an exhaustive manner the persons and authorities that can request access to the retained data:

---

[24]Privacy Commission, Advice No. 20/2009 of 1 July 2009, parliamentary proceedings, Parl.St. 53 – 2921/001, 106.

[25]Parliamentary proceedings, Parl.St. 53 – 2921/001, 106, parliamentary proceedings, Parl.St. 53 – 2921/001, 128.

- The judicial authorities in view of detecting, researching and prosecuting criminal offences if provided under the Criminal Code of Procedure;
- The intelligence—and security services to enable their intelligence operations if provided under the Act on the Intelligence and Security Services;
- Every officer of the judicial police of the Institute to investigate the abuse of the electronic communication services or networks;
- Emergency services to offer aid after an emergency call in case they are not informed of the identity or have been given incorrect details, albeit limited to 24 hours after the emergency call;
- An officer of the judicial police of the cell for missing persons in case of a worrying disappearance, albeit limited to a period of 48 hours after the data request;
- The Ombuds service for telecommunication, albeit limited to identification data in identifying a person who has maliciously abused an electronic network or service;
- An auditor of the Financial Services and Markets Authority (FSMA), albeit limited for an exhaustive list of purposes.

This meant a substantial extension of the authorities and services granted access to these data. The original Article 126 ECA only allowed access for law enforcement, and the emergency services or Ombuds service, although the latter only to identify persons who maliciously abuse a network. The access to retained data by these authorised bodies is limited to the purpose of the access, the period of access and for most enlisted bodies, the scope of data. While Article 126 ECA provides for a narrow scope of access for most authorised bodies as to the period or data that can be requested, such limitations are not mentioned for judicial authorities and intelligence and security services. Article 126 ECA refers to the applicable legislation as to the conditions and limitations of access to the retained data. Access is only legitimate if necessary for the purpose provided in the provision. For example, law enforcement can only have access to these data to detect, investigate and prosecute criminal offences or intelligence and security services to enable intelligence operations. The limitations of access and processing of these data for law enforcement and intelligence purposes are therefore to be found in the provisions regulating criminal investigation and intelligence operations.

The Code of Criminal Procedure (hereafter: CCP) provides for the rules governing the access of judicial authorities to retained data in the course of criminal proceedings.[26] The public prosecutor can request for identification data under Article 46bis CCP, while the investigating judge can request for traffic and location data under Article 88bis CCP. Both provisions specify the scope of valid data request and provide for specific material and procedural requirements for a valid data request.

Articles 46bis and 88bis CCP define which data can be requested. Based on Article 46bis CCP, the public prosecutor has access to the data to identify (1) the

[26]On these provisions pre-Digital Rights Ireland see Kerkhofs and Van Linthout (2013), pp. 387–412.

subscriber or the habitual user of an electronic communications service, (2) the electronic communication means used, and (3) the electronic communications services to which a particular person is a subscriber or that are habitually used by a particular person. The investigating judge has the competency to (1) trace traffic data of electronic communications means from which or to which electronic communications are or were made, (2) locate the origin or the destination of electronic communications based on Article 88bis CCP.

The provision does not indicate who can be the subject of a data request. As such, the data of persons other than a suspect can be requested if it is deemed useful for the criminal investigation and proportionate. Neither did these provisions stipulate a maximum period for data to be requested. As such, the investigators would be limited by the retention policy of the providers and operators in line with Article 126 ECA.

Articles 46bis and 88bis CCP provide for a broad territorial scope for data requests. The provisions stipulate that the obligation to transfer retained data upon request applies to every service provider or operator that provides or offers a service within the Belgian territory, that concerns either transmitting signals via electronic communication networks or allowing users to receive or send information via an electronic communication network.[27] This broad territorial definition followed from the Court of Cassation's judgments in the case of Yahoo!.[28] The service provider refused to communicate subscriber information upon direct request of a Belgian prosecutor stating that it was a US Internet service provider and could therefore only provide the information based on a request or warrant of the U.S. Justice Department. Yahoo! argued that the Belgian prosecutor must request the data via the mutual legal assistance treaty with the United States. The Court of Cassation, however, rejected this reasoning holding that an Internet service provider is "virtually" present in Belgium and therefore falls under the cooperation duty of Article 46bis CCP if (1) its services or economic activities target users on the Belgian territory and (2) there is a connection between the service or communication on the one hand and the Belgian territory on the other, e.g. the mail was sent from or to a person in Belgium.[29]

The access and processing of the retained data for intelligence operations is governed by Articles 18/7 and 18/8 of the Act on Intelligence and Security

[27] Act of 25 December 2016 concerning various changes to the Code of Criminal Procedure and the Criminal Code, for the purpose of improving the special investigation methods and certain investigation methods concerning internet and electronic and telecommunication, Belgian Official Journal, 17 January 2017, 2738.

[28] The Court of Cassation was requested three times to consider points of law in this case, particularly with regard to the territoriality of the cooperation duty. Cass. 4 September 2012, P.111906.N., Cass. 18 January 2011, P.101347.N. and Cass. 1 December 2015, P.15.1346.N. In a recent case, this approach has been applied to tapping orders of Skype conversations: Cass. 28 February 2019, P.17.1229.N.

[29] On this case see De Hert and Kopcheva (2011), pp. 291–297; Conings (2017), pp. 810–811 and Van de Heyning (2016b), pp. 44–47.

Services.[30] These provisions allow for the collection of identification, traffic and localisation data of telecommunication. As with the requests in criminal investigations, no period was provided for data requests.

3 Proceedings Before the Constitutional Court (2015)

The *Ordre des barreaux francophones et germanophone* (Francophone and German Bar) and the *Ligue of droits de l'homme* (Human Rights League) both started annulment proceedings against the Act of 30 July 2013 in February 2014.[31] These organisations argued that the new ECA violated the rights of defence, protection of personal data and privacy under Articles 6 and 8 ECHR and 7, 8 and 47 of the Charter[32] for the following reasons:

1. No exemption or specific protection for communication protected by legal privilege in violation of Article 6 ECHR;
2. The infringement of the protection of personal data and privacy due to the nature (bulk retention) and scope (all persons) of data retention;
3. Lack of protection of professional secrecy of journalists which could infringe upon freedom of the press and association;
4. The lack of precision as to who is provided access to the data and on what grounds can data be requested by intelligence services;
5. The absence of effective jurisdictional review over the data requests;
6. The vague notion of "criminal fact" for the requests by law enforcement would be arbitrary and disproportionate;
7. The lack of a definition of the data to be retained per category of services and requirements of the data (e.g. accuracy...);
8. The period of retention is disproportionate.

---

[30]Act of 30 November 1998 on intelligence and security services, BS 18 December 1998.

[31]Constitutional Court, 11 June 2015, No. 84/2015, available at: www.const-court.be. Accessed 12 June 2015. Summarised in English in: De Hert (2017), pp. 73–75.

[32]The Constitutional Court cannot directly check the compatibility of supranational norms with domestic legislation. However, such control is executed via the provisions 10 and 11 of the Constitution (prohibition of discrimination and right to equal treatment) read into the light of the Articles of the Charter and ECHR.

4 Decision of the Constitutional Court (2015)

During the submission of pleadings to the Constitutional Court, the CJEU had already declared the Data Retention Directive invalid in the case of *Digital Rights Ireland*.[33] As such, the Constitutional Court must judge the constitutionality of the domestic provisions implementing the directive in the light of this judgement. The Constitutional Court highlighted that both the retention of data as access to these data in itself infringe fundamental rights, particularly the protection of personal data (§ B.9). Therefore, the court reiterates in line with the CJEU's judgment that a strict proportionality test must applied to scrutinise whether infringement is proportionate to the legitimate aim of fighting serious crime. Several scholars highlighted that the Constitutional Court by this reasoning accepted that fighting serious crime in itself is a legitimate reason to limit the protection of personal data and privacy by means of data retention, albeit in so far as proportionate.[34]

To assess the proportionality, the court cited at length the CJEU's judgment and approached the constitutional review of the Belgian provisions from the main arguments in the *Digital Rights Ireland* judgment rather than considered the various objections raised by the applicants. The government argued before the court that the CJEU's judgment only affected those domestic provisions explicitly mentioning the Data Retention Directive but was without consequence for Article 126 ECA as Member States remained competent to regulate the retention of data (§ B.7). The government implied that this provision was self-standing, although it was introduced to bring the ECA in line with the Data Retention Directive. The Constitutional Court rejected this reasoning, pointing out that the domestic legislation did not differ substantially from the directive on the crucial points on the basis of which the CJEU had found the Data Retention Directive to violate the Charter (§ B.11).

First, the scope of application is the same, namely a general application to all persons and all electronic communication means, without any distinction based on the purpose of the Data Retention Directive, i.e. the fight against serious crime (§ B.10.1). As such, like the Data Retention Directive, Article 126 ECA allows for the retention of the personal data of persons who have no connection to crime. Second, the retention of these data is in no way linked to the protection of public order or security. There is no limitation as to a certain period or geographic area for the scope of protection (§ B.10.2). Third, there are no material or judicial criteria governing the access to the retained data (§ B.10.3). Fourth, Article 126 ECA makes no distinction as to the period of retention as to the categories of data from the perspective of the fight against serious crime or to the persons affected (§ B.10.4). For the above reasons, the Constitutional Court found the provision to be disproportionate and

---

[33]ECJ, 8 April 2014, *Digital Rights Ireland Ltd v. Minister for Communications, Marine and Natural Resources and Others and Kärntner Landesregierung and Others*, Joined Cases C-293/12 and C-594/12, ECLI:EU:C:2014:238.

[34]Verstraelen, annotation under Constitutional Court 11 June 2015, No. 84/2015, *NC* 2015, pp. 490–491 and Panzavolta, Royer and Severijns (2018), p. 7.

hence, in violation of Articles 7, 8 and 52, §1 of the Charter, and annulled the Belgian act.[35]

5 Consequences and Execution of Judicial Decision (2015)

Following the Constitutional Court's judgment, it was questioned what this meant for ongoing investigations and procedures that relied on data processed based on the annulled data provisions of the ECA. The Constitutional Court had not provided for a temporary preservation of the consequences of the annulled legislation.[36] Consequently, the older data retention provision as established before the Act of 2013 was revived. Therefore, telephony data were still to be retained and could be relied upon in criminal investigations or intelligences operations.

However, it was clear that this was a setback for law enforcement in investigating crime, as the availability of retained electronic communication data was substantially limited by this judgment.[37] Yet, the rules governing access to these data had not been altered by the Constitutional Court's judgment. Under Article 46bis and 88bis CCP, the public ministry and the investigating judge have the competence to request these data if retained by telecommunication service providers or operators.[38] However, the probability that these operators or service providers would reply that these data were no longer available had seriously risen. Moreover, as no Belgian electronic retention obligation would apply, the Belgian authorities would become more dependent on foreign Internet service providers in their assessment of the necessity and proportionality to provide these data.[39] As to the identification data, the loss was only partial because the ECA still allowed for electronic communication operators and services to retain those data as long as necessary for invoicing or technical operations. As such, most electronic communication operators and services will retain subscriber data for a very long period, i.e. as long as the subscriber relies on these services or network for his or her communication. Localisation and traffic data, to the contrary, will much faster be removed by operators and service providers.

[35]As it already found the act to violate the Constitution in the light of the Charter based on application of the *Ordre des barreaux francophones et germanophones*, there was no need to investigate the additional arguments raised by the *Ligue des droits de l'homme*. As such, the court did not deal with the compatibility of data retention and the freedom of expression and association.

[36]Verstraelen (2015a), pp. 492–494. Likewise, the ECJ had not followed the consideration of Advocate General Cruz Villalón who had urged for such measure. See Opinion of Advocate General Cruz Villalón, 12 December 2013, *Digital Rights Ireland Ltd* and *Kärtner Landesregierung*, Joined Cases C-293/12 and C-594/12, ECLI:EU:C:2013:845, §§ 154–158.

[37]On the discussion of the importance of data retention for law enforcement see Cameron (2017), p. 1483.

[38]Verstraelen (2015a), p. 495.

[39]Verbruggen et al. (2018).

The status of electronic communication data already relied upon in ongoing investigations and procedures was less clear. Since the act was annulled, there was no legitimate basis from the start in retaining those data. Following an annulment, the targeted norm is considered never to have been enacted.[40] The privacy act only allows for the retention of personal data based on agreement (consensual) of the owner of the personal data or based on a legal obligation, the latter now being annulled.[41] The Court of Cassation was asked whether the data obtained based on the annulled provision could still be relied on as lawful evidence in criminal procedures.[42] The court reiterated its established doctrine on the use of evidence in criminal investigations (so-called Antigoon doctrine). Evidence which has been obtained in breach of fundamental rights or a formal law should only be dismissed if the criminal procedural code explicitly provides that in breach of the procedural rule the evidence is null and void, the evidence has been rendered inaccurate or unreliable or the evidence has been obtained in violation of Article 6 ECHR. In previous case law, the Court of Cassation already outlined that Article 6 ECHR is breached and evidence should be dismissed, if the committed error against the procedural rules or fundamental right is disproportionate to the crime under investigation, the infringement has been intentional or the contaminated evidence is not material.[43]

As such, in line with the ECtHR case law on this point, a violation of the protection of privacy (Article 8 ECHR) does not necessarily result in excluding evidence.[44] Only if the evidence has been obtained in a manner that does not pass the Antigoon test that the evidence will have to be dismissed. Applied to the data obtained based on the annulled Article 126 ECA, the court found that indeed the data had been obtained in violation of fundamental rights, i.e. Article 8 ECHR. However, the Court of Cassation decided that the evidence should not be excluded as the breach of fundamental rights neither rendered the data inaccurate nor was there any violation of Article 6 ECHR. This judgment is in line with the established

[40]Verstraelen (2015b), p. 278.

[41]It should be noted that only a limited number of cases was involved since the electronic operators and service providers were only obliged to conform to the data retention provision by 9 October 2014. As such, Article 126 ECA had only been fully operative for eight months before its annulment.

[42]Cass. 19 April 2016, AR P.15.1639.N. Discussed in: Meese (2016–2017), pp. 1639–1640 and Van de Heyning (2016a), pp. 368–369.

[43]Cass. 14 oktober 2003, *RABG* 2004, 337, Cass. 23 maart 2004, *RABG* 2004, 1061 and Cass. 2 maart 2005, *JLMB* 2005, 1086. On this case law see De Wolf (2003–2004), pp. 1235–1239; Traest (2004), pp. 133–143; Reynaerts (2011), pp. 94–126; De Smet (2011), pp. 70–84; and Kuty (2008), pp. 32–47. This so-called Antigoon doctrine (Article 32 introductory chapter to the Code of Criminal Procedure) has been tested by the ECtHR and considered compatible with Article 6 ECHR. The ECtHR added an additional criterion, i.e. whether the contaminated evidence is the sole element *à charge*. ECHR, 31 January 2017, No. 40233/07, *Kalneniene v. Belgium*, § 49.

[44]On this issue see Beernaert (2014), p. 80. More critical, De Hert argued (2019, p. 29) that concerning evidence "*concern for rendering privacy, data protection and other constitutional rights effective has been absent.*"

ECtHR case law on this point whereby the Strasbourg court has repeatedly held that reliance on evidence gathered in violation of Article 8 ECHR does not automatically imply a violation of Article 6 ECHR.[45]

The Constitutional Court's judgment came as no surprise given the previous successful challenges before other constitutional courts and the annulment by the CJEU of the directive on which the Belgian legislation was based.[46] It was clear early on that no easy consensus for an alternative to the Data Retention Directive would be found.[47] Moreover, further challenges to the concept of bulk data retention were already pending before the CJEU following preliminary questions from Sweden and the United Kingdom. Nevertheless, Belgium decided to amend the ECA to restore the possibility of bulk retention and safeguard the reliance on these data in criminal investigations. It was argued in parliament that criminal investigations would be seriously handicapped if they could not rely on a normative frame allowing for bulk data retention. Certain scholars also argued that neither the Constitutional Court of the CJEU had outruled the bulk retention of communication data to fight serious crime.[48]

Instead of radically altering its approach to bulk retention of communication data, the legislator opted to further develop the safeguards of processed data and limit the reliance upon these data in criminal investigations in the Act of 29 May 2016.[49] The new Article 126 ECA still provided for a compulsory retention period of 12 months for all subscriber, traffic and localisation data. However, there was no more the possibility to extend this period by Royal Decree. Additional safeguards as to the processing, storage and security were further added to meet the demands of the Constitutional Court.

While maintaining the generalised retention of communication data for 12 months, the provisions in the Criminal Code of Procedure were fundamentally altered limiting and diversifying the timeframe for public prosecutors and investigative judges to retroactively request communication data. This amendment meant that although data might be stored based on the 12-month period under Article 126 ECA, the public prosecutor or investigating judge might not be able to request these data for a criminal investigation. The following framework was provided in the CCP (Table 1):

In addition, the legislator introduced an obligation for the public prosecutor and investigation judge to justify the proportionality and the subsidiarity of the measure. As such, these data could only be requested if no other means could be applied to obtain the same information.

---

[45]ECHR, 12 May 2000, *Khan v. the United Kingdom*, § 34; ECHR, 5 November 2002, *Allan v. the United Kingdom*, §§ 42–43; and ECHR 28 July 2009, *Lee Davies v. Belgium*, §§ 41–42.

[46]Cassart and Henrotte (2014), pp. 956–957.

[47]Conings and Verbruggen (2015), p. 1.

[48]Conings (2015), p. 912.

[49]On the new Act: Conings and De Schepper (2016–2017), pp. 12–13 and De Smet (2016–2017), p. 402.

Table 1 Data access: Competences and duration of criminal investigation

Competence	Data	Period
Public Prosecutor (46bis CCP)	Identification data	Up to 6 months prior to request for crimes punished with a prison sentence below 1 year
		Up to 12 months prior to request for crimes punished with a prison sentence of 1 year or more
Investigation judge (88bis CCP)	Localisation and traffic data	Up to 12 months prior to request for specific terrorist offences
		Up to 9 months prior to request for specific offences committed in a criminal organisation and punished with a prison sentence 5 years or more
		Up to 6 months prior to request for other offences

The new act also answered the critique that the Belgian framework of data retention did not provide sufficient protection for professional secrecy. Also, on this point the legislator amended the provisions in the criminal code concerning the request of retained data and not the retention itself. In Articles 46bis and 88bis CCP a paragraph was added protecting the professional secrecy of lawyers and doctors. The measure may only cover the electronic communications of lawyers or doctors if they are suspected of having committed or participated in one of the criminal offenses for which data can be requested, or if specific facts suggest that third parties suspected of having committed a criminal offense use their electronic communications.[50]

The Privacy Commission issued a positive advice on the new Act finding that the Belgian legislator had remedied the essential flaws of the previous law.[51] The Privacy Commission indirectly criticised the case law of the CJEU holding that it appeared difficult to conceive how data retention could be effectively targeted as to certain person, periods or geographical areas. The Privacy Commission argues that the infringement of the protection of personal data and privacy due to bulk retention is compensated by the limitation in time of the retention, the specific restrictions as to access and reliance upon these data, technical and organisational security measures as to the destruction of retained data, the control by independent authorities on the retention of data and the protection of professional secrecy.[52]

[50]This safeguard was copied from the protection of professional secrecy for wiretapping in Article 90ter CCP.

[51]Privacy Commission, Advice No. 33/2015, 9 September 2015, available at www.privacycommission.be. Accessed 12 January 2019.

[52]Privacy Commission, Advice No. 33/2015, 9 September 2015, §§ 11–12, available at www.privacycommission.be. Accessed 12 January 2019.

6 Proceedings Before the Constitutional Court (2018)

It came as no surprise that an annulment procedure was launched against the new act governing data retention by the *Ligue des droits de l'homme* and *Ordre des barreaux Francophones et Germanophone*. The parties argued that the main objection against the Belgian approach to data retention had not been remedied, i.e. bulk retention of communication data. In the meantime, the CJEU had found the national legislation allowing for bulk retention of communication data in violation of the Charter, more precisely the protection of personal data and privacy, in its *Tele2/Watson* judgment.[53] Once again, the Constitutional Court was requested to reassess the validity of the Belgian data retention framework in the light of a restricting CJEU judgment.

On the one hand, it was argued by the president of the Belgian Privacy Commission that the new legislation would pass the *Tele2/Watson* test as the legislator had considered the protection of communication data under Article 7 of the Charter and imposed a proportionate scheme with sufficient safeguards.[54] Legal scholars were, however, less convinced arguing that the CJEU clearly ruled out bulk retention of communication data.[55] The CJEU argued in this case that bulk retention touched upon the core of the right. In such interpretation, procedural safeguards could not save the provision as a core infringement does not leave any margin of discretion to Member States to balance a limitation of the right towards the public interest of fighting serious crime.

7 Decision of the Constitutional Court (2018)

Given the above, the outcome of the case was much anticipated. The Constitutional Court elaborately cited the *Tele2/Watson* judgment holding that Articles 7 and 8 of the Charter oppose:

> a national framework that regulates the protection and security of traffic data and localization data and in particular the access of national authorities to retained data without, in the context of the fight against crime, stipulating that access can only be provided to fight serious crime, that access is under prior review by a judicial or independent administrative authority, and the concerned data are stored on the sole of the European Union (§ B.6.7).

[53]ECJ, 21 December 2016, *Tele2 Sverige and Watson*, Joined Cases C-203-15 and C-698/15, ECLI: EU:C:2016:970.

[54]Privacycommissie: België heeft datawetgeving al aangepast, Europees arrest niet van toepassing, Reuters, 22 December 2001.

[55]Gosse (2017), pp. 179–204; Royer and Conings (2017), p. 1; Van de Heyning (2017), pp. 533–538; and Forget (2017), p. 233.

At the same time, the Constitutional Court also referred to the more recent ECtHR case law, particularly the case of *Centrum för Rättvisa v. Sweden*.[56] The Strasbourg court, contrary to the CJEU, argued that bulk retention *in itself* is not contrary to Article 8 ECHR, i.e. the right to privacy. The Court argued that bulk retention could be justified to fight specific crimes, particularly those cases where access to electronic communication is crucial for investigating these crimes. In such cases, and if access and reliance on these data is sufficiently protected by safeguards, the limitation of privacy by means of bulk retention can be justified.

Instead of deciding the matter based on the above case law, the Constitutional Court decided that there were still some outstanding questions on the interpretation of the protection of personal data and privacy in the light of the Charter.[57] The Constitutional Court first referred to preliminary questions pending before the CJEU as to what constitutes a legitimate interest to justify a limitation of these rights. In *Digital Rights Ireland* and *Tele2/Watson*, the CJEU had argued that fighting serious crime is a legitimate interest justifying a proportionate limitation of the protection of personal data and privacy. Therefore, it was justified for law enforcement to have access to retained data for this purpose.

The Constitutional Court was questioned how "serious crime" is to be understood.[58] The parliamentary proceedings of the Act of 29 May 2016 elaborate that the retention of data serves not only investigations into terrorism or paedophilia, but can also be relied upon for the investigation of a wide variety of crimes (§ B.3). The Constitutional Court referred to the pending question in the case of *Ministerio Fiscal* (§ B.17.2).[59] The *Audiencia provincial de Tarragona* asked the CJEU whether the sanction should be regarded as the criterion to evaluate the seriousness of a crime, or whether this condition is only fulfilled when individual or collective legal goods are concerned. The *Audiencia* further refined her question by putting forward a prison sentence of 3 years and more as threshold for finding a crime sufficiently serious to justify access to retained localisation and traffic data. The Belgian Constitutional Court decided to suspend its assessment on this issue until after the CJEU's judgment in this case.

---

[56]ECHR, 19 June 2018, No. 35252/08, *Centrum för Rättvisa v. Sweden*. At the moment of the Constitutional Court's analysis, the new ECHR judgment *Big Brother Watch* had not yet been delivered. ECHR, 13 September 2018, Nos. 58170/13, 62322/14 and 294960/15, *Big Brother Watch and others v. United Kingdom*. The latter judgment has not made the task of the Constitutional Court easier as it provides for other criteria as the ECJ to test the legitimacy of data retention. See Christakis (2018).

[57]See for analysis in English: Verbruggen et al. (2018).

[58]Given the lack of a definition of serious crime under the Data Retention Directive, the Council had urged Member States to rely on the list in the Framework decision of the European Arrest Warrant. However, it was early on clear that Member States provided for their own assessment of this notion. See Tzanou (2017), p. 69.

[59]ECJ, 2 October 2018, *Ministerio Fiscal*, C-207/16, ECLI:EU:C:2018:788. See Van de Heyning (2019), pp. 43–44.

In the meantime, the CJEU delivered its judgment applying a flexible approach. The Court highlighted that the e-Privacy Directive allows for the processing of electronic communication for the prevention, investigation, detection and prosecution of criminal offences without specifying that it only applies to "serious" crime.[60] However, the interference for this objective should be proportionate to the infringement of the protection of personal data and privacy.[61] As such, the CJEU does not intend to set a certain threshold of "seriousness" based on the category of crime or the national punishment, but rather provides a margin to the Member States to balance the interference of the fundamental rights versus the seriousness of the crime and the importance of the data to prevent, investigate, detect or prosecute it. The case only concerned access to a restricted part of retained data, namely the subscriber information enabling the identification of SIM users. The CJEU suggests that access to these data is considered a limited infringement of the protection of personal data and private life. Therefore, access to these data for less serious offences can be allowed.

However, the CJEU reiterated the *Tele2/Watson* reasoning that access to traffic and localisation data are in contrast substantial infringements of these fundamental rights and can only be therefore justified for fighting "serious" crime. The key criterion to evaluate whether or not the interference is substantial, is the question whether the data "*allow precise conclusions to be drawn concerning the private lives of the persons whose data is concerned.*"[62] The Belgian legislation (in particular Articles 46bis and 88bis BCC) appear to pass the test set in *Ministerio Fiscal*. While Article 46bis BCC does not set a minimum threshold as to penalty for access to retained identification data, Article 88bis BCC in contrast only allows the investigating judge to request traffic and localisation data for specific, more serious crimes.

The Belgian data retention legislation does not only allow the retention of and access to telecommunication data for investigating crime, but also for intelligence purposes. As such, intelligence services are equally provided access. Therefore, the question remained whether intelligence operations qualified equally as a legitimate interest justifying the limitation of Articles 7–8 of the Charter. The Constitutional Court noted that a preliminary question on this issue was already pending before the CJEU and therefore decided to postpone its decision until the Luxembourg's verdict on the matter (§ B.17.1). The Investigatory Powers Tribunal of London asked the CJEU whether requests by intelligence and security authorities fell into the ambit of the General Data Protection Regulation (GDPR) and e-Privacy Directive, and if so, whether a request by these services to operators and providers to provide bulk communication violated these norms in the light of the protection of personal data and privacy provided in the Charter.[63] The court decided to postpone its analysis on

---

[60]ECJ, 2 October 2018, *Ministerio Fiscal*, C-207/16, § 53, ECLI:EU:C:2018:788.

[61]ECJ, 2 October 2018, *Ministerio Fiscal*, C-207/16, §§ 56–57, ECLI:EU:C:2018:788.

[62]ECJ, 2 October 2018, *Ministerio Fiscal*, C-207/16, § 60, ECLI:EU:C:2018:788.

[63]ECJ, pending, *Privacy International v. Secretary of State for Foreign and Commonwealth Affairs*, Case C-623/17, 2018/C 022/41.

the matter until the CJEU had pronounced on both preliminary questions in order to decide what constitutes a legitimate interest in the view of limiting the protection of personal data and privacy.

Second, the Constitutional Court considered the central question of the case and the core of the *Tele2* judgement, namely whether the protection of personal data and privacy allowed for bulk retention of communication data if the access to these data is restricted. While the CJEU requested that data retention should be targeted and specific, the Belgian legislator had argued that a retention specific to particular persons (e.g. in protection of legal privilege), timeframe or geography is impossible (§ B.4). The Constitutional Court reaffirmed that Belgian legislation did provide for undifferentiated bulk retention of communication data, without any selection as to period, persons and geography or without an exemption of persons for whom a professional secrecy applies (§ B.19.4). This finding in combination with the cited and summarised *desiderata* of the *Tele2* case showed that the Belgian legislation is on its face incompatible with the EU law.

The Belgian government defended the regulation by highlighting that the new norms provided for a regulated framework for the retention of data that had already existed for many years to fight crime. The new norms provide for more safeguards as to the access, the security and accuracy of these data. Second, the government argued that the retention of these data benefits all actors, i.e. not only victims and authorities investigating crime but also suspects to prove their innocence. Third and finally, the Belgian government distinguished the Belgian norms from the legislation concerned in the cases of *Digital Rights Ireland* and *Tele2*, in that the legislation served a broader scope. Article 126 ECA also allowed for access to these data to follow up on calls of emergency services and to locate missing persons whose physical integrity might be in danger. The Belgian government argued that in view of the latter objectives, bulk retention was justified (§ B.20.1). Moreover, it added that a differentiated approach was simply impossible.

The Constitutional Court notifies that many Member States in addition to Belgium find difficulties in rendering their legislation in line with the CJEU case law (§ B.20.2).[64] Moreover, the Constitutional Court highlights that during the hearing the Belgian government mentioned that it is also under an obligation to conform Articles 3 and 8 ECHR to protect the physical and moral integrity of minors and vulnerable persons. The Belgian government stressed that the investigation and prosecution of cases concerning the abuse of minors, also when committed using digital communication tools, is an objective of the data retention act. The Constitutional Court therefore finds that two new constitutional questions should be referred to the CJEU putting bulk retention to the test, namely whether the protection of other rights or interests may justify undifferentiated bulk retention.

---

[64]The Constitutional Court refers to the report of the FRA (Data retention across the EU, http://fra.europa.eu/en/theme/information-society-privacy-and-data-protection/data-retention) as to a letter of the Minister of Justice of the Netherlands to parliament (2017–2018, nr. 34 537, nr. 7), available on https://zoek.officielebekendmakingen.nl/kst-34537-7.html.

Given the phrasing of the question as well as the summary provided by the Constitutional Court of *Tele2*, it appears that the court considers that bulk retention is ruled out if only for the purpose to investigate and prosecute serious crime. The Constitutional Court therefore asks the CJEU whether bulk retention can be a proportionate and therefore justified restriction of Articles 7 and 8 ECHR to protect other interests (i.e. the first preliminary question) or to safeguard positive obligations of fundamental rights protection (i.e. the second preliminary question). The Constitutional Court thereby provides the CJEU for an opportunity to restrictively interpret its *Digital Rights Ireland* and *Tele2* case law and restrict the scope and consequences.

The first question considers whether a national scheme of bulk retention, be it subject to safeguards in relation to data retention and access to these data, violates the protection of personal data and privacy in Articles 7–8 of the Charter and read into the light of the protection of safety conform Article 6 of the Charter if it does not only allow the retention for the investigation of serious crime, but also for ensuring national security, the protection of the borders and public safety, and the investigation, detection and prosecution of facts other than serious crime, the prevention of prohibited use of electronic communications, or the achievement of other objectives identified by Article 23 (1) of Regulation (EU) 2016/679. While the already pending questions consider whether access to retained data or an obligation to retain data is also allowed for objective other than the investigation and prosecution of serious crime, the question of the Constitutional Court is more far-reaching, namely whether these other objectives justify bulk retention. Remarkably, the Constitutional Court does not only refer to these fundamental rights limiting the retention of data (namely the protection of personal data and privacy), but also to a potentially conflicting fundamental rights, i.e. the right to safety.

The second preliminary question focuses on conflicting rights, namely whether bulk retention violates the protection of personal data and privacy, as well as the freedom of expression provided in the Charter, if the objective of the obligation on services providers and operators to retain traffic and location data is to safeguard the positive obligations of the Member States under Articles 4 and 8 of the Charter, namely to allow for effective criminal investigation and punishment of sexual abuse of minors and identify the perpetrators of the crime when using electronic means. With its second question, the Constitutional Court demands the CJEU to consider the critique by the Belgian government that the fight against online sexual abuse of minors is severely undermined without bulk retention of data.

The first two questions are a clear invitation for the CJEU to reconsider its case law. In the *Tele2/Watson* judgment, the CJEU had argued that bulk retention touches upon the core of the protection of personal data and privacy under Articles 7–8 of the Charter. Both rights are relative rights implying that an infringement can be justified by a conflicting legitimate interest or rights if the limitation of the right is proportionate. However, such limitation will not pass the test if it touches upon the core of the fundamental right. Therefore, the Constitutional Court could have dismissed the urge of the Belgian government to consider conflicting interests (such as intelligence surveillance) or rights (such as positive obligations under Articles 4 and 8 of the

Charter). From that perspective, the preliminary questions are an invitation to the CJEU to reconsider its case law, albeit from a broader perspective than merely the fight against serious crimes.

The Constitutional Court referred a third and final question to the CJEU as to the consequences of a potential annulment of the Belgian data retention provision. The court asked the CJEU whether a finding of incompatibility of the Belgian regulation on bulk retention would prevent the reliance on telecommunication data previously processed based on this regulation. In its 2015 judgment on the previous Article 126 ECA, the Belgian Constitutional Court had not discussed the consequences of reliance in criminal procedures on data that had been collected and processed before its judgment.

However, in the meantime questions were raised on the compatibility of the Court of Cassation's case law finding that these data could still be relied upon. Certain scholars had argued that in the case of *Webmindlicenses,* the CJEU had opened the door for a stricter doctrine of the exclusion of contaminated evidence.[65] The CJEU held that evidence gathered without consent in a parallel criminal investigation could be relied upon in a fiscal, administrative procedure if they are gathered in compliance with fundamental rights, thus including Articles 7–8 of the Charter.[66] Whether or not the CJEU had thereby also implied that evidence can only be relied upon in the criminal procedure if in line with fundamental rights was debated.[67] Therefore, the preliminary question to clarify this case law and hence, the consequences for the use of retained data in criminal procedures if the CJEU decides that the Belgian provision is incompatible with Article 7 of the Charter was required to end all speculation. The Constitutional Court explicitly requested the CJEU to consider the matter in the light of the principle of legal certainty.

8 Conclusion

The Data Retention Directive has been a gamechanger in the Belgian legal order on the retention and protection of telecommunication data. Until that moment, data retention had been limited to telephony services and lacked stringent safeguards as to oversight, security and access. For law enforcement, the implementation of the directive opened a new and important avenue for investigation in online activities. Today, digital investigation based on cooperation with Internet service providers and operators is one of the most important investigatory tools. The annulment of the act implementing the directive following the *Digital Rights Ireland* judgment was considered a serious setback. Therefore, Belgium has been an outspoken supporter

[65]ECJ, 17 December 2015, *Webmindlicenses Kft* Case C-419/14, ECLI:EU:C:2015:832.

[66]ECJ, 17 December 2015, *Webmindlicenses Kft*, Case C-419/14, § 90, ECLI:EU:C:2015:832.

[67]See in favour and against: Koning (2016), p. 400; Gnedasj (2016), p. 36; Waeterinckx and Van Heyning (2016), p. 231.

of new rules and reconsideration of the legal framework to provide for a new framework allowing for data retention.

The Belgian legislator did not await a new European initiative and designed a new approach to the retention of telecommunication data: while bulk retention of telecommunication data is maintained, additional safeguards have been included, most notably a limited access for law enforcement to these data. In reply to CJEU's request for differentiated retention, the Belgian legislator answered with differentiated access. Given the CJEU's *Tele2/Watson* ruling, these safeguards might not suffice. This judgment seemed to outrule any form of undifferentiated retention of telecommunication data as it touches upon the core of the protection of personal data. Yet, given the clear contestation by the Belgian government that without bulk retention the fight against serious forms of crime and safeguarding other objectives such as locating a missing person would become impossible, the Constitutional Court decided to provide the CJEU a new opportunity to reconsider or at least refine its approach.[68] While legislators of other Member States rather remained at the background awaiting further guidance from the European Union, the Belgian legislator opted to rethink the framework. It is to be awaited whether it will be pushed back again.

References

Beernaert M-A (2014) La recevabilité des preuves en matière pénale dans la jurisprudence de la Cour européenne des droits de l'homme: nouvel état de la question. In: Bouiokliev I, Dhaeyer P (eds) La théorie des nullités en droit pénal. Anthémis, Limal

Buono I, Taylor A (2017) Mass surveillance in the CJEU: forging a European consensus. Cambridge Law J 76(2)

Cameron I (2017) Balancing data protection and law enforcement needs: Tele2 Sverige and Watson. CML Rev 54(5)

Cassart A, Henrotte J-F (2014) L'invalidation de la directive 2006/24 sur la conservation des données de communication électronique ou la chronique d'une mort annoncée. JMLB 20

Christakis T (2018) A fragmentation of EU/ECHR law on mass surveillance: initial thoughts on the big brother watch judgment. www.europeanlawblog.eu. Accessed 20 Sept 2018

Conings C (2015), Dataretentieplicht en privacy, NJW 333

Conings C (2017) Klassiek en digitaal speuren naar strafrechtelijk bewijs. Intersentia, Antwerpen

Conings C, De Schepper K (2016–2017) Dataretentie: tweede keer, goede keer. Juristenkrant 326

Conings C, Verbruggen F (2015), Grondwettelijk Hof plaats reparateurs dataretentiewet voor moeilijke opdraht. Juristenkrant 312

De Hert P (2017) Courts, privacy and data protection in Belgium: fundamental rights that might as well be struck from the Constitution. In: Brkan M, Psychogiopoulou E (eds) Courts, Privacy and data protection in the digital environment. Edward Elgar Publishing, Cheltenham

De Hert P (2019) Belgium, Courts, Privacy and Data Protection: An Inventory of Belgian Case Law from the Pre-GDPR Regime (1995–2015) (31 January 2019). Brussels Privacy Hubworking Papervol. 5, No. 15, January 2019. Available at SSRN: https://ssrn.com/abstract=3331014 or https://doi.org/10.2139/ssrn.3331014

[68]Verbruggen et al. (2018); Van de Heyning (2019), pp. 46–47.

De Hert P, Boulet G (2016) Belgium. In: Sieber U, Mühlen N. von zur (eds) Access to Telecommunication data in criminal justice. Duncker & Humblot, Berlin

De Hert P, Kopcheva M (2011) International mutual legal assistance in criminal law made redundant: a comment on the Belgian Yahoo! case, Comput Secur Rev 27

De Smet B (2011) Nietigheden in het strafproces. Antwerpen, Intersentia

De Smet B (2016–2017) Nieuwe regels voor dataretentie van telecomoperatoren: een obstakel voor de waarheidsvinding, RW 80(11)

De Wolf D (2004) Nieuwe wending in de rechtspraak betreffende de sanctie bij onrechtmatig verkregen bewijs. RW 67(31)

Forget C (2017) L'obligation de conservation des "métadonnées", la fin d'une longue saga juridique? JT 6683

Gnedasj S (2016) Impact van het arrest WebMindLicenses op de fiscale en strafrechtelijke Antigoon-doctrines. Bescherming van grondrechten op twee snelheden of toch logica en consistentie? Een repliek op de kritiek. . ., AFT 36

Gosse A (2017) Dans quelle mesure les autorités judiciaires belges peuvent-elles contraindre des entreprises de télécommunication étrangères à collaborer à une enquête pénale en Belgique?, *Dr. pén.entr.* 3

Kerkhofs J, Van Linthout P (2013) Cybercrime. Politeia, Brussels

Koning F (2016) Mort de la transposition en matière fiscale de la jurisprudence pénale Antigone? JT 6652

Kosta E, Valcke P (2006) Retaining the data retention directive. Comput Law Secur Rev 22(5):6.2

Kuty F (2008) La sanction de l'illégalité et de irrégularité de la preuve pénale. In: Kuty F, Mougenot D (eds) La Preuve: Questions spéciales. Anthémis, Liège

Meese J (2016–2017) Dataretentie: het Hof van Justitie waakt over onze privacy, RW 41

Panzavolta M, Royer S, Severijns H (2018) Algemene dataretentie: ten minste houdbaar tot. . .?, *T. Strafr.* 1

Reynaerts B (2011) De sanctionering van het onrechtmatig verkregen bewijs voor de vonnisgerechten, NC 0

Royer S, Conings C (2017) Ook hervormde dataretentiewet staat onder druk, Juristenkrant 134

Traest P (2004) Onrechtmatig doch bruikbaar bewijs: het Hof van Cassatie zet de bakens uit. T. Strafr. 2

Tzanou M (2017) The fundamental right to data protection. Hart, Oxford

Van de Heyning C (2016a) Telecommunicatiegegevens toelaatbaar in strafrechtelijk onderzoek – Nieuwe dataretentiewet, T.Strafr. 5

Van de Heyning C (2016b) The boundaries of jurisdiction in cybercrime and constitutional protection: the European perspective. In: Pollicino O, Romeo G (eds) The internet and constitutional law. Routledge, Abingdon

Van de Heyning C (2017) Het gebruik van telecommunicatiegegevens in het strafrechtelijk onderzoek in gevaar?, RABG 7

Van de Heyning C (2019) Overzicht van rechtspraak – Het bewaren en gebruiken van telecommunicatiegegevens in het strafrechtelijk onderzoek: de hoogste hoven in dialoog, T. Strafr. 1

Verbruggen F, Royer S, Severijns H (2018) Reconsidering the blanket-data-retention-taboo, for human rights' sake? www.europeanlawblog.eu. Accessed 1 Oct 2018

Verstraelen S (2015a) De vernietiging van de Belgische Dataretentiewet met terugwerkende kracht: de bescherming van het privéleven primeert, NC 6

Verstraelen S (2015b) Rechterlijk Overgangsrecht. Intersentia, Antwerpen

Waeterinckx P, Van Heyning C (2016) Rechten van verdediging tijdens het strafonderzoek en de regeling van de rechtspleging - capita selecta. In: Conferentie D (ed) Mensenrechten in de Praktijk. Intersentia, Antwerpen

Data Retention in Bulgaria

Alexander Kashumov

Abstract The Data Retention Directive 2006/24/EC was initially transposed into the Bulgarian legal order in 2008 through a regulation enacted by the Minister of Interior and the President of the State Agency of Information Technologies and Communications. The regulation introduced a 12-month long retention period for electronic communication and allowed a unit in the Ministry of Interior direct access to the data. In December 2008, the Supreme Administrative Court held that the regulation violated Articles 32 and 34 of the Bulgarian Constitution and Article 8 of the European Convention on Human Rights. The later amendments to the data protection legislation were found in contravention of the Constitution by the Constitutional Court in 2015. The Parliament passed new provisions in line with the Constitutional Court judgment shortening the retention period to six months. Subsequently, in 2016 and 2018, the new laws on anti-terrorism and anti-corruption tend to shift the balance back to security, rather than privacy.

1 Implementation of Directive 2006/24/EC in Bulgaria

The development of technologies gave rise to the question of using communications data, exchanged by mobile and Internet providers, in combatting crime. Before the enactment of specific legislation on the subject, granting access to communications databases was one of the requirements mobile providers had to meet in order to obtain a license. In 2006, the European Parliament and the Council adopted Directive 2006/24/EC[1] on the retention of data related to the traffic of electronic

[1]Directive 2006/24/EC of the European Parliament and of the Council of 15 March 2006 on the retention of data generated or processed in connection with the provision of publicly available electronic communications services or of public communications networks and amending Directive 2002/58/EC.

A. Kashumov (✉)
Access to Information Programme, Sofia, Bulgaria
e-mail: kashumov@aip-bg.org

M. Zubik et al. (eds.), *European Constitutional Courts towards Data Retention Laws*, Law, Governance and Technology Series 45,
https://doi.org/10.1007/978-3-030-57189-4_5

communications, which obliged Member States to pass legislation ensuring the retention of data related to the traffic of electronic communications for a period between 6 and 24 months. The idea of harmonising the legislations of Member States in this regard was to guarantee that those data would be accessible in the investigation, detection, and prosecution of serious crimes, in accordance with the definition of the latter in each Member State.

In January 2008, the Directive was incorporated into Bulgarian legislation by a specific Regulation,[2] enacted jointly by the Minister of Interior and the Chairman of the State Agency for Information Technology and Communications. In contrast with the Directive, the enacted Regulation provided for a much wider scope of offences, the detection of which justified retaining and obtaining access to data, connected with the traffic of electronic communications. The Regulation specified that the retention and accessing of those data was prescribed for the broad purpose of "detection of crimes," whereas the Directive stipulated the more narrow scope of "detection of serious crimes." The other purpose of the retention and accessing of data was also formulated in general terms—"in the interests of national security."

In addition to the problem with the scope of the retained data, there was also the issue related to the access of public institutions to those data. Article 5 of Regulation No. 40/2008 allowed investigative authorities, courts, and security services to access the data upon a mere request in writing, without need of a court order. Furthermore, a Ministry of Interior Directorate was granted the right to receive unlimited direct access to the data through a computer terminal.

2 Decision of the Supreme Administrative Court (2008)

Access to Information Programme (AIP)[3] challenged Regulation No. 40/2008 before the Supreme Administrative Court (SAC), highlighting its incompatibility with the Bulgarian Constitution and the European Convention on Human Rights (ECHR). A three-member panel of the SAC declared the complaint admissible, but then dismissed it on its merits. AIP appealed the decision before a five-member panel of the SAC, which ruled that Article 5 of the Regulation, relating to the procedure for granting public authorities access to data connected with the traffic of electronic communications, should be abolished.[4]

On the provision of the Regulation granting access to traffic data to a Ministry of Interior Directorate through a computer terminal, the SAC held that it "does not pose

[2]Regulation No. 40 of 7 January 2008 on the categories of data and the mechanism of retention and transmission of data by enterprises providing public electronic communication services for the purposes of national security and the detection of crimes.

[3]An NGO created in 1996 with the mission to facilitate general access to government-held information. As the protection of personal data is the other side of the coin, the organisation also works in that field.

[4]Judgment of the Bulgarian Supreme Administrative Court, 11 December 2008, No. 13627.

any limitations on the scope of data that can be accessed through a computer terminal, and the justification 'for the purposes of detection' is too general and does not guarantee the inviolability of private life, enshrined in Article 32 § 1 of the Bulgarian Constitution. No measures have been envisaged to protect against unlawful interference with the individual's private and family life, as well as against encroachment on his honour, dignity, and good reputation."

On the stipulated right of investigative authorities, prosecution authorities, and courts to access data related to the traffic of electronic communications "in the interest of executing criminal proceedings," and the identical right of security services—"in the interest of national security," the five-member panel of the SAC held that the wording of the Regulation in this regard did not provide for any measures protecting against potential abuse of the constitutional rights of citizens. Such measures could have been, for example, referring to other legislation, such as the Criminal Procedure Code, the Special Intelligence Means Act, and the Personal Data Protection Act, which detail the conditions of allowing access to certain data, connected with the personal life and personal data of individuals. The SAC concluded that the three paragraphs of Article 5 of Regulation No. 40/2008 violated Article 32 and Article 34 of the Bulgarian Constitution and Article 8 of the ECHR.[5]

3 Consequences and Execution of the Judicial Decision (2008)

The abolition of Article 5 of Regulation No. 40/2008 provoked intensive action on clarifying the legal framework related to the retention and accessing of data, connected with the traffic of electronic communications. In January 2009, there were already debates in Parliament concerning the introduced amendments to the Electronic Communications Act (ECA). The attempts of reinstating the direct access of a Ministry of Interior Directorate to the data was rejected by a majority in Parliament. Instead, the legislators established mandatory judicial control of the access, stipulating that every request for access should be warranted by an order of the relevant regional court. The scope of offences, the detection and prosecution of which would justify granting access to traffic data, was limited to the categories of "serious offences"[6] and "computer crimes." The introduced period of data retention was 12 months.

Following the general elections in 2009, the administration of the newly-appointed Minister of Interior, Tsvetan Tsvetanov, drew up a new proposition for amendments to the ECA, aimed at facilitating the Ministry of Interior's access to data related to the traffic of electronic communications. This sparked heated

[5]See the Judgment of the SAC in Bulgarian language at: http://aip-bg.org/pdf/reshenie%2013627_december%2008.pdf.

[6]Under Article 93 § 1, item 7 of the Criminal Code "serious crimes" are those offences punishable with more than five years imprisonment.

discussions within the ministry and in Parliament, as a result of which a new version of the ECA was adopted in 2010, amending the provisions connected with the retention and accessing of data related to the traffic of electronic communications. The new ECA did not provide for direct technical access to retained data but increased the scope of institutions that could request access to such data. It was established that accessing data for detecting crimes would be granted upon obtaining an order from the relevant regional court,[7] and accessing data for investigating crimes would be regulated by the Criminal Procedure Code.[8] Once again, the scope of offences whose detection and investigation could justify accessing traffic data was widened by supplementing the category of "serious offences" with the category of "computer crimes." On the positive side, the legislators adopted some propositions of civil society organisations, among which were: the rule that only heads of competent authorities shall have the right to submit requests to mobile and Internet providers for access to traffic data; the requirement that requests for access to traffic data should contain an outline of the purposes for which the data are requested; and that Parliament would exercise monitoring functions over the Ministry of Interior with respect to accessing traffic data.

Statistical information illustrates the results of the legislative changes and their application in the period 2008–2011. According to information announced in Parliament by Michael Mikov, the Minister of Interior preceding Tsvetan Tsvetanov, in 2008 the Ministry of Interior obtained around 300,000 records containing traffic data of around 40,000 users.[9] The statistics actually reflected the period when Regulation No. 40/2008 was in force.

The 2009 amendments in ECA changed the trend imposing a strict regime requiring that a court permission be obtained prior to each individual access of an authorised public body to retained electronic communications data. However, the ECA amendments of 2010 provided for a wider scope of access to data related to the traffic of electronic communications without envisaging sufficient measures to protect individuals' rights to privacy. This is evidenced by the official report of the relevant Parliamentary sub-committee, according to which in the period between 1 January 2010 and 9 May 2010, when the 2009 ECA amendments were in force, the number of access permissions amounted to 2760, while in the period between 10 May 2010 and 31 December 2010, when the next amendments of the ECA entered into force, the number of access permissions amounted to 18,845.[10] In this later period, access to retention data was denied only in 358 cases. Some of the amendments to the ECA only provided for an opportunity to go around the

[7]Article 250c, §§ 1–3 of the ECA. Regional courts are the courts of first instance. The previous legal regime under 2009 ECA amendments provided that the higher level "district courts" are in charge.

[8]Article 250d, § 4 of the ECA.

[9]SEGA Daily, *Службите са следили незаконно 40 000 души*, 20 March 2009. Available at: http://old.segabg.com/article.php?id=407480.

[10]The matter was discussed in an article in *Dnevnik daily* written by Pavlina Jeleva: https://m.dnevnik.bg/bulgaria/2011/01/20/1028582_sledeneto_na_telefoni_i_internet_bez_sudeben_kontrol_e/.

procedures for obtaining access after a court order has been granted. As early as 2010, the Prosecutor's Office issued guidelines for the application of the law, according to which it was interpreted that a court order would not be necessary if the access to traffic data was for the investigation of serious offences and computer crimes.[11] Indeed, following the 2010 amendments, in such cases the ECA referred to the provisions of the Criminal Procedure Code (hereafter: CPC). The CPC confers on courts and investigative authorities the right to request data, including traffic data, from individuals.[12] On another hand, a court order was necessary to warrant access to the data retained only for detecting such criminal offences. According to the official report of the relevant Parliamentary Sub-committee, in 2011, access to data within the meaning of the ECA was granted under the CPC procedure in 58,702 cases (i.e. without a court order), while in 15,350 cases the access was granted under Article 250b § 1 of the ECA (following a court order).[13] The number of refusals to grant access was again very low - only 639. Following the 2010 ECA amendments, the number of access permissions increased considerably—from 20,605 in 2010 to 74,052 in 2011, or more than three times within the period of 1 year.

The data for 2013, 2014, and 2015 are derived from a report of the Parliamentary Committee for Control of the Security Services, of the Application and Use of Special Surveillance Means, and of the Access to the Data under the Electronic Communications Act. In 2013, the requests for access submitted to mobile operators alone were 116,091. For 2014 and 2015, the numbers are 108,333 and 70,406, respectively. Furthermore, in 2015, 12,948 requests for access were submitted to courts; the courts granted 12,856 permissions to access and issued 1994 refusals. According to official information, obtained by Access to Information Programme in the context of the case *Ekimdzhiev and others v. Bulgaria*, the requests to access communications data in 2016 were 57,678. To date, there is no information of any individuals ever been informed that their communications data have been unlawfully breached.

4 Proceeding Before the Constitutional Court (2015)

In April 2014, the Court of Justice of the European Union (hereafter: CJEU) declared Directive 2006/24/EC invalid.[14] The Court held that the Directive was incompatible with Article 7, Article 8, and Article 52 § 1 of the Charter of Fundamental Rights of

[11]The guidelines were not publicly available but provided on information request to *Dnevnik daily* which disclosed the said content in the article referred to above.

[12]See Article 159 of the Criminal Procedure Code.

[13]The information contained in the 2011 report of the Sub-committee was commented in an article published on the online media Praven Svjat at: http://legalworld.bg/26868.razreshenite-srs-izkustveno-namaliavat-no-horata-sreshtu-koito-se-prilagat-se-uvelichavat.html.

[14]Judgment of the Court of Justice of the European Union, 8 April 2014, case No. C-293/12 and case No. C-594/12.

the EU. The CJEU judgment was passed not long after the Federal Constitutional Court of Germany abolished the provisions incorporating the Directive within the country's national legislation.

In the same year, the Bulgarian Ombudsman, Konstantin Pentchev, lodged an application to the Constitutional Court of Bulgaria to declare the ECA provisions transposing Directive 2006/24/EC within the national legislation incompatible with the Bulgarian Constitution. State agencies and NGOs also took part in the case as interested parties. *Amicus curiae* briefs were submitted by the Supreme Court of Cassation, the Supreme Administrative Court, the Supreme Bar Council, the President, the Ministry of Interior, the Ministry of Transport, Information Technology and Communications, the Prosecutor General, the National Bureau for Control over Special Intelligence Means, the Communication Regulations Commission, the Union of Jurists in Bulgaria, Access to Information Programme, Bulgarian Lawyers for Human Rights, and the Modern Policy Institute.

The Ombudsman referred to the CJEU judgment on joint cases C-293/12 and C-594/12, with which the Court declared Directive 2006/24/EC invalid due to inconsistencies with provisions of the Charter of Fundamental Rights of the EU. In his opinion, the legislation transposing the Directive into national law was in violation of Article 5 § 4 of the Bulgarian Constitution, which states that international treaties, ratified, promulgated, and in force in Bulgaria, are considered part of the domestic law and precede any provisions that contradict them. In addition, the Ombudsman claimed that the ECA provisions were incompliant with Article 32 § 1 of the Bulgarian Constitution, which safeguards the private life of citizens, as well as with Article 34 § 1, which protects the confidentiality of correspondence and other communications. According to the Ombudsman, the nature of data collected with respect to electronic communications permitted the identification of the parties whom the user communicates with, as well as modalities, such as the location, time, and the means and frequency of communication.

In his statement, the President supported the application of the Ombudsman stating that the extension of the scope of crimes for the detection and investigation of which electronic communications traffic data could be retained and subsequently accessed by the authorised public bodies seems to contradict Article 34 of the Constitution. The latter permits interference in communication only where it is necessary for the prevention or detection of "serious crimes" and should be interpreted strictly, while most of the "computer crimes" do not fall in that category. He also raised the argument that the data retention regime applies broadly and extends to individuals who are neither suspects nor anyhow connected with the commission of a crime and even to those whose communications are subject to confidentiality. The data collection actually allows detailed profiling of individuals and there were no guarantees against abuse by public authorities. In conclusion, the President shared the opinion that the disputed ECA provisions were in violation of Articles 32 § 1 and 34 of the Bulgarian Constitution and Article 8 of the European Convention of Human Rights.

Similar considerations were expressed in the statement of the Supreme Court of Cassation (hereafter: SCC) which is the highest judicial body for criminal cases. SCC found that the compliance of the disputed ECA provisions with Article 8 of ECHR was of crucial importance in the case. The broad scope of individuals covered by the data retention just for the sake of prevention was pointed out as a problem. The lack of differentiation of the categories of the data and subsequent determination of duration of the retention for those categories was also mentioned. According to SCC, the national legislator simply reflected the content of the Data Retention Directive without taking care of the fundamental rights that are affected.

The application of the Ombudsman was also supported by all the NGOs involved in the case.

On another hand, the Ministry of Interior submitted that the provisions of the ECA transposing Directive 2006/24/EC that were challenged by the Ombudsman in fact fell within the scope of exceptions to the protection of individual rights under the Bulgarian Constitution. Therefore, the Ministry maintained that the only pertinent question for the Court to address was that of the proportionality of the measures envisaged in the said provisions. In that regard, the Ministry claimed that the ECA provisions at issue conformed to the principles of necessity and proportionality, established by the CJEU, as the 12-month period of data retention was relatively short and consistent with the legitimate aim behind the interference with citizens' rights. The Ministry of Interior further argued that the CJEU abolished Directive 2006/24/EC, but left in force Directive 2002/58/EC, which in its Article 15 stipulated that Member States could adopt measures to ensure the protection of national security, the public order, and the enforcement of domestic criminal law provisions. The Ministry stated that safeguarding the latter interests did not simply justify the proportionality of the adopted measures, but was also deemed in line with guaranteeing the right to security of individuals, enshrined in Article 6 of the European Charter of Fundamental Rights.

5 Decision of the Constitutional Court (2015)

With a judgment dated March 2015,[15] the Constitutional Court proclaimed all provisions relating to the retention and access to traffic data incompliant with the Bulgarian Constitution.[16] The Constitutional Court held that the legal framework in this regard could be amended so as to not contravene the Constitution. This objective would be achieved by regulating the state interference with traffic data by means of clear legislation that would fall within the exceptions of the Constitution, require that the interference pursues a legitimate aim and be in accordance with the public interest. The Constitutional Court further ruled that the retention of data without evidence of the subjects' involvement in criminal activities did not constitute a disproportionate measure, but the period of the retention did. The Court found the

[15]Judgment of the Constitutional Court of the Republic of Bulgaria, 12 March 2015, No. 2 on case No. 8/2014.

[16]Articles 250a–250e, 251, and 251a of the Electronic Communications Act.

latter to be too long, as "the accumulation of a communication traffic database for a period of one year would permit the use of such data not only for the building of a comprehensive personal profile (having in mind the problems this itself evokes), but also for attaining an accurate and detailed differentiation of the permanent, regular, and incidental activities of subjects, their contacts, interests (including those that form precedents in their behaviour), and reactions, as well as for systematising, by means of set criteria, the places they visit regularly or incidentally, and the persons they meet with." In conclusion, the Constitutional Court declared that there were no sufficient procedural guarantees to safeguard the rights of citizens, drawing on parallels with the legal framework governing the use of special surveillance means. Furthermore, the Constitutional Court held that the challenged legislative provision connected with eliminating the judicial control over requests for access to traffic data by investigative authorities (the hypothesis referring to the CPC) was incompliant with the standards set by the Bulgarian Constitution, the European Charter of Fundamental Rights, and the ECHR.

In a concurring opinion, three of the constitutional justices disagreed partly with the majority. They pointed that declaring the whole range of the disputed provisions unconstitutional went too far and was not consistent with the established practice of the Constitutional Court. They emphasised it was not necessary to find all the provisions contrary to the Constitution when there were concrete breaches such as the duration of the retention and the lack of requirement to access the data only after a court order in some cases. Otherwise they said, the provisions on data retention would be useful for the effective fight against serious crimes and especially terrorism. So, such legislation should exist, but in line with the Constitution. They did also point that the Constitution also permits interference with the aim to prevent serious crimes but such issues were not subject to any legislative initiative so they thought the Constitutional Court should call the legislator to act in this field.

6 Consequences and Execution of the Judicial Decision (2015)

Shortly after the Constitutional Court's judgment, the legislature adopted new ECA amendments in the area of retention and access to data related to the traffic of electronic communications.[17] The changes provided that there should be a court permission in each case of access to the electronic communications data retained.

In 2016, Parliament enacted the Countering Terrorism Act with which it amended the ECA.[18] Under these amendments, in cases of immediate danger of committing certain listed serious crimes, the electronic communications providers are obliged to provide immediate access to the retained data to the relevant public bodies. In these

[17]Electronic Communications Act, amended, published in State Gazette No. 24 of 2015.

[18]Published in State Gazette No. 103 of 27 December 2016.

cases, permission by a court is not required. The law does not specify which cases are of "immediate danger," nor how the latter is established, by whom, and by what criteria.

In 2018, Parliament enacted the Countering Corruption and Confiscation of Illegally Obtained Property Act with which it amended the ECA.[19] With these amendments, the public bodies responsible for countering corruption obtain the right to access retained data under the conditions of ECA.[20] Those bodies do not have any investigative power and obtain information about individuals occupying high-ranking posts just for the sake of data collection.

In the last years, the Parliamentary Committee responsible for the supervision of the use of special surveillance means and data retention did not publish its reports, thus changing the practice of wider publicity in the period 2010–2012.[21] Such reports are not available for the period 2017–2018 (http://www.parliament.bg/bg/parliamentarycommittees/members/2596/reports).

With judgment on criminal case No. C-61/2015, the Sofia City Court found the previous President of the SCC, Vladimira Yaneva, guilty of a criminal offence related to issuing an illegal permission for the use of special surveillance means.[22] With the same judgment, it found guilty the ex-internal security chief Todor Kostadinov. In the case, there were findings of serious abuse of the police electronic system containing registered suspects' data.[23]

In the meantime, the former Minister of Interior, Tsvetan Tsvetanov, was acquitted of crimes related to allowing illegal overtapping. The motivation of the court judgment was classified, and a journalist was denied access to it.[24]

In 2020, following the outburst of the Covid-19 pandemic, Parliament introduced new amendments to the ECA, through which the Ministry of Interior was granted the right to access the communications data of individuals in quarantine without obtaining a court permission. This increase in the scope of powers is not limited to the Covid-19 disease context. The amendments were challenged before the Constitutional Court by a group of MPs. The case is still pending.

---

[19]Published in State Gazette No. 7 of 19 January 2018.

[20]Article 251b, § 2.

[21]For example, the 2011 report was published in the periodic issue of the Supreme Bar Council: http://www.vas.bg/p/A/d/Adv10_2012_3-2147.pdf.

[22]See http://www.bta.bg/en/c/DF/id/1251794.

[23]See also: https://www.capital.bg/politika_i_ikonomika/bulgaria/2015/11/05/2643184_po_deloto_chervei_dans_izmislila_kak_da_podslushva/.

[24]See application No. 4326/2018 registered by the European Court of Human Rights—*Girginova v. Bulgaria*.

Data Retention in Cyprus in the Light of EU Data Retention Law

Christiana Markou

Abstract The chapter aims at describing the Cypriot data retention regime contained in Law 183(I)/2007, which transposes the Data Retention Directive into Cyprus law, as developed through case law from the transposition of the Directive to a very recent Supreme Court judgement. The latter judgement seems capable of putting an end to the wrong direction towards which case law has been heading so far and marking the beginning of a new era of data retention. The chapter starts with the period beginning with the introduction of Law 183(I)/2007 and ending with the 2014 CJEU ruling annulling the Data Retention Directive, and then proceeds with the period beginning with the said ruling and finishing with the 2018 Supreme Court judgement. It is demonstrated that the case law has wrongly regarded Law 183(I)/2007 as having remained unaffected by the annulling CJEU ruling and has thus continued upholding court orders allowing access to retained data even after a more recent CJEU judgement in which a general and indiscriminate data retention obligation has explicitly been stated to be incompatible with the EU Charter. The chapter finishes with a discussion on the possible practical effects of the 2018 Supreme Court judgement on data retention in Cyprus as well as on the possible upcoming amendments at national and the EU level, which should be expected to clearly set the boundaries of data retention and establish legal certainty. It should however been clarified that this chapter is based on the state of the relevant law as of April 2018. Developments have taken place during the publication process which prevented or delayed the change that the present author illustrates as possible following the 2018 Supreme Court decision. More specifically, the certiorari application filed in context of the relevant case has been withdrawn and the state of the law regarding data retention in Cyprus has remained unchanged. However, the matter is currently pending before the Supreme Court of Cyprus sitting as a full bench court and remains to be seen whether there will be a change of approach. It is hoped that a development at EU level, namely the decision of the CJEU in *C-207/16 Ministerio Fiscal* should not be taken as entailing a deviation of the European Court from its

C. Markou (✉)
European University Cyprus, C. Markou & Co LLC, Nicosia, Cyprus
e-mail: c.markou@euc.ac.cy

M. Zubik et al. (eds.), *European Constitutional Courts towards Data Retention Laws*, Law, Governance and Technology Series 45,
https://doi.org/10.1007/978-3-030-57189-4_6

previous case law; said decision concerns a very specific question relating to access to data only and the CJEU expressly emphasizes in paragraph 49 of its judgement that the question before it did not concern with the legality of the retention of the data at all.

1 Implementation of Directive 2006/24/EC in Cyprus

The Directive 2006/24/EC on data retention (the Data Retention Directive) has been a highly controversial measure. Before and even after its entry into force, commentators and privacy activists have seen in the said measure a disproportionate interference with the human rights to data protection and privacy guaranteed by the EU Charter of Human Rights. Its purpose, namely the combatting of serious crime including terrorism, was definitely a legitimate one, yet the retention of data of *all* citizens prescribed by it appeared to be an exaggerated response to the relevant problem that showed little respect to the privacy of EU citizens. The author of this article has looked into this controversy elsewhere[1] and has concluded that the relevant criticism was valid; due to problems with its provisions on data retention and because access to the retained data by enforcement authorities was left to be dealt with by the Member States, the Directive failed to strike a fair balance between security on the one hand and privacy on the other.

Despite all issues, the Directive had to be transposed into the national laws of all Member States. Cyprus, being a Member State of the EU, has, for this purpose, introduced Law 183(I)/2007 on the basis of which numerous court orders have been issued allowing the police access to traffic and location data of individuals suspected of crimes. Until 2014, the validity of several of those court orders has been challenged with no success; the Supreme Court, hearing relevant applications for certiorari, i.e. a prerogative order annulling a lower court's order on grounds of manifest illegality (or applications for leave for a certiorari application), has repeatedly opined that the court orders allowing access to retained data were in line with the data retention law. Indeed, that was true.

In 2014, however the CJEU annulled the Data Retention Directive taking a clear and strict view against it seeing a problem *not only* with the non-regulation of the issue of access to data *but also* with the data retention obligation as such. National courts (in Cyprus at least) seem not to have shared the relevant opinion of the CJEU or did not actually want to take it up. After all, despite the annulment of the Directive, the national law transposing it into the Cypriot legal order *remained* and the question as to how its validity was affected by the CJEU ruling proved not an easy one to resolve. Additionally, the said law empowered enforcement authorities in their fight against serious crime to which courts are naturally sympathetic. Moreover, Cyprus has gone as far as to amend the Constitution to accommodate

[1]Markou (2012), pp. 468–475.

the data retention law, thereby bringing it in line with it. The said move attracted negative criticism[2] and was definitely dramatic; in most cases, it is a law that must be brought in line with the Constitution, not the opposite. Thus, when the Data Retention Directive (which effectively led to this move) has been set aside, the Cypriot legal order ended up with a law that was definitely constitutional (or perfectly aligned with the Constitution) but which was based on a Directive, which has been found to be in contravention of the EU Charter of Fundamental Rights. Admittedly, Cypriot courts have found themselves in a delicate position. The ultimate result was that the pre-2014 stance of case law remained unchanged. Specifically, lower courts have been issuing access orders based on the national data retention law (Law 183(I)/2007) and the Supreme Court has been rejecting certiorari applications (and/or applications for leave for certiorari applications) in which the applicants disputed their validity on the ground that they were not in accord with the Charter, specifically with the human rights of data protection and privacy.

In the view of the present author, the overall legal position was relatively straightforward. As the present author argued elsewhere,[3] the Cypriot data retention law is effectively *a copy* of the data retention provisions of the Directive. Since that Directive has been found to be incompatible with the Charter, the relevant national law inevitably must be regarded as incompatible with the Charter, too. The supremacy of the EU law, expressly dictated in Article 1A of the Constitution, effectively means that the Charter must be given precedence over the (conflicting) national data retention law and in effect, the said law is rendered inapplicable. Put simply, no court should have applied a law that contravenes the EU Chater, thereby issuing data access orders integrally associated with the provisions relating to the retention of the data. The Supreme Court, acting as an appeal court, had to put an end to the different case law direction, and it appeared prepared to do so in 2018 in an appeal to a decision dismissing one of the applications for leave for a certiorari application against a data access order. Although the 2018 Supreme Court judgement has not in fact demolished the current Cypriot data retention regime, the Cypriot legislature will probably have to set a new one, hopefully based on a correct reading of the 2014 CJEU ruling and thus, in line with the Charter. Already relevant amendments are being discussed both at national and the EU law.

This chapter aims to describe the Cypriot data retention regime, as it has developed from the transposition of the Data Retention Directive into Cyprus law to the aforementioned 2018 Supreme Court judgement, which may mark the beginning of a new era of data retention that cannot be assessed at this stage. It will start with the period starting with introduction of the data retention (transposition) law and ending with the 2014 CJEU ruling annulling the Data Retention Directive, and then proceed with the period beginning with the said ruling and ending with the 2018 Supreme Court judgement. It will finish with a discussion on the possible practical

[2]Kombos (2015), pp. 411–427.

[3]Markou (2017).

effects of this judgement on data retention in Cyprus as well as on the possible upcoming amendments at national and the EU level, which, hopefully, will avoid mistakes and manage to clearly set the boundaries of data retention and access to retained data, thereby establishing legal certainty.

2 Decision of the Supreme Court (2011)

In 2007, Cyprus passed the Law 183(I)/2007 having the same title as that of the Data Retention Directive, thereby transposing the latter into the Cypriot legal order. The law effectively copies the provisions of the Directive regarding the obligation of electronic communications service providers to retain data, specifically traffic and location data, generated by the use of their services by individual users. On access to the retained data by enforcement authorities, the law subjects such access to the obtaining of a relevant court order addressed to relevant providers, ordering them to disclose the data to the relevant authorities. However, up to 2010, there was a constitutional obstacle to the usability of the said law, which meant that while the law existed, it could not work in practice, thereby allowing the police access to the retained data and serving its aim of facilitating the combatting of serious crime.[4] More specifically, Article 17(2) of the Constitution, as it stood up to 2010, only allowed an interference with the right to the secrecy of communications in certain very limited cases, specifically with regard to persons in custody or serving imprisonment or being under receivership/administration. Accordingly, the Constitution did not permit the access to telecommunications data of *any* person suspected to be involved in crime provided for by Law 183(I)/2007.

A decision of the Supreme Court in 2011[5] serves as a clear illustration of the aforementioned constitutional "block" to Law 183(I)/2007. It concerned a certiorari application against several court orders that enabled access to telecommunications data of four applicants who were suspected of crimes. Except for the case of one applicant who had been in prison during the period for which his data had been retained, the application succeeded and the relevant access orders were annulled on the ground that Article 17(2) of the Constitution did not permit an interference with their right to the secrecy of communication; the applicants were not in custody or in prison or under administration or receivership. Although the judgement had been seen as mirroring the Cyprus court rejecting the data retention law and in effect, the Data Retention Directive, thereby possibly having wider repercussions on the

[4]That alone meant that up to then, the data retention obligation as laid down in the Cypriot transposition law was nothing but a manifest violation of the human rights of data protection and privacy, as it could serve no legitimate purpose against which the proportionality of the restriction to human rights it entailed could be assessed. In other words, it was restricting the said human rights basically for reason. For more on this, see Markou (2017).

[5]Matsias and others (2011) 1 CLR 152.

Cypriot data retention regime,[6] that was *not* in fact the case. First, the decision did not touch upon the data retention provisions of the relevant law at all. Besides, given Article 1A of the Constitution, which specifically states that nothing in the Constitution could effectively bar compliance on the part of Cyprus with its obligations derived from the EU law, the data retention obligations of Law 183(I)/2007 could not be regarded as unconstitutional and/or invalid. The said provisions were transposition provisions introduced so that Cyprus could comply with its obligation to transpose the corresponding provisions of the Data Retention Directive. The decision thus focused on the issue of access to the retained data allowed by the court orders in dispute and annulled them by reference of Article 17(2); it did not even expressly declare the provisions on access to retained data of Law 183(I)/2007 as unconstitutional, although in the opinion of the present author, it arose that they were clearly incompatible with the Constitution. Moreover, the relevant decision was limited to the facts of that particular case and was not bound to have any wider implications on data retention in Cyprus.

Indeed, the Cyprus legislature has realised the problem and reacted to it by the Sixth Amendment of the Constitution passed in 2010, while the aforementioned case related to retained data referring to a period preceding the said constitutional amendment. The amendment clearly aimed to bring Article 17(2) of the Constitution in line with Law 183(I)/2007, as the former has, since then, expressly permitted an interference with the right to the secrecy of communication, also when the said interference is in the form of *access orders* for the prevention, investigation and prosecution of serious crime. Consequently, the relevant constitutional obstacle had been removed and no more successful certiorari applications (or annulled data access court orders) should have been expected. Indeed, following the 2010 amendment of the Constitution, *Law 183(I)/2007 became perfectly workable*; on its basis Cypriot courts have issued numerous orders allowing the police access to retained data and *all* certiorari applications seeking to challenge the validity or legality of such orders on grounds of constitutionality would have failed. It follows therefrom that the period between 2010 and 2014 was the one during which data retention law in Cyprus was working "according to plan" and without any problems being envisaged. Yet, as it later became clear, this "normality" in the data retention scene was in reality only temporary.

3 Data Retention Legislation in Cyprus *After* the 2014 CJEU Ruling

In its infamous judgement in *Digital Rights Ireland Ltd, C-293/12, 8 April 2014*, the CJEU has been clear and unequivocal:

[6]EDRi, Data retention law provisions declared unlawful in Cyprus, 9 February 2011. https://edri.org/edrigramnumber9-3data-retention-un-lawful-cyprus/.

> *Directive 2006/24/EC* of the European Parliament and of the Council of 15 March 2006 on the retention of data generated or processed in connection with the provision of publicly available electronic communications services or of public communications networks and amending Directive 2002/58/EC *is invalid.*[7]

This is how the Court concluded its judgement by which it annulled the Data Retention Directive on the ground that it contravened Articles 7 and 8 of the Charter by disproportionately interfering with the human rights to data protection and privacy guaranteed by the said two provisions of the Charter.

This blatant rejection of the Data Retention Directive by the CJEU did not however prevent the Cyprus Supreme Court from stating that it had no effect on the national data protection legislation, which remained in force as *national* law (or part of the national legal order).[8] This statement seems to have influenced subsequent case law in which certiorari applications seeking the annulment of data access court orders on the ground of the aforementioned 2014 CJEU ruling (or applications for leave for a certiorari application) were rejected.[9] Yet, as I have argued elsewhere, the said case law was misguided heading towards the wrong direction.[10] Indeed, the fact that national legislation exists does not mean that it is (or should be) applicable too. The effect of the principle of supremacy (or primacy) of the EU law as developed by the CJEU[11] is that "(...) any conflict between a Community norm and a national norm that have the same scope of application *should be solved by a non-application of conflicting national law* (...)".[12] Given Article 6 of the Treaty of the European Union, which gives the Charter "the same legal value as the Treaties", there should be no doubt that its provisions qualify as community norms and as such, they should prevail over conflicting national rules or regulations. In fact, the CJEU has recently expressly stated that national courts should refrain from applying national legislation which stands in conflict with a provision of the Charter.[13]

It follows that the crucial arising question relates to *whether the Cypriot data retention legislation is in fact incompatible with the Charter*. Understandably, if it is so, then clearly it should *not* have been applied by Cypriot courts in the issuing of data access orders. Equally clearly, the Supreme Court should not have rejected relevant certiorari applications against such orders.

It is submitted that the said question should be answered *in the affirmative* and the same view was also expressed by the minority of the Supreme Court in the

---

[7]Emphasis added.

[8]*Isaias*, Civil Appeal, 402/2012, 7/7/2014 (majority decision).

[9]See for example, *Syfantou*, Civil applications 216/14 and 36/2015, 27/10/2015.

[10]Markou (2017).

[11]*Simmenthal*, 106/77, §§ 21, 24, EU:C:1978:49; *Filipiak*, C-314/08, § 81, EU:C:2009:719; *Melki and Abdeli*, § 43, EU:C:2010:363, and the case law cited; and *Åkerberg Fransson*, C-617/10, § 45, EU:C:2013:105.

[12]Kowalik-Banczyk (2005), p. 1356.

[13]Case C-112/13, *A v. B and Others*, 11 September 2014, § 46, ECLI:EU:C:2014:2195.

aforementioned Civil Appeal, 402/2012, 7/7/2014.[14] According to the minority, since Law 183(I)/2007 has wholly been based on the annulled Data Retention Directive, its legitimising basis has been swept away, something that must hold true of the whole system of police access to retained data. In reality, although there is no (hard) rule dictating that the annulment of a Directive automatically annuls or renders inapplicable all relevant national transposition laws, yet in this particular case, common sense would dictate that Law 183(I)/2007 contravenes the Charter too and should therefore cease to be considered applicable. *This is because Law 183(1)/2007 simply copies provisions of the Directive that have expressly been found by the CJEU in Digital Rights Ireland Ltd*[15] *as contravening the Charter.*

More specifically, in paras. 57–59, 63–64, 66–68 of its judgement, the CJEU has pinpointed the following issues which render the provisions of the Directive pertaining to the obligation of electronic communications service providers to retain traffic and location data of their users, (i.e. *the provisions on data retention*) incompatible with the Charter:

- They impose a general and very wide (all-person, all-communication means and all-data) retention obligation.
- The said obligation covers the data of persons with no direct, indirect or even remote link with serious crime, including persons whose communications are subject to professional secrecy obligations.
- It is *not* limited to data pertaining to a particular period and/or a particular geographical zone and/or to a circle of particular persons likely to be involved in serious crime, or to persons who could, for other reasons, contribute, by the retention of their data, to the prevention, detection or prosecution of serious offences.
- The relevant provisions require data retention for 6 to 24 months for all data without requiring that different periods be set for different data depending on their possible usefulness in the fight against crime.
- They do not provide for sufficient safeguards to ensure effective security for the retained data (against loss and abuse); and
- They do not require the data in question to be retained within the European Union.

If one looks at Law 183(I)/2007, one can readily observe that Sections 3 and 6–14, which transpose the data retention provisions of the Directive, suffer from *all* of the above-listed "privacy deficiencies" pinpointed by the CJEU. The provisions laying down the data retention obligation and specifying the categories of data to be retained, namely Sections 3 and 6–12, comprise a copy-paste of the corresponding provisions of the Directive. Section 13 provides for a *single* data retention period (specifically, six months) for all data and Section 14 on the security of the retained

[14]Case C-112/13, *A v. B and Others*, 11 September 2014, § 46 and associated text, ECLI:EU:C:2014:2195.

[15]Case C-112/13, *A v. B and Others*, 11 September 2014, § 46, ECLI:EU:C:2014:2195.

data does not, in any way, go beyond the corresponding Article 7 of the Directive, which has been found insufficient. Finally, Law 183(I)/2007 contains no provision requiring the retention of data within the EU either. Accordingly, the conclusion that the said Law is, just like the Directive, incompatible with the Charter is essentially inevitable.

The opposite view taken by Cypriot case law is probably the result of a mistaken reading of the CJEU ruling. More specifically, apart from the aforementioned problems with the "data retention" provisions of the Directive, the CJEU also found issues with the provisions of the Directive that refer to the access to retained data by enforcement authorities. Indeed, in paras. 60–62 of its judgement, the European Court finds as problematic and/or unacceptable the fact that the Directive enables access to retained data on the general and undefined ground of "serious crime" and that such access is not made dependent on a prior review carried out by a court or by an independent administrative body. It is true that Law 183(I)/2007 does *not* suffer from these defects; Section 2 defines "serious crime" as crime punishable with imprisonment of 5 years or more and Section 5 of the said law subjects data access to the prior securing of a court order through an application to the court.[16] Importantly however, *nowhere in its relevant judgement, the CJEU hinted that if the problems with regard to data access did not exist, the Charter-incompatibility issues with regard to data retention would be swept away.* This view is reinforced by another part of the CJEU, namely paragraphs 34–35, where the Court seems to regard data retention and access to the retained data as *two separate interferences* with the rights to data protection and privacy of Articles 7 and 8 of the Charter. Logically, the disproportionality (or impermissibility) of the one interference cannot be corrected by the non-existence of the other. This is true especially when retention and access are so closely connected (or inter-related) that is difficult to envisage legitimate access to illegitimately retained data.

As already mentioned, the Cypriot courts did not share this view. The decision of the Supreme Court in *Constantinou Syfantou, Civil Applications 216/14 and 36/2015, 27/10/2015* is revealing of the different judicial approach that led to the dismissal of those and other relevant certiorari applications. More specifically, the Court relied on a reading of the CJEU ruling by the English High Court in the case of *Davis & Ors v. SSHD (2015) EWHC 2092 (Admin).* In that case, specifically in paragraph 89 of its judgement, the English High Court opined that the CJEU, in its decision annulling the Directive, must be understood as saying that if access to retained data is subject to prior review by a court in accordance with a detailed relevant regime at national level, then the general and unrestricted data retention obligation is in accord with the Charter. Yet, as it has already been illustrated, this is clearly *not* the case and the English High Court seems to have offered no convincing justification for taking this (opposite) view. Paragraph 61 of the relevant CJEU

[16]For more on this provision, see Markou (2017).

ruling[17] to which the High Court refers in paragraph 91 of its judgement, does not seem to support such view at all; it simply mentions one of the aforementioned problems found by the European Court in relation to the access (as opposed to the retention) provisions of the Directive. Moreover, contrary to the opinion of the English High Court as expressed in paragraph 89 of its judgement, the fact that the European Court stated that "the retention of data for the purpose of allowing the competent national authorities to have possible access to those data…genuinely satisfies an objective of general interest"[18] does not in any way assist in the said reading of the CJEU ruling. That data retention aims at protecting the general interest is indisputable. Yet, measures that restrict human rights in the name of the general interest must comply with the principle of proportionality, something that the European Court found was not the case in relation to the data retention obligation of the Directive. The English High Court has avoided this important detail, thereby adopting an erroneous reading the CJEU ruling.

The adoption of the particular reading of the CJEU ruling is not the only problem with the approach taken by the Cypriot Supreme Court in the aforementioned case. The Court also stated that Article 15 of the *Directive 2002/58/EC of the European Parliament and of the Council of 12 July 2002 concerning the processing of personal data and the protection of privacy in the electronic communications sector (Directive on privacy and electronic communications)* does not apply to the particular case and is irrelevant to Law 183(I)/2007. This is not right. The Directive on privacy and electronic communications specifically *prohibits* the retention of user traffic (including most location) data except for billing and interconnection payments without prejudice to Article 15(1).[19] Article 15(1) allows Member States to restrict the rights and obligations laid down by the Directive, "when such restriction constitutes a necessary, appropriate and proportionate measure within a democratic society to safeguard national security (i.e. State security), defence, public security, and the prevention, investigation, detection and prosecution of criminal offences (…)". The relevant provision adds that "To this end, Member States may, inter alia, adopt legislative measures *providing for the retention of data* for a limited period justified on the grounds laid down in this paragraph."[20] Accordingly, data retention

[17]*Digital Rights Ireland Ltd*, C-293/12, 8 April 2014, § 61: "Furthermore, Directive 2006/24 does not contain substantive and procedural conditions relating to the access of the competent national authorities to the data and to their subsequent use. Article 4 of the directive, which governs the access of those authorities to the data retained, does not expressly provide that that access and the subsequent use of the data in question must be strictly restricted to the purpose of preventing and detecting precisely defined serious offences or of conducting criminal prosecutions relating thereto; it merely provides that each Member State is to define the procedures to be followed and the conditions to be fulfilled in order to gain access to the retained data in accordance with necessity and proportionality requirements."

[18]*Digital Rights Ireland Ltd*, C-293/12, 8 April 2014, § 44.

[19]See Article 6(1) and (2) in combination with Article 2(b) and (c), Directive on privacy and electronic communications.

[20]Emphasis added.

measures aiming at safeguarding the prevention, investigation, detection and prosecution of crime, are allowed as an exception to the rule provided they meet the conditions of necessity, appropriateness and proportionality stated in Article 15(1). Most importantly, it expressly arises from the Recitals of the (annulled) Data Retention Directive that the said measure had been introduced to harmonise the national data retention measures introduced on the ground of Article 15(1) of the Directive on privacy and electronic communications.[21] Therefore, not only is Article 15(1) *not* irrelevant to Law 183(I)/2007, but also after the annulment of the Data Retention Directive, any national data retention laws (and their permissibility) inevitably have to be assessed against the criteria of necessity, appropriateness and proportionality of Article 15(1). Law 183(I)/2007, to the extent that it copies the data retention provisions of the Data Retention Directive, which have expressly been found as not meeting the said conditions, inevitably fails to meet them too and is therefore incompatible with the EU law. However, by viewing Article 15(1) as irrelevant to Law 183(I)/2007, the Cypriot Supreme Court inevitably did not assess Law 183(I)/2007 against the relevant criteria and could not therefore reach this conclusion of impermissibility and/or incompatibility.

4 Decision of the Supreme Court (2018)

More than two years after its ruling in *Digital Rights Ireland*, the CJEU issued another ruling, specifically in *Tele2 Sverige AB, C-203/15, 21/12/2016*, leaving absolutely no doubt on *both* the relevance of Article 15(1) of the Directive on privacy and electronic communications *and* the fact that Law 183(I)/2007 does *not* meet the required conditions of compatibility with the EU law. More specifically, the European Court ruled as follows:

> Article 15(1) of Directive 2002/58/EC (...) read in the light of Articles 7, 8 and 11 and Article 52(1) of the Charter of Fundamental Rights of the European Union, must be interpreted *as precluding national legislation which, for the purpose of fighting crime, provides for general and indiscriminate retention of all traffic and location data of all subscribers and registered users relating to all means of electronic communication.*[22]

The CJEU ruling in *Tele2 Sverige AB* must have placed the Cyprus Supreme Court in a difficult position but has not led to a diversion in the judicial approach followed in certiorari applications (or applications for leave for a certiorari application). Both these points can be illustrated by reference to the Supreme Court decision in the case of *Artemi Kkolou, Civil Application 1/2017, 31/1/2017*. The said case concerned a relevant application for leave for a certiorari application, which has been filed *after Tele2 Sverige AB* and yet, it has again been rejected by the court. In its decision, the court avoided referring to the aforementioned clear stance taken by the

[21]See Recitals 4, 5 and 6 of the Data Retention Directive.

[22]Emphasis added.

CJEU towards *a general and indiscriminate* data retention obligation, which is exactly what Law 183(I)/2007 lays down. Instead, it referred to another passage of the *Tele2 Sverige AB* ruling in which the European Court talks about the permissibility of *a targeted* (to specific circles of people or geographical locations) data retention obligation, which is clearly *not* what the Cypriot law imposes. Evidently, the court was troubled by the possible reduced effectiveness of a targeted or limited data retention obligation, as it referred to the example of a person with no prior criminal activity who downloads child pornography wondering how targeted data retention could lead to the detection, investigation and prosecution of the crime in that case. Yet, this is what the EU principle of proportionality and the inherent balancing of conflicting interests is all about; we could perhaps eliminate crime by *cancelling* privacy and data protection, but should we do so? After all, the CJEU has specifically addressed the relevant issue and has obviously insisted that

> (...) while the effectiveness of the fight against serious crime, in particular organised crime and terrorism, may depend to a great extent on the use of modern investigation techniques, such an objective of general interest, however fundamental it may be, cannot in itself justify that national legislation providing for the general and indiscriminate retention of all traffic and location data should be considered to be necessary for the purposes of that fight.[23]

The Cyprus Supreme Court also noted that the access order to retained data challenged in the relevant certiorari application has been issued before the European ruling in *Tele2 Sverige AB*. That was not a valid justification in rejecting the said application either. The said ruling only followed and applied the CJEU ruling in the *Digital Rights Ireland*, which preceded the challenged access order. Besides, the CJEU only interprets the EU law (including the Charter and the Directive on privacy and electronic communications) and that law was definitely in force and should have been applied at the material time.

Despite the aforementioned legal problems with the adopted judicial approach and the consequent rejection of the relevant certiorari application, the reasoning of the court has been fully adopted in criminal proceedings in which the defendants challenged the legality and hence, admissibility of their telecommunications data, which the police had accessed through a court order issued based on Law 183(I)/2007.[24] The relevant criminal court rejected the argument that the said data was essentially evidence obtained illegally, which should not therefore be considered wholly by reference to the above-discussed ruling of the Supreme Court in *Artemi Kkolou*.[25] The above-discussed case was meant to lay the foundations for the change of the judicial approach towards data retention in Cyprus and of the Cypriot data retention legislative regime. More specifically, the applicant has filed an appeal against the relevant decision which has been heard by the Cypriot Supreme Court in its capacity as an appeal court. Judgement was issued in April 2018 reversing the

[23]*Tele2 Sverige AB*, C-203/15, 21/12/2016, § 103.

[24]*Republic v. Polydorou and others*, Criminal Case 15549/16, 9/5/2017.

[25]*Republic v. Polydorou and others*, Criminal Case 15549/16, 9/5/2017.

decision to reject the application for leave for a certiorari application.[26] The Supreme Court accepted that the fact that the challenged data access order has been issued prior to the CJEU ruling in *Tele2 Sverige AB* cannot furnish the said order with legality if its issuance contravenes the Charter. By reference to the said CJEU ruling, the Court further laconically accepted that there is a *prima facie* case of illegality, which is enough for leave to be granted so that the applicant can file a certiorari application. It is in the context of that application, that the court can take a clear stance towards the legality of data access orders issued based on Law 183(I)/2007. Given the arguments unfolded earlier in this chapter, it should be expected that the certiorari application will succeed, and the relevant court order will be annulled unless perhaps said application fails on some other (unrelated) procedural ground.

5 Consequences of Judicial Decision (2018)

Given the aforementioned judgement of the Cypriot Supreme Court in 2018 and if the opinion of the court is adopted also in the context of the subsequent certiorari application, subsequent certiorari applications against court orders giving access to data retained by application of Law 183(I)/2007 will probably succeed. Any other approach would seem difficult to be reconciled with EU law and its supremacy over national law explicitly guaranteed by the Constitution.[27] Of course, consequently, Cypriot enforcement authorities will become less powerful in their fight against serious crime, something that cannot be ignored either.

Already, the office of the Attorney-General of the Republic of Cyprus is working together with the Cypriot Data Protection Commissioner on possible amendments on Law 183(I)/2007. A relevant draft amendment law has not been published yet, however, it seems that there is no other way forward than following the guidelines given by the CJEU in *Digital Rights Ireland* and even more explicitly, in *Tele2 Sverige AB*. As in Cyprus, access to the retained data is already subject to review by an independent court, it should be expected that the upcoming amendments must focus on the data retention provisions of the law. Although their exact content cannot be predicted, as much as it is clear that data retention must be targeted (rather than general and indiscriminate as is currently the case), the relevant CJEU guidelines leave Member States some room to devise one that suits their needs while complying with the principles of necessity and proportionality.[28] Importantly however, according to the CJEU, any data retention obligation must satisfy conditions, which "(. . .) must be shown to be such as actually to circumscribe, in practice, the

[26] *Artemis Kkolou*, Civil Appeal 26/2017, 26/4/2018.

[27] Article 1A of the Constitution.

[28] These guidelines are found in *Tele2 Sverige AB*, C-203/15, 21/12/2016, §§ 108–111.

extent of that measure and, thus, the public affected."[29] Accordingly, it is not permissible for one such obligation to be subject to *time limits* only, thus not being restricted to particular geographical locations or groups of persons, which would effectively limit the public to be affected. Any other reading of the CJEU ruling would probably be wrong resulting in new national data retention regimes that remain vulnerable to legality attacks because of their incompatibility with the Charter.

Such (erroneous) reading could be the result of a paragraph preceding the relevant guidelines, where the European Court states that the national legislation at stake did not restrict retention to "(i) data pertaining to a particular time period *and/or* geographical area *and/or* a group of persons likely to be involved, in one way or another, in a serious crime, or (ii) persons who could, for other reasons, contribute, through their data being retained, to fighting crime."[30] It should be emphasised however that in this passage, the CJEU only observed the limits that the national legislation at issue was lacking without making a clear statement with regard to the specific limits, which would render relevant legislation acceptable.

Given the risk of varying and most importantly, Charter-incompatible new national data retention regimes, the best solution seems to be a new data retention regime at the EU level. There is currently no proposal for a new Directive (or other measure) to replace the annulled Data Retention Directive but data retention is discussed in the draft e-Privacy Regulation intended to replace the aforementioned Directive on privacy and electronic communications.[31] It seems that there is no concrete evidence of any relevant provisions yet,[32] but if data retention is eventually spelled out in the upcoming e-Privacy Regulation (and provided that the EU legislator gets the CJEU guidelines right), the issue can be resolved soon[33] and in a harmonised way, something that is certainly desirable. Yet, it is expected that an amended data retention law in Cyprus will precede the time when such e-Privacy Regulation can become applicable and therefore, it would be very interesting to see if Cyprus will manage to introduce a Charter-compatible data retention regime.

[29] *Tele2 Sverige AB*, C-203/15, 21/12/2016, § 110.

[30] *Tele2 Sverige AB*, C-203/15, 21/12/2016, § 106.

[31] IT-Pol, EU Member States fight to retain data retention in place despite CJEU ruling, 2 May 2018, shttps://edri.org/eu-member-states-fight-to-retain-data-retention-in-place-despite-cjeu-rulings/.

[32] IT-Pol, EU Member States fight to retain data retention in place despite CJEU ruling, 2 May 2018, shttps://edri.org/eu-member-states-fight-to-retain-data-retention-in-place-despite-cjeu-rulings/.

[33] The proposed Regulation is currently being discussed before the Council which has very recently published a revised draft.

6 Conclusion

As Law 183(I)/2007 on data retention largely copies the Data Retention Directive found by the CJEU incompatible with the Charter, it must be regarded as invalid and inapplicable because it is contrary to Articles 7, 8 and 52(1) of the Charter, which being the EU law, prevails over national law. Cypriot case law has so far been developing in the wrong direction, as it has regarded Law 183(I)/2007 as having remained unaffected by the annulment of the Data Retention Directive by the CJEU. Even after the more recent *Tele2 Sverige AB* ruling, in which the CJEU has expressly stated that a general and indiscriminate data retention obligation is incompatible with the Charter, Cypriot courts continued to reject certiorari applications seeking to challenge the legality of data access orders issued based on Law 183(I)/2007.

However, since April 2018, a change in the judicial approach is on sight, as the Cypriot Supreme Court, acting as an appeal court, reversed a first instance decision concerning an application for leave for a certiorari application, opining that there is a *prima facie* case of illegality in relation to a court order allowing the police access to retained data issued based on Law 183(I)/2007. The decision opened the way for the filing of a certiorari application in which the legality of the said order will be examined; it should be expected that the order will be found to suffer from illegality and annulled on the ground that it has been issued based on a law that is incompatible with the Charter (or on the ground that it has authorized access to data retained on the basis of a law incompatible with the Charter. Any other data access orders issued recently must have the same fate if challenged through a certiorari application on relevant grounds especially if applicants carefully challenge not only the act of access to the data (leaving its retention untouched) but also the legality of the retention of said data flagging out its integral association with the access ordered by the court. That would seem to effectively close any route of escaping a court inquiry into the lawfulness of the problematic data retention provisions of Law 183 (I)/2007. As for those court orders not challenged in a similar way, it should probably be accepted that they have given access to illegally obtained data (or evidence).

Law 183(I)/2007 should be amended to provide for a narrower and targeted data retention obligation. A relevant amendment is currently being discussed in Cyprus and the draft amending law is eagerly awaited; it would be very interesting to see whether the Cypriot legislator will get the CJEU rulings right, thereby devising a Charter-compatible data retention regime leading to the issuance of data access orders that are not vulnerable to successful legal challenges. Discussions on new data retention provisions are also underway at the EU level, specifically in the draft e-Privacy Regulation. If the EU legislator manages to introduce relevant provisions that adhere to the CJEU guidelines, the matter will be effectively resolved in a harmonised way, which is certainly desirable.

References

Kombos C (2015) Cyprus Rapport: data retention in Cyprus: going beyond the call of duty. European Public Law 21(3):411–427

Kowalik-Banczyk K (2005) Should we polish it up – the polish constitutional tribunal and the idea of supremacy of EU law. German Law J 6(1355):1356

Markou C (2012) The Cyprus and other EU court rulings on data retention: the Directive as a privacy bomb. Comput Law Secur Rev 28(4):468–475

Markou C (2017) Data Retention in Cyprus after the CJEU annulment of the Data Retention Directive (conference presentation). 2nd International Conference on Regulation and Enforcement in the Digital Age – REDA 2017, 16–17 November 2017, University of Cyprus and European University Cyprus, Nicosia, Cyprus

Data Retention in the Czech Republic

Radim Polčák

Abstract The Czech Republic was among the few EU Member States that had implemented the Data Retention Directive twice. First, the statutory implementation into the Electronic Communications Act had been taken down by the Czech Constitutional Court mainly because of insufficient safeguards to the protection of privacy and personal data. The risks to privacy had been considered by the Czech Constitutional Court so severe and disproportionate that the invalidation of respective provisions had immediate effect. Second, the statutory implementation of the Data Retention Directive that contains various substantive and procedural safeguards is currently being reviewed by the Czech Constitutional Court. A decision is expected around the end of 2018.

The text provides for a systematic analysis of constitutional issues related to data retention in the Czech Republic. It focuses on reasons and impact of the first annulling decision of the Czech Constitutional Court and it offers, besides analysis of respective constitutional argumentation, broader perspective of specific understanding of proportionality of fundamental rights in a post-communist EU Member State.

1 Implementation of Directive 2006/24/EC in the Czech Republic

Data retention obligations did not emerge in the Czech Republic from the adoption of the Directive, but were previously established by national telecommunications (electronic communications) legislation. The Telecommunications Act of 2000[1] contained provisions requiring telecommunications operators to make available

[1]See Act No. 151/2000 Sb. on Telecommunications.

R. Polčák (✉)
Masaryk University, Brno, Czech Republic
e-mail: Radim.Polcak@law.muni.cz

M. Zubik et al. (eds.), *European Constitutional Courts towards Data Retention Laws*, Law, Governance and Technology Series 45,
https://doi.org/10.1007/978-3-030-57189-4_7

upon request to certain public bodies basic traffic data (dialling and dialled numbers, identification of used telecommunications service, date, time, duration and place of connection)[2] related to connections made in the past 2 months.

The Telecommunications Act of 2000 did not include detailed technical specifications of traffic data, nor did it even specify an exact period of retention. Instead, it only set a minimum requirement of 2 months while failing to establish a maximum limit.

The Telecommunications Act of 2000 was superseded by the Electronic Communications Act of 2005,[3] which took effect at the beginning of May 2005. The Telecommunications Act already contained specific provisions about data retention, specifically including a detailed definition of retained data, an express duty of operators of services of electronic communications to retain these data and a definition of subsequent duties.

The Telecommunications Act also distinguished traffic data from other localisation data. Localisation data processed in the course of providing respective service of electronic communications were treated in the same manner as other traffic data, i.e. they were to be stored by the operator and eventually made available at the request of a public body. Processing of other localisation data (i.e. those unnecessary for operators providing respective services) were either subject to anonymisation or explicit informed consent of respective users. This chapter on data retention obligations focuses specifically on data that the Electronic Communications Act defines as "traffic data" including traffic localisation data. Those localisation data that are not simultaneously considered as traffic data are not discussed here.

Obviously from the above dates, all aforementioned legislative provisions were implemented before the adoption of the Directive[4] in March 2016. While tracking legislative developments, it is important to note that the original adoption of the data retention duties in 2000 and their later extension in 2005 were not accompanied by any significant political or legal concerns. Instead, at that time service providers of electronic communications expressed only minor concerns about the reimbursement of costs related to the storage of relevant traffic data for the prescribed periods.

Although data retention laws have previously existed in the Czech Republic before the adoption of the Directive, it may seem counterintuitive that the Czech Republic used the mechanism established in Article 15 of the Directive and postponed the implementation of the Directive regarding "Internet access, Internet telephony and Internet e-mail" by 2009. Peterka[5] and subsequently Myska[6] note

[2]See § 85 of the Telecommunication Act.

[3]See Act No. 127/2005 Sb. on Electronic Communications.

[4]See Directive 2006/24/EC of the European Parliament and of the Council of 15 March 2006 on the retention of data generated or processed in connection with the provision of publicly available electronic communications services or of public communications networks and amending Directive 2002/58/EC (hereafter: the Directive).

[5]See Peterka (2009).

[6]See Myška (2013), p. 66. This monograph is up to date the only available complex Czech doctrinal study of data retention.

that most likely the postponement was not caused by politicians wanting to delay new data retention obligations and prevent their societal impact by introducing new forms of surveillance. Instead, the postponement was more likely due to public sector lobbying by those entitled to retained data. The main cause for postponement was the rules introduced by the Electronic Communication Act of 2005 and subsequent bylaws allowed for a broader scope and greater flexibility in collecting and processing traffic data than the rules established in the Directive. The delayed implementation of the Directive required electronic communications service providers to retain between 2005 and 2009 a broader variety of traffic data than was envisaged by the Directive.[7]

The data retention requirements in the Electronic Communications Act, as well as the subsequent amendment[8] of remaining elements required by the Directive were based on the general statutory definitions of traffic data defined more specifically in implementing bylaws. In particular, the distinction of particular types of traffic data, together with the form in which they were to be collected and retained, was established in Ministerial Decree No. 485/2005 Sb.[9] (This decree was quashed, together with respective parts of the Electronic Communications Act, by the decision of the Constitutional Court—see below).

Importantly, the original provisions of the Electronic Communication Act of 2005 did not require operators of electronic communications to delete retained traffic data after the expiration of the prescribed retention period. That requirement and other amendments were introduced only after the aforementioned delayed implementation of the Directive in 2009.

One issue that later formed the argumentative basis for the constitutional complaint (see below) was the mechanism of requesting retained data. The Electronic Communications Act required electronic communications service operators to make retained data available at the request of "public bodies entitled to request them upon a special statutory provision." The Electronic Communications Act also entrusted the specification of a range of traffic data to a sub-statutory legislative instrument (the aforementioned Ministerial Decree).

The Electronic Communication Act's construction of institutional entitlement is not only rooted in the lawmakers' intent to make access of retained traffic data maximally flexible. In the author's opinion, one of the reasons for entitling public sector bodies is a rather formalist interpretation of Article 2(3) of the Czech Constitution requiring that state authority *"be asserted only in cases, within the bounds, and in the manner provided for by law."*

[7]For an English language overview of the development of retention provisions in the Czech telecommunications legislation, see Polčák et al. (2016). Available also for free download at cyber.law.muni.cz. Accessed 9 April 2019.

[8]See Act No. 247/2008 Sb., amending the Electronic Communications Act.

[9]See Ministerial Decree No. 485/2005 Sb. on the scope of traffic and localisation data, retention periods and form and procedures of their transfers to entitled public sector bodies.

The constitutional limitation applicable to law enforcement, security, intelligence and other similar bodies in the Czech Republic is interpreted in the most restrictive manner, i.e. that any activity by these bodies is deemed to require explicit empowerment expressly delegated to them. Consequently, duties involving access to and maintenance of information, as in the case of data retention, are enumerated twice in Czech statutory law. The first statutory provision expressly obliges private or public entities to provide information or alternatively cooperate with respective public bodies. The second provision in statutory law (found mostly in those statutes regulating the operation and activities of relevant public bodies, e.g. the Police Act) explicitly empowers the relevant public body to request information or other assistance.

This construction is obviously redundant because both statutory provisions have practically the same regulatory content (a duty of one party automatically implies a claim of the other party). However, this way of legislating cooperative and collaborative duties involving law enforcement, security, intelligence and other similar bodies somehow became a standard in the Czech law, and similar legislative constructions remain throughout the Czech statutory law.[10]

2 Proceedings Before the Constitutional Court

Unlike other countries, namely Germany, the introduction of data retention provisions in the Czech Republic did not spark broader societal or political response. There is a good reason to believe that almost no presence of data retention in contemporary political and societal discourse was primarily caused by an overall lack of interest of the Czech society in issues related to privacy.

The fact that Czech society overall does not consider privacy a relevant topic is relatively surprising considering the country's communist history.[11] Some traces of the practices utilised by communist security forces, namely the secret police, still somewhat resonate in Czech political discourse. In addition, the generation raised during the period of so-called "normalisation" when communist authorities used privacy violations as an efficient tool for pacifying and quelling society has now matured to middle age and represents a core target group for most in the political mainstream.

Even if most people who were now between 40 and 60 years of age (meaning they were approx. 10 years younger when the data retention laws were enacted) had no personal experience with the communist security institutions' operations, practically everybody alive during the communist dictatorship was exposed to the extensive and oppressive processing of personal data. The state authorities were extremely diligent

[10]For more details, see Polčák et al. (2016).

[11]For a comprehensive overview of the impact of communist rule on the Czech society and system of law, see Bobek et al. (2009).

in assembling most private data into files that massively affected individuals' lives from kindergarten to retirement. Even at grammar schools, the worst punishment for misbehaviour or negligence was that respective incidents were "put into the file" (which could then adversely affect a person's entire personal and professional life).

Nevertheless, it seems that the Czech society has somewhat lost its sensitivity towards privacy issues and processing of personal data in little over a decade after the collapse of the communist dictatorship. There were some attempts to bring privacy into the mainstream of political debate primarily by civic society organisations[12] and also but to a lesser degree by individual politicians. However, privacy never became a major topic for mainstream political parties, and it never had, up until now, represented a relevant source of political capital.[13]

This reflects the current situation wherein privacy is more often regarded in the Czech Republic by societal elites than by the general public.[14] It also explains why the constitutional complaint against the introduction of data retention was brought by a group of deputies of the House of Representatives rather than by a popular movement.

The overall argumentative basis of the constitutional complaint was the general lack of balance between data retention obligations and fundamental rights.[15] The petitioners in general argued that this form of privacy infringement is simply disproportionate towards all envisaged positive effects. In other words, the claim was based on the argument that the infringement of fundamental rights brought by the data retention provisions of the amended Electronic Communications Act is simply too broad to justify societal benefits.

The doctrine of fundamental rights proportionality assessment practiced since the middle of the 1990s by the Czech Constitutional Court is based on Robert Alexy's three- (or respectively four-) prong test.[16] The Constitutional Court first used this doctrine in case No. Pl. US 4/94 when a group of members of the House of Representatives contested the constitutionality of newly introduced criminal procedural measures referred to as the "anonymous witness". The Constitutional Court summarised the three main elements of the proportionality test as follows:

> When considering the possibilities of restricting a basic right or freedom for the benefit of another basic right or freedom the following conditions can be stipulated governing the priority of one basic right or freedom:
>
> The first condition is their mutual comparison, the other is the requirement to examine the substance and the sense of the fundamental right or freedom being restricted (...). The

[12]See, e.g. Iuridicum Remedium, ISP: Co dělají provideři a telefonní operátoři s našimi daty? Studie praxe poskytovatelů internetových a telekomunikačních služeb (ISP). www.bigbrotherawards.cz. Accessed 20 April 2010. See also Vobořil (2011).

[13]See, e.g. Cibulka (2013).

[14]See, e.g., Pokorný (2012).

[15]See, Herzeg (2010), p. 22.

[16]Alexy (2014), p. 51.

> mutual comparison of colliding fundamental rights and freedoms is based upon the following criteria:
>
> The first is the criterion of applicability, i.e. a reply to the question whether the institute restricting a certain basic right allows the achievement of the desirable aim (the protection of another basic right). In the given case the legislator can be affirmed in that the institute of anonymous witness allows to achieve the aim, i.e. to guarantee the inviolability of his person.
>
> The second criterion for measuring basic rights and freedoms is the criterion of necessity residing in the comparison of the legislative means restricting some basic right or freedom with other provisions allowing to achieve the same objective, however, without impinging upon fundamental rights and freedoms. (. . .)
>
> The third criterion is the comparison of the importance of both conflicting basic rights. (. . .) The comparison of the importance of colliding basic rights (after having fulfilled the condition of appropriateness and necessity) resides in weighting empirical, systemic, contextual and value-oriented arguments.

The Constitutional Court elaborated on the minimisation of impact, which in Czech constitutional doctrine is referred to either as the fourth prong or as a specific output-element of the third prong of the proportionality test. The Constitutional Court summarised the minimisation requirement as follows:

> Part of comparing the relative weight of the conflicting basic rights is also considering the utilisation of legal institutes minimizing the intervention into one of them, supported by arguments. For instance, an argument disfavouring the restriction of one basic right due to the possibility of misusing such arrangement can be eliminated by minimizing such adverse impact in establishing further procedural conditions for deciding about the same. Therefore, it can be stated that in case of a conclusion about the well-foundedness of the priority of one of two conflicting basic rights a necessary condition for the final judgment is also having applied all possibilities of minimizing the impingement upon one of them. Such conclusion can be derived also from Art. 4 para 4 of the Charter of Fundamental Rights and Freedoms, and namely in the sense that the basic rights and freedoms should be preserved not only when applying provisions on the limits of basic rights and freedoms, but also, in analogy, in case of their restriction due to their conflicting with one another.

The complaint against the data retention provisions rested primarily on the ground that the mere retention of traffic data represents an intrusion into the private lives of individuals. The complaining deputies pointed out that the scope of retained data was beyond the requirements of the Directive. The complaint asserted that retained data provide personal and intimate details into an individual's private life. The complaint then implied that such serious infringement of a fundamental right must be proportionate to the envisaged protective benefits.

It was also stressed that data retention affects all users of electronic communication services. While wiretapping or other intrusive measures are used upon a suspicion or other discriminatory criteria, retention of traffic data applies generally. That should, according to the complainants, affect the assessment of proportionality of fundamental rights. This argument was based on the logic that it might be proportionate to intrude or limit privacy in cases involving a person suspected of illegal behaviour, but it is disproportionate if the same or similar extent of intrusion is used against all users of electronic communications without any particular discriminatory criteria.

The complaint also elaborated on the length of storage and access to data. In terms of length, the complainants pointed out the extensive retention period of up to 2 years and questioned its necessity (given the regular time frame of criminal investigations).

Another argument in the complaint was related to requesting and using retained data. The complaint specifically pointed out the vague and ambiguous provision in the Telecommunication Act failing to specifically enumerate bodies and institutions entitled to request the retained data. In that respect, the complainants argued that this vagueness further increases the risk of misuse or even abuse of retained data.

The Constitutional Court requested opinions from the House of Representatives (the petitioners were deputies, but in this case the Court also requested the opinion of the House as such), the Senate, and the Ombudsman. Among these institutions, only the Senate provided substantive input that was mostly in defence of the contested provisions. The Senate argued that the retention of traffic data should be considered differently in comparison to other intrusive measures. Consequently, the Senate expressed the opinion that retention of traffic data, as established in the Telecommunications Act, was proportionate and thus compliant with the Constitution and the Bill of Rights.

Quite surprisingly, the Ombudsman (the Office of Public Defender of Rights) chose not to submit substantive arguments and entirely refrained from the proceedings. Another interesting element noted by the Constitutional Court in its decision (see below) was that petitioning deputies from the House of Representatives filed the petition without trying to change or quash the law. The Constitutional Court noted that it is logically paradoxical when a deputy files a constitutional complaint rather than use its own capacity and propose through a legislative initiative, amendment, or derogation in the House.

The Constitutional Court had even stronger words where the petitioners themselves initially voted for the contested Act already containing data retention provisions and for its subsequent amendment. In that respect, the Court noted:

> In this particular case the group of complainants not only consisted mainly of representatives of the political parties who at present participate and at the time of the submission participated in the exercise of government power and who had and continue to have the majority in the Chamber of Deputies of the Parliament of the Czech Republic required to amend the contested legislation, furthermore, and the Constitutional Court cannot omit a critical comment on this issue, most of them through their participation in the process of law-making by their affirmative (!) vote directly enabled adoption of the contested legislation. The Constitutional Court would in the future in such instances of its (mis)use have to be forced to dismiss submissions filed under such circumstances.

3 Decision of the Constitutional Court

In this case, the Constitutional Court considered the annulment of a statutory act following submission of a petition by a group of deputies. Consequently, the decision was taken by the Plenary. Although the decision is relatively lengthy, given the importance and complexity of the case, the discussion and argumentation directly related to the subject matter are considerably short. Particularly, the argumentative core of the decision is between para. 45 and 54 and altogether constitute only approximately 3000 words out of the total 13,000 words of the judgment.

The Court devoted considerable attention in the judgment to general considerations regarding privacy and informational self-determination. It extensively acknowledged the existing case law of the European Court of Human Rights, and it also noted in relatively great detail the contemporary interpretive practice of other constitutional instances around Europe (see below). However, part VII of the judgment between para. 26 and 40 also contains traces of what we earlier noted—privacy (and eventually self-determination of information) did not represent an issue with which the Czech Constitutional Court would have been overly familiar.[17] Probably most symptomatic is the reference to Brandeis' dissenting opinion in Olmstead, where Brandeis mentions the "right to be let alone."[18] The problem with this citation is that Brandeis neither invented that right (it was in fact a creation of a US Judge Thomas Cooley),[19] nor was it the first case when the U.S. Supreme Court used that statement (that happened more than 30 years earlier in Union Pacific case where the Court used it in the majority opinion).[20] Another problem is its translation to Czech, which if reversed would translate literarily back into English as something like "the right to be left to one's self."

For our discussion here, the Constitutional Court's recapitulation of historical developments concerning the right to privacy and extent of factual correctness are not important. Also, it is not problematic if the Court did not get entirely correct the Czech translation for the definition of privacy. However, these lapses show that (1) the Czech Constitutional Court did not have a solid and complex understanding of privacy and, (2) the acquisition of such understanding from foreign doctrines was not entirely flawless.

It also shows that the way in which the Constitutional Court understood privacy as a regulatory concept in this case was much different from how it was approached by Cooley, the early U.S. Supreme Court or even Brandeis and Warren themselves.[21] While "being let alone" originally meant being let undisturbed (or being

[17]See Polčák (2012).

[18]See § 27 of the decision.

[19]See Cooley (1988).

[20]See the Supreme Court case *Union Pac. Ry. Co. v. Botsford*, 141 U.S. 250, 251 (1891).

[21]For a proper reference, see Warren and Brandeis (1890–1891), p. 193.

let to one's peace),[22] the Czech Constitutional Court extended the reach of this concept to something rather extreme like being left lonely.

That linguistic pettiness might illustrate more than just a different understanding of the concept of privacy by the Constitutional Court. It may point to the overall difference in understanding of the state and its powers between the US and Czech constitutional doctrine.

The Czech Constitutional Court was established at the beginning of 1990s with the teleology to become the ultimate power defending people's fundamental rights against the state. That was primarily based on an assumption that the state, meaning all three branches of power, is and will be to some extent and for a considerable time, run by actual or former communists or communist-minded officials. In consideration of this, the Constitutional Court should have served the purpose of an ultimate constitutional safeguard.

A second, but no less important, core aspect of the aforementioned institutional purpose of the Czech Constitutional Court was a general assumption that an individual inevitably stands in opposition to the state and vice versa. While this assumption proved more or less historically valid in Czechoslovakia, the history of relations between the state and the individual was rather different or more complex in the USA.

The above differences in fundamental institutional teleology might also explain the different ways in which privacy limitations are approached by Supreme Court cases in the USA and the Czech Republic. Rather strict assumptions on the allowance for privacy limitations, including the specifically emphasised role of the judiciary, were summarised in the judgment as follows:[23]

> Restrictions imposed on personal integrity and individual privacy (i.e. breaching the respect towards them) may only be applied as an absolute exception, provided it is deemed necessary in a democratic society, unless it is possible to meet the purpose pursued by the public interest in any other way and if it is acceptable from the perspective of the legal existence and respecting effective and specific guarantees against arbitrariness. Essential presumptions of a due process require that the individual be provided with sufficient guarantee against the potential abuse of power by the public authorities. Such an essential guarantee consists of the relevant legal regulations and existence of the effective means of monitoring adherence to it, represented by, above all, the supervision of the most intense infringements of the fundamental rights and freedoms of individuals performed by an independent and impartial court, since it is the courts' obligation to provide the protection of individuals' fundamental rights and freedoms (...).

The part of the judgment addressing particular constitutional concerns with the contested statutory and sub-statutory provisions is structured according to a substantive understanding of the issue by the Constitutional Court. The Court in this case used neither the standard structure of the proportionality assessment (see above) nor the structure of arguments presented in the complaint (see also above).

[22]See Polčák and Svantesson (2017).

[23]See § 36.

At first, in paras. 41–44 the Court expressed its general opinion about the extent of the data retention obligations' infringement of privacy. The court agreed with the complainants that traffic data (including traffic location data) can provide personal and intimate details into individuals' private lives. In that sense, the Court rejected the Senate's argument (see above) that traffic data be treated differently than substantive data (e.g. wiretapped communications). Particularly, the Court argued:[24]

> Although the prescribed obligation to retain traffic and location data does not apply to the content of individual messages (. . .), the data on the users, addresses, precise time, dates, places, and forms of telecommunication connection, provided that monitoring takes place over an extended period of time and when combined together, allows compiling detailed information on social or political membership, as well as personal interests, inclinations or weaknesses of individual persons. (. . .) With a degree of certainty of up to 90%, the data allow deducing, for instance whom, how often and even at what times the individual contacts, who their closest acquaintances, friends or work colleagues are, or what activities and at what times they engage in (. . .). Collecting and retaining location and traffic data thus also represents a significant infringement of the right to privacy, and for this reason, it is necessary that the scope of the protection of the fundamental right to respect of private life taking the form of the right to informational self-determination (. . .) should include not only the protection of the contents of the messages transferred via telephone communication or communication via so-called public networks, but also the traffic and location data related to them.

This assessment of the level of data retention's intrusiveness was used as a basis for further argumentation of its disproportionality. Quite interestingly, the Court did not expressly contest the fulfilment of the first and second criterion of proportionality, i.e. applicability and necessity (see above the proportionality test laid down in the case No. Pl. US 4/94). Both applicability and necessity of data retention were questioned only in *obiter dictum*. There is good reason to speculate whether the Reporting Justice originally intended to place the necessity and applicability test at the end of substantive reasoning and label it as an *obiter dictum*, or whether it was not placed there only as a matter of compromise during deliberations. In any case, the critique of the objective need for data retention as such was strongly formulated here:[25]

> Taking the form of an obiter dictum only, the Constitutional Court maintains that it is aware of the fact that owing to the development of modern information technologies and communication means, new and more sophisticated ways of commitment of crime occur, which need to be addressed accordingly. Nonetheless, the Constitutional Court expresses its doubts as to whether the very instrument of global and preventive retention of location and traffic data on almost all electronic communications may be deemed necessary and adequate from the perspective of the intensity of the intervention to the private sphere of an indefinite number of participants to electronic communications. (. . .) Similarly, the Constitutional Court expressed its doubts when also examining whether the instrument of global and preventive retention of traffic and location data may be deemed, from the perspective of the original purpose (i.e. protection against security threats and prevention of serious crime) as an effective tool, mainly due to the existence of so-called anonymous SIM cards, which

[24]See § 44.

[25]See part VIII *Obiter Dictum*, §§ 55–57.

> are beyond the extent of retained location and traffic data as anticipated within the contested legislation (. . .).

The most substantive arguments that the Constitutional Court raised within *ratio decidendi* against the contested provisions were related not to the mere mechanism of data retention but rather to the way in which it was particularly legislated into the Czech statutory law and sub-statutory law.[26] Thus, the reasons for which the Constitutional Court finally annulled the contested provisions were based mostly on the failure to demonstrate the least possible infringement of relevant fundamental rights (i.e. the fourth prong of Alexy's proportionality assessment).

Initially, the Constitutional Court noted that there is no reason for only a general statement regarding public sector bodies entitled to ask for retained data. More particular rules were laid down in a bylaw, but that solution lacked, according to the Constitutional Court, proper legitimacy. The Court noted (abstract from Para. 46):

> Although (. . .) the contested Decree specifies fulfilling the duty towards the competent authorities in individual cases, i.e. it provides a relatively detailed definition of the manner in which the data are handed over, communication mode (electronic), format, programmes used, codes, etc., the wording of the challenged provision (. . .) or even the explanatory report do not specifically imply (. . .) the competent authorities or the special legal regulations (. . .). The existing legal regulations allowing for a massive infringement of fundamental rights thus do not comply with the requirements concerning the certainty and clarity from the perspective of the state governed by the rule of law (. . .).

The Constitutional Court also criticised the relative vagueness of statutory law with respect to the purpose of data retention. Neither the provisions in the Electronic Communications Act nor those in procedural codes gave any limitations as to the purpose for which retained data might be requested and used by public sector bodies. Therefore, the Constitutional Court ruled that such substantial infringement of privacy required corresponding purpose limitation (not to allow the use of retained data in cases of marginal significance). The Court noted:[27]

> [T]he purpose under which the traffic and location data are provided to the competent authorities has not been defined clearly and precisely, which precludes assessing the challenged legal regulation from the perspective of its actual necessity (. . .). While the Data Retention Directive (. . .) was adopted in order to harmonise the regulations applied in the Member States (. . .) with the aim "to ensure that those data are available for the purpose of the investigation, detection and prosecution of serious crime" (although it fails to specify the criminal offence in more detail), the contested legislation (. . .) does not contain any such restrictions. (. . .) The absence of proper legal regulation (. . .) as demonstrated by the statistical data has in fact resulted in the situation that the instrument in the form of requesting and using the retained data (. . .) has also been used (or overused) by the bodies responsible for criminal proceedings for the purposes of investigating common (i.e. less serious) crime.

[26] For complex case comments see, e.g., Myška (2011), p. 43 or Molek (2012), p. 338.

[27] See §§ 47 to 49.

Finally, the Court pointed to insufficient statutory safeguards concerning the security of retained data. The Court stated that provisions requiring providers to adopt adequate security measures were unnecessarily and broadly vague and provide too much room for possible abuse or misuse of retained data. The Court argued:[28]

> [T]he legal regulation contested by the applicant fails to define sufficiently, or fails to define at all, unambiguous and detailed rules containing minimum requirements concerning the security of the retained data, in particular, taking the form of restricting third-party access, the procedure of maintaining data integrity and credibility, or the removal procedure. Furthermore, the contested regulation does not provide individuals with sufficient guarantees against the risk of data abuse and arbitrariness. (...) None of these obligations is provided, in more detail, with the rules and specific procedures for how to meet them; the requirements concerning the security of the retained data have not been defined in a stringent manner; it is not sufficiently clear how the data are handled, either by legal entities or natural persons collecting and retaining the location and traffic data, or by the competent public authorities when requested; and the manner in which the data are removed has not been specifically determined either. Similarly, the liability or possible sanctions for failure to comply with such duties, including the absence of the possibility for the individuals affected to seek efficient protection against potential misuse, arbitrariness or failure to comply with the relevant duties have not been defined either.

Consequently, the Constitutional Court annulled the contested provisions of the Electronic Communications Act. In addition, the Court also noted that similar defects found in the contested provisions are also in the corresponding provisions of the Code of Criminal Procedure. However, because the respective provisions of the Code of Criminal Procedure were not contested by the complainants, the Court did not annul them. It is not common for the Czech Constitutional Court to openly note a lack of constitutional compliance but leave unconstitutional provisions intact. The Constitutional Court's action was likely intended to strongly admonish lawmakers to amend the Code of Criminal Procedure to make it constitutionally compliant, but not to cause immediate harm to pending criminal proceedings that often rely heavily on different kinds of data acquired through provisions of the Electronic Communications Act.[29]

As mentioned above, privacy is not an issue often addressed by the Czech Constitutional Court. To date, relevant Czech constitutional cases have involved mostly individual issues of wiretapping or conflicts between privacy and freedom of speech. The Czech Constitutional Court, unlike its German counterpart or the European Court of Human Rights, had never previously confronted such a complex privacy issue broadly affecting societal, ethical and even economic aspects. Therefore, when the Court rendered its decision on data retention, it heavily relied on prior case law of foreign constitutional courts or similar tribunals.

Since the middle of 1990s, the Czech Constitutional Court generally seems to have gained inspiration from the German and Austrian Constitutional Courts, as well as from German constitutional doctrine. Besides geographical proximity, historical

[28]See §§ 50 and 51.

[29]See Jamborová (2012), p. 61.

links and overall similarities of the Czech, German, or Austrian national legal cultures, the sources of inspiration also stem from frequent personal contacts and scientific exchange between the Czech constitutional judiciary and its German and Austrian counterparts.

Due to the lack of its own experience together with the immediate availability of properly reasoned judicial results in similar proceedings from almost identical legal cultures, the Czech Constitutional Court extensively uses argumentative ideas from other jurisdictions.

The inspiration from foreign constitutional case law and from the case law of the European Court of Human Rights is apparent in the text of the judgment. The Court extensively cites the following foreign cases of the ECHR: *Malone v. UK* (No. 8691/79), *Niemietz v. Germany* (No. 13710/88), *Amman v. Switzerland* (No. 27798/95) *Klass and others v. Germany* (No. 5029/71), *Leander v. Spain* (No. 9248/81), *Kruslin v. France* (No. 11801/85), *Kopp v. Switzerland* (No. 23224/94) *P. G. and J. H. v. UK* (No. 44787/98) *S. and Marper v. UK* (No. 30562/04 and 30566/04), *Rotaru v. Romania* (No. 28341/95), *Hassan and Tchaouch v. Bulgaria* (No. 30985/96, 39023/97), *Weber and Saravia v. Germany* (No. 54934/00), *Liberty and others v. UK* (No. 58243/00) and *Camenzind v. Switzerl*and (No. 21353/93).

In addition to the case law of the European Court of Human Rights, the Czech Constitutional Court also extensively cited the German constitutional case law, namely BVerfGE 65, 1 (Volkszählungsurteil), BVerfGE 115, 320 (Rasterfahndungurteil II), BVerfGE 113, 348 (Vorbeugende Telekommunikationsüberwachung), BVerfGE 120, 274 (Grundrecht auf Computerschutz), 1 BvR 256/08 (Volltextveröffentlichungen), 1 BvR 263/08 and 1 BvR 586/08 (Vorratsdatenspeicherung).

When the Czech decision was rendered on 22 March 2011, there were already reported decisions about data retention from the Romanian Constitutional Court, Supreme Court of Cyprus, and the Bulgarian Supreme Administrative Court. The Czech Constitutional Court briefly noted these decisions, but neither established any particular argumentative links nor explained and compared them in detail.[30]

On the Czech Constitutional Court's contribution to the establishment of an international constitutional standard, there are no entirely new, substantive, or argumentative elements. The only relatively specific addition to what was already established by German, Romanian, Bulgarian or Cyprian courts is clear claim for particular and specific statutory provisions instead of missing or vague formulations. The Czech Constitutional Court extensively argued that the vagueness of statutory rules does not inevitably lead to particular disproportionate infringements of individual rights, but it represents a risk that must be mitigated. In other aspects, the Court mostly repeated the same sort of concerns about the length of processing, purpose limitations, or security that were previously raised by the above-referenced constitutional tribunals or supreme court cases.

[30]See, e.g. Novák (2011), p. 21.

4 Consequences and Execution of Judicial Decision

In the case of the Electronic Communications Act, the Constitutional Court obviously was not satisfied with the way in which data retention was originally legislated. Consequently, the Court annulled contested provisions including sub-statutory legislation that contained particular technical rules and requirements. As noted above, the Court did not directly contest the mechanism of data retention as such (doubts as to its necessity were raised only in *obiter dictum*), but found serious and unnecessary risks and omissions especially concerning safeguards to privacy (see above).

The effect of the annulment of the contested provisions was immediate. This immediate effect of the Constitutional Court's decision was relatively surprising and caused massive confusion. The problem was that the Court correctly noted the above-referenced disproportions and risks, but omitted to consider the larger picture of data retention.

The truth was and remains that traffic data were not retained only upon the contested and later annulled provisions of the Electronic Communications Act, but also upon consent in individual user agreements made between service providers and consumers of services of electronic communications. Moreover, traffic data were not only retained by electronic communications service providers, but also contractually by information society service providers such as webmails, social networking sites, auction platforms, etc. (These providers were not even included among the number of those obliged to retain data under the Electronic Communications Act.)

The Constitutional Court noted neither the fact that traffic data are being retained and processed upon causes other than the contested provisions nor the fact that data retention is also a common practice outside electronic communications sector. Therefore, the decision did not give any guidance as to what should follow. The decision only gave the following guidance as to the assessment of data retained to date:[31]

> General courts will have to engage in examining, in each and every individual case, the application of the already requested data for the purposes of criminal proceedings from the perspective of the proportionality of the infringement of the right to privacy. Above all, courts will have to consider the seriousness of the crime committed upon the act against which criminal proceedings have been initiated and in which the requested data should be used.

However, neither electronic communications service providers nor information society service providers were given any official advice as to how they should proceed with the technical practice of traffic data retention. On one hand, it was clear that the Court annulled only one legal provision while not addressing other legal causes for retaining and processing traffic data including transfers. On the other hand, media often referred to the decision as if the Court prohibited retention of traffic data as such. Consequently, it took a couple of months for all stakeholders including service providers, the police, State Prosecution Service, etc. to operate

[31]See § 59.

following the annulment of the unconstitutional provisions of the Electronic Communications Act and to overcome the ensuing regulatory chaos.

Nevertheless, data retention, including the processing of retained data and their transfers, technically continued even after the annulment of unconstitutional provisions of the Electronic Communications Act. Following the annulment of unconstitutional provisions, some contractual clauses had to be revised, and new methods for making data available to the police, Prosecution Service, and courts had to be established. Depending on particular service providers' circumstances, in some cases this caused a temporary disturbance of police or intelligence operations. However, a provisional status quo was mostly established even before the adoption of new legislation (see below).

The situation following the decision of the Constitutional Court is illustrated by the example of an unrecorded exchange between a major telecommunications operator (for obvious reasons, we cannot disclose its name) and the police's request for retained traffic data. The operator initially replied that no data were available because they were not being processed pursuant to the decisions of the Constitutional Court. Shortly thereafter, the police replied that the data was necessary in connection with an urgent search for a missing child. A DVD with the requested data was then swiftly available and all requested data was legally retained because the respective users originally consented to data processing and transfers in their service contracts.

5 Conclusion

Despite the legal uncertainty that it caused, the overall impact of the Constitutional Court's decision was mostly positive. Initially, the decision led to significant improvements in statutory provisions on data retention. Although not all critical notes from the Constitutional Court were properly implemented, statutory safeguards against abuse or misuse of retained data have significantly improved. Compared to the original provisions, the new rules also contain considerably less vague and metaphorical formulations making their impact more foreseeable and reviewable.

More importantly, the Constitutional Court's decision significantly helped to shift privacy of electronic communications a bit more towards mainstream political discourse. Surprisingly, privacy never represented a mainstream topic in post-communist Czech society. The Constitutional Court previously ruled on cases related to wiretapping or other forms of privacy infringements mostly in cases limited to criminal proceedings. Thus, the mainstream society, which typically is not overly concerned about various nuances in criminal proceedings, never had a practical need for understanding privacy as a matter of general constitutional concern.

In that sense, the Constitutional Court addressed the issue of privacy of electronic communications and *de facto* performed the job for the deputies who originally failed to do so when negotiating the Electronic Communications Act and its data retention amendment in the House of Representatives. Thanks to the decision of the Constitutional Court, it is probably not far from the truth that a significant part of the Czech population just learned about the retention and transfer of their personal data.

Acknowledgement This chapter is based on a research funded by project No. CZ.02.1.01/0.0/0.0/16_019/0000822.

References

Alexy R (2014) Constitutional rights and proportionality. Revus 20(22):51–65

Bobek M, Molek P, Šimíček V (eds) (2009) Komunistické právo v Československu – kapitoly z dějin bezpráví. Masarykova univerzita, Brno

Cibulka J (2013) Co o nás ví telefon? Tři dny lidského života v datech mobilního operátora. ihned.cz. Accessed 5 Feb 2013

Cooley TM (1988) Law of torts, 2nd edn. Callaghan and Company, Chicago

Herzeg J (2010) Ústavněprávní limity monitoringu telekomunikačního provozu. Bulletin advokacie 5:28

Jamborová K (2012) Provozní a lokalizační údaje, nález Ústavního soudu a § 88a TrŘ. Trestněprávní revue 3:61

Molek P (2012) Czech constitutional court: unconstitutionality of the Czech implementation of the data retention directive, decision of 22 March 2011, Pl. ÚS 24/10. Eur Const Law Rev 8(2):338

Myška M (2011) Ústavnost data retention v České republice. Revue pro právo a technologie 2 (3):42–43

Myška M (2013) Právní aspekty uchovávání provozních a lokalizačních údajů. Masarykova univerzita, Brno

Novák D (2011) Blanketní uchovávání komunikačních údajů v judikatuře evropských soudů. Časopis pro právní vědu a praxi 19(1):21–34

Peterka J (2009) Přiškrcení českého Velkého bratra. www.lupa.cz. Accessed 12 Sept 2008

Pokorný L (2012) Zpravodajské služby. Auditorium, Praha

Polčák R (2012) Internet a proměny práva. Auditorium, Praha

Polčák R, Svantesson DJB (2017) Information sovereignty. Edward Elgar Publishing, Cheltenham

Polčák R, Míšek J, Stupka V, Loutocký P, Abelovský T (2016) Interception of electronic communications in the Czech Republic and Slovakia. Masaryk University, Brno

Vobořil J (2011) Výhrady iure k novele zákona o naší komunikaci. slidilove.cz. Accessed 3 Apr 2012

Warren SD, Brandeis LD (1890–1891) The right to privacy. Harv Law Rev 4(5):193–220

Data Retention in Germany

Marion Albers

1 Introduction

The term "data retention" as such is a rather vague term. As a result, it is understood differently, especially with regard to the different fields in which "data retention" is discussed.[1] In Germany, the term is primarily used in two contexts: On the one hand, its understanding is shaped by the census judgment of the Federal Constitutional Court (FCC). In connection with the requirements of purpose determination and purpose limitation established in this judgment, the court had also laid down a strict prohibition on the collection of personal data for indefinite or not yet definable purposes.[2] According to this, "data retention" means the collection and storage of personal data for an undetermined purpose in the event that it should ever be needed for not yet specified future use. On the other hand, data retention is regularly linked to the EU Data Retention Directive (DRD)[3] and the implementing laws of the member states. In this context, it comprises the preservation of personal data that are generated in telecommunications for the purpose of enabling authorities at a later

[1]There are fields other than telecommunications, e. g. the retention of passenger name records, cf. CJEU (Grand Chamber), Opinion of 26 July 2017—1/15, curia.europa.eu; Vedaschi and Marino Noberasco (2017), or the retention of banking data to keep them available in combating money laundering and financing of terrorism, see inter alia Milaj and Kaiser (2017).

[2]See FCC, Judgment of 15 December 1983—1 BvR 209/83 et al., BVerfGE (Volume of the decisions of the FCC) 65, pp. 46 and 47.

[3]Directive 2006/24/EC of the European Parliament and of the Council of 15 March 2006 on the retention of data generated or processed in connection with the provision of publicly available electronic communications services or of public communications networks and amending Directive 2002/58/EC, OJ L 105/54.

M. Albers (✉)
Hamburg University, Hamburg, Germany
e-mail: Marion.Albers@uni-hamburg.de

M. Zubik et al. (eds.), *European Constitutional Courts towards Data Retention Laws*, Law, Governance and Technology Series 45,
https://doi.org/10.1007/978-3-030-57189-4_8

point in time to gain access to and make use of these data. The references both to the prohibition expressly highlighted in the census judgment and to the field of telecommunications, which has far-reaching implications against the background of the dynamic development of the Internet, are among the central factors that explain why "data retention" has been the subject of an enduring public discussion and of a quite strong protest movement in Germany. The laws implementing the DRD triggered the largest mass constitutional complaint in the history of the Federal Republic of Germany.

After an explanation of how the DRD was implemented in Germany, this chapter analyses the leading judgment of the FCC in 2010. Both this judgment and the decisions of the European Court of Justice (CJEU) had a strong impact on the subsequent legislation and jurisdiction which is far from over. Data retention proves to be one of the finest examples of both the new possibilities of surveillance and the emerging network of courts.

2 Implementation of Directive 2006/24/EC in Germany

The DRD was transposed into national law on 1 January 2008 by several acts amending existing laws.[4] The amendments can be systematised into three complexes. First, regulations were introduced obliging companies in the telecommunications sector to store certain personal data that are generated by their services for longer than is necessary for their business purposes.[5] Second, rules were added obliging companies to provide these data to certain authorities under certain conditions. The third complex consisted of regulations that allowed the authorities to require and receive the data to be transferred and to use the data transferred for their own purposes. For according to the requirements recognised under German law, in addition to the regulations obliging a data controller, in this case a private company, to transmit data to the authorities, further regulations are necessary that allow the authorities to query or receive the data ("double-door model").[6]

In its former version, § 113a of the Telecommunications Act (TKG) obliged the providers of publicly accessible telecommunications services, e.g. telephone services, e-mail services or Internet access services, to store certain telecommunications service data for a period of 6 months. The catalogue of data corresponded to the DRD and included among other things, the telephone number or other identification of the calling and called line, the identity of the electronic mailboxes of senders and receivers of messages, Internet Protocol addresses allocated to users of access

[4]In particular: Gesetz zur Neuregelung der Telekommunikationsüberwachung und anderer verdeckter Ermittlungsmaßnahmen sowie zur Umsetzung der Richtlinie 2006/24/EG of 21 December 2007, BGBl I 3198.

[5]As to the business purposes, § 96 TKG provides the possibility of storing and using telecommunications data to the extent necessary for purposes such as charging and invoicing the parties or recognising deficiencies of telecommunications equipment.

[6]Cf. more closely Albers (2001), p. 334 f.; Gazeas (2014), p. 228 f., 501 ff.

providers and the commencement and cessation of the use of the services with date and time. The duty of storage essentially extended to all information that is necessary to reconstruct who communicated or attempted to communicate with whom, when, from where and for how long. Telecommunications service providers that—like anonymisation services—altered the data to be stored were required to store the original and new data as well as the time at which these data were transcribed.[7] § 113a sect. 8 TKG emphasised that the contents of the communication, e.g. the details of what Internet pages visited by users, may not be stored. The data stored were to be deleted within 1 month of the end of the storage period.[8] As regards data security, the care generally necessary in the area of telecommunications had to be observed.[9]

§ 113b TKG generally defined the purposes for which the telecommunications companies were allowed to transmit stored data to public authorities. Three exclusive purposes were enumerated: the prosecution of criminal offences, the warding off of substantial dangers to public security, and the performance of intelligence service tasks. Furthermore, and under less strict conditions, the use of these data was permitted to identify Internet users to whom specific IP addresses had been assigned in order to provide necessary customer and traffic data to authorities requesting these data, e.g. for purposes of copyright protection in accordance with the relevant laws.[10]

Authorisations to access and use the data stored were to be put in concrete terms by provisions of specific branches of law passed by, due to the German federalist system, both the Federal Government and the Länder (states). The Federal Government is competent for criminal procedural provisions and federal authorities, e.g. the Federal Intelligence Service; the Länder are responsible for regulating their police forces and intelligence services. Provisions for prosecution had been laid down in § 100g of the Code of Criminal Procedure (StPO). This norm allowed the criminal prosecution authorities to collect data stored by way of precaution under § 113a TKG without the knowledge of the person concerned.[11] The authorisation was limited insofar as data access and use were necessary for investigating the facts of the case or determining the whereabouts of an accused person and only applied to "offences of considerable importance" and to offences committed via telecommunications. Data collection could only be ordered by a judge, except in cases of imminent danger.[12] The court order was only to be directed against accused persons or against persons of whom it must be assumed due to specific facts that they receive or transmit specific messages directed to the accused or originating from this person, or that the accused uses their line. The order did not authorise the authorities to

[7] § 113a sect. 6 TKG (former version).

[8] § 113a sect. 11 TKG (former version).

[9] § 113a sect. 10 TKG (former version).

[10] This means that if authorities already knew an IP address through their own investigations, they should be able to request information as to which subscriber the address belonged to.

[11] The Code of Criminal Procedure provides for duties of ex post-notification of the persons affected by measures and subsequent judicial relief.

[12] §§100g sect. 2 in conjunction with 100a sect. 3 StPO (former version).

directly access the data but obliged the service providers to filter out and transmit the data in a separate intermediate step in accordance with the requirements of the order.

Overall, the provisions of federal law were partly directive-implementing and partly directive-exceeding in character. In particular, they transposed the Directive to the extent that telecommunications service providers were required to retain data for a period of 6 months without any cause. They went beyond the Directive in fleshing out the details of the exploitation of the data stored, for instance, by concretising the purposes as the prosecution of "criminal offences of considerable importance."

3 Proceedings Before the Federal Constitutional Court

Data retention, access to telecommunications data and extracting information from these communications were highly contested in Germany. While some advanced the view that the temporary retention of metadata results in only minimal intrusions or risks, many people criticised these measures as mass surveillance without any particular cause. There was a widespread protest movement, which also organised itself on the Internet and laid the foundation for a large number of constitutional complaints. Around 34,000 complainants initiated or, mostly, joined proceedings. This led to some pressure on the political system and on the FCC as well. For its proceedings, the FCC selected several constitutional complaints that covered all aspects to be decided with regard to the complainants and to the issues to be addressed.

Most of the complainants emphasised, as users of telecommunications services, potential violations of the guarantee of the inviolability of the secrecy of telecommunications as well as, insofar as they were attorneys or journalists, of the freedom of occupation or the freedom of the press and of the right to informational self-determination. Among their key points were the arguments that the storage of traffic data was extensive and that these data were stored without specific cause or suspicion for future reference, although the probability that they would later be required for criminal prosecution or averting danger was negligible. With data retention, the complainants expressed concerns that the state is establishing an infrastructure that could destroy citizens' trust in free communication and enable further surveillance in the future. Personality, behaviour, communication and movement profiles were made possible. Both special relations of trust, such as with lawyers, journalists, doctors or counselling centres, and the core area of personal conduct were insufficiently protected. The extent to which persons are affected by the measures although they are not ultimately the targeted persons, was large and the suitability of data retention doubtful, because criminals would use prepaid and anonymisation options. The possibilities for access granted by § 100g StPO and the range of crimes defined there went too far. Finally, the complainants stated that safeguarding of data security was deficient.

Furthermore, a provider of anonymisation service software which also operated a publicly accessible server offering such services was among the complainants. This enterprise complained about the organisational and financial costs resulting from the obligations imposed on it. Beyond that, the business model of anonymisation services would be hampered or deprived of its basis if there were obligations to identify customers and their data traffic.

4 Decision of the Federal Constitutional Court

The FCC referred to and discussed all these arguments in its decision. Many of the Court's decisions are easier to understand if the complainants' criticism is read. However, the FCC is not limited to the arguments submitted, but carries out an objective examination. With a view to procedural law, the constitutional complaints are the trigger, but not the basis and limit of the examination.

Following several preliminary injunctions, the FCC reached its principal decision on 2 March 2010.[13] The FCC first had to deal with the extent to which it had jurisdiction to examine the legal complaints and whether the constitutional complaints were admissible. Then it had to identify the relevant fundamental rights of the German constitution and to flesh out their scope of protection. The focus of the judicial considerations concerned the constitutionality of the provisions of the TKG and the StPO. Here, we can highlight three central questions: Is precautionary storage without cause constitutional? Which requirements must the provisions meet? What is the situation of the providers of telecommunications and anonymisation services?

In its previous case law, the FCC had determined the scope of its own competence to examine cases distinct from the CJEU under the so-called "Solange" principle: As long as (= *Solange*) the European Union generally guarantees effective protection of fundamental rights that can be regarded as essentially equivalent to the protection of fundamental rights under the Basic Law, the FCC no longer exercises its jurisdiction to decide on the applicability of Union law cited as the legal basis for the acts of German authorities and does not review national legislation that implements mandatory provisions of Union law.[14] In March 2010, the Data Retention Directive had

[13]Judgment of the FCC of 2 March 2010, 1 BvR 256/08, 263/08, and 586/08= BVerfGE 125, 260 (with dissenting opinions of two judges). This judgment developed several new considerations but also built on the court's jurisdiction which had been developed since the census decision of 1983. See, e. g. FCC, Judgment of 14 July 1999—1 BvR 2226/94 et al. = BVerfGE 100, 313; Judgment of 3 March 2004—1 BvR 2378/98 et al. = BVerfGE 109, 279; Decision of 3 March 2004—1 BvF 3/92 = BVerfGE 110, 33; Judgment of 27 February 2008 – 1 BvR 370/07 et al. = BVerfGE 120, 274.

[14]Cf. FCC, Decision of 22 October 1986—2 BvR 197/83 = BVerfGE 73, 339; Decision of 7 June 2000—2 BvL 1/97 = BVerfGE 102, 147; Decision of 13 March 2007—1 BvF 1/05 = BVerfGE 118, 79.

not yet been declared null and void by the CJEU, which had until then only ruled on EU areas of competence.[15] Accordingly, the FCC would have only been competent to review that portion of the national regulations on the basis of German fundamental rights not stipulated by mandatory provisions of the Directive. Reviewing the provisions transposing mandatory provisions of the directive while the directive was still in force would not have been permissible. The only conceivable solution here would have been to initiate proceedings for a preliminary ruling before the CJEU.

The FCC, however, fully reviewed the contested provisions. This was initially justified succinctly by the fact that there is nothing to preclude an examination on the basis of fundamental rights if the CJEU were to declare the directive null and void by way of a preliminary ruling.[16] This reasoning can be challenged because its latter part is based solely on an assumption and remains hypothetical.[17] The initiation of a preliminary ruling proceeding was subsequently rejected on the grounds that it is not decision-relevant. The Court argued that the contents of the Directive leave broad discretion in shaping the storage of telecommunications traffic data and do not govern subsequent access to the data or their use and that, considering these contents, the implementability of the Directive as such is not called into question because the national provisions on data retention prove to be not unconstitutional under all circumstances. If this line of argument is taken as a foundation, a review of regulations determined under the Union law would always be possible if the FCC can arrive at the result that the provisions in question are compatible with the Basic Law. The former quasi-spatial control waiver rule of the *Solange* method is replaced by a functional delimitation construction: "Union law objections do not preclude from confirming the implementing national law under the Basic Law because the mere confirmation of constitutionality does not jeopardise the uniform and effective implementation of Union law."[18] In this approach, the jurisdiction of the FCC is significantly expanded again. In the particular case, the court opened up the avenue of a strategically important review of the conformity of the data retention provisions with fundamental rights, which the CJEU had not undertaken with regard to European fundamental rights.

We can highlight two reasons for this new approach. First, given the level of protest in Germany, the mass constitutional complaint and the preliminary injunction of the FCC, there was considerable political pressure for a relatively quick decision to be made. The complainants had hastened to explain that their complaint was admissible, and the FCC could hardly have waited for the CJEU's decision in the pending cases on compatibility with the EU fundamental rights. Second, in this relevant case, the court also wanted to make its own decision and elaborate constitutional guidelines and requirements intended to have an overarching impact within

[15]Judgment of the CJEU of 10 February 2009, C-301/06.

[16]Cf. Judgment of the FCC of 2 March 2010, 1 BvR 256/08, 263/08, and 586/08, § 182.

[17]Albers and Reinhardt (2010), p. 769.

[18]Britz (2015), p. 277.

the network of courts. Its strategy has proved successful, as can be seen from comparison with the later CJEU decision.

As the complainants had claimed violations of several fundamental rights, the FCC had to determine the relationship of these rights to each other and, primarily, to refine the scope of protection of the guarantee of the inviolability of the secrecy of correspondence and telecommunications. Article 10 (1) Basic Law protects the freedom and inviolability of individual communication relying on telecommunications techniques and services. It thus responds to the threats to freedom arising from the use of telecommunications or telecommunications technology and the facilities of third parties. The guarantee refers to the use of the respective communication techniques and services as a formal reference point. It covers the communication process from the sending of the message to its receipt within the recipient's sphere of control.[19] In the case of Internet-mediated communication, its scope of application must be delimited vis-à-vis Article 5 (1) 2 Basic Law which protects the freedom of broadcasting services, since Article 10 (1) Basic Law only protects individual communication, not public mass communication. However, a distinction between individual and mass communication is not possible without a link to the content of the information transmitted, which is contrary to the protective function of the fundamental right, and therefore, the FCC explained, Article 10 Basic Law applies as long as the character of the communication in the network is not discernible.[20]

Its protection is not confined to the contents of the communication.[21] The confidentiality of the closer circumstances of the communication process is also protected. This includes whether, when and how often telecommunications traffic took place or was attempted between which persons or telecommunications devices.[22] Article 10 Basic Law thus also protects the corresponding information and the pertinent data recorded. The FCC explained this in the context of the principle of proportionality: The informative value of these data can be extremely broad. Depending on the use of the telecommunications by the persons affected, and in future with increasing frequency, it is possible to create meaningful personality and mobility profiles and to draw conclusions (with a more or less reliable degree of probability) about the individual activities and the social environment of the persons, about their social or political affiliations and preferences, or about internal influence structures and decision-making processes within groups.[23]

---

[19]As to problems in determining the appropriate fundamental right in the field of telecommunications and the Internet cf. FCC, Judgment of 2 March 2006—1 BvR 2099/04 = BVerfGE 115, 166 (185 ff.). Cf. also Albers (2010b), p. 1064.

[20]Judgment of the FCC of 2 March 2010, 1 BvR 256/08, 263/08, and 586/08, § 192.

[21]It does not matter whether the communication contents are of a private nature or serve business purposes see, e.g. FCC, Judgment of 14 July 1999—1 BvR 2226/94 et al. = BVerfGE 100, 313 (358).

[22]This is settled case law, see, e.g. FCC, Decision of 20 June 1984—1 BvR 1494/78 = BVerfGE 67, 157 (172); Decision of 25 Mar 1992—1 BvR 1430/88 = BVerfGE 85, 386 (396).

[23]More closely: Judgment of the FCC of 2 March 2010, 1 BvR 256/08, 263/08, and 586/08, § 211. See also Tzanou (2017), p. 79, who highlights these considerations.

Moreover, the scope of protection of Article 10 Basic Law covers not only the cognisance of telecommunications data but extends to the subsequent information and data processing processes.[24] This means that protection extends from the gathering and storage of data to their request by authorities and any transmission of data to their further storage for security purposes and their subsequent use. The "secrecy" protection does not end as soon as data become known to providers or authorities but continues to set constitutional criteria. Article 10 Basic Law thus offers the guiding norm. Other fundamental rights, such as the freedom of the press, might be referred to in order to strengthen its protection.[25] However, the data retention decision mentioned them only marginally.[26]

After having clarified the scope of protection of Article 10 Basic Law, the FCC explained that the legal obligations of the telecommunications companies to store telecommunications data and transfer them to state authorities must be regarded not as an indirect, but as a direct infringement of the rights of those communicating. It argued that service providers, without any margin of discretion being left to them in this respect, would be used solely as auxiliaries for the performance of tasks by state authorities, so that the storage of the data is legally accountable to the legislature as a direct infringement.[27] It corresponds to the refining of the scope of protection that each legally regulated step of data processing—storage (§ 113a (1) TKG), request and transmission (§ 113b TKG), further storage and subsequent use (§ 100g StPO)—is a separate encroachment on the basic right deriving from Article 10 Basic Law.[28] The constitutional review dealt with these steps in a differentiated manner.

One of the core problems of the case was whether precautionary data retention without cause as such could be constitutional at all. The complainants invoked the famous census judgment whose grounds include a strict prohibition, in the given case addressed to the state, of precautionary collecting and storing non-anonymous data "for indefinite or not yet definable purposes."[29]

However, the FCC delimited the data retention constellation to be assessed against this strict prohibition. For the purpose of delimitation, it described this constellation as "a precautionary storage of telecommunications traffic data without cause for later transmission with cause to the authorities responsible for criminal prosecution or warding off danger or to the intelligence services."[30] It did not consider such a form of precautionary data retention to be absolutely incompatible with Article 10 Basic Law, but as only permissible in exceptional cases and subject to particularly strict requirements.

[24]Leading decision in this respect: FCC, Judgment of 14 July 1999—1 BvR 2226/94 et al. = BVerfGE 100, 313 (359).

[25]See FCC, Judgment of 14 July 1999—1 BvR 2226/94 et al. = BVerfGE 100, 313 (365).

[26]Cf. Judgment of the FCC of 2 March 2010, 1 BvR 256/08, 263/08, and 586/08, § 191, 305.

[27]Judgment of the FCC of 2 March 2010, 1 BvR 256/08, 263/08, and 586/08, § 193.

[28]Judgment of the FCC of 2 March 2010, 1 BvR 256/08, 263/08, and 586/08, § 192 ff.

[29]Judgment of the FCC of 15 December 1983, 1 BvR 209/83 et al. = BVerfGE 65, 1 (46 and 47).

[30]Judgment of the FCC of 2 March 2010, 1 BvR 256/08, 263/08, and 586/08, § 207.

The problem that the telecommunications traffic data had to be stored by the service providers without cause for 6 months was discussed not as an independent requirement for the determination of purpose[31] but as part of the proportionality test. The FCC affirmed the suitability even if it admitted that "such a storage of data cannot ensure that all telecommunications connections can reliably be assigned to specific users, and it may be possible for criminals to circumvent storage by using Wi-Fi hotspots, Internet cafés, foreign Internet telephone services or prepaid mobile telephones registered under a false name."[32] However, suitability "merely requires that the attainment of the goal is facilitated."[33] The storage was also regarded as necessary in the sense that there are no less drastic but similarly effective means.[34] The main considerations dealt with the question of whether the storage is disproportionate from the outset. The FCC classified the storage as a particularly serious encroachment. Among the criteria relevant for this classification are the extent of storage and the absence of cause as well as the far-reaching informative value of the stored data. Even without recording the contents of the communication, conclusions could be drawn, on, for example, social or political affiliations and personal preferences, inclinations and weaknesses. This included connections that are engaged in with an expectation of confidentiality. The persons concerned faced increased risks of being exposed to further investigations without themselves having given occasion for this and of being affected by an abuse of the data collected. The infringement was given particular weight by the fact that the storage of telecommunications traffic data without cause "is capable of creating a diffusely threatening feeling of being watched which can impair a free exercise of fundamental rights in many areas."[35] The aspect that "trust" is a central condition for the unbiased exercise of fundamental rights had already been emphasised by the court in its decision on the fundamental right to the guarantee of the integrity and confidentiality of information technology systems.[36]

Despite the severity of the encroachment, the court did not consider precautionary storage without cause of telecommunications traffic data to be absolutely prohibited under constitutional law. Decisive for the justifiability was how the statutory framework was shaped. First, the storage without cause was not carried out directly by the state, but through an obligation imposed on private service providers. The data are

[31]Concerning the significance of purpose determination see Albers (2005), p. 498 ff.; von Grafenstein (2018), p. 231 ff.

[32]Judgment of the FCC of 2 March 2010, 1 BvR 256/08, 263/08, and 586/08, § 207.

[33]Judgment of the FCC of 2 March 2010, 1 BvR 256/08, 263/08, and 586/08, § 207. This consideration is settled case law and is rooted in the notion that legislation should have a margin of assessment in this respect. This notion and the margin of assessment are the reference point for the now widely acknowledged duty of legislation to establish evaluations by means of which the accuracy of legislative assumptions at the time of the enactment of a law is later checked (duties of legislation to observe developments and to improve the law if necessary).

[34]Judgment of the FCC of 2 March 2010, 1 BvR 256/08, 263/08, and 586/08, § 208.

[35]Judgment of the FCC of 2 March 2010, 1 BvR 256/08, 263/08, and 586/08, § 212.

[36]FCC, Judgment of 27 February 2008—1 BvR 370/07 et al., § 181 et sqq. = BVerfGE 120, 274 (306 ff.).

thus, the court argued without mentioning the rather oligopolistic situation on the market, not yet compiled during storage itself, but remain distributed over many individual companies. The retrieval of the data by state authorities only took place in a second step and was then carried out on a case-by-case basis following legally defined criteria. "The formulation of the provisions giving permission for retrieval and further use of the stored data may ensure," the court argues, "that the storage is not made for purposes that are indefinite or cannot yet be determined."[37] The separation of storage and retrieval and their respective legal frameworks are therefore at the heart of the court's argument. The court pointed out that the storage of telecommunications traffic data does not include the contents, is limited to 6 months and is not directed towards total recording of all citizen's activities but takes up, in a manner that is still limited, the special significance of telecommunications and responds to the specific potential danger associated with them, for instance, that criminal offences operating essentially on the Internet would escape observation if telecommunications data were deleted. The court added that the precautionary storage of telecommunications traffic data without cause must remain an exception. In particular, it must not "in interaction with other existing files, lead to virtually all activities of the citizens being reconstructible."[38] Legislation aimed at precautionary storing, as comprehensively as possible, all data potentially useful for criminal prosecution or the prevention of danger would from the outset be incompatible with the constitution. The court introduced a kind of "surveillance overall accounting" as a duty of the legislator.[39] It even associated the normative statement that the exercise of freedom may not be recorded and registered in its entirety with the constitutional proviso with regard to identity asserted in the Lisbon decision.[40]

Despite these latter restraints, the grounds of the data retention decision considerably weaken the strict prohibition of precautionary collecting and storing of personal data for indefinite or not yet definable purposes, which has been emphasised since the census judgment. This prohibition follows from the principle of purpose limitation. This principle requires not only that the purposes be determinable, but also refers to the requirement that the data be necessary for the respective purposes. A determination of the purpose would be useless without the correlate of necessity. It is true that the purposes, if we follow the court's construction of "a precautionary storage of telecommunications traffic data without cause for later transmission with cause to the authorities responsible for criminal prosecution or warding off danger or to the intelligence services," might be described more closely with a view to the permitted uses by the entitled authorities. This description, however, anticipates a certain course of events from the first element of storage to the further elements of access and use which are actually relatively separate from storage (the court itself has highlighted this as a condition influencing the assessment of

[37] Judgment of the FCC of 2 March 2010, 1 BvR 256/08, 263/08, and 586/08, § 214.

[38] Judgment of the FCC of 2 March 2010, 1 BvR 256/08, 263/08, and 586/08, § 218.

[39] More closely Roßnagel (2010), p. 1240 f.

[40] Cf. FCC, Judgment of 2 March 2010, 1 BvR 256/08, 263/08, and 586/08, § 218.

constitutionality). The problem arises that the necessity of the data for preventive, criminal procedural or intelligence purposes is not certain at the time of storage. The service providers only retain the data in the event that they prove to be necessary in the future. And what is new about the storage duties at issue here is that the precautionary storage is carried out without further criteria which support the prognosis of a later necessity and which otherwise include, for example, indications or assumptions of danger or suspicion because of assessments of situations, specific findings or previous conduct of persons. It is precisely for this reason that the vast majority of data will prove to be unnecessary. The lack of more detailed criteria for precautionary storage and necessity prognosis gets, it might be thought, at the core issue of the prohibition of precautionary storage of personal data for indefinite or not yet definable purposes. But the FCC came to the conclusion that the chosen construction does not give rise to a fundamental verdict of unconstitutionality.[41] It then tried to set restrictions by means of the above-mentioned "surveillance overall accounting"—which, however, faces difficulties of operationalising cumulative effects of surveillance measures—and by means of a bundle of requirements that must be complied with for constitutionality to be granted.

Based on the principles of legal certainty and definiteness regarding norms and of proportionality, the FCC derived concrete and in part detailed constitutional requirements resulting in a network of dovetailed substantive and procedural precautions. Innovative remarks concern aspects of data security, the scope of data use, transparency, enforcement as well as control mechanisms and provisions ensuring evaluations. Also deserving special mention is the approach conceiving the individual elements as part of a coherent concept with the consequence that the constitutionality of certain elements depends on whether other elements have been formulated in accordance with the constitution.

The precautionary storage of telecommunications traffic data without cause must meet the requirements of the principle of proportionality. Considerations of suitability and necessity as well as some of the aspects relevant to the balancing of interests have already been advanced by the court in its examination of the question whether the contested data retention provisions could be constitutional at all: The data remain distributed over several private providers and the storage is limited to 6 months and to traffic or metadata which arise regularly in connection with the service and are already temporarily stored for particular purposes. Beyond that, the court emphasised that the severe encroachment constituted by such storage is only proportionate in the narrow sense if a particularly high standard of data security by means of clear and binding obligations on private service providers is guaranteed.[42] This responsibility on the part of the legislator to guarantee data security responds to the fact that the risk of illegal access to data being attractive in view of its

[41] See also the comparison with Decision no. 1258 of the Romanian Constitutional Court of 8 October 2009 in: De Vries et al. (2011), p. 13 ff.

[42] Judgment of the FCC of 2 March 2010, 1 BvR 256/08, 263/08, and 586/08, § 221 et sqq.

multifaceted informative value is high[43] and that private service providers have only limited incentives to guarantee data security on their own due to cost pressure. Data security requirements apply both to data retention and transmission, and effective safeguards are also needed to ensure data deletion. The data security standard must be designed dynamically: It must be based on the present state of development of the discussion between technical experts—for example, by resorting to legal figures under ordinary law such as the state of the art—and continuously incorporate new findings and insights. Referring to the expert statements in the written submissions and in the oral hearing of the proceedings before the court, as examples the FCC named separate storage of the data, fastidious coding, a secure access regime through more refined use of for instance the "four-eye principle" and audit-proof recording of the access to data and their deletion. In this respect, the requirements to be laid down must be specified either by sophisticated technical regulations, possibly graduated at various levels of legislation, or in a general manner and then specified in a transparent manner by binding individual decisions of the regulatory authorities addressed to the individual companies. Constitutional law also requires monitoring that is comprehensible to the public and that involves the independent data protection officer and a balanced system of sanctions which also attaches appropriate weight to violations of data security. The FCC endeavoured with these data security requirements to ensure that the data retained is not used in any other way than for the intended security purposes and not beyond the time stipulated. Finally, the constitutionality of the storage of the data depends on the regulations on subsequent access and further use being designed in such a way that they themselves meet the requirements of the principle of proportionality.[44]

The retrieval by security authorities, the transmission to them and their use of telecommunications traffic data are also subject to several requirements. To begin with, the legislator must provide for a fundamental prohibition of transmission for a confined range of telecommunications connections relying on special confidentiality, such as counselling over the phone in situations of emotional crisis.[45] Apart from that, because the analysis of retained data allows conclusions to be drawn that might pry deeply into private lives and facilitates the creation of personality or movement profiles, the use of retained data must be for the purpose of fulfilling tasks of paramount importance related to the protection of legal interests. This must be reflected in the statutory description of both the protected legal interests and the thresholds that must be reached to enable the authorities to request and then to use the data. For criminal prosecution, this means that the legislature must provide an exhaustive list of the criminal offences that are to apply here, either by having

[43] Cf. Clarke (2015), p. 128: Data retention measures and huge volumes of highly sensitive data result in a concentrated "honey-pot" which attracts attacks.

[44] Judgment of the FCC of 2 March 2010, 1 BvR 256/08, 263/08, and 586/08, § 226: "The drafting of these provisions on use, in a manner that is not disproportionate, thus not only decides on the constitutionality of these provisions, which in themselves constitute an encroachment, but has also an effect on the constitutionality of the storage as such."

[45] Judgment of the FCC of 2 March 2010, 1 BvR 256/08, 263/08, and 586/08, § 238.

recourse to existing lists or by creating a new one; a blanket clause or a mere reference to criminal offences of considerable significance is not sufficient. Furthermore, a retrieval of the data requires at least the suspicion of a listed offence based on specific facts. In the context of preventing danger, the use of the stored data may only be permitted to ward off dangers to the life, limb or freedom of a person, to the existence or security of the Federal Republic or of a *Land* or to ward off a danger to public safety. The statutory norm must provide for the threshold of "actual evidence of a concrete danger to the legal interests to be protected."[46] This means that specific given facts support the prognosis that, without intervention, damage will occur with reasonable probability in the foreseeable future. Considering the impairments for citizens associated with the use of intelligence data, these requirements also expressly apply to intelligence services, even though their tasks of informing the government and therefore elucidating particular areas of activity are not solely linked to concrete danger situations.[47] On procedural safeguards, the FCC required, except for the intelligence services,[48] the retrieval and transmission of the data to be subject to a well-defined judge's pre-emptive review,[49] although Article 10 GG does not provide for such a proviso.

The limitation to certain purposes, which reflect the outstandingly important tasks of legal protection, must also be ensured after the data have been retrieved and transferred to the authorities requesting it, and must be accompanied by procedural safeguards. In particular, the data must be analysed immediately after transmission and deleted if they are irrelevant. The retrieving authorities may, however, forward the data to other bodies insofar as this is done to perform tasks for which access to these data would also be directly permissible (the so-called "hypothetical substitute intervention").

The FCC also required the legislature to take effective precautions to ensure transparency in the use of data. Secret use of data could only be considered if the purpose of the investigation for which the data retrieval serves would otherwise be thwarted. The legislature could assume this, in principle, in cases of warding off danger and performing intelligence service tasks, but not in cases of criminal prosecution, where investigative measures are regularly carried out with the knowledge of and in the presence of the suspect. If the data subject does not have to be informed prior to querying or transmission of his or her data, the legislature must provide for a duty of subsequently notifying him or her.[50]

Furthermore, it is constitutionally required that a legal protection procedure be available to subsequently review the use of the data. Where persons affected had no

[46]Judgment of the FCC of 2 March 2010, 1 BvR 256/08, 263/08, and 586/08, § 231. Cf. also already FCC, Judgment of 27 Feb 2008—1 BvR 370/07 et al., § 247 et sqq.= BVerfGE 120, 274 (328 f.).

[47]Judgment of the FCC of 2 March 2010, 1 BvR 256/08, 263/08, and 586/08, § 233.

[48]In this respect, Article 10 (2) Basic Law allows the replacement of pre-emptive judicial supervision by supervision carried out by an agency or auxiliary agency appointed by parliament.

[49]Judgment of the FCC of 2 March 2010, 1 BvR 256/08, 263/08, and 586/08, § 247 et sqq.

[50]Judgment of the FCC of 2 March 2010, 1 BvR 256/08, 263/08, and 586/08, § 243 et sqq.

opportunity before the measure was carried out to defend themselves against the use of their telecommunications traffic data, they must be given the possibility of subsequent judicial review. Finally, a legislative formulation that is not disproportionate also requires effective sanctions for violations of rights, whether these are incorporated into the general structure of the law of criminal procedure or into current liability law, or established by more extensive provisions.

For the indirect use of data for information under § 113 (1) TKG in the form of a claim for information from service providers for the identification of IP addresses, the FCC stipulated less strict requirements.[51] In this case, the authorities are merely given personal information on what owner was registered on the Internet with regard to an IP address, and this owner is determined by the service providers by recourse to data retained. The informative value of these data is limited. Nevertheless, the respective rules influence the conditions of communication on the Internet and limit its anonymity. The FCC explained that the legislature must ensure that information may only be obtained based on a sufficient initial suspicion or of a concrete danger on the basis of facts and with a view to sufficiently weighty adverse effects on a legal interest. There is no duty to provide for a judge's pre-emptive review. The person affected has, in principle, the right to learn that this anonymity has been removed, and why.

Once it had worked out the requirements, the FCC reviewed the respective legal regulations. Closer examination showed that the contested provisions did not satisfy the developed constitutional requirements in key respects. They were incompatible with Article 10 (1) Basic Law as a whole.

§ 113a TKG required telecommunications service companies, including anonymisation services, to store and, where applicable, transmit the data listed in the law, with the costs for the necessary infrastructure to be paid by the companies. Both the restrictions on anonymisation services and the proportionality of using private companies for the fulfilment of public tasks were contested parts of the constitutional complaints, and the impairments caused by this must be measured against the standard set out in Article 12 (1) Basic Law. In a decision issued in 2003, the Austrian Constitutional Court declared the relevant Austrian provisions unconstitutional if the costs remain with the telecommunications companies; otherwise, however, it considered the commissioning to be justified.

By contrast, the FCC did not express any constitutional concerns with regard to Article 12 Basic Law.[52] It argued that § 113a (6) TKG did not make the offer of an anonymisation service de facto impossible. Rather, anonymisation services could continue to offer their users the possibility of surfing the Internet without private individuals being able to identify their IP address; anonymity would only be lifted vis-à-vis the state authorities under the narrow conditions of a permitted data retrieval. The court did not deal separately with those anonymisation service providers who themselves could not identify their users and are now obliged to ensure

[51]Judgment of the FCC of 2 March 2010, 1 BvR 256/08, 263/08, and 586/08, § 254 et sqq.

[52]Judgment of the FCC of 2 March 2010, 1 BvR 256/08, 263/08, and 586/08, § 293 et sqq.

identifiability. However, the impossibility of such an offer also constitutes (only) a regulation of the exercise of a profession which can be regarded as proportionate. Moreover, the FCC also classified neither the technical effort nor the financial burdens as a disproportionate impairment of the freedom of telecommunications service providers to exercise their profession.[53] As long as the effects are not highly restrictive, the legislature has been granted wide discretion concerning what burdens and measures to safeguard public interests, which are in need of regulation as a result of commercial activities, it imposes on market players in order to integrate the associated costs into the market and market prices.

The FCC did not consider the contested form of data retention to be unconstitutional under all circumstances. But it worked out a set of constitutional requirements. The challenged provisions did not meet these requirements and violated the guarantee of the inviolability of the secrecy of telecommunications, Article 10 Basic Law. From the point of view of the court, the constitutionality of data retention depends on how it is shaped by legal regulations and whether sufficient limits are set at the numerous points that can be identified. Data retention proves to be a complex issue embracing many aspects: Which data are involved, and which stakeholders are involved? To what extent and for what primary purposes do data already accrue for what period? What about data security measures and protection against misuse? What is the relationship between primary, secondary and possibly further purposes? For what secondary purposes do which security authorities have access to which data under what conditions and intervention thresholds and in what form? Which control mechanisms are implemented? Are there provisions ensuring appropriate evaluations to verify the assumptions underlying the establishment of data retention and the shaping of its regulation?[54]

As far as providers of telecommunications and anonymisation services are concerned, a violation of Article 12 Basic Law was rejected. The FCC even came to the conclusion that higher security standards are necessary, which can be imposed on the providers without any convincing constitutional objections.

5 Legislation and Jurisdiction in the Aftermath

The German legislator did not immediately adapt the provisions declared unconstitutional, but waited for the decision of the CJEU, as the procedure that expressly concerned the compatibility of the DRD with European fundamental rights was already pending. In April 2014, the CJEU declared the DRD invalid because it exceeded the limits imposed by compliance with the principle of proportionality in

---

[53]Judgment of the FCC of 2 March 2010, 1 BvR 256/08, 263/08, and 586/08, § 300 et sqq.

[54]Cf. Albers (2010a). See also more broadly Clarke (2015), p. 129 ff. Empirical studies are complicated and rare; see, as an example, Max Planck Institut für ausländisches und internationales Strafrecht (2011).

the light of Articles 7, 8 and 52 (1) Charter of Fundamental Rights.[55] In its statement of the grounds for this judgment, the CJEU adopted some of the considerations and requirements that the FCC had elaborated in its decision: the acknowledgement of the broad informative nature of the data stored that would allow very precise conclusions to be drawn about the private lives of persons,[56] the seriousness of the intrusions which were divided into relatively independent steps (although the essence of the relevant fundamental rights was not adversely affected)[57] and the necessity of substantive and procedural thresholds, limits and precautions for storage as well as for the authorities' access to the data and their subsequent use, especially regarding the indispensability of appropriate data security measures,[58] precautions with a view to obligations of professional secrecy,[59] the restriction to sufficiently serious criminal offences[60] and the requirement of a prior review by a court or an independent administrative body.[61] Beyond that, the CJEU pointed out that the DRD covered all persons, all means of electronic communication and traffic data without any differentiation, limitation or exception being made in the light of the objective of fighting against serious crime. The Court explained in more detail that the directive did not require any relationship between the data whose retention is provided for and a threat to public security, and that there were, in particular, no restrictions of retention in relation to data pertaining to a particular time period and/or a particular geographical zone and/or to a circle of particular persons likely to be involved in a serious crime, or to persons who could contribute, through the retention of their data, to the prevention, detection or prosecution of serious offences.[62] Another objection pointed out that the period of time for which data should be withheld was not more differentiated in terms of categories of data and their possible usefulness for the purposes or according to the persons concerned.[63] Finally, the Court criticised that the DRD did not call for data to be retained within the EU to ensure control by an independent authority.[64]

---

[55] Judgment of the CJEU (Grand Chamber) of 8 April 2014, C-293/12 and C-594/12, available under curia.europa.eu. On the difficulties caused by the limited areas of competence of the EU, which also explain why the DRD rules on access by security authorities do not go into detail, see Bignami (2011), p. 238 ff. We also must note that, at this point and in subsequent points, the judgment of the CJEU of 10 February 2009, on the one hand, and the CJEU-judgment of 8 April 2014, on the other hand, are not consistent in every respect.

[56] Judgment of the CJEU (Grand Chamber) of 8 April 2014, C-293/12 and C-594/12, §§ 27, 56. The CJEU added that the retention of the data might impact the exercise of the freedom of expression.

[57] Judgment of the CJEU (Grand Chamber) of 8 April 2014, C-293/12 and C-594/12, § 39 et sqq.

[58] Judgment of the CJEU (Grand Chamber) of 8 April 2014, C-293/12 and C-594/12, § 66 et sqq.

[59] Judgment of the CJEU (Grand Chamber) of 8 April 2014, C-293/12 and C-594/12, § 58.

[60] Judgment of the CJEU (Grand Chamber) of 8 April 2014, C-293/12 and C-594/12, § 60 et sqq.

[61] Judgment of the CJEU (Grand Chamber) of 8 April 2014, C-293/12 and C-594/12, § 62.

[62] Judgment of the CJEU (Grand Chamber) of 8 April 2014, C-293/12 and C-594/12, § 56 et sqq.

[63] Judgment of the CJEU (Grand Chamber) of 8 April 2014, C-293/12 and C-594/12, § 63.

[64] Judgment of the CJEU (Grand Chamber) of 8 April 2014, C-293/12 and C-594/12, § 68.

The extent to which this judgment required which adjustments of member state laws was (and is) not fully clear. With the nullification of the DRD, this depends on the scope, the precautions and the limitations of Directive 2002/58/EC.[65] In 2015, after heated discussions, the German parliament approved laws reintroducing data retention.[66] The provisions were supposed to be implemented by providers by 1 July 2017. The legislator claimed to comply with both the requirements of Germany's FCC and those of the CJEU. Among other things, the data to be stored were reduced, e.g. e-mail services' data were excluded, the retention periods were differentiated into between 4 and 10 weeks according to data categories, protective measures for professional secrets were provided, the provisions for data security were significantly tightened, the transmission thresholds were raised, access and use for prosecution purposes were linked to a listed catalogue of criminal offences, and various procedural safeguards were introduced.

In its Tele2 Sverige-judgment of December 2016, the CJEU then decided on questions arising in the context of Directive 2002/58.[67] Most important is the reasoning, that the contested national legislation on data retention fall within the scope of EU law, that Article 15 (1) Directive 2002/58 is exhaustive and that it allows member states to adopt legislation permitting data retention only if certain restrictions are adhered to. In this respect, the CJEU reaffirms the requirements it had already set out in its DRD-decision of 2014.

The grounds for this judgment, in conjunction with the declaration of the invalidity of the DRD, may require adjustments to national legislation.[68] In Germany, however, the legislator saw no reason to change the law already enacted. Applications for interim measures have been rejected twice by the FCC because of the complexity of the legal issues and as a result of a balancing of consequences, as is usual in proceedings for interim relief.[69] But the administrative courts are concerned with the data retention obligations as well, because they are called upon by service providers. They have delivered several preliminary and main rulings with the result that the obligations are unlawful.[70] The administrative courts highlight, in particular, the fact that the requirement to restrict in any suitable manner the circle of persons

[65]Directive 2002/58/EC of the European Parliament and of the Council of 12 July 2002 concerning the processing of personal data and the protection of privacy in the electronic communications sector (Directive on privacy and electronic communications), OJ L 201/37.

[66]Gesetz zur Einführung einer Speicherpflicht und einer Höchstspeicherfrist für Verkehrsdaten, v. 10.12.2015, BGBl. I 2218.

[67]Judgment of the CJEU (Grand Chamber) of 21 December 2016, C-203/15 and C-698/15.

[68]Cf. for an overview also the Eurojust-Report, Data retention regimes in Europe in light of the CJEU ruling of December 2016 in Joined cases C-203/15 and C-698/15, Council EU, Doc 10098/17.

[69]FCC, Ruling of 8 June 2016, 1 BvQ 42/15, and ruling of 26 March 2017, 1 BvR 3156/15.

[70]Administrative Court of Cologne, Ruling of 25 January 2017—9 L 1009/16; Higher Administrative Court of North Rhine-Westphalia, Ruling of 22 June 2017—13 B 238/17; Administrative Court of Cologne, Judgment of 20 April 2018—9 K 3859/16.

affected by data retention is not met.[71] The stages of appeals has not yet ended. The Federal Administrative Court has meanwhile referred this matter to the CJEU, questioning whether national legislators are denied any possibility of establishing data retention without cause in order to combat serious crime, even if they limit the risks of personality profiles and provide strict data security and access rules. In view of these legal uncertainties, the Federal Network Agency has provisionally suspended the providers' obligation to retain data.

At present, everyone is waiting for the new decision of the FCC in the pending main proceedings.[72] The FCC will have to assess the new law against the background of Directive 2002/58 and the jurisdiction of the CJEU. This is all the more challenging, as this jurisdiction for its part is developing dynamically: In a decision of 2018, the CJEU has set lower requirements for access to mere identification data[73]—entirely in line with the FCC.[74] All in all, the questions of whether the FCC will initiate a preliminary ruling this time and of how it will integrate European legal standards into the examination of national constitutionality is an exciting one.

6 Final Remarks

As a result of the rise of the Internet and the onli*fe* world, data collections of private companies, data retention and subsequent governmental data access and use will take on ever increasing importance as surveillance strategies. And the forms surveillance take are impacted by digitisation and by the Internet.[75] In addition, technologies are continuously advancing, particularly in the area of artificial intelligence, that are capable of analysing huge amounts of data. Retention of data generated in telecommunications is an illustrative example of how the courts are struggling to grasp protection needs and to develop appropriate legal requirements. The decision of the FCC is notable in that it did not judge the extensive precautionary data retention without cause to be unconstitutional as such. Instead, the constellation is broken down into different aspects and a bundle of interdependent requirements drawn from fundamental rights is worked out. However, the

[71] Cf. Higher Administrative Court of North Rhine-Westphalia, Ruling of 22 June 2017—13 B 238/17, § 80 et sqq.; Administrative Court of Cologne, Judgment of 20 April 2018—9 K 3859/16, § 88 et sqq.

[72] 1 BvR 141/16, 229/16, 2023/16 and 2683/16.

[73] Judgment of the CJEU (Grand Chamber) of 2 October 2018, C-207/16, § 57 et sqq., curia.europa.eu. The CJEU has explicitly excluded the question of whether the Spanish Ley 25/2007 de conservación de datos relativos a las comunicaciones electrónicas y a la redes públicas de comunicaciones that provides for obligations to retain data under the invalid DRD is consistent with the requirements laid down in Article 15(1) of Directive 2002/58.

[74] See point 3 of this chapter.

[75] Cf. Bennett et al. (2014), p. 6: Surveillance was once literally "watching"; now, it is also "seeing with data."

substantive discussion in this field is far from closed, and beyond that, the problem of data retention is not limited to this field. We will encounter it, each time in a slightly different form, in many other constellations.

Data retention is also a good example of the interactions between courts, in particular between national constitutional courts, CJEU and also member states' instance courts.[76] The judgment of the FCC taken in 2010 has developed the orientation effects in the proceedings before the CJEU, which the FCC may have expected in the case of such proceedings. In turn, by being in some respects more critical than the FCC, the CJEU has taken advantage of the opportunity to distinguish itself as an even better fundamental rights court.[77] This progress is particularly important in the light of the General Data Protection Regulation or the need for common European positions on privacy and data protection, for example vis-à-vis the USA. The role of the non-constitutional national courts, which are no longer oriented solely to the FCC, but also to the CJEU and thus gain in their relative independence, should also be emphasised. The standard of legal requirements that emerges in this interplay cannot be determined hierarchically. It differentiates itself in manifold ways at several levels and will continue to stay in flux.

Acknowledgement Thanks to Matthew Harris for a thorough proofreading of this text.

References

Albers M (2001) Die Determination polizeilicher Tätigkeit in den Bereichen der Straftatenverhütung und der Verfolgungsvorsorge. Duncker & Humblot, Berlin

Albers M (2005) Informationelle Selbstbestimmung. Nomos, Baden-Baden

Albers M (2010a) Funktionen, Entwicklungsstand und Probleme von Evaluationen im Sicherheitsrecht. In: Albers M, Weinzierl R (eds) Menschenrechtliche Standards in der Sicherheitspolitik. Beiträge zur rechtsstaatsorientierten Evaluierung von Sicherheitsgesetzen. Nomos, Baden-Baden, pp 25–54

Albers M (2010b) Grundrechtsschutz der Privatheit. Deutsches Verwaltungsblatt (DVBl) 125:1061–1069

Albers M (2012) Höchstrichterliche Rechtsfindung und Auslegung gerichtlicher Entscheidungen. In: Grundsatzfragen der Rechtsetzung und Rechtsfindung, VVDStRL, vol 71. de Gruyter, Berlin, pp 257–295

Albers M, Reinhardt J (2010) Vorratsdatenspeicherung im Mehrebenensystem: Die Entscheidung des BVerfG vom 2. 3. 2010. Zeitschrift für das juristische Studium (ZJS):767–774

Bennett CJ, Haggerty KD, Lyon D, Steeves V (2014) Transparent lives: surveillance in Canada. AU Press, Edmonton

Bignami F (2011) Privacy and law enforcement in the European Union: the data retention directive. Chicago Journal of International Law, Spring 2007, Duke Science, Technology & Innovation Paper No. 13. Available at SSRN: https://ssrn.com/abstract=955261

[76]See more closely Slaughter (2004), Maduro (2009), Voßkuhle (2010) and Albers (2012).

[77]Cf. also Kühling (2014); Granger and Irion (2014), p. 844 ff.

Britz G (2015) Grundrechtsschutz durch das Bundesverfassungsgericht und den Europäischen Gerichtshof. Europäische Grundrechte-Zeitschrift (EuGRZ) 42:275–281

Clarke R (2015) Data retention as mass surveillance: the need for an evaluative framework. Int Data Privacy Law 5(2):121–132

De Vries K, Bellanova R, De Hert P, Gutwirth S (2011) The German Constitutional Court judgment on data retention: proportionality overrides unlimited surveillance (Doesn't It?). In: Gutwirth S, Poullet Y, De Hert P, Leenes R (eds) Computers, privacy and data protection: an element of choice. Springer, Dordrecht, pp 3–23

Gazeas N (2014) Übermittlung nachrichtendienstlicher Erkenntnisse an Strafverfolgungsbehörden. Duncker & Humblot, Berlin

Granger MP, Irion K (2014) The Court of Justice and the data retention directive in *Digital Rights Ireland*. Telling off the EU legislator and teaching a lesson in privacy and data protection. Eur Law Rev 39:835–850

Kühling J (2014) Der Fall der Vorratsdatenspeicherungsrichtlinie und der Aufstieg des EuGH zum Grundrechtsgericht. Neue Zeitschrift für Verwaltungsrecht (NVwZ) 2014:681–685

Maduro MP (2009) Courts and pluralism: essay on a theory of judicial adjudication in the context of legal and constitutional pluralism. In: Dunoff L, Trachtmann JP (eds) Ruling the World? Cambridge University Press, Cambridge, pp 356–380

Max-Planck-Institut für ausländisches und internationales Strafrecht (2011) Schutzlücken durch Wegfall der Vorratsdatenspeicherung? Eine Untersuchung zu Problemen der Gefahrenabwehr und Strafverfolgung bei Fehlen gespeicherter Telekommunikationsverkehrsdaten. Gutachten im Auftrag des Bundesamtes für Justiz, 2. Aufl., Freiburg i.Br

Milaj J, Kaiser C (2017) Retention of data in the new anti-money laundering directive – "need to know" versus "nice to know". Int Data Privacy Law 7(2):115–125

Roßnagel A (2010) Die "Überwachungs-Gesamtrechnung" – Das BVerfG und die Vorratsdatenspeicherung. Neue Juristische Wochenschrift (NJW) 63:1238–1242

Slaughter A-M (2004) A new World order. Princeton University Press, Princeton

Tzanou M (2017) The fundamental right to data protection: normative value in the context of counter-terrorism surveillance. Hart Publishing, Oxford

Vedaschi A, Marino Noberasco G (2017) From DRD to PNR: looking for a new balance between privacy and security. In: Cole DD, Fabbrini F, Schulhofer S (eds) Surveillance, privacy and transatlantic relations. Hart Publishing, Oxford, pp 67–87

von Grafenstein M (2018) The principle of purpose limitation in data protection laws. Nomos, Baden-Baden

Voßkuhle A (2010) Der europäische Verfassungsgerichtsverbund. Neue Zeitschrift für Verwaltungsrecht (NVwZ):1–8

Data Retention in Ireland

David Fennelly

Abstract This chapter examines the litigation around data retention which has come before the Irish courts. In its reference to the Court of Justice in the case of *Digital Rights Ireland*, culminating in the landmark judgment of the Court of Justice, the Irish courts made an important contribution to the debate around data retention in the European Union. This chapter examines the history of this case both before and after the landmark judgment of 8 April 2014. Notwithstanding this important contribution to the data retention debate, it was only in December 2018 that the Irish High Court has delivered a substantive judgment surrounding Ireland's own data retention legislation. In the *Dwyer* case, the Court found that part of Ireland's legislation was inconsistent with the EU law on the grounds that it provided for general and indiscriminate retention of telephony data and access to such retained data without appropriate safeguards, including prior review by a court or independent administrative authority. This judgment, which is now under appeal and the subject of a reference to the Court of Justice, illustrates many of the very real challenges arising from the Court of Justice's jurisprudence in this field. Yet, for Ireland, as for other Member States, it is likely to be some time before the implications of the judgment in Digital Rights Ireland—and, even more so, the subsequent judgment in *Tele2 Sverige/Watson* and its sequelae—are fully worked out.

While the author has acted in several cases under discussion in this chapter, this chapter is written in a purely personal capacity. This contribution sets out the position as of October 2019 and, as a result, it has only been possible to note subsequent developments, including the judgments of the Supreme Court of 24 February 2020 and its reference to the Court of Justice of the European Union in Case C-140/20.

D. Fennelly (✉)
School of Law, Trinity College Dublin, the University of Dublin, Dublin, Ireland
e-mail: David.Fennelly@tcd.ie

M. Zubik et al. (eds.), *European Constitutional Courts towards Data Retention Laws*, Law, Governance and Technology Series 45,
https://doi.org/10.1007/978-3-030-57189-4_9

1 Introduction

Over the past decade, the Irish courts have become a fertile ground for litigation on data protection. From this fertile ground, the Irish courts have made references to the Court of Justice of the European Union, culminating in landmark judgments on data protection with far-reaching consequences for the EU and its citizens. One of the most important references from the Irish courts was that in *Digital Rights Ireland.*[1] It was in the context of this reference—joined with a similar reference from the Austrian Constitutional Court in *Seitlinger & Ors*—that the Court of Justice struck down the Data Retention Directive as a disproportionate infringement of the rights to privacy and data protection enshrined in Articles 7 and 8 of the Charter. In the wake of the Court of Justice's judgment in *Digital Rights Ireland*, difficult issues around data retention continue to be litigated in Ireland. The purpose of this chapter is to examine the litigation around data retention which has come before the Irish courts. It will focus on the domestic proceedings in the case of *Digital Rights Ireland* while also considering the ongoing challenges to which the Court of Justice's judgment in that case has given rise.

2 Implementation of Directive 2006/24/EC in Ireland

Before the adoption of the Data Retention Directive, there was considerable divergence across EU Member States on the regulation of data retention. Ireland was one of the Member States that enacted a data retention regime before the adoption of the Directive. Building on a number of earlier measures permitting access by authorities to telecommunications data,[2] Section 63 of the Criminal Justice (Terrorist Offences) Act 2005 (hereafter: the 2005 Act) granted the Garda Commissioner, the head of the Irish police force, the power to request a telecommunications service provider to retain, for a period of three years, traffic data or location data or both for the purposes of fighting crime and of national security.[3] Section 64 of this Act regulated access to such retained data, including for law enforcement purposes.

At the EU level, Ireland initially supported the adoption of a Data Retention Directive to harmonise Member States' rules on data retention. Indeed, in April 2004, before the enactment of its domestic legislation, and during the Irish Presidency of the EU, Ireland—along with France, Sweden and the United Kingdom—

[1]Judgment of 8 April 2014 in *Digital Rights Ireland & Others*, C-293/12 and C-594/12, ECLI:EU:C:2014:238. See also judgment of 6 October 2015, *Schrems v. Data Protection Commissioner*, Case C-362/14, ECLI:EU:C:2015:650; Case C-311/18, *Facebook Ireland and Schrems* (pending).

[2]See, in particular, Section 110(1) of the Postal Telecommunications Services Act 1983 (as amended). For a valuable discussion of the regulation of data retention in Ireland, see McIntyre (2008).

[3]The text of the 2005 Act is available on www.irishstatutebook.ie.

had proposed a draft framework decision on data retention under the Third Pillar which addressed police and judicial cooperation in criminal matters under the Treaty on European Union. This proposal was later withdrawn.[4]

Later, when the European Commission proposed the legislative measure which would ultimately become the Data Retention Directive, it did so on the basis that such legislation would have to be adopted under the First Pillar—the European Communities pillar—as an internal market harmonisation measure.[5] For its part, Ireland—along with Slovakia—opposed the adoption of the Data Retention Directive on the basis that it should have been adopted under the Third Pillar rather than under the First Pillar. Notwithstanding this opposition, the Directive was eventually adopted on 15 March 2006. From the time of its adoption, the Directive met with much criticism and controversy.

In July 2006, Ireland, supported by Slovakia, brought proceedings against the Council and Parliament seeking the annulment of the Directive on the basis that it had been adopted on the wrong legal basis. Ireland argued that, because the sole or predominant objective of the Directive was to facilitate the investigation, detection and prosecution of crime, including terrorism, it should have been adopted under the Third Pillar, not the First Pillar. In its judgment of 10 February 2009, the Grand Chamber of the Court of Justice rejected this challenge.[6] Having examined the substantive provisions of the Directive, the Court concluded that the provisions of the Directive were "essentially limited to the activities of service providers and do not govern access to data or the use thereof by the police or judicial authorities of the Member States".[7] On this basis, the Court of Justice upheld Article 95 EC, the internal market harmonisation provision, as the proper legal basis for the adoption of the Directive.[8]

Following this judgment, the European Commission began to take enforcement action against Member States which had failed to transpose the Directive into national law in a timely manner.[9] In a judgment delivered on 26 November 2009,

[4]See European Commission, Annex to the Proposal for a Directive of the European Parliament and of the Council on the retention of data processed in connection with the provision of public electronic communication services and amending Directive 2002/58/EC – Extended Impact Assessment COM(2005) 438 final/SEC/2005/1131.

[5]See European Commission, Annex to the Proposal for a Directive of the European Parliament and of the Council on the retention of data processed in connection with the provision of public electronic communication services and amending Directive 2002/58/EC – Extended Impact Assessment COM(2005) 438 final/SEC/2005/1131.

[6]Judgment of 10 February 2009, *Ireland v. Parliament and Council*, C-301/06, ECLI:EU:C:2009:68. See Herlin-Karnell (2009), p. 1667; Konstadinides (2010), p. 88; Poli (2010), p. 137.

[7]Judgment of 10 February 2009, *Ireland v. Parliament and Council*, C-301/06, para. 80, ECLI:EU:C:2009:68.

[8]Judgment of 10 February 2009, *Ireland v. Parliament and Council*, C-301/06, para. 93, ECLI:EU:C:2009:68.

[9]Judgment of 26 November 2009, *Commission v. Greece*, C-211/09, ECLI:EU:C:2009:737; Judgment of 4 February 2010, *Commission v. Sweden*, C-185/09, ECLI:EU:C:2010:59; Judgment of 29 July 2010, *Commission v. Austria*, C-189/09, ECLI:EU:C:2010:455.

the Court of Justice found that Ireland had failed to fulfil its obligations under the Data Retention Directive by failing to adopt the measures necessary to give it effect in domestic law.[10]

In the wake of this judgment, the Irish legislature enacted the Communications (Retention of Data) Act 2011 (hereafter: the 2011 Act), which transposed the Directive into Irish law.[11] The 2011 Act followed closely the provisions of the Directive, imposing an obligation on service providers to retain the relevant categories of telephony data and Internet data. The Irish legislature chose a period of two years for the retention of telephony data and a period of one year for the relevant categories of Internet data.[12] Under Section 6 of the 2011 Act, a member of the Irish police force, An Garda Síochána, not below the rank of chief superintendent, was one of the authorities given the power to make a disclosure request to a service provider of the retained data. Such a request could only be made where the designated member of An Garda Síochána was satisfied that the data were required for one of the following three purposes: (1) the prevention, detection, investigation or prosecution of a serious offence; (2) the safeguarding of the security of the State; or (3) the saving of human life. Similar powers were granted to the Defence Forces, the Revenue Commissioners and, later, the Competition and Consumer Protection Commission. While the 2011 Act made provision for a complaints procedure and an annual review of the Act's operation by a senior member of the judiciary,[13] it did not impose a requirement for prior judicial review of individual access requests.[14]

3 Proceedings Before the High Court: First Round

On 11 August 2006, just over a month after Ireland had instituted its annulment action against the Data Retention Directive before the Court of Justice, Digital Rights Ireland (DRI)—an Irish civil society organisation working on civil liberties in the digital age—began a wide-ranging challenge to both Irish and the EU data retention laws before the High Court in Dublin. Naming the Minister for Communications, Marine and Natural Resources, the Minister for Justice, Equality and Law Reform, the Commissioner of An Garda Síochána, Ireland and the Attorney General as defendants ("the Defendants"), DRI claimed that the Data Retention Directive and Irish data retention legislation—at that time, the 2005 Act, subsequently the 2011 Act—infringed the fundamental rights of DRI, its members and other citizens. In particular, DRI alleged that the Defendants had wrongfully exercised control over its data and that of its members and other mobile phone users. On this basis, it sought

[10]Judgment of 26 November 2009, *Commission v. Ireland*, C-202/09, ECLI:EU:C:2009:736.

[11]The text of the 2011 Act is available on www.irishstatutebook.ie.

[12]Section 4, Communications (Retention of Data) Act 2011.

[13]Sections 10 and 11, Communications (Retention of Data) Act 2011.

[14]See, in this regard, McIntyre (2016), p. 136.

declarations that the Irish and EU legislative measures were invalid. In advancing this case, DRI relied not only on the right to privacy but also the right to travel, the right to communicate, and the right to freedom of expression, as guaranteed under the Irish Constitution, the ECHR and the Charter of Fundamental Rights. The Defendants denied the claims.

The proceedings were the subject of several preliminary applications. First, the Defendants argued that DRI, as a limited company, lacked standing to make the claim. Second, they argued that DRI, because it had no assets, should provide security for costs based on that, if DRI were unsuccessful, it would be unable to satisfy any order for costs in favour of the Defendants. Third, for its part, DRI asked the High Court to refer to the Court of Justice the validity of the Data Retention Directive. Ireland's national human rights institution, the Irish Human Rights Commission,[15] successfully applied to be joined as an *amicus curiae* to the proceedings. These preliminary issues were heard before the High Court in July 2008 and were ultimately determined by the High Court (McKechnie J.) in a written judgment delivered on 5 May 2010.[16]

4 Decision of the High Court (2010)

First, the Court addressed the standing of DRI, as a company, to advance the claim based on fundamental rights. The Defendants argued that DRI, as a legal person, did not enjoy these fundamental rights or that, if it did, the rights were very limited in scope. They also argued that DRI could not assert the rights of natural persons, whether its own members or other members of the public. For its part, DRI asserted its standing on the basis that it was an owner of a mobile phone and, even more importantly, on the basis that the challenge affected virtually every citizen in the State and raised important questions of the EU law. In its view, this justified a relaxation of any strict requirements as to standing.

The High Court accepted DRI's standing to bring the challenge. Stating that ultimately it had "a duty to prevent the unconstitutional abuse of public power, be it through legislation or otherwise," the Court expressed the view that, where a particular act could adversely affect the fundamental rights of a plaintiff or society as a while, "a more relaxed approach to standing may be called for in order for the court to uphold that duty, and vindicate those rights."[17] The Court also accepted that, in bringing its challenge, DRI was acting *bona fide*.[18] It then proceeded to examine

[15]The Commission, established under the Human Rights Commission Act 2000, has been merged with the Equality Authority to become the Irish Human Rights and Equality Commission: see Section 44, Irish Human Rights and Equality Commission Act 2014.

[16]*Digital Rights Ireland v. Minister for Communications, Energy and Natural Resources & Ors* [2010] 3 IR 251.

[17][2010] 3 IR 251, 277–278.

[18][2010] 3 IR 251, 292.

the specific rights invoked. First, with respect to the right to privacy, the Court described it as "paramount" that companies, which were an "integral part of modern day business," could rely on the right to privacy concerning their business transactions, even if this right would "inevitably be narrower than that applicable to natural persons."[19] In reaching this conclusion, the Court referred to the jurisprudence of the Court of Justice and of the European Court of Human Rights.[20] In a similar vein, the Court concluded that DRI could rely on the right to communicate, and the corollary right to privileged communication, referring specifically to a right "not to be unjustifiably surveilled."[21] By contrast, the Court held that DRI, as a corporate person, could not rely on the right to marital privacy and the right to travel, which it considered as only capable of being enjoyed by natural persons.[22]

While this may have been sufficient to dispose of the issue of standing, the Court went even further, emphasising that DRI should be permitted to litigate the issues fully in a manner that was not limited by reference to its status as a company.[23] Recognising that there was "a significant element of public interest concern" in the proceedings being advanced, and the difficulties likely to face an individual telecommunications user in bringing such proceedings, the Court accepted that the case was a matter of "fundamental public importance" which DRI should be permitted to litigate "as what might be termed an *actio popularis*."[24]

Second, the Court rejected the defendants' application for an order for security for costs. Under Section 390 of the Companies Act 1963, the legislation then in force, where a limited company was the plaintiff in a case, and there was reason to believe that the company would be unable to pay the defendant's costs if the defendant was successful, a court enjoyed a discretion to require the company to provide sufficient security for those costs before allowing the action to proceed. In its conclusion on this issue, the Court once again emphasised the "significant public importance" of the proceedings:

> Given the rapid advance of current technology it is of great importance to define the legitimate legal limits of modern surveillance techniques used by governments, in particular with regard to telecommunications data retention; without sufficient legal safeguards the potential for abuse and unwarranted invasion of privacy is obvious. Its effect on persons, without their knowledge or consent, also raises important questions indicative of a prima facie interference with all citizens' rights to privacy and communication (Copland v. United Kingdom (App. 62617/00) (Unreported, European Court of Human Rights, 3rd April, 2007)). That is not to say that this is the case here, but the potential is in my opinion so great that a closer scrutiny of the relevant legislation is certainly merited with regards to its potential interference with important and fundamental rights of persons, both natural and legal.[25]

[19] [2010] 3 IR 251, 280.
[20] [2010] 3 IR 251, 285.
[21] [2010] 3 IR 251.
[22] [2010] 3 IR 251, 283, 288.
[23] [2010] 3 IR 251, 292.
[24] [2010] 3 IR 251, 294. See Mulligan (2016), p. 204.
[25] [2010] 3 IR 251, 298.

Thus, the significant public interest in the issues raised by DRI weighed heavily with the Court in its determination of the preliminary issues raised on behalf of the Defendants.

Finally, in the most important part of the judgment, the Court had to consider whether it should exercise its discretion to make a preliminary reference to the Court of Justice under Article 267 TFEU. Accepting that there was sufficient information before it on the basis of which it could make a reference, the Court described the case as "a challenge to specific legislative provisions which speak for themselves."[26] Because the High Court could not rule on the validity of the EU law, the Court was satisfied that a reference under Article 267 TFEU was necessary to assess the validity of the Data Retention Directive and agreed to hear further submissions from the parties as to the precise questions to be referred.[27]

5 Request for Preliminary Ruling (2012)

Ultimately, in June 2012, the High Court of Ireland formally referred three questions to the Court of Justice under Article 267 TFEU. First, the Court asked if the restrictions on the plaintiff's rights arising from Articles 3, 4 and 6 of the Data Retention Directive were proportionate. Second, the Court asked if the Directive was compatible with fundamental rights: specifically, the right of citizens to move and reside freely within the territory of the Member States laid down in Article 21 TFEU; the right to privacy as protected under Article 7 of the Charter and Article 8 ECHR; the right to protection of personal data protected in Article 8 of the Charter; the right to freedom of expression as protected under Article 11 of the Charter and Article 10 ECHR; and the right to good administration laid down in Article 41 of the Charter. Third, the Court asked about the extent to which the Treaties, and in particular the principle of loyal cooperation under the Treaties, required a national court to assess the compatibility of national implementing measures with the fundamental rights guaranteed in the EU law.

Thus, almost six years after the institution of the proceedings, the merits of DRI's data retention challenge were coming into focus. In the meantime, as already noted, the domestic legislative landscape had changed. In January 2011, the Communications (Retention of Data) Act, 2011 had been enacted to give effect to the Data Retention Directive in Irish law and to repeal Part 7 of the Criminal Justice (Terrorist Offences) Act, 2005. DRI amended its pleadings to reflect the change in the legislation. While the progress of the case was slow, this had some benign effects. In particular, as of December 2009, the Charter of Fundamental Rights had taken full legal effect within the EU legal order. The new fundamental right to data protection, enshrined in Article 8 of the Charter, allied with the right to privacy in Article 7 of

[26] [2010] 3 IR 251, 300.

[27] [2010] 3 IR 251, 300.

the Charter, were already making their presence felt in the jurisprudence of the Court of Justice. In its judgment of 9 November 2010 in the cases of *Volker und Markus Scheke and Eifert*, the Court of Justice found that certain provisions of Regulation No. 1290/2005 and Regulation No. 259/2008 in its entirety—which provided for the publication of details of beneficiaries of the European Agricultural Guarantee Fund and the European Agricultural Fund for Rural Development—were invalid by reference to the right to privacy and right to protection of personal data enshrined in Articles 7 and 8 of the Charter of Fundamental Rights.[28]

In December 2012, around six months after the reference from the Irish High Court, the Austrian Constitutional Court made a reference in proceedings brought by the Kärntner Landesregierung and by Mr Seitlinger, Mr Tschohl and 11,128 other applicants, seeking the annulment of the Austrian legislation which implemented the Data Retention Directive. In its reference, the Austrian Constitutional Court also raised the question of whether the provisions of the Directive were compatible with Articles 7, 8 and 11 of the Charter of Fundamental Rights.

The Court of Justice held a joint hearing of the Irish and Austrian references in July 2013. This hearing took place shortly after the Snowden revelations had brought to public attention the extent of surveillance carried out by the US National Security Agency and the intelligence agencies of its international partners. While these revelations were not directly relevant to the issues before the Court, they undoubtedly set the scene for the Court's formal examination of the validity of the Directive.

In its landmark judgment in the joined cases delivered on 8 April 2014, the Court of Justice struck down the Data Retention Directive as invalid on the basis that it amounted to a disproportionate interference with the rights to privacy and to data protection enshrined in Articles 7 and 8 of the Charter of Fundamental Rights. As the judgment is examined elsewhere in this collection,[29] it is not necessary to analyse it in detail in this chapter. It suffices to say that the judgment of the Court of Justice vindicated many of the concerns voiced by DRI and indeed the High Court in its judgment. In one of the most important passages in the judgment, the Court of Justice took the view that the interference with fundamental rights that the Directive entailed was "wide-ranging", "particularly serious" and—echoing the words of the Advocate General—"likely to generate in the minds of the persons concerned the feeling that their private lives are the subject of constant surveillance."[30] In light of the failure of the Directive to lay down clear and precise rules governing its scope and application and its failure to impose minimum safeguards, the Court concluded

[28]Judgment of 9 November 2010, *Volker und Markus Scheke and Eifert*, C-92/09 and C-93/09, ECLI:EU:C:2010:662. See Bobek (2011), p. 2005.

[29]See Chapter 1 in this book.

[30]Judgment of 8 April 2014 in *Digital Rights Ireland & Others*, C-293/12 and C-594/12, para. 37, ECLI:EU:C:2014:238.

that the Directive constituted a disproportionate interference with the rights to privacy and data protection.[31]

Having disposed of the references on the basis of its finding that the Directive itself was invalid, the Court of Justice did not go on to consider the third question raised by the High Court about the extent to which the Treaties and specifically the principle of loyal cooperation require a national court to assess the compatibility of national implementing measures by reference to the Charter. Nor, in contrast to the Opinion of the Advocate General,[32] did the Court of Justice refer to the question of the temporal effect of this declaration of invalidity. Only in its official press release did the Court note that, because it had not limited the temporal effect of its judgment, the declaration took effect "from the date on which the directive entered into force."[33] In time, these issues would return before the Court of Justice.

DRI, and the litigants in the Austrian proceedings, had achieved a remarkable victory in having the Data Retention Directive struck down. However, the question remained: what did this mean for the national data retention measures?

6 Consequences of the Judgment in the DRI Case

Following the judgment in *Digital Rights Ireland*, Member States took different approaches to the status of national data retention measures. Some Member States repealed or revised their data retention legislation. In other Member States, including Austria, the courts found the implementing legislation invalid. Still other Member States adopted a wait-and-see approach.[34] The European Commission did not bring forward any proposal for legislation to replace the Data Retention Directive. Across the EU, courts, politicians and officials grappled with the implications of *Digital Rights Ireland.*

In Ireland, the Government commenced a review of the 2011 Act in light of the Court of Justice's judgment.[35] However, the legislation—which applied not only to crime but also national security matters—remained in force.[36] In May 2015, over a

[31]The judgment has been the subject of a significant body of commentary. For some valuable perspectives, see e.g. Lynskey (2014), p. 1789; Fabbrini (2015), p. 65; Granger and Irion (2014), p. 835; Marin (2016).

[32]Opinion of Advocate General Cruz Villalón of 12 December 2013, paras. 154–158, ECLI:EU:C:2013:845.

[33]Court of Justice of the European Union, Press Release 54/14, 8 April 2014.

[34]For a valuable survey of the position in the immediate aftermath of the Court's judgment, see Vainio and Miettinen (2015), p. 290. For a more recent review, see Privacy International, *Report On The National Data Retention Laws Since The CJEU's Tele-2/Watson Judgment* (Sept 2017).

[35]Presentation of the Minister for Justice and Equality to the Joint Committee on Justice, Defence and Equality, 25 June 2014.

[36]For a useful commentary on the Irish position in the wake of the Court of Justice judgment, see Murphy (2014), pp. 105–115.

year after the delivery of the judgment of the CJEU, DRI gave notice of its intention to proceed with its case before the Irish courts. In November 2015, DRI brought a further preliminary application to the High Court. On this occasion, it sought to have the EU law issues in the proceedings tried in advance of the full hearing of the merits of the case. In the alternative, DRI sought a further preliminary reference to the Court of Justice, asking whether, in light of the judgment in *Digital Rights Ireland*, "a domestic legislative measure which requires indiscriminate retention of telecommunications data for a period longer than is required for the legitimate commercial purposes of the telecommunications providers, is valid."[37]

Around this time, the status of national data retention measures within the Member States post-*Digital Rights Ireland* was finding its way back to Luxembourg. In July 2014, the United Kingdom Parliament enacted the Data Retention and Investigatory Powers Act 2014, which continued to provide a legal basis for data retention in the UK following the judgment in *Digital Rights Ireland*. This legislation was challenged before the UK courts on the basis that it was incompatible with the Charter of Fundamental Rights and ECHR. In April 2015, in proceedings taken by two MPs, David Davis and Tom Watson, the Court of Appeal in England & Wales referred to the Court of Justice seeking guidance as to whether, in order to comply with Articles 7 and 8 of the Charter, the judgment in *Digital Rights Ireland* laid down mandatory requirements of the EU law applicable to a Member State's domestic regime governing access to retained data in accordance with national legislation.[38]

On 9 April 2014, the day after the delivery of the judgment in *Digital Rights Ireland*, Tele2 Sverige, a major Swedish telecommunications service provider, notified the Swedish authorities that it would cease to retain telecommunications data under the national implementing legislation. In December 2015, the Administrative Court of Appeal in Stockholm referred to the Court of Justice in the case of *Tele2 Sverige*, asking *inter alia* whether a general obligation to retain traffic data for the purpose of combating crime was compatible with Article 15(1) of Directive 2002/58/EC, considering Articles 7, 8 and 52(1) of the Charter.

While the national measures may have been adopted in the implementation of the Directive, in the wake of *Digital Rights Ireland*, there was now no EU legislation on data retention. The only provision of the EU law which in any way regulated data retention was Article 15(1) of the e-Privacy Directive. As the issues raised in the UK and Swedish references overlapped, the Court of Justice joined the cases for hearing. Considering the potential implications of the Court of Justice's judgment for the domestic proceedings in *Digital Rights Ireland*, the hearing of DRI's application was delayed pending judgment in these proceedings.

In his Opinion delivered in July 2016 in *Tele2 Sverige/Watson*, Advocate General Saugmandsgaard Øe took the view that a general data retention regime could be

[37] *Digital Rights Ireland v. Minister for Communications, Energy and Natural Resources & Ors* [2017] IEHC 307.

[38] *Secretary of State for the Home Department v Davis MP & Ors* [2015] EWCA Civ 1185.

compatible with the EU law if it was accompanied by appropriate safeguards, including the safeguards set out in the Court's judgment in *Digital Rights Ireland* which he considered to be mandatory in nature. According to the Advocate General, it was a matter for the national courts to determine whether national regimes satisfied the requirements of the EU law and, in particular, whether they were proportionate in their interference with fundamental rights.[39]

On 21 December 2016, the Court of Justice (Grand Chamber) delivered its judgment.[40] Departing from the approach proposed by the Advocate General, the Court concluded that national legislation providing for a general data retention regime was precluded by the EU law. However, according to the Court, this did not preclude Member States from adopting "legislation permitting, as a preventive measure, the targeted retention of traffic and location data, for the purpose of fighting serious crime, provided that the retention of data is limited, with respect to the categories of data to be retained, the means of communication affected, the persons concerned and the retention period adopted, to what is strictly necessary."[41] In addition, the Court of Justice addressed the safeguards that must accompany such legislation, following closely the requirements laid down in *Digital Rights Ireland*. In particular, the Court reaffirmed that "access of the competent national authorities to retained data should, as a general rule, except in cases of validly established urgency, be subject to a prior review carried out either by a court or by an independent administrative body, and that the decision of that court or body should be made following a reasoned request by those authorities submitted, inter alia, within the framework of procedures for the prevention, detection or prosecution of crime."[42] In addition, it confirmed that national authorities to whom access was granted "must notify the persons affected, under the applicable national procedures, as soon as that notification is no longer liable to jeopardise the investigations being undertaken by those authorities" so that they can exercise their right to a legal remedy under the EU data protection law.[43] According to the Court, it was the task of the national courts to determine whether and to what extent national legislation satisfied these requirements.[44]

---

[39]Opinion of 19 July 2016 in *Tele2 Sverige/Watson*, C-203/15 and C-698/15, ECLI:EU:C:2016:572.

[40]Judgment of 21 December 2016 in *Tele2 Sverige/Watson*, C-203/15 and C-698/15, ECLI:EU:C:2016:970.

[41]Judgment of 21 December 2016 in *Tele2 Sverige/Watson*, C-203/15 and C-698/15, para. 108, ECLI:EU:C:2016:970.

[42]Judgment of 21 December 2016 in *Tele2 Sverige/Watson*, C-203/15 and C-698/15, para. 120, ECLI:EU:C:2016:970.

[43]Judgment of 21 December 2016 in *Tele2 Sverige/Watson*, C-203/15 and C-698/15, para. 121, ECLI:EU:C:2016:970.

[44]Judgment of 21 December 2016 in *Tele2 Sverige/Watson*, C-203/15 and C-698/15, para. 124, ECLI:EU:C:2016:970. Upon its return, the Court of Appeal of England and Wales granted a declaration that the domestic legislation was inconsistent with the EU law to the extent that, in the prevention, investigation, detection and prosecution of criminal offences, it permitted access to

7 Proceedings Before the High Court: Second Round

Back in Ireland, DRI's application was heard before the High Court in June 2017. DRI submitted that, in light of the judgment in *Tele2 Sverige/Watson*, it was appropriate to try the EU law issues in the proceedings in advance of the full hearing of the case. DRI argued that the judgments in *Digital Rights Ireland* and *Tele2 Sverige/Watson* established five cardinal principles, namely:

- Mass retention of data is prohibited.
- A two-year retention period of data is unacceptable.
- Access by competent authorities must be monitored by a court or an independent body before affording the competent authority access to the retained data.
- The retention of data should be confined to data belonging to targeted persons.
- The domestic legislation of the Member States should ensure that the data is retained within the European Union.

It argued that the 2011 Act fell afoul of each of these five principles.[45]

8 Decision of High Court (2017)

In its written judgment on this issue, delivered in July 2017, the High Court considered whether the application met the requirements for a trial by way of preliminary issue in Irish law. These requirements included that the issue to be tried must be precisely defined, based on agreed or undisputed facts, and result in the saving of costs and expense.[46] In addition, a court would not usually direct the trial of a preliminary issue if other issues would remain to be resolved in the proceedings. The Court found that the issues in the proceedings were "complex and not straightforward" and that, no matter how strong the plaintiff's case may be, the case could not be "tried *in vacuo*", that is, in the absence of evidence or agreed or established facts.[47] The Court also concluded that the proposed preliminary issue—the trial of the EU law issues in the case—had not been defined "with sufficient precision" or by reference to any specific pleas or reliefs sought in the claim.[48] Further, the Court concluded that the trial by way of preliminary issue of the EU law issues would not result in the termination of the claim because, even if DRI was successful in this

retained data: (a) where the object pursued by that access was not restricted solely to fighting serious crime; or (b) where access was not subject to prior review by a court or an independent administrative authority: *Secretary of State for the Home Department v. Watson MP & Ors*, 2018, EWCA Civ 70.

[45] [2017] IEHC 307, para. 11.

[46] [2017] IEHC 307, para. 14.

[47] [2017] IEHC 307, para. 26.

[48] [2017] IEHC 307, para. 27.

respect, a second hearing would be required to deal with the balance of its claim.[49] Finally, the Court was not satisfied that the trial of the preliminary issue "would result in any saving of time or costs."[50] For these reasons, the High Court refused DRI's application for the trial of a preliminary issue. The claim would therefore have to proceed to trial in the ordinary way.

The Court then considered whether, in the alternative, it should refer to the Court of Justice. Noting that the decision to refer was "a matter for the discretion of the court of first instance as to whether the court believes such a reference is necessary to enable the court to resolve the case before it", and that the trial judge may decide that such a reference was necessary in light of the evidence adduced at the hearing of the action, the Court was not satisfied that a reference was required at that stage of the proceedings.[51]

Since the dismissal of this application, no further steps have been taken in the domestic proceedings which remain pending before the Irish courts. Thus, well over a decade after their institution, the domestic proceedings in *Digital Rights Ireland* have yet to reach their conclusion.

9 Consequences and Execution of Judicial Decisions

In the meantime, however, the fate of the Irish legislation has come into sharp focus both in the courts and in the political arena.

The most important challenge to the 2011 Act, besides *Digital Rights Ireland* itself, has come in the case of *Dwyer v. Commissioner of An Garda Síochána & Others*.[52] In early 2015, Graham Dwyer, the plaintiff in these proceedings, was convicted of murder of Elaine O'Hara and sentenced to life imprisonment. Mr Dwyer and Ms O'Hara had engaged in a secret sexual relationship over several years before her murder during which time they had used "master" and "slave" phones to communicate with each other. Ms O'Hara was killed in the Dublin mountains in August 2012. The phones were discarded in a reservoir some distance from this location. Ms O'Hara's disappearance was initially treated as a missing persons case. In September 2013, when water levels were particularly low after a dry summer, items were recovered from the reservoir, including the "master" and "slave" phones. Around the same time, in a remarkable coincidence, Ms O'Hara's body was found by a dog walker in the Dublin mountains. Using location data from these mobile phones, the police eventually identified Mr Dwyer as a suspect. Once identified, location data confirmed that the master phone was generally in use at the

[49] [2017] IEHC 307, para. 28.

[50] [2017] IEHC 307, para. 29.

[51] [2017] IEHC 307, para. 32.

[52] *Dwyer v. Commissioner of An Garda Síochána, Minister for Communications, Energy and Natural Resources, Ireland and the Attorney General* [2018] IEHC 685.

same location as Mr Dwyer's work phone. Combined with other evidence of Mr Dwyer's activities, this evidence played a very important role in the successful prosecution of Mr Dwyer for the murder of Ms O'Hara.[53]

At trial, the Plaintiff challenged the admissibility of this evidence on the basis that, in the wake of *Digital Rights Ireland*, it had been obtained in breach of his constitutional and Charter rights. The trial judge rejected this challenge. Mr Dwyer was convicted and sentenced after a lengthy trial. Mr Dwyer has appealed his conviction. Because he could not challenge the constitutionality of the 2011 Act within the context of the criminal trial, Mr Dwyer also brought separate proceedings challenging the legislation by reference to the Constitution, the ECHR and EU law.[54] The plaintiff's intention was to challenge the legality of the 2011 Act with a view to raising this as an argument in the context of his pending criminal appeal. The Plaintiff's case started to be heard in February 2018 and the hearing of evidence and submissions concluded in July 2018.

In its detailed written judgment delivered on 6 December 2018, the High Court upheld the Plaintiff's claim and concluded that the 2011 Act was inconsistent with the EU law.

First, the High Court concluded that Section 3 of the 2011 Act—insofar as it provided for the retention of telephony data by service providers for a period of two years—constituted general and indiscriminate retention contrary to the Court of Justice's judgment in *Tele2 Sverige/Watson*.[55] The Court considered that that judgment precluded it from carrying out its own proportionality assessment in this regard.[56]

Second, the High Court concluded that Section 6(1)(a) of the 2011 Act—which provided for access by police authorities to retained data for fighting crime—was inconsistent with the EU law "because there is no prior review by a court or an independent administrative authority for access to the telephony data" and there are "no adequate legislative guarantees against abuse."[57] In the Court's words, too much was "left to those who implement and utilise the access provisions" and the 2011 Act did not meet "the demands of a modern day democratic society to guarantee the fundamental right to privacy prescribed by EU and ECHR."[58]

Ultimately, the Court granted a declaration, with a stay, that Section 6(1)(a) of the Communications (Retention of Data) Act 2011—insofar as it relates to telephony data and which is retained on a general and indiscriminate basis under Section 3 of the Act—was inconsistent with Article 15(1) of Directive 2002/58/EC read in light of Articles 7, 8 and 52(1) of the Charter of Fundamental Rights. This left the 2011 Act intact insofar as it applied to national security and the saving of human life. The

[53] Gartland and Gleeson (2015).

[54] [2018] IEHC 685.

[55] [2018] IEHC 685, para. 363.

[56] [2018] IEHC 685, para. 366.

[57] [2018] IEHC 685, para. 3.106.

[58] [2018] IEHC 685, para. 3.106 and paras. 3–103.

judgment is now under appeal to the Supreme Court. Following a hearing in December 2019, the Supreme Court delivered judgment on 24 February 2020, deciding to refer a number of questions to the Court of Justice. This Reference is now pending before the Court of Justice as Case C-140/20. The Supreme Court's reference, and the underlying judgments, seriously engage with some of the challenges to which the Court of Justice's jurisprudence gives rise.

In contrast to *Digital Rights Ireland*, which is in essence an abstract challenge to the legislation, *Dwyer* raises important and challenging issues about data retention in the context of the facts of a real and concrete case. The case brings into sharp focus the implications of the jurisprudence of the Court of Justice for the day-to-day practice of law enforcement. First, on the substantive validity of data retention measures, the case raises the important question of whether targeted retention—of the kind envisaged in *Tele2 Sverige/Watson*—can indeed be effective. While, in light of the judgment in *Tele2 Sverige/Watson,* the High Court considered it unnecessary to address that question, this issue forms part of the Supreme Court's reference to the Court of Justice. Second, the case raises the question of the implications of such a finding for evidence gathered under domestic legislation while it is still in force, including evidence gathered before 8 April 2014, at which time Member States were still under an obligation to give effect to the Data Retention Directive. In its judgment, the High Court refused to limit the temporal effect of its declaration. It remains to be seen whether a similar approach will be adopted on appeal and this issue also forms part of the Supreme Court's reference which is pending before the Court of Justice.

While the challenges to the 2011 Act continue before the Irish courts, the legislation has also come under scrutiny within the political arena. Following a controversy about reported access by the Irish police ombudsman to journalists' telecommunications records, in January 2016, the Government asked former Chief Justice, John L. Murray, to carry out a review of the 2011 Act. While the terms of reference for the review focused on the legislative framework for access by statutory bodies to the communications data of journalists, because the 2011 Act applied in equal measure to journalists and other persons, the review addressed the legislative framework for access to retained telecommunications data, in essence the 2011 Act, more generally. In the review, Mr Justice Murray concluded that many features of the data retention scheme established by the 2011 Act were precluded by the EU law.[59]

In October 2017, at the same time as the Murray Review was published, the Minister for Justice and Equality published a general scheme for legislation to replace the 2011 Act. Within the confines of this chapter, it is not possible to provide a detailed analysis of the draft legislation. However, it is instructive to identify a few of its key features. Under Head 5 of the General Scheme of the Communications (Retention of Data) Bill 2017, the Garda Commissioner, the head of the Irish police force, may apply to the Minister for Justice for an order for the retention of (1) a

[59]Murray (2017).

category or specified categories of traffic and location data or (2) traffic and location data of a specified person, "where it is the assessment of the Garda Commissioner that such data is likely to assist in the prevention, detection, investigation or prosecution of serious offences, or the safeguarding of the security of the State". In this way, the Scheme seeks to put in place what might be considered to be a form of targeted retention. Under Head 6, the period of application of such an order shall not exceed 12 months. Head 8 of the Scheme permits members of the police to apply for authorisation for the disclosure of retained data where "he or she has reasonable grounds for believing that the data which are the subject of the application (a) relate to a person who is suspected of being or having been involved in the commission of a serious offence, and are necessary for the prevention, detection, investigation or prosecution of that offence; or (b) while not directly related to a person who is suspected of being or having been involved in the commission of the offence, are nevertheless likely to assist in the prevention, detection, investigation or prosecution of that offence." The Irish Parliament's Joint Committee on Justice and Equality carried out pre-legislative scrutiny of the General Scheme in late 2017 and heard from stakeholders, including the Department itself, Digital Rights Ireland, the Irish Council for Civil Liberties and the National Union of Journalists. In its Report published in January 2018, the Joint Committee made a series of recommendations with a view to ensuring that the "proposed data retention legislation is fully compliant with EU law and adequately reflects European Convention on Human Rights norms", including that the legislation should include special protection for journalists and their sources, a right to notification, a right to an effective judicial remedy for a person whose data is retained, and an independent monitoring authority.[60]

Across the European Union, Member States continue to grapple with the challenge of putting in place effective data retention legislation which could comply with the Court of Justice's judgment in *Tele2 Sverige/Watson*. Within the Council of the European Union, the Working Party on Information Exchange and Data Protection (DAPIX) has engaged in a reflection process on data retention issues without any clear resolution of these issues.[61] In a series of references, Member States' courts have sought further guidance from the Court of Justice. In its judgment of 2 October 2018 in the case of *Ministerio Fiscal*, the Court of Justice has confirmed that the EU law does not require that access to subscriber data be limited to the objective of fighting serious crime only.[62] In *Ordre des barreaux francophones et germanophone & Others*, the Belgian Constitutional Court has referred the question of whether a general retention obligation—laid down in legislation which has as its objective to

[60]Houses of the Oireachtas, Joint Committee on Justice and Equality, *Report on Pre-Legislative Scrutiny of the Communications (Retention of Data) Bill 2017* (January 2018), available online at https://data.oireachtas.ie/ie/oireachtas/committee/dail/32/joint_committee_on_justice_and_equality/reports/2017/2017-11-23_report-on-pre-legislative-scrutiny-of-the-general-scheme-of-the-data-protection-bill-2017_en.pdf.

[61]See, e.g., Council of the European Union, Note 7597/17, available online at http://data.consilium.europa.eu/doc/document/ST-7597-2017-INIT/en/pdf.

[62]Judgment of 2 October 2018, *Ministerio Fiscal*, C-207/16, ECLI:EU:C:2018:788.

fight serious crime and to safeguard national security and which contains safeguards for data retention and access—is precluded by the EU law. It has also asked if such legislation is precluded by the EU law even if the object of that legislation is to comply with the positive obligations under Articles 4 and 8 of the Charter which require effective investigation and punishment of child sexual abusers. Finally, the Court has queried whether, if such legislation is found to be invalid, the effects of the legislation could be maintained on a temporary basis to avoid legal uncertainty and to enable data previously collected and retained to be used for fighting serious crime and safeguarding national security.[63] In making the reference, the Court noted that the Belgian parliament had not considered that it was possible to put in place a targeted retention regime. In a similar vein, in the cases of *Quadrature du Net & Others*, the Conseil d'État in France has asked whether a general and indiscriminate retention obligation may be justified by reference to the right to security guaranteed under Article 6 of the Charter and the requirements of national security, responsibility for which falls to the Member States alone under Article 4 TEU.[64] More recently, the Estonian Supreme Court has made a further reference on its national data retention legislation.[65]

The reference from the Irish Supreme Court in Dwyer forms the latest in this long line of references on data retention. It is thus clear that, some years after the landmark judgment in *Digital Rights Ireland*, fundamental issues around data retention remain to be resolved and considerable uncertainty continues to hang over whether and, if so, in what circumstances data retention is permissible.[66] In the absence of any legislation at the EU level, it is to the Court of Justice that Member States must turn for guidance as to what is permissible, as a matter of the EU law, in the definition of their domestic data retention legislation. This is not only problematic at the level of policy and principle but also, as the *Dwyer* case illustrates, for the day-to-day practice of law enforcement.

10 Conclusion

In referring to the Court of Justice in the case of *Digital Rights Ireland*, the Irish courts made an important contribution to the debate around data retention in the European Union. This culminated in the landmark judgment of the Court of Justice striking down the Data Retention Directive. It is perhaps surprising, against this backdrop, that it is only in December 2018 that the Irish High Court has delivered a

---

[63] *Ordre des barreaux francophones et germanophone & Others*, Case C-520/18 (pending).

[64] *Quadrature du Net & Others*, Joined Cases C-511/18 and C-512/18 (pending).

[65] *H.K.*, C-746/18 (pending).

[66] See also C-623/17, *Privacy International* (pending), a reference from the United Kingdom's Investigatory Powers Tribunal, asking whether data retention in the context of national security falls within the scope of the EU law.

substantive judgment in relation to Ireland's own data retention legislation. This judgment, which is now under appeal and the subject of a further reference to the Court of Justice, illustrates many of the very real challenges arising from the Court of Justice's jurisprudence in this field. The reference in *Dwyer* may yet make a further contribution to the debate about data retention in the EU. For Ireland, as for other Member States, it is likely to be some time before the implications of the judgment in *Digital Rights Ireland*—and, even more so, the subsequent judgment in *Tele2 Sverige/Watson* and its sequelae—are fully worked out.

References

Bobek M (2011) Joined Cases C-92/09 and C-93/09, Volker und Markus Schecke GbR and Hartmut Eifert. Common Mark Law Rev 48(6):2005

Fabbrini F (2015) Human rights in the digital age: The European Court of Justice ruling in the data retention case and its lessons for privacy and surveillance in the U.S. Harv Hum Rights J 28:65

Gartland F, Gleeson C, Graham Dwyer found guilty of murdering Elaine O'Hara. Irish Times, 27 March 2015

Granger M-P, Irion K (2014) The Court of Justice and the Data Retention Directive in Digital Rights Ireland: telling off the EU legislator and teaching a lesson in privacy and data protection. Eur Law Rev 39(6):835

Herlin-Karnell E (2009) Case C-301/06, Ireland v Parliament and Council, judgment of the Court (Grand Chamber) of 10 February 2009. Common Mark Law Rev 46(5):1667

Konstadinides T (2010) Wavering between centres of gravity: comment on Ireland v Parliament and Council. Eur Law Rev 35(1):88

Lynskey O (2014) The Data Retention Directive is incompatible with the rights to privacy and data protection and is invalid in its entirety: Digital Rights Ireland. Common Mark Law Rev 51 (6):1789

Marin L (2016) The fate of the Data Retention Directive: about mass surveillance and fundamental rights in the EU legal order. In: Mitsilegas V, Bergström M, Konstadinides T (eds) Research handbook on EU criminal law. Edward Elgar Publishing, Cheltenham

McIntyre TJ (2008) Data retention: privacy, policy and proportionality. Comput Law Secur Rev 24 (4):326

McIntyre TJ (2016) Judicial oversight of surveillance: the case of Ireland in comparative perspective. In: Scheinin M, Krunke H, Aksenova M (eds) Judges as guardians of constitutionalism and human rights. Edward Elgar Publishing, Cheltenham, p 136

Mulligan A (2016) Constitutional aspects of international data transfer and mass surveillance. Irish Jurist 55:199, 204

Murphy MH (2014) Data retention in the aftermath of *Digital Rights Ireland and Seitlinger*. Irish Crim Law J 24(4):105–115

Murray JL (2017) Review of the law on the retention of and access to communications data (April 2017). http://www.justice.ie/en/JELR/Review_of_the_Law_on_Retention_of_and_Access_to_Communications_Data.pdf/Files/Review_of_the_Law_on_Retention_of_and_Access_to_Communications_Data.pdf

Poli S (2010) The legal basis of internal market measures with a security dimension: comment on case C-301/06 of 10/02/2009. Eur Constit Law Rev 6(1):137

Vainio N, Miettinen S (2015) Telecommunications data retention after Digital Rights Ireland: legislative and judicial reactions in the Member States. Int J Law Inf Technol 23(3):290

Data Retention in Poland

Jan Podkowik and Marek Zubik

Abstract On 30 July 2014, the Constitutional Tribunal delivered a long-awaited judgment in which it assessed the compatibility of particular provisions of domestic law on covert electronic surveillance with the Constitution and the Convention for the Protection of Human Rights and Fundamental Freedoms. The case was heard after seven joint motions were filed in 2011 and 2012 by the Human Rights Defender (Ombudsman) and the Attorney General. The Tribunal did not deal with the provisions imposing on telecommunication providers the obligation to retain traffic and localisation data. It assessed only the statutory provisions on police and secret services' access to retained data. The chapter discusses the roots of data retention in Poland, previous case law as well as legal effects of the Tribunal's judgment of 2014 and its implementation by the legislator.

1 Implementation of Directive 2006/24/EC in Poland

Regulations governing the retention and disclosure by operators of public telecommunication networks or providers of publicly available telecommunications services of telecommunications data for purposes related to maintaining security and investigation, detection and prosecution of criminal activities were introduced into the Polish legal system on 1 January 2001 by the Telecommunications Law of 2000,[1] which preceded Poland's accession to the European Union (EU). The obligation to retain telecommunication data concerned, among other things, data necessary to identify the subscriber or user of a telecommunications network, the data on the call or the call attempt, as well as the data on the circumstances and type of the call made.

[1]The Act of 21 July 2000 on the Telecommunications Law (Journal of Laws No. 73, item 852, as amended).

J. Podkowik · M. Zubik (✉)
Department of Constitutional Law, Faculty of Law and Administration, University of Warsaw, Warsaw, Poland

M. Zubik et al. (eds.), *European Constitutional Courts towards Data Retention Laws*, Law, Governance and Technology Series 45,
https://doi.org/10.1007/978-3-030-57189-4_10

In the light of Article 40.3 of the Telecommunications Law of 2000, the detailed rules related to the disclosure of telecommunications data to state authorities were to be defined in a regulation by the competent minister for telecommunications. The regulation was issued in 2003.[2] It imposed the obligation to gain access to retained data for the last 12 months from the date of the communication.

With the adoption of the Telecommunications Law of 2000, amendments were made to the acts regulating the surveillance measures *undertaken by the officers of the Police and* the Office for State Protection (Polish: *Urząd Ochrony Państwa*, UOP)—the civil intelligence agency at that time. Those acts directly authorised the officers of the Police and of UOP to access the telecommunications data retained by private entities. The Police could access those data for preventing and detecting all crimes (Article 20c.1 of the Act on the Police). Under Article 10 of the Act on the Office for State Protection, UOP could access the retained data for preventing or detecting crimes prosecuted under international agreements; identifying and counteracting threats to security, defence, independence, integrity and international position of the state; preventing and detecting espionage, terrorism and other crimes threatening state security, and prosecution of the perpetrators of those crimes; preventing and detecting crimes threatening the economic foundations of the state and prosecuting their perpetrators; preventing and detecting crimes of international scope or nature, including the illegal manufacture, possession and circulation of arms, ammunition and explosives, narcotic drugs, psychotropic substances or nuclear and radioactive materials and prosecution of their perpetrators; as well as identifying and counteracting breaches of state secrets. Both acts envisaged no external control over access to retained data.

The next step was the amendment of the Penal Procedure Code in 2003.[3] Based on the new amendment, Article 218 of the Penal Procedure Code authorised courts and prosecutors to request—during criminal proceedings—a list of telecommunications calls, including their times and other information related to the calls, but excluding the content of the telephone conversation.

Similar authorisations to access retained data were later granted to other police and intelligence services, including those that have ceased to exist, i.e. the tax inspection services (Polish: *kontrola skarbowa*)[4] and the Military Information Services (Polish: *Wojskowe Służby Informacyjne*, WSI).[5] The organisational changes in the police and state protection services that took place in 2005–2009 resulted in an

[2]The Regulation of the Minister of Infrastructure of 24 January 2003 on performance by operators of tasks for the benefit of defence, state security and public security and order (Journal of Laws No. 19, item 166).

[3]The Act of 10 January 2003 on amending the Act on the Penal Procedure Code, the Act on provisions implementing the Penal Procedure Code, the Act on protected witness and the Act on protection of undisclosed information (Journal of Laws No. 17, item 155).

[4]The Act of 27 June 2003 on establishment of Voivodeship Tax Boards and on amending some acts regulating the tasks and competences of authorities and organisation of organisational units subordinate to the competent minister for public finances (Journal of Laws No. 137, item 1302).

[5]The Act of 9 July 2003 on the Military Information Services (Journal of Laws No. 139, item 1326, as amended).

expansion of the scope of access to telecommunications data retained by operators and providers of telecommunications services.

Further modifications of the statutory regulation concerning telecommunications data retention took place when the new Telecommunications Law was adopted in 2004.[6] The Act introduced a statutory obligation to retain transmission data concerning subscribers and end users for 12 months and access to those data at the request of competent authorities (Article 165 of the Telecommunications Law of 2004). In 2006, an amendment was made to the Polish Telecommunications Law,[7] which took place nearly simultaneously with legislative work on Directive 2006/24/EC. The data retention obligation was extended to 2 years. During the legislative works, an amendment was submitted to the draft act that envisaged extending the data retention obligation to as much as 15 years,[8] but this amendment was finally rejected as overly interfering with individuals' freedoms and rights.

More significant changes were introduced in 2009.[9] Their goal was to adjust the Polish law to the requirements of Directive 2006/24/EC. The previous regulations were repealed and replaced by a regulation of a totally different legislative design. The newly added Article 180a of the Telecommunications Law imposed on operators of public telecommunication networks and providers of publicly available telecommunications services an obligation to retain and store data generated in the telecommunications network or processed by those operators and providers on the territory of the Republic of Poland for 24 months after the call or the unsuccessful call attempt. The data to be retained were those that were necessary to determine the network termination, the telecommunications terminal equipment, the end user initiating the call and the end user to whom the call is made. Moreover, the data required to determine the date and time of the call and its duration, the type of call and the location of the telecommunications terminal equipment were also to be retained. After the 2-year period, the data were to be destroyed.

The legislator also obliged the operators and service providers to allow access to the retained data only to competent authorities, i.e. officers of the Police, the Border Guard, the Military Gendarmerie (Polish: *Żandarmeria Wojskowa*), the tax inspection services, the Internal Security Agency (Polish: *Agencja Bezpieczeństwa Wewnętrznego*, ABW), the Central Anticorruption Bureau (Polish: *Centralne Biuro Antykorupcyjne*, CBA) and the Customs Service, as well as to courts and prosecutors. The detailed rules of access to those data are regulated by the provisions of the acts regulating the tasks and competences of particular services. Moreover,

---

[6]The Act of 16 July 2004 on the Telecommunications Law (Journal of Laws No. 171, item 1800, as amended).

[7]The Act of 29 December 2005 on amending to the Act on the Telecommunications Law and the Act on the Civil Procedure Code (Journal of Laws No. 12, item 66).

[8]The report of the standing subcommittee on communication and modern information technologies on the draft act on amending the Act on the Telecommunications Law (parliamentary document No. 51/5th term of office of the Sejm) of 7 December 2005.

[9]The Act of 24 April 2009 on amending the Act on the Telecommunications Law and some other acts (Journal of Laws No. 85, item 716).

operators and providers were obliged to protect those data against accidental or unlawful destruction, loss or alteration, unauthorised or unlawful storage, processing, access and disclosure. At the same time, the acts regulating the tasks and competences of particular services were refined to determine the rules concerning the officers' access to the obligatorily retained data. As a rule, accessing the data took place remotely via a special interface at the request of the authorised officers. The precondition for the request was, as a rule, prevention and detection of crimes or tax offences, sometimes also violations of the law that were not crimes; in the case of civil and military counterintelligence services, the data could be accessed in implementing the statutory tasks of those services, including ensuring security, counteracting terrorism and espionage, as well as analytical tasks.

As explained in the justification to the draft act, introducing the maximum data retention period of 24 months, which is the longest period envisaged by Directive 2006/24/EC, ensued from the specific safety hazards related in part to the geographic location and type of criminal activity carried out on the territory of Poland. It was argued that Poland could also be used as a logistics hub or transit point for terrorist groups. It was claimed that there was an increased risk of activity by international organised crime groups. However, this circumstance did not translate into limiting the possibility of requesting telecommunications data in the investigation, detection and prevention of the most serious crimes.

In 2013, the retention period was reduced from 24 months to 12 months.[10] In the justification to the draft act, the change was motivated by the fact that Poland was one of the few EU Member States that decided to use the maximum period of retention set out in Directive 2006/24/EC. An analysis of retained data usage contained in the annual report of the President of the Office of Electronic Communications (Polish: *Urząd Komunikacji Elektronicznej*, UKE)[11] indicated that the data from the first year were of most significance and value. This is why, considering the costs incurred by telecommunication companies in connection with the 2-year obligation of data retention, as well as the suggestions made in the report of the European Commission,[12] it was concluded that the 2-year retention obligation was not justified.

In assessing the implementation of Directive 2006/24/EC, it is worth noting that the Polish legislator implemented it in an extensive manner,[13] which was also

[10]The Act of 16 November 2012 on amending the Act on the Telecommunications Law and some other acts (Journal of Laws No. 1445).

[11]In approximately 49% of cases of 2013, retained data is requested within the first 2 months of its retention, while in 69% of cases, retained data is requested within the first 4 months of its retention. In this regard, a 12-month period of data retention could be reasonably considered as both too long and unjustified under the principle of proportionality.

[12]COM (2011) 225 final on the Data Retention Directive published by the European Commission on 18 April 2011, and the proposals presented on 29 September 2011 in *Sprawozdanie z pracy Zespołu do spraw pozyskiwania danych telekomunikacyjnych* [Report of the group on telecommunications data retention].

[13]See, e.g. Adamski (2013); Adamski (2005), p. 173.

pointed out by the Constitutional Tribunal (Polish: *Trybunał Konstytucyjny*) in its judgment of 30 July 2014 (File No. K 23/11).[14] First, the Polish legislator opted for the maximum allowed data retention period of 24 months envisaged by the directive (which was uncommon among the EU Member States). As previously mentioned, this period was reduced to 12 months only in 2013. Second, the legislator made it possible to request telecommunications data not only for investigating, detecting and prosecuting serious crimes, as envisaged by the directive, but also for counteracting low-gravity crimes or acts other than crimes, as well as in implementing the services' analytical and planning tasks. Third, the competence to request access to the retained data was granted to a relatively large group of state authorities compared to the other EU Member States. Access to those data could be obtained by all courts and prosecutors during criminal proceedings, as well as eight police and intelligence or counterintelligence state services.

2 Proceedings Before the Constitutional Tribunal

Regulations concerning retaining telecommunications data, particularly the practice of making the retained data available to competent services, provoked heated discussions on the scale of surveillance of Polish citizens.[15] These discussions were further stimulated by the annual report of the President of the Office of Electronic Communications prepared in connection with implementing Article 10 of Directive 2006/24/EC, which indicated the number of requests for telecommunications data.[16] The report indicated that the number of telecommunications data requests submitted by the competent services, prosecutors and courts was: 1.07 million in 2010, 1.399 million in 2011, 1.874 million in 2012, 1.762 million in 2013, and 1.754 million in 2014. Public opinion recognised that, compared to other EU Member States, it was generally the highest number of requests, making Poles the most invigilated citizens in Europe. It is worth noting that, as a rule, the Supreme Audit Office (Polish: *Najwyższa Izba Kontroli*, NIK)[17] positively assessed the

---

[14]See the judgment of the Constitutional Tribunal of 30 July 2014, K 23/11, OTK ZU 7A/2014, item 80.

[15]The Helsinki Foundation for Human Rights and the Panoptykon Foundation were exceptionally active in this regard.

[16]Press release on *Information for the European Commission on the provision of telecommunications data retained by telecommunications undertakings and operators in 2013*. Available at: http://en.uke.gov.pl/information-on-annual-report-on-the-provision-of-telecommunications-data-13559.

[17]See *Informacja o wynikach kontroli. Uzyskiwanie i przetwarzanie przez uprawnione podmioty danych z bilingów, informacji o lokalizacji oraz innych danych, o których mowa w art. 180c i d ustawy Prawo telekomunikacyjne, znak: KPB-P/12/191, wersja jawna, podpisana w dniu 12 czerwca 2013 r.* [Information about the results of the control. Acquisition and processing by authorised authorities of data from billings, information on location and other data referred to in Article 180c and Article 180d of the Act on the Telecommunications Law, Ref. No.: KPB-P/12/191, non-confidential version, signed on 12 June 2013].

actions of officers of the services as regards access and use of the telecommunications data.

According to the current statistical data published by the Public Prosecutor General of Poland (Polish: *Prokurator Generalny*), based on other regulations and a methodology different from the one used by UKE, in 2016 the Police, the Customs Service, the Border Guard, the Internal Security Agency, the Central Anticorruption Bureau, the Treasury Intelligence Department (Polish: *Kontrola Skarbowa*), the Military Gendarmerie Headquarters, the Military Gendarmerie Branches and the Military Counterintelligence Service (Polish: *Służba Kontrwywiadu Wojskowego*, SKW) processed a total of 1.147 million telecommunications data.[18] Out of this, 76.9% were data on calls, 13.6% were location data, 7% were user data, and 2.5% other kinds of data.

The President of UKE argued that comparing the scale of retained data requests in individual Member States is unwarranted.[19] This is because the methodology of analysis and calculation is not the same for all Member States. Moreover, the relatively high number of telecommunications data requests in Poland results from the fact that the figures include not only access to location and billing data, but also subscriber data, which are not considered in the statistics of some other Member States. This was related to the lack of a central subscriber base and the obligation to register prepaid cards. Moreover, as pointed out in the proceedings in case No. K 23/11, the large number of telecommunications data requests registered in Poland is caused by the need to request the same data twice: first, for operational and exploratory activities conducted by the services, and then by the prosecutor or the court during criminal proceedings as evidence. This practice results from the lack of sufficient legal basis to use the materials gathered at the operational and exploratory stage of criminal proceedings as evidence.

The first motion to the Constitutional Tribunal challenging, among other things, the statutory obligation imposed on operators to retain telecommunications data for 2 years and disclose them to the officers of the Police, the Border Guard, the tax inspection services, the Military Gendarmerie, the Internal Security Agency, the Central Anticorruption Bureau and the Military Intelligence Service was submitted to the Constitutional Tribunal on 28 January 2011 (File No. 2/11). The applicant was a group of deputies of an opposition party. As could be assumed, the motion was the result of a heated discussion in Poland and at the EU level on the acceptability and scope of telecommunications data retention and the judgment of the German Federal Constitutional Court (German: *Bundesverfassungsgericht*, BVerfG) of 2 March 2010, which declared that certain regulations on data retention are inconsistent with the Basic Law for the Federal Republic of Germany (German: *Grundgesetz für die Bundesrepublik Deutschland*).[20]

[18]See the parliamentary document of 30 June 2017, No. 534/11th Term of Office of the Senate.

[19]Available at: https://www.uke.gov.pl/uke-wyjasnia-sposob-liczenia-danych-retencyjnych-12250.

[20]See the judgment of the Federal Constitutional Court of Germany, 2 March 2010, 1 BvR 256/08, 1 BvR 263/08, 1 BvR 586/08.

According to the applicant, the challenged regulations interfered with his private life and confidentiality of communications in a disproportionate manner, while allowing the public authorities to obtain citizen data other than necessary in a democratic state. Furthermore, it violated the constitutional right to request the correction or removal of false, incomplete data or data collected in a manner inconsistent with the act. Their unconstitutionality was claimed to ensue from the legislative omission of procedural and institutional warranties related to the protection against the arbitrariness of the decisions of the competent services as regards acquisition and retention of information. The omission was said to be related to, among other things, the lack of regulations imposing the obligation on the services carrying out the surveillance to: obtain the court's approval to gain access to the telecommunications data, inform every individual of the acquisition of their telecommunication data, even if occurring after the termination of the proceedings, destroy the data deemed irrelevant to the proceedings, and refrain from obtaining data representing the so-called inadmissible evidence. The proceedings before the Constitutional Tribunal in this case were discontinued by the decision of the Constitutional Tribunal of 30 November 2011[21] for purely formal reasons—expiry of the term of office of the Sejm and of the applicants.

Already after case No. K 23/11 had been submitted to the Constitutional Tribunal, the Polish Commissioner for Human Rights (Polish: *Rzecznik Praw Obywatelskich*, RPO) and, at a later date, the Public Prosecutor General of Poland challenged the regulations on surveillance conducted by the Police and secret services. Seven joint motions were submitted in 2011 and 2012. The Tribunal heard the case, sitting as a full bench.

Objections were formulated against the regulations governing the operational control (including wiretapping and recording of conversations and electronic correspondence), as well as the regulations governing the disclosure of the telecommunications data referred to in Article 180c and 180d of the Telecommunications Law to officers of the Police, the tax inspection services, the Military Gendarmerie, the Internal Security Agency, the Central Anticorruption Bureau, the Military Intelligence Service and the Customs Service.

None of the applicants in case No. K 23/11 objected to the statutory obligation to retain telecommunications data by telecommunications providers or operators, including the scope of the retained data and the retention period. The applicants' objections concerned a relatively narrow problem of disclosing the retained data to the police and intelligence services. The applicants did not challenge the possibility of making the telecommunications data available at the request of a court or prosecutor. Consequently, it was the scope of the objections that determined the scope of the statements of the constitutional court.

The objections related to the regulations governing the disclosure of telecommunications data concerned four basic issues:

[21]See the order of the Constitutional Tribunal of 30 November 2011, File No. K 23/11, OTK ZU 9A/2011, item 108.

First, according to the applicants, the challenged regulations authorised the officers of the Police, the Border Guard and the Military Gendarmerie to obtain telecommunications data to prevent all criminal acts regardless of the crime's seriousness. The Treasury Intelligence Department could access such data to prevent all tax offences and offences of corruption committed by persons employed by or serving in organisational units subordinate to the competent minister for public finance, as well as violations of national and community customs rules, i.e. acts that are not considered crimes under the law, and to detect such crimes and unlawful acts. At the same time, the officers of CBA, SKW and ABW could access those data in implementing any of their statutory tasks. Consequently, the scope of those regulations is broader than the one allowed by Directive 2006/24/EC, which reserved access to those data only for prosecuting "serious crime." In this scope, the second applicant, i.e. the Public Prosecutor General of Poland, provided a specification as to which prohibited acts enumerated in the Penal Code and Tax Penal Code are considered relatively trivial, and thus do not justify gaining access to the telecommunications data to investigate, detect or prevent them.

Second, the acquisition of telecommunications data based on the challenged regulations was not subsidiary. It was allowed in each case in which the competent services requested them. Obtaining access to these data was not conditioned by exhaustion of other legal remedies—the ones that would interfere with privacy and confidentiality of communications to a smaller extent.

Third, the legislator did not envisage an obligation to obtain the consent of a court or other independent authority to acquire those data. In the opinion of the Commissioner for Human Rights, it would be a best solution to entrust competences in this regard to courts, although it was not strictly necessary. The constitutional standard would also be maintained if the control were exercised by another public authority independent of and external with respect to the executive authority.

Fourth, the acts pertaining to the Internal Security Agency, Central Anticorruption Bureau and Military Counterintelligence Service envisaged no regulations governing the verification and destruction of unnecessary data (i.e. irrelevant) for further proceedings.

The following provisions were to be used by the Constitutional Tribunal to verify the contested regulations: Article 2 of the Constitution, which expresses the principle of the democratic state ruled by law; Article 47 of the Constitution, which guarantees the right to protection of private life; Article 49 of the Constitution, which guarantees the protection of freedom and confidentiality of communication; Article 51 of the Constitution, which guarantees the so-called information autonomy; as well as Article 31.3 of the Constitution, which expresses the principle of proportionality. Additionally, the applicants pointed to Article 8 of the Convention for the Protection of Human Rights and Fundamental Freedom, which in the light of Article 188.2 of the Constitution, may be considered the reference law for monitoring statutes.

3 Decision of the Constitutional Tribunal

In its judgment of 30 July 2014,[22] after a 3-day long hearing on 1–3 April 2017, the Constitutional Tribunal supported some of the objections of the Polish Commissioner for Human Rights and the Public Prosecutor General. In point 5 of the operative part of the judgment, the Constitutional Tribunal stated that the challenged regulations granting authorisation to officers of the Police, the Border Guard, the Military Gendarmerie, the Internal Security Agency, the Central Anticorruption Bureau, the Military Counterintelligence Service and the Customs Service were unconstitutional insofar as they do not provide for independent supervision over the process of granting access to telecommunications data referred to in Article 180c and Article 180d of the Telecommunications Act. It was a circumstance that alone settled the issue of incompatibility of the challenged provision with the Constitution. The Constitutional Tribunal did not settle the remaining objections, namely: the inadmissibility of disclosing telecommunications data for purposes other than investigating, preventing or prosecuting serious crime and the lack of subsidiary character of the access to the retained data. Those issues were only referred to as peripheral to the main considerations: the Constitutional Tribunal indicated the constitutional standard binding the legislator regulating surveillance activities (see point 4 below). Moreover, in points 8 and 9 of the operative part of the judgment, the Constitutional Tribunal stated it was unconstitutional that there is no procedure related to the destruction of unnecessary telecommunications data obtained during operations undertaken by the Internal Security Agency, the Military Counterintelligence Service, the Central Anticorruption Bureau and the Customs Service.

The Constitutional Tribunal pointed out the importance of independent control over the police and intelligence services in a democratic state. Since the acquisition of telecommunications data is conducted in a covert manner, i.e. without the knowledge or permission of the data subjects and under limited control of the public opinion, lack of independent control of state authorities over this process creates a risk of fraud. It may not only contribute to unwarranted interference with freedom and human rights, but it also poses a threat to democratic mechanisms of state governance. The broader the range of competences of state authorities to covertly acquire data of individuals, the stronger the requirement to include procedural mechanisms counteracting arbitrariness in the statute. The broader the range of competences to access telecommunications data, the more restrictive the control over the process should be.

According to a legal provision applicable at that time, not all officers were authorised to access telecommunications data. The authorised officers were those who held an authorisation issued by the head of a given service. However, the legislator failed to envisage any external control that would come from outside the structure of the services or executive authority. The procedure did not even require

[22]The judgment of the Constitutional Tribunal of 30 July 2014, K 11/2014, OTK ZU 7A/23, item 80.

obtaining consent of the prosecutor, who was a legal authority independent of the state at that time. The legislature also failed to envisage basic elements of ex-post control legalising the undertaken actions. The Constitutional Tribunal did not precisely define the procedure according to which the retained data should be accessed. However, it is possible to conclude that the scope and character of control may vary depending on the type of telecommunications data acquired by the services, as well as on the individual character of the activity of particular services and situations in which those data are acquired. In the Constitutional Tribunal's opinion, it is not impossible to introduce ex-post (follow-up) control as the rule. According to the constitutional principle of the efficiency of public institutions (the introduction to the Constitution), it is necessary to create a mechanism that will make it possible for the services responsible for state protection and public order to effectively counteract threats. In some cases, the ex-ante control would reduce the effectiveness of their operation. However, the Constitutional Tribunal also pointed to arguments in favour of introducing ex-ante control in some cases. The ex-ante control should in particular concern the acquisition of data on persons carrying out professions of public trust (such as attorneys, legal counsels or journalists, who are bound by professional secrecy) and in cases in which urgent action of the services is not required. However, those issues should be adequately considered by the legislator. The requirement formulated by the Constitutional Tribunal, which was inclined towards ex-post control mechanisms, seems to depart from the standard established by the Court of Justice of the European Union (CJEU) in its judgment in the case of *Digital Rights Ireland*, in which ex-ante control was indicated as the rule and ex-post control as the exception.[23]

The Constitutional Tribunal did not consider it necessary to introduce judicial control over retained data acquisition. However, it was deemed necessary that it should be an authority independent of the government and not linked to the officers acquiring the data by any direct or indirect reporting relation.

Referring to the allegation concerning the lack of procedures governing the handling of the collected data, the Constitutional Tribunal stated that the constitutional condition for the covert acquisition of data on individuals, including their telecommunications data, is the establishment of a procedure regarding the immediate selection and destruction of irrelevant or inadmissible materials. This prevents unauthorised use by state authorities of legally collected information and their storage in case they prove useful for other purposes in the future. As indicated by the Constitutional Tribunal, it is not only one-time acquisition of data on an individual that interferes with the privacy of individuals, but also other operations on the data, including their storage or repeated use in the course of other proceedings.

The Constitutional Tribunal, to some extent, allowed differentiation to the standard of information autonomy protection between Polish citizens and non-citizens. This is motivated by Article 51.2 of the Constitution, which prohibits public

[23]See further: Podkowik (2015b), pp. 577–595; Podkowik (2015a), pp. 23–40.

authorities to gather information about its citizens other than necessary in a democratic state, and Article 37.2 of the Constitution, which justifies the possibility of introducing exceptional restrictions of freedoms and constitutional rights with respect to foreign citizens and other entities. In particular, this provision should apply in situations in which there are serious and motivated suspicions as to their engagement in an activity that threatens the security of the state, including terrorism and organised crime. At the same time, the Constitutional Tribunal warned that stronger interference with the foreign citizens' information autonomy cannot be treated as a predominant solution and, in any case, cannot result in an arbitrary differentiation of those constitutional freedoms and rights, which were not characterised as pertaining to citizens only by the legislator. The Constitution does not preclude different specification of premises for data acquisition and their handling with respect to persons not subject to the Polish law (e.g. data acquired by intelligence services about the activity of foreign entities or subjects abroad), although in each case such activity of the public authorities must meet the standards of the rule of law.

The judgment of the Constitutional Tribunal of 30 July 2014, File No. K 23/11, significantly expanded the case law on the protection of the freedom of communication and privacy of individuals in the digital era.[24] It was also an example of the dialogue of the Polish Constitutional Tribunal with other constitutional courts adjudicating on the legislation implementing Directive 2006/24/EC and the Court of Justice of the European Union.

Considering the requirements ensuing from its previous case law, as well as the standards developed by the European Court of Human Rights (ECHR) and the CJEU, the Constitutional Tribunal formed a kind of test for evaluating the regulations allowing surveillance by public authorities in a democratic state ruled by law (point III.5.3 of the justification). The requirements are as follows:

- gathering, storing and processing of data on individuals, in particular on their privacy, is admissible only based on a clear and precise provision of a statute, as an act adopted by the parliament and able to be the basis for restricting freedoms and rights of individuals;[25]
- it is necessary to precisely determine in a statute the state authorities authorised to gather and process data on an individual, including for surveillance purposes;
- in the statute the legitimate purposes for the covert acquisition of information about individuals must be precisely defined, and these are: prevention, detection

[24]The Constitutional Tribunal expressed its standpoint on covert acquisition of information about individuals in its judgments: of 20 April 2004, File No. K 45/02, OTK ZU No. 4/A/2004, item 30; of 12 December 2005, File No. K 32/04; of 23 June 2009, File No. K 54/07; and its orders of 25 January 2006, File No. S 2/06, OTK ZU No. 1/A/2006, item 13; and of 15 November 2010, File No. S 4/10, OTK ZU No. 9/A/2010, item 111.

[25]See, for example, judgments of the Constitutional Tribunal of 12 December 2005, File No. K 32/04; and of 23 June 2009, File No. K 54/07.

and prosecution of serious crimes only; the statute should indicate the types of such crimes;[26]
- the statute should define the categories of subjects with respect to whom surveillance may be undertaken;[27]
- it is recommended that the act defines the types of means of covert information acquisition and the types of information acquired with particular means;
- surveillance must be a subsidiary means of acquiring information or evidence concerning individuals in those cases in which it is impossible to acquire them in ways less distressing for the subjects;[28]
- the statute should determine the maximum period for conducting surveillance with respect to individuals, which should not exceed the necessary maximum in a democratic state ruled by law;
- it is necessary to precisely determine in the statute the procedures of managing operational and exploratory activities, including in particular the requirement to obtain the consent of an independent authority for surveillance purposes;[29]
- it is necessary to precisely determine in the statute the rules of handling the materials collected during operational and exploratory activities, in particular the rules of their use and destruction of irrelevant or inadmissible data;[30]
- it is necessary to ensure the protection of the collected data against unauthorised access by other entities or subjects;
- it is necessary to regulate the procedure of informing individuals about the covert acquisition of information pertaining to them in a reasonable period after the surveillance is completed, and to ensure—at the request of the data subject—that the legality of those activities is assessed by a court; derogation of this rule may be accepted as an exception;[31]
- it is necessary to guarantee the transparency of the scale of surveillance undertaken by particular public authorities in the form of public availability of the aggregated statistical and comparable data on the numbers and types of surveillance carried out;

[26]See, for example, the order of the Constitutional Tribunal of 15 November 2010, File No. S 4/10; the judgment of the ECHR: of 29 June 2006, *Weber and Saravia v. Germany*, Application No. 54934/00; and of 10 February 2009, *Iordachi and others v. Moldova*, Application No. 25198/02.

[27]See the judgment of the Constitutional Tribunal of 12 December 2005, File No. K 32/04; judgments of the ECHR of: 16 February 2000, *Amann v. Switzerland*, Application No. 27798/95; and of 10 February 2009, *Iordachi and others v. Moldova*, Application No. 25198/02.

[28]See the judgments of the Constitutional Tribunal of 12 December 2005, File No. K 32/04; and of 23 June 2009, File No. K 54/07.

[29]See, for example, the judgment of the Constitutional Tribunal of 12 December 2005, File No. K 32/04; the judgments of the ECHR of 29 June 2006, *Weber and Saravia v. Germany*, Application No. 54934/00; and of 2 September 2010, *Uzun v. Germany*, Application No. 35623/05.

[30]See, for example, the judgment of the Constitutional Tribunal of 12 December 2005, File No. K 32/04.

[31]See, for example, the order of the Constitutional Tribunal of 25 January 2006, File No. S 2/06.

- it is not inadmissible to differentiate the level of protection of privacy, information autonomy and confidentiality of communication between data about individuals acquired by intelligence or state protection services, on the one hand, or by police services, on the other hand.
- differentiation of the level of protection of privacy, information autonomy and confidentiality of communication may also take place between the covert acquisition of data on Polish citizens, on the one hand, and non-citizens, on the other.

In the judgment, new technologies were perceived not only as a tool facilitating communication. These technologies make it possible to purchase goods and services or to take decisions about the manner of fulfilling personal needs. The Constitutional Tribunal noticed that they play a vital role in ensuring safety to people and property by making it possible to monitor people and places and their electronic surveillance. The Internet plays a crucial role in this respect. According to the Constitutional Tribunal, it is not only a means of communication between individuals. It has become a multidimensional tool for creating, storing and transferring various types of data, as well as making it possible for an individual to function within modern society (point III.1.5 of the justification).

However, there is also a dark side of new technologies. They are also used as a tool to violate the law. They may be used to obtain unauthorised knowledge about behaviours of citizens, including content and forms of communications sent, the manner of gathering of these data for own purposes and their processing. Additionally, they may be used to commit specialist crimes threatening various goods and serve as a platform for communication or integration of criminal circles. As noted by the Constitutional Tribunal (point III.1.6 of the justification), the development of technology has resulted in the emergence of new ways of committing "traditional" offences. The Internet and means of remote communication represent an added, specialised tool in the hands of criminals, which exists in parallel to the techniques used so far. Apart from that, new and previously unknown types of offences have emerged, which can only be committed with the use of new technologies (the so-called cybercrime involving, inter alia, unauthorised access to computer data). Communicating through the new technologies and crimes committed with the use of those technologies are generally beyond the control of society. As a result, it is difficult to determine the identity of the persons violating the law, and thus prevent and detect threats. This circumstance should be considered by the legislator and the services, which are obliged to ensure security to the citizens and mechanisms of democratic and lawful governance in a state. A democratic state ruled by law cannot ignore the growing importance of new technologies or the scale of their use, sometimes for the purpose of violating the law. The services protecting those values should not only be able to detect crimes that have already been committed. On global criminal activity and cross-border terrorism or organised crime, it is also important to prevent threats whose perpetration could lead to irreversible losses for legally protected goods (point III.1.7 of the justification).

Even if the Constitution does not refer to virtual activities of individuals, according to the Constitutional Tribunal, it is necessary to reinterpret the existing constitutional provisions to ensure their protection.[32] As a consequence, the protection of constitutional freedoms and rights in connection with the use of the Internet and other electronic means of remote communication must not be different from the protection covering the traditional forms of communication or other activity. Data transferred via the Internet cannot be treated as functioning outside the constitutionally protected human activities.

Therefore, the activity of individuals in this sphere corresponds to the respective forms of traditional activity, already constitutionally protected. Correspondence by electronic means (e.g. e-mail) is covered by the same constitutional protection as sending a letter in traditional paper form (Article 47, Article 49 and Article 51). Providing information to one's counsel for the defence via the Internet or other means of electronic communication is covered by the same guarantees as providing them in a conversation in person (Article 42). The protection of confidentiality in contacts with professions of public trust is the same regardless of their form (Article 47). Expressing opinions, acquiring and disseminating information electronically are fully subject to the protection provided for in Article 54 of the Constitution. Likewise, the protection of the freedom of the press is the same regardless of the form in which one makes use of the freedom (Article 14 and Article 54). The constitutional protection of freedom of economic activity (Article 20 and Article 22) also covers undertaking business activity on the Internet or through other forms of electronic communication. The same applies to the freedom to choose and practice a profession (Article 65), freedom of artistic expression, freedom of scientific research and disseminating its results, as well as freedom of teaching and freedom to use the cultural heritage (Article 73) or the right to submit petitions, motions and complaints to public authorities (Article 63). As emphasised by the Constitutional Tribunal, at the current stage of development of electronic forms of communication, it is not admissible to contradistinguish the statutory protection of traditional correspondence from other forms of correspondence carried out through telecommunications networks (point III.1.5 of the justification).

Considering the constitutional scope of protecting privacy and information autonomy (point III.1.4. of the justification), the Tribunal—in reference to the case law of ECHR and, in particular, of the Federal Constitutional Court—pointed to the fact that the constitutional protection ensuing from Article 47, Article 49 and Article 51.1 of the Constitution covers all means and forms of communication regardless of the physical medium (e.g. in-person or telephone conversations, written correspondence, fax, text or multimedia messages, as well as electronic mail). The constitutional protection covers not only the content of the communication, but also all the circumstances of the communication process, which include the personal details of the participants in the process, information about the dialled telephone numbers, data indicating the time and frequency of calls or enabling establishing the geographical location of the participants in the conversation, as well as data on the IP address and the IMEI number. Moreover, the constitutionally guaranteed human freedom and

[32] See Zubik et al. (2018), pp. 391–492.

information autonomy includes protection against the covert surveillance of individuals and their conversations, even in public and generally available places. Additionally, it is irrelevant whether the exchange of information concerns the person's private life or professional activity.

Particular attention should be drawn to the Tribunal's observation that, in a democratic state ruled by law, the organisation of public and social life should envisage the possibility of individuals' presence in the public space in an anonymous way and should not require those individuals to disclose their identities to the state and private entities, so long as they exercise their constitutional freedoms (point III.1.4 of the justification).

The judgment extensively referred to the judgments of constitutional courts or supreme courts of other EU Member States previously forming judgments about national regulations implementing Directive 2006/24/EC and the judgments of the CJEU in the case of *Digital Rights Ireland* (point III.3 of the justification).[33] Moreover, it analysed the case law of the ECHR concerning surveillance activities undertaken with respect to individuals (point 2 of the justification). It provided the context for reconstruction of the constitutional standard referring to the protection of the freedom of communication and premises for its restriction for reasons of state security and public order (see point 4.1 above).

The Constitutional Tribunal rendered its judgment after the CJEU annulled Directive 2006/24/EC. Consequently, an issue arose as to the impact of the CJEU's judgment on the national regulations implementing the directive and the possible decision of the Polish Constitutional Tribunal as regards constitutionality of the regulations governing access to the retained data. It was assumed that the CJEU's judgment had no impact on the proceedings before the constitutional court (point III.3.2.3 of the justification). The regulations challenged in case No. K 23/11 were not a direct implementation of Directive 2006/24/EC. Consequently, the judgment in the case of *Digital Rights Ireland* has not directly bound the Constitutional Tribunal in this particular procedure of controlling the constitutionality of national regulations. Considering that the contested regulations are functionally related to Directive 2006/24/EC and that the level of privacy protection on gathering and processing of personal data by public authorities ensuing from the Constitution should not be lower than the protection guaranteed in Article 7 and Article 8 of the Charter of Fundamental Rights of the European Union, the Constitutional Tribunal considered it necessary to take this judgment into account as the background for adjudicating the constitutionality of national regulations on the disclosure of telecommunications data to the police and state protection services.

[33] See also Grabowska-Moroz (2016), p. 34–36.

4 Consequences and Execution of Judicial Decision

Under Article 190.1 of the Constitution, the Constitutional Tribunal's judgments are final and have general validity. Judgments declaring that a normative act violates the Constitution invalidate the act's binding force. The legislator additionally authorised the Constitutional Tribunal to postpone the date of the loss of binding force of the unconstitutional act by 18 months (Article 190.3 of the Constitution). The provisions of the Constitution do not specify the temporal consequences of the constitutional court's judgments in a precise way. However, it is generally assumed in the doctrine that they apply prospectively. Consequently, there are no grounds to declare an absolute voidance of an act considered unconstitutional.

By declaring the unconstitutionality of the regulations for allowing access to telecommunications data to the police and state protection services, the Constitutional Tribunal exercised its right to postpone the loss of their binding force by 18 months of publishing the judgment in the Journal of Laws of the Republic of Poland. This solution was motivated by the need to reduce the risk posed by the lack of effective mechanisms in combating threats, and consequently a growth in criminality or its lower detectability. Consequently, despite the declared unconstitutionality, the statutory basis regulating the access to telecommunications data still existed, and the regulations could be used by state authorities until 6 July 2016.

The formulation of the operative part of the judgment raised practical doubts.[34] These were in particular related to the manner in which the judgment was drafted in the section concerning the regulations authorising the services to use the retained data. In its judgment, the Constitutional Tribunal stated expressly that the regulations violated the Constitution "insofar as they do not provide for independent supervision over the process of granting access to telecommunications data referred to in Article 180c and Article 180d of the Telecommunications Act". Considering the wording of the decision, it was uncertain whether—after the expiry of the deferral period and in the case of lack of legislative changes—the regulations would lose their binding force, or whether the judgment would be binding.

In the first case, the services would be deprived of the right to request retained data from operators. This problem failed to occur since the legislator changed the regulations covered by the judgment of the Constitutional Tribunal during the deferral period.

Although the court set the maximum 18-month period for adjusting the legal situation to the constitutional requirements, the legislator did not undertake legislative action immediately. The draft act in this respect was prepared in the Senate and directed to the Sejm on 24 July 2015.[35] The solutions proposed therein, referring,

[34]See Podkowik (2015a), pp. 23–40. These doubts were also referred to in the explanatory memorandum accompanying the draft act adjusting the regulations to the constitutional requirements set out in the judgment in case No. K 23/11 (parliamentary document No. 154/8th Term of Office of the Sejm of 23 December 2016).

[35]The parliamentary document of 28 July 2015, No. 3765/8th Term of Office of the Sejm.

among other things, to the control over disclosure of telecommunications data to the services, were criticised by the public opinion, experts of the Bureau of Research (Polish: *Biuro Analiz Sejmowych*) of the Chancellery of the Sejm and external institutions issuing opinions on the bill. The bill was amended: many substantive comments and proposals were considered. Due to the approaching end of the term of office of the houses of the Polish parliament and the parliamentary elections scheduled in October 2015, as well as considering the objections concerning the unconstitutionality of the planned regulations, the legislative work was not finished.

The changes were introduced with the Act of 15 January 2016 on amending the Act on the Police and certain other acts[36] and became effective as of 7 February 2016. They were adopted not long after the beginning of the 8th term of office of the Sejm.[37] As a rule, the adopted solutions were based on the Senate bill[38] submitted in July 2015. The Act of 2016 also contained other solutions, not envisaged in the Senate bill of 24 July 2015, and not ensuing from the judgment of the Constitutional Tribunal, File No. K 23/11. These solutions included the right of the officers of the services to request access to Internet data, which include information about the start and end times of an Internet session and information about each use of a service provided electronically. The Act aroused a lot of controversy in the arena of public opinion. In connection with the publicly formulated statements that the solutions contained therein implement the judgment of the Constitutional Tribunal, File No. K 23/11, the Constitutional Tribunal published a press release recalling the scope of the requirements ensuing from its judgment[39] on its website. The press release also rectified other inconsistencies concerning the content of the judgment that appeared in public debate.

On the implementation of the judgment under File No. K 23/11, the legislator imposed judicial control over the acquisition of telecommunications data. However, contrary to the suggestions ensuring from the justification of the judgment of the Constitutional Tribunal and the judgment of the CJEU in the case of *Digital Rights Ireland*, the legislator failed to narrow down the situations in which it was possible to use telecommunications data only with respect to "serious crime". Consequently, the material scope of the admissibility of using retained data remained nearly unchanged.

In the light of the new regulations, the control over the acquisition by a given service of telecommunications, postal or Internet data was exercised by the regional court competent for the seat of the police authority (and respectively for the other services, except the Military Gendarmerie: in this case, the control is exercised by the

[36]Journal of Laws 2016, item 147.

[37]The parliamentary document of 23 December 2015, No. 154/8th Term of Office of the Sejm.

[38]A detailed analysis of the draft act can be found in the report of the Panoptykon Foundation available, for example, at: https://panoptykon.org/sites/default/files/publikacje/fp_rok_z_tzw._ustawa_inwigilacyjna_18-01-2017.pdf.

[39]See the Communication of the Office of the Constitutional Tribunal in connection with the amendment to the Act on the Police, available at: http://trybunal.gov.pl/uploads/media/Komunikat_BTK_w_zwiazku_z_nowela_ustawy_o_Policji.pdf.

military regional court competent for the seat of the authority of the Military Gendarmerie; for the Central Anticorruption Bureau: in this case, the competent court is the Regional Court in Warsaw; and for the Military Counterintelligence Service: in this case, the competent court is the Military Regional Court in Warsaw) that was granted access to the data. The competent authority of the Police (and other services) is obliged to submit a report to the competent court every 6 months, in line with the regulations on the protection of undisclosed information. The report should include: (1) the number of cases of telecommunications, postal or Internet data acquisition in the reporting period, as well as the type of those data; (2) the legal classifications of the acts in connection with which the telecommunications, postal or Internet data were requested, or information about data acquisition for the purpose of saving human life or health or supporting search and rescue operations.[40] As part of the control, the regional court may peruse the materials justifying the disclosure of the telecommunications, postal or Internet data to the Police (and to the other services, respectively). The regional court informs the police authority (and other services, respectively) about the results of the control within 30 days of its completion. Additionally, the regulations specify a case in which data acquisition is not subject to judicial control (the data collected based on Article 20cb of the Act on the Police and other acts on the remaining services, respectively). The control is to involve an analysis of the semi-annual reports submitted to the courts by the services.

The legislator did not undertake any attempt to balance the need to introduce ex-ante control. Moreover, in the case of the ex-post control, the legislator formulated it in such a way that, in practice, it can be illusory. The defectiveness of such a solution was already shown during the work on the Senate draft act. However, the comments were ignored by the legislator.

The provisions of 15 January 2016 on amending the Act on the Police and certain other acts were challenged by the Commissioner for Human Rights.[41] In the motion to the Constitutional Tribunal the Commissioner claimed that they are inconsistent with the Constitution, the European Convention on Human Rights and the Charter of Fundamental Rights of the European Union. among other things, as regards the lack of temporal restrictions or disproportionately long period of operational control, limiting the professional secrecy during the operational control, unlimited acquisition of Internet, telecommunications and postal data by the officers of the services, lack of effective control of data disclosure, and lack of subsequent notification of the data subject whose data was checked or acquired.

In 2018 the Commissioner withdrew the case, therefore the Tribunal discontinued the procedure.[42] As for the reason, he indicated the change of the formerly

---

[40] Zubik (2018), p. 391–492.

[41] The motion of RPO of 18 February 2016, K 9/16. See also the press release of the Office of the Commissioner for Human Rights available at: https://www.rpo.gov.pl/en/content/application-constitutional-tribunal-amendment-act-police.

[42] See the order of the Constitutional Tribunal of 22 March 2018, File No. K 9/16.

determined composition of the Constitutional Tribunal's adjudicating panel and the fact that the current panel includes three persons not entitled to adjudicate in the Tribunal.[43]

References

Adamski A (2005) Retencja danych o ruchu telekomunikacyjnym – polskie rozwiązania i europejskie dylematy. Acta Universitatis Wratislaviensis. Przegląd Prawa i Administracji 70:173

Adamski A (2013) The telecommunication data retention in Poland: does the legal regulation pass the proportionality test? ICT Law Rev 1

Grabowska-Moroz B (2016) Ochrona gromadzonych danych telekomunikacyjnych i zasady ich udostępniania na tle Konstytucji RP i prawa Unii Europejskiej – glosa do wyroku Trybunału Sprawiedliwości z 8.04.2014 r. w sprawach połączonych: C-293/12 i C-594/12 Digital Rights Ireland oraz do wyroku Trybunału Konstytucyjnego z 30.07.2014 r. (K 23/11). Europejski Przegląd Sądowy 1:31–36

Podkowik J (2015a) Niezależna kontrola udostępniania danych telekomunikacyjnych. Przegląd Legislacyjny 2:23–40

Podkowik J (2015b) Privacy in the digital era – Polish electronic surveillance law declared partially unconstitutional. Eur Constitutional Law Rev 3:577–595

Zubik M (2018) Ochrona prywatności informacji o zdrowiu w nowym prawodawstwie Unii Europejskiej, Przegląd Konstytucyjny 3:7–21

Zubik M, Podkowik J, Rybski R (2018) Prywatność. Wolność u progu D-day. Gdańskie Studia Prawnicze 2:391–492

[43]See also the press release of the Office of the Commissioner for Human Rights available at: https://www.rpo.gov.pl/en/content/adam-bodnar-withdrew-form-constitutional-tribunal-motion-regarding-act-10-june-2017-counter.

Data Retention in Portugal

Teresa Violante

Abstract This chapter provides a general overview of the Portuguese legislation implementing Directive 2006/24/EC and of the domestic constitutional case law on this topic. It begins with a review of the Portuguese constitutional framework on the right to privacy, then the inviolability of communications and the protection of automated data is discussed, and the Portuguese system of constitutional review and the implementation of the law are briefly analysed. Further, the relevant constitutional case law—Decisions 403/2015 and 420/2017 of the Constitutional Court—is presented. Finally, the case law is reviewed, and notice is taken of the more recent legal developments [The research leading to this chapter was concluded in April 2019. Nevertheless, two important developments have taken place afterwards: a more recent Constitutional Court decision invalidating access of intelligence officers to certain metadata (Decision 464/2019, delivered in September 2019), and a constitutionality review filed by the Ombudsperson (August 2019). These developments are briefly mentioned below in the relevant sections but could not be examined thoroughly.] concerning access to stored communications data by intelligence services.

The research leading to this paper has been funded by the German Research Foundation/Deutsche Forschungsgemeinschat (DFG) in the framework of the Emmy Noether Project on "Transnational Solidarity Conflicts" at FAU Erlangen-Nürnberg. I would like to thank Francisco Pereira Coutinho for his insightful comments and suggestions.

T. Violante (✉)
Friedrich-Alexander-Universität Erlangen-Nürnberg, Erlangen, Germany
e-mail: teresa.nunes.violante@fau.de

M. Zubik et al. (eds.), *European Constitutional Courts towards Data Retention Laws*, Law, Governance and Technology Series 45,
https://doi.org/10.1007/978-3-030-57189-4_11

1 Introduction

The Constitution of the Portuguese Republic (hereinafter: CPR or Constitution) was adopted in 1976 and has been revised five times to this day. The original version entailed an extensive catalogue of fundamental rights, both civil and political as well as economic, social and cultural rights. Due to its extension and detail, the Portuguese bill of rights has been called one of the most complete in the world, particularly as to what concerns welfare rights. The hybrid nature of the original version of the constitutional text combined the liberal democratic vision of the world with a commitment towards socialism and a class-free society. Such hybrid nature reflected the tension inherent in the political and revolutionary process during the transition to democracy. It explains the fact that some of the constitutional revisions, particularly the first and second ones (1982 and 1989), introduced significant changes to the original version. The bill of rights, however, despite its extension and comprehensiveness, was not significantly affected. Formal amendments to this catalogue have only envisaged its update and enlargement, to contemplate newly developed rights or categories of rights, rather than its restriction. One of the areas where amendments have been made relates precisely to the protection of personal data, namely data subject to automated processing.

The right to the protection of privacy of personal and family life is enshrined in Article 26 CPR. The Constitution also protects the right of inviolability of correspondence and other means of private communication in Article 34(1). Public authorities and private entities are prohibited from interfering in any way with correspondence, telecommunications or other types of communications, save in the cases in which the law so provides in matters related to criminal proceedings.

The CPR was the first to enshrine a fundamental right to the protection of personal data subject to automated processing (Article 35).[1] The original text was subsequently amended to accommodate the growing technological development. The constitutional protection encompasses the following dimensions: right of every individual to access all computerised data that concerns him or herself, as well as the right to request the necessary corrections and updates, and the right to be informed of the purpose for which they are intended, as laid down by law (Article 35(1) CPR); prohibition to use information technology to treat data concerning philosophical or political convictions, party or trade union affiliations, religious faith, private life or ethnic origins, unless there is express consent or authorisation provided for by law and with guarantees of non-discrimination, or for processing statistical data that are not individually identifiable (Article 35(3) CPR); prohibition of third-party access to personal data save in exceptional cases provided for by law (Article 35(4) CPR); prohibition of allocation of a single national number to any citizen (Article 35 (5) CPR); guarantee of free access to public-use information technology networks (Article 35(6) CPR).

[1]Castro (2005), p. 76.

The Constitution defers the definition of personal data together with the terms and conditions governing its automatised treatment to the legislature. Oversight over transmission and use of personal data are guaranteed by an independent administrative authority (Article 35(2) CPR). The *Comissão Nacional para a Proteção de Dados* (CNPD) was established in 1991 and introduced in the constitutional text in the 1997 revision.

Before we turn to the constitutional endeavours raised by the implementation of Directive 2006/24/EC of the European Parliament and of the Council of 15 March 2006 (hereinafter: Directive 2006/24/EC), some remarks on the Portuguese system of constitutional review must be made to fully understand the impact of the constitutional case law.

By the end of the period of transition to democracy (1976–1982), Portugal adopted a mixed system of constitutional review that combines concrete diffuse review with a centralised system for abstract review. Every court in Portugal can refuse to apply a norm on the grounds of its unconstitutionality (Article 204 CPR). The judicial decisions on the constitutionality of legislation may be appealed to the Constitutional Court (CC) (the appeal is mandatory in some cases for the Public Prosecutor). The decisions delivered by the CC on these proceedings are only binding *inter partes* even if they find the legislation to be unconstitutional (diffuse concrete system of constitutional review).

Abstract review of legislation follows the Austrian model. The CC is exclusively competent to perform this control (centralised abstract system of constitutional review) which includes *ex ante* review (before the bill has been promulgated by the President of the Republic) and *ex post* review (when the legislation has entered into force). Rulings delivered on *ex ante* (also called *preventive*) review have the mere force of a *pronouncement* for the unconstitutionality. Following a pronouncement for the unconstitutionality, the President of the Republic[2] must veto the bill and, in case of parliamentary bills, return it to the Parliament. The Parliament is free to redraft the bill or drop the legislative initiative. It can also confirm the unconstitutional provision by a majority that is at least equal to two-thirds of all members of the Parliament who are present and greater than an absolute majority of all the deputies in full exercise of their office.

Rulings under *ex post* abstract review have *erga omnes* effects and are binding upon the legislature. In this chapter, we will deal with two decisions of the CC: Decision 403/2015, delivered under an *ex ante* review, and Decision 402/2017, concerning a concrete review case.

[2]Or the Representative of the Republic in case of regional legislation.

2 Implementation of Directive 2006/24/EC in Portugal

Directive 2006/24/EC was transposed into the Portuguese legal order by Law 32/2008 of 17 July 2008. Law 32/2008 implements the duty to store and provide traffic and location data as well as all the relevant data required to identify the subscriber or registered user in the framework of investigation, detection and punishment of serious crimes. Data may only be retained in cases of crimes of terrorism, violent or highly organised crime, kidnapping and hostage-taking, crimes against cultural identity, personal integrity, and State security, counterfeiting of currency or coin denominated securities and crimes covered by a convention on security of air or sea navigation (Articles 3(1) and 1(g)). Access to stored data must be requested or authorised by a judge if it is indispensable to establish the facts or access to any other evidence would be impossible or very difficult to gather (Articles 3(2) and 9(1)). The authorisation can only be requested by the Prosecutor or the relevant law enforcement authority (Article 9(2)).

The data subject to the storage obligation are thoroughly detailed in Article 4 according to which providers of publicly available electronic communications services or of public communications networks must store the data needed to find and identify: (1) the source of a communication; (2) the destination of a communication; as well as the data needed to identify (3) the date, time and duration of a communication; (4) the type of communication; (5) the users' equipment, and (6) the location of the equipment.

Data can only be provided if it concerns the suspect or defendant, or a person acting as an intermediary, for whom there are reasonable grounds to believe that he or she receives or transmits messages intended or derived from suspects or defendants, or the victim of crime, subject to effective or presumed consent (Article 9(3)). Furthermore, the judicial order must comply with the principles of adequacy, necessity and proportionality (Article 9(4)).

Providers of publicly available electronic communications services or of public communications networks shall retain the relevant data for a period of one year after the end of communication (Article 6).

3 Decision 403/2015 of the Constitutional Tribunal (2015)

The implementation of Directive 2006/24/EC has not given rise to significant constitutional litigation. So far, the CC has only been called once, on a concrete review case, to assess the constitutionality of one provision of Law 32/2008 (Decision 420/2017).[3] However, in 2015, the CC delivered one important ruling on a draft

[3]All the decisions of the CC on the merits are available on its website. The collective decisions (delivered by any of the sections or the plenary) are available at http://www.tribunalconstitucional.pt/tc/acordaos/. Some decisions have an English summary available at http://www.

bill that provided for the access of intelligence services to data stored under Law 32/2008 (Decision 403/2015).[4]

The CC was requested to assess the constitutionality of a provision of a parliamentary decree (Decree 426/XII) that would have approved the regime governing the Intelligence System of the Portuguese Republic. When the bill was sent to the President of the Republic for promulgation, he filed an *ex ante* review challenging the constitutionality of Article 78(2). This provision would have allowed intelligence officers access to banking and tax data, as well as traffic and location data and any other related communication information deemed necessary to identify the subscriber or user or to identify the source, destination, date, time, duration and type of communication, as well as to identify the communications' equipment or its location, whenever such information was necessary, adequate and proportional, within a democratic society, to the enforcement of their legal competences. These competences included safeguarding national independence as well as national interests and the internal and external security of the Portuguese State; guaranteeing the security of citizens and the full and proper functioning of democratic institutions, in due respect for the principles of legality and the rule of law; preventing sabotage, espionage, terrorism, highly organised transnational crime or acts that could change or destroy the democratic state based on the rule of law.

Access would be granted upon written request to the Previous Control Commission, a newly established body comprising three judges of the Supreme Court of Justice appointed by the Superior Judiciary Council (Article 35 of the Decree). The requests should indicate the operation to be implemented as well as the facts and reasons supporting it and the required access to data. The decision should be delivered within 72 h or, in urgent cases, in 24 h. Access to the requested data would be subject to the regime of State secret and all the data and information gathered under this procedure with no link with the object or purposes of the authorisation should be immediately destroyed (Article 37(7) of the Decree). Moreover, the three-judge committee might cancel any access to data and information (Article 37(8) of the Decree).

The President's request only challenged the possibility of access, by the intelligence services, to communications metadata, i.e. to traffic, location, and other communications-related data needed to identify the subscriber or user or to find and identify the source, destination, date, time, duration and type of communication, as well as to identify the telecommunications' equipment or its location. The request

---

tribunalconstitucional.pt/tc/en/acordaos/. Both decisions analysed in this chapter have an available English summary.

[4]In August 2019, the Ombudsperson filed a review request challenging the constitutionality of the transposing law (Law 32/2008, of July 17) insofar as it establishes a widespread and undifferentiated duty, incumbent on telecommunications operators, to retain and conserve communications' data on traffic and location for the period of one year. In the Ombudsperson's opinion, the legal regime breaches the fundamental rights to privacy and the secrecy of communications, as well as the right to effective judicial protection. The review is still pending, and the request can be accessed at http://www.provedor-jus.pt/?idc=32&idi=18045 (Portuguese only).

raised two possible grounds for unconstitutionality: (1) Was access to data compatible with the requirements of Article 34(2) CPR, according to which interference with communications can only take place within criminal proceedings?; (2) Was the authorisation procedure by the Previous Control Commission equivalent to the oversight provided by criminal proceedings?

The CC considered that the contested provision breached Article 34(2) CPR. The judges qualified the data at stake as "traffic data" following previous legislation and case law. This concept also encompasses location and other communications-related data. They expressly considered that "basic data" (elements related to the function of the network such as telephone number, email or contract with the supplier) and "location data" that are not related to a concrete communication, although included in the right to the protection of privacy of personal life, are not covered by the right to the secret of communications enshrined in Article 34 CPR.

The CC considered that the data at stake is afforded extensive international protection under Article 12 of the Universal Declaration of Human Rights (UDHR), Article 17 of the International Covenant on Civil and Political Rights (ICCPR) and Article 8 of the European Convention on Human Rights (ECHR). In the EU context, the CC quoted Articles 7 and 8 of the Charter of Fundamental Rights of the European Union (CFEU), as well as the judgements of the Court of Justice of the European Union delivered on *Roquette Frères*, *Volkerund Markus Schecke* and *Digital Rights Ireland*[5] (*DRI*).

The judges recognised the constitutional protection of a "right to communicational self-determination" derived not only from the right to the protection of privacy but also from the fundamental right to the free development of personality. Communicational self-determination is protected under Article 34 CPR. As mentioned earlier, this provision establishes the inviolability of private communications. The constitutional text expressly prohibits any interference from public authorities in private communications outside criminal proceedings (Article 34(4) CPR). The CC also affirmed, following previous constitutional case law as well as foreign scholarship and foreign and EU case law, that the protection at stake is not restricted to the actual *content* of communications. Given the extension of information that the collection of metadata can provide on a certain individual, particularly when such data is combined, there is an unquestionable intrusion on the fundamental rights.

Moreover, the CC also recognised that the European Court of Human Rights (ECtHR) had already established that procedures of access to data must be governed by adequate legislation since the affected individuals cannot usually enforce their rights on this domain. That demands sufficiently clear and precise legislation, detailing the infringements that may give rise to such interference, setting a maximum duration for the access to data, and governing the conditions regulating the

[5]Respectively: Judgment of 22 October 2012, *Roquette Frères*, C-94/00, ECLI:EU:C:2002:603; Judgment of 9 November 2010, *Volkerund Markus Schecke*, C-92/09 and C-93/09, ECLI:EU:C:2010:662; and Judgment of 8 April 2014, *Digital Rights Ireland*, C-293/12 and C-594/12, ECLI:EU:C:2013:845.

access and elimination of data. The CC also quoted case law from the Spanish and German Constitutional Courts requiring sufficiently detailed legislation governing access to telephone communications and shared data bases. This would lead to the second finding of unconstitutionality as we will see below.

The fundamental question was whether access to stored data by the intelligence services, acting within the legal scopes specified in the Decree, which included the protection of national independence, the internal and external security of the State, the security of citizens and the prevention of terrorism or highly organised transnational crime, met the requirements detailed under Article 34(4) CPR. The CC easily rejected this possibility: this provision entails a prohibition of interference with communications with the only exception of cases foreseen in the law within criminal proceedings. An extensive interpretation of the expression "criminal proceedings" would not only widen the constitutional exception but would also reduce the reservation of jurisdiction set forth in the fundamental text.

The CC considered that, even though intelligence services pursue highly relevant constitutional tasks, access to traffic data could not be qualified as an act comprised in criminal law enforcement. The pre-emptive nature of intelligence activity—aimed at preventing actions before they occur—clearly separates it from the criminal investigation stage, which by nature demands a *notitia criminis* and a specific context limited to concrete facts and individuals.

The CC thus concluded that the provision at stake fell within the scope of Article 34 CPR, namely its fourth paragraph under which interference with private communications is only allowed in the framework of concrete criminal proceedings.

Furthermore, the deferral of the power to authorise access to data to a body comprised of three judges did not grant a *judicial* nature to said authorisation. The CC considered that the Previous Control Commission had a mere administrative nature which reduced the guarantees afforded by criminal proceedings where the most intrusive acts must be authorised by an Investigative Judge.

According to the CC and following case law of the ECtHR and the Spanish and German Constitutional Courts, the conditions upon which access to data could be granted were not sufficiently determined and detailed. The general allusion to the prevention of sabotage, espionage, terrorism, highly organised transnational crime or any other act that might affect or destroy the rule of law did not meet the constitutional threshold of determination and precision of situations that may lead to an authorised intrusion on the right to communicative self-determination. In this aspect, the CC drew parallelism with the regime for the access of data set forth in implementing Law 32/2008. According to the judges, Law 32/2008 provides more precise requirements since its Article 9(1) states that access to data can only be granted if there are reasons to believe that it is indispensable to determine the truth or that the evidence would in any other case too difficult or even impossible to gather within the enforcement and punishment of serious crimes. Moreover, in the context of Law 32/2008 it is not possible to grant a generalised and undetermined access to data. Under the implementing law, it is only admissible access to data on the suspect, defendant or a third person if there are strong reasons to believe that this person receives or transmits messages from or to the suspect, the defendant or the victim of a crime, if there is effective or presumed consent from such person.

This is an important *obiter dictum* from the CC on the validity of Law 32/2008. Accordingly, the Court concluded that this piece of legislation requires a determinability of the available data that was not matched by the contested bill. The intrusion upon fundamental rights in the framework of Law 32/2008 will always rely upon a duly substantiated suspicion.

Finally, the CC censored the contested provision for failing to provide a clear and explicit procedure governing the access to stored data, its duration and elimination of collected information. The Commission of Previous Control would not afford the same degree of judicial oversight provided by a criminal proceeding, unlike Law 32/2008.

Decision 403/2015 was adopted by a majority vote.[6] There was one concurring and one dissenting vote. The concurring opinion[7] agreed with the majority's view that the conditions detailing the possibility of intercepting communications data were not sufficiently clear and precise as they allowed the administration a broad leeway to establish the need for intervention. However, the judge dissented on the conclusion that access to traffic data would only be constitutionally admissible in the framework of criminal proceedings. Given the importance of the intelligence services as an administrative mechanism of protection of the Constitution, Article 34 (4) CPR should not be interpreted as prohibiting the access to traffic data outside the scope of criminal proceedings.

The dissenting opinion was signed by the original rapporteur and claimed that the protection of the Constitution entails not only the law enforcement mechanisms within criminal proceedings but also the administrative protection charged to the intelligence services for the protection of security and democracy. This "administrative protection of the Constitution" would still fall under the exception provided for in Article 34(4) CPR. Because the contested provision would not breach that constitutional standard, the interpreter would need to assess the restriction considering the general tests binding on legislative restrictions of fundamental rights, enshrined Article 18(2) CPR. These tests demand that restrictive legislation is proportional, aimed at safeguarding other constitutionally protected values, and suitable and necessary to pursue that aim. The dissenting judge concluded that the contested provision successfully passed all the tests.

[6]However, it was adopted only by seven judges because the deadline to deliver the decision expired during the holiday break.

[7]Subscribed by former judge and Vice-President of the CC, Maria Lúcia Amaral. She is the current Ombudsperson and, in that capacity, has recently faced a request to file a constitutional review proceeding on the legislation passed in 2017 granting access to communications data to intelligence services as explained in Sect. 5.

4 Decision 420/2017 of the Constitutional Tribunal (2017)

This ruling was enacted on a concrete review case following a decision of the first instance court to disapply Article 6 of Law 32/2008 for breach of Articles 18 and 34 (4) CPR. The Investigative Judge considered that, because of the decision of the CJEU in *Digital Rights Ireland*, the implementation mechanism allowing a broad, extensive, prolonged and indiscriminate retention of data should also be invalidated.

The mandatory appeal was filed by the Public Prosecutor who concluded the final allegations by claiming that the contested legal provisions—Articles 6, 4(1)(a) and 4 (2)(b) of Law 32/2008—interpreted as allowing the Prosecutor access to basic data [data necessary to identify the subscriber or registered user] in the framework of criminal proceedings are *not* unconstitutional.

Before the judgment on the merits, the CC analysed the international applicable framework, by quoting Decision 403/2015 and its review of the international and EU law standards.

The CC stated that invalidation of a directive by the CJEU does not imply an automatic invalidation of the national implementation mechanism since this mechanism holds an autonomous source of validity and legitimacy. The Court also quoted a working note[8] from the Public Prosecutor's Office on Cybercrime stating that the regime established in Law 32/2008 is not affected by the invalidity judgment delivered in *Digital Rights Ireland*. According to the Court, the CJEU specifically censored the retention of "traffic" and "location data" whereas the case at stake pertained specifically to "basic data". That conclusion had already been established in Decision 403/2015 and, according to the judges, was later strengthened by the CJEU on *Tele2 Sverige*.[9] This interpretation of the European case law allowed the national court to set the national standards as the only relevant yardstick.

As the CC clarified, the only normative dimension at stake related to the duty of the provider of publicly available electronic communications services or public communications networks to retain, for the period of one year from the date of the communication, data on the name and address of the subscriber or registered user to whom an Internet Protocol address was allocated at the time of the communication.

According to previous constitutional case law, "basic data" are not included in the protection afforded by Article 34 CPR. They are, however, covered by the right to privacy (Article 26 CPR). After establishing the relevant constitutional standard, the Court conducted a proportionality review of the challenged normative dimension and concluded that there was no constitutional breach. The regime set forth in Law 34/2008 was crucial to this outcome. As access to stored data is allowed only in

---

[8]Available at http://cibercrime.ministeriopublico.pt/sites/default/files/documentos/pdf/nota_pratica_7_retencao_de_dados.pdf.

[9]Judgment of 21 December 2016, *Tele2 Sverige*, C-203/15, ECLI:EU:C:2016:970.

when serious crimes are at stake, the requested information on the user ID proved an adequate measure to identify the suspect of crimes of child pornography. Since a less intrusive mechanism was not envisaged, the CC rejected any violation of the right to privacy.

5 Consequences and Execution of Judicial Decisions

The Portuguese top court has never faced the major question that has been haunting European and domestic law since *DRI*, on the problem of knowing whether a program that enforces a generalised system of data retention of people that use electronic communication services without their knowledge and outside any suspicion of concrete criminal acts is valid.[10] The CC was careful to say, in both of its rulings, that it was not adjudicating any mass-surveillance system. In Decision 403/2015, the judgment only concerned the possibility of access, by the intelligence services, to metadata on communications in the framework of concrete operations subject to a case-by-case analysis and review by an independent commission. Decision 402/2017 only concerned access to "basic data" during a concrete criminal proceeding, i.e., data that, according to the CC, were not subject to the invalidity rulings in *DRI* and *Tele2 Sverige*.

The discussion on the effects of *DRI* and, more recently, *Tele2 Sverige*, on implementing Law 32/2008 remains open: is the national instrument affected by the invalidity rulings of the CJEU? The Government's official position is that the Portuguese legislation on the retention of data generated or processed in connection with the provision of publicly available electronic communications services or of public communications networks complies with the case law of the CJEU since it demands "*that the retention and transmission of data take place for the exclusive purpose of investigating, detecting and prosecuting serious crimes, and always requires the intervention of the Investigative Judge, thus safeguarding the rights to data protection and privacy enshrined in the Constitution of the Portuguese Republic.*"[11]

The similar position had already been adopted by the Office of Cybercrime of the Public Prosecutor, in the working note quoted in Decision 402/2017. In this document, the Public Prosecutor's Office explicitly assumes that Law 2/2008 does not fulfil one of the conditions identified in *DRI*, as it determines the retention of data of every individual irrespectively of any concrete suspicions. However, the document states that this is a condition impossible to reach if data retention is to be

[10]That challenge was finally formulated in the Ombudsperson's review request of August 2019. See *supra*.

[11]See the contribution provided by Portugal to the General Secretariat of the Council on retention of electronic communication data. http://data.consilium.europa.eu/doc/document/ST-6726-2017-REV-1/en/pdf.

implemented. Retention which is not generalised and undifferentiated would lose any effectiveness. Although the Government's position is more restrained, it seems to share the same view, as it expressly called for a "*harmonised approach on data retention at European level (...) to avoid negative impacts on the effectiveness of criminal investigations and prosecutions, regarding the validity and admissibility of evidence in court.*"

That is not the view endorsed by the CNPD. In three specific opinions delivered in legislative drafting proceedings, the CNPD has drawn the attention to the invalidity of Law 32/2008 in light of the CJEU's case law. The first opinion[12] concerned the Decree challenged under Decision 403/2015. The unconstitutionality assessment by the CC (delivered under an *ex ante* request) prevented the President of the Republic from promulgating the bill which was returned to the Parliament to redraft the challenged provision. The second and third opinions concerned draft bills that pursued the aim of the failed initiative to allow intelligence services the possibility of acceding communication data retained under Law 32/2008.[13] In its Deliberation 641/2017 of 9 May 2017[14] the CNPD explicitly recommended the revision of Law 32/2008 to render it compatible with the case law enshrined in both *DRI* and *Tele2 Sverige*. Finally, in its Deliberation 1008/2017,[15] the independent authority decided to openly disapply Law 32/2008 in all future cases reported by the Prosecutor's Office on alleged breaches of Law 32/2008 by providers of communications services.

Upon a successful parliamentary agreement, a common bill was adopted ensuring the secret services access to stored communications data. This new regime—currently Organic Law 4/2017, of 25 August 2017—was not subject to an *ex ante* review of constitutionality as the President of the Republic considered that it enjoyed a "*large juridical consensus*"[16] regarding compliance with the conditions detailed previously by the CC in Decision 403/2015.

According to the new legislation, communications data stored by providers of electronic communications services can be accessed by intelligence services officers for the strict purpose of preventing acts of espionage or terrorism (Articles 1 and 4). They can accede "basic data" as well as "location" and "traffic data", according to the definitions provided in Article 2(2). Access must be granted by a prior judicial authorisation of a special formation comprised by judges of the criminal chambers of the Supreme Court of Justice (Article 5). The request must be decided in 48 h and, in urgent cases, this deadline can be reduced. Access to retained data must be adequate, necessary and proportional and envisage gathering information on a concrete target or that would in any other case be too difficult or impossible to obtain.

---

[12]Opinion 51/2015. https://www.cnpd.pt/bin/decisoes/Par/40_51_2015.pdf.

[13]See Opinion 24/2017, https://www.cnpd.pt/bin/decisoes/Par/40_24_2017.pdf. See also Opinion 38/2017. https://www.cnpd.pt/bin/decisoes/Par/40_38_2017.pdf.

[14]Available at https://www.cnpd.pt/bin/decisoes/Delib/20_641_2017.pdf.

[15]Available at https://www.cnpd.pt/bin/decisoes/Delib/20_1008_2017.pdf.

[16]http://www.presidencia.pt/?idc=10&idi=134159.

Law 4/2017 entered into force on 30 August 2017. However, the Government has not yet enacted the relevant regulation detailing the conditions governing access to data. In March 2018, a draft parliamentary resolution urging the Government to enact the required regulation was rejected by a majority vote. One of the reasons invoked was a pending review request on the constitutionality of the new regime filed by a group of parliamentarians. The review request was filed on 11 January 2018 and is still pending at the CC. The petitioners claim that access to communications data breaches the Constitution insofar as Article 34(2) only allows interference with communications in the framework of criminal proceedings.[17]

By the end of 2017, *D3*, a not-for profit organisation committed to the protection of digital rights, drafted a request to the Portuguese Ombudsperson, claiming the unconstitutionality of the regime enshrined in Organic Law 4/2017, and requesting her intervention.[18] Since there is no direct individual access to the CC outside judicial litigation, whenever individuals or civil society organisations wish to bring a case to the CC they must file a claim to the Ombudsperson. The Ombudsperson remains free to take the matter to the Constitutional Court or not and, in any case, the decision is expected to be publicly announced and dully grounded. *D3* filed later another complaint near the European Commission claiming that Law 32/2008 breaches Articles 7 and 8 CFEU.

More recently, the Ombudsperson sent a recommendation[19] to the Minister of Justice urging for the amendment of this legislation insofar as it breaches the EU law, in accordance with the case law of the CJEU, as well as the national Constitution. This recommendation undoubtedly recognises the invalidity of Law 32/2008 for allowing a general and undifferentiated retention of every communication data, on the one hand, and, on the other, for not granting sufficient protection of stored data.[20]

The outcome of the pending review near the CC is expected soon. If the CC follows its previous case law the new regime will be invalidated for breach of Art. 34 (2) CPR.[21] But we should not take this outcome for granted. Decision 403/2015 was

[17]http://www.pcp.pt/sites/default/files/documentos/20170111_pedido_fiscalizacao_constitucionalidade_acesso_dos_servicos_seguranca_defesa_dados_telecomunicacoes_internet.pdf. The ruling was delivered in September 2019. See below.

[18]https://www.direitosdigitais.pt/comunicacao/comunicados/38-d3-pede-a-provedora-de-justica-que-leve-metadados-ao-constitucional?highlight=WyJtZXRhZGFkb3MiXQ==.

[19]In January 2019. http://www.provedor-jus.pt/site/public/archive/doc/Rec_1B2019_2019_01_22_Recomendacao_da_Protecao_de_dados_Ministra_Justica.pdf.

[20]The recommendation was rejected by the Minister of Justice in March 2019 (the rejection is available at http://www.provedor-jus.pt/?idc=32&idi=17866—Portuguese only). This rejection prompted the Ombudsperson to request the Constitutional Court the assessment of the validity of the implementing law.

[21]Through Decision 464/2019, delivered in September 2019, the Court indeed declared the unconstitutionality of legal provisions allowing intelligence officials access to certain communications' metadata (basic and location as well as traffic data). However, the Court accepted the access to basic and location data in the context of prevention of sabotage acts, espionage, terrorism, the proliferation of weapons of mass destruction, and highly organized crime. The original version of this ruling is available at http://www.tribunalconstitucional.pt/tc/acordaos/20190464.html.

adopted by seven judges and not the full composition of the Court. Four out of those seven members have completed their mandate in 2016. Moreover, there is a broad consensus on granting intelligence officers' access to communications and a growing pressure to equip the Portuguese officers with adequate tools in the sharing of intelligence between state agencies.

There is also the possibility that the CC decides to refer the case to the CJEU. That would truly be a historic move as the CC remains one of the few European top courts that has never engaged in direct dialogue with the European Court even when the EU law is at stake.

Reference

Castro CS (2005) O direito à autodeterminação informativa e os novos desafios gerados pelo direito à liberdade e à segurança no pós 11 de setembro. In: Estudos em Homenagem ao Conselheiro José Manuel Cardoso da Costa. Coimbra Editora, Coimbra, pp 65–95

Data Retention in Romania

Simona Şandru

Abstract Until 2008, there was no legal provision on the retention of traffic and location data for law enforcement agencies in Romania. Like all other Member States of the European Union, Romania had to also transpose Directive 2006/24/EC, but the law was shortly repealed. Thus, the Romanian Constitutional Court is among the first courts in Europe that declared the national legal provisions on data retention as contrary to the Constitution. Furthermore, it may be the only court that has done so twice—first in 2009 and again in 2014. The reasoning behind those decisions is similar to that of the Court of Justice of the European Union (CJEU), in the judgment of the CJEU that invalidated Directive 2006/24/EC based on the lack of adequate safeguards for the right to privacy, confidentiality of correspondence, and freedom of expression. As a result of the decisions in 2014, the Romanian lawmaker ceased trying to enact another similar law.

1 Introduction

The concept of "data retention" in Romania was non-existent until the European Union legislation on the matter was adopted and triggered the obligation of the Member States to transpose the Data Retention Directive.[1] However, the first law transposing this directive (Law 298/2008)[2] was quite fast declared unconstitutional by the Constitutional Court's Decision 1258/2009.[3] The second law (Law 82/2012)[4]

[1]Directive 2006/24/EC of the European Parliament and of the Council of 15 March 2006 on the retention of data generated or processed in connection with the provision of publicly available electronic communications services or of public communications networks and amending Directive 2002/58/EC, OJ L 105, 13.4.2006.

[2]Official Journal of Romania, Part I, No. 780 of 21.11.2008.

[3]Official Journal of Romania, Part I, No. 798 of 23.11.2009.

[4]Official Journal of Romania, Part I, No. 406 of 18.6.2012.

S. Şandru (✉)
University of Bucharest, Bucharest, Romania

M. Zubik et al. (eds.), *European Constitutional Courts towards Data Retention Laws*, Law, Governance and Technology Series 45,
https://doi.org/10.1007/978-3-030-57189-4_12

that was subsequently passed via political consensus derived from the potential danger of an infringement procedure by the European Commission experienced the same fate and was considered unconstitutional by the Constitutional Court's Decision 440/2014.[5] The latter decision was supported by the European Court of Justice's decision annulling the Data Retention Directive,[6] rendered a few months before the Romanian Constitutional Court' decision. Although the decisions of both the European and national courts did not rule out the possibility of adopting a new legal act on data retention equipped with all the necessary safeguards for the fundamental rights, Romania has not adopted another law on this matter until the date of the present paper.

This analysis will mainly cover the Constitutional Court's decisions of 2009 and 2014 and their subsequent impact on Romanian legislation in the area of personal data protection in connection with electronic communications.

2 Implementation of Directive 2006/24/EC in Romania

In the 1980s, when the United Kingdom was more or less prepared to adopt legislation on data protection, two British journalists rightly commented that privacy was fundamental for personal integrity and remained one of the fewest means of defence available to a person in case of a conflict with public power.[7] This is all the more true when it comes to defending someone's privacy against the use of intrusive means that may reduce the confidentiality of communication by electronic tools. For instance, "electronic privacy" or "e-privacy" is one aspect of the fundamental right to "informational self-determination" according to German law.[8] In countries like Romania, where totalitarian regime had imposed broad yet subtle control over the people through the political police, the former *Securitate*, the post-communist era made it possible to enact and implement norms aimed at protecting fundamental human rights against the intrusive action of the State. From the very first article of the Romanian Constitution[9] (adopted in 1991 and revised in 2003), "human dignity, the citizens' rights and freedoms, the free development of human personality, justice and political pluralism represent supreme values, in the spirit of the democratic traditions of the Romanian people and the ideals of the Revolution of December 1989, and shall be guaranteed." Among the fundamental rights enshrined for the first time in

[5]Official Journal of Romania, Part I, No. 653 of 4.9.2014.

[6]Judgment of the Court (Grand Chamber), 8 April 2014, Joined Cases C-293/12 and C-594/12, ECLI:EU:C:2014:238.

[7]Campbell and Connor (1986), p. 12.

[8]Decision of the German Federal Constitutional Tribunal of 15 December 1983, BVerfGE 65, 1 BvR 209.

[9]The full text of the current Constitution is available in English at http://www.cdep.ro/pls/dic/site.page?den=act2_2&par1=1#t1c0s0sba1.

the Constitution is the right to intimate, family and private life (Article 26),[10] along with two other important rights in this context—inviolability of domicile and confidentiality of correspondence, in the next two articles (Articles 27[11]–28[12]). These latter two rights were previously provided for in all modern versions of the Romanian constitutions, democratic or not, since 1866 until 1965.

However, the right to protection of personal data is not expressly written as such in the current Romanian Constitution. Thus, its adoption within the national legal system is due to the implementation of the European Union norms into domestic legislation via the enactment of various directives on this subject matter. (Romania joined the European Union on 1 January 2007.)

For the purpose of this article the most relevant legal instruments are the legal framework for data protection (Law 677/2001[13] transposing Directive 95/46/EC[14]), the law on privacy in the electronic communications sector (Law 506/2004[15] transposing Directive 2002/58/EC[16]), and the laws on data retention (former Law 298/2008 and Law 82/2012 implementing Directive 2006/24/EC). The laws on data retention were very similar to the Directive provisions, requiring that electronic communications service providers and public networks retain specific data such as traffic, location and related data necessary for identifying the subscriber or registered user, generated or processed in relation to their activity, for six months, and make those data available to competent authorities for their investigations, discovery, and

[10]Article 26: (1) The public authorities shall respect and protect the intimate, family and private life. (2) Any natural person has the right to freely dispose of himself unless by this he infringes on the rights and freedoms of others, on public order or morals.

[11]Article 27: (1) The domicile and the residence are inviolable. No one shall enter or remain in the domicile or residence of a person without his consent. (2) An exemption from the provisions of paragraph (1) can operate, according to the law, for the following instances: (a) carrying into execution a warrant for arrest or a court decree; (b) removing a risk to someone's life, physical integrity, or a person's assets; (c) defending national security or public order; (d) preventing the spread of an epidemic. (3) Searches shall only be ordered by a judge and carried out under the terms and forms stipulated by the law. (4) Searches during the night shall be forbidden, except for crimes in flagrante delicto.

[12]Article 28: Secrecy of the letters, telegrams and other postal communications, of telephone conversations, and of any other legal means of communication is inviolable.

[13]Official Journal of Romania, Part I, No. 790 of 12.12.2001, no longer in force. As of the 25 May 2018, the Regulation (EU) 2016/679 of the European Parliament and of the Council of 27 April 2016 on the protection of natural persons with regard to the processing of personal data and on the free movement of such data, and repealing Directive 95/46/EC (General Data Protection Regulation) (Text with EEA relevance) is fully applicable in Romania; OJ L 119, 4.5.2016, pp. 1–88.

[14]Directive 95/46/EC of the European Parliament and of the Council of 24 October 1995 on the protection of individuals with regard to the processing of personal data and on the free movement of such data, OJ L 281, 23.11.1995.

[15]Official Journal of Romania, Part I, No. 1101 of 25.11.2004.

[16]Directive 2002/58/EC of the European Parliament and of the Council of 12 July 2002 concerning the processing of personal data and the protection of privacy in the electronic communications sector (Directive on privacy and electronic communications), OJ L 201, 31.7.2002.

prosecution of serious crimes. The transmission of retained data was mandatory based on authorisation issued by a judge.

We shall explore this legal framework operating on three levels (the European Union law, Romanian Constitution and primary laws), and analyse how the Constitutional Court considered it when deciding to declare data retention norms void.

Romania adopted Law 298/2008 after the deadline imposed by Directive 2006/24/EC (15 September 2007), and used the extension norm allowing Member States to postpone until 15 March 2009 the application of this directive on the retention of communications data relating to internet access, internet telephony and internet e-mail. The intense public debate concerning the so-called "Big Brother law" resulted in legal action further to which the law was declared unconstitutional by the Constitutional Court's Decision 1258/2009.

After a few other unsuccessful drafts, a new law on data retention was passed in 2012 (Law 82/2012) to prevent an infringement procedure initiated by the European Commission against Romania. This new law was also declared as contrary to the Constitution by the Constitutional Court's Decision 440/2014 following the annulment of the directive on data retention by the European Court of Justice. Presently, Romania has not adopted another law on data retention, but has instead implemented specific norms allowing competent law enforcement agencies to have access to personal, traffic and location data already stored by electronic communications service providers and public networks. These provisions were introduced in the text of the Law 506/2004 by amendment, specifically Law 235/2015.[17]

3 Decision of the Constitutional Court (2009)

The Romanian Constitutional Court's decision of 2009 was among the first decisions rendered by the national courts concerning domestic provisions on data retention. Furthermore, the Romanian judges declared that the retention of data *per se* contravenes the constitutional provisions on fundamental rights. This was equal to saying that the object of the Data Retention Directive violated constitutional rights. This decision was heavily debated by legal doctrine.[18]

The exception[19] was introduced before the court (Tribunalul Bucureşti—Bucharest Tribunal) by a nongovernmental organisation (Comisariatul pentru Societatea

[17]Official Journal of Romania, Part I, No. 767 of 14.10.2015.

[18]Larionescu (2010), p. 152; Toader and Safta (2010), pp. 295–299; Şandru (2011), pp. 137–153; Şandru (2013), pp. 379–399; Weber (2015), p. 27.

[19]There are two main proceedings for declaring a law unconstitutional: by way of an objection and by way of an exception. In the first case, it is about a draft law adopted by the Parliament but not yet promulgated by the Republic's President; in this case, the Constitutional Court may be notified by the President of Romania, one of the presidents of the two Chambers, the Government, the High Court of Cassation and Justice, the Advocate of the People, and a number of at least 50 deputies or at least 25 senators. In the second case, the Constitutional Court decides on exceptions as to the

Civilă—Commission for the Civil Society). Under the law,[20] the court of law sent the exception to the Romanian Constitutional Court, which is the only authority vested with the power to declare a law unconstitutional.

The main objective of the judicial proceedings[21] was to request a "presidential order" (injunction), which is an expeditious procedure before a court of law. The goal was to obtain a quick and temporary solution based on the Civil Code provisions. The facts of the case indicate that it was merely a fictitious (artificial) case because the plaintiff admittedly had no real, actual, or effective interest. A claim was filed against Orange SA, a telecom company, with respect to executed contracts, wherein traffic and location data related to the natural and legal persons involved in the contract should not have been retained or processed. The plaintiff claimed that the confidentiality of the communications made by the organisation and its members was necessary to achieve its statutory objectives. The plaintiff also claimed that its monitoring of data would discourage citizens from notifying them about public authorities' abuses of citizens' rights. Therefore, the plaintiff believed that a presidential order would prevent an imminent prejudice with consequences on the organisation's activity, and accordingly requested the immediate cessation of any future form of monitoring of phone conversations.

For its part, the defendant requested that the court reject the charge as inadmissible and unsubstantiated for the following reasons: (1) there were no contractual relationships with the plaintiff justifying the request (at a later stage, the plaintiff proved execution of a contract with the defendant); and (2) as an authorised electronic communications service provider, the defendant must observe all legal obligations, including those stipulated by Law 298/2008 on data retention, thus the request made by the plaintiff (not pertaining to this law) was unlawful and consequently inadmissible.

Moreover, the defendant called into question the plaintiff's allegations concerning the "monitoring" and "confidentiality" of conversations because Law 298/2008 does not apply to the content of the communication. Furthermore, the defendant claimed that it did not retain the content of the communications.

There were only two terms for the judicial proceedings before the tribunal. On 5 February 2009, the plaintiff invoked the exception of the unconstitutionality of Law 298/2008, and the tribunal decided to send it to the Constitutional Court and suspended the proceedings. On 17/18 December 2009 the tribunal, after publishing the Constitutional Court's decision in the Official Journal of Romania, rejected the charge as unfounded.

---

unconstitutionality of laws and Government ordinances, brought up before courts of law or commercial arbitration; the exception may also be brought up directly by the Advocate of the People (the Ombudsman).

[20]Law 47/1992 on the organisation and functioning of the Constitutional Court (Official Journal of Romania 101/22.05.1992), further amended and supplemented.

[21]Details of the case and an extract of the judgment are available in Romanian at: http://portal.just.ro/3/SitePages/Dosar.aspx?id_dosar=300000000252673&id_inst=3 and http://rolii.ro/hotarari/59a7789fe49009882e0000c6.

The tribunal concluded that the conditions of the Civil Code (urgency, provisional character of the requested measure, no pre-solving of the subject matter) for a presidential order were not satisfied in the case. In addition, the plea remained without an object following the Constitutional Court's Decision 1258/2009.

At the second term, the plaintiff stated: "(. . .) it leaves the decision up to the court, taking into consideration that the purpose for introducing the present plea was to notify the Constitutional Court with the exception of the unconstitutionality of the Law 298/2008."

This course of action is not innovative. For instance, consider the *Mangold* case,[22] where the European Court of Justice considered as admissible the request for a preliminary ruling made by a German court. That case involved the application of national provisions contrary to Community directives on the protection of workers against discrimination despite the German Government's challenge to their admissibility on the grounds that the dispute in the main proceedings was fictitious or contrived (para. 32 of the judgment).

The European Court of Justice, after reiterating the role of the national court to assess the case and issue a preliminary ruling enabling it to render a decision, states the following: "However, in the case in the main proceedings, it hardly seems arguable that the interpretation of Community law sought by the national court does actually respond to an objective need inherent in the outcome of a case pending before it. In fact, it is common ground that the contract has actually been performed and that its application raises a question of interpretation of Community law. The fact that the parties to the dispute in the main proceedings are at one in their interpretation of Paragraph 14(3) of the TzBfG cannot affect the reality of that dispute."

Both the Romanian tribunal and Constitutional Court did not consider as inadmissible the charge and the exception brought before them, thus enabling the assessment of the validity of a law clashing with constitutional provisions on basic rights.

The arguments before the Constitutional Court took place on 8 September 2009 and 8 October 2009 in the presence of the plaintiff's representative during the main proceedings. The plaintiff reiterated arguments concerning the unconstitutionality of Law 298/2008 in its entirety, and particularly of Article 1 and 15 for violating constitutional provisions guaranteeing the right to privacy and the confidentiality of correspondence. Also, the plaintiff argued that the lack of a legal definition of the term "related data" might abolish the presumption of innocence, diminish the individual's dignity, and cause competent authorities to abuse information.

Furthermore, the Criminal Procedure Code provides a special procedure for obtaining and using data concerning an individual's private life. Therefore, Law 298/2008 proved to be useless.

---

[22]Case C-144/04, Judgment of the Court (Grand Chamber) of 22 November 2005, *Werner Mangold v. Rüdiger Helm,* ECLI:EU:C:2005:709.

The fear induced by the potential identification and localisation of electronic communications services users is likely to infringe upon the right to private life, the right to free movement, and the freedom of speech. The prosecutor attending the proceedings requested that the exception be rejected because the definition of "related" data is not within the competence of the Constitutional Court, and the obligations imposed by the law in question do not apply to the content of the communications.

The tribunal of second instance concluded that Law 298/2008 was constitutional in its scope and categories of data to be retained. The Romanian Government and the Ombudsman expressed similar views, considering that Law 298/2008 provides for measures that are justified under Article 53 of the Constitution on the conditions and limitations on fundamental rights. The Ombudsman also referred to Article 148 para. 2[23] of the Constitution concerning the Romania's obligation to respect the European Union's mandatory legislation including Directive 2006/24/EC.

The Constitutional Court made its legal analysis considering first the nature and content of the fundamental rights that the plaintiff claimed had been violated. The right to privacy and the confidentiality of correspondence are complex, personal, non-patrimonial rights that have as a common element the personal, intimate space enjoyed by everyone.

The first right includes the second one, irrespective of the norms regulating their content, as separate or intrinsic to the right to privacy. Thus, "the correspondence expresses the links a person may establish in different ways of communication, with other members of the society, so this includes both telephonic calls and electronic communications."[24]

On the other hand, the Court stresses the relative character of the right to privacy, confidentiality of correspondence, and freedom of speech. In this respect, Law 298/2008 expresses the lawmaker's will to impose some limits on the exercise of those rights. However, limitations are allowed only under strict conditions provided by Article 53[25] of the Constitution and in accordance with established case law of the European Court of Human Rights[26] and of the Romanian Constitutional Court.

---

[23]Article 148(2): As a result of the accession, the provisions of the constituent treaties of the European Union, as well as the other mandatory community regulations shall take precedence over the opposite provisions of the national laws, in compliance with the provisions of the accession act.

[24]For this paper, an English version of this decision is referred to, available at http://www.legi-internet.ro/fileadmin/editor_folder/pdf/decision-constitutional-court-romania-data-retention.pdf (unofficial translation).

[25]Article 53: (1) The exercise of certain rights or freedoms may only be restricted by law, and only if necessary, as the case may be, for: the defence of national security, of public order, health, or morals, of the citizens' rights and freedoms; conducting a criminal investigation; preventing the consequences of a natural calamity, disaster, or an extremely severe catastrophe. (2) Such restriction shall only be ordered if necessary in a democratic society. The measure shall be proportional to the situation having caused it, applied without discrimination, and without infringing on the existence of such right or freedom.

[26]In this context, the Constitutional Court cited the relevant jurisprudence of the European Court of Human Rights, such as: *Klass and Others v. Germany*, application No. 5029/71, judgment of

Therefore, the legal act regulating measures that may affect the exercise of those rights must contain adequate and sufficient safeguards to protect the individual against arbitrary action by State authorities. The Constitutional Court recognised the possibility for the lawmaker to limit the exercise of certain rights and freedoms, as well as the necessity of providing modalities to give law enforcement authorities efficient and adequate tools to prevent and especially detect crimes involving terrorism and other serious crimes. Moreover, the provisions of the Criminal Procedure Code concerning the interception and recording of calls or communications made by phone or any other means of electronic communications were found to be constitutional in previous decisions of the Court.

On the application of the law in line with Directive 2006/24/EC, the Court referred to its mandatory character only concerning the legal solution and not the concrete modalities to achieve the result. These modalities are at the discretion of the Member States, which must adapt regulations according to the particularities of their local legislation and national realities.

Therefore, recognising these preliminary considerations, the Constitutional Court found that Law 298/2008 as drafted, "may affect, even in an indirect way, the exercise of the fundamental rights or freedoms, in this case of the right to intimate, private and family life, the right to the secrecy of correspondence and the freedom of expression, in a way that does not meet the requirements established by Article 53 of the Romanian Constitution."

The arguments supporting the conclusion that the law breached permissible conditions limiting basic rights are as follows:

(1) *The lack of an express definition of "related" data for identifying and locating the subscriber or registered user*

This *lacuna* opens, in the Court's view, the possibility of abuses in the activity of data retention. The limitation of the rights must be made to all recipients of a legal norm in a clear, foreseeable and unambiguous manner. Once again, the Constitutional Court refers to the European Court of Human Rights' relevant jurisprudence related to the criteria of accessibility and predictability of a legal norm.[27]

(2) *The ambiguous manner of drafting that fails to comply with the rules of the normative drafting pursuant to Article 20 of Law 298/2008*[28]

6 September 1978; *Dumitru Popescu v. Romania*, application No. 71525/01, judgment of 26 April 2007.

[27]Citations were made from the ECHR cases *Rotaru* (*Rotaru v. Romania*, application No. 28341/95, judgment of 4 May 2000) and *Sunday Times* (*The Sunday Times v. The United Kingdom*, application No. 6538/74, judgment of 26 April 1979).

[28]Article 20: For the prevention and counteracting the threats to national security, the state institutions with attributions in this field may have access, under the conditions established by the normative acts that regulate the activity of national security, to the retained data held by the electronic communication services and public networks providers.

These provisions include the margin of appreciation left to the states when transposing Directive 2006/24/EC to extend its scope. However, Article 4 of this Directive imposed procedures for allowing access to retained data only in specific cases and in accordance with the requirements of necessity and proportionality established by the European Union law and international public law—particularly by the European Convention for the Protection of Human Rights and Fundamental Freedoms as interpreted by the European Court of Human Rights.

Accordingly, the Romanian Constitutional Court concluded that the lack of a clear definition of "threats to national security" might lead to an arbitrary and abusive assessment of different actions, information or other ordinary activities. Therefore, the Court found that it was necessary to precisely define the scope of this law while considering the complex nature of the rights subject to limitations, as well as the likely consequences a public authority's abuse might have on the private life of each individual.

(3) *The continuous retention of personal data for 6 months from interception per a rule established by Law 298/2008 in its entirety is likely to nullify the principle of protection of personal data and their confidentiality as guaranteed by Law 677/2001 and Law 506/2004.*

This is in fact the core element of Decision 1258/2009, where the Constitutional Court found Law 298/2008 to be completely unconstitutional in its entirety. The court implicitly based its argument on the subject matter of Directive 2006/24/EC itself, i.e. the obligation to continuously retain data. The European Court of Justice, five years later, declared invalid the European directive chiefly for the same reason.

In its analysis, the Romanian Constitutional Court stated that, according to the European Court of Human Rights case law,[29] the individuals' rights must be concrete and effective and not theoretical or illusory. Therefore, the adopted legal norms should effectively ensure the protection of these rights. On the contrary, by making the continuous retention of personal data a legal obligation, the exception becomes the rule.

Therefore, the right to privacy and freedom of expression are negatively regulated. The continuous limitation of these two rights causes their very essence to disappear, leaving no safeguards for their exercise. By permanently interfering with these rights, the mass users of electronic communications are deprived of their free and uncensored manifestation.

On the principle of proportionality as enumerated by Article 53 of the Constitution, the Court insists that Law 298/2008 requires a constant retention of traffic data without considering the necessity for cessation of the limitation once the determinant cause has disappeared. Thus, interference with rights takes place continuously and independently of the occurrence of a justifying fact, of a determinant cause, and only for crime prevention or the discovery of serious crimes. Moreover, the interference

[29] *Prince Hans-Adam II of Liechtenstein v. Germany*, application No. 4252798, judgment of 12 July 2001.

with the right to privacy is excessive when it infringes upon the rights of an individual who might become a suspect without even knowing it.

Returning to its arguments on the matter, the Constitutional Court does not focus on how the unjustified use of data unacceptably harms the exercise of the right to privacy or the freedom of expression, but rather stresses the continuous legal obligation of data retention equally addressing all who are subject to the law, regardless of whether they have committed a crime, or whether or not they are the subject of a criminal investigation. If so, it is likely to overturn the presumption of innocence and to transform *a priori* all users of electronic communication services or public communication networks into people susceptible of committing terrorism crimes or other serious crimes.

The continuous retention of data likely generates within people a legitimate suspicion about respect for their privacy, as well as perpetration of abuses against them. The legal safeguards provided by Law 298/2008 have not been considered by the Court as adequate to remove the fear that individual personal rights are not violated.

The Court recognises the need to restrain some rights to defend public interests such as national security, public order, or criminal prevention. However, at the same time, it notes the necessity to establish appropriate guarantees to ensure a fair balance between individuals' rights and the interest of society. Otherwise, enacting surveillance measures without proper safeguards may lead to "undermining or even destroying democracy on the ground of defending it," as the European Court of Human Rights remarked in the *Klass* case cited above.

Based on all detailed arguments presented, the Constitutional Court admitted the exception introduced before the Bucharest Tribunal and declared Law 298/2008 to be completely unconstitutional.

4 Decision of the Constitutional Court (2014)

After Law 298/2008 was declared unconstitutional, no other law on data retention was passed until 2012 when Romania faced an infringement procedure commenced by the European Commission for failure to transpose Directive 2006/24/EC.

In this context, after a few other unsuccessful attempts, a new law (Law 82/2012) came into force addressing the same subject matter. Most provisions are closely similar to the previous legislative act declared unconstitutional,[30] thus its fate in a subsequent legal action was predictable.

This time, the exception was introduced by two courts of first instance—the Constanța and Târgoviște City Courts, *ex officio*. The cases focused on the authorisation for transmission of personal, traffic and location data, as requested by the

[30]For a critical analysis of this law, see Şandru (2012), pp. 468–475.

Prosecutor's Office.[31] The critical influential element that occurred between the adoption of Law 82/2012 and the rendering of Decision 440/2014 is the European Court of Justice's decision of 8 April 2014 annulling Directive 2006/24/EC.

However, although the Member States have to consider this decision when implementing the European Union law, the decision does not impose *per se* a direct obligation to revoke the domestic legislation on data retention if compliant with the standards established by CJEU case law. This is also the main argument presented by the prosecutor who attended the debates during the proceedings before the Constitutional Court when requesting a dismissal of the exception. The courts of first instance remarked that Law 82/2012 was not modified after the CJEU decision and contravenes Article 26 of the Constitution on the right to privacy because it lacks the safeguards mentioned by the CJEU.

The Romanian Constitutional Court started its analysis by making a detailed review of the arguments retained by the European Court of Justice in its decision of 8 April 2014 (paras. 23–38). Second, the Court reiterated the reasons for declaring the unconstitutionality of the previous Law 298/2008 in its Decision 1258/2009 (paras. 39–48). Thereafter, the Court compared the provisions of the two laws implementing Directive 2006/24/EC, concluding that Law 82/2012:

- extends the scope of serious crimes and the cases for which competent authorities may request the retained data,
- maintains the ambiguous notion of the "necessary data for identification of a subscriber/user,"
- maintains the unclear procedure for requesting data by intelligence services,
- maintains the obligation for continuous retention of data by providers.

The reasons expressed in the previous decision and in the CJEU decision were also applicable to Law 82/2012; therefore, the Constitutional Court found that the interference with the right to privacy, confidentiality of correspondence, and freedom of expression was of great amplitude and extremely serious. The retention and continuous use of data performed without the subscriber's/user's consent is likely to induce suspicion of constant surveillance into private life.

The retained data may lead to very precise conclusions about an individual's daily life, customs, residence, travelling, activities, and social relations. This kind of limitation upon the exercise of an individual's right to privacy, confidentiality of correspondence, and freedom of expression should occur in a clear, predictable and unambiguous manner and avoid possible abuses by public authorities.

Moreover, the Law 82/2012 does not provide objective criteria for restricting the number of persons with access to data, nor the existence of previous controls set by a court or other independent administrative entity for limiting access to information that is really useful for the declared purposes. As for the retention of data, the Court emphasised the lack of sufficient safeguards for the second phase concerning access

[31] There is no other public information concerning the judicial files where the exception was introduced.

and use by competent authorities of the retained and stored data, especially when it comes about the access via intelligence services without a judge's prior authorisation. Another issue discussed by the Court concerns the lack of adequate guarantees for carrying out real control by an independent authority such as a data protection authority, which in Romania is the National Supervisory Authority for Personal Data Processing.

Lastly, the Romanian Constitutional Court cited arguments from decisions issued by other constitutional or supreme courts, including those from Germany on 2 March 2010, Czech Republic on 22 March 2011, and Bulgaria on 11 December 2008, while adjudicating and nullifying national provisions on data retention.

The Constitutional Court admitted the exception and declared Law 82/2012 unconstitutional. Furthermore, the Court fixed the terms for both electronic communications providers and competent authorities, under which the former may store data only for commercial and billing purposes with the consent of the data subject in accordance with Directive 2002/58/EC, and the latter may no longer have access to data retained under Law 82/2012 and Law 506/2004 (for having a different purpose of processing). Nevertheless, the Court left the door open for adoption by the Parliament of a new law on data retention in compliance with constitutional provisions and exigencies as analysed in the Court's decision (para. 79).

As previously mentioned, the Constitutional Court in both of its decisions in 2009 and 2014 made significant references to the European Court of Human Rights and other European national courts to support the judges' views on the limits of interferences with fundamental rights and on the admitted appropriate safeguards in establishing the fair balance between individuals' rights and the public interest.

5 Consequences and Execution of Judicial Decision

The Constitutional Court's Decision 440/2014 was followed by two other cases applying the Court's reasoning in declaring unconstitutional the provisions of a draft law regulating obligations to obtain personal information from holders' prepay cards and from Internet users' access points (Decision 461/2014[32]—objection made by the Ombudsman) and the provisions of a draft law on cyber security of Romania (Decision 17/2015[33]—objection introduced by 69 deputies).

All the cited decisions rendered by the Constitutional Court were very well received by the populace at large, but extremely criticised by representatives of the public authorities interested in obtaining access to those data.[34]

[32] Official Journal of Romania, Part I, No. 775 of 24.10.2014.

[33] Official Journal of Romania, Part I, No. 79 of 30.1.2015.

[34] The former head of the Romanian Intelligence Service made a public statement after the last decision, in 2015, in which he declared the following: "I would like to warn very seriously about the responsability and the moral of the State, about the national security of Romanian citizens (...) and

Nevertheless, the legislative gap created after Decision 440/2014 was filled by the adoption of Law 235/2015,[35] which introduces a special procedure for judicial authorisation to receive traffic, location and personal data from electronic communications providers when these data have been stored for providing the service or for billing purposes (*retention* was replaced by *conservation.*) The procedure is also taking place under the provisions of the Criminal Procedure Code.

6 Conclusion

The Romanian "saga" concerning constitutional judicial control over legislation on data retention comprises two episodes of declaring unconstitutional national provisions implementing Directive 2006/24/EC: in 2009 and in 2014.

Thereafter, no new law has been passed for the specific purpose of imposing a general obligation on the retention of personal, traffic and location data. Perhaps it is merely a matter of time until law enforcement agencies and intelligence services will seek other legal remedies to expand existing methods of gaining access to this information, with or without a legislative "incentive" from the European Union.

References

Campbell D, Connor S (1986) On the record. Surveillance, computers and privacy – the inside story. Michael Joseph, London, p 12

Larionescu L (2010) Curtea Constituțională a României. Decizia nr. 1258 din 8 octombrie 2009. Excepție de neconstituționalitate admisă. Reținerea datelor privind telecomunicațiile. Drepturi individuale. Curierul Judiciar 3:152

Şandru S (2011) Analiză critică a jurisprudenței de contencios constituțional din România şi Germania cu privire la declararea neconstituționalității legilor naționale de transpunere a Directivei nr. 2006/24/CE privind reținerea datelor generate sau prelucrate in legătură cu furnizarea de servicii de comunicații electronice destinate publicului sau de rețele publice de comunicații, precum şi pentru modificarea Directivei nr. 2002/58/CE. Pandectele Române 4:137–153

Şandru S (2012) Noul act normativ privind reținerea datelor – între constituționalitate şi europenitate. Curierul Judiciar 8:468–475

Şandru S (2013) About data protection and data retention in Romania. Law Technol 7(2):379–399

at the moment when a catastrophic event will happen, I shall know who to point my finger on." See http://www.hotnews.ro/stiri-esential-19192755-george-maior-seful-sri-noi-critici-pntru-curtea-constitutionala-exista-raspundere-morala-undeva-stat-legatura-securitatea-cetatenilor-sper-nu-opune-sri-ului-curtea-constitutionala-considerat-exista-an.htm.

[35]This law was also challenged before the Constitutional Court, but the exception was rejected as inadmissible, the judges considering that the ordinary courts which introduced the exception *ex officio* had no procedural interest, since they already dismissed the requests for access to data (Decision 621/2016, Official Journal of Romania, Part I, No. 973 of 5.12.2016.

Toader C, Safta M (2010) Transpunerea Directivei 2006/24/CE a Parlamentului European şi a Consiliului din 15 martie 2006 privind păstrarea datelor generate sau prelucrate în legătură cu furnizarea serviciilor de comunicaţii electronice accesibile publicului sau de reţele de comunicaţii publice şi de modificare a Directivei 2002/58/CE în legislaţia română. Curierul Judiciar 5:295–299
Weber L (2015) Rethinking border control for a globalizing world: a preferred future. Routledge, p 27

Data Retention in Slovakia

Matej Gera and Martin Husovec

Abstract This contribution tells the story of the Slovak struggle with the Data Retention Directive. It explains the implementation, its constitutional challenge and the resulting outcome. After analysing the decision of the Constitutional Court which invalidates the Slovak implementation of the Directive, the article highlights the policy consequences for the legislator and their uptake by the Slovak Parliament.

1 Introduction

The Slovak Republic, one of the Member States of the EU, was obliged to implement national legislation on data retention after Directive 2006/24/EC was passed. While initially there had been very little resistance to the legislation, opposition slowly grew in 2010 and finally materialised itself in a form of constitutional review, which was initiated in October 2012.

This contribution intends to provide account of the procedure of annulling data retention legislation in Slovakia—commencing with the discussion on how data retention was implemented and continuing with the build-up to constitutional review. We will also analyse the decision of the constitutional court concerning European-wide standards for the protection of the right to privacy and data protection and conclude with an analysis of the post-annulment situation.

M. Gera
Bournemouth University, Bournemouth, UK
e-mail: mgera@bournemouth.ac.uk

M. Husovec (✉)
University of Tilburg, Tilburg, The Netherlands
e-mail: martin@husovec.eu

M. Zubik et al. (eds.), *European Constitutional Courts towards Data Retention Laws*, Law, Governance and Technology Series 45,
https://doi.org/10.1007/978-3-030-57189-4_13

2 Implementation of Directive 2006/24/EC in Slovakia

Directive 2006/24/EC[1] was implemented into the national law of the Slovak Republic within the broader framework of a set of provisions and acts establishing rights to privacy, as well as protection of personal data. The rights are regulated on the level of constitutional law, as well as on the lower level of "ordinary law."

The guarantees of *right to privacy* are present in several provisions of the Constitution.[2] First, Article 16(1) states that "the right of every individual to integrity and *privacy* shall be guaranteed"[3] and that "this right may be restricted only in cases specifically provided by a law." This provision is further extended by Article 19 (2) of the Constitution that protects "the right to be free from unjustified interference in his or her *private and family life*."[4] Article 19(1) subsequently protects similar values—human dignity and reputation, both of which are closely related to privacy.

Article 19(3) of the Constitution is a foundation for the *protection of personal data* by stating that "everyone shall have the right to be protected against unjustified collection, disclosure and other misuse of his or her *personal data*."[5] Lastly, Article 22 of the Constitution explicitly enshrines the protection of "confidentiality of letters, other communications and written messages delivered by post and of *personal data*."[6] According to the second paragraph of the provision, "no one shall violate the confidentiality of letters, neither the confidentiality of other communications and written messages kept private or delivered by post or otherwise; save in cases laid down by a law." The same is applicable to "communications delivered over telephone, telegraph or other similar equipment" (Article 22(2)).

Apart from the Constitution, the European Convention on Human Rights (ECHR) and the Charter of Fundamental Rights (CFR) of the EU complement the system of constitutional guarantees of privacy and data protection. ECHR is a binding international treaty on human rights, and it is also an integral part of the Slovak legal system. ECHR has precedence over the "ordinary" laws, but not the Constitution.[7] The Constitutional Court often interprets provisions of the Constitution, including those on privacy and data protection, in light of the ECHR and the case law of the

---

[1] Directive 2006/24/EC of the European Parliament and of the Council of 15 March 2006 on the retention of data generated or processed in connection with the provision of publicly available electronic communications services or of public communications networks and amending Directive 2002/58/EC.

[2] Act No. 460/1992 Coll., Constitution of the Slovak Republic; Finding of the Constitutional Court of the Slovak Republic of 10 September 1996, PL. ÚS 43/95; Decision of the Constitutional Court of the Slovak Republic of 29 January 2014, PL. ÚS 1/2014.

[3] Emphasis added.

[4] Emphasis added.

[5] Emphasis added.

[6] Emphasis added.

[7] The Convention does not have formal precedence over the Constitution (II. ÚS 91/99), but its content is effectively applied and imposed by the Constitutional Court (II. ÚS 48/97; PL ÚS 15/98) on all public bodies as if it were on an equal footing with it.

ECtHR. The CFR, similarly to the Convention, is qualified as an 'international treaty on human rights and fundamental freedoms' (Article 7(5)).[8] Of course, this only applies provided that the scope of its application is opened (Article 51(1) CFR).[9]

As for the "ordinary" law, values of privacy and data protection are regulated in the numerous legal acts such as the Civil Code,[10] the Data Protection Act,[11] the Penal Procedural Code,[12] the Act against Wiretapping[13] and the Act on Electronic Communications.[14]

On data retention legislation, the most appropriate legal instrument to discuss is the Act on Electronic Communications. Under the now invalid provisions of the Act on Electronic Communications, "undertakings," i.e. electronic communications providers, were obliged to store traffic data, localisation data and data about the communicating parties, implementing on the most general level the obligation established in Article 2 of Directive 2006/24/EC.[15] Within the possible retention period of six months and two years, as presupposed by Article 6 of Directive 2006/24/EC, the national implementation dictated a retention period of six months in the case internet, email or VoIP communication, and for a period of 12 months in case of other communications.[16] Under Article 5 of Directive 2006/24/EC, the stored data included data about who, for how long, when, how and from where the communication was made. Data about unsuccessful calls was also stored to the same extent. Full specification of data that the undertaking was obliged to store has been included in the Annex to the Act on Electronic Communications, and it fully reflects the extensive list of data categories included under Article 5 of Directive 2006/24/EC.[17]

Directive 2006/24/EC gave the Member States a relatively free hand in deciding on how to implement access to stored data, as long as the national regulation conforms with the limits of Article 4 of Directive 2006/24/EC. In the Slovak national law, the access to data by national bodies has been regulated in several acts—

---

[8] § 69, Finding of the Constitutional Court of the Slovak Republic of 29 April 2015, PL. ÚS 10/2014.

[9] § 69, Finding of the Constitutional Court of the Slovak Republic of 29 April 2015, PL. ÚS 10/2014.

[10] Act No. 40/1964 Coll. Civil Code.

[11] Act No. 122/2013 Coll. on Protection of Personal Data.

[12] Act No. 301/2005 Coll. Penal Procedure Code.

[13] Act No. 166/2003 Coll. on Protection of Privacy Against Illegal Use of Information-technical Instruments.

[14] Act No. 351/2011 Coll. on Electronic Communications.

[15] § 58(5) to (7) of Act No. 351/2011 Coll. on Electronic Communications, as amended by Act No. 402/2013 Coll.

[16] § 58(5) to (7) of Act No. 351/2011 Coll. on Electronic Communications, as amended by Act No. 402/2013 Coll.

[17] Annex No. 2 to the Act No. 351/2011 Coll. on Electronic Communications, as amended by Act No. 402/2013 Coll.

including the Act on Electronic Communications[18], the Penal Code[19] and the Police Force Act[20]. Although each of the permissions to access data was subject to an approval by a court, the regulation was quite lax in other areas. Most notably, the data could have been accessed in case of *any* serious crime and was not limited to a specified set of crimes. In the case of the Police Force Act, data could have been accessed even in cases of "ordinary" crimes. Curiously, the possibilities to access the data as a whole in case of data retention were much more relaxed in comparison to comparable regulation of wiretapping.[21]

3 Proceeding Before the Constitutional Court

The road leading to the Constitutional Court in the case involving data retention legislation has been somewhat long and winding. Bringing the case to the Constitutional Court can be mostly credited to civil society, namely the non-governmental organisation European Information Society Institute (EISi). Motivated by the ongoing fights against data retention legislation in other Member States and, at the same time, dissatisfied with the state of the public debate and lack of resistance to mass data collection in Slovakia, EISi started drafting a report explaining why the provisions of data retention legislation in Slovakia did not adhere to the standards set by the Constitution, the ECHR or the CFR.[22] After not being able to persuade two local authorities competent to start a proceeding before the Constitutional Court to review the constitutionality of the data retention legislation, EISi had to pursue a more complicated option requiring a petition to review the constitutionality to be supported by at least one-fifth of the Slovak Parliament—the National Council of the Slovak Republic. After two years of mostly volunteer work, EISi was able to persuade enough members of the Parliament. The submission was finally successfully submitted and filed in October 2012.[23]

The subject of the complaint included all parts of the data retention process—the obligation to collect and store data, as well as providing access to them. The crux of the arguments of the complainant consisted of the fact that, due to its massive, unabridged scale and not considering the innocence or prior behaviour of the persons subject to the data retention, the whole process of collecting data was a perceivable

[18]§ 63(6) of Act No. 351/2011 Coll. on Electronic Communications, as amended by Act No. 402/2013 Coll.

[19]§ 116 of Act No. 301/2005 Coll., the Penal Code, as amended by Act No. 307/2014 Coll.

[20]§ 76a(3) of Act No. 171/1993 Coll., the Police Force Act, as amended by Act No. 78/2015 Coll.

[21]Gera (2015).

[22]Husovec and Lukič (2014), pp. 220–223.

[23]Husovec and Lukič (2014), pp. 220–223.

interference with the private lives of Slovak citizens and inhabitants.[24] According to the complainant, the legislation in question was capable of uncovering many aspects of private lives of concerned persons, while at the same it did not respect the secrecy of certain relationships (e.g. client-attorney privilege, doctor-patient privilege, protection of journalists and their sources).[25] Because the data was actually collected and stored by private persons and not by the state, this bore a greater risk of misuse of data by private individuals.[26]

As a comparison, the complainant alleged that the neighbouring legislation on wire-tapping was much more strict in terms of the extent of persons subjected to the data retention, as well as the extent of collected data.[27] Moreover, the number of requests filed by the authorities indicates that access to data collected under data retention laws was exercised rather broadly and not only in cases involving more serious crimes. For example, in 2010, over 7400 permissions to access data have been granted.[28] In 2012, this number was allegedly over 18,000 permissions.[29]

In the section of the submission discussing the constitutionality of data retention itself, the complainant argued that it represents an interference with the right to private life. Basing the argument in the case law of ECtHR, as well as case law of the Czech Constitutional Court, the complaint stated that the object of right to private life is not merely protection against inspection of the content of private communications, but it includes meta data as well, such as dialled phone numbers or the dates and times of calls.[30] Blanket preventive collection and storage of meta data relating to phone calls or other electronic communications thus represents an interference with the right to private life. The complainant then requested application of the proportionality test as a decisive measure in establishing whether such interference with private life can be introduced in a democratic and legal state.[31]

---

[24]EISi, *The template complaint before the Slovak Constitutional Court in case of data retention*, 2012. http://www.eisionline.org/images/finish%20-%20podanie%20na%20ussr.pdf.

[25]EISi, *The template complaint before the Slovak Constitutional Court in case of data retention*, 2012. http://www.eisionline.org/images/finish%20-%20podanie%20na%20ussr.pdf.

[26]EISi, *The template complaint before the Slovak Constitutional Court in case of data retention*, 2012. http://www.eisionline.org/images/finish%20-%20podanie%20na%20ussr.pdf.

[27]EISi, *The template complaint before the Slovak Constitutional Court in case of data retention*, 2012. http://www.eisionline.org/images/finish%20-%20podanie%20na%20ussr.pdf.

[28]EISi, *The template complaint before the Slovak Constitutional Court in case of data retention*, 2012. http://www.eisionline.org/images/finish%20-%20podanie%20na%20ussr.pdf.

[29]A. Valcek, Facebook post, January 2017. https://www.facebook.com/adamvalcek/posts/10207298570254089.

[30]A. Valcek, Facebook post, January 2017. https://www.facebook.com/adamvalcek/posts/10207298570254089. Citing, inter alia, Judgment of the ECtHR of 22 September 1993, *Klaas v. Germany*, Application No. 15473/89; Judgment of the ECtHR of 3 April 2007, *Copland v. United Kingdom*, Application No. 62617/00.

[31]A. Valcek, Facebook post, January 2017. https://www.facebook.com/adamvalcek/posts/10207298570254089. Citing, inter alia, Judgment of the ECtHR of 22 September 1993, *Klaas v. Germany*, Application No. 15473/89; Judgment of the ECtHR of 3 April 2007, *Copland v. United Kingdom*, Application No. 62617/00.

The complainant reminded the Constitutional Court, referring to standards set by the *Klaas v. Germany* decision of the ECtHR, that although the ECHR gives countries a certain level of freedom to interfere with private life by introducing surveillance measures, they are not free to introduce any kind of measures by simply referring to aims such as national security or prevention of criminality. This is especially true if the nature of the measure consists in blanket and mass collection of data.[32] Therefore, any such measure must adhere to the "proportionality test"—a legal instrument well established in case law of the Slovak Constitutional Court, as well as many other European constitutional courts.[33]

Analysing each step of the test, the complainant alleged that while the legislation in question passed the first step—the test of *legitimate aim* (pointing to the fact that the purpose of legislation was to protect national security, which is a legitimate aim), it did not comply with the requirement of *necessity* as well as *proportionality stricto sensu* (i.e. weighing the positive effects of the measures in terms of achieving prescribed aims versus the negative effects on the fundamental rights or freedoms at stake). On the one hand, the complainant argued that it is doubtful whether the reviewed measures are capable of fulfilling the prescribed aim, especially when contemporary research shows that data retention does not improve the chances of solving crimes.[34]

On the other hand, in the part discussing the last step of the test—proportionality in the strict sense—the complainant pointed out, first, that there are many technological measures allowing the perpetrators of criminal activities to specifically avoid being targets of data retention.[35] Second, on the extent and level of the interference, the complainant alleged that even in case of metadata (and not having the content of electronic communications itself), these can be easily analysed, manipulated and subsequently misused, which in turn requires the reviewed measures to be classified as an extraordinarily serious interference with the right to private life.[36] Lastly, looking at the safeguards that existed against the potential misuse of data, the complainant came to the conclusion that these are also unsatisfactory from both a

[32]A. Valcek, Facebook post, January 2017. https://www.facebook.com/adamvalcek/posts/10207298570254089. Citing, inter alia, Judgment of the ECtHR of 22 September 1993, *Klaas v. Germany*, Application No. 15473/89; Judgment of the ECtHR of 3 April 2007, *Copland v. United Kingdom*, Application No. 62617/00.

[33]A. Valcek, Facebook post, January 2017. https://www.facebook.com/adamvalcek/posts/10207298570254089. Citing, inter alia, Judgment of the CJEU of 9 November 2010, *Volker und Markus Schecke*, Cases C-92/09 and C-93/09.

[34]A. Valcek, Facebook post, January 2017. https://www.facebook.com/adamvalcek/posts/10207298570254089. Citing the study Max Planck Institute, *Stutzlücken durch Wegfall der Vorratsdatenspeicherung?*, 2011. http://vds.brauchts.net/MPI_VDS_Studie.pdf.

[35]A. Valcek, Facebook post, January 2017. https://www.facebook.com/adamvalcek/posts/10207298570254089. Citing the study Max Planck Institute, *Stutzlücken durch Wegfall der Vorratsdatenspeicherung?*, 2011. http://vds.brauchts.net/MPI_VDS_Studie.pdf.

[36]A. Valcek, Facebook post, January 2017. https://www.facebook.com/adamvalcek/posts/10207298570254089. Citing the study Max Planck Institute, *Stutzlücken durch Wegfall der Vorratsdatenspeicherung?*, 2011. http://vds.brauchts.net/MPI_VDS_Studie.pdf.

technical and legal point of view. For example, the legislation did not recognise the obligation of state authorities to provide subsequent notification to persons who were the targets of data retention measures.[37]

Nor did the complainant look favourably at the evaluation of how the data was made accessible to various state authorities. When assessing the framework under the standard set forth in comparable jurisdictions such as Germany or the Czech Republic, the complainant found that it failed in terms of sufficient specificity of the regulation, specification of the aims of use of the stored data, the obligation to use data as a subsidiary measure, safeguarding technical access to data, obligation to notify, or subsequent deletion of data.[38]

4 Decision of Constitutional Court[39]

It took the Constitutional Court over one and a half years to hand down the initial ruling, which indicates it decided to first wait for the decision of the Court of the Justice of the European Union (CJEU) in the matter annulling Directive 2006/24/EC in preliminary submissions filed by the Austrian and Irish constitutional courts.[40] In April 2014, following the decision of CJEU in *Digital Rights Ireland* C-293/12 and C-594/12, the Slovak Constitutional Court first preliminarily suspended the national legislation implementing the Data Retention Directive. A year later, in April 2015, the national provisions on data retention have been officially annulled, and a full-fledged finding of the Constitutional Court has been published.[41]

In the court's decision PL. ÚS 10/2014, the court declared that the relevant national provisions on data retention (§ 58(5) to (7) and § 63(6) of Act No. 351/2011 Coll. regarding Electronic Communications, as well as § 116 of the Penal Code and § 76a(3) of the Police Force Act) were incompatible with applicable provisions of the Slovak Constitution and ECHR.[42]

In the decision, the court first summarised the complainant's arguments and gave an opportunity to the parliament, as well as the government, to provide their opinion on the constitutionality of the data retention measures. In its opinion, the government

[37] A. Valcek, Facebook post, January 2017. https://www.facebook.com/adamvalcek/posts/10207298570254089. Citing the study Max Planck Institute, *Stutzlücken durch Wegfall der Vorratsdatenspeicherung?*, 2011. http://vds.brauchts.net/MPI_VDS_Studie.pdf.

[38] A. Valcek, Facebook post, January 2017. https://www.facebook.com/adamvalcek/posts/10207298570254089. Citing the study Max Planck Institute, *Stutzlücken durch Wegfall der Vorratsdatenspeicherung?*, 2011. http://vds.brauchts.net/MPI_VDS_Studie.pdf.

[39] Part of this text are based on Husovec (2015), p. 227.

[40] Husovec and Lukič (2014), pp. 220–223.

[41] EISi, *The Slovak Constitutional Court canceled mass surveillance of citizens*, 2015. http://www.eisionline.org/index.php/en/projekty-m-2/ochrana-sukromia/109-the-slovak-constitutional-court-cancelled-mass-surveillance-of-citizens.

[42] Finding of the Constitutional Court of the Slovak Republic of 29 April 2015, PL. ÚS 10/2014.

opposed declaring the legislation unconstitutional. The opinion mostly opposed arguments provided by the complainant. The government tried to assure the court that the legislation adheres to constitutional limits, that it is sufficiently specific and provides adequate safeguards.[43] For example, it pointed to the report of the EU Commission, which, contrary to the study referred by the complainant, alleged that data retention is an effective measure for Member States in their fight against various types of criminality.[44]

The Court started its assessment by alleging that, even after Directive 2006/24/EC had already been repealed by the CJEU, the reviewed provisions of Slovak acts still represent an implementation of the EU law. This is because the provision in question are a derogation from an EU legal instrument, namely Directive 2002/58/EC (the so-called "e-Privacy Directive"). Therefore, because national data retention legislation is a derogation from Article 15 of Directive 2002/58/EC, the reviewed legislation remains within the scope of the EU law.[45]

After emphasising the principle of *pacta sunt servanda* and the need to interpret fundamental rights and freedoms in light of applicable international treaties, the court commenced assessing the issue at hand. It first examined all constitutional provisions guaranteeing a right to privacy. These consist of inviolability of a person and its privacy (Article 16(1) of the Constitution and Article 7(1) of the Charter), protection against violation of private and family life (Article 19(2) of the Constitution and Article 10(2) of the Charter), protection against collection, publication or other misuse of personal data (Article 19(3) of the Constitution and Article 10(3) of the Charter) and secrecy of mail, other messages and protection of personal data (Article 22(1) and (2) of the Constitution and Article 13 of the Charter).[46] Basing the statement in its previous case law, the court reiterated that the right to privacy is established in a number of provisions in the constitutional law, and that it includes not only protection against negative actions of the state, but also the obligation to create a standard of protection in the state.[47]

In the ensuing section of its decision, the court extensively referred to the international framework of the right to privacy, predominantly discussing the protection under Articles 8(1) and (2) of the ECHR, Article 7 and 8 of the CHR, as well

[43]Finding of the Constitutional Court of the Slovak Republic of 29 April 2015, PL. ÚS 10/2014, § 31.

[44]Report from the Commission to the Council and the European Parliament, Evaluation report on the Data Retention Directive (Directive 2006/24/EC), COM (2011) 225.

[45]Finding of the Constitutional Court of the Slovak Republic of 29 April 2015, PL. ÚS 10/2014, §§ 63–68; similarly see opinion of the complainant, see Husovec (2014).

[46]Finding of the Constitutional Court of the Slovak Republic of 29 April 2015, PL. ÚS 10/2014, §§ 77–80.

[47]Finding of the Constitutional Court of the Slovak Republic of 29 April 2015, PL. ÚS 10/2014, § 81; the referred cases of the Constitutional Court were I. ÚS 274/05, III. ÚS 331/09 and III. ÚS 133/2010.

as the applicable case law of the ECtHR and CJEU relating to the articles of ECHR and CHR in question.[48]

Analysing the compliance of reviewed legislation with the right to privacy, the court decided to take the aforementioned and well-established approach, in constitutional case law, consisting first of assessing whether there is an *interference* with the right to privacy, and second, whether the interference is *justified* under the standards set by constitutional law. The analysis was divided into two parts, first analysing the compliance of the provisions included in the Act on Electronic Communications and in the second part analysing the provisions of the Penal Code and the Police Force Act.[49]

4.1 Provisions of the Act on Electronic Communications

The court found that under the data retention provisions in the Act on Electronic Communications, there is a clear interference with the right to privacy. The court here adopted the complainant's argument and agreed that although data retention does not uncover the content of the communication itself, it amasses a large number of different categories of meta data, which effectively can uncover various aspects of private lives.[50] The legislation therefore constitutes an interference, and a serious one at that, because of the blanket nature of the data retention, creating the perception that individuals might be constantly under surveillance.[51]

The decision ensued with assessing the justification of the interference. The court established that the right to privacy might be interfered with, but only insofar as such interference considers the nature and the purpose of the right and follows a legitimate aim. In the following section of its decision, the court again came to the same conclusion as the complainant and stated that the legislation in question follows a legitimate aim, i.e. making the data available to provide assistance in uncovering or prosecuting criminal activity related to terrorism, trafficking or organised crime and therefore ultimately to protect public security.[52] Similar views have been taken in the case law of ECtHR, to which the Constitutional Court has also referred.[53]

---

[48]This part of the judgement is analysed in part 5 of this chapter.

[49]Finding of the Constitutional Court of the Slovak Republic of 29 April 2015, PL. ÚS 10/2014, Part IV.

[50]Finding of the Constitutional Court of the Slovak Republic of 29 April 2015, PL. ÚS 10/2014, §§ 105–106.

[51]Finding of the Constitutional Court of the Slovak Republic of 29 April 2015, PL. ÚS 10/2014, §§ 107–108.

[52]Finding of the Constitutional Court of the Slovak Republic of 29 April 2015, PL. ÚS 10/2014, § 114.

[53]Finding of the Constitutional Court of the Slovak Republic of 29 April 2015, PL. ÚS 10/2014, § 115.

After analysing the legitimacy of the aim of the reviewed legislation, the court continued assessing first whether the measures at issue are capable of contributing to the prescribed aim and, second, whether they do not go beyond what is necessary and required for their purpose. In assessing the necessity of the measures, the court disagreed with the argument provided by the complainant. The court considered the data retention to be a useful and effective tool for uncovering and prosecuting crimes.[54] Accordingly, even if the perpetrators of criminal activity could have avoided being detected based on data retention legislation by using precautions, this might only lessen the effectivity of the measures in question, and not make them incapable of contributing to the prescribed aim as a whole.[55]

While assessing the proportionality of the measure, the court reminded the legislature that although the aim of preventing and prosecuting serious criminality is an important one, it cannot in itself justify an interference that would go beyond what is deemed necessary.[56] The court began the assessment with an enumeration of the different types of meta data that the retention related to, as well as noticing that the measures affect almost all methods of electronic communication extensively used by the public. The legislation in question was applied indiscriminately to all persons communicating through these methods, irrespective of their relevance to a criminal proceeding, irrespective of the connection to a threat to public security, and not limited to any per-selected time frames or geographical locations. Therefore, it also affected persons who were not even in a situation indirectly related to a criminal proceeding. Moreover, no exception existed concerning conversations which are privileged under other legal frameworks (e.g. duty of discretion).[57]

Due to these specifications of the reviewed legislation, the court concluded that it is not proportional to what is necessary to achieve the prescribed aim. As a less intrusive measure, the court referred to so-called *data freezing*, which would allow for retention of data, but only after fulfilling required conditions and allowing only for collection of data related to specified persons.[58] Likewise, the court criticised the lack of appropriate safeguards against misuse of data and the lack of defensive mechanisms for affected individuals.[59] For example, the court found that the level of required technological and organisational security prescribed by law does not suffice

---

[54]Finding of the Constitutional Court of the Slovak Republic of 29 April 2015, PL. ÚS 10/2014, § 117; citing also the Judgment of the CJEU of 8 April 2014, Digital Rights Ireland, cases C-293/12 and C-594/12.

[55]Finding of the Constitutional Court of the Slovak Republic of 29 April 2015, PL. ÚS 10/2014, § 118.

[56]Finding of the Constitutional Court of the Slovak Republic of 29 April 2015, PL. ÚS 10/2014, § 119.

[57]Finding of the Constitutional Court of the Slovak Republic of 29 April 2015, PL. ÚS 10/2014, §§ 120–121.

[58]Finding of the Constitutional Court of the Slovak Republic of 29 April 2015, PL. ÚS 10/2014, § 122.

[59]Finding of the Constitutional Court of the Slovak Republic of 29 April r 2015, PL. ÚS 10/2014, § 122.

to reach the standard required by constitutional provisions.[60] The court therefore ruled that in the case of provisions of the Act on Electronic Communications, these were not proportional and therefore not in conformity with constitutional law.

4.2 *Provisions of the Penal Code and the Police Force Act*

As for the second part of the assessment pertaining to the Penal Code and the Police Force Act, the court easily concluded that provisions allowing for the collection and retention of personal data by national authorities represents an interference with the right to privacy. (Of course, the court again referred to the applicable standards set by the case law of the CJEU and the ECtHR).[61] Once again, the court applied the standard test for interference with the right to privacy, starting by assessing the legality of interference, its necessity, and finally the proportionality of the measure. The court did not see an issue in terms of legality of the measure, as well as its ability to achieve the prescribed aim. However, it again provided a more detailed analysis in establishing whether the extent of the measures was necessary to achieve the aim.

Because the provision of data to national authorities under both acts represents a negative form of interference with the right to privacy, it is required that such legislation also includes necessary guarantees against the misuse of personal data for the duration of any criminal proceeding where the data has been made available. The guarantees should be understood as setting conditions under which national authorities can access data, as well as establishing an effective scrutiny over compliance with said conditions.[62] The need for such guarantees is even more pressing when considering the vast amount of data flowing through communications of persons, which is likely to affect the private sphere of individuals.[63]

After the court looked at the text of the provisions in question, it concluded that they are not limited to certain categories of crimes, but rather relate to a more broader group of crimes. The court thereafter found that the provisions were circumscribed in a broad and vague manner. The fact that provisions were not limited only to the most serious crimes was at odds with the fact that the interference in question is serious

[60]Finding of the Constitutional Court of the Slovak Republic of 29 April 2015, PL. ÚS 10/2014, §§ 123–124.

[61]Finding of the Constitutional Court of the Slovak Republic of 29 April 2015, PL. ÚS 10/2014, §§ 127–128.

[62]Finding of the Constitutional Court of the Slovak Republic of 29 April 2015, PL. ÚS 10/2014, § 133; the court also referred to Finding of the Constitutional Court of the Czech Republic of 20 December 2011, Pl. ÚS 42/11.

[63]Finding of the Constitutional Court of the Slovak Republic of 29 April 2015, PL. ÚS 10/2014, § 133.

and does not necessarily warrant the use of data in case of less serious crimes, especially if other less intrusive measures are available to national authorities.[64]

The court also found missing clear and detailed rules regulating the minimal requirements for handling the data to guarantee that they will not be misused for purposes other than those related to criminal proceedings.[65] Among other missing features were the lack of measures ensuring that third persons cannot easily gain access to data and also the obligation to notify person whose personal data was made available to the authorities under data retention measures.[66] Lastly, the court recommended also more detailed, formal requirements for personal data requests to the court by national authorities. The Constitutional Court justified this on the grounds that the court deciding a request for access to data must have as much information as possible to fulfil its judicial duty thoroughly and effectively.[67] Due to the aforementioned reasons of incompatibility with the constitutionally recognised limits to the right to privacy, the court found that the reviewed provisions of both the Penal Code and the Police Force Act failed to comply with the fundamental right to privacy.[68]

As a Member State of the European Union and as a member of the Council of Europe, the Slovak Constitutional Court is well aware of the binding standards set by the provisions of the ECHR and the CHR, as well as by the precedents set by the CJEU and ECtHR. This has also manifested itself in the case of the data retention legislation, where the court referred to provisions of the European legal instruments and case law of European courts in various places.

The case law of the ECtHR has guided the Constitutional Court's decision in various ways, including establishing that the right to privacy includes also protection not only against negative actions of the state, but also a positive obligation to set certain level of protection.[69] The court also referred to ECtHR cases when it acknowledged that as the collection and storage of personal data is covered by Article 8 of the ECHR.[70] The court duly noted the conditions under which a right to privacy might be interfered with under the standards set by the ECHR, namely the

---

[64]Finding of the Constitutional Court of the Slovak Republic of 29 April 2015, PL. ÚS 10/2014, § 134.

[65]Finding of the Constitutional Court of the Slovak Republic of 29 April 2015, PL. ÚS 10/2014, § 136.

[66]Finding of the Constitutional Court of the Slovak Republic of 29 April 2015, PL. ÚS 10/2014, § 136.

[67]Finding of the Constitutional Court of the Slovak Republic of 29 April 2015, PL. ÚS 10/2014, § 137.

[68]Finding of the Constitutional Court of the Slovak Republic of 29 April 2015, PL. ÚS 10/2014, §§ 138–139.

[69]Judgment of the ECtHR of 13 June 1979, *Marckx v Belgium*, Application No. 6833/74.

[70]See §§ 87–88 and the decision of the ECtHR cited therein. Finding of the Constitutional Court of the Slovak Republic of 29 April 2015, PL. ÚS 10/2014.

quality of legislation, including the legitimacy and the proportionality of the measure.[71]

Likewise, when concluding that the reviewed provisions fall under the scope of the EU law, the Constitutional Court referred namely to Articles 7 and 8 of the CHR. Among other decisions of the CJEU, the Constitutional Court referred to the decisions *Volker und Markus Schecke GbR*[72] and *Land Hessen*[73] and observed the limitations on interferences with the right to privacy established by these precedents. Most importantly, the court has certainly been influenced in the present case by the decision of the CJEU in *Digital Rights Ireland*, which invalidated the Directive 2006/24/EC itself, as the court has extensively quoted the arguments from this decision.[74]

Not only did the Constitutional Court refer to 'higher' authorities of the CJEU and ECtHR, it also gained inspiration from constitutional courts in countries with similar legal traditions, namely the Czech and German constitutional courts. For example, the Constitutional Court referred to case law from the Federal Constitutional Court of Germany while establishing that the protection extends not only to the content of communications but also to the meta data from the communications.[75]

5 Consequences and Execution of Judicial Decision

After the Constitutional Court's decision was rendered, it obliged the Slovak legislature to bring the reviewed provisions into compliance with the constitutional requirements within six months as required under relevant constitutional provisions.[76]

Currently, there is effectively no blanket data retention legislation in Slovakia. The reviewed provisions of the Act on Electronic Communications have been replaced by what resembles data freezing—a technique which the Constitutional Court has denoted as a less interfering measure.[77] An undertaking is therefore now

[71]See § 90–95 and the decisions of the ECtHR cited therein.

[72]Judgment of the CJEU of 9 November 2010, *Volker und Markus Schecke*, cases C-92/09 and C-93/09.

[73]Judgment of the CJEU of 21 July 2011, *Gerhard Fuchs and Peter Köhler v Land Hessen*, cases C-159/10 and C-160/10.

[74]Judgment of the CJEU of 8 April 2014, *Digital Rights Ireland*, cases C-293/12 and C-594/12; see also §§ 100–103 of the Finding of the Constitutional Court of the Slovak Republic of 29 April 2015, PL. ÚS 10/2014.

[75]See § 89 of the Finding of the Constitutional Court of the Slovak Republic of 29 April 2015, PL. ÚS 10/2014; the referred cases were the decision of the BverfGE 113, 348 of 27 July 2005, *Vorbeugende Telekommunikationsüberwachung* and the decision of the BVerfGE 120, 274 of 27 February 2008, *Grundrecht auf Computerschutz*.

[76]Article 125(3) of the Constitution.

[77]See fn. 57.

required to store traffic, localisation and identification data only of parties to which a court order is applicable.[78] The extent of the data that should be collected and stored is again specified in the Annex to the act, and seemingly it has not changed from the previous version of the act before the court rendered its decision.[79]

Furthermore, the act presently contains more detailed specificity as to what a court request initiating data collection should contain in accordance with the court's decision. Article 63(7) to (10) of the Act on Electronic Communications now specifies that a request must identify the targeted person, the method, extent and time frame within which the data shall be provided, the justification for the data request. The request must also provide information about prior unsuccessful or ineffective attempts to uncover and monitor particular criminal activity.[80]

The provisions on accessing data included in both the Penal Code and the Police Force Act have been amended appropriately. Both acts now contain detailed specification of criminal activity where access to data might be requested.[81] Such limitations, together with more stringent conditions for data collection, seem to have reduced the number of requests and permissions to access data, as they are now at most in the hundreds instead of the thousands.[82]

6 Conclusion

Following the civil society's initial efforts and the Slovak Constitutional Court's hesitation, the story of data retention has reached a 'happy ending'. The Constitutional Court in Slovakia has largely followed the reasoning of the CJEU in *Digital Right Ireland* in annulling the data retention provision on the national level. Likewise, the Slovak legislature has largely followed the decisions of both the CJEU and the Constitutional Court. Consequently, appropriate changes have been made to the acts reviewed by the court. Following the Constitutional Court's decision, the discussion on data retention has calmed down, and it does not seem likely that in the foreseeable future the Slovak Parliament will draft and introduce new legislation for any kind of blanket data retention.[83]

---

[78] § 58(5) to (7) of Act No. 351/2011 Coll. on Electronic Communications.

[79] Annex No. 2 to the Act No. 351/2011 Coll. on Electronic Communications.

[80] § 58(5) to (7) of Act No. 351/2011 Coll. on Electronic Communications.

[81] § 116 of Act No. 301/2005 Coll., the Penal Code and § 76a(3) of Act No. 171/1993 Coll., the Police Force Act.

[82] A. Valcek, Facebook post, January 2017. https://www.facebook.com/adamvalcek/posts/10207298570254089.

[83] Compare for example with situation in Italy – ICT Legal Consulting, *The shadow of mass surveillance: Italian Parliament to approve new rules for traffic data retention*, 30 October 2017. https://ictlegalconsulting.com/eng/2017/10/30/the-shadow-of-mass-surveillance-italian-parliament-to-approve-new-rules-for-traffic-data-retention/.

The Slovak example also shows that hesitance of judges is an important element in decision-making, and that cross-country dialogue on novel issues, such as those triggered by new technologies, might be even more important than previously thought. To fully assess the scale of the consequences in the rapidly moving context requires a lot of evidence and a high-level of expertise, which is often difficult to quickly establish, particularly on the national level in smaller Member States. Therefore, dialogue appears that it will be to be critical to high-quality, intra-European, judicial decision-making.

References

Gera M (2015) Slovakia: mass surveillance of citizens is unconstitutional, EDRi. https://edri.org/slovakia-mass-surveillance-of-citizens-is-unconstitutional/

Husovec M (2014) Opinion of EISi on the scope of applicability of Digital Rights Ireland C-293/12 & C-594/12. http://www.eisionline.org/images/projekty/sukromie/OpinionCJEU-EN.pdf

Husovec M (2015) Slovakia · Slovak Constitutional Court Annuls National Data Retention Provisions. Eur Data Protect Rev 3:227

Husovec M, Lukič L (2014) The quest for privacy in Slovakia: the case of data retention. In: Global Information Society Watch 2014: Communications surveillance in the digital age, pp 220–223. http://giswatch.org/sites/default/files/gisw2014_communications_surveillance.pdf

Data Retention in Slovenia

Jurij Toplak

Abstract In 2006, Slovenia was one of the first EU Member States to introduce data retention. Based on the Electronic Communication Act, the telecommunication providers must keep certain data for 24 months, which was later shortened to 14 and 8 months. In early 2013, the Information Commissioner asked the Constitutional Court to invalidate the data retention provisions. She relied on similar decisions of other EU Member States' courts. The Court announced that it would wait until the Court of Justice of the European Union (CJEU) decides the cases C-293/12 and C-594/12. Soon after the CJEU decided these cases, the Constitutional Court unanimously invalidated the data retention provisions.

1 Implementation of Directive 2006/24/EC in Slovenia

Slovenia was one of the first to implement the Directive. In December 2006, the Electronic Communication Act was amended to include provisions, under which the service providers must keep the data for 24 months,[1] which was the longest period provided by the Directive. According to the Act, the purpose of the retention was to serve the criminal procedure, national security, constitutional order and the security, national defence, political and economic interests of the state, and assistance to the Slovenian Intelligence and Security Agency.

In 2012, the Parliament enacted a new Electronic Communication Act.[2] It shortened the retention period of the telephone use data to 14 months following the day of communication and 8 months from the day of communication "for other

[1]Article 107.a of the Electronic Communication Act (ZEKom), Official Gazette 129/2006.

[2]Electronic Communication Act (ZEKom-1), Official Gazette 109/2012.

J. Toplak (✉)
Alma Mater Europaea ECM, Maribor, Slovenia
e-mail: jurij.toplak@almamater.si

M. Zubik et al. (eds.), *European Constitutional Courts towards Data Retention Laws*, Law, Governance and Technology Series 45,
https://doi.org/10.1007/978-3-030-57189-4_14

data", which was mainly the Internet usage data.[3] The Act authorised the court to extend this period of retention under "justified circumstances." If this had occurred, the court must inform the ministry and the Information Commissioner.[4]

The Act listed the data, which the providers must retain. The data necessary to trace and identify the source of communication must be retained. This included the data concerning fixed network telephony and mobile telephony: the calling telephone number and the name and address of the subscriber or registered user, and the data concerning Internet access, electronic mail and Internet telephony: the Internet Protocol address, the user ID, the telephone number allocated to any communication entering the public telephone network, and the name and address of the subscriber or registered user to whom an Internet Protocol address, user ID or telephone number was allocated at the time of the communication. The data necessary to identify the destination of communication must be retained as well. It included the data concerning fixed network telephony and mobile telephony: the number called and, in cases involving supplementary services such as call-forwarding or call transfer, the number or numbers to which the call is routed, and the name and address of the subscriber or registered user, the data concerning Internet access, electronic mail and Internet telephony: the user ID or telephone number of the intended recipient of an Internet telephony call, the name and address of the subscriber or registered user and the user ID of the intended recipient of the communication.

The data necessary to identify the date, time and duration of a communication, must also be retained. This included the data on fixed network telephony and mobile telephony: the date and time of the start and end of the communication, the data on Internet access: the date and time of the log-in and log-off of the Internet access service, based on a certain time zone, together with the IP address, whether dynamic or static, allocated by the Internet access service provider to a communication, and the user ID of the subscriber or registered user, and the data on electronic mail and Internet telephony: the date and time of activation of the service and, for Internet telephony, the duration or time of completion of provision of the service, where the time zone shall be considered.

The law also asked the service providers to retain the data necessary to identify the type of communication, which included the data on fixed network telephony and mobile telephony: the telephone service used, and on electronic mail and Internet telephony: the Internet service used. The calling and called telephone numbers, the International Mobile Subscriber Identity of the calling and called parties, the International Mobile Equipment Identity of the calling and called parties, and in the case of pre-paid anonymous services, the date and time of the initial activation of the service and the Cell ID from which the service was activated, must also be retained. On the Internet, email, and Internet telephony, the calling telephone number for dial-up access and the digital subscriber line or other end-point of the originator of the

[3]Article 163 of the Electronic Communication Act (ZEKom-1), Official Gazette 109/2012.
[4]Article 163 of the Electronic Communication Act (ZEKom-1), Official Gazette 109/2012.

communication must be retained. The data necessary to identify the location of mobile communication equipment must also be retained.[5]

The law also ordered the communication providers to retain the data on unsuccessful call attempts. The content of the communication does not need to be retained. Operators must bear the retention costs.[6] Under the law, the operators must immediately transmit the retained data when they were asked to do so by the court.[7] Each court must maintain a collective database of its access orders, and must report to the ministry yearly.[8] The supervision over the implementation of the law, and the retention and transmission of the data was shared between the Information Commissioner and the Communications Networks and Services Agency of Slovenia.[9]

When the law was enacted, and also before it was enacted, the leading Slovenian authors agreed that not only the content data, but also the traffic data represent the personal data of the users. The traffic data are the "integral part" of the communication.[10]

2 Proceedings Before the Constitutional Court

The amendments to the Electronic Communication Act came into force in January 2013, and 2 months later the Information Commissioner initiated the proceedings before the Constitutional Court. She argued that based on the Data Retention Directive, the Republic of Slovenia imposed the obligation on service providers to retain as a precautionary measure the traffic and location data of all users, regardless of whether the users themselves gave rise to reasons for such an interference with their rights. She relied on the case law of the constitutional courts of Germany, Romania, Czech Republic, and of the High court of Ireland. She claimed that not only the content of the communication but also data which constitute an integral part of communication enjoy constitutional protection and protection under the European Convention on Human Rights. She argued that data retention inadmissibly interferes with the rights to the protection of personal data and communication privacy, the right to freedom of movement, the right to freedom of expression, and with the principle of the presumption of innocence,[11] and would not pass the proportionality test.[12]

---

[5]Article 164.

[6]Article 167.

[7]Article 166.

[8]Article 168.

[9]Article 169.

[10]Klemenčič (2002), p. 397; Klemenčič et al. (2007), p. 376.

[11]Articles 27, 32, 37, 38, 39 of the Constitution of Slovenia.

[12]The Information Commissioner of Slovenia. The Request to Review the Constitutionality. https://www.ip-rs.si/fileadmin/user_upload/Pdf/ocene_ustavnosti/ZEKom_-_Zahteva_za_oceno_

The National Assembly and the Government agreed that the data significantly interferes with the privacy of the individuals but argued that the authorities need this data. Data retention *"is an important tool for the detection and investigation of criminal offences, the defence of the state, national security, and constitutional regulation, and that such data must most often be obtained for a past period of time, which is precisely what the obligatory precautionary retention of data enables."*[13]

In September 2013, the court announced that it would wait until the European Court of Justice decides its cases on data retention.[14] Since Slovenia is a member of the European Union, according to the court, the court is bound to follow and apply the European Union law. Since the Information Commissioner had alleged that the statutory provisions, which implemented the EU Directive, were unconstitutional, she in essence alleged that the Directive was unconstitutional. The court went on to repeat that, according to the TFEU, the Court of Justice has exclusive jurisdiction to review the validity of the Directive. Since the Court of Justice has not yet decided on the validity of the Data Retention Directive from the viewpoint of its consistency with Articles 7 and 8 of the Charter, even if the cases were already pending before the European Court of Justice, the court announced that it was unable to adopt a decision on the matter until the Court of Justice decides its cases.

3 Decision of the Constitutional Court

The court stressed that the only reason for the introduction of data retention in the Slovenian legal system was the implementation of the Directive. The court emphasised that, in essence, the question is whether the Directive is in line with human rights. For this reason, the court waited for the European Court of Justice to decide the cases C-293/12 and C-594/12. Since the European Court of Justice ruled that the Directive was invalid, the states are no longer required to implement the Directive into the domestic legislation. The state, however, is still allowed to keep the retention of data in its law if it chooses so under Article 15 of the Directive 2002/58/EC. The Constitutional Court, therefore, must assess whether the data retention provisions of the Electronic Communications Act pass the proportionality test.

The court relied on the European Court of Justice's finding that *"Those data, taken as a whole, may allow very precise conclusions to be drawn concerning the private lives of the persons whose data has been detained, such as the habits of everyday life, permanent or temporary places of residence, daily or other*

ustavnosti__data_retention_.pdf. Accessed 25 Mar 2019. Order of the Constitutional Court U-I-65/13 of 26 Sept 2013, and Decision U-I-65/13 of 3 July 2014.

[13]Decision of the Constitutional Court U-I-65/13 of 3 July 2014, para. 4.

[14]Order of the Constitutional Court U-I-65/13 of 26 September 2013.

movements, the activities carried out, the social relationships of those persons and the social environments frequented by them."[15]

The retention of this data, under the established case law, entails an interference with the right to privacy under the Slovenian constitution, the Charter, and the European Convention of Human Rights. While these rights are not absolute, the court went on to the proportionality test.

When using the proportionality test, the court first assessed whether there exists a constitutionally admissible aim. Since the intention of the data retention is to ensure data available *"for the purpose of the investigation, detection and prosecution of serious crime, (...) for the purposes of ensuring the national security and the constitutional system and the security, political, and economic interests of the state, (...) as well as the defence of the state"*, the court concluded that the legislature did have constitutionally admissible aims for interfering with the constitutionally protected right to information privacy.

The court also concluded that the measures are appropriate for achieving these legitimate aims. They can, in fact, be achieved by these measures. The data can be used for the investigation, detection, and prosecution of serious crimes.

However, the court went on to say that even if a measure is both appropriate and useful, this does not mean that at the same time it is necessary. The court must assess whether, to achieve the pursued aim, no other less invasive measures that would interfere less with the human rights of individuals were available. Here the court relied on the reasons that led the European Court of Justice to its decision in the cases C-293/12 and C-594/12. Relying on the CJEU decision, the Constitutional Court concluded that just like the Directive, the Slovenian legal provisions on data retention were also not necessary. *"The precautionary and non-selective retention of data necessarily entails that it predominantly interferes with the rights of those persons who are not and will not be even indirectly connected with the purposes for which these data were primarily collected. Both the Data Retention Directive and the Slovene legislature did not limit the retention to those data that have some reasonable and objectively verifiable connection with a purpose that the legislator intends the measure to achieve."*[16]

The court also stressed that the length of the retention was an important factor in determining whether data retention was in line with the constitution. It emphasised that neither the National Assembly nor the Government could justify why they decided for the 8- and 14- month retention, and why they decided for the different lengths of retention periods for the telephone and Internet data.

The court invalidated the data retention provisions with the immediate effect, and it did so under the constitutional provision on the right to privacy (Article 38 of the Constitution). For this reason, it was not necessary for the court to evaluate whether other constitutional rights had been violated as well.

---

[15]C-293/12 and C-594/12, para. 27, cited in Constitutional Court decision U-I-65/13, para. 14.

[16]Decision of the Constitutional Court U-I-65/13 of 3 July 2014, para. 25.

4 Consequences and Execution of Judicial Decision

The decision of the Constitutional Court was effective immediately and it did not require any legal amendments. The court invalidated the statutory provisions on data retention with an immediate effect. Moreover, to prevent further interferences with the constitutional rights, the court not only invalidated the statutory provisions but also determined the matter of execution of the judgment. It ordered that the service providers must destroy the data immediately after the publication of the court decision.

The Constitutional Court's data retention case was quoted by the court in several of its subsequent decisions. Most notably, judge Jadranka Sovdat, later the president of the court, mentioned the case in her dissenting opinion on the police interference with the Internet use data without a court order. The case concerned child pornography on the user's computer. She argued that the police should not have interfered with the Internet use data without a court order. The majority of the court had not found a violation of constitutional rights, but the European Court of Human Rights subsequently did.[17]

Under the current law, the communication providers are only allowed to keep the data for the last 3 months for their own commercial needs such as billing or customer complaints. In March 2018, the Office of the State Prosecutor General and the Police informed the public that the decision of the constitutional court had hindered their work and their ability to prosecute the crimes.[18] While they had access to the data for the past 3 months, they argued that this was insufficient. They called for legislative amendments. A former Minister of Interior Vinko Gorenak, now an opposition member of the parliament, responded that police access to the data, which is only kept for communication providers' commercial use, was illegal. The Ministry of Public Administration responded that the authorities were authorised to access this data, because with the annulment of the Directive and with the Constitutional Court decision, the situation had returned to where it had been before the Directive came in power.[19] In April 2018, the European Court of Human Rights ruled that Slovenia had violated the rights of an Internet user when the police had accessed his IP address and web use data without a court order.[20] A leading Slovenian cybercrime researcher and author Miha Šepec, who analysed data retention in Slovenia and abroad, expects that the European Union will sooner or later again ask the Member States to regulate the retention of the traffic data.[21]

[17]Constitutional Court decision Up-540/11 of 27 February 2014, dissent by J. Sovdat. Judgment of ECHR of 24 Apr 2018, *Benedik v. Slovenia*, No. 62357/14.

[18]Slovenian Press Agency (STA), A. Kocjan, *Krajši rok hrambe podatkov o telekomunikacijskem prometu težava pri pregonu najtežjega kriminala*, 18 March 2018.

[19]Ibid.

[20]Judgment of ECHR of 24 April 2018, *Benedik v. Slovenia*, No. 62357/14.

[21]Šepec (2018), p. 100.

References

Klemenčič G (2002) 37 člen. In: Šturm L (ed) Komentar Ustave Republike Slovenije. FUDŠ, Ljubljana, pp 391–408
Klemenčič G, Tičar K, Makarovič B (2007) Internet in človekove pravice. In: Makarovič B, Toplišek J (eds) Pravni vodnik po internetu. GV, Ljubljana, pp 361–395
Šepec M (2018) Kibernetski kriminal. Univerzitetna založba UM, Maribor, p 100

Part III
Common European Standard of Data Retention Law in Europe

Judicial Dialogue on Data Retention Laws in Europe in the Digital Age: Concluding Remarks

Marek Zubik, Jan Podkowik, and Robert Rybski

Abstract The chapter is a summary of the analysis contained in chapters of the book regarding European constitutional courts' approach to data retention law. It presents an outline of judicial dialogue in this matter. In addition, the constitutional standard concerning both the data retention mechanism itself and the premises for providing access to retained data are indicated.

1 Introduction

Mass surveillance has been on the agenda for two decades. Numerous terrorist attacks in the USA and Europe in the beginning of the twentieth century led to the introduction of new legislation. It was aimed at acceleration and facilitation of combating and preventing terrorism and serious organised crime. Since members of terrorist or criminal groups communicate through telecommunication networks, it became clear that an effective way to track their activity is analysing telecommunications metadata. Thus, in many countries worldwide, telecommunications companies were obliged to retain data of mobile and Internet users and provide access to them to the police and intelligence services.

At the level of the European Union, a unilateral telecommunications data retention framework was introduced by the Directive 2006/24/EC.[1] Accordingly, a

[1]Cf. Directive 2006/24/EC of the European Parliament and of the Council of 15 March 2006 on the retention of data generated or processed in connection with the provision of publicly available electronic communications services or of public communications networks and amending Directive 2002/58/EC; OJ L 105, 13.4.2006, pp. 54–63.

M. Zubik · J. Podkowik · R. Rybski (✉)
Department of Constitutional Law, Faculty of Law and Administration, University of Warsaw, Warsaw, Poland

M. Zubik et al. (eds.), *European Constitutional Courts towards Data Retention Laws*, Law, Governance and Technology Series 45,
https://doi.org/10.1007/978-3-030-57189-4_15

structurally-related legal mechanism was adopted in most of the EU Member States.[2]

Although data retention mechanism was considered a necessary measure to combat terrorism and organised crime, it quickly turned out that it would pose a serious threat to privacy and freedom of communication. It is true that the data retained does not include the content of messages transmitted in the telecommunication networks and is only the "data about data" (metadata). It might, however, not only reveal much about individuals' habits and even enable profiling citizens (i.e. creating profiles of their movements and their personality), detecting journalistic sources or political opponents, but it also poses a threat to democratic mechanisms of state governance. Additionally, data retention laws originally aimed at combating terrorism and organised crime are currently used for different purposes, including combating ordinary crime.

Serious considerations on intrusive nature of the data retention mechanism have been raised, particularly its disproportionate interference with privacy, secrecy of communication or informational autonomy. From criticism expressed both in public and academic debate,[3] data retention laws were challenged before 12 European constitutional courts (in Bulgaria, Romania, Germany, Czech Republic, Cyprus, Austria, Slovenia, Poland, Slovakia, Portugal, Ireland, Belgium) and before the Court of Justice of the European Union (hereinafter 'the CJEU'). It is worth mentioning that national constitutional courts examined domestic provisions implementing the Directive. They did not contest the Directive itself.[4] In judgments issued after the judgment of the CJEU in the case of *Digital Rights Ireland*, the national courts pointed out that it does not automatically affect the validity (constitutionality) of national provisions. Reviewing the same legal mechanism—both at the EU and domestic level—created an excellent field for cooperation of constitutional courts in Europe and the CJEU, transgressing an ordinary judicial dialogue. We can even observe a sort of a constitutional courts' federation forming within the EU. Not only was this federation established without an external intervention of legislators or without changes in constitutional systems of the EU Member States, but it evolved thanks to a legislative framework (on telecommunications data retention) introduced within the EU legislation.

In this paper, we shall refer to common requirements that European constitutional courts have placed before the legislators regarding data retention. Based on the analysis of judgments of European courts, universal European standards in that matter may be distinguished, balancing privacy and national security.

---

[2]According to the Treaty on Functioning of the European Union, a directive shall be binding, as to the result to be achieved, upon each Member State to which it is addressed, but shall leave to the national authorities the choice of form and methods (Article 288.2). All Member States shall adopt all measures of national law necessary to implement legally binding Union acts (Article 291).

[3]Cf. for example, Bignami (2007), pp. 233–255; Feiler (2010); Konstadinides (2014), pp. 69–84.

[4]The Directive itself was implicitly criticised, however, by the Romanian Constitutional Court in the decision of 8 October 2009, ref. No. 1.258.

2 On the Road Towards a Harmonised European Data Retention Law

It is necessary to provide a background on how the European Union ended up with a unilateral, harmonised measure for retention and access to telecommunications data. The starting point was the 9/11. The United Nations Security Council Resolution 1368 of 12 September 2001[5] and the UN Security Council Resolution 1373(2001)[6] made way for undertaking national measures at the level of international law. However, the EU's initial response[7] to September 11 attacks did not include the adoption of any legal measures similar to the USA Patriot Act,[8] with the European Arrest Warrant as the most intrusive measure for individual citizens.[9] The tipping point for an EU action was the 2004 terrorist act in Madrid (Spain): train bombing with 192 casualties and over 2000 people injured. In its Declaration on combating terrorism of 25 March 2004, the Council of the European Union demanded adopting rules on the retention of communications data by service providers.[10] On 28 April 2004, four EU Member States (France, Ireland, Sweden and the United Kingdom) presented a proposal of a Framework Decision on the retention of data processed and stored in connection with the provision of publicly available electronic communications services or data on public communications networks for the purpose of prevention, investigation, detection and prosecution of crime and criminal offences including terrorism.[11] This proposal was however rejected by the European Commission persuading that the mechanism of data retention shall not be adopted within the third pillar of the pre-Lisbon Treaty institutional legal framework of the EU, which was intended for police and judicial co-operation in criminal matters.[12] On

[5]Resolution 1368(2001) adopted by the Security Council at its 4370th meeting on 12 September 2001. http://www.un.org/en/ga/search/view_doc.asp?symbol=S/RES/1368%20%282001%29.

[6]Resolution 1373(2001) adopted by the Security Council at its 4385th meeting on 28 September 2001. https://www.unodc.org/pdf/crime/terrorism/res_1373_english.pdf.

[7]Cf. Conclusions and Plan of Action of Extraordinary European Council Meeting on 21 September 2001. https://www.consilium.europa.eu/media/20972/140en.pdf.

[8]An act to deter and punish terrorist acts in the United States and around the world, to enhance law enforcement investigatory tools, and to serve other purposes, enacted on 26 October 2001 (Public Law 107-56). https://www.gpo.gov/fdsys/pkg/PLAW-107publ56/pdf/PLAW-107publ56.pdf.

[9]Introduced by the Council Framework Decision of 13 June 2002 on the European arrest warrant and the surrender procedures between Member States (OJ L 190, 18.7.2002, pp. 1–20). http://eur-lex.europa.eu/LexUriServ/LexUriServ.do?uri=CELEX:32002F0584:EN:HTML.

[10]Cf. The Declaration on Combating Terrorism adopted by the European Council on 25 March 2004, pp. 5–6. http://data.consilium.europa.eu/doc/document/ST-7906-2004-INIT/en/pdf.

[11]https://www.steptoe.com/images/content/4/1/v1/4149/PI5331.pdf.

[12]Cf. *Commission of the European Communities Extended Impact Assessment. Annex to the Proposal for a Directive of the European Parliament and of the Council on the retention of data processed in connection with the provision of public electronic communication services and amending Directive 2002/58/EC*, pp. 9–12. http://www.europarl.europa.eu/RegData/docs_autres_institutions/commission_europeenne/sec/2005/1131/COM_SEC(2005)1131_EN.pdf.

7 July 2005, a series of terrorist attacks took place in London. On 13 July 2005, the Council of the EU adopted a Declaration condemning terrorist attacks in London, in which it reaffirmed the need to promptly introduce the retention of traffic data in the EU.[13] On 21 September 2005, the Commission presented a Proposal for a Directive of the European Parliament and of the Council on the retention of data processed in connection with the provision of public electronic communication services and amending Directive 2002/58/EC.[14] It was based on Article 95 of the European Community Treaty concerning the establishment and functioning of the internal market—the first pillar of the European Communities—and it aimed at regulating data retention from the perspective of internal market. The proposal introduced harmonised obligations for providers concerning data retention. It is worth noting that a very broad scope of data was to be collected: besides telecommunications data, providers were to retain the data concerning Internet access, Internet e-mail and Internet telephony. The lack of an EU regulation on access potentially enabled it to those state authorities that do not fight terrorism. On the other hand, the Directive unified provisions on data retention that had already existed or were to be introduced in the EU Member States (e.g. introducing a 15-year time frame for granting access in the Polish legislation was considered).

The proposal was criticised, inter alia, by the European Data Protection Supervisor, with relation to the legal grounds chosen, proportionality of the measures, lack of harmonisation of access to the retained data; even the introduction of the mechanism itself was criticised.[15]

Despite this criticism, the Directive 2006/24/EC was adopted (however, Ireland and the Slovak Republic were against it during the vote in the Council). The Directive provided a transposition deadline for Member States—no later than 15 September 2007. However, under Article 15 section 3 of the Directive, Member States were allowed to postpone transposition of the Directive on the retention of communications data relating to Internet access, Internet telephony and Internet e-mail. By submitting appropriate declarations, 16 countries used the clause.

Worth noting are the cases of countries that transposed the Directive with delay—Austria and Sweden. The Court of Justice decided that Austria and Sweden violated their obligation to implement the Directive (C-189/09 and C-185/09). In the second case against Sweden, in its judgment of 30 May 2013 (C-270/11), the Court of Justice declared that Sweden failed to comply with its judgment C-185/09 and ordered a lump sum payment. The Court noted that Sweden had never failed to comply with any judgment previously passed by the Court under Article 258 TFEU,

[13]Cf. Press release of the Extraordinary Council meeting in Brussels, 13 July 2005, p. 6. http://www.consilium.europa.eu/ueDocs/cms_Data/docs/pressData/en/jha/85703.pdf.

[14]https://eur-lex.europa.eu/legal-content/EN/TXT/PDF/?uri=CELEX:52005PC0438&from=EN.

[15]Cf. Op*inion of the European Data Protection Supervisor on the proposal for a Directive of the European Parliament and of the Council on the retention of data processed in connection with the provision of public electronic communication services and amending Directive 2002/58/EC (COM (2005) 438 final)*, OJ C 298, 29.11.2005, pp. 1–12. http://eur-lex.europa.eu/legal-content/EN/TXT/?uri=CELEX:52005XX1129(01).

which it regarded as a manifestation of Sweden's determination not to implement the Directive. Hence, a paradox was observed: the Court of Justice defended legal grounds of the Directive in 2009 and urged the two Member States to implement the dirCctive in its three subsequent judgments; then, just one year after the last judgment against Sweden, the Court passed a judgment in which it declared the Directive null and void, and revoked it.

The EU legal acts include an obligation to evaluate them after they had been adopted. In the case of the Directive, the evaluation prescribed by its Article 14 was already conducted after the first judgment of CJEU and several constitutional courts (i.e. in Czech Republic, Germany, Romania and Bulgaria). The report of the European Commission of 18 April 2011 included a list of shortcomings of the Directive that the Commission was able to identify (inter alia, reducing categories of data to be retained or the group of authorities granted access to the retained data).[16] In the Report, the Commission announced the revision of the Directive aiming to address its shortcomings[17] without, however, questioning the data retention obligation itself. This approach was met with the criticism of the European Data Protection Supervisor who called, inter alia, for a consideration of the introduction of measures considered less privacy-intrusive, e.g. the method of data preservation (the so-called 'quick freeze').[18]

The Evaluation Report also presented the statistical data on data requests for either 2008 and/or 2009—over 2 million data requests were submitted annually, differing from less than 100 per year in Cyprus to over 1 million in Poland.[19] (On more recent data for Poland, in 2016 there were 1 million, 147,000 of telecommunications data requests and approximately 23,000 Internet data requests.)[20] It is worth pointing out that no common methodology was applied at the EU level to calculate the data retained and the ways of presenting them. Thus, the analysis of Evaluation Report clearly reveals how burdensome it is to compare this kind of data.

---

[16]Cf. *European Commission Report from the Commission to the Council and the European Parliament. Evaluation report on the Data Retention Directive (Directive 2006/24/EC)*, pp. 30–33. https://eur-lex.europa.eu/legal-content/EN/TXT/PDF/?uri=CELEX:52011DC0225&from=EN.

[17]Cf. *European Commission Report from the Commission to the Council and the European Parliament. Evaluation report on the Data Retention Directive (Directive 2006/24/EC)*, pp. 30–33. https://eur-lex.europa.eu/legal-content/EN/TXT/PDF/?uri=CELEX:52011DC0225&from=EN, pp. 32–33.

[18]Cf. *Opinion of the European Data Protection Supervisor on the Evaluation report from the Commission to the Council and the European Parliament on the Data Retention Directive (Directive 2006/24/EC)*, OJ C 279/1, 23.9.2011, p. 10, 14. https://eur-lex.europa.eu/legal-content/EN/TXT/?uri=celex%3A52011XX0923%2801%29.

[19]Cf. Cf. *Opinion of the European Data Protection Supervisor on the Evaluation report from the Commission to the Council and the European Parliament on the Data Retention Directive (Directive 2006/24/EC)*, OJ C 279/1, 23.9.2011, p. 21. https://eur-lex.europa.eu/legal-content/EN/TXT/?uri=celex%3A52011XX0923%2801%29.

[20]Cf. The parliamentary document of 30 June 2017, No. 543, 9th Term of Office of the Senate. https://www.senat.gov.pl/download/gfx/senat/pl/senatdruki/8641/druk/543.pdf.

On 6 July 2006, Ireland challenged the Directive 2006/24/EC before the Court of Justice and sought its annulment based on its adoption on the wrong legal basis. Ireland maintained that the main or predominant purpose of the Directive was to facilitate the investigation, detection and prosecution of serious crimes, including terrorism, and thus the only permissible legal base for the measures contained in the Directive was the third pillar.[21] The opinion of Advocate General Bot supported the choice of the legal basis.[22] Advocate General Bot emphasised that during the proceedings no party questioned the rationale of the obligation to retain data imposed on providers of electronic communications and he supported this approach.[23] The Court ruled against Ireland, stressing the state's very narrow challenge of the Directive. In its application to the Court, Ireland did not contest the issue of possible infringements of fundamental rights resulting from the Directive.[24] It seems that the Court accepted the legal ground chosen by the Commission mostly because the Directive 2006/24 did not regulate the access of state authorities to the retained data and concentrated solely on the obligation of service providers to retain data.[25]

3 Timeline of Judgments Regarding the Directive 2006/24/EC

The most characteristic circumstance for the Directive 2006/24/EC is a significant number of judgments of European constitutional courts concerning the national legislation that implemented Directive 2006/24/EC, as well as the CJEU judgments. The following timeline can be formulated:

[21]Cf. Summary of the complaint, OJ C 237/5, 30.9.2006. http://eur-lex.europa.eu/legal-content/en/TXT/PDF/?uri=uriserv%3AOJ.C_.2006.237.01.0005.01.ENG.

[22]Cf. *Opinion of Advocate General Bot delivered on 14 October 2006 Case C-301/06 Ireland v. European Parliament, Council of the European Union*. http://curia.europa.eu/juris/document/document.jsf?text=&docid=66649&pageIndex=0&doclang=EN&mode=req&dir=&occ=first&part=1&cid=911303.

[23]Cf. *Opinion of Advocate General Bot delivered on 14 October 2006 Case C-301/06 Ireland v. European Parliament, Council of the European Union*, § 92. http://curia.europa.eu/juris/document/document.jsf?text=&docid=66649&pageIndex=0&doclang=EN&mode=req&dir=&occ=first&part=1&cid=911303.

[24]Cf. § 57 of the judgment of the Court of 10 February 2009, *Ireland v. European Parliament*, Council of the European Union (C-301/06). http://curia.europa.eu/juris/document/document.jsf?text=&docid=72843&pageIndex=0&doclang=EN&mode=req&dir=&occ=first&part=1&cid=911303.

[25]Cf. §§ 83–86 of the judgment of the Court of 10 February 2009, *Ireland v. European Parliament*, Council of the European Union (C-301/06). http://curia.europa.eu/juris/document/document.jsf?text=&docid=72843&pageIndex=0&doclang=EN&mode=req&dir=&occ=first&part=1&cid=911303.

- 11 March 2008, the German Federal Constitutional Court, ref. No. 1 BvR 256/08, preliminary ruling;
- 28 October 2008, the German Federal Constitutional Court, ref. No. 1 BvR 256/08, second preliminary ruling;
- 11 December 2008, the Supreme Administrative Court of the Republic of Bulgaria, ref. No. 13627;
- 10 February 2009, the Court of Justice, *Ireland v. European Parliament*, Council of the European Union, ref. No. C-301/06, action for annulment of Directive dismissed;
- 8 October 2009, Romanian Constitutional Court, ref. No. 1258;
- 4 February 2010, the Court of Justice, *Commission v. Sweden*, failure to implement Directive 2006/24/EC, ref. No. C-185/09;
- 2 March 2010, the German Federal Constitutional Court, ref. Nos. 1 BvR 256/08, 1 BvR 263/08, 1 BvR 586/08;
- 5 May 2010, the High Court of Ireland, *Digital Rights Ireland Limited v. Minister for Communications, Marine and Natural Resources et al.*, granting motion for a preliminary question to the Court of Justice, ref. No. 2006 3785 P [2010] IEHC 221;
- 29 July 2010, the Court of Justice, *Commission v. Austria*, failure to implement Directive 2006/24/EC, ref. No. C-185/09;
- 1 February 2011, the Supreme Court of Cyprus, ref. Nos. 65/2009, 78/2009, 82/2009 and 15/2010-22/2010;
- 22 March 2011, the Czech Constitutional Court, ref. No. Pl. ÚS 24/2011;
- 28 November 2012, the Austrian Constitutional Court, ref. No. G-47/2012-49 et al., submission to the Court of Justice for a preliminary ruling;
- 30 May 2013, the Court of Justice, ref. No. C-270/11, penal sum on Sweden for lack of implementation of Directive;
- 8 April 2014, the Court of Justice, ref. Noa. C-293/12 and C-594/12, *Digital Rights Ireland Ltd, etc.*
- 23 April 2014, the Constitutional Court of the Slovak Republic, ref. No. 10/2014-29, preliminary ruling to suspend domestic law on data retention;
- 27 June 2014, the Austrian Constitutional Court, ref. No. G 47/2012;
- 3 July 2014, the Constitutional Court of Slovenia, ref. No. U-I-65/13;
- 8 July 2014, Romanian Constitutional Court, ref. No. 440;
- 30 July 2014, the Constitutional Tribunal of the Republic of Poland, ref. No. K 23/11;
- 12 March 2015, the Constitutional Court of Bulgaria, ref. No. 8/2014;
- 29 April 2015, Constitutional Court of the Slovak Republic, ref. No. PL. ÚS 10/2014;
- 11 June 2015, the Constitutional Court of Belgium, ref. No. 84/2015;
- 27 August 2015, the Constitutional Court of Portugal, ref. No. 403/15;
- 21 December 2016, the Court of Justice, ref. Nos. C-203/15 and C-698/15, *Tele2 Sverige AB et al.*;
- 3 May 2018, the Court of Justice, Opinion of Advocate General Saugmandsgaard Øe in the case C-207/16.

4 Privacy and Secrecy of Communication in the Digital Age

The constitutions of Member States as well as the Charter of Fundamental Rights and the European Convention do not contain explicit guarantees of privacy, secrecy of communication, and informational autonomy in the digital sphere. In most EU Member States there are constitutional provisions guaranteeing the right to privacy protection, freedom of communication or so-called information autonomy. The constitutions of the EU Member States, however, do not provide for explicit protection of individuals in the digital sphere nor their communication by electronic means (telephone, e-mail etc.), or even more what type of information are embraced by constitutional freedom of communication. With few exceptions on electronic communication (e.g. Article 10 of the Basic Law of the Federal Republic of Germany providing for the protection of telecommunications secrecy, Article 35 of the Constitution of Portugal relating to the use of information technology to process personal data, Article 37 of the Constitution of Slovenian Republic guaranteeing secrecy), correspondence and communication by other means, there are no constitutional guarantees for the protection of telecommunications metadata in the form of so-called traffic and location data within the meaning of the Directive and national provisions implementing it. Article 8 ECHR and Articles 7 and 8 of the Charter also provide for the legal protection of privacy and the confidentiality of correspondence as well as protection of personal data. There do not determine, however, whether this protection covers the sphere of digital communications, including traffic and location data.

In the judicial decisions that were the subject of our analysis—both national courts, the ECtHR and the CJEU unanimously determined that communication through new communication channels is also protected by these fundamental rights standards. Nevertheless, it is widely accepted by the referred courts that communication through new communication channels, as well as using the Internet, is subjected to constitutional protection. These new channels of communication are only a form—or rather—a new reflection, of traditional correspondence. They must, therefore, be subject to the same protection as letter correspondence or interpersonal communication (face-to-face communication). Therefore, the same constitutional guarantees as for traditional correspondence of the analogue era apply to communication by new technologies.

However, the problem arose with the assessment of whether the interference with privacy, information autonomy or the secret of communication was data retention itself and the access to metadata, so-called traffic and location data, by public authorities. These data do not concern the content of the messages transmitted, but only the circumstances related to the process of communication.

Referring to the established case law of the ECHR, some constitutional courts also considered that although a legal obligation to retain telecommunication metadata does not include the contents of conversations and transmitted messages, such metadata might allow to determine the circumstances of the communication, including its addressee and time of communication. That data, taken as a whole, allows very precise conclusions to be drawn concerning the private lives of the persons whose data has been retained, such as everyday habits, permanent or temporary places of residence, daily or other movements, the activities carried out, social relationships of those persons and social environments frequented by them.

The national constitutional courts and the CJEU pointed out that the mere retention of metadata is by itself a severe interference with privacy or secrecy of communication. If the content of conversations or messages transmitted were to be retained, it would lead to the violation of the essence of the right to privacy protection, which is unacceptable.

5 Constitutional Requirements: Towards a Common European Standard

Interference with privacy, secrecy of communication or informational autonomy is caused both by the retention of telecommunication data and subsequent access thereto by competent state authorities. Although the data retention mechanism itself does not allow the detection of all criminal activities, in many cases it becomes an effective means of combating some threats to public security, including organised crime and terrorism as well as cybercrime. Since the obtaining and processing of telecommunications data (stored by telecommunication operators) are carried out implicitly, it is necessary to introduce strong and precise procedural guarantees to protect individuals against abuse of power or unauthorised use of data. The requirements formulated by national constitutional courts and the CJEU concerned the data retention and gaining access to the data by competent state bodies.

5.1 Data Retention

Under the Directive 2006/24/EC, providers of publicly available electronic communications services or of public communications networks are obliged to retain the data necessary to trace and identify the source of communication and its destination, to identify the date, time, duration and type of a communication, to identify users' communication equipment, and to identify the location of mobile communication equipment, data which consist of, inter alia, the name and address of the subscriber or registered user, the calling telephone number, the number called and an IP address for Internet services. It did not apply to the content of electronic communications, including information consulted using an electronic communications network. These data must be retained—regardless of type—between a minimum of six months and a maximum of 24 months. The national legislatures' duty was to determine the retention period in their respective country.

The Directive contained many shortcomings such as ambiguity of its provisions and lack of appropriate procedural guarantees. This was confirmed by the precedent judgment in the DRI case[26] declaring the entire directive null and void. The imperfections of the directive itself were not only mechanically transferred but in many cases, they were overstretched and deepened, in the Member States legislation.[27]

The CJEU, in its two rulings,[28] and European constitutional courts, generally, did not undermine the data retention mechanism as a whole. The Romanian court drew attention to the systemic disadvantages of the data retention mechanism. It admitted that there is an urgent need to ensure adequate and efficient legal tools to combat terrorism and serious crime. However, bulk data collection of all citizens, regardless of their involvement in criminal activity, "is likely to overturn the presumption of innocence."[29] The Slovak court, however, took a hawkish position among the others. When assessing the proportionality of the mechanism, it pointed out that the legislator should have considered the introduction of the "quick freeze", while the Constitutional Court of Germany referring to the data freezing model concluded that the "data freezing" does not guarantee comparable effectiveness in combating serious crimes and terrorism to an ongoing data retention as regulated in the directive and national legislation.[30]

Several requirements for lawmakers, which must be met in order for data retention to be regarded as a proportional interference in privacy, were formulated by the CJEU and national constitutional courts. These are as follows:

First, the necessary, and at the same time the initial condition for the constitutionality of such intrusive interference with privacy and secrecy of communication, is the separation of the retention mechanism (done by private operators) from access to retained data (by state authorities).[31]

Second, a general obligation to store all telecommunications metadata by private entities is permissible only for a strictly specified important purpose of public

[26]Cf. the CJEU judgment of 8 April 2014, ref. No. C-293/12 and C-594/12, *Digital Rights Ireland et al.*

[27]Cf. judgment of the Constitutional Court of Bulgaria of 12 March 2015, case No. 8/2015, § 6.

[28]Cf. judgments of the CJEU of 8 April 2014, ref. Nos. C-293/12 and C-594/12; 21 December 2016, C 203/15 and C 698/15 (*Tele2*).

[29]Cf. Decision of the Constitutional Court of Romania of 8 October 2009, ref. No. 1.258.

[30]Cf. judgment of the Federal Constitutional Court of Germany of 2 March 2010, ref. No. 1 BvR 256/08, § 203.

[31]Cf. judgment of the Federal Constitutional Court of Germany of 2 March 2010, ref. No. 1 BvR 256/08.

interest (combating serious crime and threats to national security). They must be precisely specified by law[32] or even by statute issued by the parliament.[33]

Third, the most important are reasons for which state authorities can gain access to particular retained data from the pool of all stored telecommunications metadata. The first type of permission to gain access refers to cases of criminal proceedings in which there occurs a justified suspicion of commitment of a serious crime. The second type of permission to gain access is related to threat-prevention—as such it could be outstretched by state authorities, therefore some courts limited it only to cases of defence against threats to life, health or freedom of a person, survival or security of a state, as well as defence against an ordinary threat.[34] The third type of granting access has to do with attempts to grant an unrestricted access to a particular type of state authorities—mostly intelligence or counterintelligence services. It is important that no state authority should be granted unrestricted access; rather, a test shall be applied and the access granted based on the case-by-case fulfilment of (the first two above mentioned) general requirements.[35]

Fourth, the retention period should not be excessively long, because it causes the feeling of being under constant observation. The issue of the retention period was extensively discussed by the CJEU and Slovenian Constitutional Court. The CJEU did not contest the maximum retention period prescribed by the Directive but pointed out that to protect fundamental rights of individuals, it is necessary to establish an objective criteria on the basis of which metadata will not be stored for longer than absolutely necessary.[36] In addition, it is reasonable to vary the retention period depending on what kind of data are retained, the persons concerned and possible usefulness of the data in relation to the assumed objective.[37]

In some Member States, the obligation to retain telecommunications data was set to the minimum period of 6 months required by the Directive (Germany), while in others (Poland) it was up to 24 months. Some national courts directly pointed out that the 6-month retention period is the maximum justified under the proportionality principle—it seems to stem from the judgments of German, Slovenian, and Bulgarian constitutional courts. While the German court has highlighted this issue,

---

[32]Cf. judgment of the Supreme Administrative Court of the Republic of Bulgaria of 11 December 2008, ref. No. 13627; judgment of the Constitutional Court of Czech Republic of 22 March 2011, ref. No. Pl. ÚS 24/10, § 47.

[33]Cf. judgment of the Constitutional Tribunal of the Republic of Poland of 30 June 2014, ref. No. K 23/11, § 5.3.

[34]Cf. judgment of the Federal Constitutional Court of Germany of 2 March 2010, ref. No. BVerfGE 125, 260, p. 330.

[35]Cf. judgment of Federal Constitutional Court of Germany of 2 March 2010, ref. No. BVerfGE 125, 260, p. 331–332.

[36]Cf. the CJEU judgment of 8 April 2014, ref. Nos. C-293/12 and C-594/12, *Digital Rights Ireland et al*, § 64; see also: the judgment of Constitutional Court of Belgium of 11 June 2015, ref. No 84/2015, § B.10.1–10.4.

[37]Cf. the CJEU judgment of 8 April 2014, ref. No. C-293/12 and C-594/12, *Digital Rights Ireland et al.*, § 63.

the Slovenian court articulated it very clearly. Slovenian legislature diversified the retention period predicting that data regarding publicly accessible phone services must be retained for 14 months and all other data—for eight months. However, the reasons of such differentiation were not clear. As it had not been proved that periods shorter than 14 and eight months would be insufficient to achieve the goals set, the court considered the prescribed periods disproportionate and unnecessary. Similarly, the length of the retention period was criticised by the Bulgarian Constitutional Court. Bulgarian legislation provided for a 12-month data storage. According to the court, this is "disproportionately long and beyond the necessary period for achieving the defined targets."[38] The 12-month retention period leads to the risk of profiling persons and the use of data for unauthorised purposes.

The argumentation of the Polish Constitutional Court is worth noting here. Although it did not rule on the provisions regulating obligation of data retention, it pointed out in *obiter dictum* that the 12-month data retention[39] period provided for in the Polish legislation is very long; the court also did not preclude that it may be excessive. This observation is justified in the light of the information delivered by the regulatory body, according to which approximately 49% instances of data disclosure took place within the first two months of retention, and approximately 69% within the first four months. A certain increase was observed in the twelfth month (up to 8.37% of the total number of instances), which may result from the delay on the part of intelligence and police services.

Six, it is mandatory to ensure the security of the stored data. As the German court explained, an obligation of private entities to retain telecommunications data at their expense poses a threat. These entities, especially small entrepreneurs, operate on market principles and under cost pressure. This can adversely affect data security. Therefore, it is necessary to introduce strict technical and software standards as well as procedural guarantees so that the data does not fall into the hands of unauthorised third persons. Legal provisions should require such standard of guarantees that reflects the current scientific knowledge in that regard, considering the results of the most recent research. A similar position was taken by the Czech[40] and Polish[41] court.

---

[38]Cf. judgment of Bulgarian Constitutional Court of 12 March 2015, ref. No. 8/2015; § 6.

[39]Until 2013, there was a 24-month data retention period in Poland.

[40]Cf. judgment of Constitutional Court of Czech Republic of 22 March 2011, ref. No Pl. ÚS 24/10; §§ 50–51.

[41]Cf. judgment of Constitutional Tribunal of Republic of Poland of 30 June 2014, ref. No K 23/11, § 5.3.

5.2 Access to the Retained Data

The Directive 2006/24/EC stipulated that the retained data are available for the "investigation, detection and prosecution of serious crime, as defined by each Member State in its national law." Thus, the objective of the directive is rather to contribute to the fight against serious crime and, ultimately, to public security, than to harmonise the obligations of telecommunications service providers to ensure the proper functioning of the internal market. As the CJEU in the DRI ruling observed, the fight against international terrorism to maintain international peace and security constitutes an objective of general interest.[42] The same is true in combating serious crime to ensure public security. The directive did not raise any doubts as to the purpose of accessing the retained data, as the objective could justify interference with privacy and the right to personal data protection guaranteed in the Charter.

While the Directive defined the objective of granting access to the retained data quite clearly—"combating serious crime"—Member States defined it differently in their legislation. Access to metadata to combat serious crime has not always been so restricted. Bearing in mind the usefulness of the data in the operational work of the police and secret services, the access was also often allowed to combat common crimes or even for analytical activities of state authorities. Thus, the issues of specifying *serious criminal offences* and providing access to the retained data for other purposes was one of the key points before, inter alia, Romanian, Czech, Polish, Slovak and Bulgarian constitutional courts.

Polish law authorised several police services to access the retained data to prevent and detect offences or fiscal crimes and sometimes violations of non-criminal law. In turn, civil and military counterintelligence could to request the said data to perform all their statutory tasks, even those involving analyses and planning. Polish Constitutional Tribunal stressed that it is not permissible to make these data available for purposes other than preventing and combating serious crimes and threats to legally protected values,[43] which must be precisely defined by law. The court did not explain, however, what criteria should be met for a crime to be considered *serious*. Likewise, the Slovak Tribunal pointed out that it was unacceptable to provide metadata in combating common crimes. "It is the task of the legislator to determine precisely where the public interest overrides the right to privacy protection, taking into account i.e. gravity of crimes".[44] In case of less serious crimes, less intrusive measures shall be available to national authorities.

The Romanian Constitutional Court explained in its 2009 ruling that according to the domestic legislation on data retention, retained data could made be available not

[42]Cf. the CJEU judgment of 8 April 2014, ref. No. C-293/12 and C-594/12, *Digital Rights Ireland et al.*, § 41 and cited case law.

[43]Cf. judgment of Constitutional Tribunal of Republic of Poland of 30 June 2014, ref. No. K 23/11, § 5.3.

[44]Cf. judgment of the Constitutional Court of the Slovak Republic of 29 April 2015, ref. No. PL. ÚS 10/2014, § 138.

only for combating serious crimes and terrorism but also for criminal prevention. This clearly named an additional purpose of such a mass surveillance measure that was not listed in the Directive. However, this court was not in favour of such a broad purpose because it stated that such mass surveillance sufficed to generate legitimate suspicion in the conscience of the public of lacking respect for its intimacy and of abuses.

In the judgment of the Bulgarian Constitutional Court an attempt was made at defining a *serious crime*. Criminal offenses punishable by an imprisonment of more than five years and life imprisonment were considered as such.[45] As it was emphasised, the principle of proportionality caused that it is not enough to limit the cases of access to data retained to combat serious crimes. There must be a reasonable suspicion of committing such crime.[46]

Among procedural requirements for providing access to metadata, the most important is a review carried out by a court or by an independent administrative body.[47] Neither the Directive nor national legislation in most Member States implementing it stipulate the review mechanism. The approach of constitutional courts and the CJEU in this respect seems convergent. Independent judicial or administrative supervision over each case of obtaining data is a *minimum minimorum*. Some courts would also accept body of the parliament (or of other elected authority).[48] The decision of a court or of an administrative body seeks to limit access to the data and their use to what is strictly necessary in attaining the objective pursued and which intervenes following a reasoned request of those authorities submitted within the framework of procedures of prevention, detection or criminal prosecutions.[49]

Against this background, the approach of the Polish Constitutional Court is significant. Although the lack of independent review was the sole ground for unconstitutionality of domestic provisions, the court took a less restrictive position than other constitutional courts and the CJEU. It did not demand introduction of prior review (*ex ante*). The court stated that the scope and nature of such review may vary depending on the type of telecommunications data that is obtained by the services, as well as the specificity of the activities of particular services and the situations in which these data are obtained. According to the court, it is not excluded to introduce—even as a rule—a mechanism of an *ex post* review. A prior review,

---

[45]Cf. judgment of Constitutional Court of Bulgaria of 12 March 2015, case No. 8/2015, § 3.

[46]Cf. judgment of Constitutional Court of Czech Republic of 22 March 2011, ref. No. Pl. ÚS 24/10, § 47.

[47]The Portuguese Constitutional Court leans towards the idea that it is necessary to introduce control exercised by the judge not by the administrative body, although it is composed of judges. Cf. judgment of Constitutional Court of Portugal 27 of August of 2015, ref. No. 403/2015.

[48]See judgment of Federal Constitutional Court of Germany of 2 March 2010, ref. No. BVerfGE 125, 260, p. 338.

[49]Cf. judgment of the CJEU of 8 April 2014, ref. No. C-293/12 and C-594/12, *Digital Rights Ireland et al.*, § 62.

however, should be introduced in some cases, particularly where there is no need for urgent operational activities.

As part of the proportionality assessment, the German, Czech and Polish courts pointed out that it is required to ensure transparency of using telecommunication data by police and intelligence services.[50] First, it is manifested in obligation imposed on public authorities to inform the person subjected to surveillance about the fact that data concerning them have been obtained. The requirement of notification may be exempted from only by an exception (e.g. in cases of using by mistake, not to give an unnecessary effect of being prosecuted in such a case). Second, as the Polish Constitutional Court has extensively addressed, it is necessary to provide the public with aggregate statistical data about the number of data requests. Additionally, to effectively and diligently fulfil the obligation to report, the legislator should determine a common and unilateral methodology for preparing statistics, applied by all entities, which would guarantee the lack of ambiguity and which would facilitate the comparability of data disclosed to public, even with regard to previous years.[51] Third, if the person subjected to surveillance was not able to challenge those materials in a court proceeding, there should exist a court control mechanism of how obtained materials were used by state authorities.[52]

Other important standards concern prohibition of granting access by operators to state authorities on an "account basis" with an access to all data, but rather providing them on strictly limited basis. Data that a state authority obtained should not be further forwarded without limits, but the legislator should rather limit it to a similar standard. Data that were accessed should then be subject to destroying them in a manner prescribed in law.

The European legislator stipulated that access to the retained data is available to competent national authority. In some Member States, that competence was given to officers of various services such as the police, military police or fiscal police. The Bulgarian court pointed out: "it is imperative for the legitimate subject to have the competence to detect and investigate serious crimes explicitly assigned to him by law, i.e., powers relating to the legitimate aim pursued by the law."[53]

[50] Cf. judgment of the ECtHR of 25 June 2013, *Youth Initiative for Human Rights v. Serbia*, ref. No. 48135/06.

[51] Cf. judgment of Constitutional Tribunal of Republic of Poland of 30 June 2014, ref. No. K 23/11, § 5.2.6.

[52] Cf. judgment of Federal Constitutional Court of Germany of 2 March 2010, ref. No. BVerfGE 125, 260, p. 339.

[53] Cf. judgment of Constitutional Court of Bulgaria of 12 March 2015, ref. No. 8/2015, § 4.

6 Material and Institutional Basis for a Common European Standard

Within such a comparative analysis of judgments of European constitutional courts as well as of the CJEU, a particular emphasis should be put on the complex system of European and national courts, the legal systems of the EU and its Member States, and the international human rights standards. This context must understand and correctly evaluate the possible common European standards, as well as to determine their potential role in constitutional review procedures. Thus, we would like to focus on common material as well as institutional basis that influenced particular judgments.

The dialogue presented by European constitutional courts is based on two dimensions. The first one was a material one, and it is based on common (universal) standards. It is a well-known issue as a common critical approach towards data retention mechanism was common within the EU. Second dimension is an institutional one. It is much more interesting. Although it might have seemed so obvious that this crucial dimension might have been omitted.

The most obvious trail when it comes to establishing the common material fundaments of dialogue of constitutional courts leads to jurisprudence of the European Court of Human Rights. It had an influence on cases pending before constitutional courts[54] and before the CJEU. All the constitutional courts that ruled in this matter are courts of the EU members, and those countries at the same time belong to the legal system of the Council of Europe which is firmly based on the ECHR and jurisprudence of the ECtHR. This clearly constitutes a firm common standard-setting layer for cooperation of those courts. Thus, the judgments of constitutional courts must start a dialogue with the ECtHR as those constitutional courts must consider the ECHR (as well as jurisprudence of the ECtHR that sets

[54]Cf. The Romanian Constitutional Court cited the following judgments of the ECtHR: *Klass and others v. Germany*, 1978; *Dumitru Popescu v. Romania*, 2007; *Rotaru v. Romania*, 2000; *Sunday Times v. The United Kingdom*, 1979; *Prince Hans-Adam II of Liechtenstein against Germany*, 2001. The Constitutional Court of Cyprus cited following judgments of the ECtHR: *Klass and others v. Germany*, 1978; *Malone v. The United Kingdom*, 1984; *Kruslin v. France*, 1990. The High Court of Ireland cited following judgments of the ECtHR: *Niemietz v. Germany*, 1992; *Société Colas Est and Others* v. France, 2002; *Klass and others v. Germany*; *Copland v. United Kingdom*, 2007. The Czech Constitutional Court cited following judgments of the ECtHR: *Malone v. The United Kingdom*, 1984; *Niemietz v. Germany*, 1992; *Klass and others v. Germany*, 1978; *Leander v. Sweden*, 1987; *Kruslin v. France*, 1990; *Kopp v. Switzerland*, 1998; *P.G. and J.H. v. the United Kingdom*, 2001; *Amman v. Switzerland*, 2000; *S. and Marper v. the United Kingdom*, 2008; *Rotaru v. Romania*, 2000; *Hassan and Tchaouch v. Bulgaria*, 2000; *Camenzind v. Switzerland*, 1997. The Slovenian Constitutional Court cited following judgments of the ECtHR: *Leander v. Sweden*, 1987; *Amann v. Switzerland*, 2000; *Kopp v. Switzerland*, 1998; *Handyside v. UK*, 1976; S. and *Marper v. UK*, 2008. The Bulgarian Constitutional Court cited the following judgments of the ECtHR: *S. and Marper v. the United Kingdom*, 2008; *Malone v. UK*, 1984; *Weber and Saravia v. Germany*, 2006; *Amman v. Switzerland*, 2000; *Association for European Integration and Human Rights and Ekimdzhiev v. Bulgaria*, 2008.

current understanding of ECHR). Moreover, because all individuals under ECHR have the right to apply for legal protection to the Strasbourg court, there was always space for those individuals to seek legal protection by the Strasbourg court (in case domestic constitutional courts did not offer standard of human rights protection equivalent to standards arising from ECHR or if constitutional courts in other EU countries would provide much higher degree of protection against data retention mechanism). All those circumstances meant that constitutional courts must come into dialogue with the ECtHR and its jurisprudence at the earliest possible moment to avoid a situation in which standards set by them would be overruled by the ECtHR. Consequently, all the constitutional courts must come into dialogue with each other to verify whether one of the other constitutional courts did not raise standards much higher, as it posed a risk that individuals from other jurisdictions would undertake legal challenges in the Strasbourg court to obtain higher standards than those set by their own constitutional court (and equal with standards set by a particularly progressive constitutional court).

One should also consider that such a high standard for almost all the constitutional courts as well as for the CJEU was already set in 2010 by the German Constitutional Court.[55] Standards set by the German court were—more or less openly—recognised by other constitutional courts.

An analysis of the judgments of constitutional courts clearly shows an unintentional influence that the CJEU 2009 ruling had on constitutional courts. It was the CJEU 2009 ruling that gave the constitutional courts an area which they could subject to constitutional review on their own.[56] The constitutional courts were not eager to review the EU legal acts or the idea of data retention. Because the CJEU's interpretation in the 2009 ruling was based on a very narrow scope of the Directive, the courts received a confirmation that the national implementing measures regulated much more than the Directive required, and all those additional (i.e. ancillary) areas were not covered by the scope of the EU law (with the CJEU having the competence to review it). Thus, the constitutional courts were able to review those added areas of national implementing measures that were outside the

[55]Other constitutional courts did not only quote the judgment on data retention. The Czech Constitutional Court referred also to the following rulings: of 15 December 1983, ref. no BVerfGE 65, 1 (*Volkszählungsurteil*)ł of 4 April 2006, ref. no BVerfGE 115, 320 (*Rasterfahndungurteil II*); of 27 July 2005, ref. no BVerfGE 113, 348 (*Vorbeugende Telekommunikationsüberwachung*); of 27 February 2008, ref. no BVerfGE 120, 274 (*Grundrecht auf Computerschutz*). The Slovenian Constitutional Court cited the 2010 judgment on data retention. The Romanian Constitutional Court also cited the German ruling with a summary and demonstrated a similar approach towards the Czech and Bulgarian judgments. The Bulgarian Constitutional Court cited the judgment from 2nd March 2010.

[56]Cf. The Constitutional Court of Cyprus based its reasoning on the following judgment of CJEU: *Ireland v. European Parliament and Council of the European Union*, ref. no C-301/06. The High Court of Ireland based part of its reasoning on *Ireland v. European Parliament and Council of the European Union* as it refrained from establishing whether the legal basis to adopt the Directive 2006/24/EC had been invalid, and followed the CJEU on that matter. The High Court of Ireland extensively cited case law of the CJEU and used it as the basis for its reasoning.

scope of the Directive (and they did). Simultaneously, the CJEU took those ancillary activities into consideration in its 2014 ruling and decided that the standards guaranteed at the level of the Directive should apply to those areas as well. This forms an interesting case because the CJEU referred to standards developed by constitutional courts concerning those additional areas before 2014 and applied them directly to the Directive. This poses another turn in this court dialogue, because even the reasoning used by the group of courts that preferred not to cooperate with the CJEU at all was considered as the CJEU applied their standards.

Despite the lack of a mechanism for constitutional courts to formally cooperate with the ECtHR as well as with other constitutional courts, after analysis of those judgments we could diagnose in those judgments the following ways of cross-influence: (a) common standard of constitutional control, which was the ECHR; (b) authority of arguments; (c) taking arguments of particular constitutional courts by the CJEU as its own; (d) 2014 *Digital Rights Ireland* ruling of the CJEU as a confirmation of common standards of constitutional courts and of the CJEU.

Smoothly moving forward towards it is worth further analysis how we did end up with the development described in letter d) in the last paragraph. Our research leads us to the conclusion that it was a result of common institutional platform that those courts started making usage of.

Our findings show that the crucial role could have played the new legal status of the Charter of Fundamental Rights of the European Union (Charter). The Data Retention Directive as well as national implementing measures were adopted long before the Charter became the EU primary law, but the 2014 judicial review of the CJEU happened already with the new legal status of the Charter. The Charter contains in Article 52 section 3 a 'transfer clause'[57] that ensures the same meaning and scope of rights as guaranteed by the European Convention of Human Rights. It also contains a clause that obliges to conform constitutional traditions of the EU Member States while interpreting rights from the Charter. One of the aims of this transfer clause was to ensure the convergence of judiciary of the CJEU with national constitutional courts as well as with the ECtHR. Recent judgments of the CJEU show that it aims to use the transfer clause either by directly referring to it[58] or by referring to its idea that the interpretation given to a particular provision of the Charter shall safeguard a level of protection which does not fall below the level of protection established in particular corresponding provision of the ECHR, as interpreted by the European Court of Human Rights.[59] Thus, the transfer clause contained in the Charter starts to be applied as an effective mechanism for strengthening judicial dialogue.

Another element of institutionalising dialogue of constitutional courts was the well-established mechanism of preliminary questions to the CJEU. Another

[57]Cf. Terhechte (2015), p. 833.

[58]Cf. Judgment of the CJEU of 29 July 2019, Ref. No C-38/18, Gambino and Hyka, § 39.

[59]Cf. Judgment of the CJEU of 19 November 2019, Ref. No C-585/18, C-624/18 and C-625/18, *A. K. v Krajowa Rada Sądownictwa, and CP and DO v Sąd Najwyższy,* § 118.

approach that was taken as model of cooperation is based on the identification of direct cooperation between two constitutional courts and the CJEU. In an ideal world, this would be the only approach that constitutional courts would take, because the legal system of the European Union was founded on the principle of primacy of the EU law. Member States are obliged to comply with the primary and secondary legislation of the European Union. From the EU's perspective, all the legal measures in Member States should be compliant with EU law (i.e. including the Directive 2006/24/EC). This stands in a clear conflict with the idea of the constitution as the supreme legal act of every Member State. It can be bypassed, thanks to the concept of the so-called constitutional monism, where international law and legal acts adopted by an international organisation form an inherent part of the state's constitutional order. Nevertheless, once an EU legal act seems to contain provisions that could be declared unconstitutional, managing this lack of compliance becomes complicated. One procedural measure seems to fit well to resolve those matters. Under Article 267 of the Treaty on the Functioning of the European Union, every court in the European Union (i.e. also constitutional courts) is entitled to refer a case for a preliminary ruling to the Court of Justice of the European Union. Prerequisite for such a referral is that it should concern the interpretation (or validity) of the EU law.

Referring a matter to the CJEU most probably have not been considered as a golden mean from the perspective of any European constitutional court. Foremost, the CJEU has different legal grounds on the basis of which it rules—it is not the constitution of a particular Member State, but rather the EU treaties that are applied to assess another piece of EU legislation. Most recently, to those legal grounds for the CJEU belongs also the Charter of Fundamental Rights. Since the adoption of the EU Charter of Fundamental Rights, one can observe the convergence of fundamental rights protected directly at the level of EU institutions with those guaranteed by the constitutions of the Member States. However, the CJEU's docket remains filled with administrative cases, so if we consider "standard docket cases" of CJEU then human rights issues may occur sporadically. This means that the CJEU is not a full-fledged human rights court. This might have been another reason that prevented other constitutional courts (than the Irish and Austrian) from referring matters to the CJEU.

7 Final Remarks

The cooperation of constitutional courts with the CJEU played a crucial role for their national legal systems. This is because the CJEU did not quash the data retention mechanism itself, but rather questioned the EU framework within which it was formed and only quashed the Directive with the reasoning that its regulation went too far. But the CJEU did not question the idea of data retention mechanism at all, so it could be re-introduced. Thus, the governments could have argued that the implementing measures should nevertheless remain in force (as e.g. happened in the Belgian case). Yet, the constitutional courts verified the national legislative frameworks in this regard and enabled appropriate improvement of the legal system by quashing those national measures (that was already upheld). In that sense, the constitutional courts guaranteed a unilateral standard of protection of fundamental rights in their own national jurisdictions.

A judicature analysis of European constitutional courts can be positively reviewed. The standards developed by the judiciary are high. Both the EU as well as national legislatures struggle with their proper introduction back into legislation at the EU as well as at national level. Those standards developed by the judiciary might even at the end bring a result abolishing a wide re-introduction of data retention mechanisms.

After the judgment in the case of *Digital Rights Ireland*, which annulled Data Retention Directive, the European Union has not adopted any other legal act regulating rules and procedure of retaining telecommunications data. One shall not expect that such a legal act is to be adopted soon. This did not end of course the ongoing procedures for compliance assessment of using secret surveillance procedures with human rights standards in few Member States. The perspective on decision-making has changed. Once more, domestic constitutional courts, the CJUE and the ECHR need to take responsibility. Jurisprudence of CJUE and ECHR give a chance to develop standards, simultaneously for all Member States of the Council of Europe. After 2018, both courts seek responses towards new challenges,[60] but it generally follows present judiciary paths. This approach should be seen in a positive way in the context of effectiveness of protecting freedom of communications as a human right.[61]

In conclusion, it is worth noting a particularly new context for our research. Under circumstances of a global pandemic, which the whole world copes with from the beginning of 2020, occurred a new threat from using more or less openly forms of collecting and using telecommunication data of citizens by states. Measures that initially aimed at counteracting terrorism and most severe crimes started to be adopted for the sake of tracking patients infected with coronavirus. For ages, governments, as well as corporations, use more and more sophisticated technologies to track, monitor and manipulate individuals. This means however that another barrier has been crossed. Measures for secret surveillance started to be adopted to protect public health on a massive scale without balancing it with appropriate protective mechanisms, including judicial review. Social approval towards this

[60]Cf. Judgment of the ECHR of 13 September 2018, Application No. 58170/13, 62322/14 and 24960/15, *Big Brother Watch And Others v. The United Kingdom* and Judgment of the Grand Chamber of the CJUE of 6 October 2020, Ref. no C-511/18, C-512/18 and C-520/18, *La Quadrature du Net and Others v Premier ministre and Others*.

[61]Cf. Judgments of the ECHR of 28 May 2019, Application No. 173/15, 181/15, 374/15, 383/15, 386/15 and 388/15, *Liblik and Others v. Estonia*; of 6 June 2019, Application No. 40429/14, 41536/14, 42804/14 and 58379/14, *Bosak And Others v. Croatia*; of 5 December 2019, Application No. 43478/11, *Hambardzumyan v. Armenia*; of 30 January 2020, Application No. 50001/12, *Breyer v. Germany*.

new approach might also be a turning point for retaining, collecting and granting access to telecommunication data.

References

Bignami F (2007) Privacy and law enforcement in the European Union: The data retention directive. Chicago J Int Law 8(1):233–255

Feiler L (2010) The legality of the data retention directive in light of the fundamental rights to privacy and data protection. Eur J Law Technol 1(3)

Konstadinides T (2014) Mass surveillance and data protection in EU law: the data retention Directive Saga. In: Bergstrom M, Jonsson Cornell A (eds) . Hart, European police and criminal law co-operation, pp 69–84

Terhechte J (2015) Kommentar zu Artikel 52 GRC. In: Groeben H, Schwarze J, Hetje A (eds) Europäisches Unionsrecht: Vertrag über die Europäische Union: Vertrag über die Arbeitsweise der Europäischen Union: Charta Grundrechte der Europäischen Union. Band I, Baden-Baden, p 833

Annex: Judgment Extracts

The Court of Justice of the European Union: Judgment of 8 April 2014, Ref. No C-293/12 and C-594/12[1]

(. . .)

1. These requests for a preliminary ruling concern the validity of Directive 2006/24/EC of the European Parliament and of the Council of 15 March 2006 on the retention of data generated or processed in connection with the provision of publicly available electronic communications services or of public communications networks and amending Directive 2002/58/EC (OJ 2006 L 105, p. 54).

2. The request made by the High Court (Case C-293/12) concerns proceedings between (i) Digital Rights Ireland Ltd. ('Digital Rights') and (ii) the Minister for Communications, Marine and Natural Resources, the Minister for Justice, Equality and Law Reform, the Commissioner of the Garda Síochána, Ireland and the Attorney General, regarding the legality of national legislative and administrative measures concerning the retention of data relating to electronic communications.

3. The request made by the Verfassungsgerichtshof (Constitutional Court) (Case C-594/12) concerns constitutional actions brought before that court by the Kärntner Landesregierung (Government of the Province of Carinthia) and by Mr Seitlinger, Mr Tschohl and 11,128 other applicants regarding the compatibility with the Federal Constitutional Law (Bundes-Verfassungsgesetz) of the law transposing Directive 2006/24 into Austrian national law.

(. . .)

24. It follows from Article 1 and recitals 4, 5, 7 to 11, 21 and 22 of Directive 2006/24 that the main objective of that directive is to harmonise Member States'

[1]CJEU, joined cases C-293/12 and C-594/12, Digital Rights Ireland and Seitlinger and Others, ECLI:EU:C:2014:238. The judgement is available in English at the page of the Court of Justice of the European Union, https://curia.europa.eu/.

M. Zubik et al. (eds.), *European Constitutional Courts towards Data Retention Laws*, Law, Governance and Technology Series 45,
https://doi.org/10.1007/978-3-030-57189-4

provisions concerning the retention, by providers of publicly available electronic communications services or of public communications networks, of certain data which are generated or processed by them, to ensure that the data are available in the prevention, investigation, detection and prosecution of serious crime, such as organised crime and terrorism, in compliance with the rights laid down in Articles 7 and 8 of the Charter.

25. The obligation, under Article 3 of Directive 2006/24, on providers of publicly available electronic communications services or of public communications networks to retain the data listed in Article 5 of the directive to make them accessible, if necessary, to the competent national authorities raises questions relating to respect for private life and communications under Article 7 of the Charter, the protection of personal data under Article 8 of the Charter and respect for freedom of expression under Article 11 of the Charter.

26. In that regard, it should be observed that the data that providers of publicly available electronic communications services or of public communications networks must retain, under Articles 3 and 5 of Directive 2006/24, include data necessary to trace and identify the source of a communication and its destination, to identify the date, time, duration and type of a communication, to identify users' communication equipment, and to identify the location of mobile communication equipment, data which consist, inter alia, of the name and address of the subscriber or registered user, the calling telephone number, the number called and an IP address for Internet services. Those data make it possible, in particular, to know the identity of the person with whom a subscriber or registered user has communicated and by what means, and to identify the time of the communication as well as the place from which that communication took place. They also make it possible to know the frequency of the communications of the subscriber or registered user with certain persons during a given period.

27. Those data, taken as a whole, may allow very precise conclusions to be drawn concerning the private lives of the persons whose data has been retained, such as the habits of everyday life, permanent or temporary places of residence, daily or other movements, the activities carried out, the social relationships of those persons and the social environments frequented by them.

28. In such circumstances, although, as is apparent from Article 1(2) and Article 5 (2) of Directive 2006/24, the directive does not permit the retention of the content of the communication or of information consulted using an electronic communications network, it is not inconceivable that the retention of the data in question might have an effect on the use, by subscribers or registered users, of the means of communication covered by that directive and, consequently, on their exercise of the freedom of expression guaranteed by Article 11 of the Charter.

29. The retention of data for possible access to them by the competent national authorities, under Directive 2006/24, directly and specifically affects private life and, consequently, the rights guaranteed by Article 7 of the Charter. Furthermore, such a retention of data also falls under Article 8 of the Charter because it constitutes the processing of personal data within the meaning of that article and, therefore, necessarily must satisfy the data protection requirements arising from that article

(Cases C-92/09 and C-93/09 *Volker und Markus Schecke and Eifert* EU: C:2010:662, paragraph 47).

30. Whereas the references for a preliminary ruling in the present cases raise, in particular, the question of principle as to whether or not, in the light of Article 7 of the Charter, the data of subscribers and registered users may be retained, they also concern the question of principle as to whether Directive 2006/24 meets the requirements for the protection of personal data arising from Article 8 of the Charter.

31. From the foregoing considerations, it is appropriate, in answering the second question, parts (b) to (d), in Case C-293/12 and the first question in Case C-594/12, to examine the validity of the directive in the light of Articles 7 and 8 of the Charter.

Interference with the Rights Laid Down in Articles 7 and 8 of the Charter

32. By requiring the retention of the data listed in Article 5(1) of Directive 2006/24 and by allowing the competent national authorities to access those data, Directive 2006/24, as the Advocate General has pointed out, in particular, in paragraphs 39 and 40 of his Opinion, derogates from the system of protection of the right to privacy established by Directives 95/46 and 2002/58 with regard to the processing of personal data in the electronic communications sector, directives which provided for the confidentiality of communications and of traffic data as well as the obligation to erase or make those data anonymous where they are no longer needed in the transmission of a communication, unless they are necessary for billing purposes and only for as long as necessary.

33. To establish the existence of an interference with the fundamental right to privacy, it does not matter whether the information on the private lives concerned is sensitive or whether the persons concerned have been inconvenienced in any way (see, to that effect, Cases C-465/00, C-138/01 and C-139/01 *Österreichischer Rundfunk and Others* EU:C:2003:294, paragraph 75).

34. As a result, the obligation imposed by Articles 3 and 6 of Directive 2006/24 on providers of publicly available electronic communications services or of public communications networks to retain, for a certain period, data relating to a person's private life and to his communications, such as those referred to in Article 5 of the directive, constitutes in itself an interference with the rights guaranteed by Article 7 of the Charter.

35. Furthermore, the access of the competent national authorities to the data constitutes a further interference with that fundamental right (see, as regards Article 8 of the ECHR, Eur. Court H.R., *Leander v. Sweden*, 26 March 1987, § 48, Series A no 116; *Rotaru v. Romania* [GC], no. 28341/95, § 46, ECHR 2000-V; and *Weber and Saravia v. Germany* (dec.), no. 54934/00, § 79, ECHR 2006-XI). Accordingly, Articles 4 and 8 of Directive 2006/24 laying down rules relating to the access of the

competent national authorities to the data also constitute an interference with the rights guaranteed by Article 7 of the Charter.

36. Likewise, Directive 2006/24 constitutes an interference with the fundamental right to the protection of personal data guaranteed by Article 8 of the Charter because it provides for the processing of personal data.

37. It must be stated that the interference caused by Directive 2006/24 with the fundamental rights laid down in Articles 7 and 8 of the Charter is, as the Advocate General has also pointed out, in particular, in paragraphs 77 and 80 of his Opinion, wide-ranging, and it must be considered to be particularly serious. Furthermore, as the Advocate General has pointed out in paragraphs 52 and 72 of his Opinion, the fact that data are retained and subsequently used without the subscriber or registered user being informed is likely to generate in the minds of the persons concerned the feeling that their private lives are the subject of constant surveillance.

Justification of the Interference with the Rights Guaranteed by Articles 7 and 8 of the Charter

38. Article 52(1) of the Charter provides that any limitation on the exercise of the rights and freedoms laid down by the Charter must be provided for by law, respect their essence and, subject to the principle of proportionality, limitations may be made to those rights and freedoms only if they are necessary and genuinely meet objectives of general interest recognised by the Union or the need to protect the rights and freedoms of others.

39. So far as concerns the essence of the fundamental right to privacy and the other rights laid down in Article 7 of the Charter, it must be held that, although the retention of data required by Directive 2006/24 constitutes a particularly serious interference with those rights, it is not such as to adversely affect the essence of those rights given that, as follows from Article 1(2) of the directive, the directive does not permit the acquisition of knowledge of the content of the electronic communications as such.

40. Nor is that retention of data such as to adversely affect the essence of the fundamental right to the protection of personal data enshrined in Article 8 of the Charter, because Article 7 of Directive 2006/24 provides, in relation to data protection and data security, that, without prejudice to the provisions adopted under Directives 95/46 and 2002/58, certain principles of data protection and data security must be respected by providers of publicly available electronic communications services or of public communications networks. Under those principles, Member States are to ensure that appropriate technical and organisational measures are adopted against accidental or unlawful destruction, accidental loss or alteration of the data.

41. On the question of whether that interference satisfies an objective of general interest, it should be observed that, whilst Directive 2006/24 aims to harmonise

Member States' provisions concerning the obligations of those providers with respect to the retention of certain data which are generated or processed by them, the material objective of that directive is, as follows from Article 1(1) thereof, to ensure that the data are available for the investigation, detection and prosecution of serious crime, as defined by each Member State in its national law. The material objective of that directive is, therefore, to contribute to the fight against serious crime and thus, ultimately, to public security.

42. It is apparent from the case law of the Court that the fight against international terrorism to maintain international peace and security constitutes an objective of general interest (see, to that effect, Cases C-402/05 P and C-415/05 P *Kadi and Al Barakaat International Foundation* v *Council and Commission* EU:C:2008:461, paragraph 363, and Cases C-539/10 P and C-550/10 P *Al-Aqsa* v *Council* EU:C:2012:711, paragraph 130). The same is true of the fight against serious crime to ensure public security (see, to that effect, Case C-145/09 *Tsakouridis* EU:C:2010:708, paragraphs 46 and 47). Furthermore, it should be noted, in this respect, that Article 6 of the Charter lays down the right of any person not only to liberty, but also to security.

43. In this respect, it is apparent from recital 7 in the preamble to Directive 2006/24 that, because of the significant growth in the possibilities afforded by electronic communications, the Justice and Home Affairs Council of 19 December 2002 concluded that data relating to the use of electronic communications are particularly important and therefore a valuable tool in the prevention of offences and the fight against crime, in particular organised crime.

44. It must therefore be held that the retention of data in allowing the competent national authorities to have possible access to those data, as required by Directive 2006/24, genuinely satisfies an objective of general interest.

45. In those circumstances, it is necessary to verify the proportionality of the interference found to exist.

46. In that regard, under the settled case law of the Court, the principle of proportionality requires that acts of the EU institutions be appropriate for attaining the legitimate objectives pursued by the legislation at issue and do not exceed the limits of what is appropriate and necessary to achieve those objectives (see, to that effect, Case C-343/09 *Afton Chemical* EU:C:2010:419, paragraph 45; *Volker und Markus Schecke and Eifert* EU:C:2010:662, paragraph 74; Cases C-581/10 and C-629/10 *Nelson and Others* EU:C:2012:657, paragraph 71; Case C-283/11 *Sky Österreich* EU:C:2013:28, paragraph 50; and Case C-101/12 *Schaible* EU:C:2013:661, paragraph 29).

47. On judicial review of compliance with those conditions, where interferences with fundamental rights are at issue, the extent of the EU legislature's discretion may prove to be limited, depending on a number of factors, including, in particular, the area concerned, the nature of the right at issue guaranteed by the Charter, the nature and seriousness of the interference and the object pursued by the interference (see, by analogy, as regards Article 8 of the ECHR, Eur. Court H.R., S. *and Marper v. the United Kingdom* [GC], nos. 30562/04 and 30566/04, § 102, ECHR 2008-V).

48. In the present case, in view of the important role played by the protection of personal data in the light of the fundamental right to respect for private life and the extent and seriousness of the interference with that right caused by Directive 2006/24, the EU legislature's discretion is reduced, with the result that review of that discretion should be strict.

49. On the question of whether the retention of data is appropriate for attaining the objective pursued by Directive 2006/24, it must be held that, having regard to the growing importance of means of electronic communication, data which must be retained under that directive allow the national authorities which are competent for criminal prosecutions to have additional opportunities to shed light on serious crime and, in this respect, they are therefore a valuable tool for criminal investigations. Consequently, the retention of such data may be considered appropriate for attaining the objective pursued by that directive.

50. That assessment cannot be called into question by the fact relied upon in particular by Mr Tschohl and Mr Seitlinger and by the Portuguese Government in their written observations submitted to the Court that there are several methods of electronic communication which do not fall within the scope of Directive 2006/24 or which allow anonymous communication. Whilst, admittedly, that fact is such as to limit the ability of the data retention measure to attain the objective pursued, it is not, however, such as to make that measure inappropriate, as the Advocate General has pointed out in paragraph 137 of his Opinion.

51. On the necessity for the retention of data required by Directive 2006/24, it must be held that the fight against serious crime, in particular against organised crime and terrorism, is indeed of the utmost importance to ensure public security and its effectiveness may depend to a great extent on the use of modern investigation techniques. However, such an objective of general interest, however fundamental it may be, does not, in itself, justify a retention measure such as that established by Directive 2006/24 being considered to be necessary for that fight.

52. So far as concerns the right to respect for private life, the protection of that fundamental right requires, under the Court's settled case law, in any event, that derogations and limitations in relation to the protection of personal data must apply only in so far as is strictly necessary (Case C-473/12 *IPI* EU:C:2013:715, paragraph 39 and the case law cited).

53. In that regard, it should be noted that the protection of personal data resulting from the explicit obligation laid down in Article 8(1) of the Charter is especially important for the right to respect for private life enshrined in Article 7 of the Charter.

54. Consequently, the EU legislation in question must lay down clear and precise rules governing the scope and application of the measure in question and imposing minimum safeguards so that the persons whose data have been retained have sufficient guarantees to effectively protect their personal data against the risk of abuse and against any unlawful access and use of that data (see, by analogy, as regards Article 8 of the ECHR, Eur. Court H.R., *Liberty and Others v. the United Kingdom*, 1 July 2008, no. 58243/00, § 62 and 63; *Rotaru v. Romania*, § 57 to 59, and *S. and Marper v. the United Kingdom*, § 99).

55. The need for such safeguards is all the greater where, as laid down in Directive 2006/24, personal data are subjected to automatic processing and where there is a significant risk of unlawful access to those data (see, by analogy, as regards Article 8 of the ECHR, *S. and Marper v. the United Kingdom*, § 103, and *M. K. v. France*, 18 April 2013, no. 19522/09, § 35).

56. On whether the interference caused by Directive 2006/24 is limited to what is strictly necessary, it should be observed that, under Article 3 read in conjunction with Article 5(1) of that directive, the directive requires the retention of all traffic data concerning fixed telephony, mobile telephony, Internet access, Internet e-mail and Internet telephony. It therefore applies to all means of electronic communication, the use of which is very widespread and of growing importance in people's everyday lives. Furthermore, under Article 3 of Directive 2006/24, the directive covers all subscribers and registered users. It therefore entails an interference with the fundamental rights of practically the entire European population.

57. In this respect, it must be noted, first, that Directive 2006/24 covers, in a generalised manner, all persons and all means of electronic communication as well as all traffic data without any differentiation, limitation or exception being made in the light of the objective of fighting against serious crime.

58. Directive 2006/24 affects, in a comprehensive manner, all persons using electronic communications services, but without the persons whose data are retained being, even indirectly, in a situation which is liable to give rise to criminal prosecutions. It therefore applies even to persons for whom there is no evidence capable of suggesting that their conduct might have a link, even an indirect or remote one, with serious crime. Furthermore, it does not provide for any exception, with the result that it applies even to persons whose communications are subject, under the rules of national law, to the obligation of professional secrecy.

59. Moreover, whilst seeking to contribute to the fight against serious crime, Directive 2006/24 does not require any relationship between the data whose retention is provided for and a threat to public security and, in particular, it is not restricted to a retention in relation (i) to data pertaining to a particular period and/or a particular geographical zone and/or to a circle of particular persons likely to be involved, in one way or another, in a serious crime, or (ii) to persons who could, for other reasons, contribute, by the retention of their data, to the prevention, detection or prosecution of serious offences.

60. Second, not only is there a general absence of limits in Directive 2006/24 but Directive 2006/24 also fails to lay down any objective criterion by which to determine the limits of the access of the competent national authorities to the data and their subsequent use for the prevention, detection or criminal prosecutions concerning offences that, in view of the extent and seriousness of the interference with the fundamental rights enshrined in Articles 7 and 8 of the Charter, may be considered to be sufficiently serious to justify such an interference. On the contrary, Directive 2006/24 simply refers, in Article 1(1), in a general manner to serious crime, as defined by each Member State in its national law.

61. Furthermore, Directive 2006/24 does not contain substantive and procedural conditions relating to the access of the competent national authorities to the data and

to their subsequent use. Article 4 of the directive, which governs the access of those authorities to the data retained, does not expressly provide that that access and the subsequent use of the data in question must be strictly restricted to the purpose of preventing and detecting precisely defined serious offences or of conducting criminal prosecutions relating thereto; it merely provides that each Member State is to define the procedures to be followed and the conditions to be fulfilled to gain access to the retained data in accordance with necessity and proportionality requirements.

62. In particular, Directive 2006/24 does not lay down any objective criterion by which the number of persons authorised to access and subsequently use the data retained is limited to what is strictly necessary in the light of the objective pursued. Above all, the access by the competent national authorities to the data retained is not made dependent on a prior review carried out by a court or by an independent administrative body whose decision seeks to limit access to the data and their use to what is strictly necessary in attaining the objective pursued and which intervenes following a reasoned request of those authorities submitted within the framework of procedures of prevention, detection or criminal prosecutions. Nor does it lay down a specific obligation on Member States designed to establish such limits.

63. Third, so far as concerns the data retention period, Article 6 of Directive 2006/24 requires that those data be retained for a period of at least six months, without any distinction being made between the categories of data set out in Article 5 of that directive based on their possible usefulness for the objective pursued or according to the persons concerned.

64. Furthermore, that period is set at between a minimum of six months and a maximum of 24 months, but it is not stated that the determination of the period of retention must be based on objective criteria to ensure that it is limited to what is strictly necessary.

65. It follows from the above that Directive 2006/24 does not lay down clear and precise rules governing the extent of the interference with the fundamental rights enshrined in Articles 7 and 8 of the Charter. It must therefore be held that Directive 2006/24 entails a wide-ranging and particularly serious interference with those fundamental rights in the legal order of the EU, without such an interference being precisely circumscribed by provisions to ensure that it is actually limited to what is strictly necessary.

66. Moreover, as far as concerns the rules relating to the security and protection of data retained by providers of publicly available electronic communications services or of public communications networks, it must be held that Directive 2006/24 does not provide for sufficient safeguards, as required by Article 8 of the Charter, to ensure effective protection of the data retained against the risk of abuse and against any unlawful access and use of that data. In the first place, Article 7 of Directive 2006/24 does not lay down rules which are specific and adapted to (i) the vast quantity of data whose retention is required by that directive, (ii) the sensitive nature of that data and (iii) the risk of unlawful access to that data, rules which would serve, in particular, to govern the protection and security of the data in question in a clear and strict manner to ensure their full integrity and confidentiality. Furthermore, a

specific obligation on Member States to establish such rules has also not been laid down.

67. Article 7 of Directive 2006/24, read in conjunction with Article 4(1) of Directive 2002/58 and the second subparagraph of Article 17(1) of Directive 95/46, does not ensure that a particularly high level of protection and security is applied by those providers by means of technical and organisational measures, but permits those providers in particular to have regard to economic considerations when determining the level of security which they apply, as regards the costs of implementing security measures. In particular, Directive 2006/24 does not ensure the irreversible destruction of the data at the end of the data retention period.

68. In the second place, it should be added that that directive does not require the data in question to be retained within the European Union, with the result that it cannot be held that the control, explicitly required by Article 8(3) of the Charter, by an independent authority of compliance with the requirements of protection and security, as referred to in the two previous paragraphs, is fully ensured. Such a control, carried out based on the EU law, is an essential component of the protection of individuals with regard to the processing of personal data (see, to that effect, Case C-614/10 *Commission* v *Austria* EU:C:2012:631, paragraph 37).

69. Considering the foregoing, it must be held that, by adopting Directive 2006/24, the EU legislature has exceeded the limits imposed by compliance with the principle of proportionality in the light of Articles 7, 8 and 52(1) of the Charter.

70. In those circumstances, there is no need to examine the validity of Directive 2006/24 in the light of Article 11 of the Charter.

71. Consequently, the answer to the second question, parts (b) to (d), in Case C-293/12 and the first question in Case C-594/12 is that Directive 2006/24 is invalid.

The first question and the second question, parts (a) and (e), and the third question in Case C-293/12 and the second question in Case C-594/12

72. It follows from what was held in the previous paragraph that there is no need to answer the first question, the second question, parts (a) and (e), and the third question in Case C-293/12 or the second question in Case C-594/12.

(...)

On those grounds, the Court (Grand Chamber) hereby rules:

Directive 2006/24/EC of the European Parliament and of the Council of 15 March 2006 on the retention of data generated or processed in connection with the provision of publicly available electronic communications services or of public communications networks and amending Directive 2002/58/EC is invalid.

The Court of Justice of the European Union: Judgment of 21 December 2016, Ref. No C-203/15 and C-698/15[2]

(. . .)

1. These requests for a preliminary ruling concern the interpretation of Article 15 (1) of Directive 2002/58/EC of the European Parliament and of the Council of 12 July 2002 concerning the processing of personal data and the protection of privacy in the electronic communications sector (Directive on privacy and electronic communications) (OJ 2002 L 201, p. 37), as amended by Directive 2009/136/EC of the European Parliament and of the Council of 25 November 2009 (OJ 2009 L 337, p. 11) ('Directive 2002/58'), read in the light of Articles 7 and 8 and Article 52 (1) of the Charter of Fundamental Rights of the European Union ('the Charter').

2. The requests have been made in two proceedings between (i) Tele2 Sverige AB and Post- och telestyrelsen (the Swedish Post and Telecom Authority; 'PTS'), concerning an order sent by PTS to Tele2 Sverige requiring the latter to retain traffic and location data in relation to its subscribers and registered users (Case C-203/15), and (ii) Mr Tom Watson, Mr Peter Brice and Mr Geoffrey Lewis, on the one hand, and the Secretary of State for the Home Department (United Kingdom of Great Britain and Northern Ireland), on the other, concerning the conformity with EU law of Section 1 of the Data Retention and Investigatory Powers Act 2014 ('DRIPA') (Case C-698/15).

(. . .)

The Scope of Directive 2002/58

65. The Member States that have submitted written observations to the Court have differed in their opinions as to whether and to what extent national legislation on the retention of traffic and location data and access to that data by the national authorities in combating crime, falls within the scope of Directive 2002/58. Whereas, in particular, the Belgian, Danish, German and Estonian Governments, Ireland and the Netherlands Government have expressed the opinion that the answer is that it does, the Czech Government has proposed that the answer is that it does not, since the sole objective of such legislation is to combat crime. The United Kingdom Government, for its part, argues that only legislation relating to the retention of data, but not legislation relating to the access to that data by the competent national law enforcement authorities, falls within the scope of that directive.

66. As regards, finally, the Commission, while it maintained, in its written observations submitted to the Court in Case C-203/15, that the national legislation

[2]CJEU, joined cases C-203/15 and C-698/15 Tele2 Sverige AB and Others, ECLI:EU:C:2014:238. The judgement is available in English at the page of the Court of Justice of the European Union, https://curia.europa.eu/.

at issue in the main proceedings falls within the scope of Directive 2002/58, the Commission argues, in its written observations in Case C-698/15, that only national rules relating to the retention of data, and not those relating to the access of the national authorities to that data, fall within the scope of that directive. The latter rules should, however, according to the Commission, be considered to assess whether national legislation governing the retention of data by providers of electronic communications services constitutes a proportionate interference in the fundamental rights guaranteed in Articles 7 and 8 of the Charter.

67. In that regard, it must be observed that a determination of the scope of Directive 2002/58 must consider, inter alia, the general structure of that directive.

68. Article 1(1) of Directive 2002/58 indicates that the directive provides, inter alia, for the harmonisation of the provisions of national law required to ensure an equivalent level of protection of fundamental rights and freedoms, and in particular the right to privacy and confidentiality, with respect to the processing of personal data in the electronic communications sector.

69. Article 1(3) of that directive excludes from its scope 'activities of the State' in specified fields, including the activities of the State in areas of criminal law and in the areas of public security, defence and State security, including the economic well-being of the State when the activities relate to State security matters (see, by analogy, with respect to the first indent of Article 3(2) of Directive 95/46, judgments of 6 November 2003, Lindqvist, C-101/01, EU:C:2003:596, paragraph 43, and of 16 December 2008, Satakunnan Markkinapörssi and Satamedia, C-73/07, EU:C:2008:727, paragraph 41).

70. Article 3 of Directive 2002/58 states that the directive is to apply to the processing of personal data in connection with the provision of publicly available electronic communications services in public communications networks in the European Union, including public communications networks supporting data collection and identification devices ('electronic communications services'). Consequently, that directive must be regarded as regulating the activities of the providers of such services.

71. Article 15(1) of Directive 2002/58 states that Member States may adopt, subject to the conditions laid down, 'legislative measures to restrict the scope of the rights and obligations provided for in Article 5, Article 6, Article 8(1), (2), (3) and (4), and Article 9 [of that directive]'. The second sentence of Article 15(1) of that directive identifies, as an example of measures that may thus be adopted by Member States, measures 'providing for the retention of data'.

72. Admittedly, the legislative measures that are referred to in Article 15(1) of Directive 2002/58 concern activities characteristic of States or State authorities, and are unrelated to fields in which individuals are active (see, to that effect, judgment of 29 January 2008, Promusicae, C-275/06, EU:C:2008:54, paragraph 51). Moreover, the objectives that, under the provision, such measures must pursue, such as safeguarding national security, defence and public security and the prevention, investigation, detection and prosecution of criminal offences or of unauthorised use of the electronic communications system, overlap substantially with the objectives pursued by the activities referred to in Article 1(3) of that directive.

73. However, having regard to the general structure of Directive 2002/58, the factors identified in the preceding paragraph of this judgment do not permit the conclusion that the legislative measures referred to in Article 15(1) of Directive 2002/58 are excluded from the scope of that directive, for otherwise that provision would be deprived of any purpose. Indeed, Article 15(1) necessarily presupposes that the national measures referred to therein, such as those relating to the retention of data in combating crime, fall within the scope of that directive, since it expressly authorises the Member States to adopt them only if the conditions laid down in the directive are met.

74. Further, the legislative measures referred to in Article 15(1) of Directive 2002/58 govern, for the purposes mentioned in that provision, the activity of providers of electronic communications services. Accordingly, Article 15(1), read together with Article 3 of that directive, must be interpreted as meaning that such legislative measures fall within the scope of that directive.

75. The scope of that directive extends, in particular, to a legislative measure, such as that at issue in the main proceedings, that requires such providers to retain traffic and location data, since to do so necessarily involves the processing, by those providers, of personal data.

76. The scope of that directive also extends to a legislative measure relating, as in the main proceedings, to the access of the national authorities to the data retained by the providers of electronic communications services.

77. The protection of the confidentiality of electronic communications and related traffic data, guaranteed in Article 5(1) of Directive 2002/58, applies to the measures taken by all persons other than users, whether private persons or bodies or State bodies. As confirmed in recital 21 of that directive, the aim of the directive is to prevent unauthorised access to communications, including 'any data related to such communications', to protect the confidentiality of electronic communications.

78. In those circumstances, a legislative measure whereby a Member State, based on Article 15(1) of Directive 2002/58, requires providers of electronic communications services, for the purposes set out in that provision, to grant national authorities, on the conditions laid down in such a measure, access to the data retained by those providers, concerns the processing of personal data by those providers, and that processing falls within the scope of that directive.

79. Further, since data is retained only for the purpose, when necessary, of making that data accessible to the competent national authorities, national legislation that imposes the retention of data necessarily entails, in principle, the existence of provisions relating to access by the competent national authorities to the data retained by the providers of electronic communications services.

80. That interpretation is confirmed by Article 15(1b) of Directive 2002/58, which provides that providers are to establish internal procedures for responding to requests for access to users' personal data, based on provisions of national law adopted under Article 15(1) of that directive.

81. It follows from the foregoing that national legislation, such as that at issue in the main proceedings in Cases C-203/15 and C-698/15, falls within the scope of Directive 2002/58.

The Interpretation of Article 15(1) of Directive 2002/58, in the Light of Articles 7, 8, 11 and Article 52(1) of the Charter

82. It must be observed that under Article 1(2) of Directive 2002/58, the provisions of that directive 'particularise and complement' Directive 95/46. As stated in its recital 2, Directive 2002/58 seeks to ensure, in particular, full respect for the rights set out in Articles 7 and 8 of the Charter. In that regard, it is clear from the explanatory memorandum of the Proposal for a Directive of the European Parliament and of the Council concerning the processing of personal data and the protection of privacy in the electronic communications sector (COM(2000) 385 final), which led to Directive 2002/58, that the EU legislature sought 'to ensure that a high level of protection of personal data and privacy will continue to be guaranteed for all electronic communications services regardless of the technology used'.

83. To that end, Directive 2002/58 contains specific provisions designed, as is apparent from, in particular, recitals 6 and 7 of that directive, to offer to the users of electronic communications services protection against risks to their personal data and privacy that arise from new technology and the increasing capacity for automated storage and processing of data.

84. In particular, Article 5(1) of that directive provides that the Member States must ensure, by means of their national legislation, the confidentiality of communications effected by means of a public communications network and publicly available electronic communications services, and the confidentiality of the related traffic data.

85. The principle of confidentiality of communications established by Directive 2002/58 implies, inter alia, as stated in the second sentence of Article 5(1) of that directive, that, as a general rule, any person other than the users is prohibited from storing, without the consent of the users concerned, the traffic data related to electronic communications. The only exceptions relate to persons lawfully authorised under Article 15(1) of that directive and to the technical storage necessary for conveyance of a communication (see, to that effect, judgment of 29 January 2008, Promusicae, C-275/06, EU:C:2008:54, paragraph 47).

86. Accordingly, as confirmed by recitals 22 and 26 of Directive 2002/58, under Article 6 of that directive, the processing and storage of traffic data are permitted only to the extent necessary and for the time necessary for the billing and marketing of services and the provision of value added services (see, to that effect, judgment of 29 January 2008, Promusicae, C-275/06, EU:C:2008:54, paragraphs 47 and 48). As regards, in particular, the billing of services, that processing is permitted only up to the end of the period during which the bill may be lawfully challenged or legal proceedings brought to obtain payment. Once that period has elapsed, the data processed and stored must be erased or made anonymous. On location data other than traffic data, Article 9(1) of that directive provides that that data may be processed only subject to certain conditions and after it has been made anonymous or the consent of the users or subscribers obtained.

87. The scope of Article 5, Article 6 and Article 9(1) of Directive 2002/58, which seek to ensure the confidentiality of communications and related data, and to minimise the risks of misuse, must moreover be assessed in the light of recital 30 of that directive, which states: ‘Systems for the provision of electronic communications networks and services should be designed to limit the amount of personal data necessary to a strict minimum’.

88. Admittedly, Article 15(1) of Directive 2002/58 enables the Member States to introduce exceptions to the obligation of principle, laid down in Article 5(1) of that directive, to ensure the confidentiality of personal data, and to the corresponding obligations, referred to in Articles 6 and 9 of that directive (see, to that effect, judgment of 29 January 2008, Promusicae, C-275/06, EU:C:2008:54, paragraph 50).

89. Nonetheless, in so far as Article 15(1) of Directive 2002/58 enables Member States to restrict the scope of the obligation of principle to ensure the confidentiality of communications and related traffic data, that provision must, in accordance with the Court’s settled case law, be interpreted strictly (see, by analogy, judgment of 22 November 2012, Probst, C-119/12, EU:C:2012:748, paragraph 23). That provision cannot, therefore, permit the exception to that obligation of principle and, in particular, to the prohibition on storage of data, laid down in Article 5 of Directive 2002/58, to become the rule, if the latter provision is not to be rendered largely meaningless.

90. It must, in that regard, be observed that the first sentence of Article 15(1) of Directive 2002/58 provides that the objectives pursued by the legislative measures that it covers, which derogate from the principle of confidentiality of communications and related traffic data, must be ‘to safeguard national security — that is, State security — defence, public security, and the prevention, investigation, detection and prosecution of criminal offences or of unauthorised use of the electronic communication system’, or one of the other objectives specified in Article 13(1) of Directive 95/46, to which the first sentence of Article 15(1) of Directive 2002/58 refers (see, to that effect, judgment of 29 January 2008, Promusicae, C-275/06, EU:C:2008:54, paragraph 53). That list of objectives is exhaustive, as is apparent from the second sentence of Article 15(1) of Directive 2002/58, which states that the legislative measures must be justified on ‘the grounds laid down’ in the first sentence of Article 15(1) of that directive. Accordingly, the Member States cannot adopt such measures for purposes other than those listed in that latter provision.

91. Further, the third sentence of Article 15(1) of Directive 2002/58 provides that ‘[a]ll the measures referred to [in Article 15(1)] shall be in accordance with the general principles of [European Union] law, including those referred to in Article 6 (1) and (2) [EU]’, which include the general principles and fundamental rights now guaranteed by the Charter. Article 15(1) of Directive 2002/58 must, therefore, be interpreted in the light of the fundamental rights guaranteed by the Charter (see, by analogy, in relation to Directive 95/46, judgments of 20 May 2003, Österreichischer Rundfunk and Others, C-465/00, C-138/01 and C-139/01, EU:C:2003:294, paragraph 68; of 13 May 2014, Google Spain and Google, C-131/12, EU:C:2014:317, paragraph 68, and of 6 October 2015, Schrems, C-362/14, EU:C:2015:650, paragraph 38).

92. In that regard, it must be emphasised that the obligation imposed on providers of electronic communications services, by national legislation such as that at issue in the main proceedings, to retain traffic data in order, when necessary, to make that data available to the competent national authorities, raises questions relating to compatibility not only with Articles 7 and 8 of the Charter, which are expressly referred to in the questions referred for a preliminary ruling, but also with the freedom of expression guaranteed in Article 11 of the Charter (see, by analogy, in relation to Directive 2006/24, the Digital Rights judgment, paragraphs 25 and 70).

93. Accordingly, the importance both of the right to privacy, guaranteed in Article 7 of the Charter, and of the right to protection of personal data, guaranteed in Article 8 of the Charter, as derived from the Court's case law (see, to that effect, judgment of 6 October 2015, Schrems, C-362/14, EU:C:2015:650, paragraph 39 and the case law cited), must be considered in interpreting Article 15(1) of Directive 2002/58. The same is true of the right to freedom of expression in the light of the particular importance accorded to that freedom in any democratic society. That fundamental right, guaranteed in Article 11 of the Charter, constitutes one of the essential foundations of a pluralist, democratic society, and is one of the values on which, under Article 2 TEU, the Union is founded (see, to that effect, judgments of 12 June 2003, Schmidberger, C-112/00, EU:C:2003:333, paragraph 79, and of 6 September 2011, Patriciello, C-163/10, EU:C:2011:543, paragraph 31).

94. In that regard, it must be recalled that, under Article 52(1) of the Charter, any limitation on the exercise of the rights and freedoms recognised by the Charter must be provided for by law and must respect the essence of those rights and freedoms. With due regard to the principle of proportionality, limitations may be imposed on the exercise of those rights and freedoms only if they are necessary and if they genuinely meet objectives of general interest recognised by the European Union or the need to protect the rights and freedoms of others (judgment of 15 February 2016, N., C-601/15 PPU, EU:C:2016:84, paragraph 50).

95. With respect to that last issue, the first sentence of Article 15(1) of Directive 2002/58 provides that Member States may adopt a measure that derogates from the principle of confidentiality of communications and related traffic data where it is a 'necessary, appropriate and proportionate measure within a democratic society', in view of the objectives laid down in that provision. As regards recital 11 of that directive, it states that a measure of that kind must be 'strictly' proportionate to the intended purpose. In relation to, in particular, the retention of data, the requirement laid down in the second sentence of Article 15(1) of that directive is that data should be retained 'for a limited period' and be 'justified' by reference to one of the objectives stated in the first sentence of Article 15(1) of that directive.

96. Due regard to the principle of proportionality also derives from the Court's settled case law to the effect that the protection of the fundamental right to respect for private life at EU level requires that derogations from and limitations on the protection of personal data should apply only in so far as is strictly necessary (judgments of 16 December 2008, Satakunnan Markkinapörssi and Satamedia, C-73/07, EU:C:2008:727, paragraph 56; of 9 November 2010, Volker und Markus Schecke and Eifert, C-92/09 and C-93/09, EU:C:2010:662, paragraph 77; the Digital

Rights judgment, paragraph 52, and of 6 October 2015, Schrems, C-362/14, EU: C:2015:650, paragraph 92).

97. On whether national legislation, such as that at issue in Case C-203/15, satisfies those conditions, it must be observed that that legislation provides for a general and indiscriminate retention of all traffic and location data of all subscribers and registered users relating to all means of electronic communication, and that it imposes on providers of electronic communications services an obligation to retain that data systematically and continuously, with no exceptions. As stated in the order for reference, the categories of data covered by that legislation correspond, in essence, to the data whose retention was required by Directive 2006/24.

98. The data which providers of electronic communications services must therefore retain makes it possible to trace and identify the source of a communication and its destination, to identify the date, time, duration and type of a communication, to identify users' communication equipment, and to establish the location of mobile communication equipment. That data includes, inter alia, the name and address of the subscriber or registered user, the telephone number of the caller, the number called and an IP address for Internet services. That data makes it possible, in particular, to identify the person with whom a subscriber or registered user has communicated and by what means, and to identify the time of the communication as well as the place from which that communication took place. Further, that data makes it possible to know how often the subscriber or registered user communicated with certain persons in a given period (see, by analogy, with respect to Directive 2006/24, the Digital Rights judgment, paragraph 26).

99. That data, taken as a whole, is liable to allow very precise conclusions to be drawn concerning the private lives of the persons whose data has been retained, such as everyday habits, permanent or temporary places of residence, daily or other movements, the activities carried out, the social relationships of those persons and the social environments frequented by them (see, by analogy, in relation to Directive 2006/24, the Digital Rights judgment, paragraph 27). In particular, that data provides the means, as observed by the Advocate General in points 253, 254 and 257 to 259 of his Opinion, of establishing a profile of the individuals concerned, information that is no less sensitive, having regard to the right to privacy, than the actual content of communications.

100. The interference entailed by such legislation in the fundamental rights enshrined in Articles 7 and 8 of the Charter is very far-reaching and must be considered particularly serious. The fact that the data is retained without the subscriber or registered user being informed is likely to cause the persons concerned to feel that their private lives are the subject of constant surveillance (see, by analogy, in relation to Directive 2006/24, the Digital Rights judgment, paragraph 37).

101. Even if such legislation does not permit retention of the content of a communication and is not, therefore, such as to affect adversely the essence of those rights (see, by analogy, in relation to Directive 2006/24, the Digital Rights judgment, paragraph 39), the retention of traffic and location data could nonetheless have an effect on the use of means of electronic communication and, consequently, on the exercise by the users thereof of their freedom of expression, guaranteed in

Article 11 of the Charter (see, by analogy, in relation to Directive 2006/24, the Digital Rights judgment, paragraph 28).

102. Given the seriousness of the interference in the fundamental rights concerned represented by national legislation that in fighting crime provides for the retention of traffic and location data, only the objective of fighting serious crime is capable of justifying such a measure (see, by analogy, in relation to Directive 2006/24, the Digital Rights judgment, paragraph 60).

103. Further, while the effectiveness of the fight against serious crime, in particular organised crime and terrorism, may depend to a great extent on the use of modern investigation techniques, such an objective of general interest, however fundamental it may be, cannot in itself justify that national legislation providing for the general and indiscriminate retention of all traffic and location data should be considered to be necessary for that fight (see, by analogy, in relation to Directive 2006/24, the Digital Rights judgment, paragraph 51).

104. In that regard, it must be observed, first, that the effect of such legislation, in the light of its characteristic features as described in paragraph 97 of the present judgment, is that the retention of traffic and location data is the rule, whereas the system put in place by Directive 2002/58 requires the retention of data to be the exception.

105. Second, national legislation such as that at issue in the main proceedings, which covers, in a generalised manner, all subscribers and registered users and all means of electronic communication as well as all traffic data, provides for no differentiation, limitation or exception according to the objective pursued. It is comprehensive in that it affects all persons using electronic communication services, although those persons are not, even indirectly, in a situation that is liable to give rise to criminal proceedings. It therefore applies even to persons for whom there is no evidence capable of suggesting that their conduct might have a link, even an indirect or remote one, with serious criminal offences. Further, it does not provide for any exception, and consequently it applies even to persons whose communications are subject, under the rules of national law, to the obligation of professional secrecy (see, by analogy, in relation to Directive 2006/24, the Digital Rights judgment, paragraphs 57 and 58).

106. Such legislation does not require there to be any relationship between the data which must be retained and a threat to public security. In particular, it is not restricted to retention in relation to (i) data pertaining to a particular period and/or geographical area and/or a group of persons likely to be involved, in one way or another, in a serious crime, or (ii) persons who could, for other reasons, contribute, through their data being retained, to fighting crime (see, by analogy, in relation to Directive 2006/24, the Digital Rights judgment, paragraph 59).

107. National legislation such as that at issue in the main proceedings therefore exceeds the limits of what is strictly necessary and cannot be considered to be justified, within a democratic society, as required by Article 15(1) of Directive 2002/58, read in the light of Articles 7, 8 and 11 and Article 52(1) of the Charter.

108. However, Article 15(1) of Directive 2002/58, read in the light of Articles 7, 8 and 11 and Article 52(1) of the Charter, does not prevent a Member State from

adopting legislation permitting, as a preventive measure, the targeted retention of traffic and location data, in fighting serious crime, provided that the retention of data is limited, with respect to the categories of data to be retained, the means of communication affected, the persons concerned and the retention period adopted, to what is strictly necessary.

109. To satisfy the requirements set out in the preceding paragraph of the present judgment, that national legislation must, first, lay down clear and precise rules governing the scope and application of such a data retention measure and imposing minimum safeguards, so that the persons whose data has been retained have sufficient guarantees of the effective protection of their personal data against the risk of misuse. That legislation must, in particular, indicate in what circumstances and under which conditions a data retention measure may, as a preventive measure, be adopted, thereby ensuring that such a measure is limited to what is strictly necessary (see, by analogy, in relation to Directive 2006/24, the Digital Rights judgment, paragraph 54 and the case law cited).

110. Second, on the substantive conditions which must be satisfied by national legislation that authorises, in the context of fighting crime, the retention, as a preventive measure, of traffic and location data, if it is to be ensured that data retention is limited to what is strictly necessary, it must be observed that, while those conditions may vary according to the nature of the measures taken for the prevention, investigation, detection and prosecution of serious crime, the retention of data must continue nonetheless to meet objective criteria, that establish a connection between the data to be retained and the objective pursued. In particular, such conditions must be shown to be such as actually to circumscribe, in practice, the extent of that measure and, thus, the public affected.

111. On the setting of limits on such a measure with respect to the public and the situations that may potentially be affected, the national legislation must be based on objective evidence which makes it possible to identify a public whose data is likely to reveal a link, at least an indirect one, with serious criminal offences, and to contribute in one way or another to fighting serious crime or to preventing a serious risk to public security. Such limits may be set by using a geographical criterion where the competent national authorities consider, based on objective evidence, that there exists, in one or more geographical areas, a high risk of preparation for or commission of such offences.

112. Considering the foregoing, the answer to the first question referred in Case C-203/15 is that Article 15(1) of Directive 2002/58, read in the light of Articles 7, 8 and 11 and Article 52(1) of the Charter, must be interpreted as precluding national legislation that in fighting crime provides for the general and indiscriminate retention of all traffic and location data of all subscribers and registered users relating to all means of electronic communication.

The Second Question in Case C-203/15 and the First Question in Case C-698/15

113. It must, at the outset, be noted that the Kammarrätten i Stockholm (Administrative Court of Appeal, Stockholm) referred the second question in Case C-203/15 only in the event that the answer to the first question in that case was negative. That second question, however, arises irrespective of whether retention of data is generalised or targeted, as set out in paragraphs 108 to 111 of this judgment. Accordingly, the Court must answer the second question in Case C-203/15 together with the first question in Case C-698/15, which is referred regardless of the extent of the obligation to retain data that is imposed on providers of electronic communications services.

114. By the second question in Case C-203/15 and the first question in Case C-698/15, the referring courts seek, in essence, to ascertain whether Article 15(1) of Directive 2002/58, read in the light of Articles 7, 8 and Article 52(1) of the Charter, must be interpreted as precluding national legislation governing the protection and security of traffic and location data, and more particularly, the access of the competent national authorities to retained data, where that legislation does not restrict that access solely to the objective of fighting serious crime, where that access is not subject to prior review by a court or an independent administrative authority, and where there is no requirement that the data concerned should be retained within the European Union.

115. On objectives that are capable of justifying national legislation that derogates from the principle of confidentiality of electronic communications, it must be borne in mind that, since, as stated in paragraphs 90 and 102 of this judgment, the list of objectives set out in the first sentence of Article 15(1) of Directive 2002/58 is exhaustive, access to the retained data must correspond, genuinely and strictly, to one of those objectives. Further, since the objective pursued by that legislation must be proportionate to the seriousness of the interference in fundamental rights that that access entails, it follows that, in the area of prevention, investigation, detection and prosecution of criminal offences, only the objective of fighting serious crime is capable of justifying such access to the retained data.

116. On compatibility with the principle of proportionality, national legislation governing the conditions under which the providers of electronic communications services must grant the competent national authorities access to the retained data must ensure, in accordance with what was stated in paragraphs 95 and 96 of this judgment, that such access does not exceed the limits of what is strictly necessary.

117. Further, since the legislative measures referred to in Article 15(1) of Directive 2002/58 must, under recital 11 of that directive, 'be subject to adequate safeguards', a data retention measure must, as follows from the case law cited in paragraph 109 of this judgment, lay down clear and precise rules indicating in what circumstances and under which conditions the providers of electronic communications services must grant the competent national authorities access to the data. Likewise, a measure of that kind must be legally binding under domestic law.

118. To ensure that access of the competent national authorities to retained data is limited to what is strictly necessary, it is, indeed, for national law to determine the conditions under which the providers of electronic communications services must grant such access. However, the national legislation concerned cannot be limited to requiring that access should be for one of the objectives referred to in Article 15(1) of Directive 2002/58, even if that objective is to fight serious crime. That national legislation must also lay down the substantive and procedural conditions governing the access of the competent national authorities to the retained data (see, by analogy, in relation to Directive 2006/24, the Digital Rights judgment, paragraph 61).

119. Accordingly, and since general access to all retained data, regardless of whether there is any link, at least indirect, with the intended purpose, cannot be regarded as limited to what is strictly necessary, the national legislation concerned must be based on objective criteria to define the circumstances and conditions under which the competent national authorities are to be granted access to the data of subscribers or registered users. In that regard, access can, as a general rule, be granted, in relation to the objective of fighting crime, only to the data of individuals suspected of planning, committing or having committed a serious crime or of being implicated in one way or another in such a crime (see, by analogy, ECtHR, 4 December 2015, Zakharov v. Russia, CE:ECHR:2015:1204JUD004714306, § 260). However, in particular situations, where for example vital national security, defence or public security interests are threatened by terrorist activities, access to the data of other persons might also be granted where there is objective evidence from which it can be deduced that that data might, in a specific case, make an effective contribution to combating such activities.

120. To ensure, in practice, that those conditions are fully respected, it is essential that access of the competent national authorities to retained data should, as a general rule, except in cases of validly established urgency, be subject to a prior review carried out either by a court or by an independent administrative body, and that the decision of that court or body should be made following a reasoned request by those authorities submitted, inter alia, within the framework of procedures for the prevention, detection or prosecution of crime (see, by analogy, in relation to Directive 2006/24, the Digital Rights judgment, paragraph 62; see also, by analogy, in relation to Article 8 of the ECHR, EctHR, 12 January 2016, Szabó and Vissy v. Hungary, CE:ECHR:2016:0112JUD003713814, §§ 77 and 80).

121. Likewise, the competent national authorities to whom access to the retained data has been granted must notify the persons affected, under the applicable national procedures, as soon as that notification is no longer liable to jeopardise the investigations being undertaken by those authorities. That notification is, in fact, necessary to enable the persons affected to exercise, inter alia, their right to a legal remedy, expressly provided for in Article 15(2) of Directive 2002/58, read together with Article 22 of Directive 95/46, where their rights have been infringed (see, by analogy, judgments of 7 May 2009, Rijkeboer, C-553/07, EU:C:2009:293, paragraph 52, and of 6 October 2015, Schrems, C-362/14, EU:C:2015:650, paragraph 95).

122. With respect to the rules relating to the security and protection of data retained by providers of electronic communications services, it must be noted that Article 15(1) of Directive 2002/58 does not allow Member States to derogate from Article 4(1) and Article 4(1a) of that directive. Those provisions require those providers to take appropriate technical and organisational measures to ensure the effective protection of retained data against risks of misuse and against any unlawful access to that data. Given the quantity of retained data, the sensitivity of that data and the risk of unlawful access to it, the providers of electronic communications services must, to ensure the full integrity and confidentiality of that data, guarantee a particularly high level of protection and security by means of appropriate technical and organisational measures. In particular, the national legislation must make provision for the data to be retained within the European Union and for the irreversible destruction of the data at the end of the data retention period (see, by analogy, in relation to Directive 2006/24, the Digital Rights judgment, paragraphs 66 to 68).

123. In any event, the Member States must ensure review, by an independent authority, of compliance with the level of protection guaranteed by EU law with respect to the protection of individuals in relation to the processing of personal data, that control being expressly required by Article 8(3) of the Charter and constituting, in accordance with the Court's settled case law, an essential element of respect for the protection of individuals in relation to the processing of personal data. If that were not so, persons whose personal data was retained would be deprived of the right, guaranteed in Article 8(1) and (3) of the Charter, to lodge with the national supervisory authorities a claim seeking the protection of their data (see, to that effect, the Digital Rights judgment, paragraph 68, and the judgment of 6 October 2015, Schrems, C-362/14, EU:C:2015:650, paragraphs 41 and 58).

124. It is the task of the referring courts to determine whether and to what extent the national legislation at issue in the main proceedings satisfies the requirements stemming from Article 15(1) of Directive 2002/58, read in the light of Articles 7, 8 and 11 and Article 52(1) of the Charter, as set out in paragraphs 115 to 123 of this judgment, with respect to both the access of the competent national authorities to the retained data and the protection and level of security of that data.

125. Considering the foregoing, the answer to the second question in Case C-203/15 and to the first question in Case C-698/15 is that Article 15(1) of Directive 2002/58, read in the light of Articles 7, 8 and 11 and Article 52(1) of the Charter, must be interpreted as precluding national legislation governing the protection and security of traffic and location data and, in particular, access of the competent national authorities to the retained data, where the objective pursued by that access, in the context of fighting crime, is not restricted solely to fighting serious crime, where access is not subject to prior review by a court or an independent administrative authority, and where there is no requirement that the data concerned should be retained within the European Union.

The Second Question in Case C-698/15

126. By the second question in Case C-698/15, the Court of Appeal (England & Wales) (Civil Division) seeks in essence to ascertain whether, in the Digital Rights judgment, the Court interpreted Articles 7 and/or 8 of the Charter in such a way as to expand the scope conferred on Article 8 ECHR by the European Court of Human Rights.

127. As a preliminary point, it should be recalled that, whilst, as Article 6(3) TEU confirms, fundamental rights recognised by the ECHR constitute general principles of EU law, the ECHR does not constitute, as long as the European Union has not acceded to it, a legal instrument which has been formally incorporated into EU law (see, to that effect, judgment of 15 February 2016, N., C-601/15 PPU, EU:C:2016:84, paragraph 45 and the case law cited).

128. Accordingly, the interpretation of Directive 2002/58, which is at issue in this case, must be undertaken solely in the light of the fundamental rights guaranteed by the Charter (see, to that effect, judgment of 15 February 2016, N., C-601/15 PPU, EU:C:2016:84, paragraph 46 and the case law cited).

129. Further, it must be borne in mind that the explanation on Article 52 of the Charter indicates that paragraph 3 of that article is intended to ensure the necessary consistency between the Charter and the ECHR, 'without thereby adversely affecting the autonomy of Union law and ... that of the Court of Justice of the European Union' (judgment of 15 February 2016, N., C-601/15 PPU, EU:C:2016:84, paragraph 47). In particular, as expressly stated in the second sentence of Article 52(3) of the Charter, the first sentence of Article 52(3) does not preclude Union law from providing protection that is more extensive then the ECHR. It should be added, finally, that Article 8 of the Charter concerns a fundamental right which is distinct from that enshrined in Article 7 of the Charter and which has no equivalent in the ECHR.

130. However, in accordance with the Court's settled case law, the justification for making a request for a preliminary ruling is not for advisory opinions to be delivered on general or hypothetical questions, but rather that it is necessary for the effective resolution of a dispute concerning EU law (see, to that effect, judgments of 24 April 2012, Kamberaj, C-571/10, EU:C:2012:233, paragraph 41; of 26 February 2013, Åkerberg Fransson, C-617/10, EU:C:2013:105, paragraph 42, and of 27 February 2014, Pohotovosť, C-470/12, EU:C:2014:101 paragraph 29).

131. In this case, in view of the considerations set out, in particular, in paragraphs 128 and 129 of the present judgment, the question whether the protection conferred by Articles 7 and 8 of the Charter is wider than that guaranteed in Article 8 of the ECHR is not such as to affect the interpretation of Directive 2002/58, read in the light of the Charter, which is the matter in dispute in the proceedings in Case C-698/15.

132. Accordingly, it does not appear that an answer to the second question in Case C-698/15 can provide any interpretation of points of EU law that is required for the resolution, in the light of that law, of that dispute.

133. It follows that the second question in Case C-698/15 is inadmissible.

(...)

On those grounds, the Court (Grand Chamber) hereby rules:

1. Article 15(1) of Directive 2002/58/EC of the European Parliament and of the Council of 12 July 2002 concerning the processing of personal data and the protection of privacy in the electronic communications sector (Directive on privacy and electronic communications), as amended by Directive 2009/136/EC of the European Parliament and of the Council of 25 November 2009, read in the light of Articles 7, 8 and 11 and Article 52(1) of the Charter of Fundamental Rights of the European Union, must be interpreted as precluding national legislation which, for the purpose of fighting crime, provides for general and indiscriminate retention of all traffic and location data of all subscribers and registered users relating to all means of electronic communication.

2. Article 15(1) of Directive 2002/58, as amended by Directive 2009/136, read in the light of Articles 7, 8 and 11 and Article 52(1) of the Charter of Fundamental Rights, must be interpreted as precluding national legislation governing the protection and security of traffic and location data and, in particular, access of the competent national authorities to the retained data, where the objective pursued by that access, in the context of fighting crime, is not restricted solely to fighting serious crime, where access is not subject to prior review by a court or an independent administrative authority, and where there is no requirement that the data concerned should be retained within the European Union.

3. The second question referred by the Court of Appeal (England & Wales) (Civil Division) is inadmissible.

The Constitutional Court of Austria: Judgment of 27 June 2014, Ref. No G 47/2012 et al.[3]

(...)

2.1. The Constitutional Court must limit itself to the discussion of the raised issues in a proceeding to review the constitutionality of a law under Article 140 B-VG, which was initiated by an application (...). Thus, the court solely must assess from the reasons set out in the application whether the contested provision is unconstitutional (...).

(...)

2.2.2. As the Constitutional Court already held in its decision in *VfSlg. 19.702/2012* with which it requested a preliminary ruling from the Court of Justice of the European Union that the Federal Constitutional Law contains an independent fundamental right to data protection besides Article 8 ECHR. The constitutional

[3]The judgement is available in English at the page of the Verfassungsgerichtshof Österreich under: https://www.vfgh.gv.at/downloads/VfGH_G_47-2012_ua_Erk_VRDspeicherung_EN.pdf.

provision of S 1 DSG 2000 provides that every natural or legal person is entitled to the confidentiality of personal data concerning him in so far as there is an interest worthy of the protection (S 1 para. 1 DSG 2000, (...)). S 1 para. 2 DSG 2000 contains a substantive legal reservation according to which, apart from the use of personal data which is of vital interest of the affected person or with his consent, limitations of the right of confidentiality are only permissible for the protection of prevailing legitimate interests of another, namely, for the interferences of an authority only based on laws, which are necessary for the grounds mentioned in Article 8 para. 2 ECHR.

2.2.3. For the legal basis S 1 para. 2 DSG 2000 requires, going beyond Article 8 para. 2 ECHR, that the use of data which is particularly worthy of protection due to its nature is only intended for the safeguarding of important public interests and that at the same time adequate safeguards to protect the confidentiality interests of the affected persons are set out in law.

2.2.4. The Constitutional Court considered in *VfSlg. 19.702/2012* that the Data Retention Directive – this was the reason for the preliminary ruling procedure – could be implemented only by infringing the fundamental right of S 1 DSG 2000 and that as a result thereof the Constitutional Court could be precluded from reviewing the legal regulations on data retention (*cf. VfSlg. 15.427/1999*). Since there would be no room for an implementation which is constitutionally conform, the Constitutional Court is precluded from a review of the legal regulations measured against the standard of S 1 DSG 2000. The Court of Justice of the European Union declared the regulation to be invalid and, therefore, this consideration is also no longer valid so that S 1 DSG 2000 and Article 8 ECHR are in any event again the relevant measure in the legal review procedure.

(...)

2.2.7. Articles 7 and 8 Charter of Fundamental Rights may also be considered as a standard in these proceedings to review the legislation. [...] This is the case when the relevant guarantee of the Charter of Fundamental Rights is similar to the constitutionally guaranteed rights of the Austrian Federal Constitution in its formulation and determination. Legal regulations which were issued based on the implementation of the directive form at least one case of implementation of Union law (*cf. only VfSlg. 19.632/2012*). Although the Data Retention Directive has been declared invalid (with effect *ex tunc*) the contested provisions – especially those that were announced by BGBl. I 27/2011 – were only issued following the implementation of Union law because they were adopted within the scope of RL 2002/58/EG and in particular Article 15 para. 1 thereof.

(...)

2.2.8.1. Article 8 ECHR determines the interpretation of Article 7 Charter of Fundamental Rights in such a way as is evident by the comments on Article 7 Charter of Fundamental Rights that this Article 7 'corresponds' to it and therefore 'has the same meaning and scope'. (Article 52 para. 3 Charter of Fundamental Rights, the references to the jurisprudence of the European Court of Human Rights in the judgment of the Court of Justice of the European Union in *Digital Rights Ireland und Seitlinger and others*, para. 35, 47, 54 f. are also in this sense).

2.2.8.2. S 1 DSG 2000 contains a substantive legal reservation which defines the limits for interference with the fundamental rights in a much narrower sense than what Article 8 para. 2 ECHR does. Apart from the use of personal data in the vital interest of the affected person, or with his consent limitations of the right of confidentiality are only permissible for the protection of prevailing legitimate interests of another, namely, for the interferences of a governmental authority purely based on laws, which are necessary for the grounds mentioned in Article 8 para. 2 ECHR.

For the legal basis S 1 para. 2 DSG 2000 requires beyond the scope of Article 8 para. 2 ECHR that data which by its very nature are particularly worthy of protection may only be made use of to safeguard important public interests and that simultaneously adequate safeguards protecting the confidentiality interests of the individual are legally set down. Finally, these provisions explicitly prescribe that in the case of permissible limitations the interference with the fundamental right must be in a 'least intrusive and goal orientated manner'.

2.2.9. According to previous court decisions of the Constitutional Court it follows from this regulation that a stricter standard must be applied to the proportionality of the interference with the fundamental right under S 1 DSG 2000 than the one already provided under Article 8 ECHR (*VfSlg. 16.369/2001, 18.643/2008*). This level of protection is also unaffected by the Charter of Fundamental Rights in those matters where the legislator has a discretion in implementing Union law (cf. Article 53 Charter of Fundamental Rights; see above 2.2.6). Against this background the contested provisions need to be measured against the standard of the Federal Constitutional law, namely against S 1 DSG 2000 and Article 8 ECHR.

(...)

2.3.4. Under S 53 para. 3a (3) SPG, security authorities are entitled to request information concerning the name and address of a user who was assigned an IP address at a particular time from providers of public communication services if the security authorities need this data as an essential prerequisite to counter a concrete danger to the life, health or freedom of an individual in the context of the first general obligation to render assistance (S 19 SPG), a dangerous attack (S 16 para. 1 (1) SPG) or a criminal association (S 16 para. 1 (2)), 'even if the use of retained data according to S 99 para. 5 (4) in conjunction with S 102a TKG 2003 is required for this'. Under S 53 para. 3b SPG, security authorities are further entitled to require from providers of public telecommunication services information about location data and the international mobile subscriber identity (IMSI) of the carried equipment of a person in danger or a person accompanying the person in danger, 'even if the use of retained data in terms S 99 para. 5 (3) in conjunction with S 102a TKG 2003 is required for this.'

The requirement of providing information under S 53 para. 3b SPG is that there is an actual threat to the life, health or freedom of an individual which can be assumed due to the set of circumstances and that the security authorities take the necessary steps within the scope of their duty to provide assistance or to avert danger (S 53 para. 3b SPG). The actions of the security authorities under the mentioned provisions of the SPG require no judicial approval. Under S 91c para. 1 SPG, the legal protection commissioner needs to 'be notified as soon as possible' about this request for information. He is responsible for the review of such a notification (S 91c para. 1 last sentence SPG).

2.3.5. Under S 1 para. 1 DSG 2000, everyone is entitled to the confidentiality of personal data concerning him, in so far as he has a legitimate interest worthy of protection, in particular with regard to the respect of the private and family life. Limitations of this fundamental right are according to the reservation of S 1 para. 2 DSG 2000 (apart from the affected individual's vital interests in the use of personal data or his consent thereto) only permissible for interferences of a public authority only based on legislation, if they are necessary for the reasons mentioned in Article 8 para. 2 ECHR and if they are sufficiently precise so that they provide in a foreseeable manner for everyone under which conditions the determination or the use of personal data is allowed for the performance of specific administrative tasks (. . .).

Legal limitations of the fundamental right to data protection must be proportional when balancing the seriousness of the interference and the weight of the objectives pursued (. . .). Such laws may only provide for the use of data which by its very nature is worthy of protection for the safeguarding of important public interests and must simultaneously set adequate safeguards for the protection of the confidentiality interests of the affected individual (S 1 para. 2 second sentence DSG 2000).

Also, in the case of permissible limitations under Article 8 para. 2 ECHR, the interference with the fundamental rights may only be carried out in the least intrusive and goal orientated manner under the last sentence of S 1 para. 2 DSG 2000. Therefore, the respective legislator must provide for these requirements a sufficient matter-specific regulation so that the cases of permissible interferences with the fundamental right of data protection are defined and limited (. . .).

2.3.6. The fundamental right of data protection which is enshrined in S 1 DSG 2000 provides for constitutional protection against the identification of personal data (. . .). The data which needs to be stored under S 102a TKG 2003 and which needs to be provided under S 135 para. 2a StPO and S 53 para. 3a as well as S 53 para. 3b SPG is personal data as defined in S 1 para. 1 DSG 2000. In particular, all the categories of data listed in para. 2 to 4 of S 102a TKG 2003 are of such a nature that the identity of the person concerned is determined or is at least determinable. Particularly, with regard to the possibilities of linking with other information (e.g. the conclusions which can be drawn from accumulated calls of a particular subscriber number) listed by the applicants, a legitimate interest of confidentiality worthy of protection exists within the affected data as defined by S 1 para. 1 DSG 2000.

2.3.7. The providers of public communication services are obliged by S 102a para. 1 TKG 2003 to store data under para. 2 to 4 of this provision. This obligation interferes with the fundamental right of data protection enshrined in S 1 DSG 2000 as well as with the right to respect for private and family life enshrined in Article 8 ECHR of the users of public communication services (. . .).

2.3.7.1. The fact that the storage is done by providers of public communication services – i.e. by private companies – who are obliged to store data under S 102a

TKG 2003 does not change the existence of an interference with the rights in S 1 DSG 2000 and Article 8 ECHR by the legislator. A ‘communication service provider’ includes everyone who offers a communication service (S 92 para. 3 first half of the sentence in conjunction with S 3 (9) TKG 2003) but who – in contrast to the ‘operator of a communication service’ (S 3 (1) TKG 2003) –does not necessarily control all the functions of this service (. . .). The TKG 2003 assumes that ‘providers’ as well as ‘operators’ of a communication service are (private) companies (see only S 1 para. 1, S 34 ff. TKG 2003).

2.3.7.2. These companies have no margin due to the imposed obligation to store data under S 102a TKG 2003. Under S 109 para. 3 (22) TKG 2003, they would commit an administrative offence if they would act contrary to the storage obligation in S 102a TKG 2003.

2.3.8. The storage of data on the ground of the obligation under S 102a TKG 2003 and access to the data (providing information) by police and prosecution authorities – particularly under S 135 para. 2a StPO and S 53 Para. 3a (3) as well as S 53 para. 3b SPG – constitute an interference with the fundamental right of data protection (S 1 DSG 2000) and the right to respect for private and family life under Article 8 ECHR (. . .).

2.3.9. Regulations which constitute a serious violation of fundamental rights such as the contested provisions may be admissible for combating serious crimes, provided they comply with the strict requirements of S 1 DSG 2000 and Article 8 ECHR. Whether such an interference with regard to S 1 para. 2 DSG 2000 and Article 8 para. 2 ECHR is permissible depends on the requirements of the conditions of the storage of data for retention and on the requirements of their erasure as well as on the legal safeguards when determining the possibilities of official and private access to this data. The contested provisions of TKG 2003, StPO and SPG do not fulfil these requirements:

2.3.10. The provisions concerning the retention of data including the provisions on information on retained data in the StPO and SPG serve to achieve the objectives mentioned in Article 8 para. 2 ECHR, namely, in particular, the maintenance of public peace and order and the protection of rights and freedoms of others. The legislator could within his scope of discretion reasonable expect that the regulations on data retention are abstractly suitable to achieve these objectives (. . .).

2.3.11. A further requirement for the proportionality and thereby the permissibility of the interference is that the severity of the specific interference does not exceed the weight and importance of the objectives which are to be achieved through data retention.

2.3.11.1. The point of departure of the assessment of the proportionality of data retention is the idea that the fundamental right of data protection in a democratic society – in the area of protection relevant here – is directed towards the facilitating and safeguarding of confidential communication between individuals. The individual and his free personal development do not only depend on the public communication but also on the confidential communication in the community; freedom as the right of an individual and as a condition of a society are determined by the quality of the information relations (. . .).

2.3.11.2. The importance and weight of the aims pursued through data retention are significant as is expressed by legislator with the purpose in S 102a para. 1 last sentence TKG 2003. Even if the regulation under the wording of para. 1 serves an important public interest (see above 2.3.10), it is necessary that due to the 'dispersion range' of the interference, the scope and nature of the affected data (see below 2.3.14.3) and the resulting severity of the interference with the right of informational self-determination (data can be accessed which not only enables the creation of a movement profile but also that conclusions can be drawn concerning private preferences and the acquaintances of an individual in the case where data can be linked; see below 2.3.14.5), the legislator ensures with appropriate regulations that the data is only made available to police and prosecution authorities in the presence of an important public interest with comparative weight in an individual case and if it is subject to judicial control. It should be noted that state action was and is faced in many ways – not least also in the fight against crime for which data retention is intended – with special challenges by the rapid distribution of the use of 'new' communication technologies (e.g. mobile telephony, e-mail, exchange of information in the context of the World Wide Web) in the last two decades. The case law of the Constitutional Court has always considered this changed environment of police investigations (. . .). It should be noted that the expansion of technical possibilities also leads thereto, that the dangers which these expansions holds for the freedom of individuals must be countered in an adequate way.

2.3.11.3. The Court of Justice of the European Union has emphasised in its judgment in *Digital Rights Ireland und Seitlinger and others* that the Data Retention Directive provides for no objective criteria which makes it possible to limit the access of the competent national authorities to data and their subsequent use for the prevention, detection or prosecution of criminal offences which with regard to the extent and severity of the interference with the fundamental rights enshrined in Articles 7 and 8 of the Charter of Fundamental Rights can be considered as sufficiently serious to justify such interference (para. 60). On the contrary, the Data Retention Directive in Article 1 para. 1 only generally refers to the serious criminal offences determined by the national law of the Member States.

(. . .)

2.3.11.6. The proportionality of the storage of data for retention is – regardless of the reservation of the judicial approval of the providing information on retained data (S 135 para. 2a in conjunction with S 137 para. 1 StPO), the referral of the legal protection commissioner and his right of appeal under S 147 para. 1 (2a) and para. 3 second sentence StPO – already, therefore, not assured because due to S 135 para. 2a StPO in conjunction with S 102a, S 102b para. 1 TKG 2003 it is not guaranteed that retained data is only then provided if it serves the criminal prosecution and solving of the investigation which in the individual case is a serious threat to the objectives stated in Article 8 para. 2 ECHR and which justifies such interference. Therefore, S 135 para. 2a StPO is conflict with S 1 para. 2 DSG 2000.

(. . .)

2.3.14. In connection with the requirements to provide information ('providing information') S 102a TKG 2003 also proves to be unconstitutional. The provisions relating to providing information on retained data together with the provisions of TKG 2003 which require the storage of data constitute a serious violation of the constitutionally guaranteed data protection right in S 1 DSG 2000 of the 'user' (S 92 para. 3 (2) TKG 2003) of public communication services or individuals otherwise affected by the storage and thus also the second and third applicant (see above 2.3.7).

2.3.14.1. The applicants never alleged nor was it submitted in the hearing that the storage and processing of the data of the type mentioned in S 102a TKG 2003 are completely unsuitable to contribute to solving the investigation of a serious crime. The suitability of the interference with the fundamental rights needs to be examined in an abstract way, as it neither requires a specific percentage of the frequency of the application of the provisions in practice, nor a specific 'success rate' in the solving of the investigation of crimes. It is sufficient if the legislature was allowed to assume the suitability of the measure that has to serve the envisaged purpose (...). The Constitutional Court does not consider in these proceedings whether each individual date to be retained under S 102a TKG 2003 displays this suitability. It is by no means established from the outset that the storage of all the data to be stored for retention and processing under S 102a TKG 2003 in the implementation of the invalid Data Retention Directive is proportional. The mere possibility to make use of new technologies for further monitoring measures does not in advance justify an interference with the freedoms protected by S 1 DSG 2000 and Article 8 ECHR.

2.3.14.2. The Constitutional Court has already emphasised in its decision in *VfSlg. 19.702/2012* that the 'distribution range' of the unfounded storage exceeds those interferences in the legal sphere which it ever had to decide and which is protected by S 1 DSG 2000 (...). This applies to the affected category of individuals, the scope and nature of the data as well as the purposes for which it is required and the modalities of the use of data.

2.3.14.3. It needs to be considered that the storage affects primarily the users of fixed networks, mobile communication, Internet access services and e-mail services (S 92 para. 3 und 15 TKG 2003) and thus the population of Austria is affected to a large extent. At the end of 2013, every business had an average of two fixed networks and more than half of every household had such a connection. On average 1.5 SIM cards for mobile telephony can be attributed to every inhabitant. Around 60% of households and businesses had Internet access via mobile or fixed broadband and the market penetration of broadband in the framework of smartphone tariffs amounted to 87% for household and businesses (...). Hence, almost the entire population is affected by the obligation to store data under S 102a TKG 2003 (...).

2.3.14.4. The Constitutional Court has already found in its decision in *VfSlg. 19.702/2012* that the data retention includes almost exclusively those individuals who have provided no cause – in the sense that they behaved in such a manner that would require state interference – for the storage of their data (...). Rather, most of the population uses public communication services for the exercise of fundamental rights, in particular the freedom of expression, information and communication.

(...)

2.3.16.1. Considering the severity of the interference in itself, the rules regarding the data retention – (...) – lack provisions which clarify for the individuals who are under the obligation to store and who are affected by the storage that with the term 'erasure' of the retained data the recoverability of the data has to be excluded (...). Nothing can change the practice of providers who probably already out of economic considerations 'overwrite' retained data and so ultimately prevent the data's recoverability, as well as the practice of courts and authorities who 'physically' erase provided data according to the relevant submissions in the hearing before the Constitutional Court. An 'erasure' in the sense that only the access to data which continues to exist (and which can be reconstructed) is prevented does not meet the strict constitutional requirements (see above 2.2.8.2). Since this is not expressly clarified by S 102a para. 8 TKG 2003 and other provisions, the requirement of a sufficiently precise legal basis (S 1 para. 2 DSG 2000) is not fulfilled with regard to the interference exercised under S 102a para. 1 TKG 2003.

2.3.16.2. A deficiency in the legal basis is also present with regard to the obligations of the operators and authorities in connection with 'always-on service' (...). If an Internet access service is run and used as an 'always-on service' the question arises at what time the 'communication' within the meaning of S 102a para. 1 TKG 2003 is deemed as terminated. (...)

2.3.17. As a result, the applicants are, therefore, correct to the extent where they argued that the regulations are not proportional in their context. The limitations of the fundamental right of data protection according to the legal reservation in S 1 para. 2 DSG 2000 are only permissible based on laws, which are necessary for the reasons mentioned on Article 8 para. 2 ECHR and which regulate in a sufficiently precise manner that is clear to everyone, the conditions under which the investigation or use of personal data for the performance of specific administrative tasks is allowed. Legal limitations on the fundamental right of data protection must be the least invasive method to achieve the objectives and must be proportionally in the balance between the seriousness of the interference and the weight of the pursued objectives.

2.3.18. The regulations (S 135 para. 2a StPO in conjunction with S102a TKG 2003, S 53 para. 3a (3) SPG in conjunction with S 102a TKG 2003, S 53 para. 3b SPG in conjunction with S 102a TKG 2003) concerning data retention do not fulfil these requirements for the above reasons.

The Constitutional Court of Belgium: Judgment of 11 June 2015, Ref. No 84/2015[4]

(. . .)

B.5.2. As Article 2 of the disputed law states, this partially transposes the "data retention" directive and Article 15.1 of the "privacy and electronic communications" directive into Belgian law.

The presentation of the grounds of the law accordingly specifies:

"The purpose of this directive 2006/24/EC is to harmonise the provisions of Member States relating to obligations of providers of publicly available electronic communication services or public electronic communications networks in terms of retention of certain data that is generated or processed by these providers, in view of guaranteeing the availability of this data for purposes of examining, detecting, and prosecuting serious offences as they are defined by each Member State in their domestic law.

Directive 2006/24/EC should have been transposed in principle by 15 September 2007, except on retention of communication data regarding Internet access, Internet telephony and Internet e-mail, for which the transposition deadline set was 15 March 2009, as Belgium exercised the option stipulated by the directive to request postponement.

At the end of September 2012, the European Commission officially demanded that Belgium transpose the directive and drew Belgium's attention to the fines that the Court of Justice could impose upon it for incomplete transposition of the directive. It is therefore out of the question to wait longer and, particularly, to wait for possible amendment of the directive.

In view of the transposition into Belgian law of Directive 2006/24/EC, it is essential to review the wording of Article 126 of the law of 13 June 2005 relating to electronic communications which, on a certain number of points, contains provisions that do not comply with the European stipulation.

The transposition of Directive 2006/24/EC will be partially added to by modification of Article 126 of the aforementioned law of 13 June 2005, and partially by the adoption of a royal order implementing this new Article 126, so that the list of data to be retained and the requirements that this data must meet will be set by the King" (Parl. doc., Chamber, 2012-2013, DOC 53-2921/001, pp. 3-4).

(. . .)

B.9. As the Court of Justice of the European Union ruled in its aforementioned judgment of 8 April 2014 (point 34), the obligation imposed by Articles 3 and 6 of Directive 2006/24 on providers of publicly available electronic communications services or of public communications networks to retain, for a certain period, data relating to a person's private life and to his communications, such as those referred to

[4]The judgement is available at the page of the Constitutional Court of Belgium under: https://www.const-court.be. Translation ordered by the University of Warsaw.

in Article 5 of the directive, constitutes in itself an interference with rights guaranteed by Article 7 of the Charter.

The Court of Justice also ruled in point 35 of the judgment that "the access of the competent national authorities to the data constitutes a further interference with that fundamental right (. . .). Accordingly, Articles 4 and 8 of Directive 2006/24 laying down rules relating to the access of the competent national authorities to the data also constitute an interference with the rights guaranteed by Article 7 of the Charter."

This interference of the directive was qualified as particularly serious (point 37), although the directive does not permit the acquisition of knowledge of the content of the electronic communications as such (point 39).

B.10.1. As the Court of Justice noted in points 56 and 57 of its judgment, the directive imposes the retention of all traffic data regarding fixed telephony, mobile telephony, Internet access, Internet e-mail and Internet telephony, covering, in a generalised manner, all persons and all means of electronic communication without any differentiation being made in the light of the objective of fighting against serious offences that the European Union legislator intended to prosecute.

The disputed law does not distinguish itself in any way from the directive on this point. Indeed, as stated in B.8, the categories of data that must be retained are identical to those stipulated in the directive, whereas no distinction is made regarding the persons concerned or the particular rules to be established based on the objective of combating the offences described in Article 126, § 2, of the law of 13 June 2005 replaced by the disputed law. As the Court of Justice noted regarding the directive (point 58), the law therefore applies even to persons for whom there is no evidence capable of suggesting that their conduct might have a link, even an indirect or remote one, with the offences stipulated by the disputed law. Likewise, the law applies without any exception even to persons whose communications are subject to professional secrecy.

B.10.2. No more than it is the case for the directive, disputed Article 5 does not require any relationship between the data whose retention is provided for and a threat to public security. It also does not limit retention in relation to data pertaining to a particular period and/or a particular geographical zone and/or to a circle of particular persons likely to be involved in an offence referred to in the law, or to persons who could, for other reasons, contribute, by the retention of their data, to the prevention, detection or prosecution of these offences.

B.10.3. If the authorities competent to access the data retained are stipulated in Article 126, § 5, 3°, of the law of 13 June 2005, replaced by Article 5 of the disputed law, no material or procedural condition was defined by the law regarding this access.

B.10.4. Finally, regarding the data retention period, the law does not make any distinction between categories of data according to their potential usefulness for the objective pursued or according to the persons concerned.

B.11. On the same grounds as those that led the Court of Justice of the European Union to judge the "data retention" directive invalid, it must be found that by adopting Article 5 of the disputed law, the legislator exceeded the limits required to comply with the principle of proportionality with regard to Articles 7, 8 and 52.1 of the Charter of Fundamental Rights of the European Union.

Subsequently, the aforementioned Article 5 breaches Articles 10 and 11 of the Constitution read in conjunction with these provisions. The sole ground in case n° 5859 and the first ground in case n° 5859 are well founded.

B.12. Due to their indivisibility from Article 5, it is necessary to also cancel Articles 1 to 4, 6 and 7 of the disputed law of 30 July 2013 and therefore the entirety of said law.

B.13. Given that they cannot lead to more extensive cancellation, there is no need to examine other grounds in case n° 5859.

On these grounds,

the Court cancels the law of 30 July 2013 "modifying Articles 2, 126 and 145 of the law of 13 June 2005 relating to electronic communications and Article 90decies of the Belgian Code of Criminal Procedure". (...)

The Supreme Administrative Court of the Republic of Bulgaria: Judgment of 11 December 2008, Ref. No 13627[5]

[...]

The present instance finds the cassation arguments for the inaccuracy of the contested judgement well-founded about the legal arguments of the three-member panel for the compliance of Article 5 of Ordinance No. 40/07.01.2008 with the substantive law and the European Convention on Human Rights.

Under Article 5 (1) of the secondary legislation, for the operational and search activities, the undertakings-providers of public electronic communication networks and/or services provide a passive technical access through a computer terminal to the data in their storage to the Directorate of "Operational and Technical Information" at the Ministry of the Interior. The Court has wrongly understood the outlined way as a "passive technical access" of the requested body from the system of the Ministry of Interior to the stored data as a method possible only upon submission of a written request, as are the prerequisites under para 2 and para 3 for the prosecution authorities, the court and the security services. In fact, the rule does not impose any limitations on the data, accessed through a computer terminal, and the expression "for the purpose of the operational and search activities" is a general one and does not guarantee the observance of Article 32 (1) of the Constitution of the Republic of Bulgaria that the personal life of the citizens is inviolable. No method is established for observing the constitutional principle on the right to protection

[5]The judgement is available at the page of the Supreme Administrative Court of the Republic of Bulgaria under: http://aip-bg.org/pdf/reshenie%2013627_december%2008.pdf. Translation ordered by the University of Warsaw.

against unlawful interference in the personal family life of the individual, as well as against the violation of his honour, dignity, and reputation.

Article 5 (2) and (3) of the Ordinance regulates the possibility of the investigative bodies, the prosecution and the court "for the purpose of the criminal process", and the security services "in case of necessity, related to the national security" to obtain from the undertakings-providers of public electronic communication networks and/or services, access to stored data upon submission of a written request. The so formulated text does not lay down conditions preventing the abuse of the possibility of violating the constitutionally guaranteed rights of citizens. No reference is made to the special laws of the Criminal Procedures Code, the Special Intelligence Tools Act, the Personal Data Protection Act, where the prerequisites for allowing access to certain data, related to the privacy and personal data of the individual are specified.

The Supreme Administrative Court considers that the text of Article 5 of Regulation 40/2008 contradicts the provision of Article 8 of the ECHR, according to which everyone has the right to respect for his or her personal and family life, his home and the secret of his correspondence, and the intervention of public authorities in the use of this right is inadmissible. An exception to this principle is set out in Article 8.2 of the Convention in exhaustively listed hypotheses: "save in the cases, provided for by law and required in a democratic society in the interest of the national and public security or the economic well-being of the country, to prevent riots and crimes, for the protection of health and morals, or the rights and freedoms of others." The national legal norms should comply with this rule and introduce comprehensible and defined grounds for both access to citizens' private data and the procedure of their receipt. Any limitation of the right to privacy should be outlined with norms, providing sufficient guarantees against misuse of the powers of individual bodies and services for access to data, related to the private lives of citizens.

In Article 5 of Ordinance 40/2008, issued by the Minister of Interior and the Chairperson of the State Agency for Information Technologies and Communications, it is not clear whether the provision regarding the guarantee of the right to protection against illegal interference in the personal and family life of citizens, and this contradicts the provision in Article 8 of the ECHR, texts in Directive 2006/24/EC, Articles 32 and 34 of the Constitution of the Republic of Bulgaria.

The judgement of the three-member panel, insofar as it concerns the contradiction of Article 5 of the Ordinance with norms of the European law and with higher norms of internal legislation as wrong, enacted in violation of the substantive law and in case of groundlessness, on the grounds of Article 229, item 3 of the APC should be repealed. Under Article 222 (1) of the APC, in this part, the dispute should be settled in substance by the present instance, and the contested rule should be repealed in full for the reasons set out above.

(. . .)

Based on the above and on the grounds of Article 221 (2) and Article 222 (1) of the APC, the Supreme Administrative Court, by a five-member panel,

ADJUDICATED:

TO REJECT Judgement No. 8786/16.07.2008, enacted on administrative case No. 5393/2008 by a three-member panel of the Supreme Administrative Court IN

THE PART, where the appeal of the "Access to Information Program" Foundation against Article 5 of Ordinance No. 40/07.01.2008 on the categories of data and order of their storage and provision by undertakings-providers of public electronic communication networks and/or services for national security and detection of crimes, issued by the Minister of the Interior and the Chairperson of the State Agency for Information Technologies and Communications was rejected, and instead DECREES:

TO REVOKE Article 5 of Ordinance No. 40/07.01.2008 on the categories of data and the method in which they are stored and provided by the undertakings-providers of public electronic communication networks and/or services for national security and detection of crimes, issued by the Minister of the Interior and the Chairman of the State Agency for Information Technologies and Communications.

TO LEAVE IN EFFECT the remaining provisions of the Judgement.

(...)

The Constitutional Court of the Republic of Bulgaria: Judgment of 12 March 2015, Ref. No 8/2014[6]

(...)

From the review of rulemaking in the field of the preservation and storage of traffic data, the protection of fundamental rights of citizens on a national and European scale, including in the light of the outcome of judicial review procedures, several considerations which the Court has laid down in its further reflections on the merits of this constitutional dispute arise:

1. Announcing Directive 2006/24/EC invalid by the abovementioned judgement of CJEU cannot have the effect of automatically repealing or dis-applying the disputed statutory provisions of the domestic law, with which it is transposed. In its declaration of invalidity, only the obligation of the Member States to introduce its requirements into their domestic law is terminated. The adopted law shall continue to operate until it has been revoked or amended by the national legislature, or declared unconstitutional by the Constitutional Court.

2. The regime of preservation, storage, access, exploitation and destruction of traffic data, introduced by the provisions of Article 250a - Article 250e, Article 251 and Article 251a of the ECA, in its nature and essence is undoubtedly an interference with the basic, constitutionally protected rights of citizens and should therefore be treated as an exception to the rules, established by the constitutional provisions of Article 32 (1) and Article 34 (1). These rights are not absolute. Under the requirements of Article 32 (2) and Article 34(2) of the Constitution, the

[6]The judgement is available at the page of the Constitutional Court of the Republic of Bulgaria under: http://constcourt.bg/en/Acts/GetHtmlContent/00025810-e1fb-4f7d-bced-a09c85bab51e. Translation ordered by the University of Warsaw.

exceptions should be regulated by law; should be admitted only with the permission of the judiciary; and only when it is necessary to detect and prevent serious crimes. In this case, the disputed regulation is created by law and therefore formally fulfills the first constitutional requirement.

3. The provision of Article 250a (2) of the ECA regarding the purpose of storing traffic data, contradicts the Constitution, namely, for the needs of detection and investigation of crimes under Article 319a - 319f of the Criminal Code (CC), as well as for the search of persons. The exception under Article 34 (2) of the Constitution is permissible only when the intervention in the sphere of the inviolability of the freedom and confidentiality of correspondence and other communications is necessary for the detection and prevention of serious crimes, and it cannot be interpreted and extensively applied. Therefore, the provision in the "and crimes under Article 319a – 319f of the Criminal Code" part, where crimes are not serious within the meaning of Article 93, item 7 of the Criminal Code, except for the one under Article 319a (5) of the Criminal Code, as long as the punishments, provided for in the relevant sections of the particular sections of the Criminal Code, are not imprisonment for more than five years, life imprisonment or life imprisonment without substitution, is unconstitutional. This is true for the latter hypothesis - the search for persons, and this hypothesis cannot be individually included in the constitutional framework of the restriction, except in the cases, when the wanted person is a victim or a perpetrator of a serious crime.

It should be noted that the Bulgarian legislator has substantially extended and exceeded even the requirements of Directive 2006/24/EC; this Directive is highly criticised in theory and practice (Article 1, § 1), and which, discussing the access to traffic data, limits it only to "the investigation, detection and tracking of serious offenses as defined in the national law of each Member State". Undoubtedly, the norm, establishing the legal definition of the concept of "serious crime" within the meaning of the Criminal Code, is applicable. By interpreting the normative solutions adopted by the Directive under discussion, upon comparing them with the principles of the Charter and the Covenant on Civil and Criminal Matters, to substantiate its thesis of its imperfections, CJEU, in its judgement, also uses the criterion of a serious crime which includes the forms of the organised crime and terrorism.

4. The approach of extending the scope of the transposed Directive is used by the legislator in defining the subjects, who are entitled to request making an inquiry on the data under Article 250b (1) of ECA. The Constitutional Court finds this group being too broad, and the current regulation projects an essential constitutional problem. Complying with the established constitutional standard, as well as any limitation of the fundamental rights of citizens should be regulated by law, and includes not only the grounds but also the bodies and procedures under which the proper measure will be implemented. In this sense, it is imperative for the legitimate subject to have the competence to detect and investigate serious crimes explicitly assigned to him by law, i.e. powers relating to the legitimate aim pursued by the law. This requirement, however, is not met by all the subjects in the group of the ones referred to in Article 250b (1) of ECA. This justifies the assumption of the

unconstitutionality of that provision according to the criteria laid down in Article 32 (2) and Article 34 (2) of the Constitution.

5. The constitutional requirement for control by a court or other independent body is absent in the procedure, governed by Article 250a (5) of ECA. In this case, the bodies, requesting access, contact directly the undertaking providing the data and, without the corresponding authorisation, put into practice a continuation of retention for up to six months, which in itself is a significant one.

There is also a lack of normal control over the destruction of an issued inquiry on data under Article 250e (4) of ECA, which is not used for the initiation of pre-trial proceedings - Article 250e of ECA. Therefore, the provisions of Article 250a (5) and Article 250e of ECA also appear to be inconsistent with the Constitution. The imperfections of the legal control, as settled by the contested legal texts, whether and to what extent it effectively and fully fulfils its purpose of not allowing unlawful interference in the private life of citizens is a matter which the Court will deal with later.

(. . .)

It is particularly important that some of the crimes could not be convincingly detected and thoroughly investigated without the investigation and analysis of traffic data (e.g. acts relating to child pornography, trafficking of people, etc.), and it is, therefore, unacceptable to deny the measures introduced by the contested provisions. To achieve the legitimate objectives thus formulated, it is necessary and appropriate to store such data in a democratic society, whereby the interference should not be inordinate in accordance with the principle of proportionality, the substance, content and criteria of which the Constitutional Court has repeatedly dealt with (. . .).

The issue of the framework of possible and permissible interference of state in the fundamental human rights in terms of their content in the context of the essence and the different manifestations of the principle of proportionality is the subject of many judgements and a rich jurisprudence of the ECHR (. . .).

To assess whether and to what extent the measure, envisaged by the contested legislation, which is an interference with the private life of citizens, is proportionate to the objective defended, it is necessary to consider another particularly important argument in the Ombudsman's claim, supported by a large number of the opinions of the interested parties - that all data from the telecommunication traffic is absolutely subject to storage, i.e. all citizens involved in communication are practically affected, not just those for whom we have data or at least clues that they have committed a serious crime, that they are involved with international terrorist organisations, etc.

The main objection raised to this end is that the pursuit of the legitimate objective formulated cannot be attained at the cost of such a substantial interference with the fundamental rights of persons having nothing to do with the intended means for the prevention, detection, and investigation. This imbalance cannot be denied because it is true, that the data, generated by telecommunication, is subject to retention in respect of all persons, not just those of suspects or perpetrators of serious crimes. However, it is also true that there is practically no other way than the commented measure, which, on the one hand, is directed only at those whose behaviour is or could be subject to criminal prosecution and, on the other hand, can provide the necessary sufficient information about the authors of serious crimes, their links, contacts, accomplices, financing, location, devices used, movement, and mainly relating to the time before the crime for the purposes of the investigation. A case, illustrating the position of the Court on this issue, would arise in case that, for example, a perpetrator of a terrorist act who, until the time of committing the act, is not in the police database in connection with other previous criminal acts, to require verification of data from his communications, is captured at the crime scene. If the contested measure did not exist, to impose retention of data on the undertakings, providing the services, for all the traffic flow, then the generation and tracking of such data in respect of that person could only begin once the offence had already taken place, and the identity of the perpetrator was established. It is clear that, in such a case, it is impossible to gather information on the issues mentioned earlier, associated with the preparation, organisation, the very perpetration of offence and the possible accomplices, because it will only cover the period following the crime and therefore cannot serve the investigation.

In this sense, the comparison of the purpose protected and the remedy applied leads to the conclusion that, by its nature, the measure introduced is in principle relevant, necessary and appropriate, including also under the criterion of the proportionality of restriction.

That is not the case, however, with the question of the period of its operation, as set out in Article 250a (1) of ECA - 12 months, which, considering the specific socio-political situation, the Court assesses as disproportionately long and substantially beyond the necessary period for achieving the defined targets. The accumulation of a communication traffic database for one year allows the use of data not only to produce a detailed personal profile (with all the related problems), but also to achieve accurate and detailed differentiation of the permanent, ordinary, incidental manifestations of the particular person, his contacts, inclinations, interests, including the demarcation of those that are precedent in his behaviour and reactions, as well as the systematisation according to different criteria of the places he visits permanently, often, rarely or incidentally, as well as an accurate identification of the persons with whom he does so. Under the same scheme, his contacts - personal, business, professional, cultural, etc., can be categorised and distinguished, and against the specifics of data - with a high degree of accuracy about the intensity of their use. It is obvious that this term has all the signs of disproportionality with the purpose of the measure introduced, which has a major impact on the constitutional assessment of the entire legal regime of the retention, access to and possible use of the data.

For these reasons, the Constitutional Court considers that the excessively long period of retention of data alone compromises the constitutionality of the adopted measure as a whole, since in its regulation, according to the envisaged period of the restriction, it is disproportionate.

(...)

The wording of Article 250c (4) of ECA is too general, and according to which, for the criminal proceedings, the data under Article 250a (1) are submitted to the court and the bodies of the pre-trial proceedings under the terms and procedure of the

Criminal Procedure Code (CPC). The law does not specify to which specific provisions of CPC the reference is directed, but it is clear that it is the application of Article 159 of CPC. The comparative analysis of the two provisions implies the conclusion that, by the legislative technique used, the disputed provision completely derogates the constitutional requirement for judicial control when access is requested to the telecommunication traffic data. This is not foreseen either in the ECA reference rule or the specific provision of the CPC. In the present case, there is no reason to assume that, despite the grave interference in the personal lives of citizens, which unconditionally constitutes violation of privacy, freedom and the confidentiality of correspondence, there is any legal possibility of constitutional tolerance of the derogation under discussion; only because the request is made by an authority of the pre-trial proceedings.

(...)

Therefore, the Constitutional Court considers that the contested legislative decision to eliminate judicial control in the event of a request for access to traffic data by a pre-trial authority is contrary to the standards, established by the Constitution, the Charter and the Covenant on Civil and Political Rights. As far as the subject of the constitutional control, in this case, is only the text of Article 250c (4) of ECA and not that of Article 159 (1) of CPC, the Court ruling is limited only to this text, finding that it is unconstitutional.

The removal of the defect, found in the contested regulation by law is of a particular material importance because it concerns the legal regulation of judicial procedures for controlling access to data, relating to citizens' fundamental rights – private life and the freedom and confidentiality of correspondence.

Second, it is necessary to point out that there is no legal remedy at all, and, therefore, there are no grounds and procedures the persons, affected by the measures, whose data were provided to the relevant public authorities, but were not used to initiate criminal proceedings or the initiation was terminated, to be informed when and on what grounds they were subject to their application, and for what purpose they were used for.

In conclusion, the Constitutional Court considers that, although the measure discussed has been introduced as a means of achieving a legitimate objective of common interest both for the European Union and for any country, to judge this measure as necessary, appropriate and proportionate in a democratic society, the measure under discussion for collecting and retaining data from all the telecommunication traffic (generally and without reason), which undoubtedly constitutes a serious interference with the private life of citizens, should be regulated in a manner, consistent with the highest possible standards and security, not provided by the existing legal regulations. The law should contain precise, clear and predictable rules, creating assurances of protection and security (...), which, in principle, exclude the formation of a sense of threat of surveillance, as far as all citizens turn out to be users of one or more forms of existing modern communications, and in the vast part they have not given cause for their behaviour and actions to be associated with severe, in particular, the organised crime or terrorism. This could only be achieved by providing sufficient in volume and legal content, reliable, adequate and effective guarantees: (1) that the bodies, authorised for requesting access to data, will be able to exercise this power only in cases, specifically and comprehensively settled by law; (2) precisely settled grounds, authorities and procedures for obtaining a judicial sanction for access, use and destruction; (3) legal guarantees for the security of the data provided, the scope of its use, the transparency and legal protection, including the provision of specialised controls against unauthorised access to data and the possibility of making it available to third parties, other than the authorised entities; (4) their use for purposes other than the constitutionally justified, and in all possible stages - generation, preservation, storage, transmission, use, destruction by the persons who store the data; (5) Optimisation of the retention period according to the established European standards, the national and European practice; (6) ensuring a balance between the purpose, the severity of the restriction and the legal remedies envisaged to protect against unauthorised access to the stored telecommunications data, including criminal one, if created. Only upon the full and accurate execution of all the criteria discussed we could believe, that the legal framework of a measure of the kind introduced would be deemed to have passed the verification of compliance with the Constitution. Such a conclusion cannot, however, be made with regard to the disputed Ombudsman regulation.

(...)

The review of the constitutional practice of various European constitutional courts shows that the national legislative acts transposing Directive 2006/24/EC have been declared unconstitutional - all or part of these. The main considerations of the constitutional courts in Germany, Romania, the Czech Republic, Slovenia, Austria, Poland, giving arguments for the Judgements taken, prove to be quite similar, and some are quite identical to the findings of the Constitutional Court of the Republic of Bulgaria in the present case. It is obvious that the vices and imperfections of the Directive itself, which led to its invalidation by the ECJ, were not only mechanically transferred, but in many cases, they were overstretched and deepened, as is the case with the ECA. The latter explains the prevailing understanding of the said constitutional courts that the accepted text of the legal provisions in the national legislations is too general, vague, inaccurate, and the adopted laws generally do not create sufficient and reliable guarantees to protect against possible data security breaches, and are rated as contradictory to the national constitutions.

Therefore, after considering all of the above, the Constitutional Court finds that the provisions of Article 250a - Article 250e, Article 251 and Article 251a of ECA are contrary to the Constitution, and because of that the Ombudsman's claim to the Republic of Bulgaria is well founded. This requires the Constitutional Court to exercise its powers under Article 149 (1), item 2 of the Constitution and declares these norms unconstitutional.

(...)

The Supreme Court of Cyprus: Judgment of 1 February 2011, Ref. No 65/2009, 78/2009, 82/2009 and 15/2010-22/2010[7]

(. . .)

The applicants allege that the contested orders have breached their personal rights of private and family life guaranteed by the Constitution (Article 15.1) and of safeguarding the confidentiality of communications (Article 17.1). Articles 4 and 5 of the Law, on which the orders were issued, are not compatible with the above Articles of the Constitution and their constitutionality is not preserved by Article 1A of the Constitution. They also say that Directive 2006/24/EC does not impose any obligation on the Member States to enact a law relating to the chapter "prosecution of crime", to which the Directive refers. The purpose of the references made in the Directive in relation to this particular subject is only to show the cause that led the Community legislator to the adoption of the Directive and not to the specification of the purpose for which it was voted and by extension to the scope of the obligation imposed on the Member States. Basically, the position of the applicants is based on the decision of the European Court of Justice (as it was at that time) in Ireland v. European Parliament and Council of the European Union (Case C-301/06, of 10.2.09).

(. . .)

Having found that the issue of constitutionality of Articles 4 and 5 of the Law is the main matter at issue and that there is no need for the claims to be heard separately due to the events surrounding them, we decided, in agreement with the parties, that all applications be heard before the Full Plenary for purposes of better administration of justice.

Article 1 of the Directive defines its object and its scope of application.

(. . .)

The Law, which has the title, "Law providing for the Retention of Telecommunications Data for the Purpose of Investigating Serious Crimes", was enacted, as is stated in its preamble, for purposes of harmonisation with the act of the European Community, with the title – "Directive 2006/24/EC of the European Parliament and of the Council of 15th March 2006 on the retention of data generated or processed in connection with the provision of publicly available electronic communication services or of public communication networks and amending Directive 2002/58/EC" However, what arises from both the title and the content of the Law, is that the aim pursued is wider since the obligation to retain the data is not only correlated with the investigation into the concept of the law of serious criminal offences under the concept of law, but simultaneously, regulations are provided for that relate to the access of data. At the same time, by enacting Article 22* of the Law, the legislator

[7]The judgement is available at the page of the Supreme Court of Cyprus under: http://www.supremecourt.gov.cy/. Translation ordered by the University of Warsaw.

expressly expressed his willingness to retain the existing legislative regime concerning the protection of the confidentiality of private communications, not to mention, of course, the case law on matters of interpretation, etc., that had arisen in the implementation of the Law of 1966 about the Protection of Confidentiality of Private Communication (Monitoring of Conversations), Law 92/(1)/96.

(...)

The case law governing the same subject as well as other similar issues is mainly found in Police v. Georghiades (1983) 2 Supreme Court Decision 33. Police v. Giallurou (1992) 2 Supreme Court Decision 147. Police v. Airman et al. (1998) 2 Supreme Court Decision 87 and Republic v. Symianou et al. (1999) 2 Supreme Court Decision 537. In Symianos, the rationale of the Airman was adopted, where it was judged that the print out of a computer in which the telephone calls between two mobile telephones, the time of the calls and their duration were recorded, was not acceptable as testimony. One of the two telephones belonged to the accused and the other to a third person who had it at the disposal of the witness for the prosecution. What emerges is that, through case law, it was confirmed that every act of monitoring or information related to or derived from the communication of citizens who do not fall under the exceptions of Article 17.2 of the Constitution is not accepted as a testimony before the Court.

(...)

It must be stressed that the "content" of the telephone communication, which is forbidden as a testimony, also includes ".. the numbers of the calls. when it concerns telecommunication", as provided for in the definition of the relevant term - (Article 2 - of Law 92(I)/96). The exemption from the provisions of the Law, which is set out in paragraph (b) of sub-paragraph (2) of Article 3, regarding the recording of telephone numbers, is limited, as found by the Plenary, in "... the subscriber's charge, an action which is part of the contractual relationship between the subscriber and the Telecommunications Authority." Consequently, it was not necessary in our Memorandum 324 to answer the question of whether the exception was compatible with the provisions of Articles 15 - (Police v. Georghiades (1983) Cyprus Law Reports 33) - and 17 of the Constitution (Police v. Giallourou (1992) 2 Supreme Court Decision 147).

The finding, in relation to the subject-matter of the exception to the exclusion rule of the content of telephone communications, also defines, in the present case, the legal framework for the consideration of the questions which arise. As we pointed out in our decision in Memorandum 324, if the exception of the rule under Article 3 (2) (b) of the Law was not limited to the scope found, it would be necessary to examine the constitutionality of the exemption in the light of provisions of Articles 15 and 17 of the Constitution, which is essentially the question raised in paragraph 6 of this memorandum.

In this case, the testimony which was intended to be supplied was an integral part of the telephone communication, the admission of which, in any form, is forbidden by Law 92/(I)/96)".

The question now is whether the legislative adjustments made by the enactment of the Law and the incorporation of the Directive into internal law, in connection with the provisions of Article 1a of the Constitution, after the Fifth Amendment, brought about a change in the law that governs the vested personal right of confidentiality of communications of citizens so that, under conditions, the confidentiality of communication may be lifted and the access to communication data be permitted.

(...)

In this case, obviously, the enactment of the law was considered to be a necessary measure being derived from the obligations of our country as a Member State of the European Union. The question is whether this law goes beyond what is necessary and proportionate to the obligation of the Republic of Cyprus so that the legislation is considered superior to the constitutional provision guaranteeing the personal right to the confidentiality of communications.

Article 1 of the Directive (above) defines its object and its scope of application. It is clear that what is being sought by the Directive is the uniform regulation of the obligations of providers of telecommunication services by the Member States as regards the retention of certain data and to ensure that such data is made available in the investigating serious criminal offences as these are defined based on the national law of the Member States. It is not apparent from the Directive's content that any obligation to enact regulations referring to the access and/or delivery of citizens' telecommunication data to the competent investigating authorities for detecting crimes is being imposed on Member States. The regulation of this matter is left exclusively to the internal law of the Member States. This view is reinforced by the content of provisions 5 and 17 of the preamble to the Directive

(...)

From what has been said, we find that the inclusion of provisions in the Law which provide for the manner in which police investigators have access to telecommunication data which providers are obliged to retain has not been made for purposes of harmonisation with European law since such an obligation does not arise nor is imposed by the Directive. It follows that Articles 4 and 5 of the Law that are being considered are not covered by the provisions of Article 1A of the Constitution which was supplemented by the Fifth Amendment (above).

The above finding is consistent with the reasoning of Ireland v. European Parliament and Council of the European Union (above).

In that case, Ireland, supported by the Slovak Republic, appealed to the European Court of Justice requesting the annulment of the Directive because, as it claimed, it was not issued formally, etc., the European Court of Justice decided that the Directive's issue procedure (voting) was correct. However, it also made references relating to the purpose and application extent of the Directive (...)

From the above, we consider that it is rightly necessary to check the constitutionality of Articles 4 and 5 of the Law on which the disputed orders were issued.

(...)

The right of communication, which, as it has been interpreted, also includes telephone communication as one of the expressions of the individual's private life, is protected by Article 15.1 of the Constitution, which generally refers to the right of a private and family life. The same right (of communication) also has parallel protection of Article 17.1 of the Constitution, which specifically refers to this right. Of course, the same right is also protected by Article 8 of the European Convention on Human Rights which is applied as part of domestic law. From the facts relating to the present applications, we consider it sufficient to place the examination of the constitutionality of the above mentioned Articles 4 and 5 of the Law in the light of Article 17 of the Constitution, which, as has been said, specifically refers to the right of communication being considered here. In Police v. Georghiades (1983) 2 Cyprus Law Reports 33, the nature, character and scope of human rights were fundamentally determined. A similar texture and content was the case law followed in Enotiades and Another v. Police (1986) 2 Cyprus Law Reports 64, Psaras v. Republic (1987) 2 Cyprus Law Reports 132, Merthodja v. Police (1987) 2 Cyprus Law Reports 227, Parpas v. Republic (1988) 2 Cyprus Law Reports 5, and Police v. Giallourou (1992) 2 Supreme Court Decision 147. In Giallourou, it was decided that any intervention in the person's telephone communication would breach both the right of a private life and the right of communication. The following excerpt from the Decision relates to this:

"Telephone communication by its nature and character constitutes an objective aspect of private life under Article 15.1 and, at the same time, a form of communication the confidentiality of which is safeguarded by Article 17.1. The telephone conversation has the characteristics of the particular communication between the interlocutors, which pertains to their private life and simultaneously constitutes a classic form of communication, the confidentiality of which is preserved by the Constitution. No third party, unless authorised by law for the purposes of the Constitution, has the right to supervise or penetrate telephone communications between citizens. Any relaxation of the rule would be in contradiction with the absolute nature of the prohibition, as set out in Articles 15.1 and 17.1 of the Constitution, and would in the long run degenerate the effectiveness of the right guaranteed."

The case law of the Supreme Court that governs the issues being examined has been developed with the Constitution of the Republic as its central reference point and is broadly harmonised in line with the case law of the European Convention on Human Rights.

(...).

In these cases, the police, acting based on the orders, received the numbers of the telephone calls to and from the applicants from the provider, without the knowledge or consent of the applicants, an act which constitutes in principle an intervention into the right vested by the Constitution of the confidentiality of the applicants' communication. What therefore needs to be considered is whether the intervention of the police, under the given conditions of every case, constitutes a lawful restriction of the right under the details specified in Article 17.2 of the Constitution (...)

In Georghiades (above) it was decided that the following cases form an exception to the Constitutional rule:

(a) When the monitoring of the private communication occurs with the knowledge and approval of the person whose right is being affected.

(b) When the communication is being carried out by means prohibited by law.

(c) In the case of persons serving a sentence of imprisonment or who are in custody.

(d) In the case of professional correspondence and communication of the bankrupt during the administration of his assets.

(...)

The case of the applicant, Anna Athini, does not fall under any of the aforementioned exceptions of the rule since she was free, she was not bankrupt, she did not give her consent for the numbers of the calls to be delivered nor were the means she used illegal. It follows that the order to disclose her telephone numbers, as is shown in detail in the contested order, was unlawful and must be cancelled.

As far as the cases of Matsia and Alexandrou are concerned, it appears that the numbers of the telephone calls which refer to the respective orders issued, refer to calls made before the applicants were taken into custody and therefore neither do these cases fall under any of the exceptions of the rule, since neither is it proved here that the applicants in question were bankrupt or that their numbers were received with their consent or that the communications were made with unlawful means. It follows that in these cases, too, the contested orders concerning the applicants in question must be cancelled. In this case, we consider that any intervention into the confidentiality of the applicants' communication, at a time when any of the exceptions to the constitutional rule could not apply, would be a breach of the right. The fact that the orders were issued while the applicants were in custody clearly does not legitimise a retroactive restriction of the right. Such a regulation is not provided for by law nor is it covered by the Constitution.

(...)

In view of the above,

(a) the applications of the applicants Christos Matsia, Andreas Alexandrou and Anna Athinis shall be at the expense of those applicants, plus VAT, if there is any, to be calculated by the Registrar and approved by the Court. Certiorari orders are issued, which annul the disputed orders that respectively concern them.

(...)

The Constitutional Court of Czech Republic: Judgment of 22 March 2011, Ref. No Pl. ÚS 24/10[8]

(...)

26. Article 1, paragraph 1 of the Constitution of the Czech Republic incorporates the normative principle of democratic law-abiding state. The fundamental attribute of the constitutional concept of a law-abiding state and prerequisite of its functioning

[8]The judgement is available at the page of the Constitutional Court of Czech Republic under: https://www.usoud.cz/en/decisions/4/20110322-pl-us-2410-data-retention-in-telecommunications-services/.

is respect towards fundamental rights and freedoms of an individual which is explicitly specified as an attribute of the chosen constitutional concept of law-abiding state in the above mentioned constitutional provision. This constitutional provision forms the basis for the material concept of legal statehood which is characterised by public authority respecting free (autonomous) sphere of the individual defined by fundamental rights and freedoms; as a matter of principle, public authority does not intervene in this sphere, or more precisely only in cases where such intervention is justified by conflict with other fundamental rights, that is in public interest which is in conformity with the constitution and which is unambiguously defined by law providing that the intervention anticipated by law respects the proportionality principle with respect to aims that are to be attained as well as the extent of reduction of fundamental right or freedom.

27. The concept of privacy is mostly being brought into connection with Western culture, more accurately with Anglo-American cultural concept in the context of liberal political philosophy. This concept is apparently not commonly shared in terms of emphasis placed on the importance of privacy as well as the question to what extent should privacy be protected. There are different concepts in different cultures concerning the issue of level of privacy individual persons have the right to in various contexts. However as early as 1928, Judge Brandeis declares the following opinion on privacy in the frequently quoted dissent (. . .): "The makers of our Constitution understood the need to secure conditions favourable to the pursuit of happiness (. . .) and include the right (. . .) to be left alone – the most comprehensive of rights and the right most valued by civilized men." Thus, a right to privacy not explicitly mentioned by the constitution has gradually become fundamental structural element of the constitution of the U.S., safeguarding autonomy of the individual, although its exertion is still subject to disputes within the U.S. Supreme Court.

28. The need for respecting individual ways of living has become, together with the claim to respect one's life, physical and spiritual integrity, personal freedom and property, one of the central human rights claims for autonomy of individuals which has formative impact on European national (fundamental) human rights catalogues as well as their subsequent regional and universal counterparts. However, not even the original European national catalogues of fundamental rights did explicitly mention the right to privacy or private life as such, as documented by the wording of national constitutions dating back to 1940s and 1950s (e.g. the constitution of the Federal Republic of Germany, not mentioning Austria, constitutions of Denmark, Finland as well as France, Ireland and also Italy and other states). The requirement to respect privacy and privacy protection are closely linked to the development of technical and technological possibilities, which of course increase the level of freedom threatening the potential of the state.

29. As the Constitutional Court stated in judgment File No. II. ÚS 2048/09 of 2 November, 2009 (. . .): "fundamental right to undisturbed private life of an individual enjoys particular respect and protection in liberal democratic states (Article 10, paragraph 2 of the Charter of Fundamental Rights and Freedoms, No. 2/1993 Coll. (hereinafter the Charter))". The right to respect for private life functions primarily as a guarantee of space for development and self-fulfilment of

individual personality. Together with the traditional concept of privacy in terms of special dimension (protection of home in broader sense) and in connection with autonomous existence of development of social relations undisturbed by public authority (within marriage, family, society), the right to private life incorporates also a guarantee of self-determination in terms of crucial decisions being made by the individual. In other words, the right to privacy also guarantees the right of an individual to decide at one's own discretion if and to which extent, in what ways and under which circumstances should personal private facts and information be disclosed to other entities. This is an aspect of the right to privacy in form of the right to informational self-determination guaranteed explicitly by Article 10, paragraph 3 of the Charter (. . .).

30. When reviewing constitutionality of legal regulation concerning data collection and retention process for census (Volkszählung), the Federal Constitutional Court of Germany, inter alia, stated in the decision BVerfGE 65, 1 mentioned above, that in modern society characterised among others by enormous rise in the amount of information and data, individuals must be protected against unlimited collection, retention, use and disclosing of data concerning one's person and privacy within the scope of a more general right of an individual to privacy guaranteed by the constitution. Should individuals not be guaranteed the possibility to guard and control the contents as well as scope of personal data and information provided which are to be disclosed, retained or used for other than their original purposes, should they not have the possibility to identify and access reliability of their potential communication partners and adjust their actions accordingly, then this is inevitably a case of infringement or restriction of their rights and freedoms and therefore, one can in such case not speak of free and democratic society. The right to informational self-determination (informationelle Selbstbestimmung) thus represents a fundamental prerequisite not only for the free development and fulfilment of an individual within the society but also for the setup of a free and democratic communication system. In simple words, under omniscient and omnipresent state and public authority, the freedom of expression, right to privacy and free choice concerning one's behaviour and actions become basically non-existent and illusory.

31. The Charter does not guarantee the right to respect for private life under one comprehensive Article (as is the case with Article 8 of the Convention). On the contrary, the protection of private sphere of an individual is divided within the Charter and amended by further aspects of the right to privacy as declared in several passages of the Charter (e.g. Article 7, paragraph 1, Articles 10, 12 and 13 of the Charter). In the same way, the right to informational self-determination as such can be derived from Article 10, paragraph 3 of the Charter, which guarantees individuals the right to protection from unauthorised collection, disclosure or other misuse of data concerning one's person, and that together with Article 13 of the Charter, safeguarding privacy of correspondence and conveyed messages, whether kept in private or send by mail, communicated by telephone, telegraph or any other similar devices or ways. However, such "fragmentation" of legal regulation concerning aspects of privacy of an individual cannot be overestimated and the list of issues that "fall" under the right to privacy and private life cannot be regarded as exhaustive or

definitive. When interpreting single fundamental rights which reflect the right to privacy in its various dimension as specified in the Charter, it is necessary to respect the aim of the right to privacy in terms of general concept of it and constantly evolving nature as such, i.e. it is necessary to consider the right to private life within the context of the given period. Thus, the right to informational self-determination, guaranteed under Article 10, paragraph 3 and Article 13 of the Charter, must be interpreted with respect to rights guaranteed under Articles 7, 8, 10 and 12 of the Charter in particular. Given its nature and importance, the right to informational self-determination falls within the scope of fundamental human rights and freedoms, since together with personal freedom, freedom in terms of spatial dimensions (home), freedom of communication and certainly other fundamental rights guaranteed under the constitution, it creates the personal sphere of an individual, whose individual integrity must be respected and consistently protected as necessary grounds for dignified existence and development of human life as such; therefore, it is certainly justified to guarantee respect and protection of this sphere under constitutional order because – looking at this issue from a slightly different point of view – this represents the manifestation of respect for rights and freedoms of humans and citizens (Article 1 of the Constitution of the Czech Republic.)

32. It is clear, following the consistent judicature of the Constitutional Court especially in relation to the issue of wiretapping, that protection of the right to respect for private life in the form of right to informational self-determination under Article 10, paragraph 3 and Article 13 of the Charter does not only apply to the contents of messages conveyed via telephone, but to data concerning dialled numbers, dates and times of calls, duration, and in case of mobile phones, data on base stations handling calls (. . .).

33. The above mentioned judgments of the Constitutional Court are, inter alia, based on the judicature of the European Court of Human Rights (. . .) which deduces from Article 8 of the Convention, guaranteeing the right to respect for private and family life as well as home and correspondence, also the right to informational self-determination, as the Court repeatedly emphasised that data collection and retention related to private life of an individual fall within the scope of Article 8 of the Convention, since the term "private life" cannot be interpreted restrictively. From this point of view, right to privacy thus incorporates the right to protection from being monitored, watched and followed by public authority as well and that even in public areas or areas open to the public. Moreover, there is no essential reason for which to exclude professional, commercial or social activities from the term private life (. . .). As declared by the European Court of Human Rights, such extensive interpretation of the term "private life" is in accordance with the Convention for the Protection of Individuals with Regards to Automatic Processing of Personal Data (. . .), the purpose of which is to "secure in the territory of each Party for every individual (. . .) respect for his rights and fundamental freedoms, and in particular his right to privacy, with regard to automatic processing of personal data relating to him" (Article 1) while these are defined as "any information relating to an identified or identifiable natural person" (Article 2) (. . .).

34. In its judicature related to the right to respect for private life under Article 8 of the Convention, the European Court of Human Rights described actions such as data, contents of mail control and wiretapping as infringement of privacy of an individual (...), detecting telephone numbers of persons on the telephone (...), detecting data concerning telephone connection (...) or retaining DNA data in databases of individuals charged with an offence (...). In the Rotaru v. Rumania decision (No. 28341/95) of 4 May, 2000, the European Court of Human Rights deduced positive obligation of the state to discard data relating to private sphere of an individual, which were collected and processed by the state, from the right to private life manifested through the right to informational self-determination.

35. Similar approach is traceable in the judicature of constitutional courts of other countries as well. For instance the above mentioned Federal Constitutional Court of Germany guarantees – via the right to informational self-determination – protection not only of the contents of information conveyed but also external circumstances under which communication takes place – i.e. place, time, participants, type and way of communication – since such information concerning the circumstances of a given communication can, combined with other data, indicate the communicated contents as such; when inspecting and analysing this data, it is possible to create individual profiles of participants involved in the communication (...).

VII. B) Admissibility of Infringement of the Right to Informational Self-Determination

36. Protection against security threats and the need to secure the availability of such data for purposes of precaution, detection, investigation and prosecution of serious crimes carried out by public authority is usually declared as the primary purpose of legal regulation of universal and preventive collection and retention of traffic and location data on electronic communication. As previously repeatedly emphasised by the Constitutional Court, prosecution of crimes and justified punishment of offenders is a public interest approved by the Constitution, the essence of which being the delegation of the responsibility to hold offenders responsible for substantial fundamental rights and freedoms infringement by natural persons and legal entities to the state. Should the criminal law allow carrying out public interest in prosecution of criminality by means of robust instruments, the use of which results in serious infringement of personal integrity and fundamental rights and freedoms of an individual, then legal constitutional limit must be respected while such enforcement takes place. Infringement of personal integrity and privacy (i.e. absence of respect for it) can thus occur only extremely exceptionally on the part of public authority, should this be inevitable in a democratic society in case that the purpose of public interest cannot be reached in any other way and should this be acceptable in terms of legal existence and compliance with effective and specific guarantees against arbitrariness. An individual must have sufficient guarantees and warrantees against possible misuse of power on the part of public authority for essential prerequisites of a fair trial to be met. Such necessary guarantees comprise of adequate legal regulation and existence of effective control of compliance with it, this being primarily the inspection of the most significant infringement of fundamental rights and freedoms of individuals by an independent and impartial court,

since courts are bound to protect fundamental rights and freedoms of individuals (Article 4 of the Constitution of the Czech Republic) (. . .).

37. The Constitutional Court was more specific on compliance with the conditions described above in its judicature when considering the admissibility of infringing privacy of individuals on the part of public authority in form of wiretapping telecommunication (. . .). The right of an individual to privacy in the form of right to informational self-determination under Article 10, paragraph 3 and Article 13 of the Charter can on the grounds of precaution and protection against criminal activity be infringed only pursuant to imperative legal regulation which must be in compliance with requirements resulting from the principle of law-abiding state fulfilling requirements resulting from the proportionality test; should fundamental rights or freedoms be in conflict with public interest or other fundamental rights and freedoms, the purpose (aim) of such infringement must be considered with regard to instruments employed, the principle of proportionality (in its broader sense) being the criterion of such considerations. Such legal regulation must be precisely and clearly formulated as well as predictable to a satisfactory extent to provide potentially affected individuals sufficient information about circumstances and conditions under which is the public authority entitled to infringe their privacy, so that they can adequately adjust their behaviour in such a way as to avoid conflict with the present rule. Similarly, there must be a strict definition of powers delegated to the authorities in question, ways and rules of exercising it so that individuals are granted protection against arbitrary infringements. Three criteria are involved in reviewing admissibility of particular infringements in terms of the proportionality principle (in broader sense). First, the prospects to meet the purpose must be considered (or suitability); this covers reviewing whether desired purpose – being the protection of other fundamental right or public goods – can ever be attained with such measure. Second, the necessity must be assessed, considering whether the chosen measure is the most moderate one with respect to the fundamental right. Finally, adequacy must be examined (in the narrow sense), i.e. whether the fundamental right infringement is not inadequate in relation to the desired purpose, meaning that adverse effects resulting from measures infringing fundamental human rights and freedoms cannot, in case that fundamental right or freedom conflicts with public interest, exceed positive effects represented by public interest with respect to these measures (. . .).

38. Essential requirement for juridical protection of fundamental rights, in case of application of criminal law measures infringing fundamental rights and freedoms of individuals, is manifested in particular by issuing judicial warrants and supporting it with sufficient reasoning. This has to be in compliance with legal requirements and constitutional principles on which the legal provision is based in particular, or as the case may be, which in reverse limit its interpretation since applying such principle represents very serious infringement of fundamental rights and freedoms of every individual. "Judicial wiretapping and telecommunication recording warrant can be issued only in properly initiated criminal proceedings for criminal activity qualified under law and must be supported by relevant evidence which indicates justified suspicion that a crime has been committed. The warrant must be personalised in relation to a specific person that uses the telephone station. Finally, the warrant must,

at least to a certain level, specify which facts relevant for criminal proceeding are to be revealed using such means and the presumptions for thereof" (. . .).

39. In its judicature, the European Court of Human Rights advocates a similar approach. European Court of Human Rights, under Article 8, paragraph 2 of the Convention, which sets legal constitutional limits for infringement of fundamental rights and freedoms of individuals guaranteed under Article 8, paragraph 1 of the Convention, considers in every individual case primarily whether the alleged infringement or restriction of fundamental rights and freedoms can be covered by Article 8 of the Convention. Should this be the case, the alleged infringement of the right to privacy on the part of public authority must be in accordance with the law which must be accessible and sufficiently predictable, i.e. formulated with a high degree of accuracy, so that individuals can adjust their behaviour accordingly (cf. Malone v. UK, Amman v. Switzerland or Rotaru vs. Rumania). The level of accuracy required in national law, which can under no circumstances encompass all possibilities, depends to a large extent on the contents of the analysed text, area which is to be covered, and the number and status of persons for which it is intended [Hassan and Tchaouch v. Bulgaria (No. 30985/96, 39023/97) of 26 October, 2000]. The infringement of fundamental rights or freedoms, guaranteed under Article 8, paragraph 1 of the Convention, under review must in accordance with Article 8, paragraph 2 of the Convention also be essential to democratic society, follow the purpose approved by the Convention (e.g. protection of life or health of persons, national and public security, protection of rights and freedoms of others or morals, prevention of unrest and criminality or interest in economic welfare of a country), which must be relevant and given proper reasons for. The review can state that statutory provisions are in compliance with the Convention, if they under Article 13 of the Convention also provide appropriate protection against arbitrariness, and as a result of this sufficiently clearly define the scope and way of exercising powers granted to competent bodies (. . .). In other words, acts constituting evident infringement of fundamental right to private life cannot be without any direct (preventive or ex-post) judicial control (. . .).

40. The European Court of Human Rights specified the above mentioned requirements for legal regulation allowing right to private life infringement in the above mentioned decisions, which review the admissibility of such infringement on the part of public authority in the form of wiretapping telephone conversation, secret surveillance, collecting data and information concerning private (personal) sphere of an individual. European Court of Human Rights emphasised that it is particularly important to define clear and detail rules concerning the scope and use of such measures, set minimum requirements for the period, way of storing of information and data acquired, their use, access by third parties, and to anchor procedures resulting in the protection of integrity and confidentiality of the data and also discarding of such data in a way so that individuals have sufficient guarantees against the risk of misuse and arbitrariness. The necessity to have such guarantees is even higher in case of protection of personal data subject to automatic processing, especially when such data is used for police purposes and at a time when available technology becomes more and more sophisticated. National law must primarily

define that collected data are relevant indeed and not exaggerated in terms of the purpose for which they had been acquired, and further on, that they are stored in a form enabling the identification of persons during a certain period not exceeding the necessary extent to meet the purpose, for which they had been acquired (...)

(...)

41. As mentioned by the Constitutional Court above, contested provisions Section 97, subsection 3 and 4 became part of the Act No. 127/2005 Coll. based on Act No. 247/2008 Coll. amending the Act No. 127/2005 Coll., Act on Electronic Communications and on Amendment to Certain Related Acts (Electronic Communications Act) as amended. According to the explanatory report, this amendment has been adopted to implement "some articles" of the Directive 2006/24/EC of the European Parliament and of the Council of 15 March 2006 on the retention of data generated or processed in connection with the provision of publicly available electronic communications services or of public communications networks and amending Directive 2002/58/EC, which "have not been implemented into our law yet, or implemented only partially (because) the Data Retention Directive has already been transposed in the Czech Republic (...). The present legal regulation is in certain respects broader than regulation under Data Retention Directive." The Czech law regulates the issue of traffic and location data retention in a modified form since the adoption of the Electronic Communications Act No. 127/2005 Coll. itself effective from 1 May, 2005 and adoption of the contested Decree of the Ministry of Informatics No. 485/2005 Coll. on the Extent of Traffic and Location Data, the Time of Retention Thereof and the Form and Method of the Transmission Thereof to Bodies Authorised to Use such Data effective from 15 December, 2005. At that time, the EU was only preparing Data Retention Directive which was actually implemented in advance in the Czech Republic and the wording of contested provisions specifies the obligation to retain traffic and location data and provide such data upon request to authorised bodies without delay, as required by Data Retention Directive later on. The contested Decree of the Ministry of Informatics has however despite of this fact not been amended, resulting to the fact that the scope of retained data subject to the contested provisions thenceforth clearly exceeds the extent anticipated by the Data Retention Directive in question.

42. Under the contested provision Section 97, subsection 3, first and second sentence of the Electronic Communications Act, legal entities or natural persons providing public communication network or publicly available electronic communications service are obliged to retain traffic and location data generated or processed when providing public communications networks and electronic communication service, including data on abandoned calls, should this also be generated or processed and retained and recorded at the same time. Under Section 90 of the Electronic Communications Act, traffic data means "any data processed for the purposes of the transmission of a message via electronic communications network or for the billing thereof". Under Section 91 of the respective Act, location data means "any data that are processed within the electronic communications network and that define the geographical location of the terminal equipment of a user of publicly available electronic communications service". More details and the scope of

traffic and location data, the retention period and form and ways of transfer to authorised bodies shall be under the contested provision Section 97, subsection 4 specified in implementing provisions, which is the contested Decree No. 485/2005 Coll.

43. Providers of landline services and mobile communications are in particular obliged to retain virtually all available data on realised as well as (should this be recorded) abandoned calls (typically unanswered calls intended to alert the person dialled of something). The data relates in particular to the type of realised communication, incoming and dialled numbers, date and time of beginning and end of communication, indication of base station transmitting the call at the time of connection, prepaid phone card or public telephone booth identification, in case of mobile communication also data on the unique code identifying each mobile phone used in the GSM network (IMEI), its location and movement, even if there is no communication under way (the phone is only switched on), number of credits for prepaid cards and the number recharged, information on mobile device and all inserted SIM cards, etc. Even more information shall be retained under the contested provisions in connection with public packets-switched networks and their services, notably the Internet. Under the contested legal provisions, when using such service, it is required to retain in particular data on network access (e.g. time, place, duration of connection, data on users and their user accounts, computer and accessed server identifier, IP address, full domain name, volume of data transferred, etc.), further information related to electronic mail box access and transmission of electronic mail messages (in this case, virtually all information is retained with the exception of the contents itself, i.e. including address identification, volume of transmitted data, etc.) and last but not least data on server and other services [e.g. URL addresses entered, type of request, data on chatting, user net, instant messaging (e.g. ICQ) and telephony IP including identification of parties involved in communication, time and service used (e.g. file transmission or transaction)]. Exceeding the frame of Data Retention Directive, in case of Internet connection and e-mail communications services, information on the volume of data, information on coding, method and status of service requests and realisation of service as well as information on SMS sent via Internet gates and other "special-interest identifiers" is monitored and retained. In case of telephony, exceeding the frame of the Data Retention Directive, the contested legal provisions require to retain data on prepaid card identification, public telephone booth, numbers or credit coupons and the numbers recharged, all SIM cards inserted into a mobile device.

44. Although the imposed obligation to retain traffic and location data does not cover the contents of individual messages (see Article 1, paragraph 2 of the Data Retention Directive and contested provision Section 97, subsection 3, sentence four), based on the combination of the above mentioned data on users, addressees, exact times, dates, locations and forms of telecommunication connections, if monitored over a longer period, detailed information on social or political profile, as well as personal preferences, inclinations and weaknesses of individuals can be compiled. The opinion of the proposer of the Act outlined in the statement of the Senate as summarised above, stating that "this does certainly not compare with wiretapping,

let only because contents of particular telephone calls or e-mail messages are not retained", is completely incorrect, since barely based on such information, sufficient conclusions in term of the contents can be made falling within the private (personal) sphere of an individual. Based on the data specified, it can be, e.g. deducted with up to 90% reliability, whom, how often and even at what time the particular individuals meet with, who are their closest acquaintances, friends or work colleagues, or which activities and at what time do they engage in [cf. study by the Massachusetts Institute of Technology (MIT), Relationship Inference, available at http://reality.media.mit.edu/dyads.php]. Location and traffic data collection and retention thus represent a serious infringement of the right to privacy and therefore, not only protection of the contents of the message conveyed via telephone communication or public networks communication itself, but related traffic and location data as well, must fall under the scope of protection of fundamental right to respect for private life in the form of right to informational self-determination (under Article 10, paragraph 3 and Article 13 of the Charter).

(. . .)

45. The Constitutional Court therefore had to consider, whether contested legal provisions regulating the issue of universal and preventive collection and retention of the specified traffic and location data on electronic communication are in accordance with the requirements of the constitutional law as described above concerning legal regulation allowing infringement of fundamental right to privacy of individuals in the form of right to informational self-determination (under Article 10 paragraph 3 and Article 13 of the Charter). Moreover, given the intensity of such infringement, which is in this case more relevant because it applies to vast and unpredictable number of participants in a communication since this is a universal and preventive collection and retention of data, it was necessary to review the compliance with requirements mentioned above using the highest standards. The Constitutional Court concluded that contested legal provisions do not meet the requirements of constitutional law by far, and that for several reasons.

46. Contested provisions of the Electronic Communications Act, Section 97, subsection 3, sentence three only vaguely and very indefinitely specify the obligation of legal entities or natural persons, that retain traffic and location data in the extent described above, to "make such data available upon request to the bodies entitled to request them on the basis of a special legal regulation" without any delay. Although the contested Decree specifies in Article 3 how to meet such obligation in individual cases in relation to entitled bodies, i.e. it describes relatively in detail the way of data transmitting, type of communication (electronic), format, programs employed, codes, etc., it is, in the opinion of the Constitutional Court, not clear neither from the wording of provisions of the Electronic Communications Act, Section 97, subsection 3, nor the explanatory report, which entitled bodies and which special legal regulation are particularly is meant. With regard to the wording of provisions of the Electronic Communications Act, Section 97, subsection 1, which lays down the obligation for legal entities or natural persons providing public communications network or providing electronic communications service accessible to general public to, at the requesting party's expense, provide and secure interfaces at specified points

of the network to connect terminal equipment for message tapping and recording, it can only be assumed, that the obligation to transmit retained traffic and location data applies to the same entitled bodies and special regulation addressed to the bodies involved in criminal proceedings, possibly under the Criminal Code, Section 88a, Security Information Service, under Section 6 to 8a of the Act No. 154/194 Coll. on the Security Information Service as amended and military intelligence under Act No. 289/2005 Coll. on Military Service, Section 9 and 10. Such definition of legal provisions allowing massive fundamental rights infringement does not meet the requirements for clarity with respect to law-abiding state (cf. paragraph 37).

47. At the same time, the purpose of transmitting traffic and location data to entitled bodies is not clearly and precisely defined, which makes it impossible to judge in how far are the contested provisions actually necessary (it is clear that the purpose can be met, i.e. purpose set in the Directive – see below). Whereas the quoted Data Retention Directive, Article 1, paragraph 1 clearly defines that it has been adopted to harmonise Member States' provisions concerning the obligations of the providers of publicly available electronic communications services or public communications networks with respect to the retention of traffic and location data necessary to identify a participant or registered user with the aim to make such data "available for the purpose of investigation, detection and prosecution of serious crime" (although it does not define these crimes in more detail), neither the contested provisions nor quoted provision of the Criminal Code, Section 88a, subsection 1 – regulating conditions of the use of retained data for criminal proceedings – do encompass such limitations. Under this legal regulation, the legislator does thus not condition the option to use retained data in criminal proceedings by justified suspicion that a serious crime has been committed; at the same time, there is no regulation concerning the obligation of authorities involved in criminal proceeding to inform the (monitored) person thereof, not even ex-post, which does not meet the requirements resulting from the second step of proportionality test, i.e. means selected must be necessary, since it is clear from the above stated, that the most regardful means in respect to fundamental right to informational self-determination has not been used.

48. The Constitutional Court does not consider such manner of (not) defining the spectrum of entitled public authorities as well as (not) defining the purpose for which they are entitled to request retained data, sufficient and predictable. Although the use of retained data is under the quoted provision of the Criminal Code, Section 88a, paragraph 1 subject to judicial control in form of an permission issued by the presiding judge of the senate (in case of preparatory proceedings the judge), the legislator was primarily obliged to define more clearly and unambiguously circumstances and conditions of the use thereof as well as the scope of use in contested provisions or in the quoted provision of the Criminal Code, Section 88a, subsection 1, instead of using very vague definitions of terms of retained data use "on telecommunication that took place" to "clarify facts important for criminal proceeding". In particular, given the relevance and scope of the infringement of the right of individuals to privacy in form if right to informational self-determination (under Article 10, paragraph 2 and Article 13 of the Charter) represented by the use of such data, the

legislator must limit the possibility to use retained data for purposes of criminal proceeding concerning very serious crimes only and only in case the pursued purpose cannot be reached otherwise. For that matter, this is the assumption not only of the quoted Data Retention Directive, but of the Provisions of the Criminal Code, Section 88, subsection 1 regulating conditions of wiretapping and telecommunications recording order ("should the criminal proceeding concern very serious crime"), however the respective provisions of Criminal Code, Section 88a, subsection 1 as a whole diverge without any reason from this (despite of legal opinions of the Constitutional Court inherent in mentioned judgments File No. II. ÚS 502/2000 or File No. IV. ÚS 78/01 – for both see above) and set regulation which clearly contradicts opinions of the Constitutional Court.

49. As it appears from the statistical data, the absence of proper legal regulation which would be in accordance with the Constitution in its meaning, results in practice in the fact, that the measure to request and use retained data (including data on abandoned calls not mentioned by the Criminal code at all) is used (overused) by authorities involved in criminal proceedings for purposes on investigating common, i.e. less serious criminal activity, as well. For example, according to the "Report on Security Situation in the Czech Republic in 2008", there were 343,799 crimes in total identified in the territory of the Czech Republic, 127,906 crimes thereof were detected and in the same period the number of requests for traffic and location data on the part of entitled public authorities reached the number of 131,560 (...). In the following period from January to October 2009 only, according to unofficial data, location and traffic data were requested in 121,839 cases (...).

50. The Constitutional Court also believes that legal regulation contested by the petitioners does not sufficiently enough or not at all define clear and detailed rules implying minimum requirements for the security of retained data, especially in the form of preventing third persons access, defining procedure resulting in protection of integrity and confidentiality of data and procedure of discarding data. Further critique concerning the contested regulation is that affected individuals do not have sufficient guarantees against the risk of data misuse and arbitrariness. The necessity to have such guarantees with respect to the considered issue of universal and preventive data collection and retention related to electronic communications however becomes even more important for an individual today, as enormous development and existence of new and more sophisticated information technologies, system and means of communication inevitably result in gradual shifting of the boundary between private and public sphere in favour of public sphere, since in virtual space of information technology and electronic communication (in the so-called cyberspace) thousands, even millions of data, facts and information are recorded, collected and virtually made accessible every minute, especially thanks to the development of the Internet and mobile communication, infringing the private (personal) sphere of every individual although they have not intended to disclose it.

51. The Constitutional Court does certainly not consider the mere stipulation of obligation imposed on legal entities or natural persons to make sure that "the contents of messages shall not be retained together with specified data retained" (Electronic Communications Act, Section 97, subsection 3, sentence four), or

obligation to "discard them after the elapse of the time, had they not been disclosed to authorities entitled to request them pursuant to special legal provisions or should this Act specify otherwise (section 90)" (Electronic Communications Act, Section 97, subsection 3, sentence six) to be clear, detailed and adequate enough guarantees. The mere definition of retention period of "no shorter than 6 month and no longer that 12 months", given the lapse of this period influences the obligation to discard the data, can be deemed ambiguous and with respect to the scope and sensitive nature of retained data entirely insufficient. None of the obligations mentioned does describe rules or methods of meeting such rules in more detail, there is no strict definition of requirements concerning security of retained data, it is not entirely traceable how is the data handled neither on the part of legal entities or natural persons retaining traffic and location data, nor entitled public authorities after requesting the data; the way of discarding such data is not defined either. Further on, there is no definition of liability and respective sanctions in case of breach of such obligations, including missing establishment of the way how affected individuals can seek efficient protection against possible misuse, arbitrariness or non-fulfilment of defined obligations. The Electronic Communications Act (Section 87 and following provisions) envisions that The Office for Personal Data Protection (ÚOOÚ) will supervise whether "obligations are met when processing personal data", which together with defined measures of its activities and control cannot be deemed as adequate and efficient means of protection of fundamental rights of affected individuals, since they do not exercise control over it themselves (…). The above mentioned acts present evident infringement of the fundamental right of individuals to privacy in form of right to informational self-determination (under Article 10, section 3 and Article 13 of the Charter) and they are thus – due to insufficient legal regulation which does not comply with the stated requirements of constitutional law – without any direct, not even ex-post control, judicial control in particular, which was deemed necessary even by the European Court of Human Rights in quoted decision Camenzind v. Switzerland.

(…)

53. Given the above stated, the Constitutional Court declares that contested provisions of Section 97, subsection 3 and 4 of the Electronic Communications Act No. 127/2005 Coll. and on Amendment to Certain Related Acts (Electronic Communications Act), as amended, and contested Decree No. 485/2005 Coll. on the Extent of Traffic and Location Data, the Time of Retention Thereof and the Form and Method of the Transmission Thereof to Bodies Authorised to Use such Data cannot be deemed conform with the constitution, since they clearly violate the limits of constitutional law as explained above, because they do not meet requirements resulting from the principle of law-abiding state and are in collision with requirements concerning the infringement of fundamental right to privacy in the form of right to informational self-determination under Article 20, paragraph 3 and Article 13 of the Charter resulting from the principle of proportionality.

54. Apart from the above stated, the Constitutional Court deems it necessary to emphasise that described deficiencies, which led the Court to derogation of the contested legal regulation, are not even reflected in special legal regulations

indirectly envisioned by contested provisions of Section 97, subsection 3 of the Electronic Communications Act. In particular, the above mentioned provisions of the Criminal Code, Section 88a, regulating requirements for the use of retained data on realised telecommunications traffic for purposes of criminal proceedings, do, in the opinion of the Constitutional Court, not respect the described limit of constitution law by far, and therefore they are deemed by the Constitutional Court unconstitutional as well. Nevertheless given the fact that the petitioners did not contest this provision in the proposal, the Constitutional Court believes, it is necessary to appeal to the legislator to consider, with regard to derogation of contested legal provisions, the amendment of the mentioned provisions of the Criminal Code, Section 88a, to reach conformity with the constitution.

(. . .)

55. Merely in the form of obiter dicta, the Constitutional Court declares that it is clearly aware of the fact that development of modern information technology and communication media goes hand in hand with new and more sophisticated ways of criminal activities that we need to deal with. However, the Constitutional Court doubts whether the instrument of universal and preventive traffic and location data retention on almost every electronic communication alone is a necessary and appropriate instrument in terms of the level of privacy infringement affecting enormous number of individuals involved in electronic communication.

Within the area of Europe, such opinion is by far not isolated since the Data Retention Directive itself has been heavily criticised from the very beginning of its existence by Member States (e.g. governments of Ireland, the Netherlands, Austria or Sweden hesitated long or are still hesitating with its implementation, and moreover, the two last above mentioned countries do so despite a threat announced in public by the Commission to initiate European Court of Justice proceedings), as well as legislators in the European Parliament, the European Data Protection Supervisor (. . .) or the Data Protection Working Party set up under Article 29 of the Directive 95/46/EC (. . .), or non-governmental organisations (Statewatch, European Digital Rights or Arbeitskreis Vorratsdatenspeicherung – AK Vorrat among others). All the above mentioned demanded either the Data Retention Directive in question to be repealed in its full extent and the instrument of universal and preventive traffic and location data retention to be replaced by other more appropriate instruments (e.g. data freezing which makes it under certain fixed conditions possible to monitor and retain necessary and selected data of only a particular individual involved in communication determined in advance), or demanded the change thereof, in particular in the form if granting affected individuals satisfactory guarantees and means of protection and introducing stricter data retention security requirements preventing the threat of loss and misuse by third parties.

56. The Constitutional Court also has certain doubts resulting from the question whether the instrument of universal and preventive traffic and location data retention is an efficient instrument in terms of its original purpose (protection against security threats and prevention of particularly serious criminal activity), especially given the existence of so-called anonymous SIM cards, which do not fall within the anticipated scope of traffic and location data retained under the contested legal regulation and

which – according to the Police of the Czech Republic – make up to 70% of communication related to engagement in criminal activities (. . .). In this context, reference can be made to the analysis of Germany's Federal Criminal Police Office (Bundeskriminalamt) of 26 January 2011, which based on comparison of statistic data on serious crimes committed within the territory of Federal Republic of Germany during the period before and after the adoption of the respective data retention legal regulation arrived at the conclusion that the use of instrument of universal and preventive traffic and location data retention had very limited impact on the reduction of the number of serious crimes committed as well as the respective detection rate (. . .). When overlooking crime statistics for the territory of the Czech Republic published by the Police of the Czech Republic, e.g. comparing statistical data for the period between 2008 and 2010 (. . .), a similar conclusion can be drawn.

57. Despite this being mentioned at the end, the Constitutional Court deems necessary to express doubts concerning the desirability of entitling private persons (providers of Internet services and telephone and mobile communication, mobile operators and companies providing Internet access in particular) to retain all data concerning provided communication as well as customers to whom they provide services (i.e. even more data than they are legally obliged to retain under the contested legal regulations) and to use them unrestrictedly to collect their claims, develop business activities and use them for marketing purposes. The Constitutional Court considers this not to be desirable, in particular given that neither the Electronic Communications Act nor other legal regulations do not regulate such entitlement in more detail and depth, there is no strict definition of rights and duties, the scope of data retained, period and retention method or more detailed specification of requirements regarding the security of such data and controlling mechanisms.

58. Considering the above stated, the Constitutional Court therefore decided under Section 70, subsection 1 of the Constitutional Court Act to repeal contested provisions of Section 97, Subsections 3 and 4 of the Act on Electronic Communications and on Amendment to Certain Related Acts (Electronic Communications Act) No. 127/2005 Coll., as amended, and contested Decree No. 485/2005 Coll. on the Extent of Traffic and Location Data, the Time of Retention Thereof and the Form and Method of the Transmission Thereof to Bodies Authorised to Use such Data as of the day of promulgation of this judgment in the Collection of Laws (Section 58, subsection 1 of the Constitutional Court Act).

59. Courts with general jurisdiction shall now consider each individual case in which data have already been requested to be used in criminal proceedings one by one – with respect to proportionality regarding privacy rights infringement. Courts shall consider primarily the seriousness of crime committed by the act against which criminal proceedings in which the requested data should be used are held.

The Federal Constitutional Court of Germany: Judgment of 2 March 2010, Ref. No 1 BvR 256/08, 1 BvR 263/08, 1 BvR 586/08[9] (Excerpt)

[...]

4 a) § 113a TKG aims, with regard to all publicly available telecommunications services, at storing, for six months, traffic data which provide information on the lines involved in a telecommunications connection and about the time and the locations at which an act of telecommunication has taken place and to keep them available for the state's performance of its duties. In doing so, the Act takes up demands which had been made by the Bundesrat for an extended period (see Bundestag printed paper (*Bundestagsdrucksache* – BTDrucks) 14/9801, p. 8; Bundesrat printed paper (*Bundesratsdrucksache* – BRDrucks 755/03 (resolution), p. 33 et seq.; BRDrucks 406/1/04; BRDrucks 406/04 (resolution); BRDrucks 723/05 (resolution), p. 1), with which the German Bundestag concurred in 2006, making reference to the respective initiatives on the European level. The German Bundestag requested the Federal Government to approve the draft Directive 2006/24/EC and to immediately submit a draft of an implementing Act (see Bundestag printed papers 16/545, p. 4; 16/690, p. 2; Minutes of plenary proceedings of the Bundestag (BTPlenarprotokoll) 16/19, p. 1430). The Federal Government complied with the request by submitting the draft Act for the Amendment of Telecommunications Surveillance (see Bundestag printed paper 16/5846).

5 § 113a.1 sentence 1 TKG obliges the of publicly available telecommunications services to store, for a period of six months, the telecommunications service data listed in § 113a.2 to 113a.5 regarding fixed network, Internet and mobile communications, the transmission of text, multi-media and similar messages, email connections and Internet access. Under § 113a.1 sentence 2 TKG, a person who provides such services without himself creating traffic data shall ensure that the data are stored, and shall inform the Federal Network Agency (*Bundesnetzagentur*) as to who is storing these data. Apart from this, a person who provides telecommunications services and in doing so alters the information to be stored under § 113a TKG is obliged to store the original and the new information. Under § 113a.11 TKG, the data are to be deleted within one month after the end of the storage period. Under § 113a.8 TKG, the contents of the communication and data on Internet sites visited may not be stored. On data security, § 113a.10 TKG makes reference to the care necessary in the area of telecommunications and demands that access to the stored data be exclusively possible to persons specifically authorised for this purpose.

[...]

176 1. The complainants admissibly challenge a violation of Article 10.1 GG. They use different telecommunications services such as in particular telephone

---

[9]The judgement in English is available at the page of the Bundesverfassungsgerichts under: https://www.bundesverfassungsgericht.de/SharedDocs/Entscheidungen/EN/2010/03/rs20100302_1bvr025608en.html.

services, electronic mail and Internet services for private and business purposes, and they put forward that the storage and intended use of their connection data violates their fundamental right to respect of the secrecy of telecommunications. As Article 10.1 GG also protects the confidentiality of the circumstances of acts of telecommunication (see BVerfGE 67, 157 (172); 85, 386 (396); 120, 274 (307); established case law), such a violation by the challenged provisions is possible.

[. . .]

II.

188 The challenged provisions encroach upon Article 10.1 GG.

189 1. Article 10.1 GG guarantees the secrecy of telecommunications, which protects the incorporeal transmission of information to individual recipients with the aid of telecommunications traffic [. . .] against the taking of notice by state authority [. . .]. In this connection, this protection does not only relate to the contents of the communication. On the contrary, the protection also covers the confidentiality of the immediate circumstances of the process of communication, which include in particular whether, when and how often telecommunications traffic occurred or was attempted between what persons or telecommunications equipment [. . .]

190 The protection of Article 10.1 GG applies not only to the first access by which state authority takes notice of telecommunications events and contents. Its protective effect also extends to the information and data processing procedures which follow the taking of notice of protected communications events, and to the use that is made of the knowledge obtained [. . .]. An encroachment upon fundamental rights includes every taking of notice, recording and evaluation of communications data, and every analysis of their contents or other use by state authority [. . .]. The recording of telecommunications data, their storage, their comparison with other data, their evaluation, their selection for further use or their transmission to third parties are therefore each an individual encroachment upon the secrecy of telecommunications [. . .]. Consequently, an order to communications enterprises to collect and store telecommunications data and to transmit them to state agencies is in each case an encroachment upon Article 10.1 GG [. . .].

191 The right arising from Article 2.1 in conjunction with Article 1.1 GG to informational self-determination does not apply in addition to Article 10 GG. In relation to telecommunications, Article 10 GG contains a special guarantee which overrides the general provision and which gives rise to special requirements for the data that are obtained by encroachments upon the secrecy of telecommunications. In this context, however, the requirements which the Federal Constitutional Court has developed from Article 2.1 in conjunction with Article 1.1 GG may largely be transferred to the more special guarantee of Article 10 GG [. . .].

192 2. a) The storage of telecommunications traffic data imposed on the service providers under § 113a.1 TKG encroaches upon the secrecy of telecommunications. In the first instance, this applies to the duties of storage relating to telecommunications services under § 113a.2 to 113a.5 TKG and in conjunction with this under § 113a.6 and § 113a.7 TKG. The information to be stored under this provision indicates whether, when, where and how often connections were established or there was an attempt to establish connections between what telecommunications

installations. In particular, this also applies to the storage of data in the service of electronic mail under § 113a.3 TKG, whose confidentiality is also protected by Article 10.1 GG [. . .]. The fact that it is technologically easy to intercept emails does not alter their confidential character and their need for protection. In this connection, storage of the data relating to the Internet connection under § 113a.4 TKG is also an encroachment upon Article 10.1 GG. Internet access enables not only communication between individuals, which is protected by the secrecy of telecommunications, but also participation in mass communication. But since it is not possible to distinguish between individual and mass communication without referring to the contents of the information transmitted in each case, which is contrary to the protective function of the fundamental right, the very storage of the data relating to the Internet access as such is to be seen as an encroachment, even if they do not contain information on the Internet pages visited [. . .]

[. . .]

196 d) Finally, § 100g StPO is also an encroachment upon Article 10.1 GG. It enables the criminal prosecution authorities to have the data stored under § 113a TKG transmitted to themselves by the persons obliged to store them, and to use these data. § 100g.1 sentence 1 StPO itself and the exercise of this authorisation, therefore, as acts of public authority, also encroach upon the area of protection of Article 10.1 GG.

III.

[. . .]

198 1. Under Article 10.2 sentence 1 GG, restrictions of the secrecy of telecommunications may be imposed only based on a statute. First, there are no doubts in this connection with regard to § 113b TKG and § 100g StPO, which – if necessary in conjunction with other provisions – are a statutory basis for individual judicial orders, based on which access to the data takes place. § 113a TKG is also constitutionally unobjectionable in this respect; for the storage of data, it does not refer to individual judicial orders but directly orders storage itself. Article 10.2 sentence 1 GG also does not prevent restrictions of the secrecy of telecommunications that are made directly by statute [. . .].

[. . .]

IV.

204 The encroachments upon the secrecy of telecommunications are substantively constitutional if they serve legitimate purposes in the public interest and apart from this comply with the principle of proportionality [. . .], i.e., are suitable, necessary and appropriate to fulfil the purposes (see BVerfGE 109, 279 (335 et seq.); 115, 320 (345); 118, 168 (193); 120, 274 (318-19)); established case law.

205 Storage of telecommunications traffic data without cause for six months for qualified uses in the course of prosecution, the warding off of danger and intelligence service duties, as is provided by §§ 113a, 113b TKG, is therefore not in itself incompatible with Article 10 GG. [. . .]

206 1. Making criminal prosecution, warding off danger and performing the tasks of the intelligence service more effective is a legitimate purpose, which can in

principle justify encroachment upon the secrecy of telecommunications [. . .] Only the precautionary storage of personal data for purposes that are indefinite and cannot yet be determined is strictly prohibited [. . .]. However, only exceptionally is the precautionary storage of data permissible. Both its justification and its formulation, in particular also with regard to the envisaged purposes of use, are subject to especially strict requirements.

[. . .]

210 a) Admittedly, such storage constitutes a particularly serious encroachment with a broader range than anything in the legal system to date: throughout the whole six-month period, virtually all telecommunications traffic data of all citizens are stored, without a connection to culpable conduct attributable to them, or to a dangerous situation – even a merely abstract one –, or to a situation otherwise qualified. This storage relates to everyday actions which are a basic part of day-to-day interaction and which are now indispensable for taking part in social life in the modern world. Fundamentally, no form of telecommunications is as a matter of principle excluded from storage. [. . .]

211 The informative value of these data is extremely broad. Depending on the use of the telecommunications services by the persons affected, a high degree of knowledge of the social environment and the individual activities of each citizen may be obtained even from the data themselves – and all the more if the data are used as starting points for further investigations. Admittedly, storage of telecommunications traffic data, as provided for in § 113a TKG, records only the connection data (time, duration, connections involved and – in the case of mobile telephony – location), but not in addition the contents of the communication. However, it is possible to draw conclusions about contents that extend into the private sphere even from these data, if they are subjected to comprehensive and automated analysis. If recipients (the particular occupational groups, institutions or interest groups they belong to or the services they offer), dates, times and places of telephone conversations are observed for a long period, then in combination they permit detailed conclusions on social or political affiliations and personal preferences, inclinations and weaknesses of the persons whose connection data are analysed. There is no protection of confidentiality in this connection. Depending on the use of the telecommunications, and in future with increasing frequency, such storage can make it possible to create meaningful personality profiles and mobility profiles of virtually all citizens. In relation to groups and associations, the data also, in certain circumstances, may make it possible to reveal internal influence structures and decision-making processes.

212 Storage which fundamentally makes such uses possible and in particular cases is intended to make them possible constitutes a serious encroachment. In this connection, it is also significant that, independent of a legislative approach to the use of data of whatever nature, the risk of citizens considerably increases of being exposed to further investigations without themselves having given occasion for this. [. . .] Particular weight also attaches to the storage of the telecommunications data because the storage itself and the intended use of the stored data are not directly noticed by the persons affected, but at the same time they include connections which

are engaged in with an expectation of confidentiality. As a result of this, the storage of telecommunications traffic data without cause can create a diffusely threatening feeling of being watched which can impair a free exercise of fundamental rights in many areas.

213 b) Despite its extremely broad range and the weight of the encroachment associated with it, the legislature is not absolutely prohibited under constitutional law from introducing a six-month duty of storage, as provided for in § 113a TKG. However, under the established case law of the Federal Constitutional Court, the state is strictly prohibited under constitutional law from creating a collection of personal data by way of precaution and retaining it for purposes that are indefinite or that cannot yet be determined [. . .]

214 aa) The first relevant factor for this is that the storage of the telecommunications traffic data provided is realised not directly by the state, but by a duty imposed on the private service providers. In this way, the data are not yet combined at the time of storage itself but remain distributed over many individual enterprises and are not directly available to the state in their entirety. In particular, the state has no direct access to the data; this must be ensured by appropriate legislation and technical precautions. The retrieval of the data by state agencies is done only in a second stage, and then related to a specific occurrence, in accordance with criteria to be legally defined in more detail. In this connection, the formulation of the provisions giving permission for retrieval and further use of the stored data may ensure that the storage is not made for purposes that are indefinite or cannot yet be determined. Thus, if such a duty of storage is imposed, it can and must be guaranteed that an actual taking notice and use of the data remains limited by well-defined provisions in a manner that takes account of the weight of the extensive collection of data and that restricts the retrieval and the actual use of the data to the part of the data pool that is absolutely necessary. At the same time, the separation of storage and retrieval structurally promotes the transparency and supervision – to be guaranteed in more detail by legislative drafting – of the use of the data.

215 bb) Nor does a six-month storage of the telecommunications traffic data in itself cancel the principle of Article 10.1 GG; it violates neither that Article's core of human dignity (Article 1.1 GG) nor its essence (Article 19.2 GG). Despite its extraordinary breadth, it remains effectively limited. Thus, for example, the contents of the telecommunications events are excluded from the storage, which is restricted to the traffic data. In addition, the duration of the storage is restricted. Admittedly, a period of six months' storage is very long, in view of the extent and informative value of the stored data, and it is at the upper limit of what can be justified from the point of view of proportionality. After the end of this period, however, citizens may rely on their data being deleted – unless they have exceptionally been retrieved for cause – and no longer being reconstructible by anyone.

216 cc) Nor does storage of the telecommunications traffic data for six months appear to be a measure directed towards total recording of the citizens' communications or activities as a whole. Instead, it takes up, in a manner still limited, the special significance of telecommunications in the modern world and reacts to the specific potential danger associated with this. [. . .] The communication, which is

virtually without resistance, enables knowledge, readiness to act and criminal energy to be combined in a way that confronts warding off danger and criminal prosecution with novel tasks. Some criminal offences are committed directly with the help of the new technology. Integrated into a conglomeration of computers and computer networks which communicate with each other only through technology, such activities largely escape observation. At the same time, they can create new kinds of dangers, for example by attacks on third-party telecommunications. For effective criminal prosecution and warding off of danger, therefore, a reconstruction of telecommunications connections is of particular importance.

217 Another problem is that because telecommunications data are not publicly perceptible, there is also no social memory, unlike in other areas, which would permit past events to be reconstructed based on chance memories. Telecommunications data are either deleted, after which they are completely lost, or stored, after which they are completely available. Consequently, in the decision as to how far such data are to be deleted or stored, the legislature may undertake a balancing of interests and take account of the concerns of state performance of duties. In this process, it may also include in its considerations the fact that the popularity of particular forms of contract used by telecommunications services providers (such as the increase of flat-rate services) reduces the availability of such data where there is a strict duty of deletion of telecommunications traffic data which are not needed for the performance of the contract. In this respect too, the precautionary storage of telecommunications traffic data may be based on aspects which have a specific foundation in special features of modern telecommunications.

218 Conversely, the storage of the telecommunications traffic data may not be seen as a step in the direction of legislation aiming at as comprehensive as possible a storage by way of precaution of all data useful for criminal prosecution or the prevention of danger. Regardless of the structure of the provisions on use, such legislation would from the outset be incompatible with the constitution. For precautionary storage of telecommunications traffic data without cause to be constitutionally unobjectionable, this procedure must, instead, remain an exception to the rule. Nor may it, in interaction with other existing files, lead to virtually all activities of the citizens being reconstructible. It is therefore in particular essential for the justifiability of such storage that it is not made directly by state agencies, that it does not also contain the contents of the communications, and that commercial service providers are in principle prohibited from also storing details of the Internet sites visited by their customers. The introduction of the storage of telecommunications traffic data may therefore not serve as a model for the precautionary creation without cause of further data pools, but forces the legislature to exercise greater restraint in considering new duties or authorisations of storage with regard to the totality of the various data pools already in existence. It is part of the constitutional identity of the Federal Republic of Germany that the exercise of freedom of its citizens may not be totally be recorded and registered (on the constitutional identity retention principle, see BVerfG, judgment of the Second Senate of 30 June 2009 – 2 BvE 2/08 and others –, juris, marginal no. 240), and the Federal Republic of German must endeavour to preserve this in European and international contexts. [. . .]

V.

220 The formulation of the legislation on a precautionary storage of telecommunications traffic data, as provided in § 113a TKG, is subject to specific constitutional requirements, in particular with regard to data security, to the extent of the use of the data, to transparency and to legal protection. Only if sufficiently sophisticated and well-defined provisions are drafted is the encroachment constituted by such storage proportionate in the narrow sense.

[...]

225 There is a need for statutory provisions which lay down such a particularly high security standard in a qualified manner and are at all events fundamentally well-defined and legally binding. In this connection the legislature is free to entrust a regulatory agency with the technicalities of putting the prescribed standard into concrete terms. In this process, however, the legislature must ensure that the decision as to the nature and degree of the protective precautions to be taken does not ultimately lie without supervision in the hands of the respective telecommunications providers. The requirements to be made must either be laid down in sophisticated technical provisions – possibly graduated on various levels of legislation – or in a general manner and then be put in specific terms in a transparent manner by a binding individual decision of the regulatory authorities addressed to the individual enterprise. In addition, there is also a constitutional requirement of monitoring which is comprehensible to the public and which involves the independent data protection officer [...] and a balanced system of sanctions which also attaches reasonable weight to violations of data security.

226 2. Storage of telecommunications traffic data as provided by § 113a TKG also requires statutory provisions on the use of these data. The drafting of these provisions on use, in a manner that is not disproportionate, thus not only decides on the constitutionality of these provisions, which in themselves constitute an encroachment, but also has an effect on the constitutionality of the storage as such. Under the case law of the Federal Constitutional Court, the greater is the weight of the encroachment constituted by the storage, the more narrowly the requirements for the use of data and their extent must be defined in the relevant basic statutory provisions. The occasion, purpose and extent of the given encroachment and the corresponding thresholds of encroachment must here be defined by the legislature in a manner that relates to a specific area and is precise and consists of well-defined provisions [...]

227 The use of the data pools obtained from systematic storage without cause of virtually all telecommunications traffic data is therefore subject to particularly strict requirements. In particular, this use is not constitutionally permissible to the same extent as the use of telecommunications traffic data which the service providers are permitted to store under § 96 TKG, depending on the given operational and contractual circumstances, which can in part be influenced by the customers. In view of the systematic precautionary storage of traffic data for six months, which is unavoidable and complete and thus results in increased informative value, their retrieval is incomparably weightier. Since an analysis of these data permits conclusions that reach deep into private lives, and in certain circumstances makes it

possible to make detailed personality profiles and track users' movements, it cannot automatically be assumed in this connection that recourse to these data carries fundamentally less weight than the content-based monitoring of telecommunications (on retrieval under the old law see BVerfGE 107, 299 (322)). Instead, the use of such data can also only be seen as proportionate if it serves particularly high-ranking reasons of public interest. A use of the data may therefore only be considered for overridingly important tasks of the protection of legal interests, that is, to punish criminal offences which threaten legal interests of paramount importance or to ward off dangers to such legal interests.

228 a) From this it follows for the prosecution of crimes that if the data are to be retrieved, there must at least be the suspicion of a serious criminal offence, based on specific facts. Together with the obligation to store data, the legislature must provide an exhaustive list of the criminal offences that are to apply here. In this, it has scope for assessment. It may either have recourse to existing lists or create its own list, for example to include criminal offences for which telecommunications traffic data are particularly important. However, if a criminal offence is to be categorised as serious, this must be objectively expressed in the statutory definition, in particular, for example, by the range of punishment provided [...]. But a blanket clause or a mere reference to criminal offences of considerable significance is not sufficient.

229 In addition to laying down such a list of criminal offences in abstract terms, the legislature must ensure that recourse to the telecommunications traffic data stored by way of precaution is permissible only if the criminal offence prosecuted is also serious in the individual case [...]

230 b) The use of the data in question must also be effectively restricted for warding off danger. In this connection, permitting access to data with reference to lists of specific criminal offences which the use of the data is intended to prevent [...] is not a suitable legislative approach. It removes the clarity from the requirements of the degree of endangerment to legal interests and leads to uncertainty where the definitions of legal offences penalise even acts preparatory to the commission of an offence and mere endangerments of legal interests. [...]

231 It follows from weighing the encroachment constituted by the storage and use of data and the importance of effective warding off of danger that retrieval of the telecommunications traffic data stored by way of precaution may only be permitted to ward off dangers to the life, limb or freedom of a person, to the existence or the security of the Federation or of a *Land* or to ward off a danger to public safety [...]. In this connection, the enabling statute must at least require actual evidence of a concrete danger to the legal interests to be protected. This requirement means that presumptions or general principles derived from experience are not sufficient to justify access to the data. On the contrary, specific facts must have been established which support the prognosis of a concrete danger. Here, the facts of the case must be such that there is sufficient probability in the individual case that specific persons will cause damage to the interests protected by the legislation in the foreseeable future, if the state does not intervene. The statements by the Senate in this connection on the requirements for online searches apply here with the necessary modifications [...]. The concrete danger is defined by three criteria: the individual case, the

imminence of the time when a danger will become actual damage, and the relationship to individual persons who are likely to cause the damage. Admittedly, the retrieval of the data stored by way of precaution may already be justified at a time when it is not yet possible with sufficient probability to establish that the danger will arise in the near future, provided that particular facts indicate the threat of a danger to a legal interest of paramount importance. On the one hand, the facts must allow events to be identified, and it must at least be possible for the nature of these events to be put into concrete terms and for the time of their occurrence to be foreseeable, and on the other hand, the facts must indicate that particular persons will be involved, and at least enough must be known of their identity to allow the measure to be specifically targeted at them and concentrated on them. In contrast, insufficient account is taken of the weight of the encroachment upon fundamental rights if the actual occasion of the encroachment is located far in advance of a concrete danger to the interests protected by the legislation, and this concrete danger cannot yet be foreseen in concrete terms.

232 c) The constitutional requirements for the use of the data to ward off danger apply to all authorisations to encroach whose objective is preventive. They therefore also apply to the use of the data by the intelligence services. Since in all these cases the adverse effect of the encroachment is the same for those affected, there is no occasion to create different rules depending on the authority involved, for example to distinguish between police authorities and other authorities which have preventive duties, such as authorities for the protection of the constitution. The fact that police authorities and authorities for the protection of the constitution have difference duties and powers and may consequently undertake measures with different degrees of encroachment is in principle irrelevant to the weighting of a use of telecommunications traffic data stored by way of precaution comprehensively and for a long time [. . .]. Admittedly, differentiations between the authorisations of the various authorities with preventive duties may stand up to constitutional review [. . .]. However, when the legislature provides for the individual powers of security authorities whose duty is advance intelligence, it is bound by the constitutional requirements which follow from the principle of proportionality [. . .]. In the present case, these lead to the conclusion that particular requirements must be imposed for the use of data both with regard of the legal interests to be protected and with regard to the threshold of encroachment to be observed in this connection.

[. . .]

235 d) It must also be ensured that the restriction of the use of data to specific purposes also applies to the use of the data after they are retrieved and transmitted to the retrieving authorities, and there must be procedures in place to support this. In this respect it must be guaranteed by statute that after transmission the data are analysed without delay and, where they are irrelevant to the purposes of the collection, are deleted [. . .]. Apart from this, it must be provided that the data are destroyed as soon as they are no longer necessary for the purposes laid down, and that a record is made of this [. . .].

[. . .]

239 3. In addition, precautionary storage of telecommunications traffic data without cause and the use of these data are only proportionate if the legislature takes sufficient precautions to ensure the transparency of the use of data and to guarantee effective legal protection and effective sanctions.

240 a) The requirements of the constitutionally unobjectionable use of data obtained by such storage include requirements as to transparency. As far as possible, the use of the data must be open. Failing this, it is in principle necessary for the persons affected to be informed, at least subsequently. If, exceptionally, even this subsequent notification is not made, there must be a judicial decision concerning the non-notification.

241 aa) Precautionary storage without cause of all telecommunications traffic data for a period of six months is such a serious encroachment, inter alia, because it can create a sense of being permanently monitored; in an unforeseen manner, it permits a high degree of knowledge of private life, without the recourse to the data being directly perceptible by or visible to the citizen. The individual does not know which state authority knows what about him or her, but knows that the authorities may know a great deal about him or her, including highly personal matters.

242 By effective provisions on transparency, the legislature must counteract the diffuse sense of threat which may attach to data storage as a result of this. Provisions on information for the persons affected by the collection or use of data are generally among the elementary instruments of constitutional data privacy [...]. In this respect, strict requirements must be imposed on the use of the data pools resulting from precautionary storage of telecommunications traffic data without cause, which are extensive and offer a variety of information. On the one hand, these requirements must reduce a sense of threat, which arises from ignorance as to the factual relevance of the data, must counteract speculations which create a sense of insecurity, and must make it possible for those affected to address such measures in public discourse. On the other hand, such requirements may also be derived from the precept of effective legal protection under Article 10.1 GG in conjunction with Article 19.4 GG. Without knowledge, those affected may assert neither unlawful official use of the data nor any rights to deletion, correction or legal redress [...].

243 bb) The requirements for transparency include the principle that the collection and use of personal data should be open. Use of the data without the knowledge of the person affected is constitutional only if otherwise the purpose of the investigation served by the retrieval of data would be frustrated. The legislature may in principle assume that this is the case for warding off danger and carrying out the duties of the intelligence services. In contrast, in criminal prosecution there is also the possibility that data may be collected and used openly (see § 33.3 and 33.4 StPO). In this connection, investigation measures are sometimes also taken in other matters with the knowledge of and in the presence of the suspect (see for example §§ 102, 103, 106 StPO). Accordingly, persons affected must as a general rule be notified before the retrieval or transmission of their data. There may only be a provision for secret use of the data here if such use is necessary and is ordered by a judge in the individual case.

244 Insofar as the use of the data is secret, the legislature must provide for a duty of information, at least subsequently. This must guarantee that the persons to whom a request for data retrieval directly applied – whether as suspects, as persons endangering public security, or as third parties – are in principle informed, at least subsequently. The legislature may provide for exceptions in weighing the notification against constitutionally protected legal interests of third parties. However, these must be restricted to what is absolutely necessary [. . .]. It is conceivable that there may be exceptions to the duties of notification in connection with the prosecution of criminal offences, for example where knowledge of the encroachment upon the secrecy of telecommunications would result in it failing to achieve its objective, if the notification cannot be made without endangering the life and limb of a person or if the concerns of an affected person which carry more weight conflict with it, for example because the notification of a measure that has had no further consequences would increase the encroachment upon fundamental rights [. . .]. If there are compelling reasons which also exclude subsequent notification, this must be judicially confirmed and reviewed at regular intervals [. . .]. In a corresponding manner, it is also necessary to structure the duties of notification on the use of the data for warding off dangers or of intelligence service duties.

245 In contrast, it is not constitutionally required to provide for comparably strict notification duties for persons whose telecommunications traffic data were only by chance collected together with others and who are not themselves the target of the actions of the authority. [. . .]

246 b) In addition, the proportionate formulation of precautionary storage of telecommunications traffic data and of their use requires that effective legal protection and adequate sanctions be guaranteed.

247 aa) To guarantee effective legal protection, a retrieval or transmission of these data must fundamentally be made subject to judicial authority.

[. . .]

249 The legislature must make provisions defining the requirement of preemptive judicial review in a concrete form with well-defined provisions, and must combine this with strict requirements as to the contents and the grounds on the judicial order [. . .]. At the same time, it follows from this that there must be a sufficiently substantiated justification and restriction of the retrieval of the data requested; it is only this that enables the court to exercise effective supervision [. . .] The court must justify its order with substantial detail. In addition, the data to be transmitted, in compliance with the principle of proportionality, must be defined sufficiently selectively and clearly [. . .], in order that the service providers do not have to undertake their own examination of the matter. These service providers may be required and permitted to transmit data based only on clear orders on data transmission.

[. . .]

251 bb) It is also constitutionally required that a legal protection procedure be available to subsequently review the use of the data. Where persons affected had no opportunity before the measure was carried out to defend themselves against the use of their telecommunications traffic data, they must be given the possibility of subsequent judicial review.

252 cc) Finally, a legislative formulation that is not disproportionate also requires effective sanctions for violations of rights. If even serious breaches of the secrecy of telecommunications were ultimately to remain without sanction, with the result that the protection of the right of personality, even in its specific manifestation in Article 10.1 GG, atrophied in view of the intangible nature of this right (see BVerfG, order of the First Chamber of the First Senate of 11 November 2009 – 1 BvR 2853/08 –, juris, marginal no. 21; BGHZ 128, 1 (15)), this would contradict the duty of the state to enable individuals to develop their personality [. . .] and to protect them against third-party threats to the right of personality [. . .]

VI.

269 The challenged provisions do not satisfy these requirements. Admittedly, the reason why § 113a TKG conflicts with the fundamental right to protection of the secrecy of telecommunications under Article 10.1 GG is not simply that the scope of the duty of storage under §§ 113a.1 to 113a.7, 11 TKG would have to be considered disproportionate from the outset. But the provisions on data security, on the purposes and the transparency of the use of data and on legal protection do not satisfy the constitutional requirements. In consequence, the whole legislation lacks a structure complying with the principle of proportionality. §§ 113a, 113b TKG and § 100g StPO, as far as the latter permits the retrieval of the data to be stored under § 113a TKG, are therefore incompatible with Article 10.1 GG.

270 1. § 113a TKG is not unconstitutional merely because of its scope. The legislature may deem the duty of storage created by § 113a TKG, which under § 113a.1 to § 113a.7 extends without cause to virtually all traffic data of publicly accessible telecommunications services, to be suitable, necessary and proportionate in the narrow sense to increase the effectiveness of criminal prosecution and the prevention of danger (see above C IV). Despite its scope, the provision is still sufficiently restricted with regard to the extent of the data covered. As § 113.8 TKG expressly states, the contents of telephone conversations, faxes and emails may not be stored, nor may the websites or service providers which a user has contacted on the Internet. In addition, in § 113a.1, 11 TKG the legislature has provided for a period of storage which is still constitutionally acceptable, given a duration of six months and a period of one month for deletion immediately following this. Similarly, at the present time it cannot be determined that the provision, in combination with other provisions, aims at or results in the creation of a general comprehensive data pool for the greatest possible reconstruction of all activities whatsoever of the citizens. In this connection, importance attaches to the application of the principle of data economy, which in other respects pervades data protection law, and to a large number of duties of deletion, with which the legislature fundamentally endeavours to prevent the creation of avoidable data pools. In this connection, the relevant factors for this assessment are in particular, for example, §§ 11 et seq. of the Telemedia Act (*Telemediengesetz* – TMG), which fundamentally subject services providers under the Telemedia Act to an obligation to delete data which are not necessary for the statement of costs (see § 13.4 no. 2, § 15 TMG) and in this way, against private-sector incentives to prevent the contents of the use of the Internet from being recorded in general commercial data pools and thus remaining reconstructible. §

113a TKG can therefore not be understood as the expression of a general public provision of data for the future for purposes of criminal prosecution and prevention of danger, but despite its breadth remains a limited exception which attempts to take account of the particular challenges of modern telecommunications for criminal prosecution and prevention of danger.

271 2. In contrast, the guarantee of a particularly high standard of security, which is constitutionally necessary for such a data pool, is missing. In this respect, § 113a.10 TKG only provides the duty, which remains undefined, to ensure by technical and organisational measures that access to the stored data is possible solely for persons who are specially authorised, and apart from this refers only to the care which is necessary in general in the area of telecommunications. There is therefore no provision which takes account of the particularly strict standards required of the security of the extensive and informative data pool under § 113a TKG. [. . .]

272 Nor is it ensured by statutory orders or by orders of the regulatory authorities that these standards are put into specific terms. In particular, § 110 TKG does not guarantee that adequate security standards apply. Admittedly, the delegated legislation to be passed under this statute (see § 110.2 and 3 TKG) may include aspects of data security. However, this statute – which is primarily determined by technical objectives – neither contains substantive standards, nor does it otherwise assume the aspect of data security. Apart from this, even two years after the duty of storage of § 113a TKG entered into force, the Telecommunications Interception Order (*Telekommunikationsüberwachungsverordnung* – TKÜV) has not been adapted to take account of the reform of the law. [. . .]

273 Nor does § 109.3 TKG guarantee sufficient data security. Admittedly, the statute provides that operators of telecommunications equipment must appoint security officers and prepare a security policy, which must be submitted to the Federal Network Agency. In addition, the policy must be adjusted and resubmitted later if the "circumstances" on which it is based are changed. However, this does not reliably guarantee a particular high security standard. Thus, for example, the provision only applies to equipment operators, but not to all the persons targeted by § 113a TKG, which also applies to other service providers. In addition, § 109.3 TKG refers substantively only to the insufficient requirements of § 109.1 and 109.2 TKG. Nor is a continuing and verifiable adaptation of the security standard to the state of the art in technology guaranteed by well-defined provisions. [. . .] At all events, there is no obligation for a periodical updating of the security policy which could enable effective supervision in this respect.

[. . .]

275 All in all, therefore, there is no guarantee in a binding form and in well-defined provisions of a particularly high security standard for the data to be stored under § 113a TKG. Neither are the instruments cited by the experts in the present proceedings as central elements (separate storage, asymmetric encryption, the four-eyes principle in conjunction with advanced authentication procedures for access to the keys, revision-proof recording of access and deletion) imposed on the persons with a duty of storage in an enforceable manner, nor are other precautions which guarantee a comparable level of security imposed on them. Nor is there a balanced

system of sanctions that attributes no less weight to violations of data security than to violations of the duties of storage themselves. The range of administrative fines for non-compliance with the duties of storage is markedly broader than that for the violation of data security (see § 149.2 sentence 1 in conjunction with § 149.1 nos. 36 and 38 TKG). The current legal situation therefore does not satisfy the constitutional requirements of the security of a data pool as is created by § 113a TKG.

276 3. The provisions on transmission and use of the data under § 113b sentence 1 half-sentence 1 TKG do not satisfy the constitutional requirements.

277 a) First, the provisions on the use of the data for criminal prosecution are incompatible with the standards developed from the principle of proportionality.

278 aa) § 113b sentence 1 no. 1 TKG in conjunction with § 100g StPO does not satisfy the particularly stringent requirements which must be satisfied for access to the data stored under § 113a TKG to be permitted. Admittedly, in these provisions the legislature has laid down a sophisticated objective of data use for criminal prosecution which is also, under Article 74.1 no. 1 and Article 72.1, final. Here, however, the legislature permits similar standards to apply for the use of the data as have applied until now for the collection of telecommunications traffic data which the service providers were entitled to store under § 96 TKG depending on their operational and contractual requirements to a more limited extent and in such a way that the individual could in part contract out of this. This does not take sufficient account of the particularly serious encroachment constituted by the systematic precautionary data storage without cause of § 113a TKG.

279 Even § 100g.1 sentence 1 no. 1 StPO does not ensure that in general and also in the individual case only serious criminal offences may be the occasion for collecting the relevant data, but – independently of an exhaustive list – merely generally accepts criminal offences of substantial weight as sufficient. § 100g.1 sentence 1 no. 2, sentence 2 StPO satisfies the constitutional standards even less, in that it accepts every criminal offence committed by means of telecommunications, regardless of its seriousness, as the possible trigger for data retrieval, depending on a general assessment in the course of a review of proportionality. This provision makes the data stored under § 113a TKG usable on virtually all criminal offences. As a result, in view of the increasing importance of telecommunications in everyday life, the use of these data loses its exceptional character. Here, the legislature no longer confines itself to the use of data to prosecute serious criminal offences, but goes far beyond this, and thus also beyond the objective of data storage specified by EU law, which also in turn is restricted to the prosecution of serious criminal offences, without including the prevention of danger. Admittedly, a use of these data can be very useful, especially for the prosecution of criminal offences committed by means of telecommunications, and therefore restricting it may in some cases make their successful investigation more difficult or even impossible. However, it is in the nature of the guarantee of Article 10.1 GG and of the proportionality standards associated with this that not every measure that is useful, and in the individual case may also be necessary, for criminal prosecution is constitutionally permissible. Conversely, as a consequence of the standards that are decisive here, telecommunications do not in their entirety become a legal vacuum, even in the area of less

serious criminal offences: the legislature may provide that information under § 113.1 TKG – including information indirectly using the data stored under § 113a TKG – is available for the investigation of all criminal offences (see above C V 4 c). Similarly, because of this, recourse under § 100g StPO to telecommunications traffic data stored otherwise than under § 113a TKG remains possible.

280 bb) In addition, § 100g StPO fails to comply with the constitutional requirements in that it fundamentally permits retrieval of data even without the knowledge of the person affected (§ 100g.1 sentence 1 StPO). The constitutional requirements of the transparency of use of data only permit the data stored under § 113a TKG to be collected secretly if this is necessary for reasons carrying more weight which must be more precisely defined by statute, and if it is judicially ordered.

281 cc) Nor does the formulation of the duty of notification in every respect comply with the standards developed above. However, the extent of the duties of notification provided for is not as such open to any constitutional objections. §§ 101.1, 101.4 and 101.5 StPO, in conformity with the case law of the Federal Constitutional Court (see BVerfGE 109, 279 (363 et seq.)), provides for complex provisions which balance the principle of subsequent notification of the person affected, in a manner which is constitutionally workable, with predominant concerns which exceptionally arise in the individual case. Another aspect which is unobjectionable in this context is the fact that under § 101.4 sentence 4 StPO, persons affected to whom the retrieval of data did not apply are not to be notified in every case, but only in accordance with a weighing of interests. In this weighing of interests, the interests of persons indirectly affected can and must be sufficiently considered.

282 In contrast, the provisions on judicial review for cases in which a notification may be omitted are inadequate. § 101.6 StPO provides for judicial review only when notification is deferred under § 101.5 StPO, but not when there is no notification, under § 101.4 StPO. This does not take sufficient account of the high value of the notification for transparent use of the data stored under § 113a TKG. Where data retrieval relates directly to traffic data of a specific person, that person absolutely must be subsequently notified unless there is a judicial review of the relevant grounds for an exception. Such a judicial review is missing in the cases in which there is to be no notification under § 101.4 sentence 3 StPO by reason of predominant concerns of a person affected.

283 dd) In contrast, the judicial review of data retrieval and data use is itself guaranteed in a manner that complies with constitutional requirements. Under § 100g.2 sentence 1, § 100b.1 sentence 1 StPO, the collection of the data stored under § 113a TKG requires a judicial order. Nor does the judicial order authorise the authorities to have direct access to the data; instead, it obliges the service providers to filter them out and transmit them, in a separate intermediate process in compliance with the order. In addition, under § 101.1, 101.7 sentences 2 to 4 StPO there is the possibility subsequently to arrange a judicial review of the lawfulness of the measure. It is not apparent that these provisions do not, as a whole, guarantee effective legal protection.

284 However, the statutory provisions on the formal requirements of the judicial order are not formulated in sufficiently well-defined provisions. § 100g.2 in conjunction with § 100b.2 StPO merely lays down the minimum requirements of the operative part of the order; apart from this, the general obligation to give reasons for a decision applies to decisions under § 34 StPO. In revising the legislation, the legislature should consider whether it would be appropriate to emphasise the strict requirements of a substantiated justification of judicial orders [...] by way of a special and tailor-made provision. At all events, it must be ensured by statute that the extent of the data to be transmitted is described in the judicial order sufficiently selectively and unambiguously for the service providers, in a manner that satisfies the principle of proportionality.

285 b) The challenged provisions also fail to satisfy the constitutional requirements with regard to the retrieval and use of the data stored under § 113a TKG for warding off danger and for the tasks of the intelligence services. [...] In this provision, the Federal legislature contents itself with sketching in a merely general manner the fields of duty for which data retrieval is to be possible, without stating the purposes of use in concrete terms. Instead, it leaves the purposes of use to be defined in concrete terms by later legislation, including in particular *Länder* legislation. In this way the Federal legislature does not satisfy its responsibility for the constitutionally required limitation of the purposes of use. If it orders that telecommunications traffic data are to be stored, it is at the same time obliged to lay down additionally in a binding form the purposes of use and thresholds of encroachment that are necessary to constitutionally justify the storage, and to bindingly lay down the consequential provisions that are necessary to guarantee that the use is limited to specific purposes. § 113b half-sentence 1 TKG contains no such provisions. Instead, because the service providers have a duty of precautionary storage of all telecommunications traffic data, and at the same time these data are released to be used by the police and the intelligence services as part of almost all their tasks, a data pool is created open to manifold and unlimited uses to which – restricted only by broad objectives – recourse may be had, in each case from the decisions of the Federal and *Länder* legislatures. The supply of such a data pool with an open purpose removes the necessary connection between storage and purpose of storage and is incompatible with the constitution (see above C V 5 a).

[...]

292 5. In summary, neither the framework established by law for data security nor the provisions on the use of data under § 113b sentence 1 no. 1 TKG in conjunction with § 100g stop, § 113b sentences 1 nos. 2 and 3 TKG and § 113b sentence 1 half-sentence 2 TKG satisfy the constitutional requirements. Consequently, the duty of storage under § 113a TKG itself also lacks a constitutionally workable justification. The challenged provisions are therefore in their totality incompatible with Article 10.1 GG.

[...]

309 The Senate decided by four votes to four that the provisions are to be declared void under § 95.3 sentence 1 of the Federal Constitutional Court Act, and not merely incompatible with the Basic Law. Accordingly, it is not possible for the provisions to

continue in effect in a restricted scope; instead, the statutory consequence is an annulment.

[. . .]

The High Court of Ireland: Judgment of 5 May 2010, Ref. No 2006 3785 P[10]

(. . .)

6. This judgment relates to the following three matters, the first two moved by the Defendants and the third by the Plaintiff, all of which were heard by way of preliminary issues:

(. . .)

iii) Whether a reference to the Court of Justice ("CoJ") under Article 267 of the Treaty on the Functioning of the European Union ("TFEU") (formerly Article 234 of the Treaty establishing the European Communities ("TEC")) should be made.

(. . .)

7. The background to the case, as the Plaintiff alleges, is that in or around th[e] 25th April 2002 the Minister for Public Enterprise, the predecessor of the First Named Defendant, issued a direction under s. 110(1) of the Postal Telecommunications Services Act 1983 (as amended by the Interception of Postal Packets and Telecommunication Messages (regulations) Act 1993) to certain telecommunications services providers to retain telecommunications data. Such direction was to be treated as confidential. Following this direction, the First Named Defendant came into possession of, and had and exercised control over, data relating to the Plaintiff, its members and other users of mobile phones.

8. By letter dated 19 December 2002, the Data Protection Commissioner advised the Department of Communications, Marine and Natural Resources that the above-mentioned direction was ultra vires, constitutionally invalid and was in breach of the Data Protection Acts 1988/2003 and S.I. 192 of 2002; with the grounds therefor being that as the objectives sought by the direction amounted to a derogation from the then existing data protection legislative scheme, the same could only be enacted through primary legislation. The Data Protection Commissioner advised the Defendants that failing a satisfactory response he would issue judicial review proceedings to challenge the validity of any direction(s) the Minister purported to make under the Postal Telecommunications Services Act 1983.

9. Some of the concerns of the Data Protection Commissioner were addressed in Part 7 of the Criminal Justice (Terrorist Offences) Act 2005 ("CJ(TO)A 2005"), which made provision for the retention of traffic and location data, relating to

[10]The judgement in English is available at the page of the High Court of Ireland under: https://beta.courts.ie/view/document/08a2f2b3-7bc4-473c-a9f1-0caf8fec4ece/2010_IEHC_221_1.pdf/pdf.

communications transmitted by fixed line or mobile telephone, and access to such data retained for law enforcement and security purposes.

10. The Plaintiff alleges that on a date or dates unknown, following the coming into force of the above Act of 2005, the Garda Commissioner issued a direction under the provisions thereof to telecommunications service providers to retain data.

11. The European legal framework in place at the time was governed by Directive 95/46/EC ('on the protection of individuals with regard to the processing of personal data and on the free movement of such data') and Directive 97/66/EC ('concerning the processing of personal data and the protection of privacy in the telecommunications sector'), later repealed by Directive 2002/58/EC ('concerning the processing of personal data and the protection of privacy in the electronic communications sector (Directive on privacy and electronic communications)'). These Directives aimed to harmonise the position of Member States:

"[T]o ensure an equivalent level of protection of fundamental rights and freedoms, and in particular the right to privacy, with respect to the processing of personal data in the electronic communication sector and to ensure the free movement of such data and of electronic communication equipment and services in the Community" (Article 1, Dir. 2002/58/EC)

The focus of these Directives was thus the protection of privacy rights arising from data retention.

12. On 6 May 2006, Directive 2006/24/EC ('on the retention of data generated or processed in connection with the provision of publicly available electronic communications services or of public communications networks and amending Directive 2002/58/EC') was published.

(...)

13. In this case, the Plaintiff alleges that the Defendants have wrongfully exercised control over data, in that they have illegally processed and stored data relating to the Plaintiff, its members, and other mobile phone users contrary to: (i) statute, (ii) EC law, and (iii) the Constitution, particularly having regard to the Plaintiff's asserted rights to privacy, to travel and to communicate (Arts. 40.3.1°, 40.3.2° and 40.6.1°), and (iv) the European Convention on Human Rights ("ECHR"), particularly the right to private life, to family life, and to privileged communication (Arts. 6(1), 8 and 10). These allegations involve a claim that s. 63 (1) of the CJ(TO)A 2005 is invalid on the within grounds and further that Directive 2006/24/EC is contrary to the Charter of Fundamental Rights ("CFR") and the ECHR.

(...)

Article 267 of TFEU Reference:

109. The Plaintiff has brought a motion calling for a Reference to the CoJ under Article 267 of TFEU. The questions to be asked all relate to the validity of Directive 2006/24/EC, particularly rights under the EU and EC Treaties, the CFR and the ECHR. Questions relating to whether the Directive was issued under the appropriate Treaty heading were live matters at the time of the hearing as the Irish Government was then involved in ongoing litigation in the CoJ on this point. Since the hearing, the CoJ has ruled against the Irish government on the issue (Ireland v. European

Parliament and Council of the European Union (Case C-301/06) (delivered on 10 February 2009)). The Court found that Directive 2006/24/EC was properly enacted under Article 95 TEC, since it was apparent that differences between national rules adopted for the retention of data were liable to have a foreseeable direct impact on the functioning of the internal market which would become more serious over time. Further, the provisions of the Directive are essentially limited to the activities of service providers and do no not govern access to data, or its use by police or judicial authorities. However, the CoJ expressly stated that the action related solely to the choice of legal basis for the Directive, and "not to any possible infringement of fundamental rights arising from interference with the exercise of the right to privacy..." (ibid. at para. 57).

110. The Plaintiff notes that there is a complete discretion, under Article 267(2), for a judge to refer a question when he considers that a decision on it is necessary to enable it to give judgment. However, in this case the Plaintiff also seeks to ground its application under Article 267(3), which states:

"Where any such question is raised in a case pending before a court or tribunal of a Member State against whose decision there is no judicial remedy under national law, that court or tribunal shall bring the matter before the Court of Justice" (emphasis added)

The Plaintiff argues that where a question of the validity Community law is raised the national court must make a reference since there is no effective judicial remedy under national law because a national judge may not declare a Community instrument invalid (...).

111. Attention is drawn to the exceptions to the requirement to make a Reference. These are that, first, the matter is not required for the national court to rule on the matter case (...). Third, the application of Community law is so obvious as to leave no doubt to the national court (...). In the Plaintiff's opinion none of these operate in this case. A useful summary in relation to references to the CoJ can be found in Kelly v National University of Ireland [2008] IEHC 464.

112. The Defendants admit that, in relation to the Article 267 Reference, it is a matter of discretion for the Court, but argues that at this point a Reference would be premature. They say that, in circumstances where the Plaintiff has elected to bring proceedings by way of plenary action, and must therefore provide evidence, including viva voce evidence, to be examined in open court, and where this has yet to be done, there is therefore as of now, no way of evaluating what the final evidential framework will be. What evidence exists is, by definition, one-sided. In this regard, reliance is placed upon Irish Creamery Milk Suppliers Association v. Ireland (Joined Cases 36 and 71/80) [1981] ECR 735, where the CoJ stated at paragraph 6 that:

"The need to provide an interpretation of Community law which will be of use to the national court makes it essential ... to define the legal context in which the interpretation requested should be placed. From that aspect it might be convenient, in certain circumstances, for the facts in the case to be established and for questions of purely national law to be settled at the time the reference is made to the Court of Justice so as to enable the latter to take cognisance of all the features of fact and of law which may be relevant to the interpretation of Community law which it is called to give."

Thus, where the legal and factual context in the case has yet to be properly defined a Reference at this stage should be refused. The Plaintiff, the Defendants submit, fails to acknowledge that significant factual and national law issues remain to be determined concerning the nature and extent of the fundamental rights directly affected by the provisions of the Directive, as well as the extent, if any, to which any such rights are capable of being enjoyed or invoked by an artificial legal entity.

113. In relation the Article 267 Reference, I am satisfied that there is sufficient information before me to make such a Reference to the CoJ. I do not think that the application is premature; it is possible to define the context of the Reference (...). This is not a case which requires significant viva voce evidence to properly define the context or issues in the case. It is a challenge to specific legislative provisions which speak for themselves. I am also satisfied that the Reference is required since I am unable to rule on the validity of Community law (...). I would therefore grant the application for a Reference under Article 267 TFEU.

114. On the questions to be referred, I do not propose to deal with those now. Instead, I would invite the parties to submit suggestions, either individually or in the form of agreed questions between them, as to the content and wording of the questions to be referred, considering my findings in this decision.

Conclusion:

115. Thus, in summary:

i) I grant the Plaintiff locus standi to bring action *actio popularis* in respect of whether the impugned provisions violate citizens' rights to privacy and communications, but not with regards to family and marital privacy or travel;

ii) I refuse the Defendants' motion for security for costs;

iii) I grant the Plaintiff's motion for a Reference to the Court of Justice under Article 267 TFEU.

The Constitutional Tribunal of Poland: Judgment of 30 July 2014, Ref. No K 23/11[11]

(...)

The constitutional protection of the person's freedom primarily refers to the realm of his/her privacy. The constitution-maker establishes the privacy of the individual, not as a constitutionally assigned subjective right, but as a constitutionally protected freedom, with all the consequences arising therefrom. Above all, this implies the individual's discretion to act as s/he wishes within the scope of that freedom, up to

[11]The judgement in English is available at the page of the Constitutional Tribunal of Poland under: https://trybunal.gov.pl/en/hearings/judgments/art/8821-okreslenie-katalogu-zbieranych-informacji-o-jednostce-za-pomoca-srodkow-technicznych-w-dzialani.

the limits set by statute. Only a clear statutory regulation may impose restrictions within the scope of certain actions that fall within the realm of a particular freedom. What is inadmissible is to make presumptions about the competence of public authorities as regards the scope of interference in the individual's freedom. An immanent element of all constitutional freedoms of the person is the state's obligation to have them respected and protected by law, as well as any interference in the said freedoms should be refrained from by the state and private parties (. . .). The said standard refers to all constitutional freedoms of the individual, and in particular to personal freedoms of the individual which – apart from privacy – comprise, inter alia: the freedom of communication (Article 49 of the Constitution), the inviolability of the home (Article 50 of the Constitution) or the broadly-construed informational self-determination of the individual (Article 51 of the Constitution).

(. . .)

(. . .) the Constitutional Tribunal deems that the constitutional protection arising from Article 47, Article 49 and Article 51(1) of the Constitution comprises all ways of exchanging messages, in every form of communication, regardless of the actual means of communication (e.g. conversations in person and via telephone, written correspondence, fax messages, text and multimedia messages, as well as electronic mail). The constitutional protection comprises not only the content of messages, but also all circumstances related to the process of communication, which include the personal data of the participants of the process, information on dialled telephone numbers, visited Internet websites, data that specify the duration and frequency of communication, or which make it possible to determine the location of the participants of communication, as well as data about a given IP number or an IMEI number. The scope of the constitutionally guaranteed freedom of the person and his/her informational self-determination also comprises protection against the secret monitoring of individuals and conversations held by them even in places that are public and generally accessible. It is irrelevant whether a given exchange of information concerns only private life or also professional life, including economic activity. Indeed, there is no such area of personal life which would not be subject to constitutional protection, or where the said protection would be intrinsically restricted. Thus, in each of those areas of personal life, the individual enjoys a constitutionally guaranteed freedom to provide and obtain information, as well as to disclose information about him/herself.

Furthermore, the Constitutional Tribunal draws attention to one more issue; namely, in a democratic state ruled by law, the organisation of social and public life must include a possibility that individuals may act within the public realm in an anonymous way. At least within the scope of exercising their freedoms, it is not generally necessary for individuals to give up their anonymity in their relations with the state or private parties. By contrast, the situation looks different as regards the exercise of subjective rights. Indeed, the exercise of the said rights requires action to be taken by the subject of a given right, usually for verifying the granted right.

(. . .) Technological development extends the realm in which the person functions. It opens new and unknown possibilities of exercising constitutionally guaranteed rights and freedoms. New technologies in an unprecedented way make it possible to overcome the barriers of time and distance in communication, thus making it possible to transfer information on every topic in any form, regardless of a distance separating the participants of given communication. Moreover, the said technologies create new ways of acquiring goods and services or ways of deciding about the fulfilment of one's needs. At the same time, they play a vital role when it comes to enhancing the security of persons and property, by permitting the monitoring of persons and places or the electronic surveillance thereof, thanks to which – regardless of unexpected events – it is possible to geographically locate the persons and property.

In the modern world, a special role is played by the Internet. It has ceased to be merely a medium for communicating and transferring data across long distances. Instead, it has become a multi-faceted tool for creating, storing and transferring data that are varied in character, and at the same time a tool which makes it possible for the individual to function in society.

The Constitutional Tribunal emphasises that although the Constitution does not refer to the functioning of the individual in the virtual space, the protection of individuals' constitutional rights and freedoms with relation to the use of the Internet and other electronic means of distant communication in no way differs from protection that concerns the traditional forms of communication or other activity. Data transferred via the Internet may not be perceived as data that are put aside, or that exist as if on the margin of the constitutionally protected forms of the person's activity. Therefore, there are no justified reasons that would permit separating the transfer of data or communication via the Internet from the realm of constitutional rights and freedoms. Due to the complexity of a phenomenon such as the Internet, the activity of individuals in that realm corresponds to the proper forms of constitutionally protected activity. Consequently, sending messages by electronic means (e.g. email) is subject to the same constitutional protection as the posting of a letter in the traditional paper form (Articles 47, 49, and 51). The provision of information to the counsel for the defence via the Internet or by other means of electronic communication is subject to the same guarantees as providing the same information in a face-to-face conversation (Article 42). The protection of intimacy in communication with persons who hold professions in which the public repose confidence remains the same, regardless of the form of communication (Article 47). The expression of opinions, as well as the collection and dissemination of information by electronic means are entirely subject to protection under Article 54 of the Constitution. Similarly, the protection of the freedom of the press and of other means of social communication is the same, irrespective of the way of exercising that freedom (Article 14; Article 54). The scope of constitutional protection guaranteed to the freedom of economic activity (Articles 20 and 22) also comprises the carrying out of that activity via the Internet or by other means of electronic communication. The same also concerns the protection of the freedom to choose and to pursue one's occupation (Article 65), the freedom of artistic creation and scientific research as well as dissemination of the fruits thereof, the freedom to teach and to enjoy the products of culture (Article 73) or the right to submit petitions, proposals and complaints to the organs of public authority (Article 63).

Therefore, the Internet should be perceived as one of the tools that make it possible to exercise subjective rights and freedoms, and not as a separate realm or a realm that escapes constitutional protection. In this state of affairs, the evaluation of provisions that permit interference in subjective rights and freedoms, in the context of individuals' use of, inter alia, the Internet, should be carried out by considering the normative content of relevant provisions of the Constitution which guarantee the protection of fundamental rights. Such evaluation affects the limits of the freedom to interpret statutory provisions. This also pertains to regulations that refer to powers vested in the organs of the state whose task is to protect the security of the state. At the current stage of the development of the electronic forms of communication, it is not admissible - in the Tribunal's opinion - to juxtapose the statutory protection of traditional correspondence with the other forms of correspondence transferred via telecommunications networks.

(. . .)

The Tribunal draws attention to one more issue which is of significance in the age of globalisation and international crime. The organs of public authority are obliged to protect the privacy of citizens also against threats that emerge outside the state itself. Consequently, the obligation of the state also comprises ensuring that the various aspects of the private life of citizens will be safeguarded against surveillance – which includes messages exchanged via telecommunications networks – conducted by foreign entities, and in particular foreign states. Indeed, an infringement of the right to the protection of privacy, guaranteed in Article 47 of the Constitution, may take place not only by the direct actions of the organs of the Polish state that acquire information on individuals in a secret way; this will also occur in a situation where no sufficient protection is granted to citizens by the state against any interference in that freedom caused by the actions of other entities.

(. . .)

From the above findings put forward by the Constitutional Tribunal, the European Court of Human Rights as well as the Court of Justice of the European Union with regard to provisions that regulate the secret obtaining of information on individuals by public authorities in a democratic state ruled by law, the Tribunal deems it necessary to draw attention to minimum requirements that must be jointly met by provisions that restrict constitutional rights and freedoms. These are as follows:

- the collecting, storing and processing of data on individuals, and in particular data concerning the realm of their privacy, are permissible activities based only on an explicit and precise provision of a statute (. . .);

- it is necessary to precisely determine in a statute what organs of the state are authorised to collect and process data on individuals, as well as to carry out operational and investigative activities;

- a statute should specify grounds for the secret obtaining of information on individuals, which include: the detection and prosecution of only serious offences as well as the prevention thereof; a statute should determine the types of such offences (. . .);

- a statute needs to specify the categories of individuals to whom operational and investigative activities may be carried out (. . .);

- it is desirable to specify by statute the types of measures used for the secret obtaining of information, as well as the types of information obtained with particular measures;

- operational and investigative activities should constitute a subsidiary measure for the secret obtaining of information or evidence on individuals, when it is impossible to gather the information in any other way that would be less intrusive for individuals (. . .)

- a statute should specify a maximum period for carrying out operational and investigative activities on individuals, which should not exceed what is necessary in a democratic state ruled by law;

- it is necessary to precisely regulate in a statute what procedure should be applied to order operational and investigative activities, which would in particular include the requirement to obtain permission from an independent organ of public authority for the secret obtaining of information (. . .);

- a statute needs to precisely specify rules of procedure for handling material gathered during operational and investigative activities, in particular rules for using and destroying data that are redundant and inadmissible (s. . .);

- it must be ensured that collected data are protected against unauthorised access on the part of other individuals and entities;

- there is a need to regulate a procedure for notifying individuals about the secret obtaining of information related to them within a reasonable time-limit after the conclusion of operational and investigative activities; also, it should be ensured that a person in question should have a possibility to apply for a judicial review of the legality of the activities that have been carried out; a departure from this is admissible only by way of exception (. . .);

- it is necessary to guarantee that operational and investigative activities are carried out in a transparent way by given organs of public authority, which implies the transparency and availability of compiled statistical data, which are valid for drawing comparisons in terms of the number and types of operational and investigative activities that have been carried out;

- it is not ruled out that differentiation may be introduced with regard to the intensity of the protection of privacy, informational self-determination as well as the privacy of communication, depending on whether data on given persons are obtained by intelligence services and state security services or whether they are gathered by police forces;

- differentiation on the level of protection of privacy, informational self-determination and the privacy of communication may also be introduced, depending on whether the secret obtaining of information concerns Polish citizens or persons who are not Polish citizens.

(. . .)

The Constitutional Tribunal draws attention to the fact that the applicants have not challenged the provisions of the Telecommunications Act which impose, on the providers of telecommunications services or networks, an obligation to retain telecommunications data (the so-called data retention). As a consequence, what will be found outside the scope of the allegation is the issue of admissibility and proportionality of the said obligation, the scope of data that are subject to retention and a period for which they need to be retained. The applicants' reservations on the use of telecommunications data concentrate only on a relatively limited case of providing police forces and state security services – as part of operational and investigative activities – with retained telecommunications data. Hence, the scope of the allegation is relatively narrow. Also, when assessing the constitutionality of provisions governing competence which authorise the organs of public authority to use those data in the course of operational and investigative activities, the Tribunal may not ignore normative surroundings in which such provisions function, as well as a way in which they are applied by competent authorities. Nor may it overlook the significance of the judgment issued by the Court of Justice of the European Union on 8 April 2014 in the case C-293/12, in which the Court of Justice ruled that the Data Retention Directive 2006/24/EC was invalid (see part III, point 3 of this statement of reasons).

(...)

The challenged provision authorises the police to collect and process telecommunications data referred to in Article 180c and Article 180d of the Telecommunications Act, as well as it specifies premises within the scope *ratione materiae* as regards providing those data to the functionaries of the police (...).

What follows from the linguistic interpretation of Article 20c(1) of the Act on the Police is that the functionaries of the police may be provided with telecommunications data in "preventing or detecting" every prohibited act that is regarded as an offence, including – what is not definitively ruled out – also a fiscal offence. The only restriction is that the prevention of given offences, or the detection thereof, should fall within the scope of the statutory tasks of the police, as set out in Article 1 of the said Act. However, the catalogue of those tasks is broad. The legislator has determined that the tasks of the police comprise, inter alia: the protection of life and health of other people as well as property against unlawful attempts at interference with those interests (Article 1(2)(1)); the protection of public security and order, including the preservation of order in public places as well as in the means of public transportation, in road traffic and public waters (Article 1(2)(2)); and also the detection of offences and misdemeanours as well as the prosecution of the perpetrators thereof (Article 1(2)(4)). The wording of Article 1(2)(4), in particular, allows one to draw the conclusion that the tasks of the police include the detection of every prohibited act categorised as an offence in the light of the Polish law. Juxtaposing those findings with the interpretation of challenged Article 20c(1) of the Act on the Police, one would have to consequently assume that requesting access to telecommunications data will also be possible for the prevention or detection of offences. Thus, it is justified to state that the legislator specifies the purpose of providing the police with telecommunications data in a very general way.

10.4.3. The Constitutional Tribunal notes that interference in the constitutional right to the protection of privacy (Article 47) and the privacy of communication (Article 49 of the Constitution) may take place not only in the case where the organs of public authority became familiar with the content of messages exchanged between individuals, but also in a situation where authorities obtain information related to the said process (for more, see part III, point 1.4, 1.10, and 6.2. of this statement of reasons). Such a view – as it has been pointed out earlier – was also adopted by the Court of Justice of the European Union in its judgment of 8 April 2014, where the Court ruled that the Data Retention Directive 2006/24/EC was invalid. This means that providing the police with data referred to in Article 180c and Article 180d of the Telecommunications Act constitutes interference in the right to the protection of privacy and the privacy of communication. Although such interference is currently unavoidable – since the police must make use of tools that allow police officers to effectively fight crime – the admissibility of that measure depends on the fulfilment of requirements arising from the principle of proportionality (Article 31(3) of the Constitution).

10.4.4. The Constitutional Tribunal agrees with the applicants' allegations about the non-conformity of Article 20c(1) of the Act on the Police to Article 47 and Article 49 in conjunction with Article 31(3) of the Constitution.

First, the Tribunal decides to address the allegation about insufficient procedural guarantees, related to the lack of external supervision of the process of accessing telecommunications data. The said allegation remains the same on all the provisions challenged within that group. The ruling declaring the unconstitutionality thereof renders it redundant to address the other allegations formulated by the applicants with regard to the admissibility of obtaining data also for preventing and prosecuting offences that have relatively insignificant detrimental effects on society, or the lack of the premise of subsidiarity.

One of the requirements which should be met by statutory provisions that authorise the police to obtain telecommunications data is to provide a mechanism for independent supervision. Since the data are obtained in secret, without the knowledge and will of individuals about whom the police gather information, and at the same time with the limited oversight of society, the lack of independent review by the organs of the state over that process poses a risk of misuse. Not only may this cause unjustified interference with the rights and freedoms of the individual, but it may also pose a threat to democratic mechanisms for exercising power. The need for regulating procedural mechanisms by statute, for the prevention of any arbitrariness in the course of obtaining telecommunications data, is correlated with the scope of competence of state authorities for the secret obtaining of information; the broader the scope of the said competence, the greater the need for the said mechanisms to be regulated by statute. The police may obtain telecommunications data not only to counteract serious offences, but also in less significant cases, or even – as it is specified in a letter of 2 March 2012 submitted by the Marshal of the Sejm – in cases that are trivial. The examples of offences, with regard to which telecommunications data may be disclosed to the police, are set out in a letter of 21 June 2012 submitted by the Public Prosecutor-General. They include inter alia: the offence of defamation (Article 212 of the Penal Code), acquiring carcasses of game animals and hunting trophies, as well as the breeding and upkeep of pedigree greyhounds and their cross-breeds (Article 52(2) and (4) of the Hunting Act). Moreover, the legislator has not correlated the possibility of requesting data with the actual circumstances of a given case, an actual risk level, and, finally, the exhaustion of other means of obtaining information that are less intrusive for the individual. In such a situation, it is even more important to establish procedural guarantees of external supervision over the process of obtaining telecommunications data, especially telephone billing data and location data.

Neither challenged Article 20c(1) of the Act on the Police nor any other provision imposes an obligation on the police to obtain permission from a competent court (or from any other authority that would be independent of authorities that request access to such data or authorities that are superior to them) for the disclosure of data specified in Article 180c and Article 180d of the Telecommunications Act. The said procedure, as it has been stressed earlier, does not require permission from a prosecutor. Nor has the legislator provided for the general elements of *ex post facto* review that legalises undertaken action. Thus, the obtaining of telecommunications data by the functionaries of the police remains beyond any permanent supervision, conducted by an authority that is independent of the police.

The Constitutional Tribunal notes that, in the provisions of the Act on the Police, the legislator has included certain restrictions on access to telecommunications data. Indeed, not every functionary may – as part of his/her work activities – be granted access to such data. Under Article 20c(2) of the Act on the Police, telecommunications data referred to in Article 180c and Article180d of the Telecommunications Act, may be disclosed to functionaries who have received appropriate authorisation from the Head of the Polish Police or the head of the police in a given voivodeship. However, the said guarantee does not suffice to prevent any misuse. The restrictions on access to telecommunications data, included in provisions that are currently binding, although needed, do not eliminate the obligation to ensure independent supervision over the process of obtaining telecommunications data.

The Constitutional Tribunal does not determine at this point what exactly a procedure for access to telecommunications data should look like, and in particular, whether it is necessary – with regard to every type of retained data referred to in Article 180c and Article 180d of the Telecommunications Act – to obtain permission for access thereto. Not always access to the data of the same type results in the same extent of interference in the freedoms and rights of the individual. Thus, in the opinion of the Tribunal, it may not be ruled out that, on accessing telecommunications data in the course of operational and investigative activities, *ex post facto* supervision will be introduced as a rule. When regulating that mechanism, the legislator should take account, inter alia, of the special character and statutory scope of tasks of particular police forces and state security services, as well as of emergencies in which the quick obtaining of telecommunications data may be necessary for the prevention or detection of offences. Pursuant to the constitutional requirement of efficiency in the work of public institutions (the Preamble to the Constitution), a mechanism should be created which would make it possible for police forces and state security services to effectively counteract risks. Nevertheless, the Tribunal recognises arguments for the introduction of *ex ante* supervision in certain cases. In particular, what is meant here is access to the telecommunications data of persons that hold professions in which the public repose confidence. However, the said issues must be appropriately weighed up by the legislator.

At the same time, the Constitutional Tribunal does not require – referring to the argumentation put forward by the applicants and the other participants in the review proceedings – that supervision over the disclosure of telecommunications data should be exercised by courts. However, it is necessary that this would be an independent authority, and that it would not remain in a direct or indirect relation of superiority to functionaries that are obtaining data. The said requirement should be regarded as well-established in the jurisprudence of the Constitutional Tribunal, as well as that of the European Court of Human Rights and the Court of Justice of the European Union (see part III points 2 and 3 of this statement of reasons).

Considering the above, Article 20c(1) of the Act on the Police, because it does not provide for independent supervision over the process of granting access to telecommunications data referred to in Article 180c and Article 180d of the Telecommunications Act, is inconsistent with Article 47 and Article 49 in conjunction with Article 31(3) of the Constitution.

(. . .)

Under Article 51(2) of the Constitution, public authorities may not obtain, collect and disclose information about citizens other than that which is necessary in a democratic state ruled by law. As it has been pointed out in the jurisprudence of the Constitutional Tribunal, the said provision has a double significance. First, it legalises the activity of public authorities that consists in obtaining, collecting and disclosing information on individuals in a different way than when such data are provided by citizens themselves. This also includes data collected in secret by authorities without any knowledge and consent of the individual. Second, the provision, to some extent, autonomously sets out the premises of the legality (limits) of such activities, by restricting the legislator's discretion to determine the scope of tasks and competence – assigned to the organs of the state – which comprise obtaining data on citizens (. . .).

(. . .)

In Article 51(2) of the Constitution, the constitution-maker has clearly referred the prohibition expressed therein to the action of obtaining information on "citizens". This might suggest that public authorities could obtain, collect and store information on other individuals (e.g. persons who are not Polish citizens) within a much broader scope than in the case of citizens, i.e. also information which is not necessary in a democratic state ruled by law. The adoption of such a stance would entail assuming varying degrees of protection on individuals' privacy, depending on whether they hold Polish citizenship or not. The Constitutional Tribunal does not rule out such differentiation, provided that it may not be regarded as a rule, and that in no case may it result in arbitrary differentiation among the subjects of those constitutional rights and freedoms which the constitution-maker has not characterised as granted exclusively to citizens. Bearing in mind, above all, Article 30 and Article 37(1) of the Constitution, one should adopt – as a starting point – a uniform standard for interference in constitutional rights and freedoms, regardless of the fact whether the subject thereof is a Polish citizen or not. Every person who is subject to the jurisdiction of the Republic of Poland, i.e. subject to Polish law (. . .) – regardless of whether s/he holds Polish citizenship or not – may rightly expect protection against unjustified interference in the rights and freedoms that s/he is entitled to. In the context of the present case, one should in fact assume that it is necessary to establish the same standards for obtaining, collecting or storing data gathered by public authorities in the course of operational and investigative activities with regard to all persons that are subject to the jurisdiction of the Republic of Poland.

(...)

The above assumption does not rule out the admissibility of a different way of specifying grounds for obtaining and processing data in the context of persons who are not Polish citizens (e.g. data obtained by intelligence services on the activity of foreigners abroad), although in every case, such actions taken by public authorities must comply with the standards of a state ruled by law.

(...) The Constitutional Tribunal agrees with the applicant's allegations raised with regard to Article 28 of the Act on the Internal Security Agency, Article 18 of the Central Anti-Corruption Bureau Act and Article 32 of the Act on the Military Counter-Intelligence Service. As indicated above (see part III, point 5.1.3 of this statement of reasons), a prerequisite for the secret obtaining of information on individuals, including telecommunications data related to them, is to devise a procedure for the immediate selection and destruction of material that is useless and inadmissible. The said solution prevents situations where information which has been legally obtained by the organs of the state is used in an unauthorised way as well as is stored in case it proves useful for other purposes in the future. As emphasised earlier, what constitutes interference in the realm of the individual's privacy is not only one instance of obtaining data on the individual (inter alia under the procedures set out in Article 28(1) of the Act on the Internal Security Agency, Article 18(1) of the Central Anti-Corruption Bureau Act and Article 32(1) of the Act on the Military Counter-Intelligence Service), but also any further processing of those data, including storing them or re-using them in the course of other proceedings (see part III, point 1.9 of this statement of reasons).

The challenged provisions do not regulate procedures for handling telecommunications data, after they have been collected under Article 28(1) of the Act on the Internal Security Agency, Article 18(1) of the Central Anti-Corruption Bureau Act and Article 32(1) of the Act on the Military Counter-Intelligence Service. The issue of handling data collected on the said basis has not been addressed by the legislator. At the same time, there is no legal basis for the proper application of the provisions that regulate the destruction of data collected in the course of operational surveillance or the provisions of the Code of Criminal Procedure which regulate the interception and recording of conversations (Article 237 and the subsequent provisions of the said Code). This entails that in the light of Article 28(1) of the Act on the Internal Security Agency, Article 18(1) of the Central Anti-Corruption Bureau Act and Article 32(1) of the Act on the Military Counter-Intelligence Service, there are no regulations concerning the verification and destruction of useless data. Thus, it is not prohibited to store data that are irrelevant to given proceedings, in the course of which access to such data was requested, or which are useless for other constitutionally justified purposes. As aptly pointed out by the Marshal of the Sejm in his letter of 2 March 2012, the challenged provisions lead to a situation where data on individuals may be stored only because the thorough verification of the data was discontinued.

The Constitutional Tribunal does not negate the admissibility of further storage of telecommunications data (i.e. after they have been analysed and deemed irrelevant to proceedings that are pending in a given case) in the context of foreigners that are subject to the jurisdiction of the Republic of Poland, especially if there are serious and justified suspicions that they may be involved in activity undermining national security, such as terrorist activity and organised crime. Such differentiation in the degree of protection may be derived primarily from Article 51(2) and Article 37 (2) of the Constitution.

Considering the above, Article 28 of the Act on the Internal Security Agency, Article 18 of the Central Anti-Corruption Bureau Act and Article 32 of the Act on the Military Counter-Intelligence Service, insofar as they do not provide for the destruction of data that are irrelevant to given proceedings, are inconsistent with Article 51 (2) in conjunction with Article 31(3) of the Constitution.

The Constitutional Court of Portugal: Judgment of 27 August 2015, Ref. No 403/15[12]

(...)

9. The rule of Article 78, No. 2, of Decree No. 426/XII assigns to SIRP information officers the functional power to access *communication data* to allow for identification of the subscriber or user, source, destination, date, time, duration and type of communication, as well as the telecommunications equipment or its location.

Considering that the object of this appeal specifically refers to access to telecommunications data by information officers, we must first determine the type of data concerned and determine whether access to same warrants constitutional protection.

The explanatory statement accompanying the Government's draft law, which was the source of Decree No. 426/XII (c.f. Article 3 of the request), in computer language, classifies it as "metadata", usually referred to as "data on data", as it involves cases of communications, not the actual content thereof.

In a specific communication, it is possible to separate from the hard core of the information provided or transmitted a set of landmarks or reference points that give it its support and that allow for restriction of information in all its forms. Such data is "information" that is added to same and whose objective is to inform people about it, in principle, and facilitate its organisation. Being data on data ("information on

[12]The judgement is available at the page of the Constitutional Court of Portugal under: http://www.tribunalconstitucional.pt/tc/acordaos/20150403.html. Translation ordered by the University of Warsaw.

information"), it ends up providing information on location, time, type of content, origin and destination, among others, of communicational acts carried out through telecommunications or other means of communication.

As a category whose legal objective is to use the designation "*traffic data*", not only because it is the linguistic statement referred to in the rule subject to review, but above all because in our legal system there is already a legal definition of that statement.

(. . .)

It is necessary to classify the data in question in the rule relating to this appeal in one of the categories listed. With reference to "traffic data", "location data" or other "related data" of communications - as the law itself states - necessary to identify the subscriber or user or to find and identify the source, destination, date, time, duration and type of communication as well as telecommunications equipment or its location. There is no doubt whatsoever that it can be described as *traffic data*, since it respects "the actual functional elements of the communication, regarding the direction, destination, route and path of a certain message". This data identifies or allows for the identification of the communication and, once preserved, it enables the identification of communications between the sender and receiver, date, time and frequency of calls made.

(. . .)

11. In addition to the all-embracing legal framework in terms of access to data, there are still several *international instruments* that protect access to data of this type.

Although some of these instruments do not provide detailed rules expressly referring to data protection, they guarantee in several rules the protection of privacy, which irrefutably include restrictions regarding access to personal data, including communications of individuals that have actually been affirmed by bodies guaranteeing the respective instruments.

First, Article 12 of the Universal Declaration of Human Rights states that "no one shall be subjected to arbitrary interference with his privacy, family, home or correspondence (. . .)". The same wording is used by Article 17 of the International Pact on Civil and Political Rights. Both texts state that everyone has the right to protection by the law against such interventions or attacks.

Article 8 of the European Convention on Human Rights (ECHR) establishes that "everyone has the right to respect for his private and family life, his home and his correspondence". Pursuant to No. 2, "there shall be no interference by a public authority with the exercise of this right except such as is in accordance with the law and which is necessary in a democratic society in the interests of national security, public safety or the economic well-being of the country, for the prevention of disorder or crime, for the protection of health or morals, or for the protection of the rights and freedoms of others". The European Court of Human Rights (ECHR) has developed a wide range of jurisprudence on the protection of access to communications data, expressly stating that it is covered by the protection of "private and family life" contained in Article, No. 1, of the ECHR. Thus, in the *Malone against United Kingdom case*, it was stated that access to and use of data relating to communications traffic is a matter that falls within the scope of Article 8, No. 1, of the ECHR (Ruling of 02/08/1984, complaint No. 8691/79).

Finally, in the context of the European Union, mention should be made of Articles 7 and 8 of the Charter of Fundamental Rights of the European Union. It should be noted that, before it had binding effects, the Court of Justice of the European Union had already proclaimed the existence of a "general principle of Community law affording protection against arbitrary and disproportionate intervention by public authorities in the private activities of a legal person" (Ruling of 22/10/2002, *Roquette Frèrres*, Process No. C-94/00). Article 7 of the Charter of Fundamental Rights currently lays down respect for private and family life and, inspired by other international rules, states that "everyone has the right to respect for his private and family life and his communications". This right is valid under Article 52, No. 3, of the Charter, and has the same meaning as Article 8 of the ECHR. Article 8 of the Charter, for its part, contains a specific provision on the protection of personal data, which is therefore given an express and autonomous support vis-à-vis Article 7. The rule in question establishes that "everyone has the right to protection of their personal data concerning him or her". The Court of Justice stated that this right is 'inseparably linked to the right to respect for private life' (Ruling of 09/11/2010, *Volkerund Markus Schecke*, process No. C-92/09 and C-93/09). On the other hand, it clarified that the protection of communications traffic data falls within the scope of protection of this fundamental right *Digital Rights Ireland Ltd*, processes No. C-293/12 and C-594/12, which annulled Directive 2004/26/EC, for infringement of Articles 7 and 8 of the Charter of Fundamental Rights.

12. Access to data from communications actually made or attempted questions the fundamental rights of people involved in the communicational act. In addition, it is not just the invasion or intrusion on the informational content conveyed by the media (*content data*) that affects them, but also the circumstances in which the communication was made (*traffic data*).

Indeed, even if there is no access to content, the interconnection between traffic data can provide a complex and complete profile of the person in question - who else they talk to, where they go, what times, etc. (. . .) This clearly shows that illegal or illegitimate manipulation of the content and circumstances of communication may violate *the privacy* of the parties involved, jeopardising or endangering people's nuclear spheres, their lives, or dimensions of their way of being. Thus, the possibility of accessing data from the communications goes against a set of values associated with *private life* that underlie and legitimise legal-constitutional protection.

First, *freedom of action*, as part of the right to the development of one's personality, according to which, in interaction with others, the conduct of one's life is *self-contained* by its performance, which presupposes, as indicated by Gomes Canotilho and Vital Moreira, "the requirement to *prohibit interference* by public authorities (. . .) such as (. . .) "the right not to be spied on"" (*Constitution of the Portuguese Republic Annotated,* 2nd ed., Vol. I, page 465).

Then, with the *inner sphere* and the *private sphere* of the human being, either as a pretence of isolation, tranquillity and exclusion from others' access to himself (*right to solitude*), or as an impediment to the interference of others (*right to anonymity*) and in view of the insufficient protection of these dimensions, as control of the information that concerns him and of subtraction from the knowledge of others the facts revealing his way of being in the conduct of his private life (*informational self-determination*). (. . .)

These rights are now expressly stated in Article 26 of the CPR and are closely interconnected, where the reservation of the intimacy of private life constitutes a dimension of the broader right, regarding the development of personality. But although it qualifies as a special right of personality, the right to reserve the privacy of private life does not stop here, as it is constitutionally enshrined as an autonomous right. At this point, it is not confused with the right to Anglo-Saxon *privacy*, which has taken on broader lines, emerging as a paradigmatic expression of all personal rights (. . .)

(. . .) 13. (. . .) Freedom of communication encompasses the ability to communicate with security and confidence and mastery and self-control over communication as expression and externalisation of one's own person. Such freedom, as a refraction of the right to the development of personality and protection of privacy, deserved in the constitutional text a specific material cut, through empowerment, in Article 34, of the *secrecy of the private media*. One can therefore speak of a "*right to communicative self-determination*" that serves to defend various juridical-constitutional properties, among them: the right to the development of personality and the right to the privacy of private life. (. . .)

(. . .) as interaction between people at a distant location must be done through the necessary mediation of a third-party communications service provider, such operator and the regulatory state must also guarantee the *integrity* and *confidentiality* of communications systems.

(. . .) it is possible to point out a double aspect of the right to communicative self-determination, as protection of the right of privacy and as freedom of action, that is, a connection between "communication secret" and "freedom of communication.".

14. Communicational self-determination is protected in Article 34 of the CPR through the inviolability of communications (. . .) This inviolability, in paragraph 4 of that constitutional provision, *prohibits interference* by public authorities in the media, not only those vested with *public powers*, but most of all other public and private entities (Article 18, No. 1, of the CPR).

(. . .)

15. It is in view of the prohibition of interference by the public authorities in communications that the Applicant raises his first question: should access to traffic data be considered interference in telecommunications under the constitutional provision?

The answer requires prior assessment of whether the so-called "traffic data" in the aforementioned definition fall within the concept of "*telecommunications*" or "*other means of communication*" set out in Article 34, No. 4, of the CPR (. . .)

However, there is a broad consensus on doctrine and jurisprudence, otherwise there is no argument against including traffic data in the concept of communications that is constitutionally relevant to the prohibition of interference. That is to say: the scope of protection of Article 34, No. 4, covers not only the content of telecommunications but also traffic data.

(. . .) similar to the opinion of the Court of Justice of the European Union, in the Ruling of 08/04/2014, *Digital Rights Ireland Ltd*, processes No. C-293/12 and C-594/12, cited above, which cancelled Directive 2004/26/EC, pointed out that, as regards the communications traffic data, "the retention of data imposed by Directive 2006/24 constitutes particularly serious interference with those rights", although it is not "likely to affect the aforementioned content, considering that, as a result of Article 1, No. 2, therein, that Directive does not make it possible to become familiar with the content of electronic communications as such" (*paragraph 39*). (. . .)

The basic data (e.g. telephone number, email address, network connection contract) and equipment location data, where it does not support a particular communication, is not subject to protection of the right to confidentiality of communications (c.f. Ruling No. 486/2009 (. . .)

We therefore conclude by replying to the first question put by the applicant in this process, on the fact that the prohibition on interference in communications set out in Article 34 of the CPR covers traffic data.

16. Based on the fact that the traffic data is included under confidentiality of communications, it is important to answer the Applicant's second question: can the prior and compulsory authorisation of the Pre-Control Committee be considered equivalent to control in criminal proceedings?

(. . .)

17. By defining the scope of the restrictive law on the right to inviolability of communications for "criminal prosecution matters", the Constitution considered and took a position (in part) regarding the conflict between legal rights protected by that fundamental right and Community values, in particular those of security, at which the criminal proceeding is directed. (. . .)

(. . .) the reference to criminal proceedings is not only a teleological indication, but also the location of the prohibition of interference in a normatively structured area in terms of offering sufficient guarantees against abusive interference. By authorising public authorities to interfere in the media only regarding *criminal proceedings*, and not for any other purpose, the Constitution sought to ensure that, to safeguard the values of "justice" and "security", those means were accessed through a procedural instrument that also protects people's fundamental rights. (. . .) reference to the criminal proceedings implies that the restrictive intervention lacks prior judicial authorisation. Seeing that the criminal proceedings are heterocompositive through which *jurisdiction* is carried out for the filing of claims based on public rules of criminal law, the intervention of a body qualified for these functions is required (c.f. Article 202 of the CPR). (. . .)

It can therefore be concluded that, regarding prohibition of interference in communications by public authorities, the first part of Article 34, No. 4, is mainly devoted to the fact that the *exceptions* referred to in the final segment of this provision are conditioned to *criminal proceedings*. This restriction is constitutionally authorised only in these terms, and it is not appropriate to make any other interpretation that would extend the restriction to *other effects*, as if it were not specified in the constitutional text itself or if it were a purely implicit restriction that allowed other values or assets constitutionally recognised to be considered.

(. . .)

19. It remains to be seen whether the activity of the SIRP information officers, for the purposes of which they access data on traffic, location or other related communication data, pursuant to the rule in question, necessary for identifying the subscriber or user or finding and identifying the source, destination, date, time, duration and type of communication, as well as identifying the telecommunication equipment or its location, can be considered a "criminal proceedings".

In the end, it is all about knowing whether access to traffic data is an act that falls within the scope of criminal investigation.

Surely, the answer must be negative.

In fact, the purposes and interests that the SIRP is required by law to pursue, the functional powers it confers on its staff, and the enforcement and control procedures it establishes place access to traffic data outside the scope of the criminal investigation.

(. . .)

Despite the relationship that exists between information and criminal investigation, the legislator made sure that he distinguished the two activities in a material and structural sense. In fact, SIRP's endeavour to "produce information necessary for safeguarding internal and external security, independence and national interests and the unity and integrity of the State", set forth in Article 2 of Decree No. 426/XII, does not include the exercise of powers, acts and activities, "within the specific jurisdiction of the courts, the Public Prosecutor's Office or entities with police functions", as set forth in Article 5, No. 2, of the same Decree. Consequently, the intelligence services do not have any police or criminal investigations, in as much as they are not intended to ensure respect for and compliance with general laws (e.g. defence of public order), nor to investigate the commission of crimes, being legally prohibited from such activities; nor are they criminal police bodies for the purpose of the Code of Criminal Proceedings, nor do they assume the status of police authority.

(. . .)

In fact, starting the criminal proceedings with *notitia criminis*, the collection of information for this purpose must take place for a crime already committed. Therefore, collection of data on criminal proceedings always takes place in a *previously delineated* context for this procedure, only collecting information for the investigation of a *specific fact* and in relation to *specific subjects* regarded as suspects.

This differs from "preventive" action taken by information services, which allows for access to data on a much wider range of people, precisely since it is not yet pre-ordained to be used for the investigation of a specific and delimited fact. Collection and processing of information to be carried out by SIRP, due to its preventive nature, are not intended for investigating crimes committed or in process. They are not judicial police acts, intended for criminal investigation.

(. . .)

20. Further, it is not the intervention of the *Pre-Control Committee* that has the legal effect of judicialising access to traffic data. The criminal proceedings are

assigned to the competent *judicial authorities* – Public Prosecution, criminal investigation judge and trial judge (c.f. paragraph b). Article 1 of the CCP) and said Commission is an *administrative body* not legally established in the judicial organisation, despite the capacity of its members. In fact, from a formal or structural point of view, it does not exercise a *judicial function,* and, from a material point of view, it does not exercise a *jurisdictional function.* (. . .)

Not even the system of prior authorisation given by the aforementioned Commission for access and maintenance of traffic data could be equated with the control existing in criminal proceedings. (. . .) this strict control is not carried out by the aforementioned Pre-Control Committee, which merely grants a "prior authorisation" visa, after which it ceases to have any intervention during the activities of access to the data in question.

21. Actually, regardless of the question of reservation of a judge on criminal proceedings, the guarantees mentioned above are also lacking in the *action* taken by said Pre-Control Committee. In fact, the law does not sufficiently identify the *cases* or *circumstances* in which said Committee can grant authorisation to access data, nor does it clearly establish the guarantees of visas regarding the *duration* of the authorisation to access or *eliminate* the data.

(. . .)

In this regard, the European Court of Human Rights has already stated that because data access is not subject to scrutiny of target individuals, it must be compensated by a sufficiently protective fundamental rights law (. . .); that this law should use terms which are sufficiently clear to enable all citizens to be aware of the circumstances and requirements enabling the public authorities to make use of a secret measure which infringes the right to private personal and family life and correspondence (. . .); which would be contrary to the requirements of Article 8, No. 2, of the ECHR if interference in telecommunications was conferred on the public authorities by means of a broad and discretionary power and that clear and detailed rules were required, in particular because the available technology becomes increasingly sophisticated to ensure adequate protection against arbitrary interference (. . .), it reached the same conclusion, stating that the law permitting interference in communications was not sufficiently clear and precise, without mentioning the nature of the offences that can give rise to same, the establishment of a limit on the duration of the measure, as well as the conditions for access to and disposal of the data.

The foreign constitutional law is oriented in the same direction. The Spanish Constitutional Court has already stated on a number of occasions that interference in telephone communications can only be considered to be constitutionally legitimate if it is provided for in the law with a *sufficient degree of precision* (. . .); and the German Constitutional Court, in relation to a law which did not regulate how the data should be stored nor did it provide a guarantee of effective supervision, decided that in the framework of a database shared between the intelligence service and various security services with the objective of combating terrorism, the sharing or transfer of information was subject to very demanding constitutional requirements, including its detailed legal configuration (Decision of 04/24/2013, 1st Senate).

Therefore, there are several requirements from this case law for a rule that, like the present one, allows access to traffic data from communications of individuals without their consent or knowledge. First, the law must implement *sufficiently clear terms* to inform all persons of the circumstances and requirements that allow the public authorities to access the data in question. Said requirements for this purpose must be clearly determined; precise reference must be made to *specific cases* where access is required, a *maximum duration* of the measure established and the rules and terms for eliminating traffic data determined. Only then can we speak of determinable interference and guarantee legal certainty to the interested parties.

22. However, if this is the case, it must be acknowledged that, in addition to the impossibility of being compatible with the rule of Article 34, No. 4, of the CPR, the rule of Article 78, No. 2, of Decree No. 426/XII does not contain *sufficient detail* to permit the legality and defence of people's rights and interests, in the field of a restrictive law. In fact, as a counterpart of access to traffic data, the rule does not sufficiently satisfy the determinability requirements that are guaranteed in criminal matters, returning to the administrative sphere considerations that should be included in the law.

(. . .)

23. Finally, the rule in Article 78, No. 2, in the legal-systematic context in which it is inserted, does not make clear and explicit the whole *access procedure, duration of access* or *elimination* of traffic data collected.

(. . .)

24. It follows from the above that, irrespective of the specific nature of the "Pre-Trial Control Board", its conduct does not appear to be comparable to the judicial review of fundamental rights in criminal proceedings. (. . .)

Consequently, the answer to the second question put by the applicant in this process is also doubtful: the Preliminary Control Commission is an administrative body which does not have powers equivalent to an intervention in criminal proceedings.

The Constitutional Court of Portugal: Judgment of 13 July 2017, Ref. No 420/17[13]

9. The order of 19 October 2016, which rejected the request of the Public Prosecutor's Office to authorise the transmission of identification data of a user assigned a specific IP protocol address was based on the unconstitutionality of Article 6 of Law No. 32/2008, by reference to Article 4 of the same law.

[13]The judgement is available at the page of the Constitutional Court of Portugal under: http://www.tribunalconstitucional.pt/tc/acordaos/20170420.html. Translation ordered by the University of Warsaw.

This unconstitutionality is sustained by invoking the ruling of the Court of Justice *Digital Rights Ireland* (Proc. No. C-293/12 and C-594/12), which declared the invalidity of Directive 2006/24/EC of the European Parliament and of the Council of 15 March 2006 on the retention of data generated or processed in the context of the provision of public e-communications services or public communications networks. This normative act was transposed into the legal order of the Portuguese Republic by Law No. 32/2008 of 17 July, where the rule relating to this case is integrated.

It is considered in the order that most of the considerations of the Court of Justice would apply to an assessment of Law No. 32/2008. (. . .)

It therefore considers that "the retention of data is determined by Law No. 32/2008 with the same breadth, generality, lack of justification, absence of prior control over data insertion and disproportionate and excessive duration, resulting from the Directive" (P.9 of the order, pp. 43). This would result in "the contradiction (. . .) of the legal regime established by Law No. 32/2008, specifically Article 6 thereof, with the provisions of Article 8 of the European Convention on Human Rights and Articles 7 and 8 of the Charter of Fundamental Rights of the European Union, in parallel with that referred to in the Ruling of the Court of Justice, of 8 April 2014" (page 10 of the order, pp. 44). This logic would also be acceptable by reference to Articles 18 and 34 of the Constitution, specifically paragraph 4 of the latter. (. . .))

10. It starts by stating that the declaration of invalidity of a directive does not have an automatic consequence on the validity of a Portuguese legislative act that transposes it. The national legislative act, while aiming at compliance with the duty to transpose a directive, deriving from EU law (Article 4 (3) of the EU Treaty, Article 288, paragraph three, of the Treaty on the Functioning of the EU and Article 112 (8) of the Constitution) has an independent source of validity and legitimacy.

The Court of Justice does not have jurisdiction to assess the validity of the national law of the Member States, and its analysis only focused on the text of the directive. The validity of Law No. 32/2008 of 17 July cannot be called into question solely because of the fact that this normative act of the Union was declared invalid.

These considerations do not, however, prevent the validity of this Law from being checked in the light of the applicable parameters, more specifically International Law, provided for in the European Convention for the Protection of Human Rights and Fundamental Freedoms, established in the Charter of Fundamental Rights of the European Union, or national law, deriving from the Constitution. Although the reasoning of the Court of Justice must be considered in this case, that court must, however, be autonomous from that of this court.

In this case, by carrying out that task, it is not possible to follow the reasoning set out in the contested decision.

11. (. . .) In Practical Note No. 7/2015 of 30 December 2015, on the retention of traffic data and Law No. 32/2008 of 17 July, the Public Prosecutor's Cybercrime Office also clarifies (point 5):

"It is important to underline that Law No. 32/2008, in addition to the transposition of Directive 2006/24/EC, introduced a much more complex framework for regulating the data retention process (for example, rules to be observed in retention, persons entitled to access data or conditions of storage and access to data). By doing this, the national law went well beyond the requirements of the Directive. Therefore, most of the requirements that came to be made by the ruling of the CJEU were already previously considered in domestic law. For that reason, it has been understood that the decision made by the Luxembourg court does not affect the validity of the national law.

As an example of what has been said, Portuguese law stipulates conditions for access to data, requiring disclosure to be preceded by a judge's order (Article 9, No. 1 of Law No. 32/2008). This condition coincides with the requirement of the Court of Justice when it declares and draws negative implications from the fact that the Directive does not provide for the need for authorisation by an independent authority to access the data.

On the other hand, the Court has an adverse opinion of the fact that the Directive does not provide for the obligation to destroy the data after the retention period. Portuguese law establishes the exact opposite, imposing the destruction of the data after the retention period (article 7, No. 1, paragraph e, of Law No. 32/2008).

The CJEU also underlined the lack of regulatory requirements on data retention. Once again, Portuguese law provides for rules that convey important safeguards in this regard (for example, defining who is authorised to access data, strict storage conditions and others)."

Since national remedies differ from Union rules, a judgement on their constitutionality must consider those differences.

It should be noted that the judgement of the Court of Justice *Digital Rights Ireland* (. . .), invoked by the contested decision, relates in particular to the duty to preserve traffic and location data, taken as a whole (. . .), not exactly to the basic data, as in this case. (. . .)

The same conclusion can be drawn from the recent ruling of the Court of Justice *Tele2 Sverige* (. . .5).

It is therefore not correct to base the invalidity of national law on a transposition of the Court's judgement on the whole content of the directive which it transposes without carrying out a specific and independent analysis of the national rule in question and, in this case, without considering the nature of the basic data.

12. In this case, the main obstacle that the judgement of unconstitutionality of the contested order faces is the correct delimitation of the rule relating to the review of constitutionality. In fact, the rule submitted for review covers exclusively the duty of electronic communications service providers to keep the basic data for a time. It is the judgement of this specific rule that we must be concerned about.

The Constitutional Court has already had the opportunity to give a verdict, albeit indirectly, on the regime of constitutional protection of the basic data.

(. . .)

Thus, it is clear from the case law of the Constitutional Court that the protection afforded by Article 34, No. 4, of the Constitution does not cover basic data, such as that covered by the rule relating to this case. In fact, the data relating to the mere identification of a user to whom a given IP protocol address was assigned is not covered by the protection of the confidentiality of communications established in that constitutional provision since it does not presuppose a specific act of communication. Therefore, the judgement of the national court, regarding the violation of point 4 of Article 34 of the Constitution, is not followed.

13. The basic data in question is, however, subject to the protection granted by the right to privacy, established in Article 26 of the Constitution.

It is therefore necessary to determine whether the requirement that "providers of publicly available e-communications services or a public communications network" retain "for a period of one year from the date of completion of the communication", data relating to "name and address of the subscriber or registered user to whom the IP protocol address was assigned at the time of communication" constitutes a restriction of these fundamental rights and whether such restriction is disproportionate, thus violating Article 18 of the Constitution.

However, the duty to preserve such data to make it available to the authorities under the law may be regarded as a restriction on the fundamental rights mentioned above. The question therefore arises in accordance with the principle of proportionality.

(. . .) the measure in question satisfies the requirements of good standing, since the retention of basic data is an appropriate measure for identifying the registered user to whom the IP address was assigned and who is suspected of being the author of the serious crimes referred to, and the necessity of same, insofar as it is not possible to set up a less restrictive means for the competent authorities to carry out such identification.

The principle of proportionality, strictly speaking, prohibits the adoption of measures that appear excessive (disproportionate) to achieve the desired objectives. In this judgement it is necessary to consider, on the one hand, the relatively non-invasive nature of the privacy of the data in question (basic data), concerning the identity of the user, and the period of storage (one year) - after which data (Article 7, No. 1 *e*) of Law No. 32/2008) and, on the other, the particularly serious nature of the crimes in question and the centrality of this data for conducting the criminal investigation. It is also necessary to consider the regime established for access to this data, with a limitation on all holders of data subject to transmission (Article 9.3 of Law No. 32/2008) and to impose the need for prior authorisation, by reasoned order of the investigating judge, who must respect the principles of adequacy, necessity and proportionality, at the request of the Public Prosecutor's Office or the competent criminal police authority (Article 9, Nos. 1, 2 and 4, of Law No. 32/2008). For these reasons, the standard relating to this appeal does not violate the principle of proportionality arising from article 18, No. 2 of the Constitution.

The Constitutional Court of Romania: Judgment of 8 October 2009, Ref. No. 1258/2009[14]

(. . .)

Objections of the author of the exception regarding the unconstitutionality of Law No. 298/2008 regarding the retention of data generated or processed by the providers of publicly available electronic communications services or of public communications networks, as well as for the amendment of the Law No. 506/2004 regarding the processing of personal data and the protection of privacy in the electronic communications sector concern certain deficiencies of the normative act being examined, such as to interfere with the exercise of the right to free movement, the right to privacy, private and family life, and to affect the secrecy of correspondence and freedom of expression. This is because the said law authorises the retention of data necessary to determine the date, time and duration of a telephone or electronic communication, identification of the type of telephone call, equipment, location of the communication equipment, but without expressly defining what is meant by "Related data" needed to identify the registered subscriber or user, data that is also processed by the communications and telecommunication service providers.

The rights allegedly infringed in the author's opinion are non-patrimonial, complex personal rights, the common element of which consists of a person having private space. The right to respect for private and family life benefits from unanimous recognition and international protection, as enshrined in Article 12 of the Universal Declaration of Human Rights in Article 17 of the International Covenant on Civil and Political Rights in Article 8 of the Convention For the protection of human rights and fundamental freedoms, as well as of Article 26 of the Romanian Constitution. The right to respect for privacy also necessarily involves the secret of correspondence, whether this component is expressly mentioned in the same text of Article 8 of the Convention, or that it is governed distinctly, as is the case in Article 28 of the Constitution. Correspondence expresses the links that a person can establish in various ways of communicating with other members of society, including both telephone conversations and electronic communications.

These rights, including the freedom of expression expressly enshrined in Article 30 of the Constitution and Article 10 of the Convention for the Protection of Human Rights and Fundamental Freedoms, although indissolubly linked to human existence, any person having the right to exercise them freely, are, however, absolute rights, but they are conditional.

Law No. 298/2008, regulating the obligation for providers of publicly available electronic communications services or public communications networks to retain certain data generated or processed in their activity, expresses the will of the legislator to impose limits on the exercise of the right to privacy, freedom of

[14]The judgement is available at the page of the Constitutional Court of Romania under: http://www.legi-internet.ro/fileadmin/editor_folder/pdf/Decizie_curtea_constitutionala_pastrarea_datelor_de_trafic.pdf. Translation ordered by University of Warsaw.

expression and, in particular, the right to secrecy of correspondence, in the aspects outlined above. Law No. 298/2008 transposes into the national legislation the Directive 2006/24/EC of the European Parliament and of the Council of 15 March 2006 on the retention of data generated or processed in connection with the provision of publicly available electronic communications services or of public communications networks and amending Directive 2002/58/EC. The legal regime of such a Community act imposes its obligation on the Member States of the European Union with regard to the regulated legal solution, not on the concrete ways in which this result is achieved, the states having a wide margin of appreciation, adapting them to the specificities of national legislation and realities.

Neither the provisions of the Convention for the Protection of Human Rights and Fundamental Freedoms nor the Constitution of Romania prohibit the legal enshrining of interference by state authorities into the exercising of these rights, but the state intervention must observe strict rules expressly mentioned in Article 8 of the Convention, respectively, in Article 53 of the Basic Law. Legislative measures likely to affect the exercise of fundamental rights and freedoms must therefore fulfil a legitimate aim in the protection of national security, public security, the defence of public order, the prevention of criminal offences and the protection of the rights and interests of others; to be necessary in a democratic society, to be proportionate to the situation which determined them, to be applied in a non-discriminatory way and not to prejudice the existence of the right or freedom.

In addition, in accordance with the limitations of the jurisprudence of the European Court of Human Rights, (. . .), the normative act governing measures capable of producing interference in the exercise of the right to private and family life, correspondence and freedom of expression must contain adequate and sufficient safeguards to protect the person from the arbitrary arbitration of the state authorities.

The Constitutional Court recognises the possibility for the legislator to restrict the exercise of fundamental rights and freedoms and the need to regulate ways to provide organs with specific attributions in criminal investigation activity effective and appropriate tools for the prevention and detection of terrorist offences in particular, of serious crimes. The Romanian legislation regulates in the Criminal Procedure Code the ways in which public authorities can intervene in exercising their rights to privacy, to correspondence and free expression, while respecting all the guarantees that this interference imposes. By Decision No. 962 of 25 June 2009, (. . .), the Constitutional Court held that the provisions of Article 91^1 of the Criminal Procedure Code, which regulates the conditions and the cases of interception and recording of calls or communications made by telephone or by any electronic means of communication are constitutional, being justified in a democratic society threatened by an increasingly complex criminal phenomenon, the need to ensure national security, the defence of public order or the prevention of crime.

The Constitutional Court notes that Law No. 298/2008, as it is drafted, is liable to affect, even indirectly, the exercise of fundamental rights or freedoms, in particular the right to privacy and family life, the right to the secrecy of correspondence and freedom of expression, in a manner that does not meet the requirements established by Article 53 of the Romanian Constitution.

Thus, Law No. 298/2008 establishes the providers of public electronic communications services and networks intended for the public or public communications networks the obligation to store for a period of six months the traffic and location data of natural and legal persons. Under Article 3 of the Act, the data necessary for "tracking and identifying" the source, destination, date, time and duration of a communication, type of communication, communication equipment or devices used by the user, the location of the communication equipment phones. Article 1 (2) of the Act includes in the category of traffic and location data of natural and legal persons and "related data necessary to identify the registered subscriber or user" without, however, expressly defining what is meant by "related data" needed to identify the registered subscriber or user.

The Constitutional Court considers that the lack of precise legal regulation that accurately determines the scope of data necessary for the identification of users or legal entities opens the possibility of abuses in the activity of retaining, processing and using data stored by providers of publicly available electronic communications services on public communications networks. Limiting the exercise of the right to privacy and the secrecy of correspondence and freedom of expression must also take place in a clear, predictable and unequivocal manner so as to remove as far as possible the possibility of arbitrariness or abuse by the authorities in this area. The addressees of the legal norm are, in this case, the entirety of natural and legal persons in their capacity as users of publicly available electronic communications services or public communications networks, thus a broad, comprehensive range of subjects of law, members of civil society. However, they must have a clear representation of the applicable legal rules so as to adapt their conduct and foresee the consequences of their non-compliance. The jurisprudence of the European Court of Human Rights, for example in Rotaru v. Romania, 2000, stated that "a rule is" predictable "only when it is drafted with sufficient precision to allow Any person - who may call for specialist advice - to correct his behaviour", and in the Sunday Times v. The United Kingdom, 1979, he decided that "[. . .] the citizen must have sufficient information on the rules Applicable in a given case and be able to foresee, to a reasonable extent, the consequences which may result from a particular act." In short, the law must be, at the same time, accessible and predictable. The same jurisprudential practice has also the Constitutional Court, relevant in this respect Decision No. 189 of 2 March 2006, published in the Official Gazette of Romania, Part I, no. 307 of 5 April 2006.

The Constitutional Court also observes the same ambiguous drafting, inconsistent with the normative legislative norms, regarding the provisions of Article 20 of Law no. 298/2008, according to which, "In order to prevent and counteract threats to national security, The state bodies with attributions in this field may have access, under the conditions established by the normative acts that regulate the activity of accomplishing the national security, to the data retained by the providers of public electronic communications services and networks". The legislator does not define what is meant by "threats to national security", so that, in the absence of precise delimitation criteria, ordinary, routine ordinary actions, information or routine activities of individuals and legal entities can be arbitrarily abusive, as having the nature of such threats. Recipients of the law may be included in the category of suspects without knowing it and without being able to prevent, through their conduct, the consequence of applying the rigours of the law. At the same time, the use of the phrase "may have" conveys the idea that the data referred to in Law no. 298/2008 is not retained for the sole purpose of being used by state bodies with specific attributions in the protection of national security and public order, but by other persons or entities, since these "can" and do not "have" access to this data, under the law.

The observance of the normative legislative norms within the complex of rules specific to the activity of law-making is a decisive factor in the transposition of the legislator's will, so that the adopted normative act fulfils all the requirements imposed by the need to respect the fundamental human rights. Without a positive legislator, the Constitutional Court observes that the precision of the regulation pursuant to applying Law No. 298/2008 is all the more necessary given the complex nature of the rights subject to the limitation and the consequences a possible abuse of public authorities would have on the private life of its recipients, as perceived at the subjective level of each individual.

Beyond this point, the Constitutional Court notes that Law No. 298/2008 as a whole establishes a rule regarding the processing of personal data, that is to say, the continuation thereof, for a period of six months at the time they are intercepted. The obligation of providers of publicly available electronic communications services or of public communications networks is continuous. In the matter of personal rights, such as the right to privacy and free speech, as well as the processing of personal data, the unanimously recognised rule is that these are guaranteed and respected and treated confidentiality, with the State having obligations in this respect, mostly negative, to abstain, avoiding as much as possible any interference in the exercise to exercising this right or freedom. For this purpose, Directive 2002/58/EC on the processing of personal data and the protection of privacy in the public communications sector was adopted, Law No. 677/2001 on the protection of individuals with regard to the processing of personal data and the free movement of such data, and Law No. 506/2004 on the processing of personal data and the protection of privacy in the electronic communications sector. The exceptions are permitted only in the conditions expressly provided by the Constitution and the international legal acts applicable in the field. Law No. 298/2008 is such an exception, as the title itself indicates.

The obligation to withhold data regulated by Law No. 298/2008 as an exception or derogation from the principle of the protection of personal data and their confidentiality, by its nature, scope and scope, empties this principle, as it is guaranteed by Law No. 677/2001 and Law No. 506/2004. However, it is widely recognised in the jurisprudence of the European Court of Human Rights, for example the case of Prince Hans-Adam II of Liechtenstein against Germany, 2001 that the signatory states of the Convention for the Protection of Human Rights and Fundamental Freedoms have assumed obligations whose nature is to ensure that the rights guaranteed by the Convention are concrete and effective, not theoretical and illusory, with the legislative measures adopted aiming to effectively protect such rights. However, the legal obligation to impose the continued detention of personal data transforms the exception to the principle of effective protection of the right to privacy and free speech as an absolute rule. The right appears to be regulated in a negative way, its positive side losing its predominant character.

In this context, the Court notes that the provisions of Article 91[1] of the Code of Criminal Procedure respect the exceptionalness of audio and video intercepts and recordings, which are permitted under certain strict conditions, from the time of obtaining the reasoned authorisation of the judge, for a limited period and which cannot exceed a total of 120 days for the same person and the same action. On the other hand, Law No. 298/2008 establishes as a rule what the Code of Criminal Procedure regulates as a strict exception and obliges the data to be kept permanently for a period of six months from the moment of interception, which can be used, with the motivated authorisation of the judge, for a period in the past, and not for the future, which will follow. Hence, the regulation of a positive obligation that concerns the limitation of the exercise of the right to privacy life and the secrecy of correspondence in an uninterrupted way makes the essence of the law itself disappear by removing the guarantees of its exercise. Physical and legal persons, mass users of publicly available electronic communications services or public communications networks, are permanently subjected to this interference in the exercise of their privacy, secrecy of correspondence and free speech, without the possibility of free, uncensored manifestations, In the form of direct communication, excluding the main means of communication currently used.

In a natural logic of this analysis it is also necessary to examine the observance of the principle of proportionality, another imperative requirement to be observed in the cases of restriction of the exercise of certain fundamental rights or freedoms, expressly provided by Article 53 paragraph (2) of the Constitution. This principle requires that the restriction measure should be in line with the situation which has led to its application and, at the same time, cease with the disappearance of the determining cause.

For example, the provisions of Article 91[1] of the Code of Criminal Procedure fully respect the requirements of the principle of proportionality, both in terms of the extent of the limitation of the right and in terms of its termination as soon as the determinant causes disappear. On the other hand, Law no. 298/2008 imposes the obligation to keep the data on a continuous basis, from its entry into force and its application (namely 20 January 2009 and 15 March 2009, respectively, regarding the location traffic data corresponding to the access services Internet, e-mail and Internet telephony), without considering the need to end the limitation measure with the disappearance of the cause of the measure. The interference with the free exercise of the right takes place incessantly and independently of the production of a certain justifying fact, of a determining cause and only for criminal prevention or of detection after they have been committed - of serious crimes.

Another aspect that leads to the unjustified restriction of the person's right to privacy is that Law No. 298/2008 has the effect of identifying not only the person who conveys a message, information, or any other means of communication, but, as it follows from the content of Article 4 and the recipient of that information. The person being called is thus exposed to the retention of data relating to his private life, independently of an act or manifestation of his own will, but only according to the behaviour of another person - the caller - whose actions cannot censor him for to protect himself against his bad faith or the intention of blackmail, harassment, etc. Although it is a passive subject in the intercommunication relationship, the person called can become, without his will, suspicious from the perspective of the rigours under which the state authorities carry out their criminal investigation. From this point of view, the interference in the private life of the person, regulated by Law No. 298/2008, appears to be excessive.

The Constitutional Court stresses that it is not the justifiable use under the conditions laid down in Law No. 298/2008 which, in itself, adversely affects the exercise of the right to privacy or freedom of speech, but the legal obligation of a continuous, general nature applicable data storage. This operation equally concerns all the targets of the law, whether or not they have committed criminal offences or whether or not they are the subject of criminal investigations, which is likely to overturn the presumption of innocence and to transform *a priori* all users of electronic communications services or public communications networks into persons suspected of committing terrorist offences or serious crimes. However, Law No. 298/2008, although using notions and procedures specific to criminal law, has a wide applicability - practically, to all natural and legal persons publicly using available electronic communications services or public communications networks, so that it cannot be deemed to be in conformity with the provisions of the Constitution and the Convention for the Protection of Human Rights and Fundamental Freedoms regarding the guarantee of privacy rights, the secrecy of correspondence and freedom of expression.

The Constitutional Court notes that although Law No. 298/2008 refers to data of a predominantly technical nature, it is retained to provide information about the person and his/her private life. Even if, under Article 1 (3) of the Law, it does not apply to the content of the communication or information consulted during the use of an electronic communications network, the other data retained, with the purpose of identifying the caller and the called party, respectively the user and the recipient of information communicated electronically, of the source, destination, date, time and duration of a communication, communication type, communication equipment or user devices, the location of the mobile communications equipment, and other "related data" - undefined in law - are likely to prejudice and restrict the right to communication or freedom of expression. Retaining this data on a continuous basis in respect of any user of publicly available electronic communications services or public communications networks regulated as an obligation of suppliers from which they cannot deviate without being subject to the sanctions under Article 18 of Law No. 298/2008, is a sufficient operation to generate legitimate suspicion in the conscience of the public about respect for their intimacy and abuses. Legal safeguards regarding the actual use of retained data - concerning the exclusion of content as a subject of data storage, upon the motivated and prior authorisation of the president of the court competent to hear the case for which the prosecution has been initiated, under the conditions provided by Article 16 of the law and the application of the sanctions regulated in Articles 18 and 19 thereof - are not sufficient and appropriate to remove the fear that personal rights to privacy are being violated so that their manifestation takes place in an acceptable manner.

As stated above, the Constitutional Court does not deny the purpose in itself considered by the legislator when adopting Law No. 298/2008, that it is imperative to ensure adequate and efficient legal means compatible with the continuous process of modernisation and technology of the means of communication so that the criminal phenomenon can be controlled and countered. That is why individual rights cannot be exercised *ad absurdum* but may be subject to restrictions which are justified by the purpose pursued. Limiting the exercise of personal rights to collective rights and public interests, which are aimed at national security, public order or criminal prevention, has always constituted a regulatory sensitive operation so as to maintain a fair balance between individual interests and rights, on the one hand, and those of society, on the other. It is no less true, as noted by the European Court of Human Rights in Klass et al., 1978, that taking monitoring measures without adequate and sufficient safeguards can lead to the "destruction of democracy under the pretext of defending it".

In conclusion, in view of the broad applicability of Law no. 298/2008 regarding the continuing character of the obligation to retain the traffic data and locate the physical and legal persons as users of the electronic communications services to the public or to public communications networks, as well as other "related data" necessary for their identification, the Constitutional Court finds, for the above reasons, that the law being considered is unconstitutional, even if the author of the exception highlights, 1 and 15 thereof.

For the reasons set out above, under Article 146 (d) and Article 147 (4) of the Constitution, as well as Articles 1 to 3, Article 11 (1) and Article 29 of the Law No. 47/1992 and by a majority of votes,

THE CONSTITUTIONAL COURT in the name of the law DECIDES:

to accept the objection of unconstitutionality raised by the Civil Society Commissariat in File No. 2971/3/2009 of the Bucharest Tribunal - Commercial Section and notes that the provisions of Law No. 298/2008 on the retention of data generated or processed by the providers of publicly available electronic communications services or public communications networks, as well as amending Law No. 506/2004 on the processing of personal data and the protection of privacy in the electronic communications sector are unconstitutional.

(...)

The Constitutional Court of Romania: Judgment of 8 July 2014, Ref. No 440[15]

(...)

[15]The judgement is available at the page of the Constitutional Court of Romania under: http://legislatie.just.ro/Public/DetaliiDocumentAfis/161081.Translation ordered by the University of Warsaw.

23. Law No. 82/2012 on the retention of the data generated or processed by the providers of public electronic communications networks and of the providers of publicly available electronic communications services, as well as for the amendment and completion of the Law No. 506/2004 regarding the processing of personal data and the protection of privacy in the electronic communications sector is the transposition into national law of Directive 2006/24/EC of the European Parliament and of the Council of 15 March 2006 on the retention of data generated or processed in connection with the provision of publicly available electronic communications services or of communication networks and amending Directive 2002/58/EC. However, Directive 2006/24/EC was declared invalid by the judgement of the Court of Justice of the European Union of 8 April 2014 in Joined Cases C-293/12 –(. . .). By that judgement, the European Court of Justice found that the Directive under consideration violates the provisions of Article 7, Article 8 and Article 52 (1) of the Charter of Fundamental Rights of the European Union.

24. The Court of Justice of the European Union has pointed out in this respect that Directive 2006/24/EC aims primarily at harmonising Member States' legislation on the obligations of providers of publicly available electronic communications services or public communications networks to keep certain data generated or processed to ensure the availability of such data for the prevention, investigation, detection and prosecution of serious crimes such as organised crime and terrorism. It has also been found that the retention of the data in question is in the public interest, contributing to the fight against serious crime and thus to public security and that it does not affect the substance of the fundamental rights protected by the Charter. It has been concluded, however, that the measures laid down in Directive 2006/24/EC, although capable of achieving the objective pursued, constitute an interference with the rights guaranteed by Articles 7 and 8 of the Charter, which does not respect the principle of proportionality between the measures taken and the public interest protected.

25. The Court of Justice of the European Union has, in that respect, held in its judgement of 8 April 2014 that the data covered by the invalidated directive lead to very precise conclusions regarding the privacy of the persons whose data has been retained, conclusions which may cover everyday life, permanent or temporary stays, daily or other journeys, activities carried out, social relations of those persons and the social backgrounds they frequent (paragraph 27) and that, under these conditions, even if, under Article 1 (2) and Article 5 (2) of Directive 2006/24/EC, it is forbidden to retain the content of the communications and information consulted through the use of an electronic communications network, as the retention of such data may affect the use by subscribers or registered users of the means of communication provided for by this Directive and, consequently, their freedom of expression, guaranteed by Article 11 of the Charter (paragraph 28).

26. It has been established by the same judgement that the retention of data to ensure the possible access to it by competent national authorities, as provided for in Directive 2006/24/EC, directly and specifically concerns private life and consequently the rights guaranteed by Article 7 of the Charter, and that this data storage also violates the provisions of Article 8 of the Charter as it constitutes a processing of

personal data within the meaning of this Article and must meet the data protection requirements that arise of that Article (paragraph 29).

27. Where the provisions of Article 7 and Article 8 of the Charter are infringed, the European Court concluded that the obligation imposed by Articles 3 and 6 of Directive 2006/24/EC to providers of publicly available electronic communications services or public communications networks to keep data relating to a person's privacy and communications for a certain period, such as those under in Article 5 of this Directive per se constitutes an interference with the rights guaranteed by Article 7 of the Charter (paragraph 34). It has also been established that the same obligation constitutes an interference with the fundamental right to the protection of personal data guaranteed by Article 8 of the Charter as it provides for the processing of personal data (paragraph 36).

28. On the same occasion, the Court of Justice of the European Union has shown that the interference with fundamental rights enshrined in Articles 7 and 8 of the Charter, caused by the provisions of Directive 2006/24/EC, is of a large scale and must be considered as particularly grave, and the fact that data retention and subsequent use are made without the subscriber or registered user being informed of this is likely to generate in the minds of the data subjects the feeling that their private life is subject to constant supervision (paragraph 37).

29. On the proportionality of the interference, it was held in that judgement that the general interest objective of Directive 2006/24/EC, even if it is fundamental, cannot justify the need for measures such as those laid down in that directive for combating the offences referred to in paragraph 51.

30. It has also been noted that the protection of personal data, resulting from the explicit obligation under Article 8 (1) of the Charter, is of particular importance for the right to respect for private life enshrined in Article 7 of the Charter (paragraph 51), which is why the directive should contain clear and precise rules on the content and application of the retention of data and provide for a number of limitations so that persons whose data has been retained have sufficient safeguards to ensure effective protection against abuse and any unauthorised access or use (paragraph 54).

31. The Court of Justice of the European Union further held, in its judgement of 8 April 2014, that Directive 2006/24/EC concerns all persons using electronic communications services, but without the persons whose data is stored being found, indirectly, in a situation likely to trigger the initiation of criminal proceedings, the provisions of the Directive being applied even to those in respect of whom there are no indications that they may have any link, even indirectly or remotely, with the commission of serious crimes. It has been pointed out that the Directive under consideration does not provide for any exception in respect of persons whose communications are subject, under national law, to professional secrecy (paragraph 58).

32. The European Court of Justice further held that Directive 2006/24/EC does not provide for any objective criterion which allows the competent national authorities to have access to data and its subsequent use for preventing, detecting or prosecuting criminal offences that, having regard to their magnitude and the severity

of the interference with fundamental rights enshrined in Articles 7 and 8 of the Charter, may be regarded as sufficiently serious to justify such interference and that it merely refers in general to Article 1 (1), to serious offences as defined in the national law of each Member State (paragraph 60).

33. In addition, it was found that the Directive does not expressly provide that the access of competent national authorities to stored data and its subsequent use must be strictly for preventing and detecting precisely defined offences or conducting criminal prosecution in their case, but merely states that each Member State defines the procedures to be followed and the conditions to be met to obtain access to the data retained, in accordance with the requirements of necessity and proportionality (paragraph 61).

34. By the same judgement, it was also noted that Directive 2006/24/EC does not provide objective criteria limiting to the strictly necessary number of persons who have access to and subsequently use retained data, that access by national authorities to stored data is not subject to prior control by a court or an independent administrative entity to restrict that access and use them to what is strictly necessary to achieve the objective pursued and that Member States are not required to lay down such limitations (paragraph 62).

35. Concerning the duration of data retention, it was noted that Directive 2006/24/EC requires them to be stored for a period of six to 24 months, without providing objective criteria for limiting the retention of data to the strict minimum necessary and without distinguishing between categories of data depending on whether they are useful for achieving the objective pursued or by the data subjects (paragraphs 63-64).

36. It has also been noted that Directive 2006/24/EC does not provide for clear and precise rules regulating the extent of the interference with fundamental rights enshrined in Article 7 and Article 8 of the Charter, that the Directive contains a great deal of interference with these fundamental rights and that the infringement is not limited to what is strictly necessary (paragraph 65). It has also been noted that Directive 2006/24/EC does not provide sufficient safeguards under Article 8 of the Charter to ensure effective protection of data stored against unauthorised access to, or use of, such data (paragraph 66).

37. Finally, it has been shown that the Directive does not require stored data to be retained within the European Union, so that the control of compliance with the protection and security requirements laid down in paragraph 3 of Article 8 of the Charter, which is an essential element of the protection of individuals with regard to the processing of personal data is not fully guaranteed (paragraph 68).

38. For the reasons given, the Court of Justice of the European Union has ruled that the Union legislature has breached the principle of proportionality by the provisions of Directive 2006/24/EC, which contravenes Article 7, Article 8 and Article 52 (1) of the Charter (paragraph 69).

39. On the other hand, it is noted that Law No. 82/2012 was adopted by the Parliament following the pronouncement by the Constitutional Court of Decision No. 1,258 of 8 October 2009, published in the Official Gazette of Romania, Part I, no. 798 of 23 November 2009, which found that the provisions of Law No. 298/2008

regarding the retention of data generated or processed by the providers of publicly available electronic communications services or of public communications networks, as well as the amendment of the Law No. 506/2004 on the processing of personal data and the protection of privacy in the electronic communications sector are unconstitutional, Law No. 298/2008 representing the first transposition of Directive 2006/24/EC into national law.

40. By Decision No. 1,258 of 8 October 2009, the Court held that Article 1 paragraph (2) of Law No. 298/2008 also includes in the category of traffic and location data of natural and legal persons "related data necessary for the identification of the subscriber or registered user", but without expressly defining what is meant by "related data". It has been shown that the lack of precise legal regulation, which precisely determines the scope of the necessary data for the identification of the user or legal persons, opens the possibility of abuses in the activity of retaining, processing and using the data stored by the providers of publicly available electronic communications services or public communications networks and that the limitation of the exercise of the right to privacy and the secrecy of correspondence and freedom of expression must also take place in a clear, predictable and unambiguous manner so as to remove as far as possible, the eventual arbitrariness or abuse by authorities in this area.

41. The Constitutional Court also observed the same ambiguous drafting, inconsistent with the normative technical requirements, of the provisions of Article 20 of Law No. 298/2008, according to which, "In order to prevent and counteract threats to national security, State bodies with attributions in this field may have access, under the conditions established by the normative acts regulating the activity of accomplishing the national security, to the data retained by the providers of electronic communications services and networks". It has been found that the legislator does not show what is meant by "threats to national security", so that, in the absence of precise delimitation criteria, ordinary, routine actions, information or routine activities of natural and legal persons can be deemed, arbitrarily and abusively, as having the nature of such threats. At the same time, it was shown that the targets of the law can be included in the category of suspects without knowing it and without being able to prevent the consequence of applying the rigours of the law and also that the use of the phrase "may have" induces the idea that the data to which Law No. 298/2008 refers is not retained for the sole purpose of its use only by state bodies with specific attributions in the protection of national security and public order, but also by other persons or entities since they "may", and do not "have" access to this data, under the law.

42. By the same decision, the Constitutional Court found that Law No. 298/2008 establishes the rule for the continued withholding of personal data, for a period of six months from the time it is intercepted. However, in the matter of personal rights, such as the right to a private life and free speech, as well as the processing of personal data, the unanimously recognised rule is that of guaranteeing and respecting these rights, with regard to confidentiality, with the state mostly negative obligations in this regard, abstaining obligations, so as to avoid as much as possible, its interference in the exercise of a person's right or freedom. It has been pointed out

that exceptions are permitted only in the conditions expressly provided by the Constitution and the international legal acts applicable in the field, and Law No. 298/2008 is such an exception, as the title itself indicates.

43. The Court also found that the obligation to withhold data regulated by Law No. 298/2008 as an exception or derogation from the principle of the protection of personal data and its confidentiality, by its nature, scope and scope, but empties this principle, as guaranteed by the Law No. 77/2001 on the protection of individuals with regard to the processing of personal data and the free movement of this data, and Law No. 506/2004 on the processing of personal data and the protection of privacy in the electronic communications sector. However, it is unanimously recognised in the case law of the European Court of Human Rights, for example in the judgement of 12 July 2001 in the case of Prince Hans-Adam II of Liechtenstein v. Germany, paragraph 45, that the signatory States of the Convention for the Protection of Human Rights and Fundamental Freedoms of the fundamental freedoms have undertaken obligations to ensure that the rights guaranteed by the Convention are concrete and effective, not theoretical and illusory, the legislative measures adopted aiming at the effective protection of rights. The legal obligation that requires the continued detention of personal data turns the exception to the principle of effective protection of the right to privacy and free speech in absolute rule. Thus, the right appears to be regulated in a negative manner, its positive side losing its predominant character.

44. At the same time, it has been observed that the regulation of a positive obligation which concerns the constant limitation of the exercise of the right to privacy and the secrecy of correspondence makes the very essence of the law disappear, by removing the guarantees for its exercise. Physical and legal persons who are mass users of publicly available electronic communications services or public communications networks are permanently subject to this interference in the exercise of their privacy rights to correspondence and free speech, without the possibility of free, uncensored manifestations, in the form of direct communication, excluding the main means of communication currently used.

45. Also, by Decision No. 1,258 of 8 October 2009, the Court has held that the examination of the principle of proportionality, another imperative requirement to be met in cases of restriction of the exercise of rights or fundamental freedoms, expressly provided for by Article 53 (2) of the Constitution. This principle requires that the restriction measure be in line with the situation which has led to its application and also ceases with the disappearance of the determining cause Law No. 298/2008 imposes the obligation to keep the data on a continuous basis, from its entry into force and its application (namely 20 January 2009, 15 March 2009, respectively, regarding the location traffic data corresponding to the Internet access services, e-mail and Internet telephony), without considering the need to end the limitation measure with the disappearance of the cause of the measure.

46. The Constitutional Court notes that, although Law No. 298/2008 refers to data of a predominantly technical nature, they are retained to provide information about the person and his/her private life. Even if, under Article 1 (3) of the Law, this does not apply to the content of the communication or information consulted during the

use of an electronic communications network, the other data retained, with the purpose of identifying the caller and persons being called, respectively the user and the recipient of information communicated electronically, of the source, destination, date, time and duration of a communication, communication type, communication equipment or user devices, the location of the mobile communications equipment, and other "related data" - undefined in the law - were likely to prejudice or mitigate the free expression of the right to communication or expression.

47. It has been shown that the legal safeguards regarding the actual use of retained data — regarding the exclusion of the content of the communication or the information consulted, as a matter of data storage, to the motivated and prior authorisation of the president of the competent court to judge the act for which the prosecution provided for by Article 16 of Law No. 298/2008 and the application of the sanctions regulated under Article 18 and Article 19 thereof - were not sufficient and appropriate to remove the fear that privacy rights are violated so that their manifestation occurs in an acceptable manner.

48. Thus, the Constitutional Court has not denied the purpose in itself considered by the legislator when adopting Law No. 298/2008, that it is imperative to ensure adequate and efficient legal means, compatible with the continuous process of modernisation and technology of the means of communication, so that the criminal phenomenon can be controlled and countered. It has been shown that this is precisely why individual rights cannot be exercised in *ad absurdum* but may be subject to restrictions which are justified by the purpose pursued. Limiting the exercise of some personal rights, considering collective rights and public interests, concerning national security, public order or criminal prevention, has always constituted a sensitive operation in terms of regulation, and it is necessary to maintain a fair balance between individual interests and rights, on the one hand, and those of society, on the other. However, the Court held that, as noted by the European Court of Human Rights in its judgement of 6 September 1978 in Klass and others v. Germany, paragraph 49, it is no less true that the taking of supervisory measures without adequate and sufficient guarantees, can lead to "the destruction of democracy under the pretext of its defence."

49. By comparing the provisions of Law No. 82/2012 with those of Law No. 298/2008, the Court finds that in both laws the cases in which the judicial authorities or the bodies responsible for national security have access to the data generated or processed by the network providers of public electronic communications services and providers of publicly available electronic communications services are those whose scope is the prevention, investigation, discovery and prosecution of "serious crimes". It is also noted that both laws define the notion of "serious crime", but Law No. 82/2012 extends significantly the scope of the offences that are circumscribed to this notion (see Article, 2 letter e) compared to Law No. 298/2008, whose coverage was lower (see Article 2, letter f)). In addition, the law subject to this constitutionality control allows access by the judicial bodies and state bodies with tasks in the field of national security to the data retained and for the settlement of the cases with missing persons or for execution of a warrant for arrest or execution of the punishment. The Court considers that this extension was

possible, having regard to the provisions of Directive 2006/24/EC, which left it to the Member States to determine the situations to which the legal act transposing the Directive applies.

50. The Court also notes that the legislator has waived in the content of the new regulation the phrase "related data necessary to identify the subscriber or the registered user" of the norm under Article 1 paragraph (2) of the Law No. 298/2008, establishing at Article 1 paragraph (2) of the Law No. 82/2012 that this normative act "shall apply to the traffic and location data of the natural persons and the legal persons, as well as the data necessary for the identification of a registered subscriber or registered user". The removal from the regulated hypothesis of the word "related" by which the phrase "necessary related data" has been reformulated to become "necessary data" is not such as to remove the vice of unconstitutionality signalled by Decision No. 1,258 of 8 October 2009, which criticised the fact that the legislator did not expressly define what is meant by "related data necessary to identify the registered subscriber or user". The current regulation preserves the imprecision of the wording, as it does not now define what is meant by "the data needed to identify a registered subscriber or user".

51. Regarding the possibility of the state bodies with attributions in the field of preventing and counteracting the threats to the national security to have access to the data retained by the providers of public electronic communications services and networks provided by Article 20 of the Law No. 298/2008, the Court finds that the right of these state bodies to have access to retained data is found in Article 16 paragraph (1) of the Law No. 82/2012 (. . .).

52. On the continued obligation of providers of public electronic communications networks and providers of electronic communications services to keep the data in question, the Court notes that this was also maintained in the new regulation, Law No. 82/2012 establishing at Article 1 (1) "the obligation on providers of public electronic communications networks and electronic communications service providers to keep certain data generated or processed in their activity for the purpose of making them available [. . .]". However, the continued character of retaining the data generated or processed in the activity of the providers of public electronic communications networks and of the providers of publicly available electronic communications services was, from the point of view of the Constitutional Court of Appeal, expressed through the Decision No. 1,258 of 8 October 2009, a reason for finding the unconstitutionality of the provisions of Law No. 298/2008.

53. In carrying out the constitutional review of Law No. 82/2012, the Court finds that the provisions of Articles 26, 28 and 30 of the Constitution regulate the right to privacy and family life, the secrecy of correspondence, as well as freedom of expression, conditions in which the subject matter of the criticised law falls within the sphere of protection of these constitutional texts. The law criticises the problem of the protection of the constitutional rights invoked as a legislative intervention in their sphere, motivated by the very purpose of this law, which coincides at national level with that of Directive 2006/24/EC and consists in the prevention, detection, and the investigation of serious crimes by the criminal prosecution bodies, courts and

state bodies with responsibilities in the field of national security, fully realised by the law subject to constitutional control.

54. Analysing the provisions of Law No. 82/2012 as well as the principle recitals contained in the judgement of the Court of Justice of the European Union of 8 April 2014, whereby Directive 2006/24/EC was declared invalid, and in the Constitutional Court Decision No. 1,258 of 8 October 2009, the Court notes that they are also applicable in principle to Law No. 82/2012.

55. First, the interference with fundamental rights relating to privacy and family life, the secrecy of correspondence and freedom of expression is of great magnitude and must be regarded as particularly grave, and the fact that data retention and subsequent use are made without the subscriber or the registered user being informed of it is likely to imply in the conscience of the data subjects the feeling that their private life is subject to constant supervision.

56. Second, data subject to regulation, although of a predominantly technical nature, is retained to provide information about the person and his/her private life. Even if, under Article 1 (3) of the Law, it does not apply to the content of the communication or information consulted during the use of an electronic communications network, the other data retained, with the purpose of identifying the caller and the called user and the recipient of information communicated electronically, of the source, destination, date, time and duration of a communication, communication type, communication equipment or user devices, the location of the mobile communications equipment, and other "necessary data" —, undefined in law — are likely to prejudice the free expression of the right to communication or expression. In particular, the data under consideration leads to very precise conclusions about the privacy of data which have been retained, conclusions that may relate to everyday life habits, permanent or temporary place of residence, daily or other journeys, activities carried out, relationships social issues of these people and the social environments frequented by them. However, such a limitation on the exercise of the right to privacy and family life, and to the secrecy of correspondence, as well as freedom of expression, must take place in a clear, predictable and unambiguous manner so as to be removed as much as possible arbitrariness or abuse of authorities in this area.

57. Third, the criticised law does not contain clear and precise rules on the content and application of the apprehension and use measure so that persons whose data have been retained have sufficient safeguards to provide effective protection against abuse and access or illicit uses. Thus, the law does not provide for objective criteria limiting to the strictly necessary number of persons who have access to and subsequently use retained data, that the access of national authorities to the data stored is not, in all cases, conditional upon prior checking by a court; or by an independent administrative entity, to restrict that access and use it in line with what is strictly necessary to achieve the objective pursued. The legal safeguards for the actual use of retained data are not sufficient and adequate to remove the fear that privacy rights are violated so that their manifestation takes place in an acceptable manner.

58. In addition to the arguments previously put forward, the Court considers it necessary, for an accurate understanding of the data retention mechanism, to

distinguish between two different stages. Observing that the data in question mainly refers to traffic and location data for people, as well as data needed to identify a registered subscriber or user, the regulated mechanism involves two steps, the first being to retain and store data and the second, that of access to these data and their use.

59. Retaining and storing data, which is naturally the first operation in terms of chronology, is the responsibility of providers of publicly available electronic communications networks and services. This operation is a technical one, being automated based on software programmes as long as the law provides for the obligation of law enforcement providers to retain those data. Since under both Directive 2006/24/EC and Law No. 82/2012, the purpose of retaining and storing is a general one, aiming at ensuring national security, defence, and preventing, investigating, detecting and prosecuting serious offences, detention and storage are unrelated to and determined by a specific case, it is evident that the obligation of the providers of public electronic communications networks and of electronic communications services must retain this data for the entire period stipulated by the normative framework in force, respectively for a period of six months, under Law No. 82/2012. Also, at this stage, being exclusively the retention and storage of a mass of information, the identification or localisation of those who are subject to electronic communication is not realised in concrete terms, this only takes place in the second stage, once it is allowed access to and use of data.

60. The Court considers that precisely because of the nature and specificity of the first stage, since the legislator considers it necessary to retain and store the data, by itself this operation alone is not contrary to the right to privacy and family life, or to the secrecy of correspondence. Neither the Constitution nor the case law of the Constitutional Court prohibits pre-emptive storage without a specific occasion of traffic and localisation data provided that access to and use of such data is accompanied by guarantees and respecting the principle of proportionality.

61. Therefore, the Court considers that only the second stage, that of access and use of these data, raises the question of the compliance of the legal provisions with the constitutional provisions. Examining the provisions of Law No. 82/2012 on the access of judicial bodies and other state bodies with duties in the field of national security to stored data, the Court finds that the law does not provide the safeguards necessary to protect the right to privacy and family life, the secrecy of correspondence and freedom expression of people whose stored data is being accessed.

62. Thus, as stated above, from the provisions of Article 1 of the Law No. 82/2012, the criminal investigation bodies, the courts and the state bodies with powers in the field of national security, have access to the data retained under the provisions of this law. However, under Article 18 of Law No. 82/2012, only the criminal prosecution bodies are obliged to comply with the provisions of Article 152 of the Criminal Procedure Code, this obligation not being provided also for state bodies with attributions in the field of national security, who can access this data in accordance with the "special laws in the matter", as provided by Article 16 (1) of the Law No. 82/2012. Therefore, only the request by criminal prosecution bodies to providers of public electronic communications networks and providers of electronic

communications services for the retrieval of retained data is subject to the prior authorisation of the judge of rights and freedoms.

63. Requests for access to data retained for use by the State Security Authorities for law enforcement purposes are not subject to authorisation or approval by the court, thus failing to guarantee the effective protection of data retained against the risks of abuse, and against any access to and use of any such data. This circumstance is likely to constitute an interference with fundamental rights to privacy and family life and the secrecy of correspondence and is therefore contrary to the constitutional provisions which enshrine and protect these rights.

64. From the analysis of the "special laws in the matter", to which Article 16 (1) of the Law No. 82/2012 refers, the Court finds that state bodies with powers in the field of national security can access and use the stored data without there being the need for a court authorisation. Thus, Law No. 51/1991 on the national security of Romania, republished in the Official Gazette of Romania, Part I, no. 190 of 18 March 2014, establishes, at Article 8, the state bodies with attributions in the field of national security, these Being the Romanian Intelligence Service, the Foreign Intelligence Service and the Protection and Guard Service, and at Article 9 provides that the Ministry of National Defence, the Ministry of Internal Affairs and the Ministry of Justice organise information structures with attributions specific to their fields of activity. The Court also notes that under Article 13, letter e) of the law, the bodies with attributions in the field of national security may, given the existence of threats to the national security of Romania, as they are defined in Article 3 of the Law No. 51/1991 to request the generation or processing of data generated or processed by the providers of public networks, electronic communications or providers of publicly available electronic communications services other than their content, and retained by them under the law, without this article or Article 14 of the Act to provide that such a request must be authorised by the judge.

65. The Court also notes that under Article 9 of Law No. 14/1992 on the organisation and functioning of the Romanian Intelligence Service, "In order to establish the existence of the threats to the national security provided for in Article 3 of the Law No. 51/1991 on National Security of Romania, with the subsequent modifications, the intelligence services can perform, in compliance with the law, checks by: [. . .] e) obtaining data generated or processed by providers of public electronic communications networks or providers of publicly available electronic communications services other than their content and retained by them under the law." But, like the provisions of Law No. 82/2012 and of Law No. 51/1991, nor the provisions of Law No. 14/1992 do not require this information service to obtain the authorisation of the judge to access the stored data.

66. At the same time, the Court observes that Law No. 1/1998 on the organisation and functioning of the Foreign Intelligence Service, republished in the Official Gazette of Romania, Part I, no. 511 of October 18, 2000, stipulates in Article 10 (1) "The Foreign Intelligence Service is authorized to use undercover legal entities to use specific methods, to create and to have adequate means to obtain, verify, protect, evaluate, exploit and store national safety data and information", and under paragraph 3 of the same article, "The use of means of obtaining, checking and

capitalizing data and information must not in any way impair the fundamental rights or freedoms of citizens, their private life, their honour or reputation, or Subjecting them to illegal encroachment." Also, under Article 11 of Law No. 1/1998, "the Foreign Intelligence Service has the right, under the conditions stipulated by law, to request and obtain from Romanian public authorities, economic agents, other legal persons, as well as from to individuals, information, data or documents necessary for the performance of his duties ". The Court therefore finds that Law No. 1/1998 does not regulate separately the access of the Foreign Intelligence Service to data held by the providers of public electronic communications networks and the providers of publicly available electronic communications services, but this access is regulated by Article 13 of the Law No. 51/1991, without being subject to the prior authorisation of a court.

67. The lack of such authorisations was also criticised by the Court of Justice of the European Union in its judgement of 8 April 2014, which is equivalent to the lack of procedural safeguards necessary to protect the right to private life and other rights enshrined in Article 7 of the Charter of Fundamental Rights and Freedoms and the fundamental right to the protection of personal data, enshrined in Article 8 of the Charter (paragraph 62).

68. The Court also notes that, although Law No. 82/2012 establishes the contraventions that may be committed by providers of public electronic communications networks and services in connection with the process of detaining, storing and accessing data, as well as the institutions competent to detect such contraventions and to apply sanctions (National Authority for Supervision of the Processing of Personal Data and the National Authority for Administration and Regulation in Communications), the law does not provide for a genuine control mechanism, which ensures these institutions a permanent and effective verification of compliance with the legal provisions so that they can easily be notified Cases in which service providers violate the legal provisions regarding the type of data retained, the length of time they are stored, their destruction in the cases provided for by law, or the bodies and institutions to which access is granted. Therefore, the legal provisions focus mainly on the required diligence in the field of communications but relativise the safeguards pertaining to the security of data retention, since electronic communications operators are not required to provide adequate security standards that can be effectively controlled by the institutions provided by law. It is also noted that the law provides for the offence by the intentional access, alteration or transfer of the data retained under the law without authorisation, and all other unlawful acts are considered contraventions, which does not ensure in all cases adequate protection of the right to privacy and family life, as well as the secret of correspondence. The non-regulation of a real mechanism of control of the activity of the providers of public networks and of electronic communications services by an independent authority is equivalent to the lack of guarantees, as required by the provisions of Articles 26 and 28 of the Constitution, effective data protection against the risks of abuse and any unauthorised access or use of such data.

69. The decisions of other European constitutional courts are relevant from the point of view of the constitutional review carried out, expressly referring to the

decisions of the Federal Constitutional Court of Germany, the Constitutional Court of the Czech Republic and the Supreme Administrative Court of Bulgaria.

70. Thus, by the judgement of 2 March 2010, the Federal Constitutional Court of Germany declared unconstitutional the provisions of Articles 113a and 113b of the Law on the new regulation of telecommunication surveillance of 21 December 2007 and Article 100g of the Code of Criminal Procedure of Germany, that they violate Article 10 paragraph 1 of the German Constitution on Telecommunication Secrets.

71. The unconstitutionality of the provisions of Articles 113a and 113b of the New Telecommunications Supervision Act of 21 December 2007 showed that storing without a specific occasion of traffic data in telecommunications is not subject to strict prohibition of preventive storage of data within the meaning of the case law of the Federal Constitutional Court and that, if this intervention is considered and is adequately carried out, the requirements of proportionality can be met.

72. The importance of the storage of traffic data in the telecommunications sector for preventive purposes has been highlighted, but also the need for sufficiently stringent and clear regulations on data security and limitation of their use to ensure transparency and legal protection. Attention is drawn however to the fact that such storage is a large interference, even if the content of the communications is not stored, since the data thus retained make it possible to have a detailed knowledge of the person's private life, especially with regard to social affiliation or politics, preferences, inclinations and weaknesses of individuals, allowing for pertinent profiles to be drawn up and posing the risk of subjecting citizens who do not have any reason to be subjected to investigations to be exposed to such actions.

73. It has been found that the provisions of Articles 113a and 113b of the New Telecommunications Supervision Act of 21 December 2007 violate the principle of proportionality, as the constitutional requirements on data security and transparency of their use and protection of individuals are not met. In this respect, it was noted that the criticised legal provisions refer only to the diligence required in general in the field of telecommunications, but relativise the safety requirements, leaving it to the telecom operators, who are not subject to sufficiently high insurance standards of the security level and for which greater sanctions are imposed in the event of a breach of the storage obligation than in the case of a breach of data security.

74. It has also been noted that the provisions of Article 100g of the Criminal Procedure Code allow accessing data in other than individual cases, without the consent of the judge and without the knowledge of the person concerned, which is why they are unconstitutional.

75. Similarly, the Constitutional Court of the Czech Republic, by its decision of 22 March 2011, found the unconstitutionality of the provisions of section 97, paragraphs 3 and 4 of Act no. 127/2005 on electronic communications and amendments to related normative acts (Electronic Communications Act) and Decree no. 485/2005 on the retention of traffic data, the location, date and duration of communications and the form and method of supplying to the authorised authorities.

76. In the content of this decision, the Court held that the criticised texts do not provide sufficient guarantees to citizens about the risk of misuse of stored data and arbitrariness. It has found that the normative acts analysed do not define at all or

define inadequately and ambiguously the rules regarding the fulfilment of the requirements regarding the security of the data retention and the restriction of the third-party access to the retained data. The importance in the context of the current level of development of society of the retention of traffic data in the field of communications was emphasised on this occasion, but also the need to maintain a balance between the public and the individual interest. The same decision found the lack of definition of the means that should be made available to the affected persons to obtain effective protection against the arbitrary and abusive use of stored data.

77. Finally, the Supreme Administrative Court of Bulgaria, by its Decision No. 13,627 of 11 December 2008, annulled an article in the national data retention law that allowed the Ministry of the Interior access to retain data in computer terminals and also to provide access to services Security and other law enforcement agencies to these data without the authorisation of a judicial body, stating that the cancelled legal provision did not provide any guarantee for the protection of the right to privacy, and that no mechanism was established to guarantee such protection against unlawful interference, so as to avoid damaging the a person's honour, dignity or reputation.

78. On the effects of its decisions, the Court recalls their definitive and general binding nature. Therefore, in the present case, in view of the judgement of 8 April 2014 of the Court of Justice of the European Union, as well as the publication in the Official Gazette of Romania, Part I, of this decision, it is deprived of legal basis, of European and national law, the activity of retaining and using data generated or processed in connection with the provision of publicly available electronic communications services or public communications networks. Specifically, this means that since the publication of the decision of the Romanian Constitutional Court, providers of public electronic communications networks and providers of publicly available electronic communications services have neither the obligation nor the legal possibility to retain certain data generated or processed within their activity and to make them available to the judiciary and the national security authorities. By exception, only the data required for billing or interconnection payments or other processed data for marketing purposes may be retained by these providers only with the prior consent of the data subject, as provided for in Directive 2002/58/EC of the European Parliament and of the Council of 12 July 2002 concerning the processing of personal data and the protection of privacy in the electronic communications sector (Directive on privacy and electronic communications) in force.

79. Correlatively, until Parliament adopts a new data retention law that complies with constitutional requirements and requirements, as outlined in this decision, judicial and state bodies with national security responsibilities are no longer able to access Data that have already been retained and stored under Directive 2006/24/EC and Law No. 82/2012 for use in the activities defined in Article 1 paragraph (1) of Law No. 82/2012. Also, the judicial and the national security authorities have no legal and constitutional basis either for accessing and using the data retained by suppliers for billing, interconnection payments or other commercial purposes to use

for their Preventing, investigating, discovering and prosecuting serious crimes or solving cases with missing persons or executing a warrant for arrest or punishment, precisely because of their different character, nature and purpose, as Is laid down in Directive 2002/58/EC. In fact, even Law No. 82/2012 establishes in Article 11 that the last data retained are exempt from the provisions of the law, having another legal regime, being subject to the provisions of the Law No. 506/2004 on the processing of personal data and the protection of privacy in the electronic communications sector.

80. On the criticism of unconstitutionality regarding the provisions of Article 152 of the Criminal Procedure Code, the Court notes that the criticised text does not regulate the procedure of retaining and storing data generated or processed by the providers of public electronic communications networks and service providers electronic communications intended for the public to retain the data generated or processed, but merely establishes the procedure for prior authorisation by the judge of rights and freedoms of the request addressed to these providers by the criminal investigating authorities for the access and use of retained data. This text governing one of the special methods of supervision or research provided for in Chapter IV of Title IV of the Code of Criminal Procedure is the one which provides judicial control over activities governed by law, constituting precisely the procedural guarantee of the right to private, family and private life, to Article 26 of the Constitution, invoked in support of the objection of unconstitutionality. It is obvious that, in the absence of a law regulating the procedure for retaining and storing data, Article 152 of the Code of Criminal Procedure remains unenforceable, but this fact does not constitute a defect of unconstitutionality, the text to become an immediate binding once a new law on data retention is adopted.

(...)

The Constitutional Court of the Slovak Republic: Judgment of 29 April 2015, Ref. No PL. ÚS 10/2014[16]

(...)

113. On the alleged interference with the very essence of the fundamental right to respect for private life, it must be stated that, although the retention of data constitutes a particularly serious interference with that right, it is not capable of interfering with the very substance of that right because the contested legislation does not make it possible to understand with regard to the very content of electronic communications (...). The storage of traffic data, localisation data and data from the communicating parties cannot interfere with the essence of the fundamental right to the protection of personal data as a component of the right to privacy either, because the Electronic Communications Act under Section 58 (10) introduces the obligation to electronic data communication providers to observe certain principles of protection

[16]The judgement is available at the page of the Constitutional Court of the Slovak Republic under: https://www.ustavnysud.sk/vyhladavanie-rozhodnuti. Translation ordered by the University of Warsaw.

and data security, to ensure that: (a) the data collected are of the same quality and subject to the same protection and observance as data processed or stored by undertakings providing networks or services; (b) data were subject to appropriate technical measures and organisational arrangements for data protection against accidental or unlawful destruction, accidental loss or alteration, unauthorised or unlawful storage, processing, access or disclosure; (c) the data have been subject to appropriate technical measures and organisational measures to ensure that data may only be made available to authorised persons acting based on the authority or authority of the undertaking and the law enforcement agencies, the court or other State authorities and their authorised or otherwise authorised members or employees; (d) data at the end of the period set out for the storage was disposed of in addition to the data provided and secured.

114. On the question whether that interference is in the public interest objective, it must be pointed out that the purpose of the contested provisions of the Electronic Communications Act requiring an electronic communications provider to keep the traffic data, localisation data and data of the communicating parties and the obligation to provide them to law enforcement authorities, the court and other state authorities under Section 55 (6) of the Electronic Communications Act, as provided under Section 58 (7), of the Electronic Communications Act, must ensure the availability of such data in investigating, detecting and prosecuting offences related to terrorism through illicit trafficking, organised crime, the leak and threat to classified information and crimes committed by dangerous groups. The objective of the contested provisions of the Electronic Communications Act is therefore to support the fight against serious crime and, ultimately, to protect public safety.

115. Preventing crime and public safety constitute, under Article 8 (2) of the Convention, legitimate objectives that, to achieve them, are likely to interfere with the exercise of the right to privacy. According to the judicature of the Court of Justice, the fight against international terrorism, to preserve peace and international security, is an objective of general interest of the Union. The same shall apply on the fight against serious crime to secure public safety. In the light of the referred, it must be stated that the contested legislation requiring the retention of data for their possible disclosure to the competent national authorities pursues a legitimate objective that is in the general interest.

116. Under such circumstances, it is necessary to examine the adequacy (proportionality) of the stated intervention. It is necessary to examine whether the contested provisions of the Electronic Communications Act are, on the one hand, appropriate to attain legitimate objectives and, on the other hand, undeniable to achieve them, i.e. do not go beyond what is appropriate and necessary to achieve these objectives. Given the importance of the protection of personal data with regard to the fundamental right to respect for private life, it is necessary to proceed with rigorous monitoring of compliance with the proportionality criteria of the stated interference.

117. On the question whether the storage of traffic data, localisation data and data from the communicating parties for their possible disclosure to the competent authorities is appropriate to achieve the objective pursued, it should be noted that, given the significant increase in the possibilities for electronic communications to be

kept under Section 58 (5) of the Electronic Communications Act and Appendix 2 of this Act specifying the category of data retained by the competent national authorities under Article 58 (7) in conjunction with the provisions of Section 55 (6) of this Act, additional possibilities for clarifying the serious crimes exhaustively defined under Section 58 (7) of this Act, and in this regard constitute a useful instrument for investigating, detecting and prosecuting offences in question. The storage of such data can therefore be considered as a means which are appropriate and capable of achieving the objectives pursued.

118. This statement cannot be called into question by the fact that the House of Representatives points out in its proposal that there are several ways of avoiding data retention, for example by choosing another way of communication which is not yet monitored by the State, e.g. using a blog, social networks (e.g. Facebook), sites that allow you to share videos (e.g. YouTube), instant messaging (IM), IRC (Internet Relay Chat), peer-to-peer (P2P) communication, as they do not use the protocols foreseen by the Electronic Communications Act or encrypt communication, or use a telephone booth or the so-called anonymous prepaid calling cards (cards for the purchase of which the identity of the buyer does not need to be demonstrated upon purchase), or the use of commercial services, and the anonymisation of the onion browser (TOR) or JAP (JonDo) communications system, due to which the contested regulation should not be appropriate for achieving the objective of combating organised crime and terrorism, since it is the people who know the crime best how to effectively avoid data retention. While it is true that such circumstances may limit the effectiveness of the retention of data in achieving the objective pursued, it cannot lead to the inability of the measure to achieve the objective pursued.

119. On the requirement to preserve selected data to achieve public safety, it must be stated that although the effectiveness of the fight against serious crime can depend to a large extent on the use of modern investigative technologies, even if that objective of general interest is essential, in itself, justify the retention measure introduced by the contested provisions of the Electronic Communications Act being considered inapplicable for such fight.

120. On the question whether the interference represented by the contested regulation of the Electronic Communications Act is limited to the most urgent, it should be noted that that amendment, under the provisions of Section 58 (5) of the Electronic Communications Act, in conjunction with Appendix 2 of the Electronic Communications Act, requires the storage of all traffic data, localisation data and data of the communicating parties concerning fixed and mobile telephone connection, Internet connection, Internet email and Internet telephony. This applies to all means of electronic communication, the use of which is very widespread and which is of growing importance to the everyday life of an individual. This referred modification applies to all participants and registered users. The traffic data, localisation data and data of the communicating parties are generally relevant to all persons using electronic communications services without, at least indirectly, finding those persons whose data are stored in a situation that could lead to a criminal prosecution. It is also applicable to persons who have no reason to believe that their conduct may at least have an indirect or distant link to serious offences. Additionally,

it does not provide for any exception, so it also applies to persons whose communication under the relevant legislation is subject to professional secrecy or to the right of establishment or recognition of confidentiality.

122. Given the contested legislation, the Electronic Communications Act constitutes a serious interference with the right to privacy and cannot be regarded as an adjustment necessary to achieve the objective pursued. The objective pursued by the contested legislation to support the fight against serious crime and, ultimately, ensure the public safety can also be achieved by other means which constitute a less intensive interference with the right to privacy, such as a tool in the form of a comprehensive and preventive retention of the data in question. A more appropriate instrument for achieving the objectives pursued can be considered, for example, a freezing data that, when the specified conditions are met, allows you to track and store the necessary and selected data only for a specific, predetermined communications of a participant. It must also be noted that the contested legislation of the Electronic Communications Act would constitute a more appropriate instrument to achieve the objectives pursued if it provided sufficient guarantees and means of protection for individuals concerned enabling them to effectively protect personal data against the risks of their leak, abuse or any unlawful access and any unlawful use of such data.

(...)

The contested legislation does not, for instance, lay down specific rules tailored to the large amount of data the storage of which provides, the sensitive nature of those data, as well as the risk of unauthorised access to such data, which would, in a clear and restrictive manner, regulate the protection and security of the data in question to guarantee their complete integrity and confidentiality.

124. The provisions of Section 58 (10) of the Electronic Communications Act does not guarantee that electronic communications providers apply an exceptionally high level of protection and security by means of technological and organisational measures, since the provisions of Section 56 (2) of the Act allows electronic communications operators to take account of the level of security which they apply, consider the economic considerations as regards the cost of implementing security measures. The provisions of Section 56 (2) of the Electronic Communications Act requires electronic communications operators to take measures which must ensure a level of safety of services that is proportionate to the existing risk in terms of the state of the technology and the costs of their implementation.

128. The access of public authorities to such data without the consent of the users of those services, with regard to the possibility of deriving from them the information on the place, time and the participants of the communication, as well as the way of their communication, directly and significantly affects their right to privacy in the form of right to informational self-determination, since they are deprived of the possibility to decide whether or not to make this information available to others.

130. In terms of the referred criteria, it must be stated that the measure consisting of authorised law enforcement authorities to demand information on the telecommunications operation performed which are otherwise subject to telecommunications secrecy or which are covered by the protection of personal data from providers

of electronic communications which form the legal basis in the contested provisions of the Code of Criminal Procedure and the Police Force Act. However, the legal basis for permissible interference with the right to privacy must meet the condition of a certain level of material quality. From the ECtHR's doctrine, which the Constitutional Court has adopted, it follows that even intervention, which has its legal basis in the legal standard, may, in a specific case, interfere with the rights guaranteed by the Constitution or a Convention. (I. ÚS 117/07). Eligible interference with the right to privacy may be implemented under the law only in accordance with the general principles under which the constitutional law or the freedom of an individual may be restricted (PL ÚS 43/95).

131. The purpose of the authorisation of law enforcement authorities to require electronic communications providers to identify and communicate data about a telecommunication operation that is otherwise subject of a telecommunications secret or subject to the protection of personal data is in particular a need to identify or verify facts relevant to criminal proceedings in criminal proceedings for an intentional criminal offence. It should be noted that such a measure pursues a constitutionally approved public interest in the fight against crime, which is important for ensuring public safety. This purpose justifies an interference with the fundamental right. The given public interest shall also be a legitimate objective justifying an interference with the fundamental right arising under Article 8 (2) of the Convention. Article 8 (2) of the Convention allows, if it is necessary in a democratic society, to interfere with the right to respect for private life to protect the rights and freedoms of others, the national and public safety, the economic welfare of the state, the prevention of disturbances and crime, or the protection of health and morale. The purpose of the contested provisions of the Code of Criminal Procedure and the Police Force Act shall also be a purpose approved by the European Union law.

133. At the beginning of the necessity assessment, it is required to point out that the contested provisions of the Code of Criminal Procedure and the Police Force Act define not only what is the subject of the applicable law of the law enforcement authorities, i.e. require the providers of electronic communications to identify and communicate the data on the telecommunication operation carried out, but also what is not covered by such legislation. The given measure constitutes a negative interference with the right to respect for private life in the form of the right to information retrieval of electronic communications users, not only for communicating electronic communications to law enforcement authorities themselves but also for making them available to others, e.g. by making them accessible to other persons or for their misuse for other purposes. It is therefore necessary to examine whether the contested provisions of the Code of Criminal Procedure and the Police Force Act provide, from the standpoint of the fundamental right to respect for private life in the form of the right to information self-determination, the right to protection of personal data, sufficient safeguards against the misuse of such data throughout the process of criminal proceedings. These safeguards should be understood as setting out the conditions under which competent authorities should have access to, and effective monitoring of, electronic data traffic. Limiting personal integrity and privacy by public authorities can only occur under very exceptional circumstances, if it is

accepted from the point of view of legal existence and the observance of effective and concrete safeguards against libel. The necessity for such privacy interfering measures to contain such safeguards is becoming more urgent for individuals nowadays, thanks to the enormous development and emergence of new information technologies and electronic communication (the so-called cyberspace), primarily thanks to the development of Internet and mobile communication recorded every minute, collected and actually made available a huge amount of data, data and information that also affect the private sphere of each individual, although they did not want to let anyone know about it.

(...)

It is clear from the wording of the contested provisions of the Police Force Act that the authorisation of the Police Force to require electronic communications providers to detect and communicate electronic communications data in a manner allowing remote, continuous and direct access is conditional only on the fact that such a measure must be directed to the detection and documentation of criminal activities and can only be carried out to the extent necessary to fulfil the specific role of the Police Force and the time it takes to accomplish this task. The authorisation of the law enforcement authorities to request the detection and communication of electronic communication data therefore does not only concern a certain category of intentional criminal offences, as provided under Section 58 (7) of the Electronic Communications Act, i.e. terrorism-related crimes, illicit trafficking, organised crime, the leak and threat to classified information and crimes committed by dangerous groups, but any intentional crimes (in the case of the contested provision of the Code of Criminal Procedure) or criminal offences (in the case of the contested provision of the Police Force Act). According to the Constitutional Court, the so-called range of offences in investigating, detecting and prosecuting offences, which may be affected by the fundamental right to information self-determination, very broadly and indefinitely governs the limits of this fundamental right. It allows the law enforcement authorities to request and use the given data even if it is possible to find a certain connection with the ongoing intentional criminal offence. However, the degree of interference with the right to privacy caused by the retention and subsequent disclosure of electronic communications by law enforcement authorities requires that law enforcement authorities require the detection and communication of data necessary to elucidate matters of importance for criminal proceedings only related to the most serious criminal offences.

(...)

Authorisation of the law enforcement authorities to request the detection and communication of data on the communication operation made cannot be considered as a routine or routine means of preventing and detecting criminal offences, given the intensity of this fundamental right. The use of such means of combating crime can only occur if there is no other and more respectful means to achieve such objective.

(...)

136. To respect the requirement of necessity or the need, the contested legislation should also include an adjustment of the handling of such data by the law

enforcement authorities. It should include clear and detailed rules containing minimum requirements for securing retained data to ensure that stored data are not used for legitimate purposes other than those established by law. Particularly, this is to prevent access by third parties and to set up a procedure to protect the integrity and confidentiality of the stored data as well as their destruction. Effective protection against unjustifiable interference with the privacy of persons concerned should be ensured by the obligation to inform the user of electronic communications services that the traffic and localisation data and the data of the communicating parties concerning them have been communicated to the law enforcement authorities. At the same time, the persons concerned should have at their disposal a legal remedy to seek judicial review of the process of law enforcement authorities in obtaining and handling the data in question. An exception to this obligation could only be allowed for legitimate reasons, which would have an interest in preserving the confidentiality of such information. However, even in these cases, the legislator must guarantee that the assessment of the competent authorities, whether the reasons for the confidentiality of this information were not arbitrary but subject to mandatory judicial review. Finally, it should be noted that there is no reason why the scope of the statutory guarantees given in relation to the Regulation should be communicated in terms of its content, unless such differentiation arises from the nature of the matter, from the guarantees provided for in the to the regulation of the interception and recording of telecommunication traffic, since in both cases the intensity of interference with the right to privacy is comparable. Unlike the statutory regulation of the Telecommunications Tracking Regulation under Section 115 of the Code of Criminal Procedure, which contains guarantees of protection against inadmissible interference with the right to privacy, the legal regulation of the regulation for the detection and communication of data on the telecommunication operation carried out under the contested provisions of the Code of Criminal Procedure and the Police Force Act, the above guarantees are missing or do not contain guarantees comparable to those contained under the provisions of Section 115 of the Code of Criminal Procedure.

137. The legislator should finally also consider the purpose of laying down more detailed rules on the content of an order for the detection and communication of data on the communication operation being carried out and, where appropriate, establishing certain formal elements of the application of such a measure itself by the law enforcement authorities. The purpose of defining the necessary content requirements directly at the law level is to ensure that the court has in its decision all the necessary information available to law enforcement authorities without difficulty, information on the user or the owner of the user address or device if such data can be obtained from the relevant communication service provider without this endangering the purpose of the criminal proceedings. In this regard, the Constitutional Court emphasises the requirement of consistency and effectiveness of judicial review and does not presuppose the participation of the counterparty before the decision of the court is adopted. The role of the court is thus based on the nature of the proceedings, even when "balancing" the procedural situation and it is inadmissible for the court to get into the position of an "assistant" of the public

prosecution, because it must always be impartial (Judgment No. PL 789/06, paragraph 17).

138. Based on the referred facts it must be therefore concluded that the contested provisions do not obstruct the second stage of the proportionality test because they do not make it necessary for law enforcement authorities to identify data on the communication operation carried out by law enforcement authorities and do not provide effective means of control for their application, the effective protection of the fundamental right to information self-determination of the persons concerned throughout the period during which such authorities have access to the given data. For the completeness of the assessment of the constitutionality of the contested provisions, it must be pointed out that they would not even pass through the third step of the proportionality test, the essence of which is the assessment of proportionality in the narrower sense. The contested provisions do not attach any meaning to the nature and gravity of the offence for which the criminal proceedings are conducted, although these facts are already generally relevant for the outcome of the conflict in the collision between the fundamental right to information self-determination and the public interest in the prevention and prosecution of criminal offences. It is the task of the legislator to determine precisely the case of which criminal offences overrides the public interest, considering their severity in their decision. The same principles are based on the limitation of the possibility to issue an order for the interception and recording of a telecommunication operation under the provisions of Section 115 of the Code of Criminal Procedure only for the criminal proceedings on a crime, corruption, crimes of extremism, criminal act of misuse of public authority, criminal act of legalisation of a crime or for other intentional offence provided for by an international treaty.

The Constitutional Court of Slovenia: Judgment of 3 July 2014, Ref. No U-I-65/13[17]

(. . .)

14. From the challenged regulation, as a precautionary measure service providers non-selectively retain, for a determined period, exhaustively determined traffic data on all communications related to fixed network phone service, mobile phone service, Internet access, Internet e-mail service, and Internet phone service. The Government alleges that these data indicate individual facts, circumstances, dynamics, and patterns of individuals' lives. On the definition [of personal data] in point 1 of Article 6 of the Personal Data Protection Act (Official Gazette RS, No. 94/07 – official consolidated text – hereinafter referred to as the PDPA-1), which determines the system of protection of personal data, personal data is any data relating to an

[17]The judgement in English is available at the page of the Constitutional Court of Slovenia under: http://odlocitve.us-rs.si/en/odlocitev/AN03707?q=U-I-65%2F13.

individual, irrespective of the form in which it is expressed. An individual is an identified or identifiable natural person to whom personal data relates; an identifiable natural person is one who can be identified, directly or indirectly, in particular by reference to an identification number or to one or more factors specific to his physical, physiological, mental, economic, cultural or social identity, where the method of identification does not incur large costs or disproportionate effort or require a large amount of time (point 2 of Article 6 of the PDPA-1). Therefore, based on the challenged regulation, service providers are retaining data that include, from the viewpoint of privacy, information regarding identifiable individuals, who must thus enjoy the protection of personal data as guaranteed by Article 38 of the Constitution. The Constitutional Court does not deal with the question of whether absolutely all traffic data that are determined by the challenged regulation are in any event personal data in the sense of the definition mentioned above. What is key is that from these data (combined) it is possible to draw details from individuals' lives, and they must thus enjoy protection from the viewpoint of the right to privacy. Or, as stated by the Court of Justice of the European Union in the Judgment in the joined cases C-293/12 and C-594/12 (paragraph 27): "Those data, taken as a whole, may allow very precise conclusions to be drawn concerning the private lives of the persons whose data has been retained, such as the habits of everyday life, permanent or temporary places of residence, daily or other movements, the activities carried out, the social relationships of those persons and the social environments frequented by them."

15. The retention of such data (also for the purposes envisaged by the challenged regulation) entails, with regard to the established constitutional case law and also the case law of the Court of Justice of the European Union, an interference with the right to the protection of personal data guaranteed by Article 38 of the Constitution, Article 8 of the Charter, and also Article 8 of the Convention for the Protection of Human Rights and Fundamental Freedoms (Official Gazette RS, No. 33/94, MP, No. 7/94 – hereinafter referred to as the ECHR).

16. From the established constitutional case law it follows that the first paragraph of Article 38 of the Constitution guarantees the protection of personal data as a special aspect of privacy. The purpose of the protection of personal data is to ensure respect for a special aspect of human privacy – so-called information privacy. As the Constitution regulates this right specifically, it has a special place and importance in the general protection of the privacy of an individual. It also has an important place on the level of the European Union. Article 8 of the Charter also in a declaratory manner elevated the right to the protection of personal data to the level of a fundamental human right. In conformity with the established constitutional case law, any collecting and processing of personal data entails an interference with the right to the protection of privacy, i.e. with the right of individuals to keep information regarding themselves [private], because they do not want others to be acquainted therewith. The fundamental value foundation of this right is the realisation that individuals have the right to retain information regarding themselves to themselves and that as a starting point it is they who can decide how much information concerning themselves they will reveal and to whom. However, the right to

information privacy is not unlimited and absolute. Therefore, individuals must accept the limitations of information privacy, i.e. allow interferences therewith that are in the prevailing public interest and if the constitutionally determined conditions are fulfilled. [Such] an interference is admissible under the conditions determined by the third paragraph of Article 15 and Article 2 of the Constitution. In such context, the Constitutional Court must assess whether the legislature followed a constitutionally admissible aim, and if it did, also whether the limitation is in conformity with the principles of a state governed by the rule of law, namely with that principle that prohibits excessive interferences by the state (the general principle of proportionality). In the law it must be precisely determined which data may be collected and processed, and for what purpose they may be used; supervision over the collection, processing, and use of personal data must be envisaged, as well as protection of the confidentiality of the collected personal data. The purpose of the collecting of personal data must be constitutionally admissible. Only data appropriate and urgently necessary for the implementation of the statutorily defined purpose may be collected. When what is at issue is the processing of personal data for police work, the legislature must weigh the measure by which it interferes with a sensitive area of the privacy of an individual without his or her consent in an especially meticulous manner. The same also applies to the processing of personal data by other authorities of the state for the defence of the state, national security, and the constitutional system.

17. The Constitutional Court has already explained numerous times that substantively similar requirements to those included in Article 38 of the Constitution are also included in the Convention for the Protection of Individuals with regard to the Automatic Processing of Personal Data (Official Gazette RS, No. 11/94, MP, No. 3/94 – hereinafter referred to as the CPI). In addition to the fact that personal data must be obtained and processed fairly and lawfully, the CPI requires that measures be taken that will ensure that personal data will be retained for specified and legitimate purposes and that they will not be used in a way incompatible with those purposes, as well as that only data that are adequate, relevant, and not excessive in relation to the purposes for which they are retained will be processed (Article 5 in relation to Article 4 of the CPI).

18. The first condition for the admissibility of an interference with the right determined by the first paragraph of Article 38 of the Constitution is thus the existence of a constitutionally admissible aim. The fundamental purpose of the Data Retention Directive, due to which the legislature instituted the challenged regulation, was determined by the first paragraph of Article 1 [of the Directive], namely "(...) to ensure that the data are available for the purpose of the investigation, detection and prosecution of serious crime, as defined by each Member State in its national law." Similarly, also the first paragraph of Article 163 of the ECA-1 determines that "[service providers] must retain, for the purposes of obtaining data in a public communications network determined by the law that regulates criminal procedure, for the purposes of ensuring the national security and the constitutional system, and the security, political, and economic interests of the state, as determined by the law that regulates the Slovene Intelligence and Security Agency, as well as the

defence of the state, as determined by the law that regulates the defence of the state, the data determined by Article 164 of this Act, if they create or process it when providing public communications services related thereto." The prosecution of serious forms of criminal offences, the defence of the state, and the safeguarding of the security of the state with the purpose of ensuring the protection of human rights and fundamental freedoms, as well as other fundamental legal values from illegal attacks against them are constitutionally admissible aims. For the state to be able to protect human rights and fundamental freedoms on its territory (Article 5 of the Constitution), it must primarily foster the existence and efficient functioning of the institutions of a state governed by the rule of law also in such a manner that it combats the most serious forms of criminal offences, ensures the defence of the state, the national security, and the constitutional system.

19. Therefore, the legislature did have constitutionally admissible aims for interfering with the constitutionally protected right to information privacy determined by the first paragraph of Article 38 of the Constitution. From this point of view, the interference is not inadmissible.

20. The challenged measure is also appropriate for achieving the mentioned aims, because they can in fact be achieved by the measure. Undoubtedly, in certain situations the retention and subsequent use of traffic data can entail an appropriate means for the investigation, detection, and prosecution of serious criminal offences. The same applies to the purposes of the defence of the state and the safeguarding of the security of the state. Such proceeds from the statements of Member States, as follows from the Evaluation Report of the European Commission and other documents published on its website, as well as from the analysis that was submitted by the Government in the proceedings at issue. The Government alleges that these data play an important supporting role in the collection of evidence in the framework of the investigation of criminal offences, because they indicate individual facts, circumstances, relations, dynamics, and patterns that significantly contribute to the collection of fundamental evidence directly proving the suspicion that a [concrete] criminal offence has been committed. Also the Court of Justice of the European Union assessed that with regard to the increasing importance of electronic communications, the data that had to be retained based on the [now] invalid Directive provided national authorities competent for criminal prosecution additional possibilities with regard to detecting serious criminal offences and that in this regard they are a valuable means for [conducting] criminal investigations. Although from the materials submitted by the Government and the documents of the Commission it is not clearly evident whether what is at issue is the use of data that otherwise in the absence of obligatory retention as envisaged by the Data Retention Directive and the now challenged regulation would not be accessible to prosecuting authorities and other competent authorities of the state, it is at the same time also not possible to conclude that these data are manifestly inappropriate for achieving the [stated] aim. Likewise, it is not evident that the measure is inappropriate even if in certain instances due to technical circumvention or specific types of use of these communications services (e.g. falsifying the number calling, the use of unregistered prepaid mobile services, the use of a service for the anonymisation of traffic over the Internet,

etc.) it is possible to cover the digital traces behind the real user or achieve anonymous use of a mobile and fixed network phone service, as well as of Internet access, which is what the applicant otherwise draws attention to. A measure is inappropriate only when the means for achieving the aim does not have a sensible connection with that aim and when the stated aim cannot be achieved in any event by the [chosen] measure, not only that [it cannot be achieved] only to a certain degree. However, the fact that the constitutionally admissible aim can only be achieved to a certain degree by the [chosen] measure can significantly influence the assessment of the proportionality of such measure.

21. Even if a measure is both appropriate and useful, such does not mean at the same time that it is necessary, i.e. that to achieve the pursued aim no [other] less invasive measures that would interfere less with the human rights of individuals are available. In the framework of the test of the necessity of a measure, the Constitutional Court assesses whether an interference is at all necessary in the sense that the aim cannot be achieved without (any) interference at all or whether the aim can be achieved without the (concrete) interference that is being assessed by means of some other [interference] that would be milder in nature.

22. For such reason, it is necessary to assess whether the legislature could also achieve the purpose for which such personal data was retained also in a manner that would interfere less invasively with the right determined by the first paragraph of Article 38 of the Constitution. Due to the fact that with regard to the manner and scope of the retention of data, the challenged regulation is actually a transposition of the requirements from the Data Retention Directive and was thus determined in a manner such as was determined by the now no longer valid Data Retention Directive, the underlying reasons that guided the Court of Justice of the European Union in its invalidation are key also to the assessment of the challenged Act.

23. First, it must be underlined that combating serious criminal offences, especially organised crime and terrorism, the defence of the state, and ensuring national security and the constitutional system, are of fundamental importance for the functioning of a state governed by the rule of law. However, such an aim, although of fundamental importance, cannot in itself justify an unlimited interference with human rights.

24. The challenged regulation provides for the precautionary (in advance) and indiscriminate retention of traffic data [generated by] certain electronic communications. A consequence of such regulation is that service providers retain, for a determined period, the traffic data of all users of phone services in fixed and mobile networks, data on accessing the Internet and e-mail, and data on the use of phone service over an Internet protocol, such as determined by Article 164 of the ECA-1. By the precautionary and indiscriminate retention of data created daily, service providers are creating vast databases that are being retained for 14 or eight months and from which, at any moment, very detailed conclusions can be drawn concerning facts regarding the private life of every single individual that uses these services. With regard to the fact that the modern manner of communicating predominantly entails the use of the mentioned electronic communications services, such a measure in fact entails a very invasive interference with the (information) privacy of the entire

population, both with regard to the scope of the persons affected by the measure and with regard to the data that are being retained. The interference with the [mentioned] right is also exacerbated by the fact that by the creation of such an extensive database of personal data on the entire population, the risk that unauthorised persons will access the retained data or that the data will be used for unlawful purposes, despite the obligations imposed on service providers by, inter alia, Article 165 of the ECA-1, increases substantially. Such a regulation substantially interferes with the human rights and fundamental freedoms of individuals also due to the fact that the affected persons are not informed of the retention and the potential subsequent use of their data, which can in the minds of these persons generate a feeling of constant surveillance. Such an intangible feeling of constant surveillance can also influence the exercise of other rights, above all the right to free expression and public communication, as guaranteed by Article 39 of the Constitution and Article 11 of the Charter.

25. By the nature of the matter, the precautionary and non-selective retention of data necessarily entails that it predominantly interferes with the rights of those persons who are not and will not be even indirectly connected with the purposes for which these data were primarily collected. Both the Data Retention Directive and the Slovene legislature did not limit the retention to those data that have some reasonable and objectively verifiable connection with purpose that [the legislature] intends the measure to achieve. The non-selective and precautionary retention of traffic data necessarily entails that it will interfere predominantly with the rights of that part of the population that did not give rise to any reasons for such an interference. As the Court of Justice of the European Union also stressed, by the unlimited measure, also data regarding communications that would otherwise have to enjoy special protection are retained. Namely, the regulation does not allow for anonymous use of means of communication in all those instances when confidential and untraceable use of the means of communication is necessary to achieve its purpose (e.g. phone services for assistance in emotional distress). Similarly, the challenged regulation, as well as the Data Retention Directive, did not limit the retention of data to a certain period, geographical area, or circle of persons who might have a certain connection with the purpose pursued by the measure.

26. The question regarding the length of time personal data is retained is also important for the assessment of whether the interference [at issue] is necessary to achieve a constitutionally admissible aim. The retention and processing of personal data for a longer period than is necessary to achieve the purpose does not fulfil the [criterion of] proportionality. In fact, in the fifth paragraph of Article 163 of the ECA-1, the legislature envisaged a different length of time for the retention of data regarding publicly accessible phone services (14 months), on the one hand, and all other data (eight months), on the other. However, the reasons why the legislature decided [to require] retention for such duration and why it determined a different period of retention for the mentioned data are not evident from either the reply of the National Assembly nor the opinion of the Government. The analysis already mentioned above that was submitted by the Government only includes the generalised claim that if the duration of retention were shortened, "a new adaptation of

investigative procedures would be necessary." On the fact that different data are collected that have, by the nature of the matter, a different utility value with regard to the duration of retention, the legislature should have considered that and correspondingly differentiated the duration of retention with regard to the usefulness of the data or with regard to the persons concerned. From the mentioned documentation it is also not evident why a shorter period of retention (than was, for instance, determined by certain Member States) does not suffice to achieve its purpose. On the measure that includes such a broad range of different data without objective criteria being determined more precisely for such retention, it is also not possible [to carry out] a subsequent test of whether the measure only refers to what is truly necessary to achieve its purpose. Such measure does not fulfil the criterion of necessity nor the criterion of proportionality in the narrower sense, because it is not possible to weigh whether the correspondingly longer period of retention and the degree of interference with the privacy of individuals related thereto are proportionate to ensuring public safety or some other interest pursued by such measure.

27. The now invalidated Data Retention Directive limited the purpose of such retention only to the investigation, detection, and prosecution of serious criminal offences. The challenged regulation does not include such a limitation. Also in the regulations referred to by the challenged regulation (the first paragraph of Article 163 of the ECA-1), the legislature did not limit the processing of personal data only to certain acts (serious criminal offences) for which it would assess that due to their weight the retention of data or access to these data justify the interference with the privacy of individuals. Also, for such reason, the measure disproportionally interferes with the right determined by the first paragraph of Article 38 of the Constitution.

28. By determining, in the first paragraph of Article 163 of the ECA-1, the obligatory retention of traffic data, the legislature substantially interfered with the right to the protection of personal data and at the same time it did not determine in detail the circumstances on which such interference would be limited to only what is truly necessary to achieve the aim. The challenged provision thereby interfered disproportionally with the right to the protection of personal data determined by the first paragraph of Article 38 of the Constitution. Consequently, the first paragraph of Article 163 of the ECA-1, which explicitly determines the obligation to retain traffic data, is unconstitutional. The other challenged provisions of Section XIII of the ECA-1 are directly connected with this provision and do not have an independent meaning. For such reason, the Constitutional Court abrogated the challenged provisions of Section XIII in their entirety (point 1 of the operative provisions).

29. Since the challenged provisions had to be abrogated already due to the inconsistency with the right to the protection of personal data determined by Article 38 of the Constitution, the Constitutional Court did not assess the other alleged unconstitutionalities.

30. To prevent further disproportionate interferences with the right to the protection of personal data determined by the first paragraph of Article 38 of the Constitution, the Constitutional Court determined, from the second paragraph of Article

40 of the CCA, the manner of the implementation of this Decision. Based on this Article, service providers that are retaining traffic data in conformity with the first paragraph of Article 163 of the ECA-1 must immediately upon the publication of this Decision in the Official Gazette of the Republic of Slovenia destroy these data (point 2 of the operative provisions).

The manufacturer's authorised representative in the EU is Springer Nature Customer Service Centre GmbH, Europaplatz 3, 69115 Heidelberg, Germany. If you have any concerns regarding our products, please contact ProductSafety@springernature.com

Printed and bound by CPI Group (UK) Ltd, Croydon, CR0 4YY
23/09/2026
02221534-0002